CONVENTION AGAINST TORTURE AND OTHER CRUEL, INHUMAN OR DEGRADING TREATMENT OR PUNISHMENT

SELECTED DECISIONS OF THE COMMITTEE AGAINST TORTURE

Volume I

Eleventh to thirty-eighth sessions
(November 1993 – May 2007)

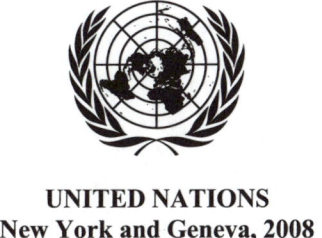

UNITED NATIONS
New York and Geneva, 2008

NOTE

The designations employed and the presentation of the material in this publication do not imply the expression of any opinion whatsoever on the part of the Secretariat of the United Nations concerning the legal status of any country, territory, city or area, or of its authorities, or concerning the delimitation of its frontiers or boundaries.

*
* *

Symbols of United Nations documents are composed of capital letters combined with figures. Mention of such a symbol indicates a reference to a United Nations document.

HR/CAT/PUB/1

UNITED NATIONS PUBLICATION
Sales N° E.08.XIV.8
ISBN 978-92-1-154185-4

CONTENTS

Page

Introduction 1

A. Inadmissibility 3
(Committee's session indicated in brackets)

N° 247/2004	[35]	A.A. v. Azerbaijan	3
N° 273/2005	[36]	T.A. v. Canada	7

B. Views under article 22 of the Convention against Torture 12

N° 8/1991	[11]	Qani Halimi-Nebzibi v. Austria	12
N° 13/1993	[12]	Balabou Mutombo v. Switzerland	15
N° 34/1995	[18]	Seid Mortesa Aemei v. Switzerland	21
N° 43/1996	[17]	Kaveh Yaragh Tala v. Sweden	27
N° 39/1996	[18]	Gorki Ernesto Tapia Páez v. Sweden	31
N° 59/1996	[20]	Encarnación Blanco Abad v. Spain	37
N° 63/1997	[23]	Josu Arkauz Arana v. France	43
N° 99/1997	[24]	T.P.S. v. Canada	51
N° 110/1998	[21]	Cecilia Rasana Núñez Chipana v. Venezuela	62
N° 113/1998	[26]	Ristic v. Yugoslavia	65
N° 120/1998	[22]	Sadiq Shek Elmi v. Australia	70
N° 161/2000	[29]	Hajrizi Dzemajl et al. v. Yugoslavia	78
N° 171/2000	[34]	Jovica Dimitrov v. Serbia and Montenegro	85
N° 172/2000	[35]	Danilo Dimitrijevic v. Serbia and Montenegro	89
N° 174/2000	[35]	Nikolić v. Serbia and Montenegro	92
N° 181/2001	[36]	Suleymane Guengueng et al. v. Senegal	99
N° 187/2001	[31]	Dhaou Belgacem Thabti v. Tunisia	107
N° 188/2001	[31]	Imed Abdelli v. Tunisia	120
N° 189/2001	[31]	Bouabdallah Ltaief v. Tunisia	133
N° 195/2002	[34]	Mafhoud Brada v. France	146
N° 207/2002	[33]	Dragan Dimitrijevic v. Serbia and Montenegro	155
N° 212/2002	[34]	Kepa Urra Guridi v. Spain	158
N° 214/2002	[32]	M.A.K. v. Germany	162
N° 219/2002	[30]	G.K. v. Switzerland	170
N° 233/2003	[34]	Ahmed Hussein Mustafa Kamil Agiza v. Sweden	177
N° 238/2003	[35]	Z.T. v. Norway	201
N° 258/2004	[35]	Mostafa Dadar v. Canada	209
N° 262/2005	[37]	V.L. v. Switzerland	215
N° 279/2005	[37]	C.T. and K.M. v. Sweden	221
N° 280/2005	[37]	Gamal El Rgeig v. Switzerland	227
N° 282/2005	[37]	S.P.A. v. Canada	231
N° 300/2006	[38]	Adel Tebourski v. France	237

Author and victim index 243

Introduction

The worldwide eradication of the practice of torture was one of the major challenges of the United Nations only a few years after it was created. To ensure adequate protection for all persons against torture and other forms of cruel, inhuman or degrading treatment or punishment, the United Nations has, over the years, adopted a number of universally applicable standards. The adoption, on 10 December 1984, of the Convention against Torture and other Cruel, Inhuman or Degrading Treatment or Punishment was a milestone in the codification process to combat torture.

In adopting this instrument, the United Nations also established a monitoring body, the Committee against Torture, whose main function is to ensure that the Convention is observed and implemented. The Committee met for the first time in April 1988 in Geneva and has since carried out numerous activities which have made it better known to the public at large.

The Convention against Torture consists of 33 articles and entered into force on 26 June 1987. By the end of 2007, 145 States had ratified the Convention or acceded to it.

The Committee against Torture was established pursuant to article 17 of the Convention. It consists of 10 experts of high moral standing and recognized competence in the field of human rights. The experts, who must be nationals of States parties, are elected by those States by secret ballot. They are elected for a term of four years and are eligible for re-election.

The Committee holds two regular sessions each year. It elects from among its members a Chairperson, three Vice-Chairpersons as well as a Rapporteur. These officers are elected for a term of two years and are eligible for re-election.

At its initial meeting in 1988, the Committee adopted its rules of procedure and set out its working methods, in conformity with the provisions of the Convention. The Committee's working methods have been fine-tuned on a number of subsequent occasions.

Like other international human rights treaties, the Convention against Torture gives individuals, under certain circumstances, the right to lodge complaints regarding the violation of one or more of the provisions of the Convention by a State party. For the Committee to be able to admit and examine individual communications against a State party, its competence in that regard must have been expressly recognized by the State concerned. Individual complaints are always examined by the Committee in closed meetings.

A communication may be submitted by any private individual who claims to be the victim of a violation of the Convention by a State party that has accepted the competence of the Committee under article 22 and which is subject to its jurisdiction. If alleged victims are not in a position to submit the communication themselves, their relatives or representatives may act on their behalf.

By 1 March 2008, the following 64 States had made the declaration under article 22 of the Convention:

> Algeria, Andorra, Argentina, Australia, Austria, Azerbaijan, Belgium, Bolivia, Bosnia and Herzegovina, Brazil, Bulgaria, Burundi, Canada, Cameroon, Chile, Costa Rica, Croatia, Cyprus, Czech Republic, Denmark, Ecuador, Finland, France, Georgia, Germany, Ghana, Greece, Guatemala, Hungary, Iceland, Ireland, Italy, Kazakhstan, Liechtenstein, Luxembourg, Malta, Mexico, Monaco, Morocco, Netherlands, New Zealand, Norway, Paraguay, Peru, Poland, Portugal, Republic of Korea, Russian Federation, Senegal, Serbia, Seychelles, Slovakia, Slovenia, South Africa, Spain, Sweden, Switzerland, the former Yugoslav Republic of Macedonia, Togo, Tunisia, Turkey, Ukraine, Uruguay, Venezuela (Bolivarian Republic of).

When considering a complaint, the Committee first examines its admissibility. Conditions for admissibility are specified in the Convention and in the Committee's rules of procedure. For a communication to be declared admissible:

- It must not be anonymous or incompatible with the provisions of the Convention.

- It must not constitute an abuse of the right to submit a communication under article 22.

- It must not have been examined (or be under examination) under another procedure of international investigation or settlement.

- The complainant must have exhausted all available and effective domestic remedies before sending the complaint to the Committee.

The Committee may request the State party concerned or the complainant to submit additional information, clarifications or observations relevant to the admissibility of the case.

If the Committee decides that a communication is admissible, after informing the complainant and transmitting its decision to the State party concerned, it will consider the merits of the case. Within six months, the State party concerned should submit to the Committee explanations or statements clarifying the case and indicating any measures that may have been taken to remedy the situation. The complainant may also submit observations or additional information to the Committee.

When registering a communication, or when considering either the admissibility or the merits of a case, and prior to any decision being taken, the Committee may, pursuant to rule 108 of its rules of procedure, request the State party concerned to take measures to avoid potential irreparable damage to the alleged victim. This provision offers persons who claim a violation of the Convention protection against any State party action or inaction that would be incompatible with that State's obligations under the Convention. At the same time, it does not prejudge the Committee's final decision.

In the light of all the information made available to it by the complainant and the State party concerned, the Committee considers the communication and adopts its Views thereon. Any member of the Committee may express an individual opinion. The Views are transmitted to the complainant and the State party, which if a violation of the Convention has been found, is invited by the Committee to inform it of any action it may take in conformity with the Views. Such follow-up information is usually requested within three months of the transmittal of the Views.

The Committee includes in its annual report a summary of the communications examined, of the explanations and statements of the State parties concerned, and of its own Views.

By the end of its 39th session in November 2007, the Committee had adopted 145 Views on individual communications submitted to it.

From the first to the end of the 39th session of the Committee, 332 communications relating to alleged violations by States parties had been registered for consideration under article 22 of the Convention. By the end of 2007, the status of these communications was as follows:

- 145 concluded by adoption of Views (47 with finding of a violation of the Convention, 98 without finding of a violation of the Convention)
- 58 declared inadmissible
- 89 discontinued or withdrawn
- 4 declared admissible and awaiting a decision on the merits
- 3 suspended
- 33 pending at the pre-admissibility stage

A. Inadmissibility

Communication N° 247/2004

Submitted by: A.A.
Alleged victim: The complainant
State party: Azerbaijan
Declared inadmissible: 25 November 2005

Subject matter: ill-treatment on death row

Procedural issues: examination by another procedure of international investigation or settlement; admissibility *ratione temporis*; exceptions to the rule of exhaustion of domestic remedies

Substantive issue: cruel, inhuman and degrading treatment

Articles of the Convention: 1, 2, 12, 13

1.1 The complainant is Mr. A.A.,[**] an Azeri national sentenced to death on 24 August 1994 by the Supreme Court of Azerbaijan. On 10 February 1998, all death sentences handed down in Azerbaijan, including the complainant's, were commuted to life imprisonment, following the abolition of the death penalty by Parliament. The complainant claims to be a victim of violation by Azerbaijan of his rights under articles 1, 2, 12 and 13, of the Convention against Torture and other Cruel, Inhuman or Degrading Treatment (the Convention). He is represented by counsel.

1.2 Azerbaijan became a State party to the Convention on 16 August 1996 (date of accession), and made the declaration under article 22 on 4 February 2002.

The facts as submitted

2.1 The complainant was a police inspector. On 24 August 1994, he was found guilty of murder, illegal storage of and port of fire arms, voluntary destruction of public property, murder with aggravating circumstances, and attempted murder. He was sentenced to death by the Supreme Court of Azerbaijan, allegedly without having been given the right to appeal against this judgement. The complainant claims that his trial did not meet the requirements of due process and was tainted by the authorities' desire to avenge the murder of a policeman. He also explains that two of the three individuals composing the court (so-called "people's assessors") had refused to countersign his death sentence.

2.2 After his conviction, the complainant was placed on death row in Baylovskaya prison (Baku), where, he allegedly shared a 6 square metres cell with "5–6" other prisoners also under sentence of death. The cell was equipped with only one bunk bed for all of them, and the prisoners had to sleep in turns. The window of the cell was obstructed by metal plates and no light could penetrate; there was only a dim lamp in the cell, which was constantly lit.

2.3 According to the complainant, on 1 October 1994, a group of prisoners escaped from Baylovskaya prison.[1] The same day, the prosecutor in charge of prisons allegedly informed the prison authorities that they were allowed to beat (to death) all prisoners "under his responsibility". After this, conditions of detention worsened. No recreation walks were authorized between 1994 and 1998. From 1994 to 1996, prisoners were obliged to take showers directly in the cells, while no bathroom existed; a collective bathroom was set up only in the summer of 1996; showers were then allowed at 20–30 days intervals, for 10–15 minutes per cell. The complainant states that more than 70 prisoners under sentences of death passed away while he was on death row from 1994 to 1998, due to the worsening conditions of detention.

2.4 The complainant explains that despite the fact that prison regulations allowed him to receive the visit of his family every month, as well as to receive a 5 kg parcel, in reality, and especially after the escaping of prisoners in October 1994, visits and parcels were "irregular".

2.5 According to the complainant, during the morning calls, all prisoners had to leave their cells, and to stand in front of the door leading to the fire squad basement. In addition, during his detention on death row, the execution chambers were cleaned on 7–8 occasions; every time thereafter, the administration threatened that a series of executions was expected.

___

[1] Throughout the text, the complainant refers to the events of October 1994 as to "escape" and "attempt to escape", without differentiation. It transpires, however, that 10 prisoners had escaped.

___

[**] Initials changed at the request of the complainant.

2.6 The complainant claims that although the law stipulated that former policemen had to be held separately, he was held together with ordinary criminals. There was allegedly an attempt to kill him while he slept, and he was severely beaten by his cell mates twice.

2.7 The complainant explains that after the "escape" in 1994, and until March 1995, no medical doctor visited the death section. Ill prisoners allegedly were held together with other prisoners, surgery was made in inadequate conditions and several prisoners died because of bad medical care.

2.8 It is further stated that immediately after the 1994 "escape", no food or water was supplied to the prisoners; when the supply was restored, rations were reduced by half. Temperatures at night were below 16° Celsius, but no covers were distributed to the prisoner between October 1994 and January 1995; covers were allowed only after an intervention by the International Committee of the Red Cross.

2.9 The complainant gives details on the allegedly bad treatment in 1994–1996: during the morning calls, prisoners were moved out of their cells, one by one, and were beaten (with wooden sticks, police batons, and electric cables, inter alia), up to the point when they fell to the ground losing conscience. Accordingly, some 45 prisoners lost their lives in such circumstances.

2.10 In May 1996, the prison administration discovered hidden documents in the complainant's cell, in which he recorded the acts of the prison authorities against him, and also listed persons who had died on death row as a consequence of ill-treatment and torture. He was severely beaten; his pens and paper were confiscated. In September 1996, a governmental delegation inspected the prison. Even though only few prisoners filed minor complaints, since they were afraid of retaliation, all those under sentence of death were severely beaten after the inspectors' departure.

2.11 In October 1996, head of the prison guards allegedly beat all prisoners, thus "celebrating" the second anniversary of the 1994 escape. The complainant was allegedly beaten for an hour and a half.

2.12 In the autumn of 1996, a prisoner who had been released allegedly met with the complainant's mother and explained to her the conditions in which her son was detained. The mother filed a complaint with the prison authorities. After this, the complainant was beaten, threatened with death, and forced to sign a disclaimer.

2.13 In early 1997, another list of deceased prisoners was discovered in the complainant's cell; he was beaten again and was confined, together with his cell-mates, to 3 days of isolation.

2.14 After the commutation of his death sentence in 1998, the complainant was allegedly held "in isolation" for another six months and was unable to meet with his family during this period.

2.15 The complainant alleges that because of the above-mentioned reasons, he was unable to, and was indeed prevented from, exhausting all available domestic remedies:

– Since 1997, his counsel has published a series of articles in different newspapers, in relation to the complainant's situation and the situation of other death row prisoners, using information provided by the complainant. However, no inquiry followed, nor was any prosecution instituted.

– In October and December 2002, several prisoners serving life sentences in Gobustan prison, including the complainant, filed complaints in the Gardaksy district court and in the Court of Appeal, denouncing the deplorable conditions of detention and the ill-treatment they had been subjected to. However, the tribunals referred to examine these complaints on the ground that the claimants' signatures had not been certified by the prison authorities. Many prisoners, such as the complainant himself, never received a reply from the courts.

– It is stated that the Ombudsman visited the prison on several occasions, but in spite of the complainant's request, he was unable to meet with her.

2.16 The complainant alleges that he believes that, in the light of the facts outlined above, any further communication with the judiciary authorities of Azerbaijan would be futile and would subject him to supplementary pressure and intimidation, or even his physical disappearance as an important witness.

2.17 According to the complainant, he had not been hospitalized during his detention. He was examined on 15 November 2003 by a Medical Commission. On 7 January 2004, he received the results and the diagnosis of the Medical Commission: "situational neurosis, elements character psychopathia". The complainant claims that on 8 January 2004, when he examined his medical record sheet, he discovered that it had been changed with new type of medical form, and that the information from his previous medical records had not been recorded. Thus, according to him, no record was kept of his illnesses in 1994–2002 (haemorrhoids, rheumatism, neurosis, "attacks", and a cerebral attack in 1999).[2] The

---

[2] According to the complainant, the medical card of his cellmate, G., who had suffered form different diseases, including tuberculosis, was completely blank.

complainant alleges that his record card was substituted to prevent any possibility for him to seek compensation for the diseases suffered.

2.18 The complainant applied to the European Court of Human Rights (application N° 34132/03 of 29 October 2003, declared inadmissible on 29 April 2005). However, according to him, the allegations before the European Court relate *only* to the period following the allegations of the present communication, i.e., *after* 10 February 1998.[3]

The claim

3.1 The complainant claims that the conditions of detention, and the manner the authorities treated him while he was on death row (1994–1998), amounted to a violation of articles 1 (1) and 2 of the Convention.

3.2 Article 2, paragraphs 1 and 3 are also said to have been violated, as the cells where he was held were allegedly overcrowded by a factor of 2 to 4 compared to the possible occupancy, and he—as a former policeman—was held together with ordinary criminals.

3.3 Allegedly, in violation of article 12 of the Convention, the authorities omitted to investigate promptly and impartially deaths of prisoners who awaited execution, "when there were reasonable grounds" that their dead was the consequence of the torture and cruel treatment they were subjected to by the prison authorities.

3.4 Finally, the complainant claims a violation of article 13, because of the State party's impossibility to secure an impartial examination of the claims of torture and cruel treatment.

State party's observations on admissibility

4. The State party contested the admissibility of the communication on 19 July 2004. It recalls that it recognized the Committee's competence to examine individual complaints on 4 February 2002, and that accordingly, the Committee is only competent to examine complaints submitted against Azerbaijan after that date. Accordingly, the State party considers the complainant's communication to be inadmissible.

Complainant's comments

5.1 By letter of 6 November 2004, the complainant concedes that the events complained of occurred before the State party's acceptance of the Committee's competence to examine individual complaints against it. According to him, however, the *ratione temporis* rule does not apply if violations continue after the date of entry into force of the procedure for the State party. As example, he refers to the jurisprudence of the Human Rights Committee (case of *K. and K.* v. *Hungary*, communication N° 520/1992, inadmissibility decision adopted on 7 April 1994, para. 6.4).

5.2 On the issue of exhaustion of domestic remedies, he reiterates that he did not believe in the effectiveness of the procedures in the State party. In support of this statement, he names five former death row prisoners who were granted new trials in 2002–2004. Allegedly, all of them had complained of torture and ill-treatment in detention, but the courts allegedly ignored all of their claims and confirmed their life sentences.[4]

5.3 According to the complainant, in 2004, one prisoner serving a life sentence sought to obtain compensation for tuberculosis he had contracted while he was on death row from 1996 to 1998, detained in an overcrowded cell together with prisoners who suffered from tuberculosis. He lost his case and his cassation appeal.[5]

Issues and proceedings before the Committee

6.1 Before considering any claims contained in a complaint, the Committee against Torture must decide whether or not it is admissible under article 22 of the Convention.

6.2 The Committee has noted, first, that the complainant's allegations (see para. 3.3 above) that the State party's authorities have consistently failed to investigate reports of deaths of prisoners on death row. It recalls that it can only examine complaints if they are submitted by the alleged victims, close relatives, or by a representative duly authorized to act on the victim's behalf. In the present case, the complainant has not presented any authorization to act on behalf of any other alleged victim. Accordingly, the Committee finds that this part of the communication is inadmissible under rule 98, paragraph 2 (c), of its rules of procedure.[6]

6.3 On the remaining parts of the complainant's claims, the Committee recalls that the State party had challenged the admissibility of the communication on the ground that the events complained of took place before its acceptance, on 4 February 2002, of the Committee's competence to deal with individual communications under article 22 of the Convention. The complainant has refuted this assertion by invoking the "continuing effect" doctrine.

---

[3] The European Convention for Human Rights entered into force for Azerbaijan on 15 April 2002.

[4] According to the complainant, only on one occasion was a life sentence commuted to 15 years of imprisonment, due to a decriminalization of an offence.

[5] It is stated however, that the Supreme Court made no decision on the case, because the plaintiff was pardoned, released and left the country.

[6] CAT/C/3/Rev.4.

6.4 The Committee recalls that a State party's obligations under the Convention apply from the date of its entry into force for that State party.[7] It considers, however, that it can examine alleged violations of the Convention which occurred before a State party's recognition of the Committee's competence to receive and consider individual communications alleging violations of the Convention (i.e., before the declaration under article 22 became effective, i.e., 4 February 2002, in the present case), if the effects of these violations continued after the declaration under article 22 became effective, and if the effects constitute in themselves a violation of the Convention. A continuing violation must be interpreted as an affirmation, after the formulation of the declaration, by act or by clear implication, of the previous violations of the State party.

6.5 The Committee has noted that in the present case, the complainant's allegations under articles 1, 2 and 13, of the Convention (see paras. 3.1, 3.2 and 3.4 above) all relate to events which occurred before the State party's recognition of the Committee's competence to consider individual complaints. According to the complainant, however, these alleged violations had effects which continued *after* the State party's acceptance of the Committee's competence under article 22.

6.6 The Committee has equally noted that the complainant filed an application in the European Court of Human Rights, regarding events which occurred after 10 February 1998, which, according to him, can be clearly distinguished from the issues submitted to the Committee. This application was declared inadmissible on 29 April 2005. The European Court held, inter alia, that the complainant's allegations of mistreatment on death row, which are identical to the claims in the present communication, were inadmissible.[8]

6.7 In this context, the Committee recalls that it shall not consider any communications from an individual under article 22, paragraph 5 (a), of the Convention, unless it has ascertained that the *same matter has not been, and is not being, examined* under another procedure of international investigation or settlement; the Committee is satisfied that examination by the European court of Human Rights constitutes an examination under such a procedure.

6.8 The Committee considers that a communication has been, and is being examined by another procedure of international investigation or settlement if the examination by the procedure relates/related to the "same matter" within the meaning of article 22, paragraph 5 (a), that must be understood as relating to the same parties, the same facts, and the same substantive rights. It observes that application N° 34132/03 was submitted to the European Court by the same complainant, was based on the same facts, and related, at least in part, to the same substantive rights as those invoked in the present communication.

6.9 Having concluded that the "same matter" has been the object of the complainant's application before the European Court and it was examined and declared inadmissible, the Committee considers that the requirements of article 22, paragraph 5 (a), have not been met in the present case. In the circumstances, the Committee decides that it is not necessary to examine the other two grounds of inadmissibility, namely on *ratione temporis* and non exhaustion of domestic remedies.

7. The Committee against Torture consequently decides:

(a) That the communication is inadmissible;

(b) That the present decision shall be communicated to the State party and to the complainant.

---

[7] See *O.R, M.M.*, and *M.S.* v. *Argentina*, communications Nos. 1, 2, and 3/1988, inadmissibility decision adopted in November 1989.

[8] The Committee has noted that the European Court, acting through a Committee of three judges, declared the application inadmissible on two grounds: partly on (a) non-exhaustion of domestic remedies (articles 3, 8, 14, and 34, of the European Convention), and (b) with regard to the applicant's remaining complaints, on the ground that the information before the Court does not reveal any violation of the applicant's rights and freedoms under the Convention.

Communication N° 273/2005

Submitted by: T.A.
Alleged victim: The complainant
State party: Canada
Declared inadmissible: 15 May 2006

Subject matter: deportation of complainant to Myanmar with alleged risk of torture and cruel, inhuman or degrading treatment or punishment

Procedural issue: non-exhaustion of domestic remedies

Substantive issues: risk of torture on deportation; risk of cruel, inhuman or degrading treatment or punishment on deportation

Articles of the Convention: 3, 16

1.1 The complainant is Mr. T.A., a Burmese national born on 8 January 1978 in Yangon, Myanmar, and currently residing in Canada, from where he faces deportation. He claims that his forcible return to Myanmar would constitute a violation by Canada of articles 3 and 16 of the Convention against Torture and Other Cruel, Inhuman or Degrading Treatment. He is represented by counsel.

1.2 In accordance with article 22, paragraph 3, of the Convention, the Committee transmitted the communication to the State party on 15 July 2005, and requested it, under rule 108, paragraph 1, of the Committee's rules of procedure, not to expel the complainant to Myanmar while his complaint is under consideration by the Committee. The request was made on the basis of the information contained in the complainant's submission and could be reviewed at the request of the State party in light of information and comments from the State party and the complainant.

1.3 By submission of 21 December 2005, the State party requested that the admissibility of the complaint be examined separately from the merits. On 26 January 2006, the Special Rapporteur on New Communications and Interim Measures granted the State party's request, pursuant to rule 109, paragraph 3, of the Committee's rules of procedure.

The facts as presented by the complainant

2.1 The complainant was involved in student demonstrations while attending the University of Hlaing, Myanmar, in 1998. In November 1998 he was involved in a demonstration where he was detained and questioned. In detention, the complainant alleges that the police made him sign a document stating that if he was caught in anti-government activities again, he would be detained indefinitely. After his release, he was interrogated on several occasions and he knew that the Government was monitoring his activities. In 2001 the complainant distributed documents relating to human rights abuses, although he did not belong to a democracy organization. He was not caught distributing these documents. In 2001 a friend of the complainant founded a soccer (football) association ('union') and asked him to join. The complainant agreed and recruited more members to play soccer. At the time in Myanmar such associations or unions were not allowed.

2.2 In January 2002 the complainant was granted a visa to study English at the Global Village School in Vancouver, Canada. He arrived in Canada on 14 December 2002, on a student visa.

2.3 In February 2003 he applied for refugee status after his mother had informed him that the Government of Myanmar was looking for him for distributing anti-government literature. She told him that the authorities had detained his father and interrogated him about the complainant's activities. His mother also told him that one of his friends had been arrested.

2.4 The complainant's application for refugee status was dismissed on 25 September 2003. Counsel explains that the complainant did not highlight that he was a member of a soccer 'union' at the time of his application for refugee status, as he thought that 'relevant organizations' for the purposes of the application meant political organizations, not sporting organizations. He did not consider at the time that he was at risk for his involvement in the soccer 'union', and only learned of a warrant for his arrest based on his involvement in the soccer 'union' at a later stage. On 20 July 2004 the complainant made submissions under the pre-removal risk assessment (PRRA) procedure, including new evidence in the form of a letter from his father and a copy of the warrant for his arrest dated 29 December 2003. The PRRA was denied on 17 September 2004. At the hearing on 29 September 2004 the complainant was advised to return by 7 October 2004 with an itinerary to return to Myanmar. He was scheduled to leave Canada on 26 October 2004.

2.5 The complainant applied for leave and judicial review of the PRRA decision before the Federal Court of Canada on 14 October 2004, which was due to be heard on 25 October 2004. In the meantime, on 22 October 2004 a consent agreement was reached between the complainant and the Minister of

Citizenship and Immigration. As part of the agreement, the complainant was required to provide new PRRA submissions by 5 November 2004, which was extended to 26 November 2004, while a stay of deportation was granted on 22 October 2004. The second PRRA was denied on 8 June 2005. The complainant was advised that he was to complete his departure requirements on 18 June 2005. An application for leave and judicial review of this PRRA decision was filed at the Federal Court on 30 June 2005. A motion to stay the removal was filed in the Federal Court on 8 July 2005. In the meantime, the complainant was notified by the Canada Border Services Agency that a travel document to Myanmar had been obtained on his behalf, and that he was scheduled to be deported on 18 July 2005.[1]

2.6 On 15 July 2005 the Federal Court granted the stay of execution of the removal order, on the basis that the officer who performed the complainant's PRRA assessment had attributed little weight to the arrest warrant and had not clearly indicated whether the warrant was genuine or not.

2.7 In light of this finding, on 3 August 2005 the Special Rapporteur on New Communications and Interim Measures of the Committee lifted the provisional interim measures previously issued by the Committee.

The complaint

3.1 The complainant argues that he would be at risk of arbitrary arrest, beatings and torture if he were returned to Myanmar, where human rights violations within the meaning of article 3, paragraph 2, of the Convention are said to be frequent.

3.2 Counsel refers to the United States Department of State Report for Burma (2004) and its reports of the human rights violations in Myanmar, including the fact that in January 2004 seven students who had formed an illegal football 'union' were given sentences ranging from seven to fifteens years imprisonment. Counsel also provides reports from non-governmental sources containing information on the human rights situation in Myanmar, and that those suspected of pro-democratic political activity are killed, arrested and detained without trial. Counsel refers to evidence from a medical training programme manager at the International Rescue Committee confirming that the Burmese Government regularly detains those deportees that it believes left Myanmar for political reasons.

3.3 The complainant highlights that he has been active in pro-democratic Burmese groups since his arrival in Canada. Specifically, he is involved in the Action Committee for Free Burma, is a supporter of the National League for Democracy, the Burmese Children Fund as well as the Myanmar Heritage Cultural Association. There is currently a warrant out for his arrest in Myanmar for his involvement with the soccer "union". In addition, the complainant argues that the fact the Canadian authorities have applied for, and received, a passport on his behalf has alerted the Myanmar authorities.

State party's observations on admissibility

4.1 On 21 December 2005, the State party contested the admissibility of the communication on two grounds. Firstly, it argues that the complainant has not exhausted domestic remedies. On 26 October 2005 the Federal Court granted the complainant's application for leave to apply for judicial review of the decision on his pre-removal risk assessment (PRRA). The hearing on the application for judicial review was scheduled for 24 January 2006. If his application is successful, the complainant will be entitled to a new PRRA assessment. If the application is not successful, the decision of the Federal Court can be appealed to the Federal Court of Appeal if the Federal Court judge certifies that the case raises a serious question of general importance, under section 74 (d) of the Immigration and Refugee Protection Act (IRPA). A decision of the Federal Court of Appeal can be appealed, with leave, to the Supreme Court of Canada. Further, if the judicial review is not successful, the complainant could also apply for a further PRRA on the basis of any new evidence that may have arisen since the last determination, although in that case he would not have the benefit of a statutory stay of removal. However, he could apply for a judicial stay of removal pending the disposition of that application. The State party refers to the jurisprudence of the Committee to find that judicial review is widely and consistently accepted to be an effective remedy.[2]

4.2 In the view of the State party, the PRRA procedure is an effective remedy which should be exhausted, contrary to the Committee's jurisprudence.[3] The State party notes that during its examination the complainant would not be removed. If successful, the complainant will become a protected person and barring serious security concerns will be eligible to apply for permanent resident status, and ultimately citizenship. It also considers that the PRRA is more comprehensive than the 'post-determination refugee claimants in

---

[1] The State party subsequently informed the Committee that the removal order had not been enforced.

[2] The State party refers to, inter alia, communication N° 183/2001 *B.S.S.* v. *Canada*, Views adopted on 12 May 2004, para. 11.6.

[3] The State party refers to communications N° 133/1999, *Falcon Ríos* v. *Canada*, Views adopted on 23 November 2004, para. 7.4, and N° 232/2003, *M.M.* v. *Canada*, admissibility decision of 7 November 2005, para. 6.4.

Canada' risk assessment, which had been considered as an effective remedy by the Human Rights Committee.[4] In the view of the State party, the Committee's decision in *Falcon Ríos* was based on the erroneous finding of fact that in the PRRA application in that case "it would only be any fresh evidence that would be taken into consideration, and otherwise the application would be rejected."[5] It is correct that pursuant to section 113 (a) of the IRPA "an application whose claim to refugee protection has been rejected may present only new evidence that arose after the rejection or was not reasonably available, or that the applicant could not reasonably have been expected in the circumstances to have presented, at the time of the rejection". However, the State party highlights that an exception has been read in by the Federal Court for those applicants whose claims for refugee protection had been rejected prior to the coming into force of the IRPA.[6] PRRA applications are considered by specially trained officers, trained to consider provisions of the Canadian Charter of Rights and Freedoms as well as of international human rights treaties. Further, the State party submits, contrary to the Committee's jurisprudence,[7] that PRRA officers are independent and impartial, referring to the jurisprudence of the Federal Court of Canada.[8] Further, PRRA is said to be a remedy governed by statutory criteria for protection, conducted pursuant to a highly regulated process and in accordance with extensive and detailed guidelines. It is subject to judicial review, and there is no authority for the proposition that a discretionary remedy cannot be an effective remedy, for purposes of admissibility.[9]

4.3 Further, the complainant has not yet filed an application on the basis of humanitarian and compassionate considerations, which the State party maintains would also be an available and effective domestic remedy. The assessment of a humanitarian and compassionate application, under section 25 of the IRPA, consists of a broad, discretionary review by an officer who determines whether a person should be granted permanent residence in Canada for humanitarian and compassionate reasons. The test is whether the person would suffer unusual, underserved or disproportionate hardship if he had to apply for a permanent resident visa from outside Canada. The assessing officer considers all the relevant information, including the person's written submissions. A humanitarian and compassionate application can be based on allegations of risk, in which case the officer assesses the risk the person may face in the country to which he would be returned. Included in the assessment are considerations of the risk of being subjected to unduly harsh or inhumane treatment, as well as current country conditions. In the event that such an application is granted, the person receives permanent residency subject to medical and security screening which can eventually lead to Canadian citizenship.

4.4 For the State party, the humanitarian and compassionate consideration application is also an effective remedy which should be exhausted, contrary to the Committee's jurisprudence.[10] The State party argues that the simple fact that a remedy is discretionary does not necessarily mean that it is not effective.[11] It invokes a judgement of the European Court of Human Rights in which the court determined that a discretionary remedy available to unsuccessful refugee claimants in Germany to prevent removal to a substantial risk of torture was adequate to fulfil Germany's obligations under article 3 of the European Convention on Human Rights.[12] Furthermore, while the decision adopted in humanitarian and compassionate applications is technically discretionary, it is in fact guided by defined standards and procedures and must be exercised in a manner consistent with the Canadian Charter of Rights and Freedoms and Canada's international obligations. In the event that the application is refused, the person can make an application for leave to apply for judicial review to

---

[4] The State party refers to communication N° 604/1994, *Nartey* v. *Canada*, inadmissibility decision of 18 July 1997, para. 6.2; communication N° 603/1994, *Badu* v. *Canada*, inadmissibility decision of 18 July 1997, para. 6.2; communication 654/1995, *Adu* v. *Canada*, inadmissibility decision of 18 July 1997, para. 6.2.
[5] Communication N° 133/1999, *Falcon Ríos* v. *Canada*, Views adopted on 23 November 2004, para. 7.5.
[6] The State party refers to *Nikolayeva* v. *Canada (Minister of Citizenship and Immigration)*, [2003] 3 F.C. 708; *Cortez* v. *Canada (Minister of Citizenship and Immigration)*, 2003 FCT 725.
[7] The State party refers to communication N° 232/2003, *M.M.* v. *Canada*, admissibility decision of 7 November 2005, para. 6.4.
[8] *Say* v. *Canada (Solicitor General)*, 2005, FC 739. The State party also refers to numerous Canadian Federal Court cases.
[9] *T.I.* v. *United Kingdom*, App. N° 43844/98, Reports of Judgements and Decisions, 2000-III; communication N° 250/2004, *A.H.* v. *Sweden*, inadmissibility decision of 15 November 2005. The State party also refers to communication N° 939/2000, *Dupuy* v. *Canada*, inadmissibility decision of 18 March 2005, para. 7.3 (HRC), concerning the effectiveness of judicial review of an application for mercy to the Minister of Justice.

[10] The State party refers, inter alia, to communication N° 133/1999, *Falcon Ríos* v. *Canada*, Views adopted on 23 November 2004, para. 7.3.
[11] The State party refers to communication N° 169/2000, *G.S.B.* v. *Canada*, discontinued by letter of the Committee dated 25 November 2005, in which a failed refugee's humanitarian and compassionate consideration application was granted.
[12] *T.I.* v. *United Kingdom*, App. N° 43844/98, Reports of Judgements and Decisions, 2000-III, para. 460.

the Federal Court on the standard of "reasonableness *simpliciter*", which means that the 'discretion' is far from absolute.

4.5 The State party challenges the Committee's reasoning in *Falcon Ríos* to the effect "that the principle of exhaustion of domestic remedies requires the petitioner to use remedies that are directly related to the risk of torture in the country to which he would be sent, not those that might allow him to stay where he is."[13] The State party argues that article 3 of the Convention obliges States not to expel, return or extradite a person to another State where there are substantial grounds for believing that he would be in danger of being subjected to torture. If an individual is permitted to stay in Canada, it follows that he will not be returned to the country where he alleges to be at risk. It should not matter on what grounds a person is not removed.[14] The State party invokes the Committee's decision in *A.R. v. Sweden* [15] where it was determined that an application for a residence permit, which could be based on humanitarian grounds but which could be decided on the grounds of a risk of torture was a remedy required to be exhausted for the purposes of admissibility. The State party argues that since a humanitarian and compassionate application may also be based and approved on the ground of risk the person may face in the country to which he would be returned, it meets the requirements set out by the Committee.

4.6 Secondly, since the complainant is not in immediate danger of removal, the communication is also inadmissible under article 22, paragraph 2, of the Convention and rule 107 (c) of the rules of procedure, as incompatible with article 3 of the Convention, and is manifestly unfounded under rule 107 (b) of the rules of procedure.

4.7 On 10 February 2006 the State party informed the Committee that the author's judicial review application was granted on 27 January 2006. Pending the completion of the new PRRA, the complainant will have the benefit of a statutory stay of removal, and is therefore not presently at risk of removal to Myanmar. Therefore, the communication is inadmissible on the basis of non-exhaustion of domestic remedies.

---

[13] Communication N° 133/1999, *Falcon Ríos* v. *Canada*, Views adopted on 23 November 2004, para. 7.4.
[14] The State party refers to *T.I.* v. *United Kingdom* (App. N° 43844/98, Reports of Judgements and Decisions, 2000-III, paras. 458–459), where the European Court of Human Rights was concerned with whether there were "procedural safeguards of any kind" protecting the applicant from removal.
[15] Communication N° 170/2000, *A.R.* v. *Sweden*, inadmissibility decision of 23 November 2001, para. 7.2.

Complainant's comments

5.1 On 12 February 2006 counsel commented on the State party's observations. She notes that the complainant submitted his humanitarian and compassionate application on 17 January 2006. Further, on 27 January 2006 the Federal Court granted the judicial review and remitted the PRRA application to be determined by a new officer. New PRRA submissions were due on 17 March 2006.

5.2 The complainant argues that the PRRA is not an effective remedy for purposes of admissibility.[16] Although PRRA officers may be considered to be specially trained, they are not experts when it comes to official documents such as warrants or summons for arrests and do make erroneous findings in such regard. The fact that, in the present case, such an error occurred during the first PRRA is evidence that such findings are not an effective remedy for those facing arrest in countries such as Myanmar. The complainant further submits that although he is now subject to a new PRRA assessment, he cannot be sure that the new PRRA officer will not make the same erroneous finding in respect of the warrant and the risk. For this reason, counsel argues that the Committee should declare the communication admissible. In the alternative, should the Committee find that the communication is inadmissible, the Committee should suspend its decision until the new PRRA determination has been made.

Issues and proceedings before the Committee

6.1 Before considering any of the allegations in a communication, the Committee against Torture must decide whether or not the communication is admissible under article 22 of the Convention. The Committee has ascertained that the same matter has not been and is not being examined under another procedure of international investigation or settlement.

6.2 In accordance with article 22, paragraph 5 (b), of the Convention, the Committee does not consider any communication unless it has ascertained that the individual has exhausted all available domestic remedies; this rule does not apply where it has been established that the application of the remedies has been unreasonably prolonged, or that it is unlikely, after a fair trial, to bring effective relief to the alleged victim.

6.3 The Committee takes note of the State party's contention that the complaint should be declared inadmissible under article 22, paragraph 5 (b), of the Convention since domestic remedies have not been exhausted, and since the complainant was granted a stay of removal and is not currently at risk of being deported. The Committee notes that the

---

[16] Referring to communication 232/2003, *M.M.* v. *Canada*, admissibility decision of 7 November 2005.

complainant's application for refugee status was refused, that pursuant to the new IRPA he has already completed two sets of PRRA procedures, and that he was granted a stay of removal each time. The Committee also notes the State party's statement that, when a refugee claim was rejected prior to the coming into force of the new IRPA, an exception has been made by the Federal Court for similar cases, which does not restrict PRRA submissions to new evidence that became available after the rejection of the refugee claim. The Committee recalls that the complainant subsequently applied for leave and judicial review of the second PRRA decision. On 15 July 2005, the Federal Court of Canada granted the stay of execution, on the grounds that the previous PRRA officer had attributed little weight to the arrest warrant and had not clearly indicated whether the warrant was genuine or not. Finally, on 27 January 2006 the Federal Court granted the judicial review and remitted the PRRA application to be determined by a new officer. In the view of the Committee, the decisions of the Federal Court support the contention that applications for leave and judicial review are not mere formalities, but that the Federal Court may, in appropriate cases, look at the substance of a case.

6.4 The Committee further notes that pursuant to section 232 of the IRPA Regulations the complainant is not at risk of deportation during the ongoing consideration of the new PRRA. It notes that the complainant has not addressed the State party's arguments about the effectiveness or availability of the PRRA, except to speculate that he cannot be sure that a third PRRA officer will not make new erroneous findings about the arrest warrant issued in Myanmar and the risks in that country. He has furnished no evidence that it would be unreasonably prolonged or unlikely to bring effective relief in his particular case. In light of this information, the Committee is satisfied with the arguments of the State party that, in this particular case, there was a remedy which was both available and effective, and which the complainant has not exhausted. Further, as the complainant is not presently at any risk of being deported, the Committee finds that the conditions in article 22, paragraph 5 (b), of the Convention have not been met.

6.5 In light of the foregoing, the Committee does not consider it necessary to address the effectiveness and availability of the humanitarian and compassionate ground application.

6.6 The Committee is therefore of the view that domestic remedies have not been exhausted, in accordance with article 22, paragraph 5 (b), of the Convention.

7. The Committee consequently decides:

(a) That the communication is inadmissible;

(b) That this decision shall be communicated to the author and to the State party.

B. Views under article 22 of the Convention against Torture

Communication N° 8/1991

Submitted by: Qani Halimi-Nedzibi
Alleged victim: The author
State party: Austria
Date of adoption of Views: 18 November 1993

Subject matter: ill-treatment during detention; evidence obtained under torture

Procedural issue: non-exhaustion of domestic remedies

Substantive issues: failure promptly to investigate allegations of torture, evidence obtained under torture

Articles of the Convention: 12, 15

1. The author of the communication is Qani Halimi-Nedzibi, a Yugoslav citizen, currently imprisoned in Austria. He claims to be a victim of a violation of articles 12 and 15 of the Convention against Torture and Other Cruel, Inhuman or Degrading Treatment or Punishment by Austria. He is represented by counsel.

The facts as submitted by the author

2.1 The author was arrested on 19 April 1988 and charged with drug trafficking. The trial at first instance opened on 23 January 1989. He was convicted on 4 July 1990 of having been in charge of an international drug-trafficking organization which allegedly operated from Austria between November 1985 and December 1987. The court of first instance (Landesgericht für Strafsachen) sentenced him to 20 years' imprisonment, plus a fine of 2 million schillings, as well as a fine of 7 million schillings in place of the customs he failed to pay. On 4 July 1991, the Court of Appeal rejected the author's appeal against his conviction, but reduced the sentence of imprisonment to a term of 18 years.

2.2 The author alleges that following his arrest in 1988 he and six named witnesses were maltreated, beaten and tortured by police inspector J.J., who was in charge of the criminal investigation. They were allegedly coerced to make incriminating statements. The author's wife, who was in her third or fourth month of pregnancy, had a miscarriage shortly after she had been interrogated by police inspector J.J. The police inspector allegedly also threatened to kill the author. The author raised these matters before the investigating judge on 5 December 1988. In particular, he stated: "I was pressured so long until I admitted that the drugs belonged to me. Inspector J.J. grabbed me by the hair and threw me against the wall; he also submerged my head in a bucket of water... I suffered an eye injury which required hospital treatment."

2.3 During the trial at first instance, author's counsel requested all statements made to inspector J.J. to be ruled inadmissible as evidence. He referred to the declaration made by Austria when ratifying the Convention against Torture in July 1987, which reads: "Austria regards article 15 of the Convention as the legal basis for the inadmissibility provided therein of the use of statements which are established to have been made as a result of torture." The court, however, ruled against his motion.

2.4 The Court of Appeal rejected counsel's plea for nullity of the judgement in first instance, taking into consideration the Austrian legislation, the non-substantiation of the allegations of ill-treatment and the fact that the evidence given by the main witnesses remained unchallenged. The Court of Appeal decided that in the circumstances the question of direct applicability (*"unmittelbare Anwendbarkeit"*) of the Convention against Torture did not arise.

The complaint

3. The author claims that the failure of the Austrian authorities promptly to investigate his allegations of torture and the refusal of the courts of first and second instance to exclude as evidence against him statements allegedly made by him and several witnesses as a result of torture constitute a violation of articles 12 and 15 of the Convention.

State party's observations and the author's comments thereon

4.1 The State party, by submission dated 27 February 1992, argued that the communication was inadmissible.

4.2 It submitted that criminal proceedings against Inspector J.J., initiated on 5 March 1990, following a complaint by the author, were still pending. The length of the investigations was attributable to the fact that difficulties had arisen in obtaining the testimonies of witnesses in the former Yugoslavia and Turkey. The State party indicated that, if Inspector J.J. would be found guilty of having ill-treated detainees in order to obtain incriminating statements, the author's case could be reopened. It argued that a retrial would constitute an effective remedy.

4.3 The State party further contended that the author could have appealed to the Constitutional Court under section 144 of the federal Constitution, as he claims to be a victim of abuse of administrative power and compulsion.

4.4 Since no appeal to the Constitutional Court had been submitted by the author and criminal proceedings against Mr. J.J. were still pending, the State party argued that the communication was inadmissible under article 22, paragraph 5 (b), of the Convention, on the ground of non-exhaustion of domestic remedies.

4.5 The State party moreover argued that the communication was inadmissible as incompatible with the provisions of the Convention. It submitted that the allegations that the witnesses had been tortured were not raised before the investigating judge, but only during the trial, after the witnesses were confronted with their statements; prior to these allegations the statements were properly deemed to be admissible evidence. Moreover, the State party argued that the witnesses gave independent, admissible evidence before the investigating judge. The State party stated that only one witness disputed the correctness of the statement made to the police; however, his statement did not incriminate the author. The correctness of other statements was not in dispute.

4.6 As concerns the author, the State party conceded that he claimed before the investigating judge to have been subjected to torture; however, according to the State party, he denied the charges against him and did not make a confession as such; thus it cannot be said that his statements were used as evidence in violation of article 15.

4.7 Finally, the State party submitted that it appears from the trial record that the jury's verdict was not based on the statements made by the witnesses who had claimed to have been subjected to torture.

5.1 In his comments on the State party's submission, counsel maintained that the communication should be declared admissible.

5.2 As regards the exhaustion of domestic remedies, counsel submitted that it was incomprehensible that the criminal proceedings against Inspector J.J. had not yet been concluded. He contended that the proceedings were unreasonably prolonged and indicated that the delay appeared to be attributable to the fact that the State party had joined the author's case with other pending matters against Inspector J.J. Thus, the difficulties in obtaining the testimony of witnesses in the former Yugoslavia and Turkey, concerning another investigation, were postponing the investigation of the author's allegations. He contended furthermore that the courts had failed to examine the allegations of torture in a timely fashion, during the criminal proceedings against the author.

5.3 Concerning the possibility of an appeal to the Constitutional Court under section 144 of the Federal Constitution, counsel argued that this appeal was not available to the author, as this procedure applies to administrative, not to criminal law. Moreover, counsel argued that, even if this appeal were available, it would not constitute an effective remedy, as criminal courts are not bound by the evaluation of evidence in the Constitutional Court.

5.4 Concerning the State party's contention that article 15 of the Convention had not been violated, counsel submitted that it is not clear from the text of article 15 how it should be established that a statement is made as a result of torture. He argued that it is sufficient that the author adduces some evidence indicating that a statement was given as a result of torture. In this connection, he referred to the difficulty for a victim to prove that he has been subjected to torture, owing to the isolation in detention and the absence of independent witnesses during interrogation. He further stated that article 15 applies to "any statement", not only to confessions or false statements, as the State party seemed to imply. He finally argued that it could not be said that the author's allegations were examined by the jury during his trial, as Inspector J.J. was not questioned on the issue, nor confronted with witnesses.

Committee's admissibility decision

6.1 At its eighth session, the Committee considered the admissibility of the communication. It ascertained that the same matter had not been or was not being examined under another procedure of international investigation or settlement, and that a case concerning the author which was pending before the European Commission of Human Rights concerned a different matter.

6.2 The Committee further considered that article 22, paragraph 5 (b), of the Convention did not, in the circumstances of the case, preclude the Committee from considering the communication on the merits. In this context, the Committee considered that there had been an unreasonable delay in the conduct of investigations into the author's allegations of torture, which were made in December 1988, and that no further effective remedies appeared to be available.

7. On 5 May 1992, the Committee therefore declared the communication admissible. It noted that the facts as presented by the author might raise issues under articles 12 and 15 and also under other provisions of the Convention.

State party's submissions on the merits and the author's comments

8.1 The State party, on 10 November 1992 and 4 January 1993, reiterates that the author made his complaint of ill-treatment months after its alleged occurrence. It submits that the author has suffered from eye trouble since childhood and that the medical records show that he complained about his left eye for the first time on 16 September 1988. As a result of examinations by the prison doctor on 14 November 1988, aphykia (the absence of the lens of the eye) and ablatio retinae (detachment of the retina) were found. Subsequently, after examinations at the Vienna Eye Hospital it was concluded that the author's left eye was blind. The State party forwarded a copy of the medical record in the author's case.

8.2 With regard to the investigations into the author's allegations, the State party states that the criminal proceedings against Inspector J.J. and a colleague were stopped by the Prosecutor's office on 6 November 1992, on the ground that following preliminary investigations the allegations were found to be totally unsubstantiated. At the preliminary hearing, the interpreter who had been present during the interrogations testified that the conduct by the police officers had been correct and that she had never witnessed any acts of torture. Only two witnesses, both co-defendants of the author, claimed to have been given one or two blows by Inspector J.J. All other witnesses gave exonerating evidence. No medical evidence was available to substantiate the allegations.

9.1 In his comments on the State party's submissions, counsel maintains his claim that the author's eye injury was caused by Inspector J.J. at the end of June or the beginning of July 1988, when the author was hit with a pistol and his head was banged against a table.

9.2 Counsel further claims that some witnesses, who could have corroborated the author's allegations, were not called by the Prosecutor during the preliminary investigations against Inspector J.J. Among these persons is the author's wife, who no longer lives in Austria.

10. On 26 April 1993, the Committee decided to request the State party to appoint, in consultation with the author's counsel, an independent expert in ophthalmology in order to determine the date of and the origin of the eye injury. It further referred to article 12 of the Convention and requested the State party to submit written explanations clarifying the delay in initiating the investigation of the author's allegations.

11.1 On 27 July 1993, the State party forwarded to the Committee an expert opinion prepared by an ophthalmologist. His report shows that the author's eye was already blind in March 1989, when he was first examined at the Eye Hospital, as a result of an old retinal detachment and that it had begun to show the first signs of an external squint. The State party concludes that the eye must have gone blind before 1988, since a blind eye does not begin to squint until after a long period of blindness.

11.2 The State party recalls that the author was arrested on 19 April 1988 on the suspicion of being involved in internationally organized heroin trafficking. On 5 December 1988, the author for the first time claimed to have been subjected to torture and threatened by Inspector J.J. Neither the *Journalrichter* nor the investigating judge had observed any signs of ill-treatment. The author repeated his allegations in a number of written submissions to the Public Prosecutor, the Attorney General and the Minister of Justice. Police Inspector J.J. and one of his colleagues were questioned on these charges by the investigating judge on 16 February 1989; they rejected the accusations made against them.

11.3 The State party submits that, since no signs of an injury could be established and the police officers denied the charges, no strong suspicion existed that an act of torture had been committed. It was therefore decided that the criminal proceedings against the author could proceed. During the trial against the author, from 8 to 11 January 1990, witnesses testified that they had been ill-treated by Inspector J.J. and his colleague. As a result, preliminary investigations against the two policemen were instituted on 5 March 1990.

12. In his comments on the State party's submission, dated 21 October 1993, counsel submits that the State party had not consulted him about the choice of the medical expert. He further states that the expert's report does not necessarily exclude the author's version of events. He emphasizes that the author received medical treatment in prison after having been ill-treated but that the records of this treatment were not kept.

Examination of the merits

13.1 The Committee has considered the communication in the light of all information made available to it by the parties, as required under article 22, paragraph 4, of the Convention.

13.2 The Committee notes that the author has claimed that he was ill-treated after his arrest and that as a consequence he suffered an eye injury. The State party has denied the alleged ill-treatment and has claimed that the author's eye injury dates from childhood. It has submitted an expert report, in which it is concluded that the author's left eye, with almost absolute certainty ("*mit an Sicherheit grenzender Wahrscheinlichkeit*") had been completely blind already in 1988, owing to retinal detachment.

13.3 The Committee observes that the competence, independence and conclusions of the specialist in ophthalmology have not been challenged. While noting with regret that the State party failed to consult with the author's counsel before appointing the specialist, as the Committee had requested in its decision of 26 April 1993, due weight must be given to his conclusions.

13.4 On the basis of the information before it, the Committee cannot conclude that the allegations of ill-treatment have been sustained. In the circumstances, the Committee finds no violation of article 15 of the Convention.

13.5 It remains to be determined whether the State party complied with its duty to proceed to a prompt and impartial investigation of the author's allegations that he had been subjected to torture, as provided in article 12 of the Convention. The Committee notes that the author made his allegations before the investigating judge on 5 December 1988. Although the investigating judge questioned the police officers about the allegations on 16 February 1989, no investigation took place until 5 March 1990, when criminal proceedings against the police officers were instituted. The Committee considers that a delay of 15 months before an investigation of allegations of torture is initiated, is unreasonably long and not in compliance with the requirement of article 12 of the Convention.

14. The Committee against Torture, acting under article 22, paragraph 7, of the Convention against Torture and Other Cruel, Inhuman or Degrading Treatment or Punishment, is of the view that the facts before it disclose a violation of article 12 of the Convention.

15. The State party is requested to ensure that similar violations do not occur in the future.

16. Pursuant to rule 111, paragraph 5, of its rules of procedure, the Committee wishes to receive information, within 90 days, on any relevant measures taken by the State party in conformity with the Committee's Views.

Communication N° 13/1993

Submitted by: Balabou Mutombo
Alleged victim: The author
State party concerned: Switzerland
Date of adoption of Views: 27 April 1994

Subject matter: deportation of complainant to the former Zaire with alleged risk of torture

Procedural issue: none

Substantive issue: risk of torture after deportation in receiving State

Article of the Convention: 3

1. The author of the communication (dated 18 October 1993) is Balabou Mutombo, a Zairian citizen, born on 24 November 1961, at present living in Switzerland and seeking recognition as a refugee. He claims to be a victim of a violation by Switzerland of article 3 of the Convention against Torture. He is represented by counsel.

The facts as submitted by the author

2.1 The author states that he has been a member of the Zairian Armed Forces since 1982. In 1988, he clandestinely became a member of the political movement Union pour la démocratie et le progrès social (UDPS), as he felt discriminated against because of his ethnic background (Luba). His father had been a member of the movement since its launch in 1982 and was allegedly forced to retire as a magistrate at the Kinshasa Magistrate's Court (Tribunal de Grande Instance) because of that affiliation. The author participated in several demonstrations and attended illegal meetings.

2.2 On 20 June 1989, the author was arrested by three members of the Division Spéciale Présidentielle, when he was about to deliver a letter from his father to Mr. Etienne Tshisekedi, a founding member and leader of the UDPS. He was detained in the military camp of Tshatsi, where he was locked up in a cell of one square metre. During the four days that followed, he was tortured by his interrogators, whom he mentions by name. He was subjected to electric shocks, beaten with a rifle, and his testicles were bruised until he lost consciousness. On 24 June 1989, he was brought before a military tribunal, found guilty of conspiracy against the State and sentenced to 15 years' imprisonment. He was transferred to the military prison of Ndolo, where he was detained for seven months. Although the author had lost part of his eyesight and suffered a head injury caused by the torture, he was not given any medical treatment. On 20 January 1990, he was released under the condition that he present himself twice a week at the Auditorat militaire of Mantete. In February 1990, he sought medical treatment for his eye injury at the General Hospital Mama Yemo.

2.3   Subsequently, the author's father and brothers suggested that he leave Kinshasa, to avoid the police finding other members of the movement by following him. They also feared for the author's security. On 30 March 1990, the author left Zaire, leaving behind his family, including his two children, who live with his father; after 15 days he arrived at Luanda, where he stayed with friends for three months. A friend provided him with a visa for Italy, where he arrived on 29 July 1990, using the passport of his friend. On 7 August 1990, he illegally crossed the border to enter Switzerland; on 8 August 1990, he applied for recognition as a refugee in Switzerland. In the course of that month he learned that his father had been detained after his departure.

2.4   The author was heard by the Cantonal Office for Asylum-seekers in Lausanne on 10 October 1990. He submitted a medical report written by a medical doctor in Switzerland indicating that the scars on his body corresponded with the alleged torture. A report by an ophthalmologist indicated that the author had an eye injury, caused by a trauma, which, according to the author, was caused by a blow to his head during the interrogation in June 1989. On 31 January 1992, the Federal Refugee Office (Office fédéral des réfugiés) rejected his application and ordered his removal from Switzerland. It considered that, even if the author had been detained in the military prison of Ndolo, it was unlikely that he had been imprisoned for political reasons, since the International Committee of the Red Cross (ICRC), which had visited the prison in November 1989, had stated that it did not visit him, since he apparently did not belong to the category of prisoners which fell under the mandate of ICRC. The Refugee Office further doubted the authenticity of the provisional release order, which the author had submitted as evidence of his detention. With regard to the author's return to Zaire, the Refugee Office considered that there were no indications that he would be exposed to punishment or treatment prohibited by article 3 of the European Convention for the Protection of Human Rights and Fundamental Freedoms.

2.5   On 6 March 1992, the author appealed the decision. On 10 August 1992, the decision to expel him was stayed, but on 2 June 1993, the Commission of Appeal in Refugee Matters (Commission suisse de recours en matière d'asile) dismissed the author's appeal. On 24 June 1993, the author was informed that he had to leave Switzerland before 15 September 1993, failing which he would be subject to expulsion. The author's request for a review of the decision, on the ground that the authorities had not sufficiently taken into account essential documents, such as a report of Amnesty International and medical reports, was dismissed on 13 September 1993. On 17 September 1993, the author received permission to stay in Switzerland until 17 October 1993.

The complaint

3.1   The author claims that a real risk exists that he would be subjected to torture or that his security would be endangered if he were to be returned to his country. It is submitted that evidence exists that there is a consistent pattern of gross and massive violations of human rights in Zaire, which, according to article 3, paragraph 2, of the Convention against Torture, are circumstances which a State party should take into account when deciding on expulsion. The author contends that on this basis alone the Swiss authorities should refrain from expelling him.

3.2   In a letter to counsel, dated 3 November 1993, Amnesty International supports the author's arguments that he would be exposed to a risk of torture upon return to Zaire. It considers the author's story credible and emphasizes that the general situation in Zaire is one of violence and repression. Amnesty International submits in particular that hundreds of soldiers suspected of sympathizing with the opposition to the rule of President Mobuto have been arrested and many of them are detained in secret places. In Amnesty International's opinion, members of the opposition are subject to repression and the simple fact of seeking recognition as a refugee is seen as a subversive act.

3.3   Since the author could be expelled at any moment, he asked the Committee to request Switzerland to take interim measures of protection and not to expel him while his communication is under consideration by the Committee.

Issues and proceedings before the Committee

4.   During its eleventh session, on 18 November 1993, the Committee decided to solicit from the State party clarifications or observations as to the admissibility of the communication, and, in the specific circumstances of the case, to request the State party, under rule 108, paragraph 9, not to expel the author while his communication was under consideration by the Committee. The State party was also invited to submit explanations or statements as to the merits of the communication, in case it had no objections to its admissibility.

5.   On 18 February 1994, the State party informed the Committee that it would comply with the Committee's request not to expel the author and

that it would not contest the admissibility of the communication, since the author had exhausted all available domestic remedies.

State party's observations on the merits of the communication

6.1 By submission of 7 March 1994, the State party recalls that the Federal Refugee Office has, on 31 January 1992, rejected the author's application to be recognized as a refugee, on the basis that there were several contradictions in his testimony, that the principal document, the provisional release order, had no legal value, that the medical certificates were not persuasive and that in general the author's allegations were not reliable. The Federal Refugee Office was of the opinion that the situation in Zaire was not one of systematic violence.

6.2 As to the author's specific claim that his expulsion would be in violation of article 3 of the Convention, the State party notes that the author has not raised this objection before any of the national authorities, but has only invoked article 3 of the European Convention for the Protection of Human Rights and Fundamental Freedoms. The State party refers to the author's argument that the existence in a State of a consistent pattern of human rights violations would by itself be sufficient reason not to return anyone to that State. The State party considers the issue raised by the author of great importance for the interpretation and application of article 3 of the Convention; it points out that, if the general situation in a country alone would suffice to conclude that substantial grounds exist for believing that someone, if returned, would be subjected to torture, the requirement of article 3, paragraph 1, that the belief concerns the individual personally, would no longer have a separate meaning. The State party concludes therefore that the interpretation as suggested by the author is incompatible with article 3 and with a systematic and teleological interpretation thereof. It submits that article 3, paragraph 1, stipulates the conditions in which a State party is precluded from expelling an individual from its territory, whereas paragraph 2 prescribes how to appreciate the evidence when determining the existence of such conditions.

6.3 The State party submits that, even if a consistent pattern of gross, flagrant or mass violations of human rights exists in a country, this should only be taken as an indication when examining all the circumstances to determine whether the person to be returned would be in concrete danger of being tortured. The existence of the "substantial grounds" of paragraph 1 has to be determined in the light of all the circumstances in a particular case. The State party argues that only in exceptional circumstances would a reference to a situation of gross violations of human rights suffice to prove the existence of substantial grounds to believe that a person would be in danger of being subjected to torture, for instance if the violations are directed against a particular group of persons in a confined territory and the individual to be returned belongs to that group. The State party submits that this is not the case with the author of the present communication.

6.4 In support of its interpretation of article 3 of the Convention, the State party refers to the jurisprudence of the European Commission of Human Rights, establishing that a decision to expel an asylum-seeker may give rise to an issue under article 3 of the European Convention for the Protection of Human Rights and Fundamental Freedoms where substantial grounds have been shown for believing that he faces a real risk of being subjected to torture. In the Commission's opinion, a reference to the general situation in a country is not sufficient to preclude the return of an individual, as it must be shown that the individual himself is at risk. The State party further refers to the decision of the European Court of Human Rights in *Vilvarajah et al. v. United Kingdom*, where it was held that a mere possibility of ill-treatment because of the general situation in a country was not in itself sufficient to give rise to a violation of article 3. The State party argues that article 3 of the Convention against Torture does not provide a wider protection than article 3 of the European Convention. It adds that the author himself is apparently of the same opinion, since he did not deem it necessary to invoke article 3 of the Convention against Torture while exhausting his domestic remedies, but only invoked article 3 of the European Convention.

6.5 The State party submits that the author of the present communication does not have substantial grounds to believe that he himself would be in danger of being subjected to torture in case of his return to Zaire. Even taking into account the general situation in Zaire, the State party claims that the evidence adduced by the author does not support his allegations. In this context, the State party submits that it has, on several occasions, contacted its embassy at Kinshasa before taking its decision not to grant the author asylum. The embassy contacted an informant from the human rights movement in Zaire, who advised the embassy that the author's story was highly unlikely. He affirmed that the provisional release order was a document without any legal value and that all released prisoners were provided with a "*fiche de libération*", which the author did not possess. Moreover, the signature on the order produced by the author does not correspond with the signature of the director of the military prison in which the author allegedly was detained. The State party further submits that the author's name does not figure in the Ndolo prison registers for 1989 and

1990 and that the author's father has declared that his son has never been detained in a military prison. It is also submitted that the drawing made by the author of the prison lacks important elements such as the desk of the prison's director and the division of the prison in two parts, one for ordinary soldiers and one for officers.

6.6 As regards the author's father, it was found that he had retired, not for political reasons, but pursuant to the applicable rules for civil servants. The leaders of the UDPS subsection to which the author's father geographically belongs have stated that he was not a UDPS member.

6.7 Moreover, the State party argues that, even if the author's story is true, it still does not indicate that a real risk exists that he will be subjected to torture upon his return. The State party argues that the fact that the author was provisionally released after seven months, while having been sentenced to 15 years' imprisonment, shows that such a risk is minimal, even if he was subjected to torture after his arrest in 1989. The State party recalls that the author has admitted having received a new military uniform upon his release. The State party further refers to the author's communication to the Committee, and concludes that he left Zaire mainly because he did not want to endanger his family and friends, not because he was personally at risk.

6.8 As regards the general situation in Zaire, the State party acknowledges that the country suffers from internal political unrest and from incidental outbursts of violence. However, it submits that this cannot lead to the conclusion that a personal risk exists for the author that he will be tortured after his return. In this context, the State party refers to a recent letter from the Office of the United Nations High Commissioner for Refugees, in which it expressed concern for the situation in Zaire and recommended great prudence in the return of persons to Zaire, but did not recommend a suspension of expulsions to Zaire altogether.

7.1 In his comments (dated 20 April 1994) on the State party's submission, counsel argues that, even if Mr. Mutombo did not invoke the Convention against Torture but only the European Convention for the Protection of Human Rights and Fundamental Freedoms before the national authorities, the Swiss authorities were, according to the Swiss legal system, nevertheless under an obligation to apply the Convention against Torture. Counsel further contests the State party's argument that article 3 of the Convention against Torture does not provide a wider protection than article 3 of the European Convention. He argues that the articles of the Convention against Torture must be interpreted in such a way as to give the most effective protection against torture. In this context, counsel notes that article 3 of the European Convention prohibits torture but does not directly deal with the issue of expulsion or *"refoulement"*. Its application to situations of expulsion has been developed only in the jurisprudence of the European Commission and the European Court on Human Rights, which have been reluctant to interpret it broadly. Since article 3 of the Convention against Torture contains an explicit protection against forced return to a country where an individual would be at risk of being subjected to torture, counsel argues that this necessarily has to lead to a different, wider interpretation.

7.2 Counsel further argues that the criteria to establish the existence of a risk that an individual, if returned, would be subjected to torture are not the same under the two conventions. The jurisprudence on the basis of article 3 of the European Convention has established that a risk must be concrete and serious to engage the applicability of article 3. Under article 3 of the Convention against Torture the existence of substantial grounds for believing that such risk exists is sufficient to prohibit the individual's return; among these grounds is the existence in the country concerned of a consistent pattern of gross, flagrant or mass violations of human rights. Counsel contests the State party's interpretation of the second paragraph of article 3, and argues that the existence of systematic human rights violations in a country sufficiently shows the existence of substantial grounds for believing that a person would be in danger of being subjected to torture, on the basis of which the person's return to that country is prohibited.

7.3 Counsel further argues that article 3 of the Convention against Torture lays the burden of proof on the State party, thereby reinforcing the protection of the individual. In this connection, counsel notes that it is difficult for an individual to prove the existence of the danger of being subjected to torture. As regards the State party's contention that Mr. Mutombo's story is not credible, and its investigation to adduce evidence to that effect, counsel notes that the secretive nature of the investigation and the use of an anonymous informant makes it impossible for him to verify the credibility and the objectivity of the information furnished. Counsel furthermore doubts that the informant would have had access to the register of the Ndolo prison, which normally would not be open to anyone from the outside. He therefore requests that the State party disclose the name of the informant and the name of the human rights movement of which he is a member, failing which the information provided by the State party should not be taken into account by the Committee. To substantiate the credibility of the author's story, counsel refers to the initial communication and the position taken by Amnesty International in support of it.

7.4 Counsel further argues that the fact that the author was conditionally released from detention does not diminish the risk of being subjected to torture upon return to the country. In this connection, counsel points out that the situation in Zaire has considerably deteriorated since 1990 and that it is the present danger facing the author upon his return to Zaire which is at issue. To support his argument, counsel refers to several reports written by non-governmental organizations and to the report concerning Zaire prepared by the Secretary-General for the United Nations Commission on Human Rights,[1] which indicate that torture and ill-treatment of detainees are common practice in Zaire and are perpetrated with impunity. Counsel argues that the State party's reference to the failure of the United Nations High Commissioner for Refugees to recommend the suspension of all expulsions to Zaire is irrelevant, because this was related to another case and had nothing to do with the author's situation. Counsel further states that the language used in the letter from the High Commissioner is strongly dissuasive of all expulsions to Zaire.

7.5 Finally, counsel refers to the medical report submitted by the author and written by a Swiss medical specialist, indicating that the author's injuries correspond with the alleged torture. He notes that the State party has rejected this report as not persuasive without even conducting a re-examination.

Decision on admissibility and examination of the merits

8. Before considering any claims contained in a communication, the Committee against Torture must decide whether or not it is admissible under article 22 of the Convention. The Committee has ascertained, as it is required to do under article 25, paragraph 5 (a), of the Convention, that the same matter has not been and is not being examined under another procedure of international investigation or settlement. The Committee notes that the State party has not raised any objections to the admissibility of the communication and that it has confirmed that the author has exhausted all available domestic remedies. The Committee therefore finds that no obstacles to the admissibility of the present communication exist and proceeds with the consideration of the merits of the communication.

9.1 The Committee observes that it is not called upon to determine whether the author's rights under the Convention have been violated by Zaire, which is not a State party to the Convention. The issue before the Committee is whether the expulsion or return of the author of the communication to Zaire would violate the obligation of Switzerland under article 3 of the Convention not to expel or return a person to another State where there are substantial grounds for believing that he would be in danger of being subjected to torture.

9.2 The Committee is aware of the concerns of the State party that the implementation of article 3 of the Convention might be abused by asylum-seekers. The Committee considers that, even if there are doubts about the facts adduced by the author, it must ensure that his security is not endangered.

9.3 The relevant provisions are contained in article 3:

"1. No State party shall expel, return ('*refouler*') or extradite a person to another State where there are substantial grounds for believing that he would be in danger of being subjected to torture.

"2. For the purpose of determining whether there are such grounds, the competent authorities shall take into account all relevant considerations including, where applicable, the existence in the State concerned of a consistent pattern of gross, flagrant or mass violations of human rights."

The Committee must decide, pursuant to paragraph 1 of article 3, whether there are substantial grounds for believing that Mr. Mutombo would be in danger of being subjected to torture. In reaching this conclusion, the Committee must take into account all relevant considerations, pursuant to paragraph 2 of article 3, including the existence of a consistent pattern of gross, flagrant or mass violations of human rights. The aim of the determination, however, is to establish whether the individual concerned would be personally at risk of being subjected to torture in the country to which he would return. It follows that the existence of a consistent pattern of gross, flagrant or mass violations of human rights in a country does not as such constitute a sufficient ground for determining that a person would be in danger of being subjected to torture upon his return to that country; additional grounds must exist that indicate that the individual concerned would be personally at risk. Similarly, the absence of a consistent pattern of gross violations of human rights does not mean that a person cannot be considered to be in danger of being subjected to torture in his specific circumstances.

9.4 The Committee considers that in the present case substantial grounds exist for believing that the author would be in danger of being subjected to torture. The Committee has noted the author's ethnic background, alleged political affiliation and detention history as well as the fact, which has not been disputed by the State party, that he appears to have deserted from the army and to have left Zaire in a clandestine manner and, when formulating an application for asylum, to have adduced arguments

---

[1] E/CN.4/1994/49.

which may be considered defamatory towards Zaire. The Committee considers that, in the present circumstances, his return to Zaire would have the foreseeable and necessary consequence of exposing him to a real risk of being detained and tortured. Moreover, the belief that "substantial grounds" exist within the meaning of article 3, paragraph 1, is strengthened by "the existence in the State concerned of a consistent pattern of gross, flagrant or mass violations of human rights", within the meaning of article 3, paragraph 2.

9.5 The Committee is aware of the serious human rights situation in Zaire, as reported, inter alia, to the United Nations Commission on Human Rights by the Secretary-General[2] and by the Commission's Special Rapporteur on extrajudicial, summary or arbitrary executions,[3] the Special Rapporteur on the question of torture[4] and the Working Group on Enforced or Involuntary Disappearances.[5] The Committee notes the serious concern expressed by the Commission in this regard, in particular in respect of the persistent practices of arbitrary arrest and detention, torture and inhuman treatment in detention centres, disappearances and summary and arbitrary executions, which prompted the Commission to decide, in March 1994, to appoint a special rapporteur specifically to examine and to report on the human rights situation in Zaire. The Committee cannot but conclude that a consistent pattern of gross, flagrant or mass violations does exist in Zaire and that the situation may be deteriorating.

9.6 Moreover, the Committee considers that, in view of the fact that Zaire is not a party to the Convention, the author would be in danger, in the event of expulsion to Zaire, not only of being subjected to torture but of no longer having the legal possibility of applying to the Committee for protection.

9.7 The Committee therefore concludes that the expulsion or return of the author to Zaire in the prevailing circumstances would constitute a violation of article 3 of the Convention against Torture and Other Cruel, Inhuman or Degrading Treatment or Punishment.

10. In the light of the above, the Committee is of the view that, in the prevailing circumstances, the State party has an obligation to refrain from expelling Balabou Mutombo to Zaire, or to any other country where he runs a real risk of being expelled or returned to Zaire or of being subjected to torture.

---

[2] Ibid.
[3] E/CN.4/1994/7, paras. 653–662.
[4] E/CN.4/1994/31, paras. 657–664.
[5] E/CN.4/1994/26, paras. 509–513.

Communication N° 34/1995

Submitted by: Seid Mortesa Aemei
Alleged victims: The author and his family
State party: Switzerland
Date of adoption of Views: 9 May 1997

Subject matter: deportation of complainant and his family to Iran with alleged risk of torture

Procedural issue: none

Substantive issue: risk of torture upon deportation

Article of the Convention: 3

1. The author of the communication is Seid Mortesa Aemei, an Iranian citizen born on 1 February 1957, currently residing in Switzerland, where he seeks asylum. He claims that his return to Iran after dismissal of his refugee claim would constitute a violation of article 3 of the Convention by Switzerland. He submits the communication also on behalf of his wife. He is represented by counsel.

The facts as submitted

2.1 The author became a People's Mojahedin activist in Iran in 1979. On 20 June 1981, after he had participated in a demonstration by the Mojahedin, he was arrested and kept in detention for 25 days. Thereafter, he had to abandon his university studies. In 1982, he threw a Molotov cocktail into the house of a senior officer of the Revolutionary Committee.

2.2 On 4 April 1983, the author was again arrested and his house was searched. He claims that he was ill-treated during the interrogations and, in particular, that he was caned after having his feet and head submerged in ice, that the next day the police officers extinguished cigarettes on his body while he was dressed only in underclothes, that he still bears the scars from those burns, and that his wife was only allowed to visit him after six months. Subsequently, he was convicted for his political activities and for stealing the licence plate of a car and sentenced to two years' imprisonment.

2.3 Seven months after his release, the author's brother-in-law fled the country, and the author was detained for three hours and questioned about the whereabouts of his brother-in-law. The author then moved to Tehran, but returned to his home town after three years. In February or March 1989, he was recognized by a client of his father's firm as the person who had thrown the Molotov cocktail seven years earlier. In panic, he fled to Tehran. He claims that his parents were visited regularly by the police and questioned about his whereabouts. After a year, he decided to leave the country, also because his son, who was born on 23 January 1984, had reached school age and he was afraid that his son's enrolment in school would lead to the police discovering his whereabouts. With a false passport he fled the country, together with his wife and their two children, and applied for asylum in Switzerland on 2 May 1990.

2.4 On 27 August 1992, his application was refused by the Federal Office for Refugees, which considered his story not credible and full of inconsistencies. It also considered that the author's wife was not aware of any political activities on the part of her husband. The Appeal Commission rejected his appeal on 26 January 1993, considering that the author's claim and story were illogical and revealed no practical experience in illegal political activities and were moreover full of contradictions.

2.5 On 26 April 1993, the author, represented by the Beratungsstelle für Asylsuchende der Region Basel, filed a request for reconsideration, based on his activities in Switzerland for the Armenian and Persian Aid Organization (APHO), which, according to the author, is considered an illegal organization in Iran. The author refers in this connection to three attempts to murder the leader of the APHO in Zurich and claims that these attempts prove that APHO members are being persecuted by Iran. The author stated that he had distributed leaflets and helped run various APHO stands, notably at a demonstration in Bern. In support of his statements he presented an APHO membership card and stand permits issued in his name, and photos showing his activities. He also said that incidents involving representatives of the Government of Iran had occurred in May 1991 (when a friend of the brother of the President of the Iranian Council of Ministers threatened APHO members with a pistol) and in June 1992 (when the Iranian consul visited the APHO stand and attempted to identify the participants). The author stated that he had reported the incident to the police the same day, in his capacity as the person in charge of the stand. In his request for review he alleged that his activity within the APHO would render him liable to treatment contrary to article 3 of the Convention if he returned to Iran.

2.6 By a decision of 5 May 1993, the Federal Office for Refugees refused to consider his request for review. The Appeals Commission also declared his application to be ill-founded by a decision of 10 August 1994. The author states that he has since been contacted by the police for the purpose of the preparation of his departure from Switzerland.

The complaint

3. The author is afraid that he will be questioned about his political activities when he returns to Iran. He adds that torture during interrogations is common in Iran. Furthermore, he is afraid that he will be charged with the Molotov cocktail attack of 1982 and that he will consequently be sentenced to a long term of imprisonment or even death. He adds that the mere act of requesting asylum in another country is considered an offence in Iran.

Procedural issues

4.1 On 22 November 1995, the Committee transmitted the communication to the State party for its observations.

4.2 In its observations of 22 January 1996, the State party contests the admissibility of the communication, stating that since the author had not, in the course of the ordinary asylum procedure before the national bodies, mentioned his fear that his political activities in Switzerland would render him liable to torture if he returned to Iran, he had not exhausted domestic remedies. The State party explains that this point should have been made during the procedure to establish the right of asylum. Since the point was not mentioned until the request for review, the authorities were not able to consider it, as the author's activities within the APHO did not constitute a new development in the light of the criteria established by the jurisprudence of the Federal Court.

4.3 In its observations, the State party nevertheless submits "that is a subjective ground under article 8 (a) of the Asylum Act, which in this connection provides that 'asylum shall not be granted to a foreigner when ... only his conduct following his departure would justify his being considered a refugee within the meaning of article 3'. According to case law and doctrine, the concept of 'subjective grounds occurring after flight from the country' covers situations in which the threat of persecution could not have been the cause of the departure of the asylum-seeker but results from his subsequent conduct. Although such grounds are not relevant to the granting of asylum under the exclusion clause of the above-mentioned article 8 (a), an applicant who invokes subjective grounds may nevertheless remain in Switzerland, by virtue of the non-return principle, if the conditions of article 45 of the Asylum Act are met. The allegation of 'subjective grounds', like the grounds which prompted the applicant to leave his country, must nevertheless satisfy the requirements of asylum procedure, among which are those relating to the obligation to cooperate. In accordance with article 12 (b) of the Asylum Act, the applicant is required to cooperate in the verification of the facts; to this end, he has in particular to explain, at his hearing, his grounds for asylum and the reasons which prompted him to request asylum."

4.4 The State party also contests Mrs. Aemei's status as author of the communication.

4.5 In a letter of 1 March 1996, counsel refutes the State party's argument contesting Mrs. Aemei's status as author of the communication on the grounds that she has not claimed any ground for asylum peculiar to herself. Counsel further states that if Mrs. Aemei were to be sent back to Iran, she would be liable to the same risks as her husband, or even greater risks, and that the State party itself has acknowledged that the applicant's subsequent conduct in Switzerland does not constitute a ground for asylum under Swiss legislation. He also maintains that the applicant had no reason to mention his political activities in Switzerland during the asylum procedures and had always been questioned about his past and about facts which could have supported his application for asylum.

4.6 Counsel points out that in any case the non-return obligation is an absolute obligation. Although the argument of the author's political activities in Switzerland was submitted late and hence, for procedural reasons, could not be taken into account in relation to the asylum decision, counsel is of the opinion that the rejection of the asylum application does not mean that the person can now be sent back to his country. He points out that Swiss legislation offers alternatives such as the possibility of a residence permit for humanitarian reasons (Asylum Act, art. 17, para. 2) or temporary admission (Asylum Act, art. 18, para. 1). Counsel also draws attention to the fact that physical integrity must not be endangered for procedural reasons. The risk that an asylum-seeker will misuse the procedure should not be overestimated, especially as few asylum-seekers can point to events as serious as those referred to by the authors in the case at hand.

4.7 After considering the observations of the parties, the Committee decided, at its sixteenth session, to suspend consideration of the communication pending the result of the author's requests for reconsideration in the light of his political activities in Switzerland. The Committee also requests information from the State party on domestic remedies and asked the applicant to provide additional information concerning his asylum applications in Switzerland on the basis of his political activities in Switzerland. The Committee also asked the State party not to expel the author and his family while their communication is under consideration.

Further observations by counsel

5.1 In a letter of 5 August 1996, counsel explains that the author did not mention his activities within the APHO in the course of the ordinary procedure for obtaining refugee status, which led to the decision of the Swiss Appeal Commission of 26 January 1993, because he had not been aware that those activities would be a determining factor. The situation changed after the decision, when he learned that he would have to return to Iran. At that point, he realized that because of his political activities in Iran before 1990 and, in particular, because of his political activities in Switzerland since 1990, he and his wife ran a very great risk of being subjected to acts contrary to article 3 of the Convention if they returned to Iran. Counsel repeats that since 1990 the author has been active in the APHO, which is considered an illegal and dissident organization in Iran and whose activities in Switzerland are monitored by the Iranian secret police. The author distributed leaflets attacking the regime in Iran, and in May 1991 he was seen and threatened by the brother of the President of the Iranian Council of Ministers. In June 1992, the Iranian consul visited the APHO stand in Bern and attempted to identify the people participating in APHO activities. Counsel concludes that the author's identity is very probably known to the Iranian authorities.

5.2 Counsel adds that on 13 May 1996 the author filed an application for temporary authorization because of his son's medical problems.

State party's observations on the admissibility and validity of the communication

6.1 In its observations of 7 August 1996, the State party informs the Committee that it no longer contests the admissibility of the communication.

6.2 The State party summarizes the "facts alleged by the author" and the domestic procedures under way. As regards the points raised by the Swiss authorities, it observes that, "under article 12 (a) of the Asylum Act, an asylum-seeker must prove—or at least make out a good case—that he is a refugee within the meaning of article 3 of the Asylum Act, i.e., that he would be likely to suffer serious harm or that he has good reason to fear that he would suffer such harm, in particular because of his political opinions", and concludes that "from that standpoint, articles 3 and 12 (a) of the Asylum Act, as interpreted by the Appeal Commission, establish criteria similar to those of article 3 of the Convention, namely, the existence of serious, concrete and personal danger of persecution (art. 3, para. 1; cf. *B. Mutombo* v. *Switzerland*, ...), in the determination of which all relevant considerations must be taken into account (art. 3, para. 2), including, in particular, the likelihood that the author's statements are true (Asylum Act, art. 12 (a)) and, where appropriate, the existence of a consistent pattern of gross, flagrant or mass violations of human rights (art. 3, para. 2)".

6.3 The State party also declares that "in the present case, the Appeal Commission confirmed the decision to reject asylum on the basis of the author's statements. It considered that the grounds invoked did not make it possible to conclude that refugee status was highly probable in the author's case. The Appeal Commission took the following points into account in making its decision:

> The author's statements about his political activity were not sufficiently substantiated, since his knowledge of the political programme of the organization in which he claims to have been active was very sketchy in essential respects;

> The circumstances in which the author claims to have resumed working with the organization are at variance with what is known about the practice of movements hostile to an established political regime. The author's explanations regarding his alleged conviction following his political activity were also considered to be at variance with the facts;

> Finally, the author's wife was unable to corroborate his statements at the hearing before the Federal Office for Refugees."

The State party concludes that Swiss legislation essentially uses the same conditions for prohibiting return as those laid down in article 3 of the Convention.

6.4 The State party refers to the text of article 3 of the Convention and the Committee's practice of considering whether there are specific grounds for believing that the individual would be in *personal* danger of being subjected to acts of torture in the country to which he would be returned. The existence of a consistent pattern of gross, flagrant or mass violations of human rights does not in itself constitute a sufficient ground for concluding that a person would be in danger of being subjected to torture on his return to that country.

6.5 The State party observes that "in the present case, the author's statements concerning his political activity with the People's Mojahedin did not appear to be sufficiently substantiated in the opinion of the competent Swiss authorities". It maintains that, "in view of the inconsistency of the author's statements, they were not sufficiently plausible to cause the Swiss authorities to consider that refugee status was highly probable in the case of the author of the communication. The allegation of a risk of inhuman treatment if the author were to return to Iran, which is based principally, if not exclusively, on the consequences of his political activity cannot seriously be taken into account when it has never been established that he engaged in the political activities in question, or even that he was a member of a party that opposed the existing political regime".

The State party further submits "that the author of the present communication has produced no document with evidentiary value, either in the course of the domestic proceedings or before the Committee against Torture, relating to his political activities for the Mojahedin, or any medical certificate attesting to his having been subjected to treatment prohibited by the Convention". In the opinion of the State party, "at this stage already, the author's communication appears to be manifestly ill-founded as regards the existence of a personal, serious and concrete danger of treatment contrary to article 3 of the Convention, to which the author claims he would be exposed if he were sent back to his country".

6.6 The Swiss authorities further consider that some of the author's statements do not correspond to the facts and, because they show a lack of familiarity with established practice with regard to illegal political activities, describe them as "totally unrealistic". In particular, the author's statement that he was sentenced to only two years' imprisonment because of the judge's respect for his origins contradicts information gathered by the Swiss authorities in the course of asylum proceedings concerning Mojahedin.

6.7 Finally, the State party notes that the author's wife did not corroborate his statements about his political activities. The State party therefore concludes that the author's fear appears to be manifestly ill-founded.

6.8 With regard to the author's activities in Switzerland, the State party is not able to confirm the author's allegation that his identity is very probably known to the Iranian authorities because of the events that occurred in May 1991 and June 1992. In particular, the Bern police are not aware of the participation of the brother of President Rafsanjani in the May 1991 incident. As regards the Iranian consul's visit to the APHO stand, the Swiss Government has stated that, "a member of the city of Bern police force recalls that there was a skirmish between Iranians in June 1992, but does not know whether it involved members of the Iranian consulate and APHO activists, because the incident was already over by the time the police arrived, when only APHO members were present. In the light of this information, the Swiss Government considers it at least doubtful whether the events in question occurred so they cannot automatically be considered to constitute a decisive ground in respect of article 3 of the Convention".

6.9 As to the author's allegation that the filing of an application for asylum is in itself a relevant ground within the meaning of article 3, paragraph 1, of the Convention, the State party observes that the author adduces no evidence in support of this argument. The State party further notes, "such an argument cannot be sufficient in respect of article 3, paragraph 1, of the Convention since the prohibition laid down in this provision is dependent on the proven existence of substantial grounds for persecution". The State party maintains that it has no information to substantiate the specific danger of persecution as a result of filing an application for asylum in Switzerland.

6.10 The State party considers that the author's statements do not enable the conclusion to be drawn that there are substantial and proven grounds for believing that he would be in danger of being tortured if he returned to Iran. Finally, it observes that "the European Commission of Human Rights has deemed that the general situation in Iran was not characterized by mass violations of human rights [application N° 21649/93, DR, 75/282]" and that, "the author himself does not claim that there is a consistent pattern of human rights violations in Iran".

Counsel's comments on State party's observations

7.1 In a letter of 30 October 1996, counsel reiterates the points made in his initial communication. As regards the State party's argument that the author's statements about his political activity within the People's Mojahedin did not appear to be sufficiently substantiated, counsel submits that it is normal for a sympathizer not to be as well informed about an organization as one of its members. He explains that the author was motivated by hostility towards the regime rather than the Mojahedin's political ideas. Counsel notes that the author is not in a position to produce documents in support of his allegations concerning the events that took place in Iran, and states that after his release the author was no longer active within the Mojahedin.

7.2 Counsel acknowledges that the security measures taken by the author's group in Iran were not sufficient, but rejects the conclusion that the author's statements are unrealistic. He also maintains that merely distributing leaflets can lead to life imprisonment and explains that the fact that the author was only sentenced to two years' imprisonment in April 1983 was due, inter alia, to the author's origin as a descendant of Muhammad. Concerning the alleged contradictions, counsel affirms that the author's statements are not contradictory on essential points, and that the discrepancies with the information provided by his wife are not relevant. Mrs. Aemei has lived in great fear for years, which would explain the fact that she wanted to know as little as possible about her husband's political activities. In any case, she first heard about them in April 1983.

7.3 Counsel is of the opinion that the author's statements about his political activities are true, which is also proved by the fact that the Swiss Government admits in its observations that there was an APHO stand in June 1992 and that a skirmish between Iranians did indeed take place. He further submits that the Swiss authorities' refusal to consider the author's request for reconsideration, based on his activities in the APHO, is a serious procedural error and contrary to the author's right to have his fear of being tortured considered by the competent authorities.

7.4 Counsel reiterates the fact, already mentioned by the author in his appeal of 24 September 1992, that the mere act of requesting asylum can constitute a relevant ground within the meaning of article 3, paragraph 1, of the Convention against Torture, and refers in this connection to documentation of the Schweizerisches Flüchtlingswerk.

Decision on admissibility and examination of the merits

8. The Committee notes with appreciation the information given by the State party that the author and his family will not be expelled while the communication is under consideration by the Committee (rules of procedure, art. 108, para. 9).

9.1 Before considering any claim contained in a communication, the Committee against Torture must decide whether or not it is admissible under article 22 of the Convention. The Committee has ascertained, as it is required to do under article 22, paragraph 5 (a), of the Convention, that the same matter has not been, and is not being examined under another international investigation or settlement procedure. The Committee notes that the State party has not raised any objection to the admissibility of the communication (see State party's observations dated 7 August 1996). The Committee therefore finds that no obstacle to the admissibility of the communication exists and proceeds with the examination of the merits of the communication.

9.2 The Committee reiterates that it is by no means its responsibility to determine whether the author's rights as recognized by the Convention *have been violated* by Iran, the country to which he risks being expelled, regardless of whether or not this State is a party to the Convention. The question before the Committee is whether expulsion, return or extradition to the latter country would violate Switzerland's obligation, under article 3 of the Convention, not to expel or return an individual to a State where there are substantial grounds for believing that he would be in danger of being subjected to torture.

9.3 In accordance with article 3, paragraph 1, of the Convention, the Committee has to determine whether there are substantial grounds for believing that Mr. Aemei and the members of his family would be in danger of being subjected to torture if they returned to Iran. In order to do this, the Committee must, in accordance with article 3, paragraph 2, take into account all relevant considerations, including the existence of a consistent pattern of gross, flagrant or mass violations of human rights. In other words, the existence of a consistent pattern of violations of human rights within the meaning of article 3, paragraph 2, lends force to the Committee's belief that substantial grounds exist within the meaning of paragraph 1.

9.4 However, the Committee has to determine whether the person concerned would be *personally* at risk of being subjected to torture in the country to which he would be expelled. Consequently, the existence of a consistent pattern of gross, flagrant or mass violations of human rights in a particular country does not in itself constitute a sufficient ground for concluding that a particular person would be in danger of being subjected to torture after returning to his country; additional grounds must exist in order to conclude that the person concerned is personally at risk. Similarly, the absence of a consistent pattern of flagrant violations of human rights does not mean that a person cannot be considered to be at risk of being subjected to torture in his specific circumstances.

9.5 In the present case, therefore, the Committee has to determine whether the expulsion of Mr. Aemei (and his family) to Iran would have the *foreseeable* consequence of exposing him to a *real and personal risk* of being arrested and tortured. It observes that the "substantial grounds" for believing that return or expulsion would expose the applicant to the risk of being subjected to torture may be based not only on acts committed in the country of origin, in other words *before* his flight from the country, but also on activities undertaken by him in the receiving country: in fact, the wording of article 3 does not distinguish between the commission of acts, which might later expose the applicant to the risk of torture, in the country of origin or in the receiving country. In other words, even if the activities of which the author is accused in Iran were insufficient for article 3 to apply, his subsequent activities in the receiving country could prove sufficient for application of that article.

9.6 The Committee certainly does not take lightly concern on the part of the State party that article 3 of the Convention might be improperly invoked by asylum-seekers. However, the Committee is of the opinion that, even though there may be some remaining doubt as to the veracity of the facts adduced by the author of a communication, it must ensure that his security is not endangered.[1] In order

---

[1] See Views on communication N° 13/1993 (*Mutombo* v. *Switzerland*), adopted on 27 April 1994, para. 9.2.

to do this, it is not necessary that all the facts invoked by the author should be proved; it is sufficient that the Committee should consider them to be sufficiently substantiated and reliable.

9.7 In the case of the author of the present communication, the Committee considers that his membership of the People's Mojahedin organization, his participation in the activities of that organization and his record of detention in 1981 and 1983 must be taken into consideration in order to determine whether he would be in danger of being subjected to torture if he returned to his country. The State party has pointed to inconsistencies and contradictions in the author's statements, which in its opinion cast doubt on the veracity of his allegations. The Committee considers that although there may indeed be some doubt about the nature of the author's political activities in his country of origin, there can be no doubt about the nature of the activities he engaged in Switzerland for the APHO, which is considered an illegal organization in Iran. The State party confirms these activities by the author and does not deny that skirmishes occurred between APHO representatives and other Iranian nationals in Bern in June 1992. The State party does not say whether it investigated these skirmishes, but the material submitted to the Committee gives the impression that no such investigation took place. In the circumstances, the Committee must take seriously the author's statement that individuals close to the Iranian authorities threatened the APHO members and the author himself on two occasions, in May 1991 and June 1992. The State party simply noted that Mr. Aemei's activities within the APHO did not constitute a new development vis-à-vis the criteria established by the case law of the Federal Tribunal and that consequently the competent authorities could not take up the matter of the author's application for reconsideration.

9.8 The Committee is not convinced by the State party's explanations in so far as they refer to Mr. Aemei's activities in Switzerland. It would recall that the protection accorded by article 3 of the Convention is absolute. Whenever there are substantial grounds for believing that a particular person would be in danger of being subjected to torture if he was expelled to another State, the State party is required not to return that person to that State. The nature of the activities in which the person engaged is not a relevant consideration in the taking of a decision in accordance with article 3 of the Convention.[2] In the present case, the refusal of the competent Swiss authorities to take up the author's request for review, based on reasoning of a procedural nature, does not appear justified in the light of article 3 of the Convention.

9.9 Lastly, the Committee is aware of the serious human rights situation in Iran, as reported inter alia to the United Nations Commission on Human Rights by the Commission's Special Representative on the situation of human rights in the Islamic Republic of Iran. The Committee notes, in particular, the concern expressed by the Commission, especially about the large number of cases of cruel, inhuman or degrading treatment or punishment.

9.10 In the light of the content of the preceding paragraphs, the Committee considers that substantial grounds exist for believing that the author and his family would be in danger of being subjected to torture if they were sent back to Iran.

10. Taking account of the above, the Committee is of the view that, in the present circumstances, the State party has an obligation to refrain from forcibly returning the author and his family to Iran, or to any other country where they would run a real risk of being expelled or returned to Iran.

11. The Committee's finding of a violation of article 3 of the Convention in no way affects the decision(s) of the competent national authorities concerning the granting or refusal of asylum. The finding of a violation of article 3 has a *declaratory character*. Consequently, the State party is not required to modify its decision(s) concerning the granting of asylum; on the other hand, it does have a responsibility to find solutions that will enable it to take all necessary measures to comply with the provisions of article 3 of the Convention. These solutions may be of a legal nature (e.g., decision to admit the applicant temporarily), but also of a political nature (e.g., action to find a third State willing to admit the applicant to its territory and undertaking not to return or expel him in its turn).

---

[2] See Views in communication N° 39/1996 (*Tapia Páez* v. *Sweden*), adopted on 28 April 1997, para. 14.5.

Communication N° 43/1996

Submitted by: Kaveh Yaragh Tala
Alleged victim: The author
State party: Sweden
Date of adoption of Views: 15 November 1996

Subject matter: deportation of complainant to Iran with alleged risk of torture

Procedural issue: none

Substantive issue: risk of torture after deportation to receiving State

Article of the Convention: 3

1. The author of the communication is Mr. Kaveh Yaragh Tala, an Iranian citizen born on 18 August 1969, currently residing in Sweden. He claims that his return to Iran would constitute a violation of article 3 of the Convention against Torture by Sweden. He is represented by counsel.

The facts as presented by the author

2.1 The author states that he became politically aware in the summer of 1985, and through a friend of the family started to become involved with the People's Mujahedin Organization of Iran (PMOI). He took part in activities such as painting slogans and distributing leaflets late at night. From September 1986 on, he also acted as a contact between the friend and two army officers. At the end of 1986, he began listening to PMOI broadcasts in order to write down messages to certain codes and to hand them to a contact person.

2.2 In February 1987, the author was forced to perform his military service. He was assigned to the maintenance section of the Revolutionary Guards headquarters. After some time he began to deliver information, such as transport routes for ammunition and armaments and location of ammunition and underground storage, to the PMOI. The author also stole and delivered to the PMOI some 20 blank passes with which vehicles could move around freely without being checked at checkpoints.

2.3 In March 1989, the author was stopped when leaving the quarters and found with two blank passes on him. He was arrested, beaten and kicked and was brought to the underground prison N° 59 of the security service of the Revolutionary Guards. There he stayed for three and a half months, during which period he was interrogated about 25 times. During each interrogation he was maltreated and tortured. During the last interrogation, he was told to lie down on his stomach and then felt a hot metal object against his thighs before he passed out. When his wounds became infected, he was brought to Khatam-al-anbia hospital, where he stayed under guard for four weeks.

2.4 After being released from hospital, he was moved to prison N° 66 of the Revolutionary Guards. There he managed to get a message out to his parents, and on 11 August 1989 he was released awaiting trial. Apparently, his father had bribed the man in charge into accepting the registration papers of the family house as bail; the author adds that normally political prisoners are not released on bail. The author had to report at the prison every third day.

2.5 After about a week, he received a message from his contact in the PMOI which he interpreted as a warning. He went into hiding in Shiraz and later in Boosher. After about six months, he contacted his brother-in-law through a friend and learned that he was wanted by the Revolutionary Guards and that they had searched the family house and arrested his parents for questioning. Apparently, the Revolutionary Guards also found some secret material that the author had hidden and arrested his contact man. The author then decided to leave the country, contacted a smuggler, and, at the end of June 1990, left from Bandar Abbas by boat to Dubai and from there by plane to Stockholm, via Amsterdam and Copenhagen.

3.1 The author arrived in Sweden on 7 July 1990 and requested asylum. He was briefly interrogated by the police. On 3 September 1990, the author was again interrogated by the police, at which occasion he told them about his activities for the PMOI, but not about the torture and maltreatment and the circumstances of his release. On 26 November 1990, the Immigration Board decided to refuse the author's application for asylum and ordered his expulsion from Sweden because of the contradictions in his statements.

3.2 During the appeal, the author applied to the Government for a change of counsel because of unsatisfactory cooperation. This was granted on 19 March 1991. According to the author, the new counsel was the first one who really listened to him. In his plea, he gives the true story of the author, including the torture, and he presented a doctor's certificate. Nevertheless, the Aliens Appeal Board rejected the author's appeal on 3 July 1992. The Board acknowledged that the author had now given a full and consistent description of his political activities, detention and torture, but it considered that he lacked credibility, since he changed his story regarding his route to Sweden, the passport used and his arrest and military service.

3.3 The author's new application to the Immigration Board, explaining how the contradictions had resulted from misunderstandings with his first counsel and submitting a new medical certificate, was rejected on 1 October 1992, since the Board considered that he had not invoked any new circumstances.

3.4 On 10 August 1995, the author submitted a new application to the Aliens Appeal Board. New evidence was presented, such as a certificate from Mujahedin Sweden that the author had been a Mujahedin activist and medical evidence from the Centre for Torture and Trauma Survivors in Stockholm testifying that the scars and marks on the author's body are in conformity with his allegations of torture and that the author suffers from post-traumatic stress disorder. The Aliens Appeal Board rejected the application on 25 August 1995, reasoning that the author had to a large extent invoked circumstances that had already been considered. The Board pointed out inconsistencies in the author's explanations as to how the injuries from torture had been caused. According to the Board, the author's scars and marks did not show that the author had been tortured in prison. With this decision, counsel argues, all domestic remedies have been exhausted.

The complaint

4.1 The author's counsel argues that, given the absolute prohibition to expel a person to a country where he risks being subjected to torture and given that, if the author's story is true, he will without doubt be subjected to torture upon his return, he should only be returned to Iran if it is beyond reasonable doubt that the author's claim is false. In this context, counsel explains that the Swedish authorities expect an applicant to give the full story of his claim the day he arrives in Sweden. Counsel states that this demand is not justified for persons who flee persecution, who for years have been living in a climate of distrust. Asylum-seekers, counsel states, behave initially in an irrational and inadequate way, do not trust anybody and are only ready to tell their true and complete story after having been in the country for some time. Counsel therefore considers absurd the Government's opinion that since the person has had his chance at the beginning, whatever he invokes later on is not trustworthy, and argues that in some cases new statements have to be accepted as trustworthy in spite of the fact that the story was incoherent, inconsistent and contradictory in the beginning.

4.2 In the instant case, counsel acknowledges that inconsistencies in the author's story exist. Nevertheless, she points out that in his very first interview with the police he already gave the core of his story, namely, that he was afraid of being arrested by the Revolutionary Guards because he had cooperated with persons suspected to be opponents. Since his first counsel did not gain the author's confidence, the inconsistencies continued. Only later did the author understand that he should tell the complete story, and he was able to do so once he found counsel who he could trust.

4.3 Counsel recalls that the medical findings confirm the author's story that he had been tortured, but that the Appeal Board, although not denying the existence of the scars, concluded that they were not caused by torture in prison. Counsel points out that the author's injuries are not of the kind that one could receive in an accident, and is at a loss to understand how the Appeal Board thinks they have been inflicted. Counsel acknowledges that, without a credible eyewitness or a video recording of the torture, it is impossible to establish with full certainty that scars and marks on a person's body are indeed a result of torture, but argues that the judgement thereof should be entrusted to medical experts, not to persons who have no qualifications to judge medical findings.

4.4 The author claims that there is a real risk that he would be subjected to torture or that his security would be endangered if he were to be returned to his country. He recalls that he had been working for the Mujahedin, the opposition group most hated and feared in Iran. According to reports the mere possession of a Mujahedin leaflet is sufficient reason for arrest and persecution. From 1987 to 1989 he had been leaking classified information to the Mujahedin. Although the authorities suspected this, they did not have enough proof at the time they detained him. However, by the time he left the country, the Revolutionary Guards had searched his home and found all the proof they wanted. If the author is forcibly returned to Iran without passport, he will be arrested to establish his identity and to check his record. Then his political background will be revealed and his life will be in danger.

4.5 In this context, the author claims that a consistent pattern of gross and massive violations of human rights exists in Iran, which according to article 3, paragraph 2, of the Convention should be taken into account by a State party when deciding on expulsion. The author refers to reports by the Special Representative of the Commission on Human Rights, which attest to a continuing violation of all basic human rights.

State party's submission and counsel's comments

5.1 By submission of 30 May 1996, the State party informs the Committee that, following its request under rule 108, paragraph 9, the Swedish Immigration Board has decided to stay the expulsion order against the author.

5.2   As regards the domestic procedure, the State party explains that the basic provisions concerning the right of aliens to enter and to remain in Sweden are found in the 1989 Aliens Act. For the determination of refugee status there are normally two instances, the Swedish Immigration Board and the Alien Appeals Board. In exceptional cases, an application is referred to the Government by either of the two boards. Chapter 8, section 1, of the Act corresponds with article 3 of the Convention against Torture and states that an alien who has been refused entry or who is to be expelled may never be sent to a country where there is firm reason to believe that he or she would be in danger of suffering capital or corporal punishment or of being subjected to torture, nor to a country where he is not protected from being sent on to a country where he would be in such danger. Further, under chapter 2, section 5, subsection 3, of the Act, an alien who is to be refused entry or expelled, can apply for a residence permit if the application is based on circumstances which have not previously been examined in the case and if either the alien is entitled to asylum in Sweden or it will otherwise be in conflict with humanitarian requirements to enforce the decision on refusal of entry or expulsion.

5.3   As to the facts of the instant case, the State party explains that the author arrived in Sweden on 7 July 1990 and applied for asylum when interrogated by the police. He had no passport and his identity was unclear. He stated that he had not been politically active but that he had carried out propaganda for the royalists when fulfilling his military service. He also said that he had travelled from Iran through Turkey to Sweden. The day after his arrival, a letter was found at the airport addressed to the author at a Swiss address, containing a false Spanish passport with the author's photograph in it. When questioned, the author stated that it could have been the passport used for him by the person who helped him to get to Stockholm. The person and he were allegedly separated at the airport in Copenhagen. No further explanations were given by the author about the Swiss address.

5.4   Since then, the State party submits, the grounds invoked by the author for political asylum have changed considerably. The State party submits that his statements at different points in time have been inconsistent and contradictory. Furthermore, it was not until his appeal that he made any statements regarding having been tortured. The State party emphasizes that all interrogations took place with an interpreter in the author's mother tongue.

6.   The State party argues that the communication is inadmissible for being incompatible with the provisions of the Convention. It also contends that an argument can be made that domestic remedies have only been exhausted once the expulsion order has been carried out.

7.1   On the merits of the communication, the State party refers to the Committee's jurisprudence in the case of *Mutombo* v. *Switzerland*[1] and the criteria established by the Committee, first, that a person must personally be at risk of being subjected to torture, and, second, that such torture must be a necessary and foreseeable consequence of the return of the person to his or her country.

7.2   The State party refers to its own legislation which reflects the same principle as that of article 3 of the Convention. The State party's authorities thus apply the same test as the Committee in deciding on the return of a person to his or her country. The State party recalls that the mere possibility that a person would be subjected to torture in his or her country of origin does not suffice to prohibit his or her return as being incompatible with article 3 of the Convention.

7.3   The State party is aware that Iran is reported to be a major violator of human rights and that there is no indication of improvement. It leaves it for the Committee to determine whether the situation in Iran amounts to a consistent pattern of gross, flagrant or mass violations of human rights.

7.4   As regards its assessment of whether or not the author would be personally at risk of being subjected to torture when returned to Iran, the State party relies on the evaluation of the facts and evidence made by its Immigration Board and the Appeals Board. The Swedish Immigration Board, in its decision of 26 November 1990, found that the elements provided by the author were inconsistent and therefore not trustworthy. The Alien Appeals Board, on 3 July 1992, also found that the circumstances invoked by the author at the appeal were not trustworthy. It noted that the author had changed his story several times and that he now for the first time alleged that he had been tortured.

7.5   On 11 August 1995, the author filed an additional new application with the Alien Appeals Board. In support he invoked a certificate from the Mujahedin's Sympathizers Association, a copy of an alleged notice obliging him to report and an examination report by the Centre for Torture and Trauma Survivors. At the hearing, the author stated that he ceased to cooperate with the Mujahedin's Sympathizers Association because it had collaborators in its organization. The Appeal Board, after having made an overall assessment of the author's statements, found that he was not trustworthy in his claim for a right to asylum.

---

[1] See Views on communication N° 13/1993 (*Mutombo* v. *Switzerland*), adopted on 27 April 1994.

7.6 As regards the medical evidence, the Board noted that the author had given contradictory statements as to how the injuries were caused, whether by a hot metal object or by a gas burner, whether by a key or a knife. The Board concluded that "against the background that Yaragh Tala on several occasions has given very detailed and exhaustive statements regarding the torture he claims to have been exposed to, the contradictory statements may, in the Board's opinion, indicate that the injuries have been caused in another way than he has stated. Although the injuries per se are documented, they do not in the Board's opinion, show that Yaragh Tala has been tortured when in detention".

7.7 The State party submits that on the basis of the above-mentioned decisions, it has concluded that the author is of no interest to the military or police authorities in Iran and that the facts he has invoked do not substantiate his assertion that he has been exposed to torture and that he risks torture upon his return to Iran.

7.8 The State party concludes that, in the circumstances of the present case, the author's return to Iran would not have the foreseeable and necessary consequence of exposing him to a real risk of torture. An enforcement of the expulsion order against the author would therefore not constitute a violation of article 3 of the Convention.

8.1 In her comments on the State party's submission, counsel for the author takes issue with the State party's suggestion that domestic remedies are not exhausted until the author has actually been deported. She states that it would then be too late to seek any effective remedy. She further argues that the elements provided by the author make his communication compatible with the provisions of the Convention.

8.2 Counsel points out that the Alien Appeals Board apparently had some hesitations as to the author's political background and requested the Swedish embassy in Tehran to verify the facts as presented by the author, including the sketches he had made of the Revolutionary Guards' headquarters. In its reply, the embassy refused to judge the personal trustworthiness of the author but confirmed that it might well be possible to bribe oneself out of prison even in political cases. Counsel argues that where the Appeal Board had real doubts about the author's expulsion, he should have benefited from those doubts, especially since at the appeal he had presented a credible, consistent, detailed and thorough description of his asylum claim. It is argued that the authorities have used the untrue statements given by the author in the beginning to completely disqualify him for asylum in Sweden regardless of what he later presented and contrary to UNHCR's *Handbook*, article 199, which states that untrue statements by themselves are not a reason for refusal of refugee status and that it is the examiner's responsibility to evaluate such statements in the light of all the circumstances of the case.

8.3 Counsel further refers to article 198 of the *Handbook*, which indicates that persons who have been persecuted may be afraid to give a full account to the authorities. Counsel acknowledges that the author's case depends completely on his credibility. He gave untrue statements and his statements were also contradictory and inconsistent. She states that only the human and psychological factor might explain his conduct. "A man fleeing from a cruel and relentless regime against which he has been fighting and which had subjected him to cruel torture cannot be expected to behave in a rational way once he has managed to escape from his tormentors. It will take time for him to collect himself enough to understand that he is spoiling his right for protection and that he must come up with his complete and true story."

8.4 Counsel contends that in spite of the initial doubts regarding the author's trustworthiness, he thereafter provided a credible, consistent, thorough and detailed description. Considering his history of torture and persecution, counsel argues that his initial failure is explainable and excusable.

8.5 Counsel concludes that the return of the author to Iran would have the foreseeable and necessary consequence of exposing him to a real risk of being detained and tortured.

Issues and proceedings before the Committee

9. Before considering any claims contained in a communication, the Committee against Torture must decide whether or not it is admissible under article 22 of the Convention. The Committee has ascertained, as it is required to do under article 22, paragraph 5 (a), of the Convention, that the same matter has not been and is not being examined under another procedure of international investigation or settlement. The Committee is further of the opinion that all domestic remedies available to the author have been exhausted. The Committee finds that no further obstacles to the admissibility of the communication exist and proceeds with the consideration of the merits of the communication.

10.1 The Committee must decide, pursuant to article 3, paragraph 1, whether there are substantial grounds for believing that Mr. Tala would be in danger of being subjected to torture upon return to Iran. In reaching this decision, the Committee must take into account all relevant considerations, pursuant to article 3, paragraph 2, including the existence of a consistent pattern of gross, flagrant or mass violations of human rights. The aim of the determination, however, is to establish whether the individual concerned would be personally at risk of being subjected to torture in the country to which he or she would return. It follows that the existence of a consistent pattern of gross, flagrant or mass violations of human rights in a country does not as such constitute a sufficient ground for determining that a particular person would be in danger of being subjected to torture upon his return to that country; additional grounds must exist to show that the individual concerned would be personally at risk. Similarly, the absence of a consistent pattern of gross violations of human rights does not mean that a person cannot be considered to be in danger of being subjected to torture in his or her specific circumstances.

10.2 The Committee has noted the State party's assertion that its authorities apply practically the same test as prescribed by article 3 of the Convention when determining whether or not a person can be deported. The Committee, however, notes that the text of the decisions taken by the Immigration Board (26 November 1990) and the Aliens Appeal Board (3 July 1992 and 25 August 1995) in the author's case does not show that the test as required by article 3 of the Convention (and as reflected in chapter 8, section 1, of the 1989 Aliens Act) was in fact applied to the author's case.

10.3 In the present case, the Committee considers that the author's political affiliation with the People's Mujahedin Organization and activities, his history of detention and torture should be taken into account when determining whether he would be in danger of being subjected to torture upon his return. The State party has pointed to contradictions and inconsistencies in the author's story, but the Committee considers that complete accuracy is seldom to be expected by victims of torture and that the inconsistencies that exist in the author's presentation of the facts do not raise doubts about the general veracity of his claims, especially since it has been demonstrated that the author suffers from post-traumatic stress disorder. Further, the Committee has noted from the medical evidence that the scars on the author's thighs could only have been caused by a burn and that this burn could only have been inflicted intentionally by a person other than the author himself.

10.4 The Committee is aware of the serious human rights situation in Iran, as reported, inter alia, to the Commission on Human Rights by the Commission's Special Representative on the situation of human rights in Iran. The Committee notes the concern expressed by the Commission, in particular in respect of the high number of executions, instances of torture and cruel, inhuman or degrading treatment or punishment.

10.5 In the circumstances, the Committee considers that substantial grounds exist for believing that the author would be in danger of being subjected to torture if returned to Iran.

11. In the light of the above, the Committee is of the view that, in the prevailing circumstances, the State party has an obligation to refrain from forcibly returning Mr. Kaveh Yaragh Tala to Iran or to any other country where he runs a real risk of being expelled or returned to Iran.

Communication N° 39/1996

Submitted by: Gorki Ernesto Tapia Páez
Alleged victim: The author
State party: Sweden
Date of adoption of Views: 28 April 1997

Subject matter: deportation of complainant to Peru with alleged risk of torture

Procedural issue: none

Substantive issues: risk of torture after deportation to receiving State; exception for serious crimes

Article of the Convention: 3

1. The author of the communication is Mr. Gorki Ernesto Tapia Páez, a Peruvian citizen, born on 5 October 1965, at present residing in Sweden, where he is seeking recognition as a refugee. He claims that his forced return to Peru would constitute a violation by Sweden of article 3 of the Convention against Torture and Other Cruel, Inhuman or Degrading Treatment or Punishment. He is represented by counsel.

The facts as submitted by the author

2.1 The author states that since 1989 he has been a member of Shining Path, an organization of the Communist Party of Peru. On 2 April 1989, he was arrested during a razzia at the university where he was studying. He was taken to the police station for identification and released after 24 hours. On 1 November 1989, the author participated in a demonstration at which he handed out leaflets and handmade bombs. The police arrested about 40 persons, among them the leader of the author's cell. According to the author, this person was forced to reveal the names of the other cell members. The same day, the author's house was allegedly searched by the police and the author decided to go into hiding until 24 June 1990, when he left Peru with a valid passport issued on 5 April 1990.

2.2 The author states that he is a cousin of José Abel Malpartida Páez, a member of Shining Path, who was arrested and allegedly killed by the police in 1989, and of Ernesto Castillo Páez, who disappeared on 21 October 1990. The author's mother and the father of the missing Ernesto Castillo Páez obtained assistance from a Peruvian lawyer to investigate his whereabouts. The lawyer subsequently received a letter bomb, which seriously injured him, upon which he fled the country and was granted asylum in Sweden. Several members of the author's family have fled Peru; some of them were granted asylum in Sweden or the Netherlands. His brother's application was refused in Sweden, while his mother and two sisters have been granted asylum as de facto refugees. The author's brother has filed an application with the European Commission of Human Rights, which was declared admissible on 18 April 1996. On 6 December 1996, the Commission adopted its report in which it found that the applicant's expulsion to Peru would not violate article 3 of the Convention.

2.3 The author arrived in Sweden on 26 June 1990 and applied for political asylum on 6 August 1990. On 30 March 1993, the Swedish Board of Immigration rejected his application for political asylum, considering that the author had participated in serious non-political criminality. On 16 December 1994, the Aliens Appeal Board found that the author had undoubtedly been politically active but that he could not be regarded as a refugee according to chapter 3, paragraph 2, of the Aliens Law. The Appeal Board considered that, although the author could be seen as a de facto refugee, his armed political activities fell within the framework of article 1 F. of the 1951 Convention relating to the Status of Refugees, and therefore particular reasons existed not to grant him asylum. The Appeal Board forwarded the case to the Swedish Government for decision. On 12 October 1995, the Government confirmed the earlier decision not to grant the author asylum.

The complaint

3.1 The author claims that his return to Peru would constitute a violation by Sweden of article 3 of the Convention; the author states that the police usually torture people in cases concerning "terrorism and treason". The author asks the Committee to request Sweden not to expel him while his communication is under consideration by the Committee.

3.2 In support of the author's claim, reference is made to an enclosed letter, dated 18 August 1994, from the Office of the United Nations High Commissioner for Refugees' regional office concerning the author's mother. The letter states that the mother's "subjective fear of persecution can be supported by objective elements". Reference is also made to a letter by Human Rights Watch of 26 October 1995, concerning another Peruvian refugee claimant, which states that "returnees from Sweden are now considered to be de facto Shining Path guerrillas". Finally, reference is made to an enclosed copy of a July 1995 report by Human Rights Watch attesting to the practice of torture in Peru.

State party's observations

4. On 15 February 1996, the Committee, through its Special Rapporteur, transmitted the communication to the State party for comments and requested it not to expel the author while his communication was under consideration by the Committee.

5.1 By submission of 12 April 1996, the State party challenges the admissibility of the communication but also addresses the merits of the case. It requests the Committee, should it not find the communication inadmissible, to examine the communication on its merits as soon as possible. It informs the Committee that its national Immigration Board has stayed the enforcement of the expulsion order against the author until 25 May 1996.

5.2 As regards domestic procedures, the State party explains that the basic provisions concerning the right of aliens to enter and to remain in Sweden are contained in the 1989 Aliens Act. For the determination of refugee status there are normally two instances, the Swedish Immigration Board and the Alien Appeals Board. In exceptional cases, an application is referred to the Government by either of the two boards. Chapter 8, section 1, of the Act corresponds to article 3 of the Convention against Torture and states that an alien who has been refused entry or who is to be expelled may never be sent to a country where there is firm reason to believe that he or she would be in danger of suffering capital or corporal punishment or of being subjected to torture, nor to a country where he is not protected from being sent on to a country where he would be in such danger. Further, under chapter 2, section 5, subsection 3, of the Act, an alien who is to be refused entry or expelled can apply for a residence permit if the application is based on circumstances which have not previously been examined in the case and if either the alien is entitled to asylum in Sweden or it will otherwise be in conflict with humanitarian requirements to enforce the decision on refusal of entry or expulsion.

5.3 As regards the facts of the author's story, the State party emphasizes that he was able to leave his country with a valid passport, issued after the police allegedly were looking for him. The author has never claimed to have bribed officials into giving him a passport, indicating, according to the State party, that the author was not being sought by the police when he legally left the country in June 1990. Further, the State party emphasizes that according to the author's own statements, he was never arrested, detained, prosecuted or sentenced for his activities for Shining Path. The only time he was arrested, in April 1989, he was released after 24 hours without having been tortured.

5.4 The State party explains that the Government, when deciding that the author should not be granted asylum in Sweden, also took into account whether the enforcement of the expulsion order would violate chapter 8, section 1, of the Aliens Act. The Government, after having carefully examined all elements of the author's case, concluded that it would not.

5.5 The State party argues that the communication is inadmissible as incompatible with the provisions of the Convention, for lacking the necessary substantiation.

6.1 On the merits of the communication, the State party refers to the Committee's jurisprudence in the case of *Mutombo* v. *Switzerland*, and the criteria established by the Committee, first, that a person must personally be at risk of being subjected to torture and, second, that such torture must be a necessary and foreseeable consequence of the return of the person to his or her country.

6.2 As regards the general situation of human rights in Peru, the State party, aware of the information collected by international human rights organizations, submits that political violence in the country has decreased. The State party further submits that a number of refugee claimants, allegedly members of Shining Path, have been deported to Peru from Sweden and that no substantiated reports of torture or ill-treatment of those persons upon their return to Peru exist. In this connection, the State party points out that its embassy in Lima has been in contact with some of the deportees and that no incidents have been reported. The State party argues that the author will not be in a worse situation than that of those who were deported earlier. The State party notes that no consistent pattern of gross, flagrant or mass violations of human rights exists in Peru.

6.3 The State party further recalls the terrorist character of Shining Path and contends that crimes committed in the name of that organization should not constitute a reason for granting asylum. The State party refers in this context to article 1 F. of the 1951 Convention relating to the Status of Refugees.

6.4 The State party refers to its own legislation, which reflects the same principle as that of article 3 of the Convention. The State party's authorities thus apply the same test as the Committee in deciding on the return of a person to his or her country. The State party recalls that the mere possibility of a person being subjected to torture in his or her country of origin does not suffice to prohibit his or her return as being incompatible with article 3 of the Convention.

6.5 The State party explains its reasons for concluding that there are no substantial grounds for believing that the author would personally be at risk of being subjected to torture upon his return to Peru. It recalls that the author has been arrested only once, in April 1989 and was released after 24 hours, and that there are no indications that he was subjected to torture. Further, the author was able to obtain a valid passport and to use it to leave Peru. It appears that he is not wanted by the police for terrorist or other acts. There is no indication that his activities for Shining Path are known to the authorities. Moreover, the State party argues that even someone wanted by the police for criminal acts does not necessarily risk being subjected to torture. According to the State party's sources, such a person will be arrested at the airport upon arrival, transported to a detention centre and placed under the supervision of a public prosecutor. The State party submits that the risk of torture in a detention centre is very limited. Finally, the State party explains that the author is free to leave Sweden at any time to a country of his choice.

6.6 With reference to the arguments summarized above, the State party argues that no sufficient evidence exists to demonstrate that the risk of the author being tortured is a foreseeable and necessary consequence of his return.

Counsel's comments

7.1 In her comments on the State party's submission, counsel challenges the State party's interpretation of article 1 F. of the 1951 Convention relating to the Status of Refugees and argues that the author's membership of Shining Path does not suffice to exclude him from the protection of that Convention.

7.2 As regards the general situation of human rights in Peru, counsel refers to the United States Department of State Country Report on Human Rights Practices for 1995, which states that torture and brutal treatment of detainees are common and that Government security forces still routinely torture suspected subversives at military and police detention centres.

7.3 As regards the author's valid passport, counsel states that this was indeed obtained through bribes, without further specifying her contention. She claims that it is possible to obtain a passport and leave the country despite serious problems with the authorities.

7.4 As regards the State party's statement that it is not aware of any case in which reliable information exists that a person was tortured upon being returned from Sweden to Peru, counsel refers to the case of Napoleon Aponte Inga, who, upon his return, was arrested at the airport and accused of having been a terrorist ambassador in Europe. He was brought to trial, acquitted after four months and then released. According to counsel, during his detention he was subjected to torture.

7.5 Counsel concludes that the State party underestimates the risk of the author being subjected to torture upon his return. She refers to reports indicating that torture is widely practised in Peru and states that the author belongs to a well-known family, one of his cousins having been killed by security forces and another cousin having disappeared.

The Committee's admissibility decision

8. At its sixteenth session, the Committee considered the admissibility of the communication and found that no obstacles to the admissibility of the communication existed.

9. The Committee noted that both the State party and author's counsel forwarded observations on the merits of the communication and that the State party had requested the Committee, if it were to find the communication admissible, to proceed to the examination of the merits of the communication. Nevertheless, the Committee considered that the information before it was not sufficient to enable it to adopt its Views.

10.1 In particular, the Committee wished to receive from author's counsel more precise and detailed information and substantiation of the claim that the author's house was searched by the police on 1 November 1989, in particular whether there were witnesses to this search and how the author found out about it. The Committee also wished to be informed whether the police returned to the house to look for the author on further occasions and when and under what circumstances the author went into hiding.

10.2 With regard to the author's passport, counsel was requested to elaborate on how the author obtained his passport on 1 April 1990 and by whom the passport was issued. The Committee further appreciated receiving information as to the precise date on which the author left his country and his means of transportation. Counsel was requested to explain whether the author took any precautions and, if so, what ones, so as to not be stopped at the border, since he was travelling under his own name. Finally, the Committee wished to know what indications the author had that the police were looking for him at the present time and why he believed that if he were returned he would be in danger of being subjected to torture.

10.3 The Committee also wished to receive from the State party more detailed information regarding its statement that it was not aware of returnees from Sweden being tortured or ill-treated upon return. The Committee would appreciate it if the State party would clarify why the author's mother and his sisters were allowed to stay in Sweden but not the author. In particular, the Committee would like to know whether the distinction between the author and his mother and sisters was based solely on the exception under article 1 F. of the 1951 Convention relating to the Status of Refugees, or whether additional grounds existed to give the mother and sisters protection, but not the author.

11. Accordingly, on 8 May 1996, the Committee declared the communication admissible.

State party's observations on the merits

12.1 By its submission of 12 September 1996, the State party explains that its conclusion that no consistent pattern of gross, flagrant or mass violations of human rights exists in Peru is based on recent information received from the embassy in Lima. The embassy referred, inter alia, to the 1995 report of the local Peruvian human rights organization, La Coordinadora, which supports the State party's conclusion that it is mostly poor people, peasants and young criminals who are exposed to torture during police interrogations.

12.2 The State party reiterates that there are no substantial grounds for believing that the author personally would be at risk of being subjected to torture upon his return to Peru, and states that this conclusion is based on information from its embassy in Lima with regard to the treatment of returned Peruvians, who have unsuccessfully requested asylum abroad by referring to activities they carried out for the benefit of Sendero Luminoso. The embassy has obtained this information through interviews and contacts with well-informed persons and human rights organizations in Peru. The State party does not reveal its sources for reasons of protection.

12.3 The State party acknowledges that the author's mother and sisters have been given de facto refugee status because they belong to a family the members of which have been involved with Sendero Luminoso. The State party adds that the author's mother and sisters had been given the benefit of the doubt. The author, however, has himself been active for Sendero Luminoso, an organization to which article 1 F. of the 1951 Convention relating to the Status of Refugees applies. In this context, the State party explains that it was not the membership of Sendero Luminoso that was decisive but the author's own statements according to which he had handed out home-made bombs in November 1989, which were actually used against the police. According to the State party, there was no reason why the author should be allowed to stay in the country and there were no obstacles to the enforcement of the expulsion order.

12.4 The State party reiterates that there is no indication that the authorities attempted to prevent the author from leaving Peru, which supports the State party's view that he is of no interest to the Peruvian police. The State party submits that it has requested its embassy in Lima to investigate the matter and that the embassy, on 14 August 1996, reported that the author has not been and is not wanted by the police for terrorist or similar acts in Peru.

12.5 The State party further questions the author's trustworthiness, since he has not been able to mention his cell leader's name or the name of the friend who informed him that he was wanted by the police.

12.6 The State party maintains that the author has not substantiated his assertion that an enforcement of the expulsion order to Peru would violate article 3 of the Convention. In this context, the State party observes that it is a general principle that the burden of proof lies with the person submitting a claim.

Observations by counsel

13.1 By submission of 16 September 1996, counsel explains that on 1 November 1990, when the author's home was searched, his mother and his brother were present. At 7 p.m., the door was banged on by two men in civilian clothes who asked for the author. When they were told that he was not at home, they searched his room and took books and other documents with them. During the search, a car without registration plates was parked outside the house, occupied by two armed men. When the men left, they told the author's mother to tell him to present himself the following day at DIRCOTE, the anti-terrorist police force, as they wanted to question him about his university friends. They added that if he did not appear, things would be worse for him. After the police left, the author's brother went to see the author's friends and asked them to tell him not to return home. Counsel adds that the police did not come again to the house to look for the author.

13.2 As regards the author's passport, counsel states that it was issued by the Dirección de Migraciones in Lima and that the author's friend did all the work for him. Counsel explains that, at the time, everybody could obtain a legal passport without a problem. One could also use tramitadores, who would apply for passports in the name of others for a fixed fee. Counsel refers to a letter from Amnesty International, Swedish section, of 10 May 1995, addressed to the Swedish Government, which stated that the fact that a Peruvian asylum-seeker has left the country legally with a passport should not be considered very important when considering his case.

13.3 The author left the country on 24 June 1990 by plane (Aeroflot). Friends bribed a person at the airport, and for protection the author was accompanied by a member of parliament (of the Unión de Izquierda Revolucionaria) and former member of the Comisión de Justicia y Derechos Humanos in Peru.

13.4 Counsel maintains that the author would be in danger if returned to Peru. She bases this on the fact that two of his cousins have been victims of severe persecutions. In this context, counsel recalls that one of the author's cousins disappeared and another was killed. Since he belongs to a politically active family, the author has every reason to fear for his security if he were to return to Peru.

13.5 Counsel adds that the author's fears have grown because of newspaper articles in Peru about the case of his brother which is before the European Commission of Human Rights, in which it is mentioned that his brother is a member of Sendero Luminoso.

13.6 In a further submission of 24 October 1996, counsel refers to a publication by Human Rights Watch/Helsinki of September 1996, entitled "Swedish asylum policy in a global human rights perspective". In the publication, criticism is expressed about Swedish policy towards Peruvian asylum-seekers. According to Human Rights Watch, reforms in Peru have been minimal, travel documents can be easily obtained by bribing officials and faceless courts continue to prosecute civilians.

13.7 According to counsel, the Human Rights Watch/Helsinki reports show how badly informed the Swedish authorities are about the situation in Peru. She refers to three cases of refoulement which suggest, according to counsel, that the primary aim of the Swedish policy is to limit immigration.

13.8 As regards the State party's claim that the author would not be in danger of being tortured upon his return to Peru, counsel notes that the State party bases itself on unrevealed sources. Counsel argues that the State party's mere reference to a non-provided report does not suffice as proof and requests a copy of the written report by the embassy, with the name of the sources deleted if necessary.

13.9 Counsel also refers to information provided by the Swedish embassy in Lima in the case of the author's mother, which proved to be wrong on the facts. This, she claims, means that information provided by the Swedish embassy must be treated with caution. Counsel also refers to the case of Napoleon Aponte Inga (who was tortured upon his return to Peru), of which the Swedish embassy seems to be unaware, although he was finally granted de facto asylum in Sweden.

13.10 Counsel submits that, while the situation in Peru may have improved as regards disappearances and judicial killings, the use of torture is still widespread and systematic. She refers to a report of Human Rights Watch/Americas of August 1996, which indicates that torture is generally practised in cases involving terrorism and thus contradicts the State party's argument that it is mainly poor people, peasants and young criminals who suffer torture.

13.11 Counsel contests the State party's argument that the author is untrustworthy because he cannot name the leader of his cell. She refers to her submission of 7 November 1990 to the Immigration Board in which she disclosed the name of the cell leader.

13.12 Finally, the author refers to the importance attached by the Office of the United Nations High Commissioner for Refugees to the experience of relatives. In this context, she recalls that two of the author's cousins were killed for political reasons and another cousin was granted political asylum in the Netherlands. Counsel also submits that although the author has been active for Sendero Luminoso, he himself never committed any crime against peace, a war crime or a crime against humanity, and therefore he should not be excluded from protection under article 1 F. of the 1951 Convention relating to the Status of Refugees.

Issues and proceedings before the Committee

14.1 The Committee has considered the communication in the light of all the information made available to it by the parties, in accordance with article 22, paragraph 4, of the Convention.

14.2 The Committee must decide, pursuant to article 3, paragraph 1, whether there are substantial grounds for believing that Mr. Tapia Páez would be in danger of being subjected to torture upon return to Peru. In reaching this decision, the Committee must take into account all relevant considerations, pursuant to article 3, paragraph 2, including the existence of a consistent pattern of gross, flagrant or mass violations of human rights. The aim of the determination, however, is to establish whether the individual concerned would be personally at risk of being subjected to torture in the country to which he or she would return. It follows that the existence of a consistent pattern of gross, flagrant or mass violations of human rights in a country does not as such constitute a sufficient ground for determining that a particular person would be in danger of being subjected to torture upon his return to that country; additional grounds must exist to show that the individual concerned would be personally at risk. Similarly, the absence of a consistent pattern of gross violations of human rights does not mean that a person cannot be considered to be in danger of being subjected to torture in his or her specific circumstances.

14.3 The Committee notes that the facts on which the author's asylum claim is based are not in dispute. The author is a member of Sendero Luminoso and on 1 November 1989 participated in a demonstration where he handed out leaflets and distributed handmade bombs. Subsequently, the police searched his house and the author went into hiding and left the country to seek asylum in Sweden. It is, further, beyond dispute that the author comes from a politically active family, that one of his cousins disappeared and another was killed for political reasons, and that his mother and sisters have been granted de facto refugee status by Sweden.

14.4 It appears from the State party's submission and from the decisions by the immigration authorities in the instant case, that the refusal to grant the author asylum in Sweden is based on the exception clause of article 1 F. of the 1951 Convention relating to the Status of Refugees. This is illustrated by the fact that the author's mother and sisters were granted de facto asylum in Sweden, since it was feared that they may be subjected to persecution because they belong to a family which is connected to Sendero Luminoso. No ground has been invoked by the State party for its distinction between the author, on the one hand, and his mother and sisters, on the other, other than the author's activities for Sendero Luminoso.

14.5 The Committee considers that the test of article 3 of the Convention is absolute. Whenever substantial grounds exist for believing that an individual would be in danger of being subjected to torture upon expulsion to another State, the State party is under obligation not to return the person concerned to that State. The nature of the activities in which the person concerned engaged cannot be a material consideration when making a determination under article 3 of the Convention.

14.6 In the circumstances of the instant case, as set out in paragraph 14.3 above, the Committee considers that the grounds invoked by the State party to justify its decision to return the author to Peru do not meet the requirements of article 3 of the Convention.

15. In the light of the above, the Committee is of the view that, in the prevailing circumstances, the State party has an obligation to refrain from forcibly returning Mr. Gorki Ernesto Tapia Páez to Peru.

Communication N° 59/1996

Submitted by: Encarnación Blanco Abad
Alleged victim: The author
State party: Spain
Date of adoption of Views: 14 May 1998

Subject matter: ill-treatment during detention under anti-terrorist legislation

Procedural issue: none

Substantive issues: failure to promptly investigate allegations of torture; admissibility of evidence obtained under torture

Articles of the Convention: 12, 13, 15

1. The author of the communication is Encarnación Blanco Abad,[1] a Spanish citizen. She claims to be the victim of violations by Spain of articles 12, 13 and 15 of the Convention against Torture and Other Cruel, Inhuman or Degrading Treatment or Punishment. She is represented by counsel.

The facts as submitted by the author

2.1 The author was detained along with her husband, Josu Eguskiza, on 29 January 1992 by officers of the Guardia Civil for alleged involvement in activities on behalf of the armed gang ETA. She alleges that she was mistreated between 29 January and 2 February 1992, when she was kept incommunicado under anti-terrorist legislation.

2.2 Brought before Madrid Court of Criminal Investigation N° 44 for preliminary investigation N° 205/92 on 13 March 1992, the author described the mistreatment and torture to which she had been subjected while in the custody of the Guardia Civil. The preliminary investigation had been instituted by the court upon receiving, from the Director of Carabanchel Women's Penitentiary Centre, the report of the doctor who had examined the author and observed bruises upon her entry into the Centre on 3 February 1992.

2.3 On 2 February 1993 the court ordered a stay of proceedings, not considering the incident reported to be a penal offence. Following an appeal, Court N° 44 granted permission on 13 October 1994 to continue with criminal proceedings. The judge handed down an order dated 4 April 1994 to shelve proceedings definitively. The Provincial High Court confirmed this decision by order dated 5 September 1995. An application for remedy of *amparo* filed with the Constitutional Court against the Provincial High Court's order was dismissed on 29 January 1996.

State party's observations on admissibility

3.1 In its submission of 17 January 1997, the State party pointed out that since 3 February 1992 Mrs. Blanco Abad had been assigned up to seven lawyers to represent and defend her. Despite this, Mrs. Blanco Abad had not formally reported any mistreatment. It submitted that the legal proceedings were set in train by the official transmission to the court of the report of the medical check-up on the author conducted when she entered the Madrid Penitentiary Centre on 3 February 1992. That is, the only legal investigations of alleged mistreatment were instituted not in response to a report by the individual concerned, nor by her family, nor by any of her seven lawyers, but rather as the result of an official procedure enshrined in the regulations to safeguard human rights. Not until 30 May 1994, two years and three months after the event, did the author send a written communication to Court of Investigation N° 44 designating three legal representatives.

3.2 The State party admitted that, with the decision of the Constitutional Court on 29 January 1996, all domestic remedies had been exhausted.

3.3 In reference to article 13 of the Convention, the State party confirmed that by letter of 9 September 1994, Mrs. Blanco Abad's counsel had appealed against the stay of the officially instituted investigations. On 13 October 1994 Court N° 44

---

[1] An earlier communication submitted on behalf of the author and her husband (communication N° 10/1993) was declared inadmissible by the Committee on 14 November 1994 for failure to exhaust domestic remedies.

annulled the stay of proceedings, allowing them to continue, and called for an expert report to be prepared. Mrs. Blanco Abad did not appeal against the examination authorized; neither did she insist on other investigations. The medical examiner submitted his report on 22 November 1994. On 4 April 1995, Court N° 44 issued an order which gave a detailed account of the medical tests conducted and concluded with the decision to shelve the proceedings definitively.

3.4 The State party submitted that from 9 September 1994, when Mrs. Blanco Abad applied in writing for the stay to be revoked, up to the aforementioned order to shelve the case definitively, the record shows not a single written communication from Mrs. Blanco Abad calling for an investigation or presenting any evidence.

3.5 On 19 April 1995, Mrs. Blanco Abad applied for reconsideration of the earlier decision to shelve the proceedings. On 19 May 1995 Court N° 44 turned the application down. On 5 September 1995 the Provincial High Court in Madrid also rejected the appeal. On 6 October 1995 Mrs. Blanco Abad applied for a remedy of *amparo* before the Constitutional Court, emphasizing the subjective evaluation of the medical examinations. The Constitutional Court considered the judicial decisions in question and pronounced them well-founded, with reasoning that could "not be challenged as manifestly unreasonable or arbitrary".

3.6 The State party pointed out that less than 15 months had elapsed between the reopening of the investigation and the Constitutional Court's decision. The investigation had been reopened for six months, and during those six months Mrs. Blanco Abad neither took any action nor submitted anything at all in writing. The remaining nine months were taken up with the application for reconsideration, the appeal before the High Court and the *amparo* proceedings before the Constitutional Court.

3.7 For the above reasons, it was submitted that Mrs. Blanco Abad's representations, over two years after the event, in investigations instituted in response to an official act, had been promptly and impartially examined. The State party therefore submits that no violation of article 13 of the Convention has occurred.

Author's comments

4.1 In her comments on the State party's submission, the author stated that by decision of the National High Court dated 26 December 1995, she was sentenced to seven years' ordinary imprisonment and a fine. The judgement observes:

"The defence initially sought annulment and suspension of the judgement on the grounds of the torture undergone by the accused during detention and while being held at the police stations. The Criminal Division, in view of the abundant and always detailed testimony offered not only by the accused but also by the witnesses called, acknowledges that this might have occurred. Hence its decision to take no account of the statements to the police, which are invalid."

4.2 The author argued that the only evidence against her were the pleas entered by two co-defendants, her husband, Mr. Josu Eguskiza, and Mr. Juan Ramón Rojo, which incriminated her, and that, notwithstanding the view of the National High Court, which found them valid, they were obtained by means of mistreatment and torture, and stemmed directly from the statements to the police that had been declared void.

4.3 The author indicated that on 2 February 1992, she made a statement to the investigating magistrate without being able to consult a lawyer, not even the duty counsel, and that although the official record mentioned the lawyer designated by her, he was not able to attend until the accused's statement had been finalized. The record showed that, responding to the first question put to her, she "neither said nor confirmed in her statement to the Guardia Civil", that she belonged to or had collaborated with ETA. She also related that while on Guardia Civil premises she was mistreated. In particular, she said she had been struck with a telephone directory, had a bag put over her head and electrodes on her body, had been forced to undress and had been threatened with rape. She also claimed to have been forced to stand for long periods against a wall with her arms raised and legs apart while being struck from time to time about the head and genitals, and receiving all manner of insults.

4.4 The author submitted that the medical examinations she underwent while detained incommunicado were superficial checks, and that not even her vital signs were measured. There was no assessment of her nervous state, and she was not asked about the kind of threats and insults to which she had been subjected; the conclusion was that she bore no signs of violence. The doctor put in her report that the detainee reported not having slept, having been beaten, and having been forced to remain naked. Despite this, she concluded that the author was in a suitable physical and mental condition to make a statement. Only on 3 February 1992, in prison, the author said, was any medical evidence of maltreatment found on her person, when three bruises were discovered. In this connection, the author refers to a June 1994 report by the European Committee for the Prevention of Torture illustrating the superficiality of the reports drawn up by doctors attached to the National High Court.

4.5 The author stated that there was no impartial and independent inquiry during the conduct of the preliminary investigation, which was instituted as a result of what she had told the doctor at the penitentiary centre. The three specialized medical reports ordered by the court were clearly at odds over the dating of her bruises by their colour (between four hours and six days), which was crucial to the outcome of the inquiry. She said that no statements were taken from those who might have been responsible for the alleged offence.

4.6 The only investigation that was done after the partial retraction of the stay of proceedings ordered as a result of the remedy filed by the author on 9 September 1994 took the form of a third specialized report by the medical examiner attached to the Court of Investigation on whether the mistreatment alleged by the author would have left traces that could be detected by a doctor on examination, hours or days later. This last medical report, dated 22 November 1994, stated that "the acts of aggression reported should have left objectively observable injuries in the parts of the body allegedly concerned, particularly the scalp and the genitals, unless the injuries were extremely slight. When a person is beaten unconscious, there will very probably be subsequent injuries, not only to the back and shoulders but to other areas as well." This opinion, combined with the National High Court doctor's lack of rigour in estimating the date of her injuries, led the court to declare the case definitively shelved.

4.7 The author pointed out that the shelving order referred to the impossibility of furnishing proof of any of the acts of aggression recounted, which included blows to the head, kicks to the genitals, hair-pulling and loss of consciousness. She emphasized that the kinds of violence she related do not leave physical marks on the victim, and that neither any of the kinds of psychological and sexual torture she alleged, nor most of the physical torture ("bagging", "hooding" and low-voltage electric shocks), leaves external signs of injury on the body. She submitted that, while a victim's testimony was not in itself always enough to secure a conviction, it was nonetheless true that such testimony, in cases where objective tests were not possible and there was no reason to doubt its veracity, had sufficed in many instances to bring in a guilty verdict when the following stipulations had been met: absence of reasonable doubt, verisimilitude corroborated by circumstantial evidence, and consistency in the charges. She stressed that no statements were taken from the officers on guard, and that the person who had shared the cell with her while she was being held incommunicado had not even been called as a witness to describe how she had been held in custody.

4.8 The author concluded that there had been breaches of articles 12 and 13 of the Convention against Torture. She submitted that current "anti-terrorist" legislation encouraged torture, infringing the basic right to counsel, hampering the collection of evidence that torture had been employed and, ultimately, guaranteeing that torture would go unpunished. In her view, that legislation runs counter to the spirit of article 2 of the Convention against Torture.

4.9 Finally, the author also submitted that the action taken against her on account of her presumed involvement with an armed gang served to show that the only evidence against her was that obtained under torture and duress from Mr. Eguskiza and Mr. Rojo, in breach of article 15 of the Convention against Torture.

The Committee's admissibility decision

5.1 At its eighteenth session the Committee considered the admissibility of the communication and ascertained that the same matter had not been, and was not being, examined under another procedure of international investigation or settlement. It observed that the State party had raised no objection regarding admissibility and considered that the available domestic remedies had been exhausted.

5.2 The Committee considered that the communication might raise issues under articles 12 and 13 of the Convention, notably in relation to the period of over a month that elapsed between when the court received the medical report and when it heard the author, and what the court was doing during the almost 11 months that separated the author's statement from the stay of proceedings.

5.3 As to the author's allegation that her conviction violated article 15 of the Convention, the Committee noted the comment in the judgement of the National High Court that the statements made to the police by the accused (including the author) had not been taken into consideration because of the possibility that torture had been used. The author's convention was based on other, uncompromised, voluntary statements made when the accused had been accompanied by counsel of their own choosing. In the circumstances, the Committee found that the author's claim of a violation of article 15 lacked the requisite corroboration, rendering it incompatible with article 22 of the Convention.

5.4 The Committee therefore decided that the communication was admissible inasmuch as it raised issues relating to articles 12 and 13 of the Convention.

State party's merits submission

6.1 On 10 November 1997, the State party reiterated that, although the author had been assisted by seven lawyers in the proceedings against her, not a single complaint or report of maltreatment had been presented via the domestic means of redress and that Court N° 44 had initiated the investigation without any application from the individual concerned, who was not even represented in court as an interested party when the compulsory offer of recourse was made to her. This attitude on the part of the author was curious since at the same time she reported the alleged maltreatment to several international bodies. From 9 September 1994, the date on which she requested the revocation of the stay of proceedings, until 4 April 1995, when the shelving order was made, the author did not request any investigation or produce any evidence. Her report of alleged maltreatment was inconsistent with this passive behaviour—not taking any action via the domestic means of redress, not being represented as a party directly involved in the official investigation, and reactivating an investigation but taking no part in it for six months.

6.2 The State party submitted, with respect to article 13 of the Convention, that in so far as this article refers to the right to complain, its application in the present case would be limited to the period beginning with the author's representations to Court of Investigation N° 44 following the order for a stay of proceedings, representations which marked the reopening of the investigation. Less than 15 months elapsed between the reopening of the investigation and the decision of the Constitutional Court. The investigation was in progress for six of these months, and during theses six months the author, assisted by lawyers, did not submit a single document to the Court and did not produce or propose any evidence. In the remaining nine months after the shelving order, the applications to the Court of Investigation, the Provincial High Court and the Constitutional Court were submitted, heard and ruled upon. Accordingly, the State party did not fail to fulfil its obligations under article 13 of the Convention.

6.3 With regard to article 12 of the Convention, the State party submitted that the Spanish system of protection against maltreatment has procedures for safeguarding that right, including in cases, such as the present one, when the party concerned takes no action. When the author entered the Penitentiary Centre on 3 February 1992, she was given a medical examination. The findings of this examination reached the High Court of Madrid on 13 February for distribution. On 17 February they were delivered to Court of Investigation N° 44. On 21 February Court N° 44 issued an order to begin a preliminary investigation and sent an official letter to the Director of the Penitentiary Centre ordering the author to appear on 7 March. She did not appear on that date, and on 9 March a new summons was issued for 13 March. On 13 March the author made a statement and the offer of recourse was made to her. On that same date the Judge authorized an application to Central Court of Investigation N° 2 of the National High Court for official copies of the records of the medical examinations carried out by the forensic medicine staff of that Court. On 30 April, when these copies had still not been received, the Judge sent an urgent reminder. The papers were delivered on 13 May. On 2 June the Judge requested the medical examiner of her Court to make a report; this report was delivered on 28 July. On 3 August the Judge summoned the medical examiner who had attended the author during her detention. On 30 October the Judge set the date of 17 November for receipt of the statement of the medical examiner and also authorized an application for information from the Penitentiary Centre about the time at which the author had been examined and the development of the injuries. On 23 December the Penitentiary Centre delivered the requested information. On 2 February the Judge issued the shelving order.

6.4 These facts show that there was no tardiness or delay in the conduct of the investigation. At no time did the author complain through the domestic channels about delays in the preliminary investigation, either before or after the temporary shelving order, once she had become represented in the proceedings.

Author's comments

7.1 In her comments on the State party's submission, the author maintains that in the five forensic examinations she underwent during the more than 100 hours for which she was held incommunicado she indicated that she had been subjected to maltreatment. The author encloses copies of the five medical reports which were prepared. In the first it is stated that "she does not mention physical ill-treatment, although she was kept hooded for many hours". According to the second, "she does not mention physical ill-treatment although does speak of threats and insults". In the third "the person concerned says that she is very nervous, has not slept and has not received food. She mentions having received ill-treatment consisting of blows to the head, but there are no signs of violence". The fourth says that "she mentions ill-treatment consisting of blows, but there are no signs of violence". In the fifth "she mentions ill-treatment consisting of blows and of having been kept undressed. No signs of violence are apparent upon examination".

7.2 In her statement to Court of Investigation N° 2 of the National High Court on 2 February 1992, the author spoke of having sustained many blows, having had a bag put over her head until she nearly suffocated, of the use of electrodes, threats and insults, and of having been forced to undress.

Notwithstanding, the judge did not automatically arrange for the competent judicial authorities to investigate the complaints.

7.3 The action of Court of Investigation N° 44 consisted in issuing various instructions for the medical reports on the examinations carried out during the period of incommunicado detention, as well details of the examination conducted in prison, to be entered in the record. In addition, two expert appraisals were obtained on 28 July and 20 November 1992, respectively. The first was by the forensic physician of the examining court and the second by the official forensic expert of Court of Investigation N° 2.

7.4 The author indicated that the forensic reports made available by Court of Investigation N° 2 did not include the one for 31 January 1992, which is not to be found in the record and has therefore not been appraised by the experts. The judicial proceedings also failed to determine the exact time of the prison medical examination on 3 February, although the certificate sent by the penitentiary centre to the author's counsel suggests that it took place in the morning.

7.5 The order definitively shelving the proceedings states that "it is necessary to establish, on the one hand, the impossibility of furnishing proof of any of the acts of aggression recounted by the complainant, i.e., blows to the head, the placing of a plastic bag over the head, kicks to the genitals, hair-pulling and loss of consciousness, since they were not confirmed in any medical examination and yet should have left some kind of palpable injury, according to the forensic medical report, and, on the other hand, the existence of other injuries as described for the first time in the medical report of 3 February". It also indicates that it is not possible to reach any conclusion regarding whether the cause of the injuries described "was accidental, intentional or self-inflicted, since the three possibilities are compatible with the objective findings, and the statement of the complainant, which constitutes the other source of information, is not supported by the chronology of the injuries established by the existing medical reports. In view of the impossibility of establishing the cause of the injuries, no offence can be said to have been committed and the proceedings must therefore be shelved".

7.6 This decision was challenged by appeal based, among other things, on the following arguments:

— With regard to virtually all the acts of aggression described by the author (blows to the head, kicks to the genitals, hair-pulling and loss of consciousness), it was argued that these involved the use of methods intended to leave no physical marks on the victim. Neither the alleged forms of psychological or sexual torture, nor most of the physical torture ("bagging", "hooding" and low-voltage electric shocks) left external signs of injury on the body;

— With regard to the dating of the various bruises, the complainant adduced the theory put forward by the first expert, defining two of them as between two and six days old, while the other two were said to be more recent. The fact that the bruises had not been detected earlier could have been due to a defective physical examination or to the poor light;

— With regard to the value of the victim's testimony considering the lack of objective evidence, reference was made to the case law of the Supreme Court, according to which account should be taken of the absence of reasonable doubt, verisimilitude corroborated by circumstantial evidence, and consistency in the charges. Furthermore, in the course of the police raid on 29 January 1992 many detainees complained of ill-treatment to the forensic physician and the examining magis-trate. The complainant therefore called for statements to be taken from the person with whom she had shared a cell while in detention, as well as from the officers on guard.

7.7 On 5 September 1995 the Provincial High Court dismissed the appeal. On 28 September 1995 the author made an application for *amparo* to the Constitutional Court as she considered that the Provincial High Court's decision violated articles 15 (right to physical and moral integrity) and 24 (right to the protection of the courts) of the Constitution, the latter on the ground of failure to allow the submission of evidence proposed by the author, namely, a statement by the prison doctor who noted the injuries and statements by the members of the Guardia Civil responsible for custody.

7.8 On 29 January 1996, the Constitutional Court rejected the application for *amparo*, holding that "the right to bring an action at law does not in turn imply an absolute right to the institution and full conduct of a criminal proceeding, but entails only the right to a reasoned judicial decision on the claims made, which may well be to stay or dismiss the proceedings or, indeed, to declare the complaint inadmissible".

Examination on the merits

8.1 The Committee has considered the communication in the light of all the information made available to it by the parties, in accordance with article 22, paragraph 4, of the Convention.

8.2 The Committee observes that, under article 12 of the Convention, the authorities have the obligation to proceed to an investigation ex officio, wherever there are reasonable grounds to believe that acts of torture or ill-treatment have been committed and whatever the origin of the suspicion. Article 12 also requires that the investigation should be prompt and impartial. The Committee observes that promptness is essential both to ensure that the victim cannot continue to be subjected to such acts and also because in general, unless the methods employed have permanent or serious effects, the physical traces of torture, and especially of cruel, inhuman or degrading treatment, soon disappear.

8.3 The Committee observes that when she appeared before the National High Court on 2 February 1992, after having been held incommunicado since 29 January, the author stated that she had been subjected to physical and mental ill-treatment, including the threat of rape. The Court had before it five reports of the forensic physician attached to the National High Court who had examined her daily, the first four examinations having taken place on Guardia Civil premises and the last on the premises of the National High Court prior to the above-mentioned court appearance. These reports note that the author complained of having been subjected to ill-treatment consisting of insults, threats and blows, of having been kept hooded for many hours and of having been forced to remain naked, although she displayed no signs of violence. The Committee considers that these elements should have sufficed for the initiation of an investigation, which did not however take place.

8.4 The Committee also observes that when, on 3 February 1992, the physician of the penitentiary centre noted bruises and contusions on the author's body, this fact was brought to the attention of the judicial authorities. However, the competent judge did not take up the matter until 17 February and Court N° 44 initiated preliminary proceedings only on 21 February.

8.5 The Committee finds that the lack of investigation of the author's allegations, which were made first to the forensic physician after the first examination and during the subsequent examinations she underwent, and then repeated before the judge of the National High Court, and the amount of time which passed between the reporting of the facts and the initiation of proceedings by Court N° 44 are incompatible with the obligation to proceed to a prompt investigation, as provided for in article 12 of the Convention.

8.6 The Committee observes that article 13 of the Convention does not require either the formal lodging of a complaint of torture under the procedure laid down in national law or an express statement of intent to institute and sustain a criminal action arising from the offence, and that it is enough for the victim simply to bring the facts to the attention of an authority of the State for the latter to be obliged to consider it as a tacit but unequivocal expression of the victim's wish that the facts should be promptly and impartially investigated, as prescribed by this provision of the Convention.

8.7 The Committee notes, as stated above, that the author's complaint to the judge of the National High Court was not examined and that, while Court N° 44 examined the complaint, it did not do so with the requisite promptness. Indeed, more than three weeks passed from the time that the court received the medical report from the penitentiary centre on 17 February 1992 until the author was brought to court and made her statement on 13 March. On that same date the court called for Section 2 of the National High Court to provide the findings of the medical examinations of the author by the forensic physician of that court, but more than two months elapsed before on 13 May they were added to the case file. On 2 June the judge requested the court's own forensic physician to report thereon, and this was done on 28 July. On 3 August the judge summoned the forensic physician of Court N° 2 who had conducted the said examinations. This physician's statement was taken on 17 November. On that same date the court requested the penitentiary centre to indicate the time at which the author had been examined in that institution and how the injuries had developed; this information was transmitted to the court on 23 December. Contrary to the State party's contention, as cited in paragraph 6.4, that there had been "no tardiness or delay in the conduct of the investigation", the Committee considers that the above chronology shows the investigative measures not to have satisfied the requirement for promptness in examining complaints, as prescribed by article 13 of the Convention, a defect that cannot be excused by the lack of any protest from the author for such a long period.

8.8 The Committee also observes that during the preliminary proceedings, up to the time when they were discontinued on 12 February 1993, the court took no steps to identify and question any of the Guardia Civil officers who might have taken part in the acts complained of by the author. The Committee finds this omission inexcusable, since a criminal investigation must seek both to determine the nature and circumstances of the alleged acts and to establish the identity of any person who might have been involved therein, as required by the State party's own domestic legislation (article 789 of the Criminal Procedure Act). Furthermore, the Committee observes that, when the proceedings resumed as of October 1994, the author requested the judge on at least two occasions to allow the submission of evidence additional to that of the medical experts, i.e., she requested the hearing of witnesses as well as the possible perpetrators of the ill-treatment, but these hearings were not ordered.

The Committee nevertheless believes that such evidence was entirely pertinent since, although forensic medical reports are important as evidence of acts of torture, they are often insufficient and have to be compared with and supplemented by other information. The Committee has found no justification in this case for the refusal of the judicial authorities to allow other evidence and, in particular, that proposed by the author. The Committee considers these omissions to be incompatible with the obligation to proceed to an impartial investigation, as provided for in article 13 of the Convention.

9. The Committee against Torture, acting under article 22, paragraph 7, of the Convention, is of the view that the facts before it reveal a violation of articles 12 and 13 of the Convention.

10. Pursuant to rule 111, paragraph 5, of its rules of procedure, the Committee would wish to receive, within 90 days, information on any relevant measures taken by the State party in accordance with the Committee's Views.

Communication N° 63/1997

Submitted by: Josu Arkauz Arana
Alleged victim: The author
State party: France
Date of adoption of Views: 9 November 1999

Subject matter: deportation of complainant to Spain with alleged risk of torture or cruel, inhuman or degrading treatment

Procedural issue: exhaustion of domestic remedies

Substantive issues: risk of torture after deportation; risk of cruel, inhuman or degrading treatment or punishment after deportation

Articles of the Convention: 3, 16

1.1 The author of the communication is Josu Arkauz Arana, a Spanish national. He is represented by counsel. Mr. Arkauz applied to the Committee on 16 December 1996 claiming to be a victim of violations by France of articles 3 and 16 of the Convention against Torture and Other Cruel, Inhuman or Degrading Treatment or Punishment because of his deportation to Spain.

1.2 In accordance with article 22, paragraph 3, of the Convention, the Committee brought the communication to the attention of the State party on 13 January 1997. At the same time, acting under rule 108, paragraph 9, of its rules of procedure, the Committee requested the State party not to expel Mr. Arkauz to Spain while his communication was being considered.

The facts as submitted by the author

2.1 The author, who is of Basque origin, states that he left Spain in 1983 following numerous arrests of persons reportedly belonging to ETA, the Basque separatist movement, by the security forces in his native village and nearby. Many of the persons arrested, some of whom were his childhood friends, were subjected to torture. During the interrogations and torture sessions, the name of Josu Arkauz Arana had been one of those most frequently mentioned. Sensing that he was a wanted person and in order to avoid being tortured, he fled. In 1984 his brother was arrested. In the course of several torture sessions the members of the security forces asked the latter questions about the author and said that Josu Arkauz Arana would be executed by the Anti-Terrorist Liberation Groups (GAL).

2.2 Several murders of Basque refugees and attempts on the lives of others took place close to where the author was working in Bayonne. The author further states that the officer in charge of the Biarritz police station summoned him in late 1984 to notify him of his fears that an attempt on his life was being prepared and that the author's administrative file, which contained all the information necessary to locate him, had been stolen. He was therefore obliged to leave his work and lead a clandestine existence. Throughout the period of his concealment, his relatives and friends were continually harassed by the Spanish security forces. In June 1987 his brother-in-law was arrested and tortured in an effort to make him reveal the author's whereabouts.

2.3 In March 1991, the author was arrested on the charge of belonging to ETA and sentenced to eight years' imprisonment for criminal conspiracy ("association de malfaiteurs"). He began serving his sentence in Saint-Maur prison and was due to be released on 13 January 1997. However, on 10 July

1992, he was further sentenced to a three-year ban from French territory. He filed an appeal against the decision to ban him with the Paris Court of Major Jurisdiction in October 1996, but no action was taken.

2.4 On 15 November 1996, the Ministry of the Interior commenced a proceeding for the author's deportation from French territory. A deportation order can be enforced by the administration ex officio and means that the person concerned is automatically taken to the border. The author applied to the Administrative Court of Limoges on 13 December 1996 requesting the annulment of the deportation order which might be made out against him and a stay of execution of such an order if it were to be issued. However, his application for a stay of execution was rejected by a ruling of 15 January 1997, the court having taken the view that handing over the author would not be likely to have irreversible consequences for him. An appeal from this ruling was not possible because the deportation measure had already been implemented.

2.5 On 10 December 1996, the author began a hunger strike to protest against his deportation. Later, because of his deteriorating health, the author was transferred to the local prison at Fresnes, in the Paris region, where he again went on strike, refusing to take liquids.

2.6 On 17 December 1996, the author was informed that the Deportation Board of the Indre Prefecture had rendered an opinion in favour of his deportation, considering that his presence in French territory constituted a serious threat to public order. The Board did, however, remind the Ministry of the Interior of the law stipulating that an alien could not be removed to another country where his life or liberty might be threatened or where he could be exposed to treatment contrary to article 3 of the European Convention on Human Rights. Following this opinion, a ministerial deportation order was issued on 13 January 1997 and communicated that day to the author. He was at the same time notified of a decision indicating that the order of deportation to Spain was being put into effect. The deportation measure was implemented the same day, after a medical examination had concluded that Mr. Arkauz could be transported by car to the Spanish border.

2.7 By a letter of 17 March 1997, the author informed the Committee that his deportation to Spain had taken place on 13 January 1997. He reported having been ill-treated and threatened by the French police and described the incidents which occurred in Spain after his deportation.

2.8 The author claims to have suffered greatly during the journey to Spain because of his extreme weakness. He states that while being driven from Fresnes to the Spanish border, a distance of nearly 1,000 kilometres covered in seven hours, he was seated between two police officers, with his hands cuffed behind his back, and he experienced very considerable back pain because he suffers from degenerative discopathy. The police officers are said to have stopped at one point and ordered Mr. Arkauz to get out of the vehicle. Since he was unable to move, the police officers reportedly threw him to the ground and beat him. He adds that the police officers intimidated him throughout the journey and that the treatment to which he was subjected is contrary to article 16 of the Convention.

2.9 As soon as he had been handed over to the Spanish Civil Guard he was placed in incommunicado detention. A forensic physician is said to have examined him and pronounced him fit to travel on to Madrid under certain conditions, since his health had been very much affected by the hunger strike. He states that he was slapped on the ears and about the head during the journey of about 500 kilometres to Madrid. He also claims to have been constantly told that he would later be tortured and killed. On entering Madrid, the officials are said to have thrust his head between his knees so that he would not know where he was being taken, namely to the Civil Guard Headquarters in Madrid. He says that he fainted from exhaustion. When revived, he was reportedly subjected to long interrogation sessions. He was allegedly forced to remain seated, with his legs apart, in a position that caused him very considerable back pain. With his eyes covered, he was reportedly slapped all over his body. He was also allegedly subjected to loud hand claps and whistling close to his ears and told in detail about the methods and long sessions of torture that would be inflicted on him. At one point, the guards are said to have ripped his clothes off, while continuing to beat him. Later, with some guards holding his legs and others his arms, he was allegedly subjected to "*la bolsa*"[1] and at the same time beaten on the testicles. He reportedly then lost consciousness. When revived and still masked, he was reportedly again seated on a chair, with his legs spread apart and his arms held to his legs. The guards allegedly brought electrodes close to him. As he tried to move away, he reportedly received a direct shock.

2.10 Some officials reportedly tried to persuade him to cooperate with them, using emotional arguments concerning his wife and two children, but the author says that he refused to cooperate. He was reportedly then examined by a doctor. After the doctor left, he was reportedly masked again and beaten about the ears and the head. Another examination was made by a doctor, who reportedly stated that the author was close to suffering from

---

[1] This form of torture consists in covering the head with a plastic bag to cause asphyxia.

tachycardia. The interrogations and threats continued and a third visit was made by the doctor some hours later. Meanwhile, his wife met the judge on 15 January 1997. She expressed fears concerning her husband's state of health and asked to see him, but this request was denied. On the forensic physician's advice, the author was transferred to a hospital. After being injected with serum and undergoing various tests, he was returned to Civil Guard Headquarters. During the day of 16 January, out of fear of reprisals, he signed a statement before a designated lawyer which the Civil Guard officers had themselves dictated. That evening he was brought before the judge, who had just lifted the incommunicado order. He was also examined by a forensic physician appointed by the family. This physician concluded that the allegations of ill-treatment represented coherent testimony. [2] On 17 January 1997, Mr. Arkauz was visited by a delegation of the European Committee for the Prevention of Torture and Inhuman or Degrading Treatment or Punishment (CPT)[3] in Soto del Real prison. On 10 March 1997, he filed a complaint of torture.

The complaint

3.1 In his communication of 16 December 1996, the author stated that his forcible return to Spain and handing over to the Spanish security forces constituted a violation by France of articles 3 and 16 of the Convention against Torture.

3.2 The author referred to article 22, paragraph 5 (b), of the Convention and claimed that the domestic remedies available against warrants of deportation were neither useful nor effective, since they had no suspensive effect and the courts would reach a decision long after the deportation had been carried out. In addition, the procedures were unreasonably prolonged. The admissibility requirement of exhaustion of domestic remedies was therefore said not to be applicable in the case.

3.3 The author submitted that his origin, political affiliation and conviction in France and the threats directed against him, his family and friends provided substantial grounds for fearing that he would be mistreated in custody and that the Spanish police would use every possible means, including torture, to obtain information about ETA activities from him. The danger was all the more real because the author had been portrayed in the press by the Spanish authorities as an ETA leader.

3.4 The handing-over of the author to the Spanish security forces allegedly was a "disguised extradition" for the purpose of his incarceration and conviction in Spain. It was an administrative procedure that did not arise from an extradition request made by the Spanish judicial authorities. The five days of police custody and incommunicado detention to which Mr. Arkauz could be subjected under the Spanish law on terrorism would be used to obtain from him the confessions needed for him to be charged. During this period he would not be given the protection of the judicial authorities to which he would have been entitled had he been extradited. The lack of jurisdictional guarantees thus increased the risk of torture.

3.5 In support of his claims, the author mentioned the cases of several Basque prisoners who had allegedly been tortured by the Spanish police between 1986 and 1996 after being expelled from French territory and handed over to the Spanish security forces at the border. In addition, he cited the reports of various international bodies and non-governmental organizations which had expressed their concern at the use of torture and ill-treatment in Spain and at the Spanish legislation enabling persons suspected of belonging to or collaborating with armed groups to be held incommunicado for five days, as well as regarding the impunity apparently enjoyed by the perpetrators of acts of torture. The combination of these various factors (existence of an administrative practice, serious deficiencies in the protection of persons deprived of their liberty and lack of punishment for officials employing torture) provided substantial grounds for believing that the author was in real danger of being subjected to torture. Lastly, he expressed his fears regarding the conditions of detention to which he would be submitted if he was imprisoned in Spain.

3.6 On 16 December 1996, the author also stated that during his transfer to the border there was a risk that he would be subjected to ill-treatment contrary to article 16 of the Convention, since the police could use force and he would be completely isolated from family and counsel.

3.7 On 17 March 1997, the author reiterates that there was a violation of articles 3 and 16 of the Convention and, subsidiarily, articles 2 and 22. In seeking to justify his surrender to the Spanish security forces, France is said to have violated article 2 of the Convention. France reportedly sought to justify that action on the basis of necessary solidarity between European States and cooperation against terrorism. However, neither the situation of acute conflict prevailing in the Basque country, nor solidarity between European States, nor the fight against terrorism can justify the practice of torture by the Spanish security forces.

3.8 The author further submits that, by proceeding with his deportation and surrendering him to the Spanish security forces, despite the Committee's

---

[2] A copy of the medical report is attached to the communication.
[3] As of the time of adoption of these Views the CPT report on this visit had not been published.

request not to expel him, the State party violated article 22 of the Convention because the individual remedy provided for by that article was rendered inoperative. He believes that the State party's attitude under those circumstances amounts to a denial of the binding nature of the Convention.

3.9 The author also criticizes the French authorities for the late notification of the deportation order and its immediate execution, the sole purpose of which, in his view, was to deprive him of any contact with his family and counsel, to prevent him from effectively preparing his defence and to place him at a psychological disadvantage. He submits that it was consequently impossible in practice for him to enter any appeal between the time of notification of the deportation order and its immediate execution.

State party's admissibility observations

4.1 On 31 October 1997, the State party disputes the admissibility of the communication. It indicates that on 13 January 1997, the day on which the deportation order was issued and carried out, it had not known of the Committee's request for a stay of execution, which was received on 14 January 1997, and it therefore could not have taken it into consideration. It adds that the immediate and rapid expulsion was necessary for reasons of public order.

4.2 The State party considers that the communication is inadmissible for non-exhaustion of domestic remedies. If, in view of the nature of the alleged violation, the Committee were nevertheless to consider that the remedies actually sought before the administrative and judicial courts were not useful since they had no suspensive effect, it should be pointed out that other channels of recourse were open to the author. When notified of the deportation order and the order indicating Spain as the country of return, he could have applied to the administrative court for a stay of execution or for effect to be given to article L.10 of the Code of Administrative Courts and Administrative Courts of Appeal. The author could also, when notified of the two orders, have complained of a flagrant irregularity ("voie de fait") to the judicial court if he believed that his transfer to Spain had no legal justification and violated a fundamental freedom. According to the State party, such a remedy could have proved effective in view of the rapidity with which the judicial court is required to act and its recognized authority to put an end to a situation which constitutes a flagrant irregularity.

4.3 The State party further specifies that, in order to obtain a rapid decision, the complainant could have applied to the interim relief judge on the basis of article 485 of the new Code of Civil Procedure.[4] It grants that an application for interim relief is admissible only in support of an application in the main action, but argues that such an application could in the present case have been made for damages for the injury suffered as a result of the irregularity. Furthermore, the Prefect who signed the orders of deportation and return to Spain could not have opposed consideration of such an application by the judicial court pursuant to article 136 of the Code of Criminal Procedure.[5]

Author's comments

5.1 In his comments, the author recalls the facts and procedures explained in the previous communication and reiterates his observations concerning the admissibility of the communication. With regard to the merits of the case, he recalls his claims concerning the personal threat to him of his being deported to Spain, and the torture and ill-treatment he underwent.

5.2 With reference to the request for a stay of execution of the deportation order made by the Committee on 13 January 1997, the author disputes the State party's claim that it had not received the request until 14 January 1997 and therefore did not have time to take it into consideration. In fact, the Government's representative was informed by fax of the request made by the Committee on 13 January 1997, well before the author was notified of the deportation order late on 13 January 1997. The author adds that he was handed over to the Civil Guard by the French police only on 14 January 1997. During the transfer, the French Government could, according to the author, have contacted its officials and deferred deportation.

5.3 The author further argues that even if the French Government had not received the Committee's request until 14 January 1997, it had the obligation, on receiving it, under article 3 of the Convention, to intercede with the Spanish authorities, through diplomatic channels, for example, to ensure that the author was protected against any possible ill-treatment. He specifies that he was tortured continuously up to 16 January 1997, long after the French authorities had received the Committee's request.

---

[4] This article states that "an application for interim relief is made by way of summons to a hearing held on the customary day and at the customary time for such proceedings. If greater speed is required, however, the interim relief judge may allow a summons to be given effect at the time indicated, even on public holidays or non-working days, either in chambers or at his place of residence, in an open hearing".

[5] This article states that "in all cases of infringement of the freedom of the individual, the dispute cannot be taken up by the administrative authority and the judicial courts always have exclusive jurisdiction".

5.4 The author contests the State party's claim that his immediate and rapid deportation was necessary for reasons of public order. Although he was in Fresnes prison, the French authorities chose to have him taken to the Franco-Spanish border, which was the furthest from Paris, yet as a European citizen Mr. Arkauz was entitled to stay and move freely in any part of the European Union, including countries with much less distant borders. According to the author, this is further evidence of the fact that the French authorities deliberately and consciously put him in the hands of the Spanish security forces.

5.5 With regard to domestic remedies, the author submits that the requirement of exhaustion of domestic remedies concerns available, i.e., accessible, remedies. However, he was prevented from having access to the available remedies. The deportation order was carried out immediately by the French police, who allegedly forbade him to warn his wife and counsel. It would thus have been physically impossible for him to communicate with them to inform them that he had been notified of the deportation order and to ask them to file an immediate appeal against his deportation. Furthermore, the French authorities allegedly refused to give them any information on what had happened to him.

5.6 Mr. Arkauz argues that, under article 22, paragraph 5 (b), of the Convention, the rule of the exhaustion of domestic remedies does not apply when their application is unreasonably prolonged. He adds that domestic remedies against deportation must have an immediate and suspensive effect. In the present case, however, no judge could have made a ruling within a "reasonable" time, since the decisions in question were enforced immediately the person concerned had been notified of them.

5.7 Thirdly, Mr. Arkauz submits that, under article 22, paragraph 5 (b), the rule of the exhaustion of remedies concerns effective and adequate remedies, and therefore does not apply if the remedies are unlikely to bring relief to the individual concerned. In the present case, neither the administrative remedy nor the judicial remedy proposed by the State party can be considered effective or adequate.

5.8 As regards the administrative remedy, the author points out that, as a preventive measure, he had applied to the Administrative Court of Limoges against his deportation and that the court had reached a decision on that application only after the deportation had been carried out. In response to the State party's argument that he could have reapplied to the administrative court, on being notified of the deportation order and of the order indicating Spain as the country of return, for a stay of execution or for the application of article L.10 of the Code of Administrative Courts and Administrative Courts of Appeal, Mr. Arkauz states that this remedy would have been no more effective than its predecessor.

5.9 As regards the judicial remedy, the author contests the theory of flagrant irregularity put forward by the State party. He states that this theory is applicable in French law only under exceptional circumstances, in particular when the administration has taken a decision which manifestly cannot be related to a power conferred upon it or when it has enforced a decision of its own volition although it manifestly did not have the authority to do so, which is not the case in the present instance. Mr. Arkauz quotes rulings of the Court of Conflicts to the effect that neither a deportation decision, even if illegal, nor a decision to enforce it may be termed flagrant irregularities, and hence only the administrative courts have jurisdiction in such matters.

The Committee's admissibility decision

6.1 At its twentieth session the Committee considered the question of the admissibility of the communication. It ascertained that the same matter had not been, and was not being, examined under another procedure of international investigation or settlement. In so far as the exhaustion of domestic remedies is concerned, the Committee noted that no decision regarding the application to the administrative court requesting the suspension of the deportation measure which might have been taken against the author had been reached when the measure was enforced. Furthermore, an appeal against the ministerial deportation order issued in respect of the complainant on 13 January 1997 would not have been effective or even possible, since it would not have had a suspensive effect and the deportation measure was enforced immediately following notification thereof, leaving the person concerned no time to seek a remedy. The Committee therefore found that article 22, paragraph 5 (b), did not preclude it from declaring the communication admissible.

6.2 Accordingly, on 19 May 1998, the Committee declared the communication admissible.

State party's observations on the Committee's admissibility decision

7.1 On 4 January 1999, the State party provides further information concerning the question of the exhaustion of domestic remedies. It maintains that the author's application to the Administrative Court of Limoges cannot be considered to be relevant, since it does not concern the decision challenged before the Committee. That application, filed on 16 December 1996 in the court registry, was directed not against the deportation measure in dispute, which had not yet been taken, but against a deportation measure that "might" have been taken.

That wording alone was sufficient to make the complaint of Mr. Arkauz inadmissible, as the practice of the administrative courts consistently requires complainants to challenge current and existing decisions. Therefore, the fact that no ruling had been made on the complaint by 13 January 1997, when the deportation order was issued, does not appear to be decisive in the present case. The judgement was given two days later, i.e., less than a month after registration of the application. The rendering of this court decision was obviously not a matter of the greatest urgency, since it related not to a current but to a possible measure.

7.2 The author failed to lodge an appeal against the ministerial order of 13 January 1997 calling for his deportation from French territory and against the decision specifying Spain as the country of destination. An application for a stay of execution under article L.10 of the Code of Administrative Courts and Administrative Courts of Appeal, a possibility of which the complainant was clearly aware, was both an appropriate and available remedy. It was not, however, used. The State party therefore submits that the Committee should declare the communication inadmissible under rule 110, paragraph 6, of the rules of procedure.

7.3 The State party argues that the execution of the deportation measure in question in no way resulted from a desire of the Government to obviate the right of recourse available to the person concerned, both at national and international level. It was physically impossible for the Government to have known on 13 January 1997, the day on which the deportation order was issued and implemented, of the request for a stay of execution made by the Committee in its letter of 13 January 1997, that letter having been received the following day by the State party, as attested by the stamp placed on the said document when it arrived. It was therefore impossible for the request to be taken into consideration before the execution of the measure.

7.4 The deportation measure was implemented on 13 January 1997, since on that date the author had paid the sum he owed to the Treasury following his court conviction and there was then no reason, bearing in mind the threat that his presence would represent for public order after his release, to defer a decision to call for and proceed with his deportation. Although the author claims that it was physically impossible for him to enter an appeal, he offers no proof of this, and he certainly does not deny that the notice of the deportation order, which he refused to sign, included information about the procedures and time limits for an appeal.

Further comments by the author

8.1 The author states that when he was notified of the deportation order and of the decision indicating Spain as the country of destination, he was prevented by the authorities from communicating with his wife and counsel. Furthermore, when the latter asked the authorities for news about the author, no information was given to them. Thus, contrary to the State party's contention, it was made impossible for the author, after notification of the deportation order and before its execution, to apply for a remedy, to be brought before a person capable of receiving such an application or to communicate with persons who could have acted in his place.

8.2 The author indicates that the applications made to the Administrative Court of Limoges were referred, on 27 July 1998, for consideration by the Administrative Court of Pau, which rendered its judgement on 4 February 1999. The judgement states that while at the time of its submission the request was premature, the issuance of the orders of 13 January 1997 calling for the deportation of Mr. Arkauz and his return to Spain had the effect of regularizing the request. The Court also found the handing over of the author to the Spanish security forces to be illegal and therefore annulled that measure. However, an appeal to a French administrative court has no suspensive effect and the Administrative Court of Pau did not reach a decision on the author's request until two years after the actual implementation of the deportation order. The finding of the author's surrender to be illegal therefore has only a symbolic effect in the circumstances of the present case.

State party's merits observations

9.1 The State party notes that, on arrival in France, the author was given temporary permits to stay as an asylum-seeker but the French Office for the Protection of Refugees and Stateless Persons (OFPRA) and the Refugee Appeals Board rejected his asylum request in 1981. Thereafter, he neither reapplied for refugee status, as he could have done, nor looked for another country prepared to accept him, although his situation was irregular and he knew that he might be subject to an enforceable measure of banishment. In 1992 he was sentenced to eight years' imprisonment, a ten-year prohibition on residence and a three-year ban from French territory for conspiring with others to commit one or more offences, as well as for illegally bearing weapons, keeping explosives and munitions and using false administrative documents. That conviction automatically gave rise to the possibility of deportation.

9.2 The State party indicates that the real risks mentioned by the author were evaluated by the national authorities prior to implementation of the deportation procedure, according to the criteria defined in article 3, paragraph 2, of the Convention.

9.3 Two points led the administration to believe that there was nothing to prevent implementation of the deportation measure. Firstly, the specialized bodies responsible for determining eligibility for political refugee status had rejected the author's application in 1981, feeling that the fears of persecution alleged by him were unfounded. Secondly, in view of the commitments made by Spain regarding the protection of fundamental freedoms, the French Government, although certainly not unaware that the person concerned might be subject to criminal prosecution in that country, could legitimately feel that there were no substantial grounds for believing that the author was in danger of being tortured. The legitimacy of that position was confirmed by the European Commission of Human Rights, which, in its inadmissibility decisions of 1998 in two cases where the points of fact and law were perfectly comparable, considered that the French Government had no substantial grounds for believing that the complainants would be subjected to torture in Spain. The Commission noted that there was a presumption favourable to that country concerning respect for human rights, in particular on account of its accession to the European Convention, the International Covenant on Civil and Political Rights and the Optional Protocol thereto. It also made reference to the report of the European Committee for the Prevention of Torture, which stated that torture could not be regarded as common practice in Spain.

9.4 The State party indicates that, before being taken to the border, Mr. Arkauz underwent a medical examination, which concluded that he was in a fit state to be deported, and that after his arrest and detention by the Spanish authorities he was again seen by a doctor. Furthermore, the procedure initiated in Spain was conducted in accordance with the instructions of the examining magistrate who had issued international arrest warrants and authorized the transfer of Mr. Arkauz to Civil Guard Headquarters in Madrid, so that he could be heard in the presence of a lawyer.

9.5 If the author had indeed been the victim of acts contrary to article 3 of the Convention, a supposition which might be verified by the proceedings under way in Spain, those acts could only be regarded as having been committed by isolated individuals in breach of the guidelines laid down by the Spain. As such, they could not have been foreseen and the French Government cannot be blamed for having neither suspected nor prevented such an outcome.

9.6 For the above reasons, no failure to comply with the provisions of article 3 of the Convention can be established.

9.7 As to the claim of a violation of article 16 of the Convention, the State party submits that the author cannot invoke this article, because the territory in which the alleged violations of article 3 of the Convention were committed is not under French jurisdiction.

Author's further comments

10.1 The author reiterates that there were substantial grounds for believing that he would be in personal danger of being subjected to torture if deported to Spain. The existence of such a danger was confirmed by the following facts: the author and his family had been the targets of threats and harassment; the Anti-Terrorist Liberation Groups (GAL) were preparing an attempt on his life; and he had been handed over by the French police to Civil Guard personnel from the anti-terrorist sections of the Intxaurrondo barracks, which had been publicly accused, inter alia, of committing acts of torture. Furthermore, during his interrogation in January 1997 the Civil Guard personnel confirmed to him that they had prepared an assassination attempt against him while he was living in Bayonne; and he had been portrayed by the Spanish authorities as an important figure in the ETA.

10.2 The author reiterates that the length and conditions of the police custody are conducive to the practice of torture and other forms of ill-treatment by the Spanish security forces and that the machinery for supervision and forensic medical assistance for detainees are seriously inadequate. Inquiries into the circumstances of torture are very difficult and when, on occasion, they are completed, the procedures are very long.

10.3 The State party maintains that the author should have requested political refugee status on the grounds of the risks to his life and liberty in the event of his return to Spain. However, for political reasons, the French Government no longer grants such status to Basques applying for it. Furthermore, the protection arising under article 3 of the Convention concerns "everyone" and not just persons applying for or having the status of refugee.

10.4 According to the author, the State party is making an erroneous interpretation of the findings of the European Committee for the Prevention of Torture (CPT). The latter actually stated that "it would be premature to conclude that the phenomenon of torture and severe ill-treatment had been eradicated" in Spain.[6]

10.5 The fact that Spain is a party to the Convention and has recognized the competence of

---

[6] Reports to the Spanish Government on the visits which took place from 1 to 12 April 1991, 10 to 22 April 1994 and 10 to 14 June 1994, CPT/Inf (96) 9, paras. 25 and 206.

the Committee under article 22 does not, in the present case, constitute a sufficient guarantee of the author's safety.

10.6 In so far as the violation of article 16 of the Convention is concerned, the State party has not denied that the author was subjected to ill-treatment during his transfer to the border post. Those acts should have been the subject of a prompt and impartial investigation by the competent authorities, in accordance with article 12 of the Convention. However, no such investigation was held. The State party does not dispute the fact that the author was illegally handed over to the Spanish security forces while in a state of extreme weakness, after 35 days of a hunger strike and five days of refusing to take liquids. The fact of handing over a person under such circumstances for prolonged interrogation in itself constitutes cruel, inhuman and degrading treatment. In addition, at the time of the deportation, the medical file of the person concerned was transmitted by the French police to the Spanish Civil Guard officers. Moreover, the medical details contained in this file, and in particular the fact that the author was suffering from degenerative discopathy, were used during the police custody to aggravate the author's suffering, notably by forcing him to adopt postures designed to increase his back pain. The fact of having supplied the medical file also constitutes cruel, inhuman and degrading treatment.

Issues and proceedings before the Committee

11.1 In accordance with rule 110, paragraph 6, of its rules of procedure, the Committee reconsidered the question of admissibility in the light of the observations made by the State party concerning the Committee's decision declaring the communication admissible. The Committee notes, however, that the application made by the author to the Administrative Court of Limoges was relevant even if, at the time of its submission, the deportation measure had not yet been taken. This was confirmed by the judgement of the Administrative Court of Pau, which stated that the issuance of the orders of 13 January 1997 calling for the deportation of Mr. Arkauz and his return to Spain had the effect of regularizing the author's application. The Committee accordingly found no reason to revoke its decision.

11.2 The Committee has noted the author's allegations that he was ill-treated by French police officers while being driven to the Spanish border. The Committee considers, however, that the author has not exhausted domestic remedies available in this respect. It therefore declares that this part of the communication is inadmissible.

11.3 With regard to the substance of the communication, the Committee must determine whether the author's deportation to Spain violated the obligation of the State party, under article 3, paragraph 1, of the Convention, not to expel or return a person to another State where there are substantial grounds for believing that he would be in danger of being subjected to torture. In so doing, the Committee must take into account all relevant considerations with a view to determining whether the person concerned is in personal danger.

11.4 The Committee recalls that during the consideration of the third periodic report submitted by Spain under article 19 of the Convention, it expressed its concern about complaints of acts of torture and ill-treatment. It also noted that, notwithstanding the legal guarantees as to the conditions under which it could be imposed, there were cases of prolonged detention incommunicado, when the detainee could not receive the assistance of a lawyer of his choice, which seemed to facilitate the practice of torture. Most complaints received concerned torture inflicted during such periods.[7] Similar concerns had already been expressed during the consideration of the second periodic report by the Committee,[8] as well as in the concluding observations of the Human Rights Committee regarding the fourth periodic report submitted by Spain under article 40 of the International Covenant on Civil and Political Rights.[9] Furthermore, the European Committee for the Prevention of Torture (CPT) had also reported complaints of torture or ill-treatment received during its visits to Spain in 1991 and 1994, in particular from persons detained for terrorist activities. The CPT concluded that it would be premature to affirm that torture and severe ill-treatment had been eradicated in Spain.[10]

11.5 The Committee notes the specific circumstances under which the author's deportation took place. First, the author had been convicted in France for his links with ETA, had been sought by the Spanish police and had been suspected, according to the press, of holding an important position within that organization. There had also been suspicions, expressed in particular by some non-governmental organizations, that other persons in the same circumstances as the author had been subjected to torture on being returned to Spain and during their incommunicado detention. The deportation was effected under an administrative procedure, which the Administrative Court of Pau had later found to be illegal, entailing a direct handover from police to police,[11] without the

---

[7] A/53/44, paras. 129 and 131.
[8] A/48/44, paras. 456 and 457.
[9] CCPR/C/79/Add.61 of 3 April 1996.
[10] CPT/Inf (96) 9, paras. 208–209.
[11] At the time of the consideration of the second periodic report submitted by France pursuant to article 19 of the Convention, the Committee expressed its concern at the practice whereby the police hand over individuals to their counterparts in another country (A/53/44, para. 143).

intervention of a judicial authority and without any possibility for the author to contact his family or his lawyer. That meant that a detainee's rights had not been respected and had placed the author in a situation where he was particularly vulnerable to possible abuse. The Committee recognizes the need for close cooperation between States in the fight against crime and for effective measures to be agreed upon for that purpose. It believes, however, that such measures must fully respect the rights and fundamental freedoms of the individuals concerned.

12. In the light of the foregoing, the Committee is of the view that the author's expulsion to Spain, in the circumstances in which it took place, constitutes a violation by the State party of article 3 of the Convention.

13. Pursuant to rule 111, paragraph 5, of its rules of procedure, the Committee would wish to receive, within 90 days, information on any measure taken by the State party in accordance with these Views.

Communication N° 99/1997

Submitted by: T.P.S. (name withheld)
Alleged victim: The author
State party: Canada
Date of adoption of Views: 16 May 2000

Subject matter: deportation of complainant to India and exposure to alleged risk of torture

Procedural issues: exhaustion of domestic remedies; failure to comply with request for interim measures

Substantive issues: risk of torture after deportation; exception for serious crimes (art. 1F of Refugee Convention)

Article of the Convention: 3

1. The author of the communication is Mr. T.P.S., an Indian citizen born in 1952 who was seeking asylum in Canada at the time the communication was registered. He claimed that his forcible return to India would constitute a violation by Canada of article 3 of the Convention against Torture. He is represented by counsel.

The facts as presented by the author

2.1 In January 1986, the author and four co-accused were convicted by a Pakistani court of hijacking an Indian Airlines plane in September 1981 and sentenced to life imprisonment. Counsel explains that no violence was used during the hijacking and that the plane, which was on its way from New Delhi to Amritsar, landed safely in Lahore, where it was diverted. There were no reports that any passenger had been mistreated. The purpose of the hijacking was to draw attention to the general maltreatment of Sikhs by the Indian Government. The author states that he was arrested within hours of the plane landing and forced to sign a confession at gunpoint. He also states that he was held in pretrial detention for four years without access to counsel. It is not clear whether he claims to be innocent, but he argues that his trial was unfair and the ensuing conviction unlawful.

2.2 In October 1994, the Government of Pakistan released the author and his co-accused on the condition that they leave the country. The author states that he could not return to India for fear of persecution. With the assistance of an agent and using a false name and passport, he arrived in Canada in May 1995. Upon arrival he applied for refugee status under his false name and did not reveal his true identity and history. In September 1995, the author was arrested and kept in detention by Immigration authorities. He was later released on the condition that he reports once a week to a Vancouver immigration office.

2.3 At the end of 1995, an immigration inquiry was opened against the author to determine whether he had committed an offence outside Canada which, if committed in Canada, would constitute an offence punishable by a maximum prison term of 10 years or more. His refugee application was suspended. In the beginning of 1996, an adjudicator decided that the author had committed such an offence and, as a result, a conditional deportation order was issued against him. At the same time the Canadian Minister of Immigration was requested to render an opinion whether the author constituted a danger to the Canadian public. Such a finding by the Minister would prevent the author from having his refugee claim heard and would remove his avenues of appeal under the Immigration Act.

2.4 The author successfully appealed the adjudicator's decision and a new inquiry was

51

ordered by the Federal Court of Canada. As a result of the second inquiry the author was again issued with a conditional deportation order. No appeal against the decision was filed for lack of funds. The Minister was again requested to render an opinion as to whether the author constituted a danger to the public. The Minister issued a certificate so stating and the author was detained with a view to his removal.

The complaint

3. The author states that the use of torture against suspected Sikh militants in India is well documented. He provides the Committee with articles and reports in that respect. He claims that he has serious grounds to believe that he will be subjected to torture upon return to India. Moreover, there is evidence that the Indian and Pakistani Governments have been actively cooperating with Canadian enforcement officials to have the author expelled. Given that he has already served his sentence, rightfully or wrongfully, and that he faces no charges for which he could be extradited, he believes that the Indian Government's interest in having him returned is for purely extrajudicial reasons.

State party's admissibility observations

4.1 On 18 December 1997 the Committee, acting through its Special Rapporteur for new communications, transmitted the communication to the State party for comments and requested the State party not to expel or deport the author to India while his communication was under consideration by the Committee. On 29 December 1997 the State party informed the Committee that the author had been removed from Canada to India on 23 December 1997. In reaching that decision the authorities had concluded that there were no substantial grounds for believing that the author would be in danger of being subjected to torture in India.

4.2 In a further submission dated 11 May 1998 the State party refers to the inquiries undertaken by the Canadian authorities. The author's refugee application was referred by a Senior Immigration Officer to the Convention Refugee Determination Division of the Canadian Immigration and Refugee Board on 26 May 1995. During his first interview with immigration officers the author used a false name and stated that he had never committed nor been convicted of a crime or offence. He based his refugee claim on religious persecution and cited one incident of mistreatment by the Indian police.

4.3 Subsequently, the Department of Citizenship and Immigration Canada (CIC) discovered his true identity and a report was issued stating that the author was suspected of belonging to a category considered inadmissible under the Immigration Act because he had engaged in acts of terrorism. On 21 September 1995 he was arrested. When interviewed by a CIC Immigration Investigator and two officers of the Canadian Security Intelligence Service (CSIS), he acknowledged that he was an active member of the Dal Khalsa terrorist group and had participated in the hijacking of the Indian Airlines flight. The State party also mentions that in an article dated 19 October 1994 published in the Pakistani press the author had pledged to continue the struggle for Khalistan.

4.4 In November 1995, another report concluded that the author belonged to another inadmissible category, namely persons for who there are reasonable grounds to believe had been convicted outside Canada of an offence that, if committed in Canada, would constitute an offence punishable by a term of at least 10 years' imprisonment. As a result of the two reports an adjudicator conducted an inquiry and concluded that the author had in fact been convicted of an offence that, if committed in Canada, would be punishable by a term of at least 10 years' imprisonment.

4.5 The author applied for leave for judicial review of this decision. The Government of Canada consented to his application after it was determined that the adjudicator had erred in the process of determining that the author was inadmissible. The Federal Court Trial Division ordered that a new inquiry be held. The adjudicator in charge of the second inquiry found, in a decision dated 30 May 1997, that the author was known for criminality and terrorism. As a result, a conditional deportation order was issued. The author did not seek leave for judicial review of this decision.

4.6 By letter dated 5 June 1997, the author was informed that CIC intended to request an opinion from the Minister of Citizenship and Immigration to the effect that it would be contrary to the public interest to have his refugee claim heard. The author was also apprised that as part of this procedure the Minister would consider any humanitarian and compassionate circumstances pertinent to his situation, including any possibility that he would be at risk should he be removed to India. The author was required to present submissions to the Minister, which he did.

4.7 On 3 December 1997, the CIC addressed a memorandum, to which the author's submissions were attached, to the Minister, evaluating the risk of returning him to India in the light of the documentary evidence of the human rights situation in India and the personal circumstances of the author. It was concluded that the author might face a minimal risk upon return to India, but that this minimal risk needed to be weighed against the impact of Canada providing refuge to an individual who had been convicted of hijacking, a terrorist act.

On 8 December 1997 the Minister rendered her opinion that it would be contrary to the public interest to have the author's refugee claim heard.

4.8 On 18 December 1997 the author applied for leave for judicial review of the Minister's decision. He also applied for an interim order staying the execution of the deportation order. On the same day the Government of Canada became aware, through a conversation with the author's counsel, that the author had filed a communication in September 1997 with the Committee and that the Committee had requested on 18 December 1997 that the author not be expelled pending its consideration of the communication. The Committee's letter informing the State party of the author's communication and the request for interim measures was received on 19 December 1997.

4.9 On 22 December 1997, the Federal Court Trial Division dismissed the author's application regarding the deportation order. The Court emphasized that the author would be excluded from Convention refugee status owing to his past terrorist activities and that Canada should not be nor be seen to be a haven for terrorists. It noted that the author had had ample opportunity to suggest another country of removal than India, that India did not have a policy of or encourage police brutality, and that the author's high profile would provide him with protection against any alleged possible ill-treatment by Indian authorities.

4.10 On 23 December 1997, the Court issued a supplementary decision with respect to the author's request that the Court certify the question whether a person's rights under the Canadian Charter of Rights and Freedoms are infringed in case of removal to a country where there is a reasonable possibility that the individual would be subjected to torture, pursuant to an opinion by the Minister that it would be contrary to the public interest to have the individual's refugee claim heard. The Court determined that the author's question should not be certified. In rendering its decision the Court found that the author had not shown that it would be demonstrably probable that he would face torture upon return to India.

4.11 On 23 December 1997, the author was removed from Canada. He was escorted to New Delhi by one CIC officer and one police officer. Upon arrival the author was dealt with in a normal fashion and was not treated by the Indian police any differently from other individuals removed to India.

4.12 On 9 March 1998, the author's application for leave for judicial review of the Minister's opinion concerning his refugee claim was dismissed by the Federal Court Trial Division for failure of the author to file an application record within the prescribed period.

4.13 The State party argues that the communication before the Committee is inadmissible for failure to exhaust domestic remedies. First of all, the author did not seek leave for judicial review of the 30 May 1997 decision of the adjudicator that he was inadmissible on the basis of terrorism and criminality under the Immigration Act. If leave had been sought and granted, that decision would have been reviewed by the Federal Court Trial Division. A successful review application would have resulted in an order that a new inquiry be held and a decision rendered consistent with the reasons of the Court. If it was determined that the petitioner did not fall within an inadmissible category, there would be no basis for excluding him from the refugee determination process and he would not have been removed from Canada pending consideration of his refugee claim. Moreover, the author could have sought an extension of the time required for the filing of the application for leave for judicial review. Such extensions are frequently granted and would have allowed the author to file a late application.

4.14 The author alleges that he did not appeal or seek judicial review for lack of funds. In fact, there is no charge for submitting an application for leave for judicial review and it is a comparatively inexpensive procedure. The author clearly found the financial means to retain counsel—or his counsel had acted pro bono—with respect to several previous and subsequent proceedings, including proceedings before the Committee. The author has not provided any evidence that he had sought legal aid or that legal aid had been denied.

4.15 Secondly, the author did apply for leave for judicial review with respect to the Minister's opinion that it would be contrary to the public interest to allow the author's refugee claim to be heard. However, the author failed to perfect this application by filing an application record within the prescribed period. As a result, the author's application was dismissed. If the author had filed an application record and leave had been granted, the Minister's opinion would have been scrutinized by the Federal Court Trial Division. If the application had been successful the Court would have returned the matter to the Minister for a decision in accordance with the reasons of the Court.

Counsel's comments

5.1 In a submission of 20 January 1998, counsel claimed that the State party, in its response of 29 December 1997, failed to indicate how the Canadian authorities arrived at their conclusion regarding the risk facing the author. The author was never afforded an opportunity to have his refugee claim heard, nor was he ever afforded the benefit of an oral hearing before an independent tribunal where he could give his personal testimony concerning his fears. The only opportunity that the author had to provide documentation regarding the risk he faced was when the Minister of Immigration was requested to render an opinion as to whether it would be contrary to the public interest to allow the author to proceed with his refugee claim. Once that documentation had been provided, the entire decision-making process was conducted by the immigration officials. Counsel was not even advised of what other materials the authorities would be considering; consequently, he never had an opportunity to comment upon or respond to all materials that might have been before the Minister.

5.2 Counsel refers to the memorandum to the Minister which she purportedly relied upon in taking her decision that it would be contrary to the public interest to allow the author to proceed with his refugee claim. According to counsel, the memorandum was evidence that there was absolutely no analysis of the particular risk facing the author in India given his past and current profile. It mainly focused on the author's past history and Canada's international obligations regarding the treatment of so-called terrorists; however, there was little reference to Canada's numerous international obligations under human rights treaties, including the 1951 Convention relating to the Status of Refugees.

5.3 Counsel also provided an affidavit by the author's niece who was in India when the author arrived from Canada. She states that upon his arrival, the author was subjected to interrogation for about six hours and that he was verbally threatened by officers from the Central Bureau of Investigation. She expressed concern that he would eventually be subjected to torture or extrajudicial execution. Further information submitted to the Committee by the niece indicates that the intimidation of the author and his family by the police has continued and that the author has informed the Human Rights Commission of Punjab about it.

5.4 With respect to the admissibility of the communication, counsel argues, in a submission of 11 June 1998, that at the time the decision of the adjudicator was rendered, it was not absolutely necessary for the author to seek leave for judicial review in order for him to be able to proceed with a refugee claim. The cost of the legal proceedings was only one factor, which guided the author's decision not to seek review. His main interest was to avoid any further delays in proceeding with his refugee claim. He had been in Canada for almost two years and was anxious to present his refugee claim to the Canadian authorities. He did not wish to delay this process by launching another judicial review. Secondly, there was little likelihood of success at any judicial review.

5.5 The State party stated that if it had determined that the petitioner did not fall within an inadmissible category, there would be no basis for excluding him from the refugee determination process and he would not have been removed pending consideration of his refugee claim. This statement is extremely misleading. In fact, the finding of the adjudicator resulted in the issuance of a conditional deportation order. This result does not necessarily mean that an individual will not be afforded the opportunity to proceed with his refugee claim; it provides that the deportation is conditional upon the outcome of the refugee claim.

5.6 Although it is acknowledged that the adjudicator's finding does provide immigration authorities with an avenue to seek the Minister's opinion with respect to whether the refugee process should remain open to such a person, there is no guarantee that such an avenue will be pursued. There was no obligation on the part of Canadian immigration authorities, or even the Minister, to prevent the author from proceeding with his refugee claim. The author's access to the refugee process was halted for political, not judicial or quasi-judicial, reasons. His refugee claim could have proceeded in spite of the adjudicator's finding.

5.7 The State party seems to be arguing that due diligence requires that a person ought to protect himself from every eventuality that might occur. Counsel argues that this is not the standard required by article 22 (5) of the Convention. A person who is anxious to proceed with telling his life story to authorities in order to secure their protection should not be blamed for not wishing to extend his agony by undertaking yet another judicial review when the refugee process remains open to him.

5.8 Regarding the author's failure to perfect an application for leave for judicial review of the Minister's opinion, counsel contends that the deadline would have been near the end of January 1998. However, the author was removed on 23 December 1997. This damage could not be undone regardless of the outcome of any judicial review application. The author had every intention of proceeding with an application for judicial review of the Minister's decision and counsel appeared in Federal Court on 20 December 1997 to seek a stay of the removal pending the outcome of this application. Unfortunately, the Federal Court chose to render a decision on what counsel views as the merits of the author's claim to refugee status. The result was that the author was deported three days later. The State party has failed to mention what procedure would be used to bring the author safely back to Canada had the Minister been compelled by the Court to render another decision.

Further State party's admissibility observations

6.1 In a further submission dated 9 October 1998, the State party contends that upon receiving a decision like that of the adjudicator in the instant case, a refugee claimant represented by counsel would not have assumed that he could proceed with his refugee claim. The adjudicator determined that the author was a person who had been convicted outside of Canada of an offence that if committed in Canada would constitute an offence punishable by a maximum term of imprisonment of 10 years or more and was also a person for whom there were reasonable grounds to believe had engaged in terrorism. A reasonable person represented by counsel receiving such a determination would have anticipated that action would be taken to have the individual excluded from the refugee determination process. Indeed, such a determination would suggest that the claimant might be excluded from the definition of a Convention refugee in section F of article 1 of the Convention relating to the Status of Refugees, which was incorporated by reference into the Canadian Immigration Act.

6.2 Moreover, the author had been advised, subsequent to the first inquiry held, that CIC intended to seek the Minister's opinion that the author constituted a danger to the public, the consequence upon issuance of such opinion being that he would be excluded from the refugee determination process. The author sought judicial review of this earlier determination and was therefore aware of the potential consequences of an adjudicator's finding that he was inadmissible.

Counsel's comments

7. Counsel argues that the adjudicator's finding was very specific (i.e., that the author had been convicted of an offence and that there were reasonable grounds to believe he had engaged in acts of terrorism). The scope for judicial review of such a finding is limited to whether the adjudicator made an error in law or whether his findings of fact were perverse, capricious or patently unreasonable. Whether or not the author agreed with the decision, it was not possible to attack it on any of these grounds based on the evidence presented. Counsel's duty is to determine whether it is in the client's best interest to pursue an appeal when there is little merit in doing so. Counsel would hesitate to launch a frivolous application before the courts simply to delay further proceedings.

State party's comments on the failure to observe the Committee's interim measures request

8.1 On 24 June 1998, the Committee invited the State party to submit written comments on the failure to observe the request not to expel the author to India while his communication is under consideration by the Committee.

8.2 In its response, the State party indicates that an interim measures request is a recommendation to a State to take certain measures, not an order. Support for this proposition may be found not only in the word employed ("request") in rule 108, paragraph 9, but also in the European Court of Human Rights judgement in *Cruz Varas and Others v. Sweden*. The Court stated the following with respect to the legal status of an interim measures request: "Firstly, it must be observed that rule 36 [regarding interim measures] has only the status of a rule of procedure drawn up by the Commission ... In the absence of a provision in the Convention for interim measures an indication given under rule 36 cannot be considered to give rise to a binding obligation on Contracting Parties."

8.3 Pursuant to rule 108, paragraph 9, an interim measures request may be issued in order to avoid "irreparable damage" to an author. The State party submits that the examination of possible irreparable harm should be a rigorous one, particularly when the individual concerned was found to represent a danger to the public or, as in the author's case, whose continued presence in the State was determined to be contrary to the public interest. On the basis of the documentary evidence submitted by the author as well as their own evidence regarding the author's risk upon removal to India, the authorities concluded that the risk was minimal. Moreover, a judge of the Federal Court Trial Division determined that the risk to the author was not sufficient to justify a stay of his removal.

8.4 The Government of Canada first became aware that the petitioner had submitted a communication, including a request for interim measures, when the author's counsel alluded to the Committee's granting of the request during a discussion with a CIC official on 18 December 1997, three months after the Committee had received the author's communication and request for interim measures. The record before the Committee reveals that the interim measures request was issued, after several appeals by the author's counsel to the Committee, a few days before his scheduled removal. The Government of Canada was not aware of these appeals nor was it given the opportunity to comment on these *ex parte* communications with the Committee.

8.5 In summary, irrespective of their legal status, interim measures requests received from the Committee are given serious consideration by the State party. However, the State party determined that the present case was not an appropriate one for a stay to be granted in light of the above-mentioned factors and in particular: (a) the prima facie absence of substantial personal risk to the author, as determined by the risk assessment conducted; (b) the fact that the continued presence in Canada of a convicted terrorist would be contrary to the public interest; and (c) the non-binding nature of the Committee's request.

Counsel's comments

9.1 Counsel contends that it has never been his position that the State party was legally obliged to comply with the Committee's interim measures request. He does argue, however, that the Canadian public would normally expect its Government to comply with a request from the United Nations. This is consistent with convention, past practice and the State party's self-image as a humanitarian member of the international community.

9.2 The State party could not possibly have given serious consideration to the interim measures request, in view of the fact that after learning of the request on 18 December 1997 it continued to act single-mindedly to effect the author's removal by opposing an application for a stay of deportation pending a review of the Minister's finding that it would be contrary to the public interest to allow the author to proceed with his refugee claim. The State party chose to rely on its position that the Minister had already conducted a risk assessment with respect to the author and that nothing further was required. The author was not able to do anything but make preliminary written submissions. There was no oral hearing, no ability to call or cross-examine witnesses, no proper disclosure of "internal State documents", and so on. The State party justifies its actions on the basis that the Federal Court dismissed the author's application for a stay of removal. However, the Federal Court's finding with respect to the stay application was not subject to review. It is the finding of one judge, with whom the author disagrees. If the author had appeared before any number of other judges in the Federal Court the result of the stay application might have been different.

Committee's admissibility decision

10.1 At its twenty-first session, the Committee considered the question of the admissibility of the communication and ascertained that the same matter had not been and was not being examined under another procedure of international investigation or settlement. With regard to the exhaustion of domestic remedies, the Committee noted that the author applied for an interim order staying the execution of the deportation order which was dismissed by the Federal Court Trial Division on 22 December 1997. As a result of a further request from the author the Court issued a supplementary decision according to which the author had not shown that it would be demonstrably probable that he would face torture upon return to India. The author also applied for leave for judicial review of the Minister's decision that it would be contrary to the public interest to have his refugee claim heard. However, the author was expelled before the deadline for perfecting the application. The Committee also noted that the author failed to seek leave for judicial review of the adjudicator's decision that he belonged to an inadmissible category. However, the Committee was not convinced that this remedy would have been an effective and necessary one, in view of the fact that the other remedies, mentioned above, were available and, indeed, utilized.

10.2 The Committee therefore decided that the communication was admissible.

State party's observations on the merits

11.1 In its submission of 12 May 1998, the State party states that according to the principle laid down in the case *Seid Mortesa Aemei* v. *Switzerland*,[1] the Committee has to determine "whether there are substantial grounds for believing that [the author] would be in danger of being subjected to torture [in the country to which he is being returned]" and "whether he would be personally at risk". It also recalls that the burden of proof is on the part of the author to establish that there are substantial grounds to believe that he or she would be personally at risk of being subjected to torture.

11.2 The State party submits that since the protection provided by article 3 is, according to the Committee's jurisprudence, absolute, irrespective of the author's past conduct, the determination of risk must be particularly rigorous. To that purpose, reference is made to a decision of the European Court of Human Rights (*Vilvarajah and others* v. *United Kingdom*), where it is stated, with regard to article 3 of the European Convention on Human Rights, that "the Court's examination of the existence of a risk of ill-treatment in breach of Article 3 at the relevant time must necessarily be a rigorous one in view of the absolute character of this provision".

11.3 In order to assess the risk of torture faced by the author, the State party contends that the following factors are pertinent: (a) whether the State concerned is one in which there is evidence of a consistent pattern of gross, flagrant or mass violation of human rights; (b) whether the author has been tortured or maltreated by or with the acquiescence of a public official in the past, (c) whether the situation referred to in (a) has changed; and (d) whether the author has engaged in political or other activity within or outside the State concerned which would

---

[1] Communication N° 34/1995, Views adopted on 9 May 1997.

appear to make him particularly vulnerable to the risk of being tortured.

11.4 The State party acknowledges that the human rights record of India is of concern but underlines that the situation, particularly in the Punjab, has improved significantly over the two years preceding the State party's submission.

11.5 According to the State party, several measures have been taken to ensure greater respect for human rights in India since the Government took office in June 1996. The signing by India of the Convention against Torture and Other Cruel, Inhuman or Degrading Treatment or Punishment on 14 October 1997, indicates its intention to take steps to prevent and sanction any acts of torture occurring in the territory. Even though the State party acknowledges the human rights abuses, including "disappearances", perpetrated by the Punjab police between 1984 and 1995, reliable sources of information attest to significant progress since 1995 in "reigning in" the Punjab police and providing redress to victims of earlier abuses. According to the United States Department of State, *"the pattern of disappearances prevalent in the early 1990s appears to be at end"* and action has been taken against several of the police officials implicated.[2]

11.6 The State party also refers to other documentation supporting the contention that while in the late 1980s and early 1990s human rights violations by the police were tolerated and overlooked by the Government, steps have since been taken to ensure that perpetrators do not go unpunished.[3] An indication of this change is the revival of many cases against Punjab police officers which had been pending before the Supreme Court for many years and the initiation of recent investigations led by the Central Bureau of Investigation (CBI). These actions confirm that impunity for the Punjab police has come to an end and although some violations might still occur, the probability of future cases of disappearances involving the Punjab police is very small.[4] It is finally noted that judicial protection for detained or arrested persons has improved. A person who claims to have been arrested arbitrarily will be able to inform a lawyer and have access to the courts.

11.7 With reference to the above-mentioned sources, the State party considers that torture is not currently prevalent in Punjab. The same documentary evidence also demonstrates that torture is not practised in all parts of India and that the author would therefore not be at risk.

11.8 The State party further argues that there is no evidence that the author has been tortured by Indian authorities in the past or since his return to India. It refers to press articles stating that the author has not been subjected to torture during questioning, Indian authorities being very conscious of the international scrutiny of their treatment of the author.[5]

11.9 It is also submitted by the State party that Indian authorities would not have any opportunity to torture the author since he has already been convicted and served his sentence. India has indeed assimilated the principle of *non bis in idem* both in its Constitution and by adhering to the International Covenant on Civil and Political Rights which sets out the principle in article 14 (7). The fact that there are no new charges against the author is also consistent with the fact that India has not requested the author's extradition. Finally, the State party mentions that the Deputy Commissioner of Police has confirmed in the press that no action could be taken against the author since he has already been convicted and served his sentence.

11.10 With regard to the affidavit of the author's niece, the State party claims that it constitutes hearsay in that she repeats statements she believes the author made. Furthermore, the statement of the niece that *"the CBI investigator then threatened [her] uncle that they would stay around him"*, even if true, would not be totally unreasonable given the past history of the author and does not demonstrate a risk of torture. Moreover, the State party argues that the facts presented in the affidavit do not amount to "mental torture" as they do not meet the requirements of article 1, paragraph 1, of the Convention. The Indian authorities have indeed not committed any act with the intention of causing the author severe mental pain or suffering.

11.11 Concerning the reference in the original communication to the 1990 killing of two acquitted hijackers who attempted to enter India, the State party does not see the relevance of this event to the present case and does not see any similarity between them. The State party emphasizes the absence of similarity between the cases in that the author has not presented evidence of any risk to his family members whereas in the other case, the family had suffered continuous harassment by the Indian authorities. The author quotes a Canadian CIC case officer according to whom the author would be *"dealt with harshly, possibly because of hijacking of the Indian plane"* if he were to return to India. The

---

[2] United States State Department, India-Country Report on Human Rights Practices for 1996.
[3] Documentation, Information and Research Branch, Immigration and Refugee Board, "India: Information from Four Specialists on the Punjab", Ottawa, 17 February 1997.
[4] Ibid.

[5] "Hijacker OK in the old country: An Indo-Canada newspaper reports an assurance that Tejinder Pal Singh will be safe in India", *Vancouver Sun*, 5 January 1998.

State party states that the comment was made in the context of a decision review hearing in which it was the officer's duty to raise concerns about the potential risk that the author would flee, but she was not commenting nor had she sufficient information to determine the level of risk run by the author in case of return.

11.12 Finally, the State party underlines that the evidence of risk that the author could face when returning to India has been carefully reviewed by the Minister of Citizenship and Immigration and that the risk has been deemed minimal. That assessment was confirmed by the Federal Court Trial Division. It is submitted that the Committee should give considerable weight to the findings of the Minister and the Court.

11.13 For the above reasons, the State party is of the opinion that there is no element showing that the author would be put at risk of torture should he return to India.

Author's merits comments

12.1 In a submission dated 11 June 1998, the author argues that the assessment made by the State party of the human rights situation in India on the basis of the documentation submitted to the Committee [6] is misleading. The State party cites remarks out of context but fails to mention information from the same sources which confirm that abuses continue to occur.

12.2 The author also draws the attention of the Committee to the fact that one of the supporting documents referred to by the State party states: "*I began by asking if someone who had fled India during the early 1990s, at the height of the troubles, would have reason to fear returning to Punjab now. I also asked if it was possible for someone on the run to hide within an existing community of Sikhs in a city or region outside the Punjab. The answer to both these questions, and a constant theme of the interview, was that only the highest profile fugitives, which they said would number a handful, would have reason to fear, or to be pursued outside the Punjab.*"[7] The author also draws attention to the fact that these comments were made prior to the elections of February 1997, before the human rights situation degenerated.

12.3 To support his statements on the current human rights situation in Punjab, the author refers to information from the Research Directorate of the Immigration and Refugee Board in Ottawa which reports that torture in custody remains a problem in India, and particularly in Punjab. Moreover, it asserts that the recent prosecutions against police officers are not indicative of a real change in the respect for human rights and constitutional guarantees. Finally, it states that the persons who are in danger are those who are still part of active nationalist groups or who refuse demands imposed by the State, including police pressure to become an informant, which, the author observes, is exactly what happened in his case. The author also refers to the Response to Information request from the Research Directorate of the Immigration and Refugee Board prepared for the United States Immigration and Naturalization Service on the situation in Punjab in 1997, indicating that despite a general improvement over the years and "*although militants and close affiliates of militants are the key category of individuals at risk, political activists and also human rights activists may also have well founded fears of persecution in India.*"[8]

12.4 In the light of the above, the author draws the attention of the Committee to the inconsistency of the State party in its assessment of the risk run by the author of being subjected to torture in India. The author argues that when deciding that the author would be denied refugee status, the Canadian authorities portrayed him as a high-profile militant terrorist and Sikh nationalist. However, when considering the author's return to India and the risks he would run, the State party no longer portrayed him as such.

12.5 Regarding the risk of being subjected to torture, it is noted that ascertaining a risk of torture in the future does not require evidence of torture in the past, particularly since the author has not been in India since his imprisonment in Pakistan. At this stage, the only evidence of risk available is the author's niece's affidavit. As was underlined by the author, although there was no evidence of actual torture, the affidavit should be considered as demonstrating the risk of such treatment. Moreover, the fact that there is no legal basis to arrest the author at present is of even more concern since the human rights record of India is filled with examples of extrajudicial behaviour.

12.6 The author further insists on the similarity between his case and that of Gurvinder Singh, referred to in the initial communication. The latter was tried with eight other persons and acquitted of a 1984 hijacking of a plane travelling from India to Pakistan. He was later shot at the border with Pakistan while he was trying to return to India. The author was tried with four others for a 1981 hijacking. In all, 14 persons have been labelled by Indian authorities as terrorists and have consistently been linked together, regardless of the differences

---

[6] United States State Department, op. cit.; Human Rights World Report 1997.

[7] See supra, note 3.

[8] Documents IND26992.E of the Research Directorate of the Immigration and Refugee Board in Ottawa, p. 3.

between the circumstances of the hijackings or whether they were acquitted or convicted. This is illustrated by a letter from the Indian CBI to the Canadian High Commission in New Delhi dated 24 July 1995 referring to a collection of photographs of each of the alleged hijackers. This is not only an indication that these 14 persons are regarded in the same way, but also that the Indian authorities are particularly interested in their return in India and that the State party has cooperated with the Indian Government since at least 1995. The Committee should therefore take into consideration anything that has happened to any of the 14 persons in its assessment of the author's risk.

Additional State party comments

13.1 In submissions dated 9 October 1998, 7 June 1999, 30 September 1998 and 28 February 2000, the State party transmitted additional observations on the merits.

13.2 It argues that although high-profile militants may be at risk in India, the author does not fall within this category, which would include a perceived leader of a militant organization, someone suspected of a terrorist attack, or someone suspected of anti-State activities. The author cannot be characterized as any of these. Although he committed the hijacking of 1981, he was convicted for his crime, served his sentence, and was presumably not involved in militant activities during his time in prison nor is he currently involved in such activities. In a further submission, the State party states that it has never disputed that the author could be considered as "high-profile". However, it does not consider that the author falls into the small category of "high-profile militants" at risk.

13.3 The State party requests the Committee to give little weight to the "section 27 report" because it is a document prepared by a junior immigration officer which only indicates that the person may be inadmissible to Canada. The definitive decision is going to be taken by a senior immigration officer and only that is subject to judicial review. Furthermore, the "section 27 report" merely mentions that the author is a member of the Dal Khalsa. It is submitted that the mere membership of a terrorist organization does not make a person a "high-profile militant".

13.4 The State party strongly denies that it has cooperated with the Indian authorities in the search for the author and confirms that it did not receive any request from India to return the author. The correspondence mentioned by the author in its previous submission does not indicate that the Indian authorities were searching for the latter but rather that the State party was concerned by the possible arrival of released hijackers on its territory and wanted to identify them. Contrary to the assertions of the author that India was interested in his return, the State party has never received any indication of such interest. Even if India had shown interest in the return of the author, that would not have proved that he was at risk of torture.

13.5 With regard to the arrival of the author at the airport in Delhi, where it was stated that there were over 40 police and army officers waiting, the State party reiterates that the accompanying officer confirmed that the author was dealt with in a normal fashion.

13.6 The State party argues that the letter presented by the author to the Committee referring to his experience in India since his arrival is only an expression of his views and does not therefore constitute sworn or tested evidence. The Committee should give little weight to this document. It is also submitted that the alleged harassment endured by the author does not constitute evidence that he is at risk of torture. Moreover, at the time of the submission, the author had been back in India for almost two years and it seems that there was no change in the manner in which he had been treated by the authorities.

13.7 The State party notes that the author alleges that he is at risk of "persecution". Even though this expression may be a simple oversight on the part of the author, the State party recalls that the issue before the Committee is whether the author is at risk of "torture", not "persecution". It is contended that the risk of torture as defined in the Convention imposes a higher and more precise standard than the risk of persecution as defined in the 1951 Convention relating to the Status of Refugees. In the present case, the State party reiterates its view that the author is not at risk of torture.

Additional comments by the author

14.1 In further submissions dated 28 October 1998, 30 May 1999, 14 July 1999 and 26 November 1999, the author states that it is the policy of the State party to restrict the number of refugees entering its territory, so that since 1996 the rates of acceptance of refugee claimants has dropped dramatically, particularly for asylum-seekers from Punjab. Even though the author acknowledges the need to combat abuse from economic migrants and fraudulent claimants, that does not justify the unrealistically favourable portrayal of the situation in Punjab.

14.2 The author's counsel requests the Committee to consider a letter, dated 2 December 1998, written by the author, revealing the difficulties he has experienced since his return to India. The author states that he received threats from the police upon arrival from Canada for not having given them the information they wanted. He and his family have been harassed by the police so that he is not able to see them anymore. After he filed a complaint with the Punjab Human Rights Committee, he was forced to sign a statement absolving the police of any wrongdoing. According to counsel, these acts constitute "slow, methodical mental torture" and there is no need to wait for evidence of physical torture.

14.3 It is also disputed by counsel that the actions of the Indian CBI on his return to India do not constitute "mental torture". It is argued that the State party has to consider these actions together with the other difficulties faced by the author and his family since his arrival and the general human rights situation in India. Secondly, it is inappropriate for the State party to use ex post facto elements, i.e., that the author has not been tortured since his return to India, to justify its decision to expel the author. Counsel contends that the author is currently a victim of torture; but that even if that were not the case, the Committee should determine if the author was at substantial risk of torture at the time of his deportation from Canada.

14.4 Counsel argues that the author has provided enough evidence by his letter and his niece's affidavit that he has been at substantial risk of torture since he arrived in India and that the Indian authorities maintain a high level of interest in him. It is reaffirmed that the deportation of the author was a disguised extradition even though there was no request for one.

14.5 Counsel draws the attention of the Committee to additional sources that dispute the State party's assertion that the human rights situation in Punjab has improved.[9] Counsel submits that the sources confirm that the situation of human rights activists deteriorated at the end of 1998. Counsel also refers to information indicating that persons who have presented complaints before the People's Commission have been visited by the police and threatened with death or arrest on false charges.

14.6 Counsel develops the argumentation that the State party has not been consistent in its risk assessment. While it is currently portraying the author as a person of no interest to the Indian authorities, it has previously qualified him as a high-profile militant, including pointing to his links with the Dal Khalsa, a known pro-Khalistan organization, the fact that he had intimated to the immigration authorities that he could "crush anyone with his thumb", as well as evidence of him having made pro-Khalistan, anti-Indian Government statements. The present contention of the State party that the author is not a high-profile militant is, therefore,

---

[9] Documents IND30759.EX and IND26992.E of the Research Directorate of the Immigration and Refugee Board in Ottawa.

fallacious. Counsel further presents additional information demonstrating that the author is indeed a "high-profile militant". One is a comment made by the BBC in May 1982 characterizing the Dal Khalsa, as an anti-national, secessionist, extremist organization. The other is an article from *The News International* of October 1994 on the author himself, qualifying him clearly as a militant. Counsel finally refers to information contained in the Canadian Government's own file relating to the removal of the author from Canada ("section 27 report"), dated 30 November 1995, indicating that the author "is a member of the Dal Khalsa, a known terrorist organization". Counsel emphasizes the use of the present tense in the sentence to demonstrate that neither the existence of the Dal Khalsa nor the affiliation of the author belongs to the past. According to counsel, these elements are a clear indication that the State party was indeed considering the author as a high-profile militant and therefore knew of the risk of returning him to India.

Issues and proceedings before the Committee

15.1 The Committee must decide, pursuant to article 3, paragraph 1, of the Convention, whether there are substantial grounds for believing that the author would be in danger of being subjected to torture upon return to India. In reaching this decision, the Committee must take into account all relevant considerations, pursuant to article 3, paragraph 2, of the Convention, including the existence of a consistent pattern of gross, flagrant or mass violations of human rights. The aim of the determination, however, is to establish whether the individual concerned would be personally at risk of being subjected to torture in the country to which he or she would return. It follows that the existence of a consistent pattern of gross, flagrant or mass violations of human rights in a country does not as such constitute a sufficient ground for determining that a particular person would be in danger of being subjected to torture upon his return to that country; additional grounds must exist to show that the individual concerned would be personally at risk. Similarly, the absence of a consistent pattern of gross violations of human rights does not mean that a person cannot be considered to be in danger of being subjected to torture in his or her specific circumstances.

15.2 The Committee first notes that the author was removed to India on 23 December 1997 despite a request for interim measures pursuant to rule 108 (9) of the rules of procedure according to which the State party was requested not to remove the author while his communication was pending before the Committee.

15.3 One of the overriding factors behind the speedy deportation was the claim by the State party that the "author's continued presence in Canada represents a danger to the public". The Committee, however is not convinced that an extension of his stay in Canada for a few more months would have been contrary to the public interest. In this regard, the Committee refers to a case before the European Court of Human Rights (*Chapel* v. *United Kingdom*) in which the Court maintained that scrutiny of the claim "must be carried out without regard to what the person may have done to warrant expulsion or to any perceived threat to the national security of the expelling State".

15.4 On the merits of the communication, the Committee notes that the author has been living in India for more than two years. During this time, although he claims to have been harassed and threatened, along with his family, on several occasions by the police, it seems that there has been no change in the manner in which he has been treated by the authorities. In these circumstances, and given the substantial period of time that has elapsed since the author's removal, giving ample time for the fears of the author to have been realized, the Committee cannot but conclude that his allegations were unfounded.

15.5 The Committee is of the opinion that after a period of nearly two and a half years, it is unlikely that the author is still at risk of being subjected to acts of torture.

15.6 The Committee considers that the State party, in ratifying the Convention and voluntarily accepting the Committee's competence under article 22, undertook to cooperate with it in good faith in applying the procedure. Compliance with the provisional measures called for by the Committee in cases it considers reasonable is essential in order to protect the person in question from irreparable harm, which could, moreover, nullify the end result of the proceedings before the Committee. The Committee is deeply concerned by the fact that the State party did not accede to its request for interim measures under rule 108, paragraph 3, of its rules of procedure and removed the author to India.

15.7 The Committee against Torture, acting under article 22, paragraph 7, of the Convention against Torture and Other Cruel, Inhuman or Degrading Treatment or Punishment, concludes that the author's removal to India by the State party does not constitute a breach of article 3 of the Convention.

Appendix

Individual opinion (dissenting) of Committee member Guibril Camara

Under rule 108, paragraph 9, of its rules of procedure, the Committee against Torture may take steps to avoid a violation of the Convention and, therefore, an irreparable damage. This provision is a logical attribute of the competence bestowed on the Committee under article 22 of the Convention, concerning which the State party has made a declaration. By invoking article 22, the author of a communication submits an enforceable decision to the Committee's judgement, with due regard to the requirement for the exhaustion of domestic remedies. Therefore, if such decision is enforced despite the Committee's request for suspension, the State party renders article 22 meaningless. This particular case is basically a matter of lack of respect, if not for the letter, then at any rate for the spirit of article 22.

Moreover, it is clear from the terms of article 3 of the Convention that the time to assess whether "there are substantial grounds for believing that [the author] would be in danger of being subjected to torture" is at the moment of expulsion, return or extradition. The facts clearly show that, at the time of his expulsion to India, there were substantial grounds for believing that the author would be subjected to torture. The State party therefore violated article 3 of the Convention in acting to expel the author.

Lastly, the fact that in this case the author was not subsequently subjected to torture has no bearing on whether the State party violated the Convention in expelling him. The question of whether the risk—in this case, of acts of torture—actually materializes is of relevance only to any reparation or damages sought by the victim or by other persons entitled to claim.

The competence of the Committee against Torture should also be exercised in the interests of prevention. In cases relating to article 3, it would surely be unreasonable to wait for a violation to occur before taking note of it.

Communication N° 110/1998

Submitted by: Cecilia Rosana Núñez Chipana
Alleged victim: The author
State party: Venezuela
Date of adoption of Views: 10 November 1998

Subject matter: deportation of complainant to Peru with alleged risk of torture

Procedural issue: failure to comply with request for interim measures

Substantive issue: risk of torture after deportation

Article of the Convention: 3

1. The author of the communication is Cecilia Rosana Núñez Chipana, a Peruvian citizen detained in Venezuela and subject to extradition proceedings at the request of the Government of Peru. She claims that her forced return to Peru would be a violation by Venezuela of article 3 of the Convention. She is represented by counsel.

The facts as submitted by the author

2.1 The Committee received the first letter from the author on 30 April 1998. She stated that she was arrested in Caracas on 16 February 1998 by officials of the Intelligence and Prevention Services Department (DISIP). The Government of Peru requested her extradition on 26 February 1998, and extradition proceedings were instituted in the Criminal Chamber of the Supreme Court.

2.2 The author maintained that the nature of the accusations against her would place her in the group of persons liable to be subjected to torture. The Peruvian authorities accused her of the offence of disturbing public order (terrorism against the State) and being a member of the subversive movement Sendero Luminoso. The main evidence in support of these accusations was testimony by two persons under the repentance legislation (a legal device for the benefit of persons who are involved in acts of terrorism and who provide useful information to the authorities) in which they stated that they recognized the author in a photograph, as well as the police reports stating that subversive propaganda had been found in the place where the witnesses say the author carried out the acts of which she was accused. According to the author, the witnesses did not meet the requirements for being regarded as competent witnesses in accordance with the State party's procedural legislation because they were co-defendants in the proceedings against her. She also pointed out that her sister had been arrested in 1992, tried for her alleged involvement in subversive acts and kept in prison for four years until an appeal court declared her innocent.

2.3 The author denied the charges, although she admitted that she belonged to the lawful organization "United Left Movement" and to lawful community organizations such as the "Glass of Milk Committees" and the "Popular Libraries Committees". She said she had worked as an instructor in literacy campaigns for low-income groups in Peru. She also said she fled her country as a result of well-founded fears that her freedom and physical integrity were in danger, when she learned in the press that she was being accused of terrorism; she recognized that she used legal identity documents belonging to her sister to enter and stay in Venezuela. She also said she had not applied for political asylum in the State party, where she was working as a teacher, because she did not know the law and was afraid because she was undocumented.

2.4 If the Supreme Court of Justice authorized the extradition, it would take place within a few hours under an Executive order by which the Supreme Court would notify the Ministry of Justice, which would in turn notify the Ministry of Foreign Affairs, which would establish contact with the Government of Peru to make arrangements for the person's return to Peru.

2.5 In an earlier communication, the author informed the Committee that the Supreme Court had agreed to extradition in a decision published on 16 June 1998. It was subject to the following conditions: (a) that the author should not be liable to life imprisonment or the death penalty; (b) that she should not be liable to more than 30 years' imprisonment; and (c) that she should not be liable to detention incommunicado, isolation, torture or any other procedure that would cause physical or mental suffering while she was on trial or serving her sentence. The author's counsel filed an application for constitutional *amparo* which was declared inadmissible by the Supreme Court. Extradition took place on 3 July 1998.

2.6 The author also informed the Committee that, on 24 March 1998, she formally submitted her application for asylum in writing and that, on 12 June 1998, her counsel formally requested that the Office of the United Nations High Commissioner for Refugees accept her as a candidate for refugee status.

The complaint

3.1 The author maintained that her forced return to Peru would place her in danger of being subjected to torture. Such a situation had to be borne in mind, particularly in the context of the existence in Peru of a consistent pattern of violations of human rights, an aspect of which was the frequent use of torture against persons accused of belonging to insurgent organizations, as noted by United Nations bodies, the Organization of American States and non-governmental organizations. The author therefore asked the Committee to request the State party to refrain from carrying out her forced return to Peru while her communication was being considered by the Committee.

3.2 She also maintained that, if she was extradited, proceedings would be brought against her that would not guarantee the fundamental principles of due process, since serious irregularities were committed every day in Peru during the trial of persons accused of belonging to an insurgent organization. Such irregularities were contrary to the provisions of the international human rights instruments ratified by Peru and by the State party.

State party's observations

4.1 Through its Special Rapporteur on New Communications, the Committee transmitted the communication to the State party on 11 May 1998, requesting it to submit its observations on the admissibility and, if it did not object thereto, on the merits of the communication. It also requested the State party to refrain from expelling or extraditing the author while her communication was being considered by the Committee.

4.2 On 2 July 1998, the State party informed the Committee that the Supreme Court's decision had been adopted in accordance with domestic legislation, particularly the Penal Code and the Code of Criminal Procedure, and the 1928 Convention on Private International Law, to which Peru and Venezuela were parties. The activities attributed to the author, namely, involvement in manufacturing and planting car bombs for later attacks which killed and wounded a large number of people, constituted a serious ordinary offence, not a political offence. The State party also indicated that the defence had not provided any factual evidence to indicate whether or not article 3, paragraph 1, of the Convention against Torture was applicable. The statements by witnesses who accused the author and whom the defence claimed had been subjected to torture had been made without any coercion, as shown by the fact that they had been given in the presence of representatives of the Public Prosecutor's Department and the defence lawyers.

Author's comments

5.1 In her comments on the observations by the State party, the author maintained that the extradition took place even though legal remedies had not been exhausted, at the time when the Supreme Court was considering an application for *amparo* with a request for precautionary measures against the decision granting extradition. The extradition took place on 3 July and only on 7 July 1998 did the Court rule on the application for *amparo*, declaring it inadmissible, together with the precautionary measure requested. In addition, the transfer to Peru took place by surprise, since the date was not communicated in advance either to the author or to her counsel.

5.2 The Supreme Court decision did not refer at all to the content of the reports submitted by the defence, but did refer at length to the opinion in favour of extradition issued by the Attorney-General of the Republic. The decision also did not refer to the provisional measures requested by the Committee, even though they were invoked by the defence. Only the dissenting judge referred to those measures, also noting that there were no grounds for convicting the author of the charges against her, that conditions in Peru did not guarantee due process and that international organizations had stated their views on flagrant human rights violations in Peru. As an argument against the opinion of the Supreme Court, the author also referred to the political nature of the offences with which she was charged in Peru.

5.3 The author said that neither she nor her counsel had received any reply in respect of the application for asylum, contrary to what the Minister for Foreign Affairs had stated when questioned by the Chamber of Deputies' Standing Committee on Domestic Policy. According to what he said, the Minister had informed the author, in a letter dated 27 March 1998, that the application for asylum did not contain evidence of political persecution and that the final decision lay with the Supreme Court.

5.4 He said that the State party had ratified the 1951 Convention relating to the Status of Refugees and the 1967 Protocol relating to the Status of Refugees, which provided that States had an obligation to set up the necessary machinery for their implementation. There were, however, no procedures or authorities in the State party to guarantee that asylum-seekers would be guaranteed that right. Moreover, the Executive authorities of the State party had said that they could take a decision on asylum only after the Supreme Court had ruled on extradition. That argument was wrong, however, because asylum and extradition are two different and autonomous legal institutions.

5.5 The author reported to the Committee that, following her extradition, she was sentenced in Peru to 25 years' imprisonment on 10 August 1998, after a trial without proper guarantees. At present, she is being held in a maximum security prison, where, inter alia, she is confined to her cell for the first year (23 hours in her cell and 1 hour outside each day) and can receive family visits in a visiting room for only one hour a week.

5.6 The author recognizes that States and the international community are entitled to take action to combat terrorism. However, such action cannot be carried out in breach of the rule of law and international human rights standards. The right not to be returned to a country where a person's life, liberty and integrity are threatened would be seriously jeopardized if the requesting State had only to claim that there was a charge of terrorism against the person wanted for extradition. Such a situation is even worse if the accusation is made on the basis of national anti-terrorist legislation, with open-ended criminal penalties, broad definitions of "terrorist acts" and judicial systems of doubtful independence.

5.7 The author maintains that the State party has violated the obligation "to refrain" imposed on it by article 3 of the Convention. This makes it an obligation for the State party to take measures to prevent acts of torture from being committed against the author for the duration of the custodial penalty imposed by the Peruvian authorities or for as long as the Peruvian Government in any way prohibits her from leaving the country as a result of the charges which led to the proceedings against her. The State party therefore has to establish suitable machinery to follow up the conditions which it imposed and which were accepted by the Peruvian authorities.

Issues and proceedings before the Committee

6.1 Before examining any complaint contained in a communication, the Committee against Torture must determine whether it is admissible under article 22 of the Convention. The Committee has ascertained that, as required under article 22, paragraph 5 (a), the same matter has not been, and is not being, examined under another procedure of international investigation or settlement. The Committee notes that the State party has not submitted objections to the admissibility of the communication and is of the opinion that, in view of the Supreme Court's decision declaring inadmissible the application for *amparo* against the sentence of extradition, all available domestic remedies have been exhausted. The Committee therefore concludes that there are no reasons why the communication should not be declared admissible. Since both the State party and the author have submitted observations on the merits of the communication, the Committee will consider it as to the merits.

6.2 The question that must be elucidated by the Committee is whether the author's extradition to Peru would violate the obligation assumed by the State party under article 3 of the Convention not to extradite a person to another State where there are substantial grounds for believing that he would be in danger of being subjected to torture.

6.3 The Committee must then decide whether there are well-founded reasons for believing that the author would be in danger of being subjected to torture on her return to Peru. In accordance with article 3, paragraph 2, of the Convention, the Committee should take account, for the purpose of determining whether there are such grounds, of all relevant considerations, including, where applicable, the existence in the State concerned of a consistent pattern of gross, flagrant or mass violations of human rights. However, the existence of a pattern of this nature does not in itself constitute a sufficient reason for deciding whether the person in question is in danger of being subjected to torture on her return to this country; there must be specific reasons for believing that the person concerned is personally in danger. Similarly, the absence of this pattern does not mean that a person is not in danger of being subjected to torture in her specific case.

6.4 When considering the periodic reports of Peru (A/50/44, paras. 62–73, and A/53/44, paras. 197–205), the Committee received numerous allegations from reliable sources concerning the use of torture by law enforcement officials in connection with the investigation of the offences of terrorism and treason with a view to obtaining information or a confession. The Committee therefore considers that, in view of the nature of the accusations made by the Peruvian authorities in requesting the extradition and the type of evidence on which they based their request, as described by the parties, the author was in a situation where she was in danger of being placed in police custody and tortured on her return to Peru.

7. In the light of the above, the Committee, acting in accordance with article 22, paragraph 7, of the Convention against Torture and Other Cruel, Inhuman or Degrading Treatment or Punishment, considers that the State party failed to fulfil its obligation not to extradite the author, which constitutes a violation of article 3 of the Convention.

8. Furthermore, the Committee is deeply concerned by the fact that the State party did not accede to the request made by the Committee under rule 108, paragraph 3, of its rules of procedure that it should refrain from expelling or extraditing the author while her communication was being considered by the Committee and thereby failed to comply with the spirit of the Convention. The Committee considers that the State party, in ratifying the Convention and voluntarily accepting the Committee's competence under article 22, undertook to cooperate with it in good faith in applying the

procedure. Compliance with the provisional measures called for by the Committee in cases it considers reasonable is essential in order to protect the person in question from irreparable harm, which could, moreover, nullify the end result of the proceedings before the Committee.

Communication N° 113/1998

Submitted by: Radivoje Ristic
Alleged victim: Milan Ristic (deceased)
State party: Yugoslavia
Date of adoption of Views: 11 May 2001

Subject matter: murder of complainant's son by police officers

Procedural issue: none

Substantive issues: failure to promptly investigate allegations of torture, right to complain, right to obtain compensation

Articles of the Convention: 12, 13, 14

1. The author of the communication, dated 22 July 1998, is Mr. Radivoje Ristic, a citizen of Yugoslavia, currently residing in Šabac, Yugoslavia. He claims that an act of torture resulting in the death of his son, Milan Ristic, was committed by the police and that the authorities have failed to carry out a prompt and impartial investigation. The communication was transmitted to the Committee, on behalf of Mr. Ristic, by the Humanitarian Law Center, a non-governmental organization based in Belgrade.

The facts as submitted by the author

2.1 The author alleges that on 13 February 1995 three policemen (Dragan Riznic, Uglješa Ivanovic and Dragan Novakovic) arrested Milan Ristic in Šabac while looking for a murder suspect. One of the officers struck his son with a blunt object, presumably a pistol or rifle butt, behind the left ear, killing him instantly. The officers moved the body and, with a blunt instrument, broke both thighbones. It was only then that they called an ambulance and the on-duty police investigation team, which included a forensic technician.

2.2 The policemen told the investigators that Milan Ristic had committed suicide by jumping from the roof of a nearby building and that they had an eyewitness to that effect (Dragan Markovic). The medical doctor who came with the ambulance pronounced Milan Ristic dead. The ambulance then left, leaving the body to be collected by a mortuary van. The author claims that after the departure of the ambulance the policemen struck the deceased on the chin, causing injury to his face.

2.3 The author provides a copy of the autopsy report, which concluded that the death was violent and caused by an injury to the brain as a result of a fall on a hard surface. The fall also explained the fractures described in the report. The author also provides a copy of the report by the doctor who came with the ambulance. That report says: "By exterior examination I found weak bleeding from the injury behind the left ear. Through the trousers above the right knee an open fracture of thighbone could be seen with small blood signs; around the wound there were no traces of blood."

2.4 The author contends that the medical reports do not fully tally with each other. The ambulance doctor explicitly states that he noticed no injuries on the face while the autopsy report lists a laceration and bruise on the chin. He challenges the reports, noting that it is hardly possible that a person could fall from a height of 14.65 metres without suffering any injury to the face, heels, pelvis, spine or internal organs and without internal haemorrhaging, leaving only bruises on the left elbow and behind the left ear. Moreover, he notes that there was no blood on the ground.

2.5 At the request of the parents, two forensic experts examined the autopsy report and found it superficial and contradictory, especially in the part referring to the cause of death. According to their report, the autopsy was not performed in accordance with the principles of forensic and medical science and practice and the conclusion is not in agreement with the findings. They proposed the exhumation of the remains and another autopsy by a forensic expert. The author further states that on 16 May 1995 they spoke with the pathologist who had performed the autopsy and visited the alleged scene of the incident. They noted that the autopsy report and the scene had nothing in common, which suggested that the body had been moved. In a written statement dated 18

July 1995 addressed to the Public Attorney's Office, the pathologist agreed that the remains should be exhumed for forensic examination and pointed out that, as he was not a specialist in forensic medicine, he might have made a mistake or missed some details.

2.6 The parents of the victim filed criminal charges against a number of police officers before the Public Prosecutor in Šabac. On 19 February 1996, the Public Prosecutor dismissed the charges. Under Yugoslav law, following dismissal of a criminal complaint, the victim or the person acting on his behalf may either request the institution of investigative proceedings or file an indictment and proceed directly to trial. In the present case, the parents presented their own indictment on 25 February 1996.

2.7 The investigating judge questioned the policemen allegedly involved as well as witnesses and found no grounds for believing that the alleged criminal offence had been committed. The Criminal Bench of the Šabac District Court endorsed the investigating judge's decision. The Court did not find it necessary to hear the testimony of the two forensic experts and did not consider the possibility of ordering an exhumation and a new autopsy. Besides, the investigating judge delivered to the parents an unsigned statement which the pathologist allegedly made in court when they were not present and which contradicts the one he had made in writing on 18 July 1995. The author further explains that, in addition to the medical contradictions, there were many other conflicting facts that the judicial investigation failed to clarify.

2.8 The parents appealed the decision of the District Court to the Serbian Supreme Court, which on 29 October 1996 dismissed the appeal as unfounded. According to the ruling, the testimony of Dragan Markovic showed without any doubt that Milan Ristic was alive at the time when police officers Sinisa Isailovic and Zoran Jeftic appeared in front of the building in which Mr. Markovic lived. They were responding to a telephone call from a person named Zoran Markovic who had noticed a man at the edge of the terrace from whose behaviour it could be concluded that he was about to commit suicide. Dragan Markovic and the two policemen actually saw Milan Ristic jump from the terrace. There was nothing they could do to stop him.

2.9 The parents again tried to bring the case before the judiciary, but on 10 February 1997 the Šabac District Court ruled that prosecution was no longer possible in view of the decision of the Supreme Court of Serbia. On 18 March 1997, the Supreme Court dismissed their further appeal and confirmed the District Court's ruling.

The complaint

3.1 The author considers that first the police and, subsequently, the judicial authorities failed to ensure a prompt and impartial investigation. All domestic remedies were exhausted without the court ever having ordered or formally instituted proper investigative proceedings. The preliminary investigation by the investigating judge, which consisted of questioning of the accused and some witnesses, did not produce sufficient information to clarify the circumstances of the death and the court never ordered a forensic examination. The court did not order either the hearing of other witnesses, such as the employees of the funeral home, whose testimony could have been relevant to establish the chronology of events. The author further contends that the investigation was not carried out in accordance with the provisions of the Criminal Procedure Code. For instance, the police failed to inform the investigating judge immediately of the incident, although obliged to do so by article 154. The entire on-site investigation was therefore conducted by the police without the presence of a judge. The author further contends that every action aimed at clarifying the incident was initiated by the parents of Milan Ristic and that the competent government bodies failed to take any effective steps to that end.

3.2 On the basis of the above, the author claims that the State party has violated several articles of the Convention, in particular articles 12, 13 and 14. He states that although the parents had the possibility of seeking compensation, the prospect of their being awarded damages was de facto non-existent in the absence of a criminal court judgement.

Observations by the State party

4. On 26 October 1998 the State party informed the Committee that, although all domestic remedies had been exhausted, the communication does not fulfil other necessary conditions provided for by the Convention. It stated, in particular, that no act of torture had been committed, since the deceased did not have any contact at all with State authorities—the police. Accordingly, the communication was not admissible.

The Committee's admissibility decision

[5.] At its twenty-second session, in April-May 1999, the Committee considered the admissibility of the communication and ascertained that the same matter had not been and was not being examined under another procedure of international investigation or settlement. The Committee noted the State party's statement that all domestic remedies had been exhausted, and considered that the communication was not an abuse of the right of submission or incompatible with the provisions of the Convention. The Committee therefore decided, on 30 April 1999, that the communication was admissible.

State party's merits observations

[6.1] In a submission dated 15 December 1999, the State party gave to the Committee its observations on the merits of the communication.

[6.2] The State party reiterates its opinion that the alleged victim was not subjected to torture because he had at no time been in contact with the law enforcement officers, i.e., the police officers. It therefore considers that there is no violation of the Convention whatsoever.

[6.3] The State party also underlines that the courts of its country operate independently and have concluded rightfully and in accordance with the law that no investigation should be initiated against the alleged authors of the acts of torture. It points in this regard to the fact that the author of the communication has not submitted all the court decisions and other judicial documents that may bring some additional light to the Committee's consideration of the communication. The said documents were submitted to that effect by the State party.

[6.4] The State party then gave its version of the facts. First, it alleges that the alleged victim took alcohol and drugs (Bromazepan) and had already tried to commit suicide some time before. During the afternoon preceding his death, on 12 February 1995, the alleged victim had taken some drugs (in the form of pills) and was in a very bad mood because of an argument he had had with his mother. These elements were, according to the State party, confirmed by four of his friends who spent the afternoon of 12 February 1995 with the alleged victim. The State party also notes that the parents and girlfriend of the alleged victim stated exactly the contrary.

[6.5] With respect to the events surrounding the death of the alleged victim, the State party refers to the statement made by the eyewitness, Dragan Markovic, who explained that he had seen the victim standing on the edge of the terrace, 15 metres from the ground and immediately called the police. When the police arrived, the victim jumped from the terrace and neither Dragan Markovic nor the police could prevent it. The State party notes also that the three policemen who are accused of the alleged murder of the victim arrived on the premises after the victim had jumped and therefore concludes that none of them could have taken any action.

[6.6] The above elements demonstrate, according to the State party, that the death of the alleged victim was the result of a suicide and that no acts of torture had therefore been committed.

[6.7] Moreover, the State party notes that the impartiality of witness Dragan Markovic, as well as of S. Isailovic and Z. Jetvic, the two police officers who arrived first on the scene, is indisputable and confirmed by the fact that the request for an investigation filed by the author of the communication was directed not against these persons but others.

[6.8] Concerning the judicial proceedings that followed the death of the victim, the State party recalls the various steps of the procedure and notes that the main reason that an investigation had not been ordered was the lack of strong evidence to prove a causal link between the behaviour of the three defendant police officers and the death of the victim. The State party contends that the procedure has been scrupulously respected at all steps and that the complaint has been carefully considered by all the magistrates who have had to deal with the case.

[6.9] Finally, the State party emphasizes that certain omissions that may have occurred during the events immediately following the death of the alleged victim and that have been referred to by the author of the communication were not important because they do not prove that the alleged victim died as a result of torture.

Author's comments on the merits

[7.1] In a submission dated 4 January 1999, the author refers to relevant jurisprudence of the European Court of Human Rights. In a further submission dated 19 April 2000, the author confirmed the assertions he had made in his communication and gave to the Committee additional observations on the merits of the communication.

[7.2] The author first makes some remarks on specific issues raised or ignored by the State party in its observations. In this regard, the author mainly points to the fact that the State party limited itself to arguing that the three police officers allegedly responsible for the murder were not involved in the death of the alleged victim and fails to address the main issue of the communication, which is the failure to carry out a prompt, impartial and comprehensive investigation.

[7.3] The author focuses on the following factual elements supporting his claim:

(a) The inspector in charge of the case took three months to collect the information needed for the investigation;

(b) The District Court was only requested to initiate an investigation seven months after the death of the alleged victim;

(c) The District Court failed to take as a starting point for establishing the relevant facts the police report that had been made at the time of the death;

(d) The eyewitness Dragan Markovic did mention in his only statement the presence at the scene of police officers Z. Jeftic and S. Isailovic and not the presence of the three defendant police officers;

(e) The Šabac Police Department failed to provide the photographs taken at the scene of the incident, as a result of which the investigating judge transmitted incomplete documentation to the public prosecutor;

(f) When the parents of the alleged victim proceeded in the capacity of private prosecutor, the investigating judge failed to order the exhumation of the body of the alleged victim and a new autopsy, at the same time agreeing that the original autopsy "had not been performed in line with all the rules of forensic medicine";

(g) Yugoslav prosecuting authorities failed to hear numerous other witnesses proposed by the author.

[7.4] Regarding the State party's contention that the alleged victim had previously attempted to commit suicide, the author indicates that the State party does not substantiate its claim with medical records or police reports, which are usually available in such cases. With regard to other rumours concerning the alleged victim, inter alia that he was addicted to drugs, the author notes that they have always been denied by the family. The author does not know when or whether the four friends of his son were interrogated and neither he nor his lawyer was ever notified of such an interrogation. Moreover, the author notes that three of these witnesses may have been subjected to pressure and influenced for various reasons.

[7.5] Concerning the obligation to investigate incidents of torture and cruel, inhuman or degrading treatment or punishment, the author refers to the jurisprudence of the Committee in the case *Encarnación Blanco Abad* v. *Spain* (CAT/C/20/D/59/1996), where the Committee observed that "under article 12 of the Convention, the authorities have the obligation to proceed to an investigation ex officio, wherever there are reasonable grounds to believe that acts of torture or ill-treatment have been committed and whatever the origin of the suspicion". He also refers to the decision in the case *Henri Unai Parot* v. *Spain* (CAT/C/14/D/6/1990), according to which the obligation of a prompt and impartial investigation exists even when torture has merely been alleged by the victim, without the existence of a formal complaint. The same jurisprudence is confirmed by the European Court of Human Rights (*Assenov and Others* v. *Bulgaria* (90/1997/874/1086)).

[7.6] Concerning the principle of prompt investigation of incidents of alleged torture or other ill-treatment, the author refers to the Committee's jurisprudence stating that a delay of 15 months before the initiation of an investigation is unreasonable and contrary to article 12 of the Convention (*Qani Halimi-Nedzibi* v. *Austria*, CAT/C/11/D/8/1991).

[7.7] Concerning the principle of the impartiality of the judicial authorities, the author states that a body cannot be impartial if it is not sufficiently independent. He refers to the case law of the European Court of Human Rights to define both the impartiality and the independence of a judicial body in accordance with article 6 (1) and 13 of the European Convention on Human Rights and underlines that the authority capable of providing a remedy should be "sufficiently independent" from the alleged responsible author of the violation.

[7.8] Concerning the existence of reasonable grounds to believe that an act of torture or other ill-treatment has been committed, the author, again relying on the jurisprudence of the European Court of Human Rights, points to "the existence of facts or information which would satisfy an objective observer that the person concerned may have committed the offence".

[7.9] Concerning the principle of compensation and rehabilitation for an act of torture or other ill-treatment, the author mentions that an effective remedy entails also the payment of compensation.

[7.10] The author stresses that, at the time of his submission, five years had already elapsed since his son's death. He contends that, notwithstanding strong indication that grave police brutality had caused the death of Milan Ristic, the Yugoslav authorities have failed to conduct a prompt, impartial and comprehensive investigation able to lead to the identification and punishment of those responsible, and have thus failed to provide the author with any redress.

[7.11] Relying on a significant amount of sources, the author explains that police brutality in Yugoslavia is systematic and considers that public prosecutors are not independent and rarely institute criminal proceedings against police officers accused of violence and/or misconduct towards citizens. In such cases, the action is very often limited to a request for information directed to the police authorities alone and the use of dilatory tactics is common.

[7.12] Finally, the author specifically refers to the most recent examination of the periodic report submitted by Yugoslavia to the Committee and the latter's subsequent concluding observations, in which it stated that it was "extremely concerned over the numerous accounts of the use of torture by the State police forces that it has received from non-governmental organizations" (A/54/44, para. 46) and "gravely concerned over the lack of sufficient investigation, prosecution and punishment by the competent authorities ... of suspected torturers or those breaching article 16 of the Convention, as well as with the insufficient reaction to the complaints of such abused persons, resulting in the de facto impunity of the perpetrators of acts of torture" (ibid., para. 47).

Issues and proceedings before the Committee

[8.1] The Committee has considered the communication in the light of all information made available to it by the parties concerned, in accordance with article 22, paragraph 4, of the Convention. It regrets in this regard that the State party has only provided the Committee with a different account of the event, and notes that more precise information concerning the conduct of the investigation was necessary, including an explanation of why a new autopsy was not carried out.

[8.2] It also notes that the author of the communication claims that the State party has violated articles 2, 12, 13, 14 and 16 of the Convention.

[8.3] With regard to articles 2 and 16, the Committee first considers that it does not fall under its mandate to assess the guilt of persons who have allegedly committed acts of torture or police brutality. Its competence is limited to considering whether the State party has failed to comply with any of the provisions of the Convention. In the present case, the Committee will therefore not pronounce itself on the existence of torture or ill-treatment.

[8.4] With regard to articles 12 and 13 of the Convention, the Committee notes the following elements, on which both parties have been able to submit observations:

(a) There are apparent differences and inconsistencies between the statement made on 18 August 1995 by the doctor who came with the ambulance as to the premise of the cause of death of the alleged victim, the autopsy report of 13 February 1995 and the report made on 20 March 1995 by two forensic experts at the request of the parents of the alleged victim;

(b) Although the investigating judge in charge of the case when the parents of the alleged victim proceeded in the capacity of private prosecutor stated that the autopsy "had not been performed in line with all the rules of forensic medicine", there was no order of exhumation of the body for a new forensic examination;

(c) There is a difference between the statement made on 13 February 1995 by one of the three police officers allegedly responsible for the death of the alleged victim according to which the Police Department had been called for a person who *had committed* suicide and the statements made by another of the above-mentioned police officers, as well as by two other police officers and the witness D. Markovic, according to which the Police Department had been called for a person who *might jump* from the roof of a building;

(d) The police did not immediately inform the investigating judge on duty of the incident in order for him to oversee the on-site investigation in compliance with article 154 of the Code of Criminal Procedure of the State party.

[8.5] Moreover, the Committee is especially concerned by the fact that the doctor who carried out the autopsy admitted in a statement dated 18 July 1995 that he was not a specialist in forensic medicine.

[8.6] Noting the above elements, the Committee considers that the investigation that was conducted by the State party's authorities was neither effective nor thorough. A proper investigation would indeed have entailed an exhumation and a new autopsy, which would in turn have allowed the cause of death to be medically established with a satisfactory degree of certainty.

[8.7] Moreover, the Committee notes that six years have elapsed since the incident took place. The State party has had ample time to conduct a proper investigation.

[8.8] In the circumstances, the Committee finds that the State party has violated its obligations under articles 12 and 13 of the Convention to investigate promptly and effectively allegations of torture or severe police brutality.

[8.9] With regard to allegations of a violation of article 14, the Committee finds that in the absence of proper criminal investigation, it is not possible to determine whether the rights to compensation of the alleged victim or his family have been violated. Such an assessment can only be made after the conclusion of proper investigations. The Committee therefore urges the State party to carry out such investigations without delay.

[9.] In pursuance of rule 111, paragraph 5, of its rules of procedure, the Committee urges the State party to provide the author of the communication with an appropriate remedy, and to inform it, within 90 days from the date of the transmittal of this decision, of the steps it has taken in response to the observations made above.

Communication N° 120/1998

Submitted by: Sadiq Shek Elmi
Alleged victim: The author
State party: Australia
Date of adoption of Views: 14 May 1999

Subject matter: deportation of complainant to Somalia involving risk of torture by non-State entities

Procedural issue: none

Substantive issue: risk of torture after deportation

Article of the Convention: 3

1. The author of the communication is Mr. Sadiq Shek Elmi, a Somali national from the Shikal clan, currently residing in Australia, where he has applied for asylum and is at risk of expulsion. He alleges that his expulsion would constitute a violation by Australia of article 3 of the Convention against Torture and Other Cruel, Inhuman or Degrading Treatment or Punishment. He is represented by counsel.

The facts as submitted by the author

2.1 The author was born on 10 July 1960 in Mogadishu. Before the war he worked as a goldsmith in Mogadishu, where his father was an elder of the Shikal clan. The author states that members of the Shikal clan, of Arabic descent, are identifiable by their lighter coloured skin and discernable accent. The clan is known for having brought Islam to Somalia, for its religious leadership and relative wealth. The author claims that the clan has not been directly involved in the fighting, however it has been targeted by other clans owing to its wealth and its refusal to join or support economically the Hawiye militia. In the lead up to the ousting of President Barre in late 1990, the author's father, as one of the elders of his clan, was approached by leaders of the Hawiye clan seeking Shikal financial support and fighters for the Hawiye militia.

2.2 The author further states that upon refusal to provide support to the Hawiye militia in general, and in particular to provide one of his sons to fight for the militia, his father was shot and killed in front of his shop. The author's brother was also killed by the militia when a bomb detonated inside his home, and his sister was raped three times by members of the Hawiye militia, precipitating her suicide in 1994.

2.3 The author claims that on a number of occasions he barely escaped the same fate as his family members, and that his life continues to be threatened, particularly by members of the Hawiye clan who, at present, control most of Mogadishu. From 1991 until he left Somalia in 1997, he continuously moved around the country for reasons of security, travelling to places that he thought would be safer. He avoided checkpoints and main roads and travelled through small streams and the bush on foot.

2.4 The author arrived in Australia on 2 October 1997 without valid travel documents and has been held in detention since his arrival. On 8 October 1997, he made an application for a protection visa to the Department of Immigration and Multicultural Affairs. Following an interview with the author held on 12 November 1997, the application was rejected on 25 March 1998. On 30 March 1998, he sought review of the negative decision before the Refugee Review Tribunal (RRT), which turned down his request for a review on 21 May 1998. The author subsequently appealed to the Minister for Immigration and Multicultural Affairs who under the Migration Act has the personal, non-compellable and non-reviewable power to intervene and set aside decisions of RRT where it is in the "public interest" to do so. This request was denied on 22 July 1998.

2.5 On 22 October 1998, the author was informed that he was to be returned to Mogadishu, via Johannesburg. Amnesty International intervened in the case and, in a letter dated 28 October 1998, urged the Minister for Immigration and Multicultural Affairs to use his powers not to remove the author as planned. In addition, the same day the author submitted a request to the Minister to lodge a second application for a protection visa. In the absence of the exercise of the Minister's discretion, the lodging of a new application for refugee status is prohibited.

2.6 On 29 October 1998, the author was taken to Melbourne Airport to be deported, escorted by guards from the Immigration Detention Centre. However, the author refused to board the plane. As a result, the captain of the aircraft refused to take him on board. The author was then taken back to the detention centre. On the same day he addressed an additional plea to the Minister in support of his previous requests not to be removed from Australia; it was rejected. On 30 October 1998, the author was informed that his removal would be carried out the following day. On the same date he sought an interim injunction from Justice Haynes at the High Court of Australia to restrain the Minister from continuing the removal procedure. Justice Haynes dismissed the author's application on 16 November 1998, in view of the fact that the circumstances did not raise a "serious question to be tried". Special leave was sought to appeal to the full bench of the High Court, but that request was also dismissed.

2.7 The author states that he has exhausted all available domestic remedies and underlines that, while he could still technically seek special leave from the High Court, his imminent removal would stymie any such application. He further indicates that the legal representatives initially provided to him by the authorities clearly failed to act in their client's best interest. As the submitted documents reveal, the initial statement and the subsequent legal submissions to RRT were undoubtedly inadequate and the representatives failed to be present during the author's hearing with the Tribunal in order to ensure a thorough investigation into his history and the consequences of his membership of the Shikal clan.

The complaint

3.1 The author claims that his forced return to Somalia would constitute a violation of article 3 of the Convention by the State party and that his background and clan membership would render him personally at risk of being subjected to torture. He fears that the Hawiye clan will be controlling the airport on his arrival in Mogadishu and that they will immediately ascertain his clan membership and the fact that he is the son of a former Shikal elder. They will then detain, torture and possibly execute him. He is also fearful that the Hawiye clan will assume that the author, being a Shikal and having been abroad, will have money, which they will attempt to extort by torture and other means.

3.2 It is emphasized that in addition to the particular circumstances pertaining to the author's individual case, Somalia is a country where there exists a pattern of gross, flagrant or mass violations of human rights. In expressing its opinion in the author's case, the Regional Office of UNHCR for Australia, New Zealand, Papua New Guinea and the South Pacific stated that "(w)hile it is true that UNHCR facilitates voluntary repatriation to so-called Somaliland, we neither promote nor encourage repatriation to any part of Somalia. In respect of rejected asylum-seekers from Somalia, this office does urge States to exercise the utmost caution in effecting return to Somalia."[1] Reference is also made to the large number of sources indicating the persisting existence of torture in Somalia, which would support the author's position that his forced return would constitute a violation of article 3 of the Convention.

State party's observations

4.1 On 18 November 1998, the Committee, acting through its Special Rapporteur on new communications, transmitted the communication to the State party for comment and requested the State party not to expel the author while his communication was under consideration by the Committee.

4.2 By submission of 16 March 1999, the State party challenged the admissibility of the communication, but also addressed the merits of the case. It informed the Committee that, following its request under rule 108, paragraph 9, the expulsion order against the author has been stayed while his communication is pending consideration by the Committee.

A. Observations on admissibility

4.3 As regards the domestic procedures, the State party submits that although it considers that domestic remedies are still available to the author it does not wish to contest the admissibility of the communication on the ground of non-exhaustion of domestic remedies.

4.4 The State party contends that this communication is inadmissible *ratione materiae* on the basis that the Convention is not applicable to the facts alleged. In particular, the kind of acts the author fears that he will be subjected to if he is returned to Somalia do not fall within the definition of "torture" set out in article 1 of the Convention. Article 1 requires that the act of torture be "committed by, or at the instigation of, or with the consent or acquiescence of a public official or any other person acting in an official capacity". The author alleges that he will be subjected to torture by members of armed Somali clans. These members, however, are not "public officials" and do not act in an "official capacity".

4.5 The Australian Government refers to the Committee's decision in *G.R.B.* v. *Sweden*, in which the Committee stated that "a State party's obligation under article 3 to refrain from forcibly returning a person to another State where there were substantial grounds to believe that he or she would be in danger of being subjected to torture was directly linked to the definition of torture as found in article 1 of the Convention."[2]

4.6 The State party further submits that the definition of torture in article 1 was the subject of lengthy debates during the negotiations for the Convention. On the issue of which perpetrators the Convention should cover, a number of views were expressed. For example, the delegation of France

---

[1] Letter dated 7 September 1998 addressed to the author's counsel.

[2] Communication N° 83/1997, *G.R.B.* v. *Sweden*, 15 May 1998, para. 6.5.

argued that "the definition of the act of torture should be a definition of the intrinsic nature of the act of torture itself, irrespective of the status of the perpetrator."[3] There was little support for the French view although most States did agree that "the Convention should not only be applicable to acts committed by public officials, but also to acts for which the public authorities could otherwise be considered to have some responsibility."[4]

4.7 The delegation of the United Kingdom of Great Britain and Northern Ireland made an alternative suggestion that the Convention refer to a "public official or any other agent of the State."[5] By contrast, the delegation of the Federal Republic of Germany "felt that it should be made clear that the term 'public official' referred not only to persons who, regardless of their legal status, have been assigned public authority by State organs on a permanent basis or in an individual case, but also to persons who, in certain regions or under particular conditions actually hold and exercise authority over others and whose authority is comparable to government authority or—be it only temporarily—has replaced government authority or whose authority has been derived from such persons."[6]

4.8 According to the State party it was ultimately "generally agreed that the definition should be extended to cover acts committed by, or at the instigation of, or with the consent or acquiescence of a public official or any other person acting in an official capacity."[7] It was not agreed that the definition should extend to private individuals acting in a non-official capacity, such as members of Somali armed bands.

B. Observations on the merits

4.9 In addition to contesting the admissibility the State party argues, in relation to the merits, that there are no substantial grounds to believe that the author would be subjected to torture if returned to Somalia. The author has failed to substantiate his claim that he would be subjected to torture by members of the Hawiye and other armed clans in Somalia, or that the risk alleged is a risk of torture as defined in the Convention.

4.10 The State party points to the existing domestic safeguards which ensure that genuine applicants for asylum and for visas on humanitarian grounds are given protection and through which the author has been given ample possibilities to present his case, as described below. In the primary stage of processing an application for a protection visa, a case officer from the Federal Department of Immigration and Multicultural Affairs (DIMA) examines the claim against the provisions of the Convention relating to the Status of Refugees. When there are claims which relate to the Convention against Torture and further clarification is required, the officer may seek an interview, using an interpreter if necessary. Applicants must be given the opportunity to comment on any adverse information, which will be taken into account when their claim is considered. Assessments of claims for refugee protection are made on an individual basis using all available and relevant information concerning the human rights situation in the applicant's home country. Submissions from migration agents or solicitors can also form part of the material to be assessed.

4.11 The State party further explains that if an application for a protection visa is refused at the primary stage, a person can seek review of the decision by the Refugee Review Tribunal (RRT), an independent body with the power to grant a protection visa. RRT also examines claims against the Convention relating to the Status of Refugees. If RRT intends making a decision that is unfavourable to the applicant on written evidence alone, it must give the applicant the opportunity of a personal hearing. Where there is a perceived error of law in the RRT decision, a further appeal may be made to the Federal Court for judicial review.

4.12 DIMA provides for application assistance to be given to eligible protection visa applicants. Under this scheme, all asylum-seekers in detention have access to contracted service providers who assist with the preparation of the application form and exposition of their claims, and attend any interview. If the primary decision by DIMA is to refuse a protection visa, the service providers may assist with any further submissions to DIMA and any review applications to RRT.

4.13 The State party draws the attention of the Committee to the fact that, in the present case, the author had the assistance of a migration agent in making his initial application and that an interview was conducted with him by an officer of DIMA with the assistance of an interpreter. In addition, during the course of the review by RRT of the primary decision, the author attended two days of hearings before RRT, during which he was also assisted by an interpreter. He was not represented by a migration agent at the RRT hearing, but the State party takes the view that legal representation before RRT is not necessary, as its proceedings are non-adversarial in nature.

---

[3] Herman Burgers and Hans Danelius, *The United Nations Convention against Torture: A Handbook on the Convention against Torture and Other Cruel, Inhuman or Degrading Treatment or Punishment* (1988).
[4] Ibid.
[5] Ibid.
[6] Ibid.
[7] E/CN.4/L.1470, 12 March 1979, para. 18.

4.14 The State party submits that neither DIMA nor RRT was satisfied that the author had a well-founded fear of persecution, because he failed to show that he would be persecuted for a reason pertaining to the Convention relating to the Status of Refugees. In particular, although RRT accepted that the author was a member of the Shikal clan and that, at the beginning of the conflict in Somalia, his father and one brother had been killed and one sister had committed suicide, it found that the author had not shown that he would be targeted personally if returned to Somalia. It found that the alleged victim had, at times, had to flee the civil war in Somalia but that this was not sufficient to show persecution for a reason pertaining to the Convention relating to the Status of Refugees.

4.15 The alleged victim sought judicial review of the RRT decision in the High Court of Australia, on the basis that RRT had erred in law and that its decision was unreasonable. He also sought an order restraining the Minister for Immigration and Multicultural Affairs from removing him from Australia until his application was decided. On 16 November 1998, Justice Hayne of the High Court dismissed all the grounds of appeal, rejecting the argument that RRT had erred in law or that its decision was unreasonable. Further, he rejected the application to restrain the Minister of Immigration and Multicultural Affairs from removing the author. Subsequently, on 17 November 1998, the author lodged a communication with the Committee. The Committee requested the State party not to remove the author until his case had been examined. Following such request, the State party interrupted the author's removal. The State party understands that on 25 November 1998 the author applied for special leave to appeal the decision of Justice Hayne to the Full Bench of the High Court of Australia.

4.16 In addition to the procedures established to deal with claims of asylum pursuant to Australia's obligations under the Convention relating to the Status of Refugees, the Minister for Immigration and Multicultural Affairs has a discretion to substitute a decision of RRT with a decision which is more favourable to the applicant, for reasons of public interest. All cases which are unsuccessful on review by RRT are assessed by the Department of Immigration and Multicultural Affairs on humanitarian grounds, to determine if they should be referred to the Minister for consideration of the exercise of his or her humanitarian stay discretion. Cases are also referred to the Minister under this section on request by the applicant or a third party on behalf of the applicant. In the present case, the Minister was requested to exercise his discretion in favour of the author, but the Minister declined to do so. The author also requested that the Minister exercise his discretion to allow him to lodge a fresh application for a protection visa, but, on the recommendation of DIMA, the Minister again declined to consider exercising his discretion.

4.17 The State party notes that in the course of the asylum procedure, the author has not provided factual evidence to support his claims. Furthermore, the State party does not accept that, even if those assertions were correct, they necessarily would lead to the conclusion that he would be subjected to "torture" as defined in the Convention. In making this assessment, the State party has taken into account the jurisprudence of the Committee establishing that a person must show that he or she faces a real, foreseeable and personal risk of being subjected to torture, as well as the existence of a consistent pattern of gross, flagrant or mass violations of human rights.

4.18 The State party does not deny that the attacks on the author's father, brother and sister occurred as described by the author, nor that at that time and immediately afterwards the author may have felt particularly vulnerable to attacks by the Hawiye clan and that this fear may have caused the author to flee Mogadishu (but not Somalia). However, there is no evidence that the author, at present, would face a threat from the Hawiye clan if he were returned to Somalia. Moreover, in the absence of any details or corroborating evidence of his alleged escapes and in the absence of any evidence or allegations to the effect that the author has previously been tortured, it must be concluded that the author remained in Somalia in relative safety throughout the conflict. The State party points out that it is incumbent upon the author of a communication to present a factual basis for his allegations. In the present case the author has failed to adduce sufficient evidence of an ongoing and real threat of torture by the Hawiye against him and other members of the Shikal clan.

4.19 The State party accepts that there has been a consistent pattern of gross, flagrant or mass violations of human rights in Somalia and that, throughout the armed conflict, members of small, unaligned and unarmed clans, like the Shikal, have been more vulnerable to human rights violations than members of the larger clans. However, through diplomatic channels, the State party has been informed that the general situation in Somalia has improved over the past year and, although random violence and human rights violations continue and living conditions remain difficult, civilians are largely able to go about their daily business. The State party has also been informed by its embassy in Nairobi that a small community of Shikal still resides in Mogadishu and that its members are apparently able to practise their trade and have no fear of being attacked by stronger clans. However, as an unarmed clan, they are particularly vulnerable to looters. Although the Shikal, including members of the author's family, may have been targeted by the Hawiye in the early stages of the Somali conflict, they have at present a harmonious relationship with the Hawiye in Mogadishu and elsewhere, affording a measure of protection to Shikal living there.

4.20 The State party points out that it has also considered the issue of whether the author would risk being targeted by other clans than the Hawiye. It states that it is prepared to accept that certain members of unarmed clans and others in Somalia suffer abuse at the hands of other Somali inhabitants. Further, the author may be more vulnerable to such attacks as he is a member of an unarmed clan whose members are generally believed to be wealthy. However, the State party does not believe that the author's membership of such a clan is sufficient to put him at a greater risk than other Somali civilians. In fact, the State party believes that many Somalis face the same risk. That view is supported by the report of its embassy in Nairobi, which states that "(a)ll Somalis in Somalia are vulnerable because of lack of a functioning central government authority and an effective rule of law. [The author's] situation, were he to return to Somalia, would not be exceptional".

4.21 In the event that the Committee disagrees with the State party's assessment that the risk faced by the author is not a real, foreseeable and personal one, the State party contends that such risk is not a risk of "torture" as defined in article 1 of the Convention. Although the State party accepts that the political situation in Somalia makes it possible that the author may face violations of his human rights, it argues that such violations will not necessarily involve the kind of acts contemplated in article 1 of the Convention. For example, even though the acts of extortion anticipated by the author may be committed for one of the purposes referred to in the definition of torture, such acts would not necessarily entail the intentional infliction of severe pain or suffering. In addition, the author's claims that he will risk detention, torture and possibly execution have not been sufficiently substantiated.

4.22 Finally, the State party reiterates its reasoning as to the admissibility of the case and also as to the merits.

Counsel's comments

5.1 As regards the *ratione materiae* admissibility of the communication, counsel submits that despite the lack of a central government, certain armed clans in effective control of territories within Somalia are covered by the terms "public official" or "other person acting in an official capacity" as required by article 1 of the Convention. In fact, the absence of a central government in a State increases the likelihood that other entities will exercise quasi-governmental powers.

5.2 Counsel further emphasizes that the reason for limiting the definition of torture to the acts of public officials or other persons acting in an official capacity was that the purpose of the Convention was to provide protection against acts committed on behalf of, or at least tolerated by, the public authorities, whereas the State would normally be expected to take action, in accordance with its criminal law, against private persons having committed acts of torture against other persons. Therefore, the assumption underlying this limitation was that, in all other cases, States were under the obligation by customary international law to punish acts of torture by "non-public officials". It is consistent with the above that the Committee stated, in *G.R.B.* v. *Sweden*, that "whether the State party has an obligation to refrain from expelling a person who might risk pain or suffering inflicted by a non-governmental entity, without the consent or acquiescence of the Government, falls outside the scope of article 3 of the Convention". However, the present case is distinguishable from the latter as it concerns return to a territory where non-governmental entities themselves are in effective control in the absence of a central government, from which protection cannot be sought.

5.3 Counsel submits that when the Convention was drafted there was agreement by all States to extend the scope of the perpetrator of the act from the "public official" referred to in the Declaration on the Protection of All Persons from Being Subjected to Torture and Other Cruel, Inhuman or Degrading Treatment or Punishment, to include "other person[s] acting in an official capacity". This would include persons who, in certain regions or under particular conditions, actually hold and exercise authority over others and whose authority is comparable to government authority.

5.4 According to a general principle of international law and international public policy, international and national courts and human rights supervisory bodies should give effect to the *realities* of administrative actions in a territory, no matter what may be the strict legal position, where those actions affect the everyday activities of private citizens. In *Ahmed* v. *Austria*, the European Court of Human Rights, in deciding that deportation to Somalia would breach article 3 of the European Convention on Human Rights, which prohibits torture, stated that "fighting was going on between a number of clans vying with each other for control of the country. There was no indication that the dangers to which the applicant would have been exposed to had ceased to exist or that any public authority would be able to protect [the applicant]."[8]

---

[8] *Ahmed* v. *Austria*, case N° 71/1995/577/663, 27 November 1996.

5.5 In relation to Somalia, there is abundant evidence that the clans, at least since 1991, have, in certain regions, fulfilled the role, or exercised the semblance, of an authority that is comparable to government authority. These clans, in relation to their regions, have prescribed their own laws and law enforcement mechanisms and have provided their own education, health and taxation systems. The report of the independent expert of the Commission on Human Rights illustrates that States and international organizations have accepted that these activities are comparable to governmental authorities and that "[t]he international community is still negotiating with the warring factions, who ironically serve as the interlocutors of the Somali people with the outside world."[9]

5.6 Counsel notes that the State party does not wish to contest admissibility on the basis of the non-exhaustion of domestic remedies, but nevertheless wishes to emphasize that the author's communication of 17 November 1998 was submitted in good faith, all domestic remedies available to the author having been exhausted. The subsequent application by the author for special leave to appeal, which is currently pending before the Full Bench of the High Court of Australia, does not provide a basis for injunctive relief to prevent the expulsion of the author. Further, following an intervention by Amnesty International in the author's case, the Minister for Immigration and Multicultural Affairs stated that "[a]s an unlawful non-citizen who had exhausted all legal avenues to remain in Australia, my Department was required under law to remove [the author] as soon as reasonably practicable."

5.7 As to the merits of the communication, the author must establish grounds that go beyond mere "theory or suspicion"[10] that he will be in danger of being tortured. As the primary object of the Convention is to provide safeguards against torture, it is submitted that the author is not required to prove all of his claims[11] and that a "benefit of the doubt" principle may be applied. There is sufficient evidence that the author faces personal risk of being subjected to torture upon his return owing to his membership of the Shikal clan and his belonging to a particular family.

5.8 Counsel contests the State party's argument that the author had in fact been able to live in Somalia since the outbreak of the war in "relative safety" and submits an affidavit from the author stating that, as an elder of the Shikal clan, his father had been prosecuted by the Hawiye clan, especially since he had categorically refused to provide money and manpower for the war. Even before the outbreak of the war there had been attempts on the author's father's life by the Hawiye clan. The family was told by the Hawiye that they would suffer the consequences of their refusal to provide support to the clan, once the Hawiye came into power in Mogadishu. The author states that he was staying at a friend's house when the violence broke out in December 1990 and he learnt that his father had been killed during an attack by the Hawiye clan. Only hours after his father's death, the Hawiye planted and detonated a bomb under the family home, killing one of the author's brothers. The author's mother, other brothers and his sisters had already fled the house.

5.9 The author also states that, together with the remaining family members, he escaped to the town of Medina, where he stayed during 1991. The Hawiye clan attacked Medina on a number of occasions and killed Shikal members in brutal and degrading ways. The author states that hot oil was poured over their heads, scalding their bodies. Sometimes, when they received warnings about Hawiye raids, the family would flee Medina for short periods of time. On one occasion, upon returning after such a flight, the author learnt that the Hawiye militia had searched the town with a list of names of people they were looking for, including the author and his family. After one year of constant fear the family fled to Afgoi. On the day of the flight, the Hawiye attacked again and the author's sister was raped for the second time by a member of the militia. In December 1992, the author heard that the United Nations was sending troops to Somalia and that the family would be protected if they returned to Mogadishu. However, the author and his family only returned as far as Medina, since they heard that the situation in Mogadishu had in fact not changed.

5.10 After another year in Medina, the family once again fled to Afgoi and from there to Ugunji, where they stayed for two years in relative peace before the Hawiye arrived in the area and enslaved the members of minority clans and peasants living there, including the author. The indigenous villagers also had pale skin, therefore the militia never questioned the author and his family about their background. However, when the family learnt that Hawiye elders were coming to the village they once again fled, knowing that they would be recognized. In the course of the following months the author went back and forth between Medina and Afgoi. Finally, the family managed to leave the country by truck to Kenya.

5.11 In addition to the grounds previously mentioned, the risk to the author is increased by the

---

[9] Report of the independent expert of the Commission on Human Rights, Ms. Mona Rishmawi, on the situation of human rights in Somalia (E/CN.4/1999/103), para. 154.
[10] Communication N° 101/1997, *Halil Haydin* v. *Sweden*, 16 December 1998, para. 6.5.
[11] Communication N° 34/1995, *Seid Mortesa Aemei* v. *Switzerland*, para. 9.6.

national and international publicity which his particular case has received. For example, Amnesty International has issued an Urgent Action in the name of the author; Reuters news agency, the BBC Somali Service and other international media have reported on the suspension of the author's expulsion following the request of the Committee; the independent expert of the Commission on Human Rights on the situation of human rights in Somalia has appealed in the author's case and made reference to it both in her report to the Commission on Human Rights and in oral statements, indicating that "[a] case currently pending in Australia concerning a forced return to Mogadishu of a Somali national is particularly alarming, due to the precedent it will create in returning individuals to areas undergoing active conflict."[12]

5.12 Counsel also submits that the danger of torture faced by the author is further aggravated owing to the manner in which the State party intends to carry out his return. According to the return plan, the author is to be delivered into the custody of private security "escorts" in order to be flown to Nairobi via Johannesburg and then continue unescorted from Nairobi to Mogadishu. Counsel submits that if the author were to arrive unescorted in North Mogadishu, at an airport which tends to be used only by humanitarian relief agencies, warlords and smugglers and which is controlled by one of the clans hostile to the Shikal, he would be immediately identifiable as an outsider and would be at increased risk of torture. In this context counsel refers to written interventions from various non-governmental sources stating that a Somali arriving in Mogadishu without escort or help to get through the so-called "authorities" would in itself give rise to scrutiny.

5.13 With reference to the State party's comments regarding the author's credibility, counsel underlines that throughout the author's application for refugee status, the credibility of the author or his claims have never been an issue. RRT accepted the author's case as claimed and clearly found the applicant a credible witness.

5.14 Counsel underlines that there is evidence of a consistent pattern of gross, flagrant or mass violations of human rights in Somalia, although the lack of security has seriously compromised the ability of human rights monitors to document comprehensively individual cases of human rights abuses, including torture. The absence of case studies concerning torture of persons with similar "risk characteristics" as the author cannot therefore lead to the conclusion that such abuses do not occur, in accordance with reports from inter alia the independent expert of the Commission on Human Rights on the situation of human rights in Somalia, UNHCR, the Office for the Coordination of Humanitarian Affairs of the United Nations and Amnesty International. Counsel further underlines that the author is a member of a minority clan and hence is recognized by all sources as belonging to a group at particular risk of becoming the victim of violations of human rights. The State party's indication of the existence of an agreement between the Shikal and Hawiye clans affording some sort of protection to the Shikal is categorically refuted by counsel on the basis of information provided by reliable sources, and is considered as unreliable and impossible to corroborate.

5.15 Finally, counsel draws the attention of the author to the fact that although Somalia acceded to the Convention on 24 January 1990, it has not yet recognized the competence of the Committee to receive and consider communications from or on behalf of individuals under article 22. If returned to Somalia, the author would no longer have the possibility of applying to the Committee for protection.

Issues and proceedings before the Committee

6.1 The Committee notes the information from the State party that the return of the author has been suspended, in accordance with the Committee's request under rule 108, paragraph 9, of its rules of procedure.

6.2 Before considering any claims contained in a communication, the Committee against Torture must decide whether or not it is admissible under article 22 of the Convention. In this respect the Committee has ascertained, as it is required to do under article 22, paragraph 5 (a), of the Convention, that the same matter has not been and is not being examined under another procedure of international investigation or settlement. The Committee also notes that the exhaustion of domestic remedies is not contested by the State party. It further notes the State party's view that the communication should be declared inadmissible *ratione materiae* on the basis that the Convention is not applicable to the facts alleged, since the acts the author will allegedly face if he is returned to Somalia do not fall within the definition of "torture" set out in article 1 of the Convention. The Committee, however, is of the opinion that the State party's argument raises a substantive issue which should be dealt with at the merits and not the admissibility stage. Since the Committee sees no further obstacles to admissibility, it declares the communication admissible.

6.3 Both the author and the State party have provided observations on the merits of the communication. The Committee will therefore proceed to examine those merits.

---

[12] Oral statement on the situation of human rights in Somalia, delivered on 22 April 1999 before the Commission on Human Rights.

6.4 The Committee must decide whether the forced return of the author to Somalia would violate the State party's obligation, under article 3, paragraph 1, of the Convention, not to expel or return (*refouler*) an individual to another State where there are substantial grounds for believing that he would be in danger of being subjected to torture. In order to reach its conclusion the Committee must take into account all relevant considerations, including the existence in the State concerned of a consistent pattern of gross, flagrant or mass violations of human rights. The aim, however, is to determine whether the individual concerned would personally risk torture in the country to which he or she would return. It follows that the existence of a consistent pattern of gross, flagrant or mass violations of human rights in a country does not as such constitute sufficient grounds for determining whether the particular person would be in danger of being subjected to torture upon his return to that country; additional grounds must be adduced to show that the individual concerned would be personally at risk. Similarly, the absence of a consistent pattern of gross violations of human rights does not mean that a person cannot be considered to be in danger of being subjected to torture in his or her specific circumstances.

6.5 The Committee does not share the State party's view that the Convention is not applicable in the present case since, according to the State party, the acts of torture the author fears he would be subjected to in Somalia would not fall within the definition of torture set out in article 1 (i.e., pain or suffering inflicted by or at the instigation of or with the consent or acquiescence of a public official or other person acting in an official capacity, in this instance for discriminatory purposes). The Committee notes that for a number of years Somalia has been without a central government, that the international community negotiates with the warring factions and that some of the factions operating in Mogadishu have set up quasi-governmental institutions and are negotiating the establishment of a common administration. It follows then that, de facto, those factions exercise certain prerogatives that are comparable to those normally exercised by legitimate governments. Accordingly, the members of those factions can fall, for the purposes of the application of the Convention, within the phrase "public officials or other persons acting in an official capacity" contained in article 1.

6.6 The State party does not dispute the fact that gross, flagrant or mass violations of human rights have been committed in Somalia. Furthermore, the independent expert on the situation of human rights in Somalia, appointed by the Commission on Human Rights, described in her latest report[13] the severity of those violations, the situation of chaos prevailing in the country, the importance of clan identity and the vulnerability of small, unarmed clans such as the Shikal, the clan to which the author belongs.

6.7 The Committee further notes, on the basis of the information before it, that the area of Mogadishu where the Shikal mainly reside, and where the author is likely to reside if he ever reaches Mogadishu, is under the effective control of the Hawiye clan, which has established quasi-governmental institutions and provides a number of public services. Furthermore, reliable sources emphasize that there is no public or informal agreement of protection between the Hawiye and the Shikal clans and that the Shikal remain at the mercy of the armed factions.

6.8 In addition to the above, the Committee considers that two factors support the author's case that he is particularly vulnerable to the kind of acts referred to in article 1 of the Convention. First, the State party has not denied the veracity of the author's claims that his family was particularly targeted in the past by the Hawiye clan, as a result of which his father and brother were executed, his sister raped and the rest of the family was forced to flee and constantly move from one part of the country to another in order to hide. Second, his case has received wide publicity and, therefore, if returned to Somalia the author could be accused of damaging the reputation of the Hawiye.

6.9 In the light of the above the Committee considers that substantial grounds exist for believing that the author would be in danger of being subjected to torture if returned to Somalia.

7. Accordingly, the Committee is of the view that, in the prevailing circumstances, the State party has an obligation, in accordance with article 3 of the Convention, to refrain from forcibly returning the author to Somalia or to any other country where he runs a risk of being expelled or returned to Somalia.

8. Pursuant to rule 111, paragraph 5, of its rules of procedure, the Committee would wish to receive, within 90 days, information on any relevant measures taken by the State party in accordance with the Committee's present Views.

---

[13] E/CN.4/1999/103.

Communication N° 161/2000

Submitted by: Hajrizi Dzemajl et al.
Alleged victim: The authors
State party: Yugoslavia
Date of adoption of Views: 21 November 2002

Subject matter: violent expulsion of complainants from Roma settlement

Procedural issue: none

Substantive issues: failure promptly to investigate allegations of cruel, inhuman and degrading treatment; right to complain; right to compensation

Articles of the Convention: 12, 13, 14, 16

1.1 The complainants are 65 persons, all of Romani origin and nationals of the (former) Federal Republic of Yugoslavia. They claim that Yugoslavia has violated articles 1, paragraph 1, 2, paragraph 1, 12, 13, 14 and 16, paragraph 1, of the Convention. They are represented by Mr. Dragan Prelevic, attorney at law, the Humanitarian Law Center, an NGO based in Yugoslavia, and the European Roma Rights Center, an NGO based in Hungary.

1.2 In accordance with article 22, paragraph 3, of the Convention, the Committee transmitted the complaint to the State party on 13 April 2000.

The facts as presented by the complainants

2.1 On 14 April 1995 at around 10 p.m., the Danilovgrad Police Department received a report indicating that two Romani minors had raped S.B., a minor ethnic Montenegrin girl. In response to this report, around midnight, the police entered and searched a number of houses in the Bozova Glavica Roma settlement and took into custody all of the young male Romani men present in the settlement (all of them presently among the complainants to this Committee).

2.2 The same day, around midnight, two hundred ethnic Montenegrins, led by relatives and neighbours of the raped girl, assembled in front of the police station and publicly demanded that the Municipal Assembly adopt a decision expelling all Roma from Danilovgrad. The crowd shouted slogans addressed to the Roma, threatening to "exterminate" them and "burn down" their houses.

2.3 Later, two Romani minors confessed under duress. On 15 April, between 4 and 5 a.m., all of the detainees except those who confessed were released from police custody. Before their release, they were warned by the police to leave Danilovgrad immediately with their families because they would be at risk of being lynched by their non-Roma neighbours.

2.4 At the same time, police officer Ljubo Radovic came to the Bozova Glavica Roma settlement and told the Romani residents of the settlement that they must evacuate the settlement immediately. The officer's announcement caused panic. Most residents of the settlement fled towards a nearby highway, where they could take buses for Podgorica. Only a few men and women remained in the settlement to safeguard their homes and livestock. At approximately 5 a.m., police officer Ljubo Radovic returned to the settlement, accompanied by police inspector Branko Micanovic. The officers told the remaining Roma still in their homes (including some of the complainants) to leave Danilovgrad immediately, as no one could guarantee their safety or provide them with protection.

2.5 The same day, at around 8 a.m., a group of non-Roma residents of Danilovgrad entered the Bozova Glavica Roma settlement, hurling stones and breaking windows of houses owned by the complainants. Those Roma who had still not left the settlement (all of them presently among the complainants to this Committee) were hidden in the cellar of one of the houses from which they eventually managed to flee through the fields and woods towards Podgorica.

2.6 In the course of the morning of 15 April, a police car repeatedly patrolled the deserted Bozova Glavica settlement. Groups of non-Roma residents of Danilovgrad gathered in different locations in the town and in the surrounding villages. Around 2 p.m. the non-Roma crowd arrived in the Bozova Glavica settlement—in cars and on foot. Soon a crowd of at least several hundred non-Roma (according to different sources, between 400 and 3,000 persons were present) assembled in the then deserted Roma settlement.

2.7 Between 2 and 3 p.m., the crowd continued to grow and some began to shout: "We shall evict them!" "We shall burn down the settlement!" "We shall raze the settlement!" Shortly after 3 p.m., the demolition of the settlement began. The mob, with stones and other objects, first broke windows of cars and houses belonging to Roma and then set them on fire. The crowd also destroyed and set fire to the haystacks, farming and other machines, animal feed sheds, stables, as well as all other objects belonging to the Roma. They hurled explosive devices and "Molotov" cocktails that they had prepared beforehand, and threw burning cloths and foam rubbers into houses through the broken windows. Shots and explosions could be heard amid the sounds of destruction. At the same time, valuables were looted and cattle slaughtered. The pogrom endured unhindered for hours.

2.8 Throughout the course of this pogrom, police officers present failed to act in accordance with their legal obligations. Shortly after the attack began, rather than intervening to halt the violence, these officers simply moved their police car to a safe distance and reported to their superior officer. As the violence and destruction unfolded, police officers did no more than feebly seek to persuade some of the attackers to calm down pending a final decision of the Municipal Assembly with respect to a popular request to evict Roma from the Bozova Glavica settlement.

2.9 The outcome of the anti-Roma rage was that the whole settlement was levelled and all properties belonging to its Roma residents burnt or completely destroyed. Although the police did nothing to halt the destruction of the Roma settlement, they did ensure that the fire did not spread to any of the surrounding buildings, which belonged to the non-Roma.

2.10 The police and the investigating magistrate of the Basic Court in Danilovgrad subsequently drew up an on-site investigation report regarding the damage caused by those who took part in the pogrom.

2.11 Official police documents, as well as statements given by a number of police officers and other witnesses alike, both before the court and in the initial stage of the investigation, indicate that the following non-Roma residents of Danilovgrad were among those who took part in the destruction of the Bozova Glavica Roma settlement: Veselin Popovic, Dragisa Makocevic, Gojko Popovic, Bosko Mitrovic, Joksim Bobicic, Darko Janjusevic, Vlatko Cacic, Radojica Makocevic.

2.12 Moreover, there is evidence that police officers Miladin Dragas, Rajko Radulovic, Dragan Buric, Djordjije Stankovic and Vuk Radovic were all present as the violence unfolded and did nothing or not enough to protect the Roma residents of Bozova Glavica or their property.

2.13 Several days following the incident, the debris of the Roma settlement was completely cleared away by heavy construction machines of the Public Utility Company. All traces of the existence of the Roma in Danilovgrad were obliterated.

2.14 Following the pogrom, and pursuant to the relevant domestic legislation, on 17 April 1995, the Podgorica Police Department filed a criminal complaint with the Basic Public Prosecutor's Office in Podgorica. The complaint alleged that a number of unknown perpetrators had committed the criminal offence of causing public danger under article 164 of the Montenegrin Criminal Code and, inter alia, explicitly stated that there are "reasonable grounds to believe that, in an organized manner and by using open flames... they caused a fire to break out... on 15 April 1995... which completely consumed dwellings... and other propert[ies] belonging to persons who used to reside in... [the Bozova Glavica] settlement".

2.15 On 17 April 1995 the police brought in 20 individuals for questioning. On 18 April 1995, a memorandum was drawn up by the Podgorica Police Department which quoted the statement of Veselin Popovic as follows: "... I noticed flames in a hut which led me to conclude that the crowd had started setting fire to huts so I found several pieces of foam rubber which I lit with a lighter I had on me and threw them, alight, into two huts, one of which caught fire."

2.16 On the basis of this testimony and the official police memorandum, the Podgorica Police Department ordered, on 18 April 1995, that Veselin Popovic be remanded into custody, on the grounds that there were reasons to believe that he had committed the criminal offence of causing public danger in the sense of article 164 of the Montenegrin Criminal Code.

2.17 On 25 April 1995, and with respect to the incident at the origin of this complaint, the Public Prosecutor instituted proceedings against one person only—Veselin Popovic.

2.18 Veselin Popovic was charged under article 164 of the Montenegrin Criminal Code. The same indictment charged Dragisa Makocevic with illegally obtaining firearms in 1993—an offence unrelated to the incident at issue notwithstanding the evidence implicating him in the destruction of the Roma Bozova Glavica settlement.

2.19 Throughout the investigation, the investigating magistrate of the Basic Court of Danilovgrad heard a number of witnesses all of whom stated that they had been present as the violence unfolded but were not able to identify a single perpetrator. On 22 June 1995, the investigating magistrate of the Basic Court of Danilovgrad heard officer Miladin Dragas. Contrary to the official memorandum he had personally drawn up on 16 April 1995, officer Dragas now stated that he had not seen anyone throwing an inflammable device, nor could he identify any of the individuals involved.

2.20 On 25 October 1995, the Basic Public Prosecutor in Podgorica requested that the investigating magistrate of the Basic Court of Danilovgrad undertake additional investigation into the facts of the case. Specifically, the prosecutor proposed that new witnesses be heard, including officers from the Danilovgrad Police Department who had been entrusted with protecting the Bozova Glavica Roma settlement. The investigating magistrate of the Basic Court of Danilovgrad then heard the additional witnesses, all of whom stated that they had seen none of the individuals who had caused the fire. The investigating magistrate took no further action.

2.21 Due to the "lack of evidence", the Basic Public Prosecutor in Podgorica dropped all charges against Veselin Popovic on 23 January 1996. On 8 February 1996, the investigating magistrate of the Basic Court of Danilovgrad issued a decision to discontinue the investigation. From February 1996 up to and including the date of filing of this complaint, the authorities took no further steps to identify and/or punish those individuals responsible for the incident at issue—"civilians" and police officers alike.

2.22 In violation of domestic legislation, the complainants were not served with the court decision of 8 February 1996 to discontinue the investigation. They were thus prevented from assuming the capacity of a private prosecutor and to continue with the prosecution of the case.

2.23 Even prior to the closing of the proceedings, on 18 and 21 September 1995, the investigating magistrate, while hearing witnesses (among them a number of the complainants), failed to advise them of their right to assume the prosecution of the case in the event that the Public Prosecutor should decide to drop the charges. This contravened domestic legislation which explicitly provides that the Court is under an obligation to advise ignorant parties of avenues of legal redress available for the protection of their interests.

2.24 On 6 September 1996, all 71 complainants filed a civil claim for damages, pecuniary and non-pecuniary, with the first instance court in Podgorica—each plaintiff claiming approximately US$ 100,000. The pecuniary damages claim was based on the complete destruction of all properties belonging to the plaintiffs, while the non-pecuniary damages claim was based on the pain and suffering of the plaintiffs associated with the fear they were subjected to, and the violation of their honour, reputation, freedom of movement and the right to choose their own place of residence. The plaintiffs addressed these claims against the Republic of Montenegro and cited articles 154, 180 (1), 200, and 203 of the Federal Law on Obligations. More than five years after the submission of their claim, the civil proceedings for damages are still pending.

2.25 On 15 August 1996, eight of the Danilovgrad Roma, all of them among the complainants in the instant case, who were dismissed by their employers for failing to report to work, filed a law suit requesting that the court order their return to work. Throughout the proceedings, the plaintiffs argued that their failure to appear at work during the relevant time period was justified by their reasonable fear that their lives would have been endangered had they come to work so soon after the incident. On 26 February 1997, the Podgorica first instance court rendered its decision dismissing the claims of the plaintiffs on the grounds that they had been absent from work for five consecutive days without justification. In doing so the court cited article 75, paragraph 2, of the Federal Labour Code which inter alia provides that "if a person fails to report to work for five consecutive days without proper justification his employment will be terminated". On 11 June 1997, the plaintiffs appealed this decision and almost five months later, on 29 October 1997, the second instance court in Podgorica quashed the first instance ruling and ordered a retrial. The reasoning underlying the second instance decision was based on the fact that the plaintiffs had apparently not been properly served with their employer's decision to terminate their employment.

2.26 In the meantime, the case went again up to the Montenegrin Supreme Court which ordered another retrial before the fist instance court in Podgorica. The case is still pending.

2.27 The complainants, having been driven out of their homes and their property having been completely destroyed, fled to the outskirts of Podgorica, the Montenegrin capital, where during the first few weeks following the incident they hid in parks and abandoned houses. Local Roma from Podgorica supplied them with basic food and told them that groups of angry non-Roma men had been looking for them in the Roma suburbs in Podgorica. From this time on, the banished Danilovgrad Roma have continued to live in Podgorica in abject poverty, makeshift shelters or abandoned houses, and have been forced to work at the Podgorica city dump or to beg for a living.

The complaint

3.1 The complainants submit that the State party has violated articles 2, paragraph 1, read in conjunction with article 1, 16, paragraph 1, and 12, 13, 14 taken alone or together with article 16, paragraph 1, of the Convention.

3.2 With regard to the admissibility of the complaint, and more particularly the exhaustion of local remedies, the complainants submit that, given the level of wrongs suffered, and alongside the jurisprudence of the European Court of Human Rights,[1] only a criminal remedy would be effective

---

[1] See *Assenov* v. *Bulgaria*, Judgement of 28 October 1998, paras. 102, 117; *Aksoy* v. *Turkey*, Judgement of 18 December 1996; *Aydin* v. *Turkey*, Judgement of 29

in the instant case. Civil and/or administrative remedies do not provide sufficient redress in this case.

3.3 The complainants note further that the authorities had the obligation to investigate, or at least to continue their investigation if they considered the available evidence insufficient. Moreover, even though they acknowledge that they have never filed a criminal complaint against individuals responsible for the pogrom, they contend that both the police and the prosecuting authorities were sufficiently aware of the facts to initiate and conduct the investigation ex officio. The complainants therefore conclude that there is no effective remedy.

3.4 The complainants also note that since there is no effective remedy in respect of the alleged breach of the Convention, the issue of exhaustion of domestic remedies should be dealt with together with the merits of the case since there is a claim of violation of articles 13 and 14 of the Convention.

3.5 Referring to a number of excerpts from NGO and governmental sources, the complainants first request that the complaint be considered taking into account the situation of the Roma in Yugoslavia as victims of systematic police brutality and dire human rights situation in general.

3.6 The complainants allege that Yugoslav authorities have violated the Convention under either article 2, paragraph 1, read in conjunction with article 1, because, during the events described previously, the police stood by and watched as the events unfolded, or article 16, paragraph 1, for the same reasons. In this regard, the complainants consider that the particularly vulnerable character of the Roma minority has to be taken into account in assessing the level of ill-treatment that has been committed. They suggest that "a given level of physical abuse is more likely to constitute 'degrading or inhuman treatment or punishment' when motivated by racial animus".

3.7 With regard to the fact that the acts have mostly been committed by non-State actors, the complainants rely on a review of international jurisprudence on the principle of "due diligence" and remind the current state of international law with regard to "positive" obligations that are incumbent on States. They submit that the purpose of the provisions of the Convention is not limited to negative obligations for States parties but include positive steps that have to be taken in order to avoid that torture and other related acts are committed by private persons.

3.8 The complainants further contend that the acts of violence occurred with the "consent or acquiescence" of the police whose duty under the law was to secure their safety and afford them protection.

3.9 The complainants then allege a violation of article 12 read alone or, if the acts committed do not amount to torture, taken together with article 16, paragraph 1, because the authorities failed to conduct a prompt, impartial, and comprehensive investigation capable of leading to the identification and punishment of those responsible. Considering the jurisprudence of the Committee against Torture, it is submitted that the State party had the obligation to conduct "not just any investigation" but a proper investigation, even in the absence of the formal submission of a complaint, since they were in possession of abundant evidence.[2] The complainants further suggest that the impartiality of the same investigation depends on the level of independence of the body conducting it. In this case, it is alleged that the level of independence of the investigative magistrate was not sufficient.

3.10 The complainants finally allege a violation of article 13 read alone and/or taken together with article 16, paragraph 1, because "their right to complain and to have [their] case promptly and impartially examined by [the] competent authorities" was violated. They also allege a violation of article 14 read alone and/or taken together with article 16, paragraph 1, because of the absence of redress and of fair and adequate compensation.

State party's admissibility observations

4. In a submission dated 9 November 1998, the State party contended that the complaint was inadmissible because the case had been conducted according to the Yugoslavian legislation and because all available legal remedies had not been exhausted.

Comments by the complainants

5. In a submission dated 20 September 2000, the complainants reiterated their main arguments with regard to the admissibility of the complaint and underlined that the State party had not explained what domestic remedies would still be available which the complainants should still exhaust. In addition, they consider that since the State party has failed to put forward any other objections in that respect, it has in effect waived its right to contest other admissibility criteria.

Admissibility decision

6. At its twenty-fifth session, the Committee considered the admissibility of the complaint. The

---

September 1997; *X and Y* v. *Netherlands*, 8 EHRR 235 (1985), paras. 21–30.

[2] See *Encarnación Blanco Abad* v. *Spain*, para. 8.2; *Henri Unai Parot* v. *Spain*, 2 May 1995, CAT/C/14/D/6/1990.

Committee ascertained, as it is required to do under article 22, paragraph 5 (a), of the Convention, that the same matter had not been and was not being examined under another procedure of international investigation or settlement. Regarding the exhaustion of domestic remedies, the Committee took note of the arguments made by the complainants and noted that it had not received any argumentation or information from the State party on this issue. Referring to rule 108, paragraph 7, of its rules of procedure, the Committee declared the complaint admissible on 23 November 2000.

State party's merits observations

7. Notwithstanding the Committee's call for observations on the merits, transmitted by a note of 5 December 2000, and two reminders of 9 October 2001 and 11 February 2002, the State party did not make any further submission.

Complainants' additional merits comments

8.1 By a letter of 6 December 2001, the complainants transmitted to the Committee additional information and comments on the merits of the case. In the same submission, the complainants have transmitted detailed information on different questions that were asked by the Committee, namely, on the presence and behaviour of the police during the events, the actions that have been taken towards the local population, the relations between the different ethnic groups, and their respective titles of property.

8.2 With regard to the presence and behaviour of the police during the events and the actions that have been taken towards the local population, the complainants give a detailed description of the facts referred to in paragraphs 2.1 to 2.29 above.

8.3 With regard to the general situation of the Roma minority in the Federal Republic of Yugoslavia, the complainants contend that the situation has remained largely unchanged after the departure of President Milosevic. Referring to a report that was earlier submitted by the Humanitarian Law Center to the Committee against Torture and to the 2001 Annual Report of Human Rights Watch, the complainants submit that the situation of Roma in the State party is today very preoccupying and emphasize that there have been a number of serious incidents against Roma over the last few years while no significant measures to find or prosecute the perpetrators or to compensate the victims have been taken by the authorities.

8.4 With regard to the property titles, the complainants explain that most were lost or destroyed during the events of 14 and 15 April 1995 and that this was not challenged by the State party's authorities during the civil proceedings.

8.5 The complainants then make a thorough analysis of the scope of application of articles 1, paragraph 1, and 16, paragraph 1, of the Convention. They first submit that the European Court of Human Rights has ascertained in *Ireland* v. *United Kingdom* and in the *Greek* case, that article 3 of the European Convention on Human Rights also covered "the infliction of mental suffering by creating a state of anguish and stress by means other than bodily assault."[3]

8.6 Moreover, the complainants reiterate that the assessment of the level of ill-treatment also depends on the vulnerability of the victim and should thus also take into account the sex, age, state of health or ethnicity of the victim. As a result, the Committee should consider the Romani ethnicity of the victims in their appreciation of the violations committed, particularly in Yugoslavia. In the same line, they reiterate that a given level of physical abuse is more likely to constitute a treatment prohibited by article 16 of the Convention if it is motivated by racial considerations.

8.7 Concerning the devastation of human settlements, the complainants refer to two cases that were decided by the European Court of Human Rights and whose factual circumstances were similar to the one at issue.[4] The European Court considered in both cases that the burning and destruction of homes as well as the eviction of their inhabitants from the village constituted acts that were contrary to article 3 of the European Convention.

8.8 Concerning the perpetrators of the alleged violations of articles 1 and 16 of the Convention, the complainants submit that although only a public official or a person acting in an official capacity could be the perpetrator of an act in the sense of either of the above provisions, both provisions state that the act of torture or of other ill-treatment may also be inflicted with the consent or acquiescence of a public official. Therefore, while they do not dispute that the acts have not been committed by the police officers or that the latter have not instigated them, the complainants consider that they have been committed with their consent and acquiescence. The police were informed of what was going to happen on 15 April 1995 and were present on the scene at the time when the pogrom took place but did not prevent the perpetrators from committing their wrongdoing.

8.9 With regard to the positive obligations of States to prevent and suppress acts of violence committed by private individuals, the complainants

---

[3] Report of 5 November 1969, Yearbook XII; the *Greek* case (1969), p. 461.
[4] *Mentes and Others* v. *Turkey*, 58/1996/677/867 and *Selcuk and Asker* v. *Turkey*, 12/1997/796/998–999.

refer to General Comment 20 of the Human Rights Committee on article 7 of the International Covenant on Civil and Political Rights according to which this provision covers acts that are committed by private individuals, which implies a duty for States to take appropriate measures to protect everyone against such acts. The complainants also refer to the United Nations Code of Conduct for Law Enforcement Officials, the Basic Principles on the Use of Force and Firearms by law Enforcement Officials and the Council of Europe's Framework Convention for the Protection of National Minorities, which have provisions with a similar purpose.

8.10 On the same issue, the complainants cite a decision of the Inter-American Court of Human Rights in *Velásquez Rodríguez* v. *Honduras*, according to which:

> [a]n illegal act which violates human rights and which is initially not directly imputable to a State (for example, because it is the act of a private person or because the person responsible has not been identified) can lead to international responsibility of the State, not because of the act itself but because of the lack of due diligence to prevent the violation or to respond to it as required by the Convention.[5]

Similarly, the European Court of Human Rights addressed the issue in *Osman* v. *United Kingdom* and stated that:

> [a]rticle 2 of the Convention may also imply in certain well-defined circumstances a positive obligation on the authorities to take preventive operational measures to protect an individual whose life is at risk from the criminal acts of another individual ... [W]here there is an allegation that the authorities have violated their positive obligation to protect the right to life in the context of their above-mentioned duty to prevent and suppress offences against the person ... it must be established to its satisfaction that the authorities knew or ought to have known at the time of the existence of a real and immediate risk to the life of an identified individual or individuals from the criminal acts of a third party and that they failed to take measures within the scope of their powers which, judged reasonably, might have been expected to avoid that risk ... [H]aving regard to the nature of the right protected by article 2, a right fundamental in the scheme of the Convention, it is sufficient for an applicant to show that the authorities did not do all that could be reasonably expected of them to avoid a real and immediate risk to life of which they have or ought to have knowledge.[6]

8.11 The complainants further contend that the extent of the obligation to take preventive measures may increase with the immediacy of the risk to life. In support of this argument, they extensively rely on the judgement of the European Court of Human Rights in *Mahmut Kaya* v. *Turkey* where the Court laid down the obligations of States as follows: first, States have an obligation to take every reasonable step in order to prevent a real and immediate threat to the life and integrity of a person when the actions could be perpetrated by a person or group of persons with the consent or acquiescence of public authorities; second, States have an obligation to provide an effective remedy, including a proper and effective investigation, with regard to actions committed by non-State actors undertaken with the consent or acquiescence of public authorities.

8.12 The complainants also underline that the obligation of the States under the European Convention on Human Rights goes well beyond mere criminal sanctions for private individuals who have committed acts contrary to article 3 of the said Convention. In *Z.* v. *United Kingdom*, the European Commission on Human Rights held that

> the authorities were aware of the serious ill-treatment and neglect suffered by the applicants over a period of years at the hands of their parents and failed, despite the means reasonably available to them, to take any effective steps to bring it to an end... [The State had therefore] failed in its positive obligation under article 3 of the Convention to provide the applicants with adequate protection against inhuman and degrading treatment.[7]

8.13 In conclusion, the complainants submit that "they were indeed subjected to acts of community violence inflicting on them great physical and mental suffering amounting to torture and/or cruel, inhuman and degrading treatment or punishment". They further state that "this happened for the purpose of punishing them for an act committed by a third person (the rape of S.B.), and that the community violence (or rather the racist pogrom) at issue took place in the presence of, and thus with the 'consent or acquiescence' of, the police whose duty under law was precisely the opposite—to secure their safety and afford them protection".

---

[5] *Velásquez Rodríguez* v. *Honduras*, Judgement of 29 July 1988, p. 291.

[6] *Osman* v. *United Kingdom*, paras. 115–116.

[7] *Z.* v. *United Kingdom*, para. 98.

8.14 Finally, concerning the absence of observations by the State party on the merits, the complainants refer to rule 108 (6) of the Committee's rules of procedure and consider that such principle should be equally applicable during the phase of the merits. Relying on the jurisprudence of the European Court of Human Rights and of the Human Rights Committee, the complainants further argue that, by not contesting the facts or the legal arguments developed in the complaint and further submissions, the State party has tacitly accepted the claims at issue.

Issues and proceedings before the Committee

9.1 The Committee has considered the complaint in the light of all information made available to it by the parties concerned, in accordance with article 22, paragraph 4, of the Convention. Moreover, in the absence of any submission from the State party following the Committee's decision on admissibility, the Committee relies on the detailed submissions made by the complainants. The Committee recalls in this respect that a State party has an obligation under article 22, paragraph 3, of the Convention to cooperate with the Committee and to submit written explanations or statements clarifying the matter and the remedy, if any, that may have been granted.

9.2 As to the legal qualification of the facts that have occurred on 15 April 1995, as they were described by the complainants, the Committee first considers that the burning and destruction of houses constitute, in the circumstances, acts of cruel, inhuman or degrading treatment or punishment. The nature of these acts is further aggravated by the fact that some of the complainants were still hidden in the settlement when the houses were burnt and destroyed, the particular vulnerability of the alleged victims and the fact that the acts were committed with a significant level of racial motivation. Moreover, the Committee considers that the complainants have sufficiently demonstrated that the police (public officials), although they had been informed of the immediate risk that the complainants were facing and had been present at the scene of the events, did not take any appropriate steps in order to protect the complainants, thus implying "acquiescence" in the sense of article 16 of the Convention. In this respect, the Committee has reiterated on many instances its concerns about "inaction by police and law-enforcement officials who fail to provide adequate protection against racially motivated attacks when such groups have been threatened" (Concluding observations on the initial report of Slovakia, A/56/44 (2001), para. 104; see also Concluding observations on the second periodic report of the Czech Republic, A/56/44 (2001), para. 113 and Concluding observations on the second periodic report of Georgia, A/56/44 (2001), para. 81). Although the acts referred to by the complainants were not committed by public officials themselves, the Committee considers that they were committed with their acquiescence and constitute therefore a violation of article 16, paragraph 1, of the Convention by the State party.

9.3 Having considered that the facts described by the complainants constitute acts within the meaning of article 16, paragraph 1, of the Convention, the Committee will analyse other alleged violations in the light of that finding.

9.4 Concerning the alleged violation of article 12 of the Convention, the Committee, as it has underlined in previous cases (see inter alia *Encarnación Blanco Abad* v. *Spain*, N° 59/1996, decided on 14 May 1998), is of the opinion that a criminal investigation must seek both to determine the nature and circumstances of the alleged acts and to establish the identity of any person who might have been involved therein. In the present case, the Committee notes that, despite the participation of at least several hundred non-Roma in the events of 15 April 1995 and the presence of a number of police officers both at the time and at the scene of those events, no person nor any member of the police forces has been tried by the courts of the State party. In these circumstances, the Committee is of the view that the investigation conducted by the authorities of the State party did not satisfy the requirements of article 12 of the Convention.

9.5 Concerning the alleged violation of article 13 of the Convention, the Committee considers that the absence of an investigation as described in the previous paragraph also constitutes a violation of article 13 of the Convention. Moreover, the Committee is of the view that the State party's failure to inform the complainants of the results of the investigation by, inter alia, not serving on them the decision to discontinue the investigation, effectively prevented them from assuming "private prosecution" of their case. In the circumstances, the Committee finds that this constitutes a further violation of article 13 of the Convention.

9.6 Concerning the alleged violation of article 14 of the Convention, the Committee notes that the scope of application of the said provision only refers to torture in the sense of article 1 of the Convention and does not cover other forms of ill-treatment. Moreover, article 16, paragraph 1, of the Convention while specifically referring to articles 10, 11, 12, and 13, does not mention article 14 of the Convention. Nevertheless, article 14 of the Convention does not mean that the State party is not obliged to grant redress and fair and adequate compensation to the victim of an act in breach of article 16 of the Convention. The positive obligations that flow from the first sentence of article 16 of the Convention include an obligation to grant redress and compensate the victims of an act in breach of that provision. The Committee is therefore of the view that the State party has failed to observe its obligations under article 16 of the Convention by failing to enable the complainants to obtain redress and to provide them with fair and adequate compensation.

10. The Committee, acting under article 22, paragraph 7, of the Convention, is of the view that the facts before it disclose a violation of articles 16, paragraph 1, 12 and 13 of the Convention against Torture and Other Cruel, Inhuman or Degrading Treatment or Punishment.

11. In pursuance of rule 111, paragraph 5, of its rules of procedure, the Committee urges the State party to conduct a proper investigation into the facts that occurred on 15 April 1995, prosecute and punish the persons responsible for those acts and provide the complainants with redress, including fair and adequate compensation and to inform it, within 90 days from the date of the transmittal of this decision, of the steps it has taken in response to the Views expressed above.

Communication N° 171/2000

Submitted by: Jovica Dimitrov
Alleged victim: The complainant
State party: Serbia and Montenegro
Date of adoption of Views: 3 May 2005

Subject matter: torture and/or ill-treatment of the complainant in detention

Procedural issue: exhaustion of domestic remedies

Substantive issues: failure promptly to investigate allegations of torture; right to complain; right to compensation

Articles of the Convention: 12, 13, 14

1. The complainant is Jovica Dimitrov, a Serbian citizen of Roma origin, residing in Serbia and Montenegro. He claims to be a victim of violations of article 2, paragraph 1, read in connection with articles 1; 16, paragraph, 1; and articles 12, and 13 and 14 taken alone and/or read in connection with article 16, paragraph 1, by Serbia and Montenegro, of the Convention against Torture and Other Cruel, Inhuman or Degrading Treatment or Punishment. He is represented by the Humanitarian Law Center (HLC), based in Belgrade and by the European Roma Rights Center (ERRC), based in Budapest, both non-governmental organizations.

The facts as presented by the complainant

2.1 In the early hours of 5 February 1996, the complainant was arrested at his home in Novi Sad, in the Serbian province of Vojvodina, and taken to the police station in Kraljevica Marka Street. The arresting officer presented no arrest warrant nor did he inform the complainant why he was being taken into custody. The complainant himself made no attempt to resist arrest. During the ensuing interrogation, the arresting officer struck the complainant repeatedly with a baseball bat and a steel cable, and kicked and punched him all over his body. The complainant lost consciousness on several occasions. Apart from brief breaks, the ill-treatment lasted from 6.30 a.m. to 7.30 p.m., leaving the complainant with numerous injuries on his buttocks and left shoulder. After 7.30 p.m., the complainant was released, again without being given an arrest warrant or a release order; nor was he told of the reason for his arrest and detention. According to the complainant, this was in contravention of articles 192 (3), 195 and 196 (3) of the Criminal Procedure Code (CPC), which deals with police powers of arrest and detention.

2.2 Following his release, the complainant returned home and spent the next 10 days in bed, being nursed by his sister. On 9 February 1996, he went to see a doctor who examined him and ordered continued bed rest. He prepared a report describing his injuries as follows: "Left upper arm: livid-red and brown discoloration 10 x 8 cm with slightly raised red edges; right shoulder blade and shoulder: livid-red discolorations in the form of stripes 3 x 11 cm, and 4 x 6 cm on the shoulders; gluteal part of the body: blue-livid discolorations of the size of a man's palm on both sides; outside of the left mid-thigh: distinct red stripe 3x5 cm; inside of right knee: light blue swelling 5x5 cm; area around ankle and soles (both legs): slight, light blue swelling." The conclusions and opinion was that the "Patient should be referred to a neurologist and a laboratory for tests." The complainant also provides a statement from his sister, who states that he was arrested at

6.30 in the morning on 5 February, held in detention until 7.30 pm, and that upon return his face was swollen, and he had bruises on his shoulders, back, legs and over his kidneys. There was clotted blood on his legs and his backside was dark blue all over. He had to stay in bed for ten days and put on compresses, and take pills for the pain. He told her that he had been beaten with a steel wire and baseball bats and fainted from the beating.

2.3 Fearing possible reprisals by police and not fully aware of his legal rights, the complainant did not file a criminal complaint with the Novi Sad Municipal Public Prosecutor's Office until 7 November 1996, in which he alleged that an unidentified police officer had committed the crime of extracting a statement by force in violation of 65 of the Serbian Criminal Code (SCC). According to the complainant, he had been arrested several times prior to the incident in question and had been interrogated about several unrelated criminal offences. The complainant considers that the ill-treatment to which he was subjected was intended to obtain his confession for one or more of these crimes.

2.4 The complaint was immediately registered by the Public Prosecutor's Office. But only on 17 September 1999 (more than three and a half years (43 months) following the incident at issue and 34 months since the complainant filed the criminal complaint) did the Public Prosecutor's Office request the investigating judge of the Novi Sad Municipal Court to undertake preliminary "investigatory actions". Such investigation precedes the possible subsequent institution of formal judicial investigations, for which the identity of the suspect must be ascertained. The investigating judge of the Novi Sad Municipal Court accepted the public prosecutor's request and opened a case file. Since that date, the prosecuting authorities have taken no concrete steps, with a view to identifying the police officer concerned. According to the complainant, if the intent of the investigating judge was really to identify the police in question, he could have heard other police officers present in the police station at the time of the abuse, and especially the on-duty shift commander who must have known the names of all officers working that particular shift. Finally, the complainant indicated in his criminal complaint that during his detention in the police station he was taken to the Homicide Division, which in and of itself could have served as one of the starting points for an official investigation into the incident at issue. No investigation has been undertaken.

2.5 According to the complainant, under article 153 (1) of the CPC, if the public prosecutor finds on the basis of the evidence, that there is reasonable suspicion that a certain person has committed a criminal offence, he should request the investigating judge to institute a formal judicial investigation further to articles 157 and 158 of the CPC. If he decides that there is no basis for the institution of a formal judicial investigation, he should inform the complainant of this decision, who can then exercise his prerogative to take over the prosecution of the case on his own behalf—i.e., in his capacity of a "private prosecutor". As the Public Prosecutor failed formally to dismiss his complaint, the complainant concludes that he was denied the right personally to take over the prosecution of the case. As the CPC sets no time limit in which the public prosecutor must decide whether or not to request a formal judicial investigation into the incident, this legal provision is open to abuse.

The complaint

3.1 The complainant claims that he has exhausted all available criminal domestic remedies by having filed a complaint with the Public Prosecutor's Office. In the complainant's view, civil/ administrative remedies would not provide sufficient redress in his case.[1]

3.2 The complainant submits that the allegations of violations of the Convention should be interpreted against a backdrop of systematic police brutality to which the Roma and others in the State party are subjected, as well as the generally poor human rights situation in the State party.[2] He claims a violation of article 2, paragraph 1, read in connection with articles 1, and 16, paragraph 1, for having been subjected to ill-treatment for the purposes of obtaining a confession, or otherwise intimidating or punishing him.[3]

3.3 He claims a violation of article 12 alone and/or read in connection with 16, paragraph 1, as the State party's authorities failed to conduct an official investigation into the incident, which gave rise to this complaint for more than three and a half years following the incident in question, and almost 34 months since the complainant filed a criminal complaint with the Public Prosecutor's Office. To date, the officer remains unidentified and

---

[1] He refers to international jurisprudence to support this claim.

[2] In this context, the complainant provides reports from various national and international non-governmental organizations and the Concluding Observations of CAT of 1998, A/54/44, paras. 35–52.

[3] To support his argument that the treatment he received was torture, cruel, inhuman and/or degrading treatment or punishment, he refers to the United Nations Code of Conduct for Law Enforcement Officials, the United Nations Body of Principles for the protection of All Persons under Any Form of Detention or Imprisonment, the United Nations Basic Principles on the Use of Force and Firearms by Law Enforcement Officials, the Council of Europe's Declaration on the Police and the European Court of Human Rights.

consequently the institution of formal judicial investigations is impossible. Since the public prosecutor's office has failed formally to dismiss the complainant's criminal complaint, he cannot personally take over the prosecution of the case in his capacity of a "private prosecutor". The complainant also alleges that the public prosecutors in Serbia and Montenegro seldom institute criminal proceedings against police officers accused of misconduct and delay the dismissal of complaints, sometimes by years, thereby denying the injured party the right to prosecute his/her own case.

3.4 The complainant claims a violation of articles 13 alone or read in connection with article 16 of the Convention, as despite exhausting all criminal domestic remedies, 54 months following the incident and almost 34 months after the submission of his criminal complaint he has received no redress for the violation of his rights. To date, the State party's authorities have not even identified the police officer concerned.[4]

3.5 Article 14 is said to be violated since the complainant was denied a criminal remedy and has thus been barred from obtaining fair and adequate compensation in a civil lawsuit. The complainant explains that under domestic law, there are two different procedures, through which compensation for criminal offences may be pursued: by criminal proceedings under article 103 of the CPC following criminal proceedings, or/and by civil action for damages under articles 154 and 200 of the Law on Obligations. The first avenue was not an option, as no criminal proceedings were instituted and the second was not availed of by the complainant, as it is the practice of the State party's courts to suspend civil proceedings for damages arising from criminal offences until prior completion of the respective criminal proceedings. Even if the complainant had attempted to avail of this recourse, he would have been prevented from pursuing it, as under articles 186 and 106 of the Civil Procedure Code he would have to identify the name of the respondent. Since the complainant to date remains unaware of the name of the officer against whom he is claiming violations of his rights the institution of a civil action would have been impossible.

State party's submission on admissibility and merits and complainant's comments

4.1 On 14 January 2003, the State party provided its submission on the admissibility and merits of the complaint. It contests the complainant's allegations and submits that police officers of the Secretariat of Internal Affairs in Novi Sad attempted three times to deliver a request for an interview to the complainant to discuss the contents of his complaint. As the complainant was never at home at the time of delivery, these requests were delivered to the complainant's wife. The complainant failed to contact the Secretariat of Internal Affairs.

4.2 The State party submits that the Municipal State Prosecutor's Office in Novi Sad received a report from the Secretariat of Internal Affairs of Novi Sad, on 2 October 1997, which confirmed that after checking its files, it was established that the complainant had not been brought to nor detained in any of its premises. The Secretariat of Internal Affairs provided the same information on 4 February 1999, at the request of the Municipal State Prosecutor's Office of 23 December 1998.

4.3 Finally, the State party submits that the complainant and two other persons had perpetrated 38 offences in the Czech Republic, for which they were sentenced to 10 years of imprisonment. The Municipal Court of Novi Sad ordered that the complainant's name be placed on a list of wanted persons, to serve prison sentence N° I.K. 265/97 of 5 May 1998.[5] It submits that, on 25 September 2002, the complainant was still in the Czech Republic.[6]

5.1 On 25 November 2003, the complainant commented on the State party's submission and argues that it suggests that as a convicted criminal he is not entitled to complain against police ill-treatment, and that given the circumstances, the investigating authorities did everything to investigate the incident at issue and provide redress. He recalls that the authorities did not interview anyone connected with the incident and ignored the medical certificate documenting the injuries sustained by the complainant. It did not interview the complainant's sister, who had nursed him after the incident, the doctor who examined him, the police officers on duty the day the incident occurred, or the complainant's lawyers. Neither did they request the Czech authorities through inter-State legal assistance to interview the complainant.

5.2 He submits that apart from the State party's failure to investigate the incident, it has failed to provide the Committee with a plausible alternative explanation as to how the victim's injuries could have been inflicted other than through acts of its agents. In the complainant's view, by failing seriously to contest the facts and/or the legal arguments put forward, the State party has in effect expressed its tacit, yet clear, acceptance of both.[7]

---

[4] The complainant refers to communication N° 59/1996, *Encarnación Blanco Abad* v. *Spain,* Views adopted on 14 May 1998.

[5] No further information is provided on this conviction.
[6] It does not state for how long the complainant has been in the Czech Republic.
[7] In this regard, he refers to decisions of the Human Rights Committee in particular communication N° 88/1981,

Issues and proceedings before the Committee

Consideration of admissibility

6. Before considering any claim contained in a complaint, the Committee must decide whether or not it is admissible under article 22 of the Convention. The Committee has ascertained, as it is required to do under article 22, paragraph 5 (a), of the Convention that the same matter has not been and is not being examined under another procedure of international investigation or settlement. With respect to the exhaustion of domestic remedies, the Committee took note of the information provided by the complainant about the criminal complaint which he filed with the public prosecutor. The Committee considers that the insurmountable procedural impediments faced by the complainant as a result of the inaction of the competent authorities rendered the application of a remedy that may bring effective relief to the complainant highly unlikely. In the absence of pertinent information from the State party, the Committee concludes that in any event, domestic proceedings, if any, have been unreasonably prolonged. With reference to article 22, paragraph 4, of the Convention and rule 107 of the Committee's rules of procedure the Committee finds no other obstacle to the admissibility of the complaint. Accordingly, it declares the complaint admissible and proceeds to its examination on the merits.

Consideration of the merits

7.1 The complainant alleges violations by the State party of article 2, paragraph 1, in connection with article 1, and of article 16, paragraph 1, of the Convention. The Committee notes the complainant's description of the treatment to which he was subjected during his detention, which can be characterized as severe pain or suffering intentionally inflicted by public officials in the context of the investigation of a crime, as well as his sister's statement and medical report. It also notes the State party's failure to adequately address this claim and respond to the complainant's allegations. In the circumstances, the Committee concludes that due weight must be given to the complainant's allegations and that the facts, as submitted, constitute torture within the meaning of article 1 of the Convention.

7.2 Concerning the alleged violation of articles 12 and 13 of the Convention, the Committee notes that the Public Prosecutor did not request the judge to initiate a preliminary investigation until 34 months after filing the criminal complaint, and that no further action was taken by the State party to investigate the complainant's allegations after the criminal complaint was filed on 7 November 1996. The State party has not contested this claim. The Committee also notes that the failure to inform the complainant of the results of any investigation effectively prevented him from pursuing a "private prosecution" of his case before a judge. In these circumstances, the Committee considers that the State party has failed to comply with its obligation, under article 12 of the Convention, to carry out a prompt and impartial investigation wherever there is reasonable ground to believe that an act of torture has been committed. In the same vein, it also disregarded its obligation, under article 13, to ensure the complainant's right to complain and to have his case promptly and impartially examined by the competent authorities.

7.3 As for the alleged violation of article 14 of the Convention, the Committee notes the complainant's allegations that the absence of criminal proceedings deprived him of the possibility of filing a civil suit for compensation. In view of the fact that the State party has not contested this allegation and given the passage of time since the complainant initiated legal proceedings at the domestic level, the Committee concludes that the State party has also violated its obligations under article 14 of the Convention in the present case.

8. The Committee, acting under article 22, paragraph 7, of the Convention, is of the view that the facts before it disclose a violation of articles 2, paragraph 1, in connection with articles 1, 12, and 13, and 14 of the Convention.

9. The Committee urges the State party to conduct a proper investigation into the facts alleged by the complainant and, in accordance with rule 112, paragraph 5, of its rules of procedure, to inform it, within 90 days from the date of the transmittal of this decision, of the steps taken in response to the Views expressed above.

Gustavo Raul Larrosa Bequio v. *Uruguay*, Views adopted on 29 March 1983, para. 10.1.

Communication N° 172/2000

Submitted by: Danilo Dimitrijevic
Alleged victim: The complainant
State party: Serbia and Montenegro
Date of adoption of Views: 16 November 2005

Subject matter: torture and/or ill-treatment of the complainant in detention.

Procedural issue: exhaustion of domestic remedies

Substantive issues: failure promptly to investigate allegations of torture; right to complain; right to compensation

Articles of the Convention: 12, 13, 14

1. The complainant is Danilo Dimitrijevic, a Serbian citizen of Roma origin, residing in Serbia and Montenegro. He claims to be a victim of violations of article 2, paragraph 1, read in connection with articles 1 and 16, paragraph 1; article 14 alone; and articles 12 and 13 taken alone and/or read in connection with article 16, paragraph 1, by Serbia and Montenegro of the Convention against Torture and Other Cruel, Inhuman or Degrading Treatment or Punishment. He is represented by the Humanitarian Law Center (HLC), based in Belgrade, and by the European Roma Rights Center (ERRC), based in Budapest, both non-governmental organizations.

The facts as presented by the complainant

2.1 At around noon on 14 November 1997, the complainant was arrested at his home in Novi Sad, in the Serbian province of Vojvodina, and taken to the police station in Kraljevica Marka Street. The arresting officer presented no arrest warrant; nor did he inform the complainant why he was being taken into custody. However, since a criminal case was already pending against him, in which he was charged with several counts of larceny, the complainant assumed that this was the reason for his arrest. He made no attempt to resist arrest. At the police station, he was locked into one of the offices. Half an hour later, an unknown man in civilian clothes entered the office, ordered him to strip to his underwear, handcuffed him to a metal bar attached to a wall and proceeded to beat him with a police club for approximately one hour from 12.30 to 13.30. He sustained numerous injuries, in particular on his thighs and back. The complainant assumes that the man was a plain-clothes police officer. During the beating an officer, whom the complainant knew by name, also entered the room and, while he did not take part in the abuse, he did not stop it.

2.2 The complainant spent the next three days, from 14 to 17 November 1997, during the day, in the same room where he had been beaten. During that time, he was denied food and water, and the possibility of using the lavatory. Although the complainant requested medical attention, and his injuries visibly required such attention, he was not provided with any. During the night, he was taken from the police station to the Novi Sad District Prison in the Klisa neighbourhood. He was not ill-treated there. At no time was he told why he had been brought to the police station, in contravention of articles 192 (3), 195 and 196 (3) of the Criminal Procedure Code (CPC), which deals with police powers of arrest and detention.

2.3 On 17 November 1997, the complainant was brought before the investigating judge of the Novi Sad District Court, Savo Durdić, for a hearing on the charges of larceny against him, in accordance with Article 165 of the Serbian Criminal Code (Case file No. Kri. 922/97). Upon noticing the complainant's injuries, the judge issued a written decision ordering the police immediately to escort him to a forensic specialist for the purpose of establishing their nature and severity.[1] In particular, the judge ordered that a forensic medial expert examine the "injuries visible in the form of bruises on the outside of the suspect's legs...." The judge did not inform the public prosecutor of the complainant's injuries, even though, according to the complainant, he should have done so in accordance with Article 165 (2) of the CPC. Rather than taking the complainant to a specialist, as instructed, the police presented him with a release order, on which the required internal registration number was missing and which incorrectly stated that his detention started at 11 p.m. on 14 November 1997, although he had been taken into custody eleven hours earlier.[2] In the complainant's view, this was an effort to evade responsibility for subjecting him to the physical abuse he had been subjected to during that period.

2.4 Upon his release, and being ignorant of his rights under the law and frightened by his experiences in the preceding three days, the complainant did not seek immediate medical assistance. He did, however, go to a privately owned photographic studio and had photographs taken of his injuries. He has provided these photos, dated 19 November 1997. On 24 November 1997, and having consulted a lawyer, the complainant attended the Clinical Centre of the Novi Sad Forensic Medicine

---

[1] This order has been provided.

[2] This release order has been provided.

Institute for an examination. However, he never received the report and was told that it had been sent to the investigating judge. The case file (No. Kri. 922/97) was examined on several occasions by the complainant's counsel but did not contain the report. In response to queries from counsel, the Medical Institute stated in a letter, dated 30 September 1999, that the report had been forwarded to the judge of the Novi Sad District Court.[3] To date this report has not been found in the case file.

2.5 Also on 24 November 1997, the complainant filed a criminal complaint with the Municipal Public Prosecutor's Office in Novi Sad. He gave a detailed account of the incident and alleged that the following crimes had been committed "extraction of statements, civil injury and slight bodily harm." He also submitted a medial certificate allegedly relating to injuries caused to the complainant by police violence in 1994 (unrelated to the incident in question), a medical report dated 18 November 1997, the police release order, the Novi Sad District Court Order, and photographs of his injuries. Despite many inquiries as to the status of his complaint, including a letter from the complainant's lawyer, dated 3 March 1999, the Novi Sad Municipal Public Prosecutor's Office, has failed to date to respond in any way to the complaint. Criminal proceedings against the complainant with respect to the charges against him for larceny (Case file No. Kri. 922/97) also remain pending. The complainant is currently serving a four-year prison term for larceny in the Sremska Mitrovica Penitentiary, unrelated to case file, No. Kri 922/97.

2.6 According to the complainant, under article 153 (1) of the CPC, if the public prosecutor finds on the basis of the evidence, that there is reasonable suspicion that a certain person has committed a criminal offence, he should request the investigating judge to institute a formal judicial investigation further to articles 157 and 158 of the CPC. If he decides that there is no basis for the institution of a formal judicial investigation, he should inform the complainant of this decision, who can then exercise his prerogative to take over the prosecution of the case on his own behalf—i.e., in his capacity of a "private prosecutor". As the Public Prosecutor did not formally dismiss his complaint, the complainant concludes that he was denied the right personally to take over prosecution of the case. As the CPC sets no time limit in which the public prosecutor must decide whether or not to request a formal judicial investigation into the incident, this provision is open to abuse.

The complaint

3.1 The complainant claims that he has exhausted all available criminal domestic remedies by having filed a complaint with the Public Prosecutor's Office. In the complainant's view, civil/administrative remedies would not provide sufficient redress in his case.[4]

3.2 The complainant submits that the allegations of violations of the Convention should be interpreted against a backdrop of systematic police brutality to which the Roma and others in the State party are subjected, as well as the generally poor human rights situation in the State party.[5] He claims a violation of article 2, paragraph 1, read in connection with articles 1, and 16, paragraph 1, for having been subjected to police brutality inflicting on him great physical and mental suffering amounting to torture, cruel, inhuman and/or degrading treatment or punishment, for the purposes of obtaining a confession, or otherwise intimidating or punishing him.[6]

3.3 He claims a violation of article 12 alone and/or read in connection with 16, paragraph 1, as the State party's authorities failed to conduct an official investigation into the incident, which gave rise to this complaint and failed to respond to queries on the status of the complaint. Since the public prosecutor's office failed formally to dismiss his criminal complaint, he cannot personally take over the prosecution of the case. The complainant alleges that public prosecutors in Serbia and Montenegro seldom institute criminal proceedings against police officers accused of misconduct and delay the dismissal of complaints, sometimes by years, thereby denying the injured party the right to prosecute his/her own case.

3.4 The complainant claims a violation of articles 13 alone or read in connection with article 16 of the Convention, as despite exhaustion of domestic remedies all criminal domestic remedies, he has received no redress for the violation of his rights.

---

[3] This letter has been provided.

[4] He refers to international jurisprudence to support this claim.

[5] In this context, the complainant provides reports from various national and international non-governmental organizations and the Concluding Observations of CAT of 1998, A/54/44, paras. 35–52.

[6] To support his argument that the treatment he received was torture, cruel, inhuman and/or degrading treatment or punishment, he refers to the United Nations Code of Conduct for Law Enforcement Officials, the United Nations Body of Principles for the protection of All Persons under Any Form of Detention or Imprisonment, the United Nations Basic Principles on the Use of Force and Firearms by Law Enforcement Officials, the Council of Europe's Declaration on the Police and the European Court of Human Rights.

The State party's authorities have not even identified the police officer concerned.[7]

3.5 Article 14 is also said to be violated, since the complainant was denied a criminal remedy and has thus been barred from obtaining fair and adequate compensation in a civil lawsuit. The complainant explains that under domestic law, two different procedures exist, through which compensation for criminal offences may be pursued: by criminal proceedings under article 103 of the CPC following criminal proceedings, or/and by civil action for damages under articles 154 and 200 of the Law on Obligations. The first avenue was not an option, as no criminal proceedings were instituted and the second was not availed of by the complainant, as it is the practice of the State party's courts to suspend civil proceedings for damages arising from criminal offences until prior completion of the respective criminal proceedings. Even if the complainant had attempted to avail of this recourse, he would have been prevented from pursuing it, as under articles 186 and 106 of the Civil Procedure Code he would have to identify the name of the respondent. Since the complainant to date remains unaware of the name of the officer against whom he is claiming violations of his rights the institution of a civil action would have been impossible.

State party's submission on admissibility and merits and complainant's comments

4. On 14 January 2003, the State party provided a submission, merely stating that it "accepts" the complaint. Following a request for clarification from the Secretariat, the State party made another submission, on 20 October 2003, in which it states that the "acceptance" of the complaint implied that the State party recognized the competence of the Committee to consider the complaint, "but not the responsibility of the State concerning the complaint in question". In addition, it submitted that the Ministry on Human and Minority Rights of Serbia and Montenegro is still in the process of collecting data from the relevant authorities of the Republic of Serbia for the purposes of giving a response on the merits. The State party has provided no further information since that date.

5. On 25 November 2003, the complainant commented on the State party's submissions. He submits that by failing seriously to contest the facts and/or his claims, the State party has in effect expressed its tacit acceptance of both.[8]

---

[7] The complainant refers to communication N° 59/1996, *Encarnación Blanco Abad* v. *Spain,* Views adopted on 14 May 1998.

[8] In this regard, he refers to decisions of the Human Rights Committee, in particular communication N° 88/1981,

Issues and proceedings before the Committee

Consideration of admissibility

6.1 The Committee notes the State party's failure to provide information with regard to the admissibility or merits of the complaint. In the circumstances, the Committee, acting under rule 109, paragraph 7, of its rules of procedure, is obliged to consider the admissibility and the merits of the complaint in the light of the available information, due weight being given to the complainant's allegations to the extent that they have been sufficiently substantiated.

6.2 Before considering any claim contained in a complaint, the Committee must decide whether or not it is admissible under article 22 of the Convention. The Committee has ascertained, as it is required to do under article 22, paragraph 5 (a), of the Convention that the same matter has not been, and is not being examined under another procedure of international investigation or settlement. With respect to the exhaustion of domestic remedies, the Committee has taken note of the information provided by the complainant about the criminal complaint, which he filed with the public prosecutor. It considers that the insurmountable procedural impediments faced by the complainant due to the inaction of the competent authorities made recourse to a remedy that may bring effective relief to the complainant highly unlikely. In the absence of pertinent information from the State party, the Committee concludes that in any event, domestic proceedings, if any, have been unreasonably prolonged since the end of November 1997. With reference to article 22, paragraph 4, of the Convention and rule 107 of the Committee's rules of procedure the Committee finds no other obstacle to the admissibility of the complaint. Accordingly, it declares the complaint admissible and proceeds to its examination on the merits.

Consideration of the merits

7.1 The complainant alleges violations by the State party of article 2, paragraph 1, in connection with article 1, and of article 16, paragraph 1, of the Convention. The Committee notes in this respect the complainant's description of the treatment he was subjected to while in detention, which can be characterized as severe pain or suffering intentionally inflicted by public officials for such purposes as obtaining from him information or a confession or punishing him for an act he has committed, or intimidating or coercing him for any reason based on discrimination of any kind in the context of the investigation of a crime. The Committee also notes the observations of the

---

Gustavo Raul Larrosa Bequio v. *Uruguay*, Views adopted on 29 March 1983, para. 10.1.

investigating judge with respect to his injuries, and photographs of his injuries provided by the complainant. It observes that the State party has not contested the facts as presented by the complainant, which took place more than seven years ago, and observes that the medical report prepared after the examination of the complainant and pursuant to an order of the Novi Sad District Court Judge, has not been integrated into the complaint file and could not be consulted by the complainant or his counsel. In the circumstances, the Committee concludes that due weight must be given to the complainant's allegations and that the facts, as submitted, constitute torture within the meaning of article 1 of the Convention.

7.2 In light of the above finding of a violation of article 1 of the Convention, the Committee need not consider whether there was a violation of article 16, paragraph 1, as the treatment suffered by the complainant under article 1 exceeds the treatment encompassed in article 16 of the Convention.

7.3 Concerning the alleged violation of articles 12 and 13 of the Convention, the Committee notes that the public prosecutor never informed the complainant whether an investigation was being or had been conducted after the criminal complaint was filed on 24 November 1997. It also notes that the failure to inform the complainant of the results of such investigation, if any, effectively prevented him from pursuing a "private prosecution" of his case. In these circumstances, the Committee considers that the State party has failed to comply with its obligation, under article 12 of the Convention, to carry out a prompt and impartial investigation whenever there is reasonable ground to believe that an act of torture has been committed. The State party also failed to comply with its obligation, under article 13, to ensure the complainant's right to complain and to have his case promptly and impartially examined by the competent authorities.

7.4 As for the alleged violation of article 14 of the Convention, the Committee notes the complainant's allegations that the absence of criminal proceedings deprived him of the possibility of filing a civil suit for compensation. In view of the fact that the State party has not contested this allegation and given the passage of time since the complainant initiated legal proceedings at the domestic level, the Committee concludes that the State party has also violated its obligations under article 14 of the Convention in the present case.

8. The Committee, acting under article 22, paragraph 7, of the Convention, is of the view that the facts before it disclose a violation of articles 2, paragraph 1, in connection with article 1; 12; 13; and 14 of the Convention against Torture.

9. The Committee urges the State party to prosecute those responsible for the violations found and to provide compensation to the complainant, in accordance with rule 112, paragraph 5, of its rules of procedure, to inform it, within 90 days from the date of the transmittal of this decision, of the steps taken in response to the Views expressed above.

Communication N° 174/2000

Submitted by: Mr. Slobodan Nikolić; Mrs. Ljiljana Nikolić
Alleged victims: The complainants' son, N.N. (deceased); the complainants
State party: Serbia and Montenegro
Date of adoption of Views: 24 November 2005

Subject matter: police arrest with violence resulting in death of victim

Procedural issue: none

Substantive issues: failure promptly to investigate allegations of torture; right to complain; right to compensation

Articles of the Convention: 12, 13, 14

1. The complainants are Mr. Slobodan Nikolić and his wife, Mrs. Ljiljana Nikolić, nationals of Serbia and Montenegro, born on 20 December 1947 and on 5 August 1951, respectively. They claim that the State party's alleged failure to proceed to a prompt and impartial investigation of the circumstances of their son's death constitutes a violation by Serbia and Montenegro of articles 12, 13 and 14 of the Convention. The complainants are represented by counsel.

The facts as submitted by the complainants

2.1 On 19 April 1994, the complainants' son, N.N., born on 19 April 1972, died in Belgrade. The post-mortem examination of his corpse was carried out on 25 April 1994 by a medical team of the Institute for Forensic Medicine of the Faculty of

Medicine in Belgrade. The autopsy report states that the death was caused by damage to vital brain centres caused by the fracture of cranial bones and haemorrhage from the rupture of the aorta and the torn blood vessels surrounding the multiple bone fractures. These injuries "were inflicted with a brandished, blunt and heavy object".

2.2 According to the police report, the complainants' son was found dead on the sidewalk in front of building N° 2 at Pariske Komune Street in Novi Beograd on 19 April 1994. He had fallen out of the window of apartment N° 82 on the 10th floor of the same building at 9.40 a.m. In an attempt to escape his arrest by the police, he had connected several cables and had tied them to a radiator. When trying to descend to the subjacent window on the ninth floor, the cables broke apart and N.N. fell on the concrete pavement.

2.3 According to police inspector J.J., this incident was preceded by the following events: On 19 April 1994, he and two other inspectors, Z.P. and M.L., went to apartment N° 82 at 2, Pariske Komune Street to arrest the complainant on the basis of a warrant, as he was suspected of having committed several property-related offences. Through a slit above the threshold of the entrance door, they noticed a shadow in the corridor. Assuming that N.N. was in the apartment, they unsuccessfully called on him to open the door. After having ordered an intervention team to break the entrance door, inspector J.J. warned N.N. that the police would forcibly enter the flat, if he continued to refuse opening the door. J.J. then went to the eleventh floor and entered the flat located directly above apartment N° 82. From a window, he saw N.N. looking out of the window below. After having returned to apartment N° 82, J.J. again called on N.N. to surrender, promising that he would not be subjected to physical violence. The intervention team then broke the door of the apartment, where they only found M.K., the girlfriend of the deceased, who was crying and stated that N.N. had fallen out of the window. Looking out of the window, J.J. saw the body of a man lying on the sidewalk.

2.4 The deceased was identified as N.N., based on documents found in one of his pockets, as well as by M.K., and his death was established by a physician of the Secretariat for Internal Affairs. At around 10:30 a.m., the investigating judge of the Belgrade District Court, D.B., arrived together with the deputy public prosecutor of the District of Belgrade (hereafter "deputy public prosecutor"), V.M., inspected "the scene of the crime",[1] interviewed M.K. and ordered that the body of the deceased be sent to the Institute of Forensic Medicine for an autopsy.

2.5 The report of the investigating judge states that several police officers informed him that N.N. had "categorically declined" to unlock the door after having argued with the police for some time. When they entered the flat, the deceased "had just jumped out of the window." M.K. confirmed that N.N. had refused to open the door. When she tried to snatch the keys of the apartment from his pocket, he told her that he would rather escape through the window than to open the door. Although she did not see what happened in the room from where N.N. had tried to escape, M.K. concluded from his absence that he had jumped out of the window, when the policemen entered the flat. She stated that there was no physical contact between N.N. and the members of the police intervention team. Apart from the cables tied to the radiator, the report mentions that a white three-socket extension cable was hanging on a tree above the sidewalk where the corpse of the deceased was lying. One single- and one double-wire of around 2.5 metres length each were tied to the socket box—probably the missing ends that had been torn from the cables tied to the radiator. Lastly, the report states that the investigating judge ordered the police to interview all witnesses of the incident.

2.6 On 22 April 1994, the deputy public prosecutor advised the complainants that he considered that their son's death had been caused by an accident and that, accordingly, no criminal investigation would be initiated.

2.7 On 18 July 1994, the complainants brought charges of murder against unknown perpetrators, asking for a criminal investigation to be initiated by the Belgrade public prosecutor's office. They claimed that the police clubbed their son with a blunt metal object, thereby causing his death, and subsequently threw his corpse out of the window to conceal the act. On 12 August and on 5 December 1994, the deputy public prosecutor informed the complainants that no sufficient grounds existed for instituting criminal proceedings, and advised them to file a criminal report with the public prosecutor's office, submitting the evidence on which their suspicion was based.

2.8 In the meantime, the investigating judge had requested a commission of medical experts of the Belgrade Institute of Forensic Medicine, composed of the same doctors who had conducted the autopsy, to prepare an expert opinion on the death of N.N. In their report dated 22 November 1994, the experts concluded on the basis of the autopsy report, as well as other documents, that the location, distribution and types of injuries observed on N.N. indicated that they were the result of the fall of his body from a considerable height on a wide, flat concrete surface.

---

[1] The term "scene of the crime" is used in the police report dated 19 April 1994.

The "signs of the injury reactions (inhalation of blood and [...] bruisès around the wounds and torn tissues)" indicated that N.N. was alive at the moment when he incurred the injuries.

2.9 On 13 and 24 January 1995, the complainants challenged inconsistencies in the medical findings of the expert commission, as well as in the autopsy report, and requested the Belgrade District Court to order another forensic expertise from a different institution at their expense.

2.10 On 27 June 1995, the complainants sought the intervention of the Public Prosecutor of the Republic, who, by reference to the forensic expertise of the expert commission, affirmed the position of the deputy public prosecutor. Similarly, the Deputy Federal Public Prosecutor, by letter of 8 January 1996, advised the complainants that there were no grounds for him to intervene.

2.11 At the complainants' request, Dr. Z.S., a pathologist from the Institute of Forensic Medicine of the Belgrade Military Hospital, evaluated the autopsy report of 19 April 1994 and the expert commission's forensic findings of 22 November 1994. In a letter of 21 March 1996, he informed the complainants that, although the described injuries could be the result of the fall of the body of the deceased from a considerable height, it could not be excluded that some of the injuries had been inflicted prior to the fall. He criticized (a) that the autopsy had been carried out six days after the death of N.N.; (b) that the reports did not describe any decomposition changes of the body; (c) that the autopsy report stated that the brain membranes and brain tissue of the deceased were intact, while at the same time noting the presence of brain tissue on the front side of his sweatshirt; (d) the contradiction between the size of the rupture of the aorta (3 cm x 1 cm) and the relatively small quantity of blood found in the chest cavity (800 ccm); (e) the expert commission's finding that the first contact of the deceased's body with the ground was with his feet, resulting in transverse fractures of the lower leg bones instead of diagonal fractures, which would usually result from a similar fall; (f) the unclear description by the expert commission of the mechanism of injuries, i.e., "that the first contact of the body was with the feet which caused feet and lower leg fractures, which was followed by *bending* and twisting (*extension* and rotation) of the thorax", given that *extension* means *stretching* of the body rather than bending; and (g) that the autopsy report diagnosed *decollement*, i.e., the separation of the skin of subcutaneous tissue from the muscle membrane, on the external side of the left thigh, although such an injury was usually "inflicted by a strong blow with a brandished blunt weapon", i.e., "the blow of the body on the ground", which was unlikely to occur after a fall on the feet and a fracture of both lower leg bones.

2.12 By letter of 28 August 1996, the complainant's lawyer requested the Belgrade Public Prosecutor's Office to order another forensic expertise, to be conducted by the Institute of Forensic Medicine of either the Belgrade Military Hospital or the Faculty of Medicine of Novi Sad, and, for that purpose, to exhume the body of N.N. at the expense of the complainants to address the doubts expressed by Dr. Z.S. In addition, he requested clarification of the following questions: (a) The time and place of death; (b) whether the contusions of the brain and the wound on the lower forehead of the deceased could have been the consequence of injuries inflicted by blows before the fall; (c) whether the small quantity of blood found in the chest cavity indicated that N.N. was already dead at the time of the fall, given that a living person discharges about 70 millilitres of blood from the left auricle into the aorta with every heartbeat (totalling about 4.9 litres per minute); (d) how it could be explained that the autopsy report did not establish any circular fractures of the bones of the base of the cranium after a fall from a height of 20 to 30 metres; and (e) which parts of the body would usually be damaged after a fall from this height, based on the weight of the body, its free movement during, as well as the velocity of the fall.

2.13 On 2 October 1996, the complainants' lawyer requested the Belgrade Public Prosecutor's Office that several potential witnesses be interviewed either by the Serbian Ministry of the Interior or by the Secretariat for Internal Affairs of Novi Sad: (a) The complainants, to find out whether M.K., when delivering the tragic news of their son's death, said: "Aunt Ljilja, they have killed Nikolica—they have killed Dumpling!"; (b) R.J. and Z.T., colleagues of the mother, who were present when M.K. told the mother that her son had died; (c) M.K., to establish whether she saw N.N. tying the cables to the radiator; whether he had been sleeping and, if so, whether he was already dressed when the police arrived at the door; how it was possible that she did not see N.N. jump out of the window, if she was in the same room; or, alternatively, how she could claim that there was no contact between N.N. and the policemen, if she was in another room; (d) neighbours in building N° 2, Pariske Komune Street, in particular D.N., the tenant of the flat above apartment N° 82, and S.L., who removed the biological traces in front of the building, to ask him what exactly he removed and whether he did this before or after the end of the in situ investigation; (e) several friends of the deceased, to find out whether N.N. had a fight with M.K. prior to 19 April 1994 and whether M.K. had threatened that she would "fix him"; (f) officials of the Belgrade Central Prison, to elucidate whether N.N. had escaped from prison, but was subsequently released on probation by decision of 23 July 1993 of the deputy public prosecutor; and (g) A.N., the sister of

N.N., to ask her whether an intervention team of the Belgrade Secretariat for Internal Affairs came to her flat in January 1994, threatening that they would throw N.N. from the sixth floor, should they capture him.

2.14 In a report dated 27 November 1996, the same medical experts who prepared the autopsy report and the first forensic expertise dated 22 November 1994, while dismissing the questions asked by the complainants' lawyer (para. 2.12) as too vague, addressed the objections raised by Dr. Z.S. (para. 2.11), observing (a) that it was not customary to state the time and place of death in an autopsy report, as this information was already contained in the report of the doctor establishing the death and in the police report; (b) that the reason for the late autopsy was that the blood of the deceased (presumably a drug addict) was tested for HIV and that the results were received late on Friday, 22 April 1994, so that the autopsy could not be carried out before Monday, 25 April; (c) that the corpse had been kept in a refrigerator and only started to decompose during the autopsy and its subsequent cleaning and transport to the hospital chapel; (d) that the purpose of the autopsy report was to record the injuries and changes of the body of the deceased, rather than to explain how the brain tissue came on his sweatshirt; it could have passed through his nose or mouth, as the front skull cavity, which forms the roof of the nose cavity and of the pharynx, displayed numerous fractures of the skull base bones, which were always accompanied by ruptures of the attached hard brain tissue; (e) that the little amount of blood found in the chest cavity of the deceased was not due to death prior to the fall but to the considerable blood loss resulting from his injuries; (f) that Dr. Z.S. himself did not rule out that a fall on the feet could cause transversal fractures of the leg bones; (g) that the bending of the body following the contact of the feet with the ground did not exclude that numerous injuries, such as the aorta rupture, led to hyperextension of the body; (h) that the mechanism of the fall first on the feet and, in a second phase, on the left side of the body and the head explained the *decollement* in the region of the left thigh, the fissure on the lower left forehead, the fracture of the skull bones, and the brain contusions; and (i) that the fall on the feet reduced the body's impact on the ground, which explained why the autopsy report recorded neither protrusion of the thigh bone heads through pelvic bones, nor circular fractures of the skull base.

2.15 On 26 February and 18 June 1997, the complainants' lawyer requested the district public prosecutor to resubmit his questions (para. 2.12) to the commission of forensic experts to seek clarification of the contradictions between the experts' findings and the findings of Dr. Z.S.

2.16 On 21 August 1997, Dr. Z.S. commented on the experts' second forensic report (para. 2.14), criticizing (a) that the experts had not provided a satisfactory explanation as to why the result of the HIV test had not been included in the autopsy report; (b) the contradiction between the experts' finding that the brain tissue on the deceased's clothes came through his nose and mouth and the statement in the autopsy report that the mucous membrane of the lips and mouth cavity were "examined in detail" but that "no signs of injuries [were] observed", and that no "foreign content", i.e., traces of brain tissue, was found in the nose and mouth; (c) the experts' failure to identify the part of the brain from which brain tissue was missing; (d) their failure to explain why such a small amount of blood was found in the thoracic cavities, given that the complainants' son probably continued to breath for some time following the infliction of the injuries, that the total blood flow of an adult is 5000 ml per minute, and that blood pressure is the highest near the heart where the 3 x 1 cm aorta fissure was located; (e) the experts' superficial and contradictory description of the bone fractures; and (f) their conclusion that all recorded injuries resulted from the body's fall on the concrete ground, ignoring the possibility that some injuries could have been inflicted with a blunt mechanical weapon before the fall.

2.17 In a letter of 29 August 1997 to the Department for the Control of Legality of the Belgrade City Secretariat for Internal Affairs, the complainants drew attention to the fact that inspector J.J. reportedly was crying when the investigating magistrate arrived at Pariske Komune Street N° 2 and that he went on vacation the following day. They referred to the case of N.L., who had allegedly been forced to wear a bullet proof vest, on which he received blows with a baseball bat during his interrogation by, inter alia, inspector J.J., leaving few traces and causing a slow and painful death after two weeks.[2]

2.18 On 30 August 1997, the complainants brought charges of murder against police inspectors J.J., Z.P. and M.L., alleging that they had maltreated their son with hard round objects (such as a baseball bat), inflicting a number of grave injuries to his body, thereby voluntarily causing his death. Assuming that the transversal fractures of the lower legs had been inflicted prior to the fall, it could be ruled out that the injured had tried to escape through the window. The complainants also claimed that the police had breached the Code of Criminal Procedure (a) by forcibly entering the flat without the presence of a neutral witness; (b) by calling the investigating magistrate 30 minutes after the incident, rather than

---

[2] See a newspaper article submitted by the authors in *VREME Magazine*, 9 March 1996, "The deadly bat".

immediately, allegedly to remove incriminating evidence and to put M.K. on tranquilizers; (c) by interviewing no other witnesses than the police inspectors; (d) by having the deceased's body identified by M.K. rather than by his family; (e) by failing to seal the door or to return the keys of the apartment to the complainants; and (f) by sending M.K. to deliver the tragic news to the complainants. The complainants also informed the district prosecutor that several witnesses could testify that the police had previously shot at and threatened their son. They challenged the deputy public prosecutor for bias, since he had already indicated that he would reject any criminal charges.

2.19 After the District Public Prosecutor had decided, on 24 September 1997, not to initiate criminal proceedings against inspectors J.J., Z.P. and M.L., the complainants, on 4 October 1997, filed a request for an investigation of their son's alleged murder with the Belgrade District Court.[3] In particular, they requested the investigating judge to interrogate J.J., Z.P. and M.L. in the capacity of accused, to detain them on remand in order to prevent any interference with witnesses, to summon and examine certain witnesses, including the complainants themselves, and to seek clarification of the remaining forensic inconsistencies. By letter of 28 January to the President of the District Court, the complainants criticized that only one of their requests, i.e., the interrogation of the police inspectors, had been complied with. They also challenged that the authorities persistently refused to state the time of their son's death, that no explanation had been given for the numerous bruises on the deceased's body, that the Institute of Forensic Medicine had refused to hand out any photographs of the deceased and that its forensic findings were intended to conceal their son's abuse by the police, that M.K. had given three different versions of the incident to the investigating judge, the complainants, and her friends, respectively, and that not a single pedestrian on the busy streets facing apartment N° 82 had witnessed their son jumping out of the window.

2.20 By decision of 17 February 1998,[4] the Belgrade District Court found that the absence of any physical contact between the police inspectors and the deceased had been established on the basis of the concurring statements of J.J., Z.P. and M.L., the report of the investigating judge, as well as the police report of 19 April 1994, and the findings and opinions of the experts from the Institute of Forensic Medicine of the Belgrade Faculty of Medicine dated 22 November 1994 and 27 November 1996. It concluded that there were no grounds for conducting an investigation against the charged police inspectors for the criminal offence of murder.

2.21 On 13 March 1998, the complainants appealed to the Supreme Court of Serbia and Montenegro and, on 23 March, they supplemented their reasons of appeal. They challenged that the District Court had failed to address their arguments or the objections raised by Prof. Dr. Z.S., an internationally renowned expert selected by the United Nations for autopsies conducted on the territory of the former Yugoslavia, while merely relying on the contradictory findings of the commission of forensic experts and on the un-scrutinized statements of M.K., as well as of the charged inspectors themselves, against one of whom criminal proceedings had previously been instituted for similar conduct. No fingerprints of the deceased had been found in apartment N° 82; the cables attached to the radiator had not even been examined for his biological traces.

2.22 By decision of 21 May 1998,[5] the Supreme Court of Serbia in Belgrade rejected the complainants' appeal as unfounded. It endorsed the findings of the Belgrade District Court, considering that the commission of experts, in its supplementary findings and opinions of 27 November 1996, responded to all objections raised by the complainants' lawyer and by Dr. Z.S. in a precise manner.

The complaint

3.1 The complainants claim that the State party failed to proceed to a prompt an impartial investigation of their son's death and alleged prior torture, in violation of article 12, although the forensic evidence submitted by the complainants strongly suggested that their son was the victim of an act of torture within the meaning of article 1 of the Convention.

3.2 They submit that other inconsistencies further supported their suspicion, inter alia: (a) the fact that N.N. was explicitly told that he would not be subjected to physical force, if he opened the door of apartment N° 82; (b) that the search warrant issued on 19 April 1994 only authorized the police to enter the apartment to "search for goods related to criminal offences", rather than to arrest N.N., and that it stated 11 a.m. as the time of the entry,

---

[3] In accordance with Section 60 of the Code of Criminal Procedure of the State party, the injured party may apply for criminal proceedings to be instituted, if the public prosecutor finds that there are no sufficient grounds to initiate criminal proceedings ex officio. If the investigating judge rejects the request for the initiation of criminal proceedings, a special chamber of the competent court decides whether such proceedings shall be initiated. See ibid., Section 159.

[4] See Belgrade District Court, Decision of 17 February 1998, Ki. N° 898/97 (Kv. N° 99/98).

[5] See Supreme Court of Serbia in Belgrade, Decision of 21 May 1998, Kž. II 224/98.

although the police report stated 9.40 a.m. as the time of death; and (c) that it was unreasonable to expect that anyone would risk his life by trying to climb from the tenth to the ninth floor of a high-rise, only secured by some electric cables, break the window and enter the apartment on the ninth floor, only in order to find himself in the same situation as before, assuming that the police had plenty of time to reach the (presumably locked) door of the apartment on the ninth floor before this could be opened from inside.

3.3 The complainants claim that the dismissal of all their motions to initiate criminal proceedings, and of their subsequent appeals, raises doubts about the impartiality of the Serbian authorities' investigation into N.N.'s death and alleged prior torture, thus disclosing a violation of article 13 of the Convention. Thus, the investigating judge had never initiated an investigation or even heard the complainants; none of the witnesses named by the complainants' lawyer was ever heard or cross-examined.

3.4 The complainants submit an amicus curiae by Human Rights Watch/Helsinki dated 24 November 1997, which states that the "[i]nconsistencies in the various police and medical reports could only be adequately addressed in a court of law."

3.5 For the complainants, the State party's failure to investigate the circumstances of their son's death de facto prevents them from exercising their right to a fair and adequate compensation, guaranteed in article 14 of the Convention, as the legal successors of their son and as indirect victims of the acts of torture that he had presumably been subjected to. They refer to a similar case, in which the European Court of Human Rights found that the disappearance of the applicant's son amounted to inhuman and degrading treatment within the meaning of article 3 of the European Convention, and awarded £15,000 compensation for the disappeared son's pain and suffering and an additional £20,000 for the applicants' own anguish and distress.[6]

3.6 The complainants submit that the same matter has not been and is not being examined under another procedure of international investigation or settlement, and that they have exhausted all available domestic remedies.

Committee's request for State party's observations

4.1 By notes verbales of 2 November 2000, 19 April 2002 and 12 December 2002, the Committee requested the State party to submit its observations on the admissibility and merits of the communication. On 14 January 2003, the State party informed the Committee that it "accepts the individual complaint N° 174/2000".

4.2 After consultations with the Secretariat, the State party, on 20 October 2003, explained that "the acceptance", in its note verbale of 14 January 2003, "implies that Serbia and Montenegro recognizes the competence of the Committee against Torture to consider the aforementioned [complaint], but not the responsibility of the State concerning the individual [complaint] in question."

4.3 At the same time, the State party advised the Committee that it was still in the process of collecting data from the relevant authorities in order to prepare its observations on the merits of the complaint. No such information has been received to date.

Issues and proceedings before the Committee

5. Before considering any claim contained in a communication, the Committee against Torture must decide whether or not it is admissible under article 22 of the Convention. The Committee has ascertained, as it is required to do under article 22, paragraphs 5 (a) and (b), of the Convention, that the same matter has not been, and is not being, examined under another procedure of international investigation or settlement, and that the complainants have exhausted all available domestic remedies. It therefore considers that the complainant's claims under articles 12, 13 and 14 of the Convention are admissible and proceeds to their examination on the merits.

6.1 The Committee has considered the communication in the light of all information made available to it, in accordance with article 22, paragraph 4, of the Convention. It regrets that the State party has not submitted any observations on the substance of the complaint and observes that, in the absence of any such observations, due weight must be given to the complainants' allegations, to the extent that they are substantiated.

6.2 The Committee must decide, pursuant to article 12 of the Convention, whether there are reasonable grounds to believe that an act of torture has been committed against the complainants' son prior to his death and, if so, whether the State party's authorities complied with their obligation to proceed to a prompt and impartial investigation.

6.3 The Committee considers that the following elements cast doubts on the sequence of events leading to the death of the complainants' son, as established by the State party's authorities:

(a) The fact that the autopsy report states that the injuries "were inflicted with a brandished, blunt and heavy object," thus suggesting that N.N. had

---

[6] See European Court of Human Rights, *Kurt* v. *Turkey*, Judgement of 25 May 1998.

been tortured prior to his fall from the window of apartment N° 82.

(b) The statement by inspector J.J. that he promised N.N. that he would not be subjected to physical violence, if he opened the door of apartment N° 82;

(c) The fact that the search warrant issued on 19 April 1994 did not explicitly authorize the police to arrest N.N., and that it states 11 a.m. as the time of entry into the apartment, although the death of N.N. occurred at 9.40 a.m., according to the police report;

(d) The contradiction between the police report and the report of the investigating judge (both dated 19 April 1994) as to the voluntary nature of the death of N.N., describing it as an accident resulting from the deceased's attempt to escape his arrest (police report) or as the result of what appears to have been a suicide (investigation report: "Nikolić had just jumped out of the window");

(e) The absence of witnesses who would have confirmed that N.N. jumped out of the window of apartment N° 82;

(f) The alleged inconsistencies in the testimony of M.K. (paras. 2.5 and 2.19);

(g) The fact that the investigating judged arrived at Pariske Komune Street N° 2 only at 10.30 a.m., apparently because he had not been informed of the death until 30 minutes after the incident, and that, despite his order to interview all witnesses, allegedly only the concerned police inspectors were interviewed;

(h) The alleged inconsistencies in the autopsy report and in the forensic findings of the expert commission and, in particular, the objections raised by Dr. Z.S., particularly his statement that it could not be excluded that some of the injuries had been inflicted prior to the fall, which in turn might have been inflicted by treatment in violation of the Convention;

(i) The alleged prior involvement of inspector J.J. in an act of torture; and

(j) The uncertainty about prior threats by the police and attempts to arrest N.N., allegedly involving the use of firearms by the police.

6.4 On the basis of these elements, the Committee considers that there were reasonable grounds for the State party to investigate the complainants' allegation that their son was tortured prior to his death.

6.5 The question therefore arises whether the investigative measures taken by the State party's authorities, in particular by the Belgrade deputy public prosecutor, were commensurate to the requirement of article 12 of the Convention to proceed to a prompt and impartial investigation of the events preceding the death of N.N. In this regard, the Committee notes the complainants' uncontested claim that the deputy public prosecutor advised them already on 22 April 1994, i.e., three days before the autopsy, that he would not initiate criminal proceedings ex officio, as he considered their son's death an accident, and that he did not examine any of the witnesses named by their lawyer. It also notes that the investigating judge entrusted the same forensic experts, who had conducted the autopsy, with the preparation of both expert opinions, with a view to addressing the alleged inconsistencies in their own autopsy report, despite several requests by the complainants to order a forensic expertise from another institution. The Committee concludes that the investigation of the circumstances of the death of the complainants' son was not impartial and therefore in violation of article 12 of the Convention.

6.6 With regard to the alleged violation of article 13, the Committee observes that, although the complainants were entitled to complain to the courts after the deputy public prosecutor had decided not to institute criminal proceedings against J.J., Z.P. and M.L., both the Belgrade District Court and the Supreme Court based their finding that there had been no physical contact between the police and N.N. exclusively on evidence that had been challenged by the complainants and which, according to them, was flawed by numerous inconsistencies.[7] Both courts dismissed the complainants' appeals without addressing their arguments. The Committee therefore considers that the State party's courts failed to examine the case impartially, thereby violating article 13 of the Convention.

7. The Committee against Torture, acting under article 22, paragraph 7, of the Convention against Torture and Other Cruel, Inhuman or Degrading Treatment or Punishment, concludes that the State party's failure to proceed to an impartial investigation of the death of the complainants' son constitutes a violation of articles 12 and 13 of the Convention.

8. Concerning the alleged violation of article 14 of the Convention, the Committee postpones its consideration until receipt of the information requested from the State party in paragraph 9 below.

9. Pursuant to rule 112, paragraph 5, of its rules of procedure, the Committee wishes to receive from the State party, within 90 days, information on the measures taken to give effect to the Committee's Views, in particular on the initiation and the results of an impartial investigation of the circumstances of the death of the complainants' son.

---

[7] See paras. 2.20–2.22 above.

Communication N° 181/2001

Submitted by: Suleymane Guengueng et al.
Alleged victims: The complainants
State party: Senegal
Date of adoption of Views: 17 May 2006

Subject matter: prosecution of former Chadian President Hissène Habré for acts of torture in Chad

Procedural issue: jurisdiction over complainants

Substantive issues: jurisdiction over torture offences; duty to prosecute or to extradite

Articles of the Convention: 5, paragraph 2; 7

1.1 The complainants are Suleymane Guengueng, Zakaria Fadoul Khidir, Issac Haroun, Younous Mahadjir, Valentin Neatobet Bidi, Ramadane Souleymane and Samuel Togoto Lamaye (hereinafter "the complainants"), all of Chadian nationality and living in Chad. They claim to be victims of a violation by Senegal of article 5, paragraph 2, and article 7 of the Convention against Torture and Other Cruel, Inhuman or Degrading Treatment or Punishment (hereinafter "the Convention").

1.2 Senegal ratified the Convention on 21 August 1986 and made the declaration under article 22 of the Convention on 16 October 1996.

1.3 In accordance with article 22, paragraph 3, of the Convention, the Committee brought the communication to the attention of the State party on 20 April 2001. At the same time, the Committee, acting under article 108, paragraph 9, of its rules of procedure, requested the State party, as an interim measure, not to expel Hissène Habré and to take all necessary measures to prevent him from leaving the territory other than under an extradition procedure. The State party acceded to this request.

The facts as submitted by the complainants

2.1 Between 1982 and 1990, when Hissène Habré was President of Chad, the complainants were purportedly tortured by agents of the Chadian State answerable directly to President Hissène Habré. The acts of torture committed during this period formed the subject of a report by the National Commission of Inquiry established by the Chadian Ministry of Justice; according to that report 40,000 political murders and systematic acts of torture were committed by the Habré regime.

2.2 The complainants have submitted to the Committee a detailed description of the torture and other forms of ill-treatment that they claim to have suffered. Moreover, relatives of two of them, Valentin Neatobet Bidi and Ramadane Souleymane, have disappeared: on the basis of developments in international law and the case law of various international bodies, the complainants consider this equivalent to torture and other inhuman and degrading treatment, both for the disappeared persons and, in particular, for their relations.

2.3 After being ousted by the current President of Chad, Idriss Déby, in December 1990, Hissène Habré took refuge in Senegal, where he has since resided. In January 2000, the complainants lodged a complaint against him with an examining magistrate in Dakar. On 3 February 2000, the examining magistrate charged Hissène Habré with being an accomplice to acts of torture, placed him under house arrest and opened an inquiry against a person or persons unknown for crimes against humanity.

2.4 On 18 February 2000, Hissène Habré applied to the Indictment Division of the Dakar Court of Appeal for the charge against him to be dismissed. The complainants consider that, thereafter, political pressure was brought to bear to influence the course of the proceedings. They allege in particular that, following this application, the examining magistrate who had indicted Hissène Habré was transferred from his position by the Supreme Council of Justice and that the President of the Indictment Division before which the appeal of Hissène Habré was pending was transferred to the Council of State.

2.5 On 4 July 2000, the Indictment Division dismissed the charge against Hissène Habré and the related proceedings on the grounds of lack of jurisdiction, affirming that "Senegalese courts cannot take cognizance of acts of torture committed by a foreigner outside Senegalese territory, regardless of the nationality of the victims: the wording of article 669 of the Code of Criminal Procedure excludes any such jurisdiction." Following this ruling, the Special Rapporteurs on the question of torture and on the independence of judges and lawyers of the United Nations Commission on Human Rights expressed their concerns in a press release dated 2 August 2000.[1]

---

[1] According to the press release, "[t]he Special Rapporteur on the independence of judges and lawyers, Mr. Dato Param Cumaraswamy, and the Special Rapporteur on the question of torture, Sir Nigel Rodley, have expressed their concern to the Government of Senegal over the circumstances surrounding the recent dismissal of charges against Hissène Habré, the former President of Chad. [...]

2.6 On 7 July 2000, the complainants filed an appeal with Senegal's Court of Cassation against the ruling of the Indictment Division, calling for the proceedings against Hissène Habré to be reopened. They maintained that the ruling of the Indictment Division was contrary to the Convention against Torture and that a domestic law could not be invoked to justify failure to apply the Convention.

2.7 On 20 March 2001, the Senegalese Court of Cassation confirmed the ruling of the Indictment Division, stating inter alia that "no procedural text confers on Senegalese courts a universal jurisdiction to prosecute and judge, if they are found on the territory of the Republic, presumed perpetrators of or accomplices in acts [of torture] ... when these acts have been committed outside Senegal by foreigners; the presence in Senegal of Hissène Habré cannot in itself justify the proceedings brought against him".

2.8 On 19 September 2005, after four years of investigation, a Belgian judge issued an international arrest warrant against Hissène Habré, charging him with genocide, crimes against humanity, war crimes, torture and other serious violations of international humanitarian law. On the same date, Belgium made an extradition request to Senegal, citing, inter alia, the Convention against Torture.

2.9 In response to the extradition request, the Senegalese authorities arrested Hissène Habré on 15 November 2005.

2.10 On 25 November 2005, the Indictment Division of the Dakar Court of Appeal stated that it lacked jurisdiction to rule on the extradition request. Nevertheless, on 26 November, the Senegalese Minister of the Interior placed Hissène Habré "at the disposal of the President of the African Union" and announced that Hissène Habré would be expelled to Nigeria within 48 hours. On 27 November, the Senegalese Minister for Foreign Affairs stated that Hissène Habré would remain in Senegal and that, following a discussion between the Presidents of Senegal and Nigeria, it had been agreed that the case would be brought to the attention of the next Summit of Heads of State and Government of the African Union, which would be held in Khartoum on 23 and 24 January 2006.

2.11 At its Sixth Ordinary Session, held on 24 January 2006, the Assembly of the African Union decided to set up a committee of eminent African jurists, who would be appointed by the Chairman of the African Union in consultation with the Chairman of the African Union Commission, to consider all aspects and implications of the Hissène Habré case and the possible options for his trial, and report to the African Union at its next ordinary session in June 2006.

The complaint

3.1 The complainants allege a violation by Senegal of article 5, paragraph 2, and article 7 of the Convention and seek in this regard various forms of compensation.

Violation of article 5, paragraph 2, of the Convention

3.2 The complainants point out that, in its ruling of 20 March 2001, the Court of Cassation stated that "article 79 of the Constitution [which stipulates that international treaties are directly applicable within the Senegalese legal order and can accordingly be invoked directly before Senegalese courts] cannot apply when compliance with the Convention requires prior legislative measures to be taken by Senegal" and "article 669 of the Code of Criminal Procedure [which enumerates the cases in which proceedings can be brought against foreigners in Senegal for acts committed abroad] has not been amended". They also note that, while the State party has adopted legislation to include the crime of torture in its Criminal Code in accordance with article 4 of the Convention, it has not adopted any legislation relating to article 5, paragraph 2, despite the fact that this provision is the "cornerstone" of the Convention, referring in this connection to the *travaux préparatoires*.

3.3 Moreover, the complainants point out, whereas the Court of Cassation states that "the presence in Senegal of Hissène Habré cannot in itself justify the proceedings", it is precisely the presence of the offender in Senegalese territory, that constitutes the basis under article 5 of the Convention for establishing the jurisdiction of the country concerned.

3.4 The complainants consider that the ruling of the Court of Cassation is contrary to the main purpose of the Convention and to the assurance given by the State party to the Committee against Torture, that no internal legal provision in any way hinders the prosecution of torture offences committed abroad.[2]

The Special Rapporteurs reminded the Government of Senegal of its obligations under the Convention against Torture and Other Cruel, Inhuman or Degrading Treatment or Punishment, to which it is party. They also draw its attention to the resolution adopted this year by the Commission on Human Rights on the question of torture (resolution 2000/43), in which the Commission stressed the general responsibility of all States to examine all allegations of torture and to ensure that those who encourage, order, tolerate or perpetrate such acts be held responsible and severely punished".

---

[2] See the second periodic report of Senegal to the Committee against Torture (CAT/C/17/Add.14, para. 42).

3.5 The complainants note that, irrespective of article 79 of the Constitution, under which the Convention is directly an integral part of internal Senegalese legislation, it was incumbent on the authorities of the State party to take any additional legislative measures necessary to prevent all ambiguities such as those pointed out by the Court of Cassation.

3.6 The complainants observe that members of the Committee regularly emphasize the need for States parties to take appropriate legislative measures to establish universal jurisdiction in cases of torture. During its consideration of the second periodic report submitted by the State party under article 19 of the Convention, the Committee underlined the importance of article 79 of the Senegalese Constitution, stressing that it should be implemented unreservedly.[3] The State party had, moreover, expressly affirmed in its final statement that it "intended to honour its commitments, in the light of the Committee's conclusions and in view of the primacy of international law over internal law".[4]

3.7 The complainants therefore consider that the State party's failure to make its legislation comply with article 5, paragraph 2, of the Convention constitutes a violation of this provision.

Violation of article 7 of the Convention

3.8 On the basis of several concordant opinions expressed by members of the British House of Lords in the Pinochet case, the complainants argue that the essential aim of the Convention is to ensure that no one suspected of torture can evade justice simply by moving to another country and that article 7 is precisely the expression of the principle *aut dedere aut punire*, which not only allows but obliges any State party to the Convention to declare it has jurisdiction over torture, wherever committed. Similarly, the complainants refer to Cherif Bassiouni and Edward Wise, who maintain that article 7 expresses the principle *aut dedere aut judicare*.[5] They also cite a legal opinion according to which "the Convention's main jurisdictional feature is thus that it does not impose a solely legislative and territorial obligation, in the manner of previous human rights conventions, drawing as it does on the models of collective security of Tokyo and The Hague, dominated by the principle of jurisdictional freedom, *aut dedere aut prosequi*, as well as by the obligation to prosecute."[6]

3.9 The complainants stress that the Committee itself, when considering the third periodic report of the United Kingdom concerning the Pinochet case, recommended "initiating criminal proceedings in England, in the event that the decision is made not to extradite him. This would satisfy the State party's obligations under articles 4 to 7 of the Convention and article 27 of the Vienna Convention on the Law of Treaties of 1969."[7]

3.10 While in its second periodic report to the Committee it described in detail the mechanism for implementing article 7 in its territory, the State party has neither prosecuted nor extradited Hissène Habré, and this the complainants consequently regard as a violation of article 7 of the Convention.

Compensation

3.11 The complainants state that they have been working for over 10 years to prepare a case against Hissène Habré and that the latter's presence in the State party together with the existence of international commitments binding upon Senegal have been decisive factors in the institution of proceedings against him. The decision by the authorities of the State party to drop these proceedings has therefore caused great injury to the complainants, for which they are entitled to seek compensation.

3.12 In particular, the complainants request the Committee to find that:

– By discontinuing the proceedings against Hissène Habré, the State party has violated article 5, paragraph 2, and article 7 of the Convention;

– The State party should take all necessary steps to ensure that Senegalese legislation complies with the obligations deriving from the above-mentioned provisions. The complainants note in this connection that, while the findings of the Committee are only declaratory in character and do not affect the decisions of the competent national authorities, they also carry with them "a responsibility on the part of the State to find solutions that will enable it to take all necessary measures to

---

[3] See the concluding observations of the Committee against Torture (A/51/44, para. 117).
[4] CAT/C/SR.249, para. 44.
[5] Cherif Bassiouni and Edward Wise, *Aut Dedere Aut Judicare: The Duty to Extradite or Prosecute in International Law* (Martinus Nijhoff Publishers, 1997), p. 159.

[6] Marc Henzelin, *Le principe de l'universalité en droit pénal international. Droit et obligation pour les Etats de poursuivre et juger selon le principe de l'universalité*, Helbing and Lichtenhahn, eds. (Bruylant, 2000), p. 349.
[7] Concluding observations of the Committee against Torture (A/54/44, para. 77 (f)).

comply with the Convention,"[8] measures that may be political or legislative;

– The State party should either extradite Hissène Habré or submit the case to the competent authorities for the institution of criminal proceedings;

– If the State party neither tries nor extradites Hissène Habré, it should compensate the complainants for the injury suffered, by virtue inter alia of article 14 of the Convention. The complainants also consider that, if necessary, the State party should itself pay this compensation in lieu of Hissène Habré, following the principle established by the European Court of Human Rights in the case of *Osman* v. *United Kingdom*;[9]

– The State party should compensate the complainants for the costs they have incurred in the proceedings in Senegal; and

– Pursuant to article 111, paragraph 5, of the Committee's rules of procedure, the State party should inform the Committee within 90 days of the action it has taken in response to the Committee's views.

The State party's admissibility observations

4. On 19 June 2001, the State party transmitted to the Committee its observations on the admissibility of the communication. It maintains that the communication could be considered by the Committee only if the complainants were subject to the jurisdiction of Senegal. The torture referred to by the complainants was suffered by nationals of Chad and is presumed to have been committed in Chad by a Chadian. The complainants are not, therefore, subject to the jurisdiction of the State party within the meaning of article 22, paragraph 1, of the Convention since, under Senegalese law, in particular article 699 of the Code of Criminal Procedure, a complaint lodged in Senegal against such acts cannot be dealt with by the Senegalese courts, whatever the nationality of the victims. The State party is consequently of the opinion that the communication should be declared inadmissible.

The complainants' comments

5.1 In a letter dated 19 July 2001, the complainants first stress that, contrary to what is indicated by the State party, the substance of the alleged violation by Senegal is not the torture they underwent in Chad but the refusal of the Senegalese courts to act upon the complaint lodged against Hissène Habré. The incidents of torture were presented to the Committee solely for the purpose of describing the background to the complaints lodged in Senegal.

5.2 The complainants go on to observe that the State party's interpretation of the expression "subject to its jurisdiction", appearing in article 22 of the Convention would effectively render any appeal to the Committee on Torture meaningless.

5.3 In this connection, the complainants point out that article 1 of the Optional Protocol to the International Covenant on Civil and Political Rights is drafted in the same terms as article 22 of the Convention and has on several occasions been discussed by the Human Rights Committee, which has interpreted the clause in an objective, functional manner: an individual should be considered subject to the jurisdiction of a State if the alleged violations result from an action by that State. It matters little whether the author of the communication is, for example, a national of that State or resides in its territory.[10] In the *Ibrahima Gueye et al.* v. *France* case, the complainants, of Senegalese nationality and living in Senegal, were found by the Human Rights Committee to be subject to French jurisdiction in the matter of pensions payable to retired soldiers of Senegalese nationality who had served in the French army prior to the independence of Senegal, although the authors were not generally subject to French jurisdiction.[11] The fact of being subject to the jurisdiction of a State within the meaning of article 22 of the Convention must be determined solely on the basis of consideration of the facts alleged in the complaint.[12]

5.4 It follows, in the present case, that the complainants should be considered subject to the jurisdiction of the State party inasmuch as the facts alleged against Senegal under the Convention concern judicial proceedings before the Senegalese courts. Thus, contrary to the contention of the State party, it matters little that the torture occurred in another country or that the victims are not Senegalese nationals. To establish that the complainants are subject to Senegalese jurisdiction in the present instance, one has only to establish that the communication concerns acts that fell under

---

[8] Communication N° 34/1995, *Seid Mortesa* v. *Switzerland* (para. 11).
[9] ECHR/87/1997/871/1083, 28 October 1998.
[10] See *Primo Jose Essono Mika Miha* v. *Equatorial Guinea*, communication N° 414/1990 submitted to the Human Rights Committee, A/49/40, vol. II (1994), annex IX, part O (pp. 96–100). The complainants also point out that the nationality of the author of a communication is not sufficient to establish that the author is subject to that State's jurisdiction (see *H.v.d.P.* v. *Netherlands*, communication N° 217/1986, A/42/40 (1987), annex IX, part C (pp. 185–186), para. 3.2.
[11] Communication N° 196/1985, A/44/40 (1989), annex X, part B (pp. 189–195).
[12] See *Sophie Vidal Martins* v. *Uruguay*, communication N° 57/1979, A/37/40 (1982), annex XIII (pp. 157–160).

Senegal's jurisdiction, since as only Senegal can decide whether to continue with the legal proceedings instituted by the complainants in Senegal. By instituting proceedings in the Senegalese courts, the complainants came under the jurisdiction of the State party for the purposes of those proceedings.

5.5 The complainants also make the subordinate point that, under Senegalese law, foreigners instituting judicial proceedings in the State party must accept Senegalese jurisdiction. This shows that, even if Senegal's restrictive interpretation is accepted, the complainants do indeed come under the State party's jurisdiction.

5.6 Lastly, the authors argue that the State party cannot invoke domestic law to claim that they are not subject to its jurisdiction since that would be tantamount to taking advantage of its failure to comply with article 5, paragraph 2, of the Convention, under which States parties are obliged to take such measures as may be necessary to establish their jurisdiction over the offences referred to in article 4 of the Convention. In invoking this argument, the State party is disregarding both customary law and international law. The principle of *nemo auditur propriam turpitudinem allegans* is applied in most legal systems and prevents anyone asserting a right acquired by fraud. Moreover, under article 27 of the Vienna Convention on the Law of Treaties, "a party may not invoke the provisions of its internal law as justification for its failure to perform a treaty". The complainants point out that the Vienna Convention thus reaffirms the principle that, regardless of the arrangements under internal law for the implementation of a treaty at the national level, such arrangements cannot detract from the State's obligation at an international level to ensure the implementation of and assume international responsibility for the treaty.

The Committee's admissibility decision

6.1 At its twenty-seventh session, the Committee considered the admissibility of the complaint. It ascertained that the matter had not been and was not being examined under another procedure of international investigation or settlement, and considered that the communication did not constitute an abuse of the right to submit such communications and was not incompatible with the provisions of the Convention.

6.2 The Committee took note of the State party's argument that the communication should be found inadmissible since the complainants are not subject to Senegal's jurisdiction within the meaning of article 22 of the Convention.

6.3 To establish whether a complainant is effectively subject to the jurisdiction of the State party against which a communication has been submitted within the meaning of article 22, the Committee must take into account various factors that are not confined to the author's nationality. The Committee observes that the alleged violations of the Convention concern the refusal of the Senegalese authorities to prosecute Hissène Habré despite their obligation to establish universal jurisdiction in accordance with article 5, paragraph 2, and article 7 of the Convention. The Committee also observes that the State party does not dispute that the authors were the plaintiffs in the proceedings brought against Hissène Habré in Senegal. Moreover, the Committee notes, the complainants in this case accepted Senegalese jurisdiction in order to pursue the proceedings against Hissène Habré which they instituted. On the basis of these elements, the Committee is of the opinion that the authors are indeed subject to the jurisdiction of Senegal in the dispute to which this communication refers.

6.4 The Committee also considers that the principle of universal jurisdiction enunciated in article 5, paragraph 2, and article 7 of the Convention implies that the jurisdiction of States parties must extend to *potential* complainants in circumstances similar to the complainants'.

6.5 Accordingly, the Committee against Torture declared the communication admissible on 13 November 2001.

The State party's merits observations

7.1 The State party transmitted its observations on the merits by note verbale dated 31 March 2002.

7.2 The State party points out that, in accordance with the rules of criminal procedure, judicial proceedings in Senegal opened on 27 January 2000 with an application from the public prosecutor's office in Dakar for criminal proceedings to be brought against Hissène Habré as an accessory to torture and acts of barbarism and against a person or persons unknown for torture, acts of barbarism and crimes against humanity. Hissène Habré was charged on both counts on 3 February 2000 and placed under house arrest. On 18 February 2000, Hissène Habré submitted an application for the proceedings to be dismissed on the grounds that the Senegalese courts were not competent, that the charges had no basis in law, and that the alleged offences were time-barred.

7.3 On 4 July 2000, the Indictment Division of the Court of Appeal dismissed the proceedings. On 20 March 2001, the Court of Cassation rejected the appeal lodged by the complainants (plaintiffs). That ruling, handed down by the highest court in Senegal, thus brought the proceedings to an end.

7.4 Regarding the allegations that the executive put pressure on the judiciary, in particular by transferring and/or removing the judges trying the case, namely the chief examining magistrate and the President of the Indictment Division, the State party reminds the Committee that the President of the Indictment Division is *primus inter pares* in a three-person court and is thus in no position to impose his or her views. The other two members of the Indictment Division were not affected by the reassignment of judges, which in any case was an across-the-board measure.

7.5 It is also important to bear in mind that any country is free to organize its institutions as it sees fit in order to ensure their proper functioning.

7.6 The independence of the judiciary is guaranteed by the Constitution and the law. One such guarantee is oversight of the profession and rules of conduct of the judiciary by the Higher Council of the Judiciary, whose members are judges, some of them elected and others appointed. Appeals may be lodged when the appointing authority is accused of having violated the principle of the independence of the judiciary.

7.7 A basic element of judicial independence is that judges may appeal against decisions affecting them, and that the executive is duty-bound not to interfere in the work of the courts. Judges' right of appeal is not merely theoretical.

7.8 The Council of State did indeed revoke a number of judges' appointments on 13 September 2001, considering that they failed to apply a basic safeguard designed to protect trial judges and thereby ensure their independence, namely the obligation to obtain people's prior consent before assigning them to new positions, even by means of promotion.

7.9 It must be acknowledged that the Senegalese judiciary is genuinely independent. Criminal proceedings necessarily culminate in decisions which, unfortunately, cannot satisfy all the parties. The judicial investigation is a component of criminal procedure and, by its very nature, is subject to all the safeguards provided for in international instruments. In the present case, the parties benefited from conditions recognized as ensuring fair dispensation of justice. Where no legal provision exists, proceedings cannot be pursued without violating the principle of legality; that was confirmed by the Court of Cassation in its ruling of 20 March 2001.

On the violation of article 5, paragraph 2, of the Convention

7.10 In its ruling on the Hissène Habré case, the Court of Cassation considered that "duly ratified treaties or agreements have, once they are published, an authority higher than that of laws, subject to implementation, in the case of each agreement or treaty, by the other party", and that the Convention cannot be applied as long as Senegal has not taken prior legislative measures. The Court adds that ratification of the Convention obliges each State party to take such measures as may be necessary to establish its jurisdiction over the offences referred to in article 4, or to extradite perpetrators of torture.

7.11 Proceedings were brought against Hissène Habré. However, since the Convention against Torture is not self-executing, Senegal, in order to comply with its commitments, promulgated Act N° 96-16 of 28 August 1996 enacting article 295 of the Criminal Code. The principle *aut dedere aut judicare* comprises the obligation to prosecute or to extradite in an efficient and fair manner. In this regard, Senegalese legislators have endorsed the argument of Professor Bassiouni, according to whom "[t]he obligation to prosecute or extradite must, in the absence of a specific convention stipulating such an obligation, and in spite of specialists' arguments to this effect, be proved to be part of customary international law".

7.12 Pursuant to article 4 of the Convention, torture is classified in the Senegalese Criminal Code as an international crime arising from *jus cogens*. It should be noted that Senegal is aware of the need to amend its legislation; however, under the Convention a State party is not bound to meet its obligations within a specific time frame.

On the violation of article 7 of the Convention

7.13 Since the Convention is not self-executing, in order to establish universal jurisdiction over acts of torture it is necessary to pass a law establishing the relevant procedure and substantive rules.

7.14 While the Committee has stressed the need for States parties to take appropriate legislative measures to ensure universal jurisdiction over crimes of torture, the manner in which this procedure is accomplished cannot be dictated. Senegal is engaged in a very complex process that must take account of its status as a developing State and the ability of its judicial system to apply the rule of law.

7.15 The State party points out that the difficulty of ensuring the absolute application of universal jurisdiction is commonly acknowledged. It is therefore normal to provide for different stages of its application.

7.16 However, the absence of domestic codification of universal jurisdiction has not allowed Hissène Habré complete impunity. Senegal applies the principle *aut dedere aut judicare*. Any request for judicial assistance or cooperation is considered benignly and granted in so far as the law permits, particularly when the request relates to the implementation of an international treaty obligation.

7.17 In the case of Hissène Habré, Senegal is applying article 7 of the Convention. The obligation to extradite, unless raised at another level, has never posed any difficulties. Consequently, if a request is made for application of the other option under the principle *aut dedere aut judicare*, there is no doubt that Senegal will fulfil its obligations.

On the request for financial compensation

7.18 In violation of the principle *Electa una via non datur recursus ad alteram* (once a course of action is chosen, there is no recourse to another), the complainants have also instituted proceedings against Hissène Habré in the Belgian courts. The State party believes that, in the circumstances, to ask Senegal to consider financial compensation would be a complete injustice.

7.19 The Belgian Act of 16 June 1993 (as amended by the Act of 23 April 2003) relating to the suppression of serious violations of international humanitarian law introduces significant departures from Belgian criminal law in both procedure and substance. A Belgian examining magistrate has been assigned, and pretrial measures have been requested, just as they had been in Senegal. The State party maintains that it is advisable to let these proceedings follow their course before considering compensation of any kind.

Complainants' observations on the merits

8.1 In a letter dated 1 July 2002, the complainants submitted their observations on the merits.

On the violation of article 5, paragraph 2, of the Convention

8.2 With regard to the State party's argument that there is no specific time frame for complying with its obligations under the Convention, the complainants' principal contention is that the State party was bound by the Convention from the date of its ratification.

8.3 According to article 16 of the Vienna Convention on the Law of Treaties (hereinafter "the Vienna Convention"), "unless the treaty otherwise provides, instruments of ratification, acceptance, approval or accession establish the consent of a State to be bound by a treaty upon: […] (b) their deposit with the depositary […]". The *travaux préparatoires* relating to this provision confirm that the State party is immediately bound by the obligations arising from the treaty, from the moment the instrument of ratification is deposited.

8.4 According to the complainants, the State party's arguments call into question the very meaning of the act of ratification and would lead to a situation in which no State would have to answer for a failure to comply with its treaty obligations.

8.5 With regard to the specific legislative measures that a State must take in order to meet its treaty obligations, the complainants maintain that the manner in which the State in question fulfils its obligations is of little importance from the standpoint of international law. Moreover, they believe that international law is moving towards the elimination of the formalities of national law relating to ratification, on the principle that the norms of international law should be considered binding in the internal and international legal order as soon as a treaty has entered into force. The complainants add that the State party could have taken the opportunity to amend its national legislation even before it ratified the Convention.

8.6 Finally, the complainants recall that article 27 of the Vienna Convention prohibits the State party from invoking the provisions of its internal law as a justification for its failure to perform its treaty obligations. This provision has been interpreted by the Committee on Economic, Social and Cultural Rights as an obligation for States to "modify the domestic legal order as necessary in order to give effect to their treaty obligations".[13]

8.7 As a subsidiary argument, the complainants maintain that, even if one considers that the State party was not bound by its obligations from the moment the treaty was ratified, it has committed a violation of article 5 by not adopting appropriate legislation to comply with the Convention within a reasonable time frame.

8.8 Article 26 of the Vienna Convention establishes the obligation of parties to perform their obligations under international treaties in good faith; the complainants point out that, since it ratified the Convention against Torture on 21 August 1986, the State party had 15 years before the submission of the present communication to implement the Convention, but did not do so.

8.9 In this regard, the Committee, in its concluding observations on the second periodic report of Senegal, had already recommended that "the State party should, during its current legislative reform, consider introducing explicitly in national legislation the following provisions: (a) The definition of torture set forth in article 1 of the Convention and the classification of torture as a general offence, in accordance with article 4 of the Convention, which would, inter alia, permit the State party to exercise universal jurisdiction as provided in articles 5 et seq. of the Convention; […]".[14] The State party has not followed up this recommendation and has unreasonably delayed adoption of the

---

[13] General Comment 9 (E/C.12/1998/24, para. 3).
[14] See A/51/44, para. 114.

legislation necessary for implementing the Convention.

On the violation of article 7 of the Convention

8.10 With regard to the argument that article 7 has not been violated because the State was prepared, if necessary, to extradite Hissène Habré, the complainants maintain that the obligation under article 7 to prosecute Hissène Habré is not linked to the existence of an extradition request.

8.11 The complainants appreciate the fact that Senegal was prepared to extradite Hissène Habré and in this connection point out that on 27 September 2001 President Wade had stated that "if a country capable of holding a fair trial—we are talking about Belgium—wishes to do so, I do not see anything to prevent it". Nevertheless, this suggestion was purely hypothetical at the time of the present observations since no extradition request had yet been made.

8.12 On the basis of a detailed examination of the *travaux préparatoires*, the complainants refute the argument that the State party appears to be propounding, namely that there would be an obligation to prosecute under article 7 only after an extradition request had been made and refused. They also condense long passages from an academic work[15] to demonstrate that the State's obligation to prosecute a perpetrator of torture under article 7 does not depend on the existence of an extradition request.

On the request for financial compensation

8.13 The complainants reject the State party's claim that they have instituted proceedings in Belgian courts. It is, in fact, other former victims of Hissène Habré who have applied to the Belgian courts. The complainants are not parties to those proceedings.

8.14 The complainants also maintain that there is no risk of double compensation because Hissène Habré can be tried only in one place.

Committee's considerations on the merits

9.1 The Committee notes, first of all, that its consideration on the merits has been delayed at the explicit wish of the parties because of judicial proceedings pending in Belgium for the extradition of Hissène Habré.

9.2 The Committee also notes that, despite its note verbale of 24 November 2005 requesting the State party to update its observations on the merits before 31 January 2006, the State party has not acceded to that request.

9.3 On the merits, the Committee must determine whether the State party violated article 5, paragraph 2, and article 7 of the Convention. It finds—and this has not been challenged—that Hissène Habré has been in the territory of the State party since December 1990. In January 2000, the complainants lodged with an examining magistrate in Dakar a complaint against Hissène Habré alleging torture. On 20 March 2001, upon completion of judicial proceedings, the Court of Cassation of Senegal ruled that "no procedural text confers on Senegalese courts a universal jurisdiction to prosecute and judge, if they are found on the territory of the Republic, presumed perpetrators of or accomplices in acts [of torture] … when these acts have been committed outside Senegal by foreigners; the presence in Senegal of Hissène Habré cannot in itself justify the proceedings brought against him". The courts of the State party have not ruled on the merits of the allegations of torture that the complainants raised in their complaint.

9.4 The Committee also notes that, on 25 November 2005, the Indictment Division of the Dakar Court of Appeal stated that it lacked jurisdiction to rule on Belgium's request for the extradition of Hissène Habré.

9.5 The Committee recalls that, in accordance with article 5, paragraph 2, of the Convention, "each State Party shall […] take such measures as may be necessary to establish its jurisdiction over such offences in cases where the alleged offender is present in any territory under its jurisdiction and it does not extradite him […]". It notes that, in its observations on the merits, the State party has not contested the fact that it had not taken "such measures as may be necessary" in keeping with article 5, paragraph 2, of the Convention, and observes that the Court of Cassation itself considered that the State party had not taken such measures. It also considers that the reasonable time frame within which the State party should have complied with this obligation has been considerably exceeded.

9.6 The Committee is consequently of the opinion that the State party has not fulfilled its obligations under article 5, paragraph 2, of the Convention.

9.7 The Committee recalls that, under article 7 of the Convention, "the State Party in the territory under whose jurisdiction a person alleged to have committed any offence referred to in article 4 is found shall in the cases contemplated in article 5, if it does not extradite him, submit the case to its competent authorities for the purpose of prosecution". It notes that the obligation to prosecute the alleged perpetrator of acts of torture does not depend on the prior existence of a request for his extradition. The alternative available to the State party under article 7 of the Convention exists only when a request for extradition has been made and puts the State party in the position of having to choose between (a) proceeding with extradition or (b)

---
[15] Henzelin, op. cit.

submitting the case to its own judicial authorities for the institution of criminal proceedings, the objective of the provision being to prevent any act of torture from going unpunished.

9.8 The Committee considers that the State party cannot invoke the complexity of its judicial proceedings or other reasons stemming from domestic law to justify its failure to comply with these obligations under the Convention. It is of the opinion that the State party was obliged to prosecute Hissène Habré for alleged acts of torture unless it could show that there was not sufficient evidence to prosecute, at least at the time when the complainants submitted their complaint in January 2000. Yet, by its decision of 20 March 2001, which is not subject to appeal, the Court of Cassation put an end to any possibility of prosecuting Hissène Habré in Senegal.

9.9 Consequently and notwithstanding the time that has elapsed since the initial submission of the communication, the Committee is of the opinion that the State party has not fulfilled its obligations under article 7 of the Convention.

9.10 Moreover, the Committee finds that, since 19 September 2005, the State party has been in another situation covered under article 7, because on that date Belgium made a formal extradition request. At that time, the State party had the choice of proceeding with extradition if it decided not to submit the case to its own judicial authorities for the purpose of prosecuting Hissène Habré.

9.11 The Committee considers that, by refusing to comply with the extradition request, the State party has again failed to perform its obligations under article 7 of the Convention.

9.12 The Committee against Torture, acting under article 22, paragraph 7, of the Convention, concludes that the State party has violated article 5, paragraph 2, and article 7 of the Convention.

10. In accordance with article 5, paragraph 2, of the Convention, the State party is obliged to adopt the necessary measures, including legislative measures, to establish its jurisdiction over the acts referred to in the present communication. Moreover, under article 7 of the Convention, the State party is obliged to submit the present case to its competent authorities for the purpose of prosecution or, failing that, since Belgium has made an extradition request, to comply with that request, or, should the case arise, with any other extradition request made by another State, in accordance with the Convention. This decision in no way influences the possibility of the complainants' obtaining compensation through the domestic courts for the State party's failure to comply with its obligations under the Convention.

11. Bearing in mind that, in making the declaration under article 22 of the Convention, the State party recognized the competence of the Committee to decide whether or not there has been a violation of the Convention, the Committee wishes to receive information from the State party within 90 days on the measures it has taken to give effect to its recommendations.

Communication N° 187/2001

Submitted by: Mr. Dhaou Belgacem THABTI (represented by the non-governmental organization Vérité-Action)
Alleged victim: The complainant
State party: Tunisia
Declared admissible: 20 November 2002
Date of adoption of Views: 14 November 2003

Subject matter: torture of complainant by police and intelligence services

Procedural issues: exhaustion of domestic remedies; abuse of right to lodge a complaint

Substantive issues: failure to take effective measures to prevent torture; failure to ensure all acts of torture are offences under its criminal law; use of evidence obtained as a result of torture; failure to institute legal proceedings against those responsible for torture; lack of investigation of the acts of torture and examination of the allegations of torture; hindrance to the right to make a complaint, right to redress and rehabilitation; sentence based on a confession obtained as a result of torture; cruel, inhuman and degrading treatment or punishment

Articles of the Convention: 1, 2 (1), 4, 5, 12, 13, 14, 15, 16

1.1 The complainant is Mr. Dhaou Belgacem Thabti, a Tunisian citizen, born on 4 July 1955 in Tataouine, Tunisia, and resident in Switzerland since 25 May 1998, where he has refugee status. He claims to have been the victim of violations by Tunisia of the provisions of article 1, article 2, paragraph 1, article 4, article 5, article 12, article 13, article 14, article 15 and article 16 of the Convention. He is represented by the non-governmental organization Vérité-Action.

1.2 Tunisia ratified the Convention against Torture and Other Cruel Inhuman or Degrading Treatment or Punishment and made the declaration under article 22 of the Convention on 23 September 1988.

The facts as submitted by the complainant

2.1 The complainant states that he was an active member of the Islamist organization ENNAHDA (formerly MTI). Following a wave of arrests in Tunisia, which commenced in 1990 and was targeted in particular against members of this organization, he went into hiding from 27 February 1991. On 6 April 1991, at 1 a.m., he was arrested and severely beaten by the police, who kicked, slapped and punched him and struck him with truncheons.

2.2 Incarcerated in the basement cells in the Interior Ministry (DST) building in Tunis and deprived of sleep, the complainant was taken, the following morning, to the office of the Director of State Security, Ezzedine Jneyeh. According to the complainant, this official personally ordered his interrogation under torture.

2.3 The complainant provides a detailed description, accompanied by sketches, of the different types of torture to which he was subjected until 4 June 1991 in the premises of the Interior Ministry (DST).

2.4 The complainant describes what is customarily known as the "roast chicken" position, in which the victim is stripped naked, his hands tied and his legs folded between his arms, with an iron bar placed behind his knees, from which he is then suspended between two tables. In this position he was subjected to beatings, in particular on the soles of his feet, until he passed out. The complainant adds that the policemen inflicting this torture would then bring him round by throwing cold water over his body and by applying ether to sensitive areas, such as his buttocks and testicles.

2.5 The complainant also claims to have been tortured in the "upside-down" position, whereby the victim is stripped, hands tied behind his back and suspended from the ceiling by a rope tied to one or both of his feet, with his head hanging downwards. In this position he was kicked and struck with sticks and whips until he passed out. He adds that his torturers tied a piece of string to his penis which they then repeatedly tugged, as if to tear his penis off.

2.6 The complainant claims to have been subjected to immersion torture, in which the victim is suspended upside-down from a hoist and immersed in a tank of water mixed with soap powder, bleach and sometimes even urine and salt; the victim is unable to breathe and is therefore forced to keep swallowing this mixture until his stomach is full. He states that he was then kicked in the stomach until he vomited.

2.7 The complainant also maintains that he was tortured in the "scorpion" position, in which the victim is stripped, his hands and feet tied behind his back, and then lifted by his torturers, face downwards, with a chain hoist, while pressure is applied to his spine. He states that, in this position, he was beaten and whipped on his legs, arms, stomach and genitals.

2.8 The complainant also claims to have been subjected to "table torture", in which he was stripped, made to lie flat on his back or stomach on a long table, with his arms and legs tied down, and was then beaten.

2.9 In support of his claims of torture and the effects of torture, the complainant submits a certificate from a Swiss physiotherapist, a report by a neurological specialist in Fribourg and a certificate of psychiatric treatment from the medical service of a Swiss insurance company. He also cites an observation mission report by the International Federation for Human Rights, stating that, during proceedings initiated on 9 July 1992 against Islamist militants, including the complainant, all the defendants that were interviewed complained that they had been subjected to serious physical abuse whilst in police custody.

2.10 The complainant provides a list of persons who subjected him to torture during this period, namely, Ezzedine Jneieh, Director of DST; Abderrahmen El Guesmi; El Hamrouni; Ben Amor, Inspector of Police; and Mahmoud El Jaouadi, Slah Eddine Tarzi and Mohamed Ennacer-Hleiss, all of Bouchoucha Intelligence Service. He adds that his torturers were assisted by two doctors and that he witnessed torture being inflicted on his fellow detainees.

2.11 On 4 June 1991, the complainant appeared before the military examining magistrate, Major Ayed Ben Kayed. The complainant states that, during the hearing, he denied the charges against him of having attempted a coup d'état, and that he was refused the assistance of counsel.

2.12 The complainant claims that he was then placed in solitary confinement in the premises of the Ministry of the Interior (DST), from 4 June to 28

July 1991, and refused all visits, mail, medicine and necessary medical attention, except for one visit, on 18 July 1991, by Dr. Moncef Marzouki, President of the Tunisian Human Rights League. The complainant adds that he was not fed properly, that he was denied the right to practise his religion and that he was once again subjected to torture.

2.13 From 28 July 1991, when his period of police custody ended, the complainant was repeatedly transferred between different prison establishments in the country—in Tunis, Borj Erroumi (Bizerte), Mahdia, Sousse, Elhaoireb and Rejim Maatoug—which transfers, he maintains, were designed to prevent him having any contact with his family.

2.14 The complainant describes the bad conditions in these detention facilities, such as overcrowding, with 60–80 persons in the small cells in which he was held, and the poor hygiene, which caused sickness: he maintains that, as a result, he developed asthma and suffered skin allergies and that his feet are now disfigured. He states that on several occasions he was placed in solitary confinement, partly because of the hunger strikes he mounted in the 9 April prison in Tunis over 12 days in July 1992, and in Mahdia over 8 days in October 1995 and 10 days in March 1996, as a protest against the conditions in which he was being held and the ill-treatment to which he was subjected, and partly by arbitrary decision of the prison warders. He also stresses that he was stripped naked and beaten in public.

2.15 On 9 July 1992 the complainant's case was heard by the Bouchoucha military court in Tunis. He maintains that he was only able to have one meeting with his counsel, on 20 July 1992, and that it was conducted under the surveillance of the prison warders. On 28 August 1992, he was sentenced to a term of six years' imprisonment.

2.16 On completion of his sentence on 27 May 1997, as indicated in the prison discharge papers he submits, the complainant was placed under administrative supervision for a period of five years, which effectively meant that he was placed under house arrest in Remada, 600 kilometres from Tunis, where his wife and children were living. Four months later, on 1 October 1997, he fled Tunisia for Libya then made his way to Switzerland, where he obtained political refugee status on 15 January 1999. In support of his statements, the complainant submits a copy of the report issued on 10 March 1996 by the Tunisian Committee for Human Rights and Freedoms, describing his condition after his release, and a certificate from the Swiss Federal Office for Refugees, on the granting of his political refugee status. The complainant adds that, after he had fled from the country, he was sentenced in absentia to 12 years' non-suspended imprisonment.

2.17 Finally, the complainant states that members of his family, in particular his wife and their five children, have been the victims of harassment (night-time raids, systematic searches of their home, intimidation, threats of rape, confiscation of property and money, detention and interrogation, constant surveillance), and of ill-treatment (the complainant's son Ezzedinne has been detained and severely beaten) by the police throughout the period of his detention and after he fled the country, continuing until 1998.

2.18 As to whether all domestic remedies have been exhausted, the complainant states that he complained of acts of torture committed against him to the Bouchoucha military court, in the presence of the national press and international human rights observers. He maintains that the president of the court tried to ignore him but, when he insisted, replied that nothing had been established. In addition, the judge refused outright the complainant's request for a medical check.

2.19 The complainant adds that, after the hearing and his return to prison, he was threatened with torture if he repeated his claims of torture to the court.

2.20 The complainant maintains in addition that, from 27 May 1997, the date of his release, his house arrest prevented him from lodging a complaint. He explains that the Remada police and gendarmerie took part a continuing process of harassment and intimidation against him during the daily visits he made for the purposes of administrative supervision. According to the complainant, the mere fact of submitting a complaint would have caused increased pressure to be applied against him, even to the point of his being returned to prison. Being under house arrest, he was also unable to apply to the authorities at his legal place of residence, in Tunis.

2.21 The complainant maintains that, while Tunisian law might make provision for the possibility of complaints against acts of torture, in practice, any victim submitting a complaint will become the target of intolerable police harassment, which acts as a disincentive to the use of this remedy. According to the complainant, any remedies are therefore ineffective and non-existent.

The complaint

3. The complainant maintains that the Tunisian Government has breached the following articles of the Convention against Torture and Other Cruel, Inhuman or Degrading Treatment or Punishment:

> Article 1. The practices described above, such as the "roast chicken" position, the "upside-down" position, the "scorpion" position, immersion torture, "table torture" and solitary confinement, to which the

complainant was subjected, constitute acts of torture.

Article 2, paragraph 1. Not only has the State party failed to take effective measures to prevent torture, it has even mobilized its administrative machinery and, in particular, its police force as an instrument of torture against the complainant.

Article 4. The State party has not ensured that all the acts of torture to which the complainant has been subjected are offences under its criminal law.

Article 5. The State party has instituted no legal proceedings against those responsible for torturing the complainant.

Article 12. The State party has not carried out an investigation of the acts of torture committed against the complainant.

Article 13. The State party has not undertaken any examination of the allegations of torture made by the complainant at the beginning of his trial; instead, these have been dismissed.

Article 14. The State party has ignored the complainant's right to make a complaint and has thereby deprived him of his right to redress and rehabilitation.

Article 15. The complainant was sentenced on 28 August 1992 to a prison sentence on the basis of a confession obtained as a result of torture.

Article 16. The repressive measures and practices described above, such as violation of the right to medical care and medicine and the right to send and receive mail, restriction of the right to property and the right to visits by family members and lawyers, house arrest and harassment of the family, applied by the State party against the complainant constitute cruel, inhuman and degrading treatment or punishment.

State party's admissibility observations

4.1 On 4 December 2001, the State party challenged the admissibility of the complaint on the grounds that the complainant has neither resorted to nor exhausted available domestic remedies.

4.2 The State party maintains that the complainant may still have recourse to the available domestic remedies, since, under Tunisian law, the limitation period for acts alleged to be, and characterized as, serious offences is 10 years.

4.3 The State party explains that, under the criminal justice system, the complainant may submit a complaint, from within Tunisia or abroad, to a representative of the Public Prosecutor's Office with jurisdiction in the area in question. He may also authorize a Tunisian lawyer of his own choice to submit the complaint or request a foreign lawyer to do so with the assistance of a Tunisian colleague.

4.4 Under the same rules of criminal procedure, the Public Prosecutor will receive the complaint and institute a judicial enquiry. In accordance with article 53 of the Code of Criminal Procedure, the examining magistrate to whom the case is referred will hear the author of the complaint. In the light of this hearing, he may decide to hear witnesses, question suspects, undertake on-site investigations and seize physical evidence. He may order expert studies and carry out any actions which he deems necessary for the uncovering of evidence, both in favour of and against the complainant, with a view to discovering the truth and verifying facts on which the trial court will be able to base its decision.

4.5 The State party explains that the complainant may, in addition, lodge with the examining magistrate during the pretrial proceedings an application for criminal indemnification for any harm suffered, over and above the criminal charges brought against those responsible for the offences against him.

4.6 If the examining magistrate deems that the public right of action is not exercisable, that the acts do not constitute a violation or that there is no prima facie case against the accused, he shall rule that there are no grounds for prosecution. If, on the other hand, the magistrate deems that the acts constitute an offence punishable by imprisonment, he shall send the accused before a competent court—which in the present instance, where a serious offence has been committed, would be the indictment chamber. All rulings by the examining magistrate are immediately communicated to all the parties to the proceedings, including the complainant who brought the criminal indemnification proceedings. Having been thus notified within a period of 48 hours, the complainant may, within four days, lodge an appeal against any ruling prejudicial to his interests. This appeal, submitted in writing or orally, is received by the clerk of the court. If there is prima facie evidence of the commission of an offence, the indictment chamber sends the accused before the competent court (criminal court or criminal division of a court of first instance), having given rulings on all the counts established during the proceedings. If it chooses, it may also order further information to be provided by one of its assessors or by the examining magistrate; it may also institute new proceedings, or conduct or order an inquiry into matters which have not yet been the subject of an examination. The decisions of the indictment chamber are subject to immediate enforcement.

4.7 A complainant seeking criminal indemnification may appeal on a point of law against a decision of the indictment chamber once it has been notified. This remedy is admissible when the indictment chamber rules that there are no grounds for prosecution; when it has ruled that the application for criminal indemnification is inadmissible, or that the prosecution is time-barred; when it has deemed the court to which the case has been referred to lack jurisdiction; or when it has omitted to make a ruling on one of the counts.

4.8 The State party stresses that, in conformity with article 7 of the Code of Criminal Procedure, the complainant may bring criminal indemnification proceedings before the court to which the case has been referred (criminal court or criminal division of the court of first instance) and, as appropriate, may lodge an appeal, either with the Court of Appeal if the offence in question is an ordinary offence, or with the criminal division of the Court of Appeal if it is a serious offence. The complainant may also appeal to the Court of Cassation.

4.9 The State party maintains that the domestic remedies are effective.

4.10 According to the State party, the Tunisian courts have systematically and consistently acted to remedy deficiencies in the law, and stiff sentences have been handed down on those responsible for abuses and violations of the law. The State party says that, between 1 January 1988 and 31 March 1995, judgements were handed down in 302 cases involving members of the police or the national guard under a variety of counts, 227 of which fell into the category of abuse of authority. The penalties imposed varied from fines to terms of imprisonment of several years.[1]

4.11 The State party maintains that, given the complainant's "political and partisan" motives and his "offensive and defamatory" remarks, his complaint may be considered an abuse of the right to submit complaints.

4.12 The State party explains that the ideology and the political platform of the "movement" of which the complainant was an active member are based exclusively on religious principles, promoting an extremist view of religion which negates democratic rights and the rights of women. This is an illegal "movement", fomenting religious and racial hatred and employing violence. According to the State party, this "movement" perpetrated terrorist attacks which caused material damage and loss of life over the period 1990–1991. For that reason, and also because it is in breach of the Constitution and the law on political parties, this "movement" has not been recognized by the authorities.

4.13 The State party explains that the complainant is making serious accusations, not genuinely substantiated by any evidence, against the judicial authorities by claiming that judges accept confessions as evidence and hand down judgements on the basis of such evidence.

Complainant's comments on the State party's observations

5.1 In a letter dated 6 May 2002, the complainant challenges the State party's argument that he was supposedly unwilling to turn to the Tunisian justice system and make use of domestic remedies.

5.2 In this context, the complainant recalls his statements concerning the torture to which he had been subjected and his request for a medical check made to the judge of the military court, all of which were ignored and not acted upon, and his reports of violations of articles 13 and 14 of the Convention against Torture, as well as his contention that placing him under administrative supervision impeded due process. According to the complainant, the practice described above is routinely applied by judges, particularly against political prisoners. In support of his arguments, he cites extracts from reports by the Tunisian Committee for Human Rights and Freedoms, the International Federation for Human Rights and the Tunisian Human Rights League. He also refers to the annual reports of such international organizations as Amnesty International and Human Rights Watch, which have denounced the practices described by the complainant.

5.3 The complainant also challenges the explanations by the State party regarding the possibility of promptly instituting legal proceedings, the existence of an effective remedy and the possibility of bringing criminal indemnification proceedings.

5.4 The complainant argues that the State party has confined itself to repeating the procedure described in the Code of Criminal Procedure, which is far from being applied in reality, particularly where political prisoners are concerned. In support of his argument, he cites reports by Amnesty International, Human Rights Watch, the World Organization against Torture, the National Consultative Commission on Human Rights in France and the National Council for Fundamental Freedoms in Tunisia. He also refers to the Committee against Torture's final observations on Tunisia, dated 19 November 1998. The complainant stresses that the Committee against Torture recommended, among other things, that the State party should, first, ensure the right of victims of torture to lodge a complaint without the fear of being

---

[1] The examples cited by the State are available for information in the file.

subjected to any kind of reprisal, harassment, harsh treatment or prosecution, even if the outcome of the investigation does not prove their allegations, and to seek and obtain redress if these allegations are proven correct; second, ensure that medical examinations are automatically provided following allegations of abuse and an autopsy is performed following any death in custody; and third, ensure that the findings of all investigations concerning cases of torture are made public and that this information includes details of any offences committed, the names of the offenders, the dates, places and circumstances of the incidents and the punishment received by those who were found guilty. The Committee also noted that many of the regulations existing in Tunisia for the protection of arrested persons were not adhered to in practice. It also expressed its concern over the wide gap that existed between law and practice with regard to the protection of human rights, and was particularly disturbed by the reported widespread practice of torture and other cruel and degrading treatment perpetrated by security forces and the police, which, in certain cases, resulted in death in custody. In addition, the complainant mentions the decision by the Committee against Torture relating to communication N° 60/1996, *Faisal Baraket* v. *Tunisia*. The complainant believes that the State party's statement regarding the possibility of ensuring an effective remedy constitutes political propaganda without any legal relevance. He explains that the cases cited by the State party (para. 4.10) relate to Tunisian citizens who were not arrested for political reasons, whereas the authorities reserve special treatment for cases involving political prisoners.

5.5 The complainant also challenges the State party's argument that a Tunisian lawyer can be instructed from abroad to lodge a complaint.

5.6 The complainant maintains that this procedure is a dead letter and has never been respected in political cases. According to him, lawyers who dare to defend such causes are subject to harassment and other forms of serious encroachment on the free and independent exercise of their profession, including prison sentences.

5.7 The complainant maintains that his situation as a political refugee in Switzerland precludes him from successfully concluding any proceedings that he might initiate, given the restrictions placed on contacts between refugees and the authorities in their own countries. He explains that severance of all relations with the country of origin is one of the conditions on which refugee status is granted, and that it plays an important role when consideration is being given to withdrawing asylum. According to the complainant, such asylum would effectively end if the refugee should once again, of his own volition, seek the protection of his country of origin, for example by maintaining close contacts with the authorities or paying regular visits to the country.

5.8 Lastly, the complainant believes that the State party's comments regarding his membership of the ENNAHDA movement and the aspersions cast upon it demonstrate the continued discrimination against the opposition, which is still considered illegal. According to the complainant, with its references in this context to terrorism, the State party is demonstrating its bias and any further talk of ensuring effective domestic remedies is therefore pure fiction. He also stresses that the prohibition of torture and inhuman or degrading treatment is a provision which admits of no exception, including for terrorists.[2]

5.9 Finally, in the light of his previous explanations, the complainant rejects the observation by the State party to the effect that the present complaint constitutes an abuse of the right to submit complaints.

Additional observations from the State party on admissibility

6. On 8 November 2002 the State party again challenged the admissibility of the complaint. It maintains, first, that the complainant's claims about recourse to the Tunisian justice system and the use of domestic remedies are baseless and unsupported by any evidence. It adds that proceedings in relation to the allegations made in the complaint are not time-barred, since the time limit for bringing proceedings in such cases is 10 years. It argues that the complainant offers no evidence in support of his claims that the Tunisian authorities' customary practice makes it difficult to initiate prompt legal action or apply for criminal indemnification. It adds that the complainant's refugee status does not deprive him of his right to lay complaints before the Tunisian courts. Third, it maintains that, contrary to the complainant's allegations, it is open to him to instruct a lawyer of his choice to lodge a complaint from abroad. Lastly, the State party reaffirms that the complaint is not based on any specific incident and cites no evidence, and constitutes an abuse of the right to submit complaints.

Committee's admissibility decision

7.1 At its twenty-ninth session, the Committee considered the admissibility of the complaint, and on 20 November 2002 declared it admissible.

---

[2] The complainant also refers to communication N° 91/1997, *A.* v. *Netherlands*, concerning which the Committee against Torture upheld the complaint of a Tunisian asylum-seeker who was a member of the opposition because of the serious risk that he would be tortured if he returned to Tunisia.

7.2   With regard to the issue of the exhaustion of domestic remedies, the Committee noted that the State party challenged the admissibility of the complaint on the grounds that the available and effective domestic remedies had not been exhausted. In the present case, the Committee noted that the State party had provided a detailed description both of the remedies available, under law, to any complainant and of cases where such remedies had been applied against those responsible for abuses and for violations of the law. The Committee considered, nevertheless, that the State party had not sufficiently demonstrated the relevance of its arguments to the specific circumstances of the case of this complainant, who claims to have suffered violations of his rights. It made clear that it did not doubt the information provided by the State party about members of the security forces being prosecuted and convicted for a variety of abuses. But the Committee pointed out that it could not lose sight of the fact that the case at issue dates from 1991 and that, given a statute of limitations of 10 years, the question arose of whether, failing interruption or suspension of the statute of limitations—a matter on which the State party had provided no information—action before the Tunisian courts would be disallowed. The Committee noted, moreover, that the complainant's allegations related to facts that had already been reported publicly to the judicial authorities in the presence of international observers. The Committee pointed out that to date it remained unaware of any investigations voluntarily undertaken by the State party. The Committee therefore considered it very unlikely in the present case that the complainant would obtain satisfaction by exhausting domestic remedies, and decided to proceed in accordance with article 22, paragraph 5 (b), of the Convention.

7.3   The Committee noted, in addition, the argument by the State party to the effect that the complainant's claim was tantamount to abuse of the right to lodge a complaint. The Committee considered that any report of torture was a serious matter and that only through consideration of the merits could it be determined whether or not the allegations were defamatory. Furthermore, the Committee believed that the complainant's political and partisan commitment adduced by the State party did not impede consideration of this complaint, in accordance with the provisions of article 22, paragraph 2, of the Convention.

State party's merits observations

8.1   In its observations of 3 April 2003 and 25 September 2003, the State party challenges the complainant's allegations and reiterates its position regarding admissibility.

8.2   In relation to the allegations concerning the State party's "complicity" and inertia vis-à-vis "practices of torture", the State party indicates that it has set up preventive[3] and dissuasive[4] machinery to combat torture so as to prevent any act which might violate the dignity and physical integrity of any individual.

8.3   Concerning the allegations relating to the "practice of torture" and the "impunity of the perpetrators of torture", the State party considers that the complainant has not presented any evidence to support his claims. It emphasizes that, contrary to the complainant's allegations, Tunisia has taken all necessary legal and practical steps, in judicial and administrative bodies, to prevent the practice of torture and prosecute any offenders, in accordance with articles 4, 5 and 13 of the Convention. Equally, according to the State party, the complainant has offered no grounds for his inertia and failure to act to take advantage of the effective legal opportunities available to him to bring his case before the judicial and administrative authorities (see para. 6). Concerning the Committee's decision on admissibility, the State party emphasizes that the complainant cites not only "incidents" dating back to 1991, but also "incidents" dating from 1995 and 1996, that is, a time when the Convention against Torture was fully incorporated into Tunisian domestic law and when he reports "ill-treatment" that he claims to have suffered while being held in "Mahdia prison". Hence the statute of limitations has not expired, and the complainant should urgently act to interrupt the limitation period, either by contacting the judicial authorities directly, or by performing an act which has the effect of interrupting the limitation. The State party also mentions the scope for the complainant to lodge an appeal for compensation for any serious injury caused by a public official in the performance of his

---

[3] This includes instruction in human rights values in training schools for the security forces, the Higher Institute of the Judiciary and the National School for training and retraining of staff and supervisors in prisons and correctional institutions; a human-rights-related code of conduct aimed at senior law enforcement officials; and the transfer of responsibility for prisons and correctional institutions from the Ministry of the Interior to the Ministry of Justice and Human Rights.

[4] A legislative reference system has been set up: contrary to the complainant's allegation that the Tunisian authorities have not criminalized acts of torture, the State party indicates that it has ratified the Convention against Torture without reservations, and that the Convention forms an integral part of Tunisian domestic law and may be invoked before the courts. The provisions of criminal law relating to torture are severe and precise (Criminal Code, art. 101 bis).

duties,[5] noting that the limitation period stands at 15 years.[6] The State party points out that the Tunisian courts have always acted systematically to remedy deficiencies in the law on acts of torture (see para. 4.10).

8.4 As for the allegations of failure to respect guarantees relating to judicial procedure, the State party regards them as unfounded. According to the State party, the authorities did not prevent the complainant from lodging a complaint before the courts—on the contrary, he opted not to make use of domestic remedies. As for the "obligation" of judges to ignore statements made as a result of torture, the State party cites article 15 of the Convention against Torture, and considers that it is incumbent on the accused to provide the judge with at least basic evidence that his statement has been made in an unlawful manner. In this way he would confirm the truth of his allegations by presenting a medical report or a certificate proving that he had lodged a complaint with the public prosecutor's office, or even by displaying obvious traces of torture or ill-treatment to the court. However, the State party points out that although, in the case relating to Mr. Thabti, the court had ordered a medical check for all the prisoners who so wished, the complainant voluntarily opted not to make such a request, preferring to reiterate his allegations of "ill-treatment" to the court, for the purpose of focusing on himself the attention of the observers attending the hearing. The complainant justifies his refusal to undergo the medical examination ordered by the court on the grounds that the doctors would behave in a "compliant" manner. The State party replies that the doctors are appointed by the examining magistrate or the court from among the doctors working in the prison administration and doctors who have no connection with it and who enjoy a reputation and integrity above all suspicion. Lastly, according to the State party, the complainant did not deem it necessary to lodge a complaint either during his detention or during his trial, and his refusal to undergo a medical examination illustrates the baselessness of his allegations and the fact that his actions form part of a strategy adopted by the "ENNAHDA" illegal extremist movement in order to discredit Tunisian institutions by alleging acts of torture and ill-treatment but not making use of available remedies.

8.5 Concerning the allegations relating to the trial, according to the State party, although the complainant acknowledges that two previous cases against him in 1983 and 1986 were dismissed for lack of evidence, he continues nevertheless to accuse the legal authorities systematically of bias. In addition, contrary to the complainant's allegations that during his trial and during questioning the examining magistrate attached to the Tunis military court denied him the assistance of counsel, the State party points out that Mr. Thabti himself refused such assistance. According to the State party, the examining magistrate, in accordance with the applicable legislation, reminded the complainant of his right not to reply except in the presence of his counsel, but the accused opted to do without such assistance, while refusing to answer the examining magistrate's questions. Given the complainant's silence, the magistrate warned him, in accordance with article 74 of the Code of Criminal Procedure, that he would embark on examination proceedings, and noted this warning in the record. Concerning the complainant's claim that he was found guilty on the sole basis of his confession, the State party points out that, under the last paragraph of article 69 and article 152 of the Code of Criminal Procedure, a confession on the part of the accused cannot relieve the judge of the obligation to seek other evidence, while confessions, like all items of evidence, are a matter for the independent appreciation of the judge. On that basis, it is a constant of Tunisian case law that an accused cannot be found guilty on the sole basis of a confession.[7] In the case in question, the basis for the court's decision, in addition to the confessions made by the complainant throughout the judicial proceedings, was statements by witnesses, testimony by his accomplices and items of evidence.

8.6 Concerning the allegations relating to prison conditions, and in particular the transfers between one prison and another, which the complainant considers an abuse, the State party points out that, in keeping with the applicable regulations, transfers are decided upon in the light of the different stages of the proceedings, the number of cases and the courts which have competence for specific areas. The prisons are grouped in three categories: for persons held awaiting trial; for persons serving custodial sentences; and semi-open prisons for persons found guilty of ordinary offences, which are authorized to organize agricultural labour. According to the State party, as the status of the complainant had changed

---

[5] Under the Administrative Court Act of 1 June 1972, the State may be held responsible even when it is performing a sovereign act if its representatives, agents or officials have caused material or moral injury to a third person. The injured party may demand from the State compensation for the injury suffered, under article 84 of the Code of Obligations and Contracts, without prejudice to the direct liability of its officials vis-à-vis the injured parties.

[6] Administrative Court – judgement N° 1013 of 10 May 1003 and judgement N° 21816 of 24 January 1997.

[7] Judgement N° 4692 of 30 July 1996, published in the Revue de Jurisprudence et Législation (R.J.L.); judgement N° 8616 of 25 February 1974 R.J.L. 1975; and judgement N° 7943 of 3 September 1973 R.J.L. 1974.

from that of remand prisoner to that of a prisoner serving a custodial sentence, and bearing in mind the requirements as to investigations in his case or in other similar cases, he was transferred from one prison to another, in accordance with the applicable regulations. Moreover, the conditions in which the complainant was held, wherever he was held, were in keeping with the prison regulations governing conditions for holding prisoners in order to ensure prisoners' physical and moral safety. The State party also considers baseless the complainant's allegations improperly equating the conditions in which he was held with degrading treatment. It points out that prisoners' rights are scrupulously protected in Tunisia, without any discrimination, whatever the status of the prisoner, in a context of respect for human dignity, in accordance with international standards and Tunisian legislation. Medical, psychological and social supervision is provided, and family visits are allowed.

8.7 Contrary to the allegations that the medical consequences suffered by the complainant are due to torture, the State party rejects any causal link. Moreover, according to the State party, the complainant was treated for everyday medical problems and received appropriate care. Lastly, following an examination by the prison doctor, the complainant was taken to see an ophthalmologist, who prescribed a pair of glasses on 21 January 1997.

8.8 Concerning the allegations that he was denied visits, according to the State party the complainant regularly received visits from his wife, Aicha Thabti, and his brother Mohamed Thabti, in accordance with the prison regulations, as demonstrated by the visitors' records in the prisons in which he was held.

8.9 Concerning the allegations relating to administrative supervision and the social position of Mr. Thabti's family, according to the State party, the administrative supervision to which the complainant was subject after having served his prison term, and which he equates with ill-treatment, is in fact an additional punishment for which provision is made in article 5 of the Criminal Code. The State party therefore considers that the punishment cannot be regarded as ill-treatment under the Convention against Torture. Lastly, contrary to the complainant's allegations, the State party maintains that the complainant's family is not suffering from any form of harassment or restrictions, and that his wife and his children are in possession of their passports.

Observations by the complainant

9.1 In his observations dated 20 May 2003, the complainant seeks to respond to each of the points contained in the above observations by the State party.

9.2 Concerning the preventive arrangements for combating torture, the complainant considers that the State party has confined itself to listing an arsenal of laws and measures of an administrative and political nature which, he says, are not put into effect in any way. To support this assertion he cites reports prepared by the non-governmental organization "National Council for Fundamental Freedoms in Tunisia" (CNLT).[8]

9.3 In relation to the establishment of a legislative reference system to combat torture, the complainant considers that article 101 bis of the Code of Criminal Procedure was adopted belatedly in 1999, in particular in response to the concern expressed by the Committee against Torture at the fact that the wording of article 101 of the Criminal Code could be used to justify serious abuses involving violence during questioning. He also claims that this new article is not applied, and attaches a list of the victims of repression in Tunisia between 1991 and 1998 prepared by the non-governmental organization "Vérité-Action". He also points out that the cases cited by the State party to demonstrate its willingness to act to combat torture relate only to accusations of abuse of authority and violence and assault, as well as offences under the ordinary law, and not to cases of torture leading to death or cases involving physical and moral harm suffered by the victims of torture.

9.4 Concerning the practice of torture and impunity, the complainant maintains that torturers do enjoy impunity, and that in particular no serious investigation has been carried out into those suspected of committing crimes of torture. Contrary to the claims made by the State party, he states that he endeavoured to lodge a complaint with the military court on several occasions, but that the president of the court always ignored his statements relating to torture on the grounds that he had no medical report in his possession. According to the reports prepared by CNLT, the court heard from the various accused and their counsel a long account of the atrocities committed by the officials of the State security division. According to the complainant, from among the total number of 170 prisoners scheduled to be tried before the Bouchoucha military court, the prison authorities selected only 25 to be given medical checks by military doctors. He claims that he was not informed of this check when he was being held in remand, but learned of it only in court. According to the complainant, the president ignored the fact that the other accused had not had medical checks, and it is false to claim that he himself freely

---

[8] "Le procès-Tournant : A propos des procès militaires de Bouchoucha et de Bab Saadoun en 1992", October 1992; "Pour la réhabilitation de l'indépendance de la justice", April 2000–December 2001.

opted not to demand one. When apprised of this fact, the president simply ignored the objections of the prisoners and their counsel, including the complainant, in flagrant breach of the provisions of the law relating to the prisoners' right to a medical report and their constitutional right to be heard, as the CNLT report confirms. According to the complainant, this is proved by the State party's acknowledgement that during the hearing he raised allegations of ill-treatment. In addition, according to the complainant, whereas a State governed by the rule of law should automatically follow up any report of a criminal act which may be regarded as a serious offence, the Tunisian authorities have always contented themselves with dismissing the claims as "false, contradictory and defamatory", without taking the trouble to launch investigations to determine the facts in accordance with the requirements of Tunisian criminal procedure. The complainant considers that his allegations are at the very least plausible in terms of the detail of the torture he suffered (names, places and treatment inflicted), but the State party contents itself with a blanket denial. The complainant did not mention torturers because of their membership of the security forces, but because of specific and repeated attacks on his physical and moral integrity and his private and family life. The initiation of an investigation designed to check whether a person belonging to the security forces has committed acts of torture or other acts does not constitute a violation of the presumption of innocence but a legal step which is vital in order to investigate a case and, if appropriate, place it before the judicial authorities for decision. In relation to appeals before the courts, the complainant considers that the State party has confined itself to repeating the description of legal options open to victims set out in its previous submissions without responding to the last two sentences of paragraph 7.2 of the decision on admissibility. He reiterates that the theoretical legal options described by the State party are inoperative, while listing in support of this conclusion cases in which the rights of the victims were ignored. He points out that the case law cited by the State party relates to cases tried under ordinary law and not to prisoners of opinion.

9.5 Concerning the complainant's inertia and lack of action, he considers that the State party is inconsistent in holding that acts of torture are regarded as serious offences in Tunisian law and accordingly prosecuted automatically, while awaiting a complaint by the victim before taking action. He also re-emphasizes his serious efforts described above to demand a medical examination and an investigation into the torture he had suffered. With particular reference to a report prepared by CNLT,[9] he mentions the circumstances surrounding the medical examinations of 25 prisoners, carried out with the aim of giving an appearance of respect for procedural guarantees, and the lack of integrity of the appointed doctors.[10] He points out that video recordings were made of the hearings in the Bouchoucha military court, which could then be replayed to check each complainant's statements.

9.6 Concerning the allegations relating to the trial, the complainant points out, first, that the dismissal of proceedings against him in 1983 and 1986 took place in a political context of détente (in 1983 and 1984, the phased release of the leaders of the Mouvement de la Tendance Islamique, which became ENNAHDA in 1989) and the legitimization of a new regime (a presidential amnesty was proclaimed after the 1987 coup d'état), and illustrated the fact that the courts were dependent on the executive branch (as shown in reports prepared by non-governmental organizations).[11] Second, in relation to his refusal of the assistance of counsel, the complainant provides the following corrections and produces a report prepared by CNLT.[12] Appearing before examining magistrate Ayed Ben Gueyid, attached to the Tunis military court, the complainant reiterated his request to be assisted by a court-appointed lawyer or one instructed by his family. The complainant designated Mr. Najib ben Youssef, who had been contacted by his family. This lawyer advised him to consult Mr. Moustafa El-Gharbi, who was able to assist the complainant only from the fourth week of the trial onwards, and was able to pay him only one or two visits in the 9 April prison, under close surveillance by prison guards. In response to the complainant's request for the assistance of a lawyer, the military examining magistrate replied "No lawyer", prompting the complainant to say "No lawyer, no statement". Following this declaration, the complainant reports that he was violently beaten by military policemen, in a room next to the office of the military examining magistrate, during a break which was imposed and ordered by the magistrate. The complainant was then placed in solitary confinement in the 9 April prison in Tunis for two months. Following this punishment, the examining magistrate's file was missing from the first hearing attended by the complainant, a matter which the

---

[9] Available for information in the file.

[10] "The role played by some of the doctors was no less serious, in the sense of what they did during the torture by assisting the torturers [to assess] the state of the victim and the degree of torture the victim could bear [...] information gathered from the torture victims or from analyses carried out in which famous doctors knowingly concealed the truth about the causes of the injuries suffered by the accused during episodes of physical torture" – CNLT report, October 2002.

[11] International Commission of Jurists, report on Tunisia, 12 March 2003.

[12] Available for information in the file.

complainant explained to the president of the court by describing what had happened before the military examining magistrate.

9.7 Concerning the allegations relating to his confession, the complainant maintains that his confession was extracted under torture, and, citing the reports of CNLT, states that such methods are used in political trials and sometimes in trials involving offences under ordinary law. Concerning the testimony of the prosecution witness Mohamed Ben Ali Ben Romdhane, his fellow prisoner, the complainant states that he does not know this person, and that he was not among the 297 persons who were tried in Bouchoucha court, and calls on the State party to produce the transcript of the testimony provided by this person, together with the court file, to make it possible to check whether the court took its decision on the basis of a confession obtained as a result of torture. According to the complainant, the reference to this witness is pure invention on the part of the torturers. Secondly, the complainant points out that, even if a prosecution witness had appeared, the accused should have had an opportunity to challenge his testimony or to confront him, which did not happen.

9.8 Concerning the conditions in which he was held, and concerning visits, the complainant considers that the State party has once again confined itself to brief and general observations in response to his plentiful, specific and substantiated evidence. He explains that he was transferred for purposes of punishment, and not for any matter related to cases pending before the courts, and in that connection provides the following chronology:

> 6 April 1991 Arrested and held in the basement of the Interior Ministry; 13 May 1991, transferred to Mornag prison incommunicado.
>
> 4 June 1991 Handed over to the political police to sign the transcript of the interrogation, without being informed of its content; handed over to the military examining magistrate, then at 11 p.m. transferred to the 9 April prison in Tunis, where he was held until the end of November 1991 (including two months in solitary confinement).
>
> 1 December 1991 Transferred to Borj Erroumi prison in Bizerte (70 kilometres from his family home).
>
> 4 July 1992 Transferred to the 9 April prison in Tunis, where he was held until 15 September 1992; this period corresponded to that of the court hearings.
>
> 28 August 1992 Sentenced to six years' non-suspended imprisonment and five years' administrative supervision.
>
> 15 September 1992 Transferred to Borj Erroumi prison in Bizerte, where he was held until 4 July 1993.
>
> 4 July 1993 Transferred to Mahdia prison (200 kilometres from his home), where he was held until 19 September 1993.
>
> 19 September 1993 Transferred to Sousse prison (160 kilometres from his home), where he was held until 4 April 1994.
>
> 4 April 1994 Transferred to Mahdia prison, where he was held until the end of December 1994.
>
> End of December 1994 Transferred to 9 April prison in Tunis; interrogated and tortured at the Interior Ministry for four consecutive days.
>
> End of December 1995 Transferred to Mahdia prison; hunger strike from the middle to the end of February 1996 to support a demand for better prison conditions.
>
> End of February 1996 Transferred to El Houerib prison in Kairouan (250 kilometres from his home) following his hunger strike.
>
> 20 March 1996 Transfer to Sousse prison; three weeks' hunger strike in January 1997 to support a demand for better prison conditions.
>
> 7 February 1997 Transferred to Rejim Maatoug prison (600 kilometres from his home, in the middle of the desert).
>
> 27 February 1997 Transfer to Sousse prison.
>
> 27 May 1997 Released, placed under administrative supervision for five years and house arrest at Nekrif-Remada (630 kilometres from his family home).
>
> 1 October 1997 Fled Tunisia.

9.9 The complainant explains that each time he was transferred, his family was obliged to spend two or three months ascertaining his new place of detention, since the prison administration provided such information only very sparingly. According to the complainant, the purpose of these transfers was to deprive him of the psychological and moral support of his family, and thus to punish him. He points out that the prison entry and exit logs can confirm his claims. He explains that denial of visits constituted a form of revenge against him each time he sought to exercise a right and took action to that end, for example in the form of a hunger strike. In addition, the complainant's family found it difficult to exercise the right to visit him because of the many transfers, the remoteness of the places of detention and the conditions imposed on the visitors—the complainant's wife was ill-treated to make her remove her scarf, and guards were permanently present between two sheets of wire mesh about one metre apart separating her from the complainant.

9.10 Concerning the allegations relating to the provision of care, the complainant repeats that he was denied the right to consult a doctor to diagnose the consequences of the torture he had suffered, and draws the Committee's attention to the medical certificate contained in his file. Concerning the treatment cited by the State party, the complainant points out that the medical check was carried out three weeks after his hunger strike, that glasses were prescribed for him when he was in danger of going blind, and that they were supplied only after a delay of about two months.

9.11 In relation to administrative supervision, the complainant considers that any punishment, including those provided for in the Tunisian Criminal Code, may be characterized as inhuman and degrading if the goal pursued is neither the "rehabilitation of the offender" nor his reconciliation with his social environment. He explains that he was forced to undergo administrative supervision 650 kilometres from his family home, in other words placed under house arrest, which was not stipulated in his sentence. He adds that each time he reported to the police station to sign the supervision log, he was ill-treated, sometimes beaten and humiliated by the police officers. According to the complainant, who produces a CNLT report,[13] administrative supervision serves only to bolster the police's stranglehold over the freedom of movement of former prisoners.

9.12 Concerning the situation of his family, the complainant records the suffering caused by the police surveillance and various forms of intimidation. He mentions that his eldest son was repeatedly slapped in front of his brothers and mother at the door of their home when he returned from school, and questioned at the regional police station about what his family was living on. In addition, the members of the family received their passports only after the complainant arrived in Switzerland on 25 May 1998 and was granted asylum. And the first members of the family received their passports only seven months later, on 9 December 1998.

9.13 In relation to the ENNAHDA movement, the complainant maintains that the organization is well known for its democratic ideals and its opposition to dictatorship and impunity, contrary to the State party's explanations. In addition, he challenges the accusations of terrorism levelled by the State party.

9.14 Lastly, according to the complainant, the State party is endeavouring to place the entire burden of proof on the victim, accusing him of inertia and failure to act, seeking protection behind a panoply of legal measures which theoretically enable victims to lodge complaints and evading its duty to ensure that those responsible for crimes, including that of torture, are automatically prosecuted. According to the complainant, the State party is thus knowingly ignoring the fact that international law and practice in relation to torture place greater emphasis on the role of States and their duties in order to enable proceedings to be completed. The complainant notes that the State party places the burden of proof on the victim alone, even though the supporting evidence, such as legal files, registers of police custody and visits, and so on, is in the sole hands of the State party and unavailable to the complainant. Referring to European case law,[14] the complainant points out that the European Court and Commission call on States parties, in the case of allegations of torture or ill-treatment, to conduct an effective investigation into the allegations of ill-treatment and not to content themselves with citing the theoretical arsenal of options available to the victim to lodge a complaint.

Consideration of the merits

10.1 The Committee examined the complaint, taking due account of all the information provided to it by the parties, in accordance with article 22, paragraph 4, of the Convention.

10.2 The Committee took note of the State party's observations of 3 April 2003 challenging the admissibility of the complaint. It notes that the points raised by the State party are not such as to prompt reconsideration of the Committee's decision on admissibility, notably owing to the lack of new or additional information from the State party on the matter of the investigations voluntarily carried out by the State party (see para. 7.2). The Committee therefore does not consider that it should review its decision on admissibility.

10.3 The Committee therefore proceeds to examine the merits of the complaint, and notes that the complainant alleges violations by the State party of article 1; article 2, paragraph 1; article 4; article 5; article 12; article 13; article 14; article 15; and article 16 of the Convention.

10.4 On article 12 of the Convention, the Committee notes that article 12 places an obligation on the authorities to proceed automatically to a prompt and impartial investigation whenever there is

---

[13] Available for information in the file.

[14] Guide to Jurisprudence on Torture and Ill-Treatment – Article 3 of the European Convention for the Protection of Human Rights, Debra Long (APT); *Ribitsch* v. *Austria*; *Assenov* v. *Bulgaria*.

reasonable ground to believe that an act of torture or ill-treatment has been committed, no special importance being attached to the grounds for the suspicion.[15]

10.5 The Committee notes that the complainant complained of acts of torture committed against him to the Bouchoucha military court at his trial from 9 July 1992 onwards, in the presence of the national press and international human rights observers. It also notes that the State party acknowledges that the complainant reiterated his allegations of ill-treatment several times before the court, in order, according to the State party, to focus the attention of the observers attending the hearing. The Committee also takes note of the detailed and substantiated information provided by the complainant regarding his hunger strikes in the 9 April prison over 12 days in July 1992 in Tunis, and in Mahdia over 8 days in October 1995 and 10 days in March 1996, as a protest against the conditions in which he was being held and the ill-treatment to which he was subjected. The Committee notes that the State party did not comment on this information, and considers that these elements, taken together, should have been enough to trigger an investigation, which was not held, in breach of the obligation to proceed to a prompt and impartial investigation under article 12 of the Convention.

10.6 The Committee observes that article 13 of the Convention does not require either the formal lodging of a complaint of torture under the procedure laid down in national law or an express statement of intent to institute and sustain a criminal action arising from the offence, and that it is enough for the victim simply to bring the facts to the attention of an authority of the State for the latter to be obliged to consider it as a tacit but unequivocal expression of the victim's wish that the facts should be promptly and impartially investigated, as prescribed by this provision of the Convention.[16]

10.7 The Committee notes, as already indicated, that the complainant did complain of ill-treatment to the Bouchoucha military court, and resorted to hunger strikes in protest at the conditions imposed on him. Yet, notwithstanding the jurisprudence under article 13 of the Convention, the Committee notes the State party's position maintaining that the complainant should have made formal use of domestic remedies in order to lodge his complaint, for example by presenting to the court a certificate proving that a complaint had been lodged with the office of the public prosecutor, or displaying obvious traces of torture or ill-treatment, or submitting a medical report. On this latter point, to which the Committee wishes to draw its attention, it is clear that the complainant maintains that the president of the Bouchoucha court ignored his complaints of torture on the grounds that he had no medical report in his possession, that the complainant was informed only during his trial of the medical checks carried out on a portion of the accused during remand, and that the president of the court ignored his demands for his right to a medical report to be respected. On the other hand, the State party maintains that the complainant voluntarily opted not to request a medical examination although the court had ordered such examinations for all prisoners who wished to undergo one. The Committee refers to its consideration of the report submitted by Tunisia in 1997, at which time it recommended that the State party should ensure that medical examinations are provided automatically following allegations of abuse, and thus without any need for the alleged victim to make a formal request to that effect.

10.8 In the light of its practice relating to article 13 and the observations set out above, the Committee considers that the breaches enumerated are incompatible with the obligation stipulated in article 13 to proceed to a prompt investigation.

10.9 Finally, the Committee considers that there are insufficient elements to make a finding on the alleged violation of other provisions of the Convention raised by the complainant at the time of adoption of this decision.

11. The Committee against Torture, acting under article 22, paragraph 7, of the Convention, is of the view that the facts before it disclose a violation of articles 12 and 13 of the Convention against Torture and Other Cruel, Inhuman or Degrading Treatment or Punishment.

12. Pursuant to rule 112, paragraph 5, of its rules of procedure, the Committee urges the State party to conduct an investigation into the complainant's allegations of torture and ill-treatment, and to inform it, within 90 days from the date of the transmittal of this decision, of the steps it has taken in response to the views expressed above.

---

[15] Communication N° 59/1996 (*Encarnación Blanco Abad v. Spain*).
[16] Communications N° 6/1990 (*Henri Unai Parot v. Spain*) and N° 59/1996 (*Encarnación Blanco Abad v. Spain*).

Communication N° 188/2001

Submitted by: Mr. Imed ABDELLI (represented by the non-governmental organization Vérité-Action)
Alleged victim: The complainant
State party: Tunisia
Declared admissible: 20 November 2002
Date of adoption of Views: 14 November 2003

Subject matter: torture of complainant by police and intelligence services

Procedural issues: exhaustion of domestic remedies; abuse of the right to lodge a complaint

Substantive issues: failure to take effective measures to prevent torture; failure to ensure that acts of torture are offences under State party criminal law; failure to institute legal proceedings against those responsible for torture; use of evidence obtained as a result of torture; lack of investigation of the acts of torture and examination of the allegations of torture; sentence based on a confession obtained as a result of torture; cruel, inhuman and degrading treatment or punishment

Articles of the Convention: 1, 2 (1), 4, 5, 11, 12, 13, 14, 15, 16

1.1 The complainant is Mr. Imed Abdelli, a Tunisian citizen, born on 3 March 1966 in Tunis and resident in Switzerland since 7 July 1998, where he has refugee status. He claims to be the victim of violations by Tunisia of the provisions of article 1, article 2, paragraph 1, article 4, article 5, article 11, article 12, article 13, article 14, article 15 and article 16 of the Convention. He is represented by the non-governmental organization Vérité-Action.

1.2 Tunisia ratified the Convention against Torture and Other Cruel, Inhuman or Degrading Treatment or Punishment and made the Declaration under article 22 of the Convention on 23 September 1988.

The facts as submitted by the complainant

2.1 The complainant states that he was an active member of the Islamist organization ENNAHDA (formerly MTI). One day in July 1987, at 1.30 a.m., the complainant was arrested at his home, on the grounds that he belonged to an unauthorized association. He says that, while he was being arrested, the police manhandled his mother and beat two of his brothers with their truncheons. The complainant was held for 2 days at the district police station in a dirty cellar with no water; for 10 days in the holding cells in El Gorjani, from where he was taken daily to the Jebel Jelloud district police headquarters for questioning; and for one month at the Bouchoucha detention centre.

2.2 The complainant provides a detailed description of the different types of torture to which he was subjected.

2.3 The complainant describes what is customarily known as the "roast chicken" position, in which the victim is stripped naked, his hands tied and his legs folded between his arms, with an iron bar placed behind his knees, from which he is then suspended between two tables and beaten, in particular on the soles of his feet, his knees and his head. The complainant says that he was subjected to this torture for two sessions lasting more than one hour each. He adds that, during one of these sessions, his torturers also masturbated him to humiliate him and leave him exhausted.

2.4 The complainant also claims that he was subjected to "chair" torture, in which the victim is forced to kneel and to hold a chair as high as possible above his head, and is then whipped whenever he starts to lower the chair.

2.5 Following this, for one month, in the detention centre of the intelligence service in Bouchoucha, the complainant was subjected to interrogation under torture, namely, the "roast chicken" position, until he passed out. He adds that, every day, when being escorted from his cell to the offices, he was struck across the face and hit with truncheons. In addition, according to the complainant, his family was unable to obtain any information about him and his mother was detained, for an entire day, in the premises of the Ministry of the Interior for having requested a meeting with her son. The complainant asserts that he witnessed torture being inflicted on other detainees, such as Zoussef Bouthelja and Moncef Zarrouk, the latter having died in his cell on 13 August 1987 as a result of the ill-treatment to which he had been subjected.

2.6 From the end of August to 25 October 1987, the complainant was detained in Tunis prison in an overcrowded cell with no facilities.

2.7 On 25 October 1987, the complainant was placed in Mornag prison, after being sentenced to two years' immediate imprisonment. When the indictment against him was quashed, he was released on 24 December 1987.

2.8 Two months later, the complainant was questioned by the police for possession of a video cassette showing the bloodshed of 1987 committed

120

by the State security services of Sousse governorate. The complainant was held for 15 days at the headquarters of the Ministry of the Interior and was subjected to interrogation accompanied by slaps, beatings and intimidation. He was released on 30 March 1988.

2.9 According to the complainant, following the April 1989 elections, he stopped coming back to his family home because of a wave of arrests being conducted at the time, targeted in particular against opposition party members and sympathizers. The complainant claims that in 1990 his family was subjected to harassment (night-time raids, summonses for questioning and confiscation of passports). In May 1991, the complainant's brothers Lofti and Nabil were detained and tortured in order to get information about the complainant.

2.10 On 20 November 1991, at 7 a.m., the complainant was detained by the State security services. He maintains that, for the next 25 days he was subjected to various forms of torture. The complainant mentions the practice of "balanco", in which the victim is held upside down and immersed in dirty water with an admixture of bleach and other chemicals until he chokes. The victim adds that his torturers tied a piece of string to his penis which they then repeatedly tugged in all directions, until it started emitting a mixture of blood and sperm.

2.11 The complainant was also placed on a table where he was masturbated and then beaten on his erect penis. The complainant claims that he was given injections in his testicles, which caused first strong arousal and then intolerable pain. He adds that he was subjected to sessions of beatings administered by experts, in which he was struck on both ears at the same time until he passed out, and claims that his hearing has been permanently damaged as a result. He also claims that his torturers were assisted by a doctor, to ensure that torture was applied in the most effective doses.

2.12 According to the complainant, on the twenty-fifth day, the Director of State Security, Ezzedine Djmail, stubbed out cigarettes on his body, notably in the region of his genitalia.

2.13 On 13 January 1992, the complainant was taken to Tunis central prison.

2.14 After appearing briefly before the judge, on 12 March 1992, the complainant was sentenced to two years' immediate imprisonment and three years' administrative supervision for helping to support an unauthorized association, and this verdict was upheld on appeal on 7 July 1992. The complainant submits a statement by a representative of the non-governmental organization Human Rights Watch, who attended one session of the trial and states that his case was disturbing.

2.15 The complainant states that his request for a medical check was refused and that he was even threatened by a member of the prison service with further torture if he dared complain of his treatment to the judge.

2.16 After six months in Tunis central prison, the complainant was repeatedly transferred between different penal institutions in the country, including El Kef prison, from 19 July to 15 October 1992; Kasserine, from 15 to 18 October 1992; and then Gafsa, and others, which transfers, he maintains, were designed to prevent him from having any contact with his family. The complainant says that he was treated like an "untouchable", in other words, he was barred from speaking with or being helped by other detainees; his mail and family visits were obstructed. The complainant says that his mother was always abused when she visited the prison—her headscarf was ripped off and she was summoned for questioning after the visits.

2.17 On leaving Gafsa prison on 11 January 1994, the complainant was taken to the governorate security headquarters to fill in a report sheet and to answer questions about the activities of other prisoners and his future plans. He was ordered to report at Gorjani district police headquarters as soon as he arrived in Tunis.

2.18 The complainant was also required to report for administrative supervision twice a day, at 10 a.m. and 4 p.m. at the local police station, and to report daily to the district police headquarters. According to the complainant, these supervision arrangements had the practical effect of house arrest, accompanied by a prohibition on employment. In addition, several weeks after his release, the complainant was required to report for questioning by various security bodies, including the national guard station on route X in Bardo, the national guard investigation centre in Bardo, the intelligence service, the State security service and the national guard barracks in Aouina. These bodies all subjected him to questioning and demanded that he collaborate with them in monitoring members of the opposition, on pain of continued harassment against him and his family, through such measures as night-time raids and summonses for questioning.

2.19 The complainant claims that, after he threatened to defy the administrative supervision arrangements, he was able to resume his university studies, but these were still severely disrupted by the repeated summonses to Sijoumi police headquarters for questioning, because of his refusal to collaborate.

2.20 In spring 1995, the complainant was rearrested on the grounds that he had attempted to flee the country. He was held for 10 days and subjected to ill-treatment, comprising beatings, slaps and threats of sexual abuse, in an endeavour to force him to collaborate. Under this coercion, the complainant signed a minuted record on 12 April 1995, certifying that he was an active member of the unauthorized organization ENNAHDA.

2.21 The complainant was then sentenced, on 18 May 1995, by the court of first instance in Tunis to three years' immediate imprisonment and five years' administrative supervision; this verdict was upheld on appeal on 31 May 1996.

2.22 The complainant says that he requested the judge at the court of first instance in Tunis to protect him from the torture to which he was subjected daily in prison, and also informed him that he had been on hunger strike for a week. According to the complainant, the police then escorted him from the courtroom in the presence of the judge, who did not react.

2.23 While held in Tunis central prison from 13 April 1995 to 31 August 1996, the complainant was subjected to torture which, on this occasion, comprised the practice of "falka", in which the torturers tie the victim's legs to a bar and raise his feet in the air so that they can whip the soles of his feet. The complainant explains that the deputy director of the prison personally participated in these torture sessions, tying him, for example, to the door of his cell before hitting him on the head with a truncheon until he passed out. At the end of August and beginning of September 1995, the complainant was placed in solitary confinement and deprived of washing facilities. He then went on a hunger strike, demanding medical attention and an end to the discriminatory treatment against him.

2.24 After being transferred to Grombalia prison, the complainant continued his hunger strike from 28 November to 13 December 1997 and, once again, was beaten on the orders of the director.

2.25 The complainant states that, during his years of detention, he was only ever able to have one meeting with his lawyers, and that was in the presence of a prison officer.

2.26 After his release on 12 April 1998, the complainant was subjected to harassment, in the form of summonses for questioning, interrogation and daily supervision, until he fled the country for Switzerland on 22 June 1998, where he was granted refugee status in December 1998.

2.27 The complainant states that, since he fled the country, members of his family have been subjected to interrogation and other forms of humiliation, including a refusal to issue a passport to his mother.

2.28 The complainant provides a list of people who committed acts of torture against him, namely, Ezzeddine Jnaieh, Director of State Security in 1991; Mohamed Ennaceur, Director of General Intelligence in 1995; Moncef Ben Gbila, senior officer in the State Security Service in 1987; Mojahid Farhi, lieutenant colonel; Belhassen Kilani, full lieutenant; Salim Boughnia, full lieutenant; Faouzi El Attrouss, major; Hédi Ezzitouni, full lieutenant; Abderrahman Guesmi, Interior Ministry official; Faycal Redissi, Interior Ministry official; Tahar Dlaiguia, Bouchoucha detention centre official; Mohamed Ben Amor, State Security; Hassen Khemiri, warrant officer; Mohamed Kassem, deputy director of Messadine prison in 1997; Habib Haoula, prison wing supervisor at Messadine prison; and Mohamed Zrelli, prison wing supervisor at Grombalia prison. The complainant adds that the then Minister for Internal Affairs, Abdallah Kallel, should be held responsible for the treatment to which he was subjected since, at a press conference held on 22 May 1991, the minister named him as the person responsible for a campaign of terror.

2.29 The complainant describes the after-effects of his torture and the conditions in which he was held, which include hearing problems (he submits a certificate from a Swiss ear, nose and throat specialist), rheumatism, skin disorders, an ulcer and mental problems.

2.30 As to whether all domestic remedies have been exhausted, the complainant argues that, although such remedies are provided in Tunisian law, they are unavailable in practice because of the bias of judges and the impunity granted to those responsible for violations. He adds that the regulations governing the activities of bodies which play a role in upholding human rights, such as the Higher Committee for Human Rights and Fundamental Freedoms and the Constitutional Council, prevent them from supporting complaints of torture. To back up his argument, he cites the reports of such non-governmental organizations as Amnesty International.

The complaint

3.1 The complainant maintains that the Tunisian Government has breached the following articles of the Convention against Torture and Other Cruel, Inhuman or Degrading Treatment or Punishment:

> Article 1. The practices described above, such as "falka", the "roast chicken" position, "balanco", the "chair", etc., to which the complainant was subjected, constitute acts of torture.
>
> Article 2, paragraph 1. It is alleged that the State party not only failed to take effective measures to prevent torture, but even mobilized its administrative machinery and, in particular, its police force as an instrument of torture against the complainant.

Article 4. It is alleged that the State party has not ensured that all the acts of torture to which the complainant has been subjected are offences under its criminal law.

Article 5. It is alleged that the State party has instituted no legal proceedings against those responsible for torturing the complainant.

Article 11. It is alleged that the authorities have not used their supervisory powers to prevent torture; instead, specific instructions have been given that torture is to be applied.

Article 12. It is alleged that the State party has not carried out an investigation of the acts of torture committed against the complainant.

Article 13. It is alleged that the State party has not effectively upheld the complainant's right to lodge a complaint with the competent authorities.

Article 14. It is alleged that the State party has ignored the complainant's right to make a complaint and has thereby deprived him of his right to redress and rehabilitation.

Article 15. It is alleged that the complainant was sentenced in 1992 and 1995 to prison sentences on the basis of confessions obtained as a result of torture.

Article 16. The repressive measures and practices described above, such as solitary confinement, violation of the right to medical care and medicine and the right to send and receive mail, restriction of family visits, house arrest and harassment of his family, applied by the State party against the complainant constitute cruel, inhuman and degrading treatment or punishment.

3.2 The complainant also alleges that his right to practise his religion while in detention, his freedom of movement and his right to work were infringed by the administrative supervision measures applied against him, as was his right to continue his studies. He seeks redress for the harm inflicted on him and on his family, including cessation of the daily harassment of his family by the local police, and requests that they be granted passports.

State party's admissibility observations

4.1 On 4 December 2001, the State party challenged the admissibility of the complaint on the grounds that the complainant had neither employed nor exhausted available domestic remedies. It maintains, first, that the complainant may still have recourse to the available domestic remedies, since, under Tunisian law, the limitation period for acts alleged to be, and characterized as, serious offences is 10 years.

4.2 The State party explains that, under the criminal justice system, the complainant may submit a complaint, from within Tunisia or abroad, to a representative of the Public Prosecutor's Office with jurisdiction in the area in question. He may also authorize a Tunisian lawyer of his own choice to submit such a complaint or request a foreign lawyer to do so with the assistance of a Tunisian colleague.

4.3 Under the same rules of criminal procedure, the Public Prosecutor will receive the said complaint and institute a judicial inquiry. In accordance with article 53 of the Code of Criminal Procedure, the examining magistrate to whom the case is referred will hear the author of the complaint. In the light of this hearing, he may decide to hear witnesses, question suspects, undertake on-site investigations and seize physical evidence. He may also order expert studies and carry out any actions which he deems necessary for the uncovering of evidence, both in favour of and against the complainant, with a view to discovering the truth and verifying facts on which the trial court will be able to base its decision.

4.4 The State party explains that the complainant may, in addition, lodge with the examining magistrate during the pretrial proceedings an application for criminal indemnification for any harm suffered, over and above the criminal charges brought against those responsible for the offences against him.

4.5 If the examining magistrate deems that the public right of action is not exercisable, that the acts do not constitute a violation or that there is no prima facie case against the accused, he shall rule that there are no grounds for prosecution. If, on the other hand, the magistrate deems that the acts constitute an offence punishable by imprisonment, he shall send the accused before a competent court—which in the present instance, where a serious offence has been committed, would be the indictment chamber. All rulings by the examining magistrate are immediately communicated to all the parties to the proceedings, including the complainant who brought the criminal indemnification proceedings. Having been thus notified within a period of 48 hours, the complainant may, within four days, lodge an appeal against any ruling prejudicial to his interests. This appeal, submitted in writing or orally, is received by the clerk of the court. If there is prima facie evidence of the commission of an offence, the indictment chamber sends the accused before the competent court (criminal court or criminal division of a court of first instance), having given rulings on all the counts established during the proceedings. If it chooses, it may also order further information to be provided by one of its assessors or by the examining magistrate; it may also institute new proceedings, or conduct or order an inquiry into matters which have not yet been the subject of an examination. The decisions of the indictment chamber are subject to immediate enforcement.

4.6 A complainant seeking criminal indemnification may appeal on a point of law against a decision of the indictment chamber once it has been notified. This remedy is admissible when the indictment chamber rules that there are no grounds for prosecution; when it has ruled that the application for criminal indemnification is inadmissible, or that the prosecution is time-barred; when it has deemed the court to which the case has been referred to lack jurisdiction; or when it has omitted to make a ruling on one of the counts.

4.7 The State party stresses that, in conformity with article 7 of the Code of Criminal Procedure, the complainant may bring criminal indemnification proceedings before the court to which the case has been referred (criminal court or criminal division of the court of first instance) and, as appropriate, may lodge an appeal, either with the Court of Appeal if the offence in question is an ordinary offence, or with the criminal division of the Court of Appeal if it is a serious offence. The complainant may also appeal to the Court of Cassation.

4.8 Second, the State party maintains that the domestic remedies are effective. According to the State party, the Tunisian courts have systematically and consistently acted to remedy deficiencies in the law, and stiff sentences have been handed down on those responsible for abuses and violations of the law. The State party says that, between 1 January 1988 and 31 March 1995, judgements were handed down in 302 cases involving members of the police or the national guard under a variety of counts, 227 of which fell into the category of abuse of authority. The penalties imposed varied from fines to terms of imprisonment of up to several years.[1]

4.9 Third, the State party maintains that, given the complainant's "political and partisan" motives and his "offensive and defamatory" remarks, his complaint may be considered an abuse of the right to submit complaints.

4.10 The State party explains that the ideology and the political platform of the "movement" of which the complainant was an active member are based exclusively on religious principles, promoting an extremist view of religion which negates democratic rights and the rights of women. This is an illegal "movement", fomenting religious and racial hatred and employing violence. According to the State party, this "movement" perpetrated terrorist attacks which caused material damage and loss of life over the period 1990–1991. For that reason, and also because it is in breach of the Constitution and the law on political parties, this "movement" has not been recognized by the authorities.

4.11 The State party indicates that the complainant is making unsubstantiated allegations to the effect that "the Tunisian authorities have not criminalized these acts of torture …". According to the State party, this allegation is given the lie by Act N° 99-89 of 2 August 1999, whereby the legislature amended and transposed a number of provisions of the Criminal Code and incorporated the definition of torture as set out in the Convention against Torture.

Complainant's comments on State party's observations

5.1 In a letter of 7 May 2002, the complainant challenged the State party's argument that he was supposedly unwilling to turn to the Tunisian justice system and make use of domestic remedies.

5.2 The complainant believes that the recourse procedures are excessively protracted. He notes, in this context, that the appeal procedure against his conviction in 1995 comprised 18 sessions, lasting from June 1995 to the end of May 1996. According to the complainant, these delays were entirely due to the authorities, who repeatedly postponed consideration of his appeal because they were embarrassed to have to convict a person—who, to make matters worse, was a political opponent—for illegally attempting to leave the country. He says that this conviction would in itself be harmful to the image of the regime and that this made it harder to hand down a stiff sentence. He believes that this delay in a simple appeal procedure demonstrates that the lodging of a complaint of torture—even assuming that such a complaint would be accepted—would be an even more protracted process. The complainant also describes how, when his name appeared in various reports by non-governmental organizations, including after his conviction in 1995, the authorities reacted by worsening the conditions in which he was held, subjecting him to mental and corporal punishment and transferring him to prisons far from his family home, and harassing his family, who were placed under stricter supervision. In support of his arguments, he cites the case of Mr. Abderraouf Khémais Ben Sadok Laribi, who died in police custody as a result of ill-treatment. According to the complainant, even though the dead man's family lodged a complaint of intentional homicide against the Minister of the Interior on 9 August 1991, and even though the case received extensive media coverage, as a result of which his family received material compensation and an interview was granted with an adviser of the President, the case was closed without any effective

---

[1] The examples cited by the State party are available for information in the file.

investigation, while the minister in office at the time was given full protection by the Government.

5.3 The complainant believes that the recourse procedures would not lead to any satisfactory remedies. He enumerates the efforts he made, to no avail, in 1992 to seek a medical examination and, in 1995, to secure protection from the judicial authorities against the ill-treatment to which he was being subjected. For that reason, it seemed unlikely to the complainant that he would obtain satisfaction from the judicial authorities. The complainant explains that his case with the magistrate was not an isolated instance and, in that context, submits an extract from a report by the Tunisian Committee for Human Rights and Freedoms. He maintains that the judicial system is not independent and gave him no protection when he was convicted in 1992 and 1995. He says that he has been a victim of the "culture of torture" in Tunisia and that it was psychologically very difficult for him to submit his complaint to the Committee against Torture for fear of reprisals against his family. He adds, lastly, that his hunger strikes against his ill-treatment failed to bring any results, apart from some material concessions. Similarly, the letters he wrote to the administration of the prisons following these hunger strikes also proved unavailing. In addition, the transfer of the prison service to the Ministry of Justice has done nothing to change the complicity of the service in such practices. The complainant cites extracts from reports by the International Federation for Human Rights and the Tunisian Committee for Human Rights and Freedoms in support of his observation that complaints of torture do not succeed and that the authorities exert pressure to prevent the lodging of such complaints. He also maintains that the administrative supervision under which he was placed, which involved constant supervision by eight different authorities, accompanied by acts of intimidation, meant that lodging a complaint would have placed him in danger.

5.4 The complainant challenges the State party's arguments that a Tunisian lawyer can be instructed from abroad to lodge a complaint.

5.5 The complainant describes serious encroachments by the authorities on the free and independent exercise of the legal profession. According to the complainant, lawyers who dare to defend complaints of torture are subject to harassment and other abuses, including prison sentences. As an example, he cites the cases of the lawyers Néjib Hosny, Béchir Essid and Anouar Kosri, and quotes extracts from reports and statements by Amnesty International, the World Organization against Torture, the International Federation for Human Rights and the International Commission of Jurists. He adds, also on the basis of these reports by non-governmental organizations, that none of the complaints lodged by victims of torture over recent years, particularly following the promulgation in 1988 of article 13 bis of the Code of Criminal Procedure, providing for the possibility of medical visits, have been followed up. He also explains that, in certain cases, medical checks have been allowed after a long delay, once all traces of torture have disappeared, and that the checks are sometimes carried out by compliant doctors who will fail to find anything wrong with the detainees' physical condition, even if there are traces of torture. The complainant believes that, in these circumstances, it would not make much difference to appoint a lawyer.

5.6 The complainant cites as an obstacle the fact that not only is legal aid not an established practice in Tunisia, but that the procedures involved are not accompanied by the necessary safeguards.

5.7 The complainant stresses that the lodging of a complaint from abroad with the Tunisian authorities is likely to be covered by article 305, paragraph 3, of the Tunisian Code of Criminal Procedure, which provides that "any Tunisian who commits any of the offences mentioned in section 52 bis of the Criminal Code abroad may be prosecuted and brought to trial, even if the aforementioned offences are not punishable under the legislation of the State in which they were committed". The complainant believes that a complaint submitted by him from abroad could be construed as an insult against the regime, given that the State party has declared him to be a terrorist.

5.8 The complainant explains that his situation as a political refugee in Switzerland precludes him from successfully concluding any proceedings that he might initiate, given the restrictions placed on contacts between refugees and the authorities in their own countries. He explains that severance of all relations with the country of origin is one of the conditions on which the status of refugee is granted, and that it plays an important role when consideration is being given to withdrawing asylum. According to the complainant, such asylum would effectively end if the refugee should once again, of his own volition, seek the protection of his country of origin, for example by maintaining close contacts with the authorities or paying regular visits to the country.

5.9 The complainant challenges the affirmation by the State party of the existence of available remedies. He argues that the State party has confined itself to repeating the procedure described in the Code of Criminal Procedure, which is far from being applied in reality, particularly where political prisoners are concerned. In support of his argument, the complainant cites reports by Amnesty International, Human Rights Watch, the World Organization against Torture, the National Consultative Commission on Human Rights in France and the National Council for Fundamental Freedoms in Tunisia. The complainant also refers to the Committee against Torture's concluding observations on Tunisia, dated 19 November 1998. He stresses that the Committee against Torture recommended, among other things, that the State party should, first, ensure the right of victims of torture to lodge a complaint without the fear of being subject to any kind of reprisal, harassment, harsh treatment or prosecution, even if the outcome of the investigation does not prove their allegations, and to seek and obtain redress if those allegations are proven correct; second, ensure that medical examinations are automatically provided following allegations of abuse and that autopsies are performed following any deaths in custody; and third, ensure that the findings of all investigations concerning cases of torture are made public and that such information includes details of any offences committed, the names of the offenders, the dates, places and circumstances of the incidents and the punishment received by those found guilty. The Committee also noted that many of the regulations existing in Tunisia for the protection of arrested persons were not adhered to in practice. It also expressed its concern over the wide gap that existed between law and practice with regard to the protection of human rights, and was particularly disturbed by the reported widespread practice of torture and other cruel and degrading treatment perpetrated by security forces and the police, which, in certain cases, resulted in death in custody.

5.10 The complainant notes the lack of independence of the judicial system and the bodies set up to monitor application of the law. Lastly, he emphasizes that the State party's reply, in the current case, shows that no domestic investigation has been held into the rather detailed information contained in the complaint under consideration.

5.11 The complainant also challenges the State party's argument that the domestic remedies are effective.

5.12 With regard to the 302 cases involving police or national guard officers against whom, according to the State party, sentences have been handed down, the complainant points out that there is no tangible proof that these cases, which have not been published or made public in any way, actually took place; that the 277 cases cited by the State party as examples of abuse of authority are not relevant to the case in question; and that the State party refers only to cases which do not tarnish the image of Tunisia and therefore include no case of inhuman or degrading treatment. He explains that the cases adduced by the State party took place during the period 1988–1995 and were covered by the concluding observations of the Committee against Torture mentioned above.

5.13 Lastly, the complainant believes that the State party's comments regarding his membership of the ENNAHDA movement and the aspersions cast upon it demonstrate the continued discrimination against the opposition, which is still considered illegal. According to the complainant, with its references in this context to terrorism, the State party is demonstrating its bias and, by extension, the impossibility of obtaining any remedy in Tunisia. He also stresses that the prohibition of torture and inhuman or degrading treatment is a provision which admits of no exception, including for terrorists.

5.14 Finally, in the light of his previous explanations, the complainant rejects the observation by the State party to the effect that the present complaint constitutes an abuse of the right to submit complaints, an argument which, the complainant believes, shows that the State party has decided to resort to a political manoeuvre which has no legal relevance.

Additional State party admissibility observations

6. On 8 November 2002 the State party again challenged the admissibility of the complaint. It maintains, first, that the complainant's claims about recourse to the Tunisian justice system and the use of domestic remedies are baseless and unsupported by any evidence. It adds that appeal procedures do not take an unreasonable time, and that proceedings in respect of the allegations made in the complaint are not time-barred, since the time limit for bringing proceedings in such cases is 10 years. Second, the State party considers that the complainant's claims that a complaint lodged from abroad with the Tunisian authorities is might be covered by article 305, paragraph 3, of the Code of Criminal Procedure, which permits the prosecution of those guilty of terrorist acts, are baseless. Third, the State party affirms that, contrary to the complainant's allegations, it is open to him to instruct a lawyer of his choice to lodge a complaint from abroad. The State party adds that the complainant's refugee status does not deprive him of his right to lay complaints before the Tunisian courts. Fourth, it maintains that domestic remedies before the Tunisian judicial authorities are not only possible in the current case but effective, as shown by the fact that victims of violations in Tunisia have obtained satisfaction. Lastly, the State party indicates that its reply of 4 December 2001 was not intended to be defamatory to the complainant, who is, nonetheless, abusing the right to submit complaints.

Committee's admissibility decision

7.1 At its twenty-ninth session, the Committee considered the admissibility of the complaint, and on 20 November 2002 declared it admissible.

7.2 With regard to the issue of the exhaustion of domestic remedies, the Committee noted that the State party challenged the admissibility of the complaint on the grounds that available and effective domestic remedies had not been exhausted. In the present case, the Committee noted that the State party had provided a detailed description both of the remedies available, under law, to any complainant and of cases where such remedies had been applied against those responsible for abuses and for violations of the law. The Committee considered, nevertheless, that the State party had not sufficiently demonstrated the relevance of its arguments to the specific circumstances of the case of this complainant, who claims to have suffered violations of his rights. It made clear that it did not doubt the information provided by the State party about members of the security forces being prosecuted and convicted for a variety of abuses. But the Committee pointed out that it could not lose sight of the fact that the case at issue dates from 1987 and that, given a statute of limitations of 10 years, the question arose in the present case of whether, failing interruption or suspension of the statute of limitations—a matter on which the State party had provided no information—action before the Tunisian courts would be disallowed. The Committee noted, moreover, that the complainant's allegations related to facts that had already been reported publicly to the authorities. The Committee pointed out that to date it remained unaware of any investigations voluntarily undertaken by the State party. The Committee therefore considered it very unlikely in the present case that the complainant would obtain satisfaction by exhausting domestic remedies, and decided to proceed in accordance with article 22, paragraph 5 (b), of the Convention.

7.3 The Committee noted, in addition, the argument by the State party to the effect that the complainant's claim was tantamount to abuse of the right to lodge a complaint. The Committee considered that any report of torture was a serious matter and that only through consideration of the merits could it be determined whether or not the allegations were defamatory. Furthermore, the Committee believed that the complainant's political and partisan commitment adduced by the State party did not impede consideration of this complaint, in accordance with the provisions of article 22, paragraph 2, of the Convention.

State party's merits observations

8.1 In its observations of 3 April 2003 and 25 September 2003, the State party challenges the complainant's allegations and reiterates its position regarding admissibility.

8.2 In relation to the allegations concerning the State party's "complicity" and inertia vis-à-vis "practices of torture", the State party indicates that it has set up preventive[2] and dissuasive[3] machinery to combat torture so as to prevent any act which might violate the dignity and physical integrity of any individual.

8.3 Concerning the allegations relating to the "practice of torture" and the "impunity of the perpetrators of torture", the State party considers that the complainant has not presented any evidence to support his claims. It emphasizes that, contrary to the complainant's allegations, Tunisia has taken all necessary legal and practical steps, in judicial and administrative bodies, to prevent the practice of torture and prosecute any offenders, in accordance with articles 4, 5 and 13 of the Convention. Equally, according to the State party, the complainant has offered no grounds for his inertia and failure to act to take advantage of the effective legal opportunities available to him to bring his case before the judicial and administrative authorities (see para. 6). Concerning the Committee's decision on admissibility, the State party emphasizes that the complainant cites not only "incidents" dating back to 1987, but also "incidents" dating from 1995, 1996 and 1997, that is, a time when the Convention against Torture was fully incorporated into Tunisian domestic law and when he reports "ill-treatment" that he claims to have suffered while being held in "Tunis central prison" and "Grombalia prison". Hence the statute of limitations has not expired, and the complainant should urgently act to interrupt the limitation period, either by contacting the judicial authorities directly, or by performing an act which has the effect of interrupting the limitation. The State party also mentions the scope for the complainant to lodge an appeal for compensation for any serious injury caused by a public official in the performance

---

[2] This includes instruction in human rights values in training schools for the security forces, the Higher Institute of the Judiciary and the National School for training and retraining of staff and supervisors in prisons and correctional institutions; a human-rights-related code of conduct aimed at senior law enforcement officials; and the transfer of responsibility for prisons and correctional institutions from the Ministry of the Interior to the Ministry of Justice and Human Rights.

[3] A legislative reference system has been set up: contrary to the complainant's allegation that the Tunisian authorities have not criminalized acts of torture, the State party indicates that it has ratified the Convention against Torture without reservations, and that the Convention forms an integral part of Tunisian domestic law and may be invoked before the courts. The provisions of criminal law relating to torture are severe and precise (Criminal Code, art. 101 bis).

of his duties,[4] noting that the limitation period stands at 15 years.[5] The State party points out that the Tunisian courts have always acted systematically to remedy deficiencies in the law on acts of torture (see para. 4.10).

8.4 As for the allegations of failure to respect guarantees relating to judicial procedure, the State party regards them as unfounded. According to the State party, the authorities did not prevent the complainant from lodging a complaint before the courts—on the contrary, he opted not to make use of domestic remedies. As for the "obligation" of judges to ignore statements made as a result of torture, the State party cites article 15 of the Convention against Torture, and considers that it is incumbent on the accused to provide the judge with at least basic evidence that his statement has been made in an unlawful manner. In this way he would confirm the truth of his allegations by presenting a medical report or a certificate proving that he had lodged a complaint with the public prosecutor's office, or even by displaying obvious traces of torture or ill-treatment to the court. However, the State party points out that the complainant did not deem it necessary to lodge a complaint either during his detention or during his trial; this formed part of a strategy adopted by the "ENNAHDA" illegal extremist movement in order to discredit Tunisian institutions by systematically alleging acts of torture and ill-treatment but not making use of available remedies.

8.5 Concerning the allegations relating to his confession, the State party considers baseless the complainant's claim that he was found guilty on the sole basis of his confession. It points out that, under the last paragraph of article 69 and article 152 of the Code of Criminal Procedure, a confession on the part of the accused cannot relieve the judge of the obligation to seek other evidence, while confessions, like all items of evidence, are a matter for the independent appreciation of the judge. On that basis, it is a constant of Tunisian case law that an accused cannot be found guilty on the sole basis of a confession.[6] In the case in question, the basis for the court's decision, in addition to the confessions made by the complainant throughout the judicial proceedings, was testimony by his accomplices. The State party also rejects as baseless the complainant's allegation that he had signed a transcript without being aware of its content, pointing out that the law requires that the transcript be read to the accused before signature, and that this was done. Concerning the complainant's allegations that the proceedings in his case were both summary and protracted, the State party indicates that the length of the proceedings is dictated by respect for the right to a defence. In addition, with the aim of preventing counsel or even the prosecution from engaging in delaying tactics and seeking the postponement of hearings, the State party points out that rulings by judges are always accompanied by a statement of grounds, as are rulings postponing hearings relating to the criminal proceedings against the complainant.

8.6 Concerning the allegations relating to prison conditions, and in particular the comparison of prisons to "concentration centres", the State party considers them unfounded. Concerning the arrangements for transfers between one prison and another, which the complainant considers to constitute an abuse, the State party points out that, in keeping with the applicable regulations, transfers are decided upon in the light of the different stages of the proceedings, the number of cases and the courts which have competence for specific areas. The prisons are grouped in three categories: for persons held awaiting trial; for persons serving custodial sentences; and semi-open prisons for persons found guilty of ordinary offences, which are authorized to organize agricultural labour. According to the State party, as the status of the complainant had changed from that of remand prisoner to that of a prisoner serving a custodial sentence, and bearing in mind the requirements as to investigations in his case or in other similar cases, he was transferred from one prison to another, in accordance with the applicable regulations. Moreover, the conditions in which the complainant was held, wherever he was held, were in keeping with the prison regulations governing conditions for holding prisoners in order to ensure prisoners' physical and moral safety. The State party points out that prisoners' rights are scrupulously protected in Tunisia, without any discrimination, whatever the status of the prisoner, in a context of respect for human dignity, in accordance with international standards and Tunisian legislation. Medical, psychological and social supervision is provided, and family visits are allowed.

8.7 Contrary to the allegations that the medical consequences suffered by the complainant are due to torture, the State party rejects any causal link. Moreover, according to the State party, contrary to the complainant's allegations that his request for a

---

[4] Under the Administrative Court Act of 1 June 1972, the State may be held responsible even when it is performing a sovereign act if its representatives, agents or officials have caused material or moral injury to a third person. The injured party may demand from the State compensation for the injury suffered, under article 84 of the Code of Obligations and Contracts, without prejudice to the direct liability of its officials vis-à-vis the injured parties.
[5] Administrative Court – judgement N° 1013 of 10 May 1003 and judgement N° 21816 of 24 January 1997.
[6] Judgement N° 4692 of 30 July 1996, published in the Revue de Jurisprudence et Législation (R.J.L.); judgement N° 8616 of 25 February 1974 R.J.L. 1975; and judgement N° 7943 of 3 September 1973 R.J.L. 1974.

medical examination was refused (see para. 2.15), he enjoyed appropriate care and proper medical supervision, as stipulated in the prison regulations, throughout his stay in prison.

8.8 Concerning the allegations that he was denied visits, according to the State party the complainant regularly received visits from his brother Belhassen Abdelli, in accordance with the prison regulations, as demonstrated by the visitors' records in the prisons in which he was held.

8.9 Concerning the allegations relating to article 11 of the Convention, the State party rejects them and refers to systematic monitoring[7] of compliance with rules, instructions, methods and practices of interrogation and provisions relating to the holding[8] and treatment of persons who have been arrested, detained or imprisoned.[9]

8.10 Concerning the allegations relating to administrative supervision and the social situation of Mr. Abdelli's family, the State party explains that administrative supervision cannot be equated with ill-treatment under the Convention against Torture because it is in fact an additional punishment for which provision is made in article 5 of the Criminal Code. According to the State party, the application of this measure did not prevent the complainant from continuing to live a normal life, and in particular to pursue his studies following his release in 1994. It is pointed out that the fact that it was not possible for those studies to be completed could not constitute proof of alleged restrictions imposed within the framework of administrative supervision. According to the State party, the allegations of abuse are unfounded, and the summonses produced by the complainant do not constitute ill-treatment or an abuse of the administrative supervision procedure. In addition, the State party indicates that the summons dating from 1998 constitutes irrefutable evidence that the complainant's allegations are false. It also maintains that the complainant's family is not suffering from any form of harassment or restrictions, that the complainant's mother is receiving a pension following the death of her husband, and that the family is living in decent circumstances.

Observations by the complainant

9.1 In his observations dated 20 May 2003, the complainant sought to respond to each of the points contained in the above observations by the State party.

9.2 Concerning the preventive arrangements for combating torture, the complainant considers that the State party has confined itself to listing an arsenal of laws and measures of an administrative and political nature which, he says, are not put into effect in any way. To support this assertion he cites reports prepared by the non-governmental organization "National Council for Fundamental Freedoms in Tunisia" (CNLT).[10]

9.3 In relation to the establishment of a legislative reference system to combat torture, the complainant considers that article 101 bis of the Code of Criminal Procedure was adopted belatedly in 1999, in particular in response to the concern expressed by the Committee against Torture at the fact that the wording of article 101 of the Criminal Code could be used to justify serious abuses involving violence during questioning. He also claims that this new article is not applied, and attaches a list of the victims of repression in Tunisia between 1991 and 1998 prepared by the non-governmental organization "Vérité-Action". He also points out that the cases cited by the State party to demonstrate its willingness to act to combat torture relate only to accusations" of abuse of authority and violence and assault, as well as offences under the ordinary law, and not to cases of torture leading to death or cases involving physical and moral harm suffered by the victims of torture.

---

[7] In addition to legislation, protective institutional machinery has been set up by stages, including surprise visits to prisons by the Chairman of the Higher Committee for Human Rights and Fundamental Freedoms, and the creation on 31 July 2000 of a post of "judge for the enforcement of sentences" who is responsible for closely monitoring the enforcement of custodial sentences and conducting periodic visits to prisons.

[8] Act N° 99-90 of 2 August 1999 amended and supplemented a number of provisions of the Code of Criminal Procedure, and in particular reduced the length of police custody to three days, renewable once only for a further three days. Under the Act, criminal investigation officers may not hold a suspect for more than three days; they must notify the public prosecutor, who may, by written decision, extend the length of police custody once only for a further three days. The criminal investigation officer must inform the suspect of the measure being taken against him and its duration, and his rights under the law, notably the possibility of undergoing a medical examination during his period in custody. The officer must also inform one of the suspect's parents or children, brothers or sisters or spouse, as selected by him, of the measure being taken against him. These safeguards were further strengthened under the constitutional reform of 26 May 2002, which granted constitutional status to supervision of police custody by the judiciary, stipulating that this custodial measure could be imposed only by order of a court.

[9] The Act of 24 April 2001 on conditions for the imprisonment and treatment of detainees strengthened safeguards for the protection of prisoners and provided for prisoners to be prepared for a working life by offering them opportunities for paid employment.

[10] "Le procès-Tournant : A propos des procès militaires de Bouchoucha et de Bab Saadoun en 1992", October 1992; "Pour la réhabilitation de l'indépendance de la justice", April 2000–December 2001.

9.4 Concerning the practice of torture and impunity, the complainant maintains that torturers do enjoy impunity, and that in particular no serious investigation has been carried out into those suspected of committing crimes of torture. He considers that, in his own case, the State party's observations display a selective approach to the facts by shifting from 1987 to 1996, whereas the most serious violations occurred in 1991. The complainant also states that, whereas a State governed by the rule of law should automatically follow up any report of a criminal act which may be regarded as a serious offence, the Tunisian authorities are content to accuse the alleged victims of terrorism and manipulation. The complainant considers that his allegations are at the very least plausible in terms of the detail of the torture he suffered (names, places and treatment inflicted), but the State party contents itself with a blanket denial. The complainant did not mention torturers because of their membership of the security forces, but because of specific and repeated attacks on his physical and moral integrity and his private and family life. The initiation of an investigation designed to check whether a person belonging to the security forces has committed acts of torture or other acts does not constitute a violation of the presumption of innocence but a legal step which is vital in order to investigate a case and, if appropriate, place it before the judicial authorities for decision. In relation to appeals before the courts, the complainant considers that the State party has confined itself to repeating the description of legal options open to victims set out in its previous submissions without responding to the last two sentences of paragraph 7.2 of the decision on admissibility. He reiterates that the theoretical legal options described by the State party are inoperative, while listing in support of this conclusion cases in which the rights of the victims were ignored.

9.5 Concerning the complainant's inertia and lack of action, he considers that the State party is inconsistent in holding that acts of torture are regarded as serious offences in Tunisian law and accordingly prosecuted automatically, while awaiting a complaint by the victim before taking action. He also re-emphasizes his serious efforts to demand a medical examination and an investigation into the torture he had suffered.

9.6 Concerning the allegations relating to the trial, the complainant considers that the State party remains silent concerning the conditions in which his trial took place, and has failed to embark on any investigation to check the allegations of torture that he made before the judge.

9.7 Concerning the allegations relating to his confession, the complainant maintains that his confession was extracted under torture, and, citing the reports of CNLT, states that such methods are used in political trials and sometimes in trials involving offences under ordinary law. Concerning the length of the trials, the complainant states that the 1992 trial was summary in nature because it formed part of a spate of trials aimed at putting as many members of the ENNAHDA movement as possible behind bars, while the 1995 trial was protracted since the lawyers insisted on the principle of double jeopardy. The complainant also notes that the State party is silent about his arrest a few months after the Presidential pardon of 1987.

9.8 Concerning the conditions in which he was held, the complainant considers that the State party is taking refuge behind legal texts in order to dismiss the detailed information he provides. He points out that the question of transferring him for the purposes of the investigation never arose, and calls on the State party to prove the contrary.

9.9 In relation to visits, the complainant explains that each time he was transferred, his family had difficulty discovering his new place of detention. He considers that denial of visits constituted a form of revenge against him each time he sought to exercise a right and took action to that end, for example in the form of hunger strikes. He points out that the prison entry and exit logs can confirm his claims. In addition, the complainant's family found it difficult to exercise the right to visit him because of the conditions imposed on the visitors—the complainant's mother was ill-treated to make her remove her scarf, and was made to wait many hours for a visit lasting a few minutes.

9.10 Concerning the allegations relating to the provision of care, the complainant draws the Committee's attention to the medical certificate contained in his file. Concerning the treatment cited by the State party, the complainant demands the production of his medical file by the State party.

9.11 In relation to administrative supervision, the complainant considers that any punishment, including those provided for in the Tunisian Criminal Code, may be characterized as inhuman and degrading if the goal pursued does not include the reconciliation of the offender with his social environment. He points out in particular that his resumption of his studies prompted a tightening of the administrative supervision, including imposition of an obligation to report to the police twice a day, insistent surveillance by the university police and a ban on contacts with the other students. Concerning his summonses, the complainant states that the three years which elapsed between his two summonses in 1995 and 1998 corresponded to the period he spent in prison after being arrested again in 1995. According to the complainant, administrative supervision serves only to bolster the police's stranglehold over the freedom of movement of former prisoners.

9.12 Concerning the situation of his family, the complainant records the suffering caused by the police surveillance and various forms of intimidation. He mentions that two of his brothers (Nabil and Lofti) were imprisoned in advance of his arrest, and that his mother was detained for a whole day. In addition, according to the complainant, the authorities' deliberate decision to move him far from his family affected the pattern of the visits.

9.13 Concerning the application of article 11 of the Convention, the complainant considers that the State party once again contents itself with a theoretical description of its legal arsenal and a reference to the activities of the Higher Committee on Human Rights and Fundamental Freedoms, a non-independent institution. Citing documents issued by non-governmental organizations,[11] the complainant notes violations relating to the supervision of detention and police custody, such as manipulation of the dates when arrests were recorded, and incommunicado detention. He notes that the State party has not responded to his precise allegations relating to his detention for over a month in 1987, for 56 days in 1991 and for 18 days in 1995.

9.14 In relation to the ENNAHDA movement, the complainant maintains that the organization is well known for its democratic ideals and its opposition to dictatorship and impunity, contrary to the State party's explanations. In addition, he challenges the accusations of terrorism levelled by the State party, which in fact form part of a complete fabrication.

9.15 Lastly, according to the complainant, the State party is endeavouring to place the entire burden of proof on the victim, accusing him of inertia and failure to act, seeking protection behind a panoply of legal measures which theoretically enable victims to lodge complaints and evading its duty to ensure that those responsible for crimes, including that of torture, are automatically prosecuted. According to the complainant, the State party is thus knowingly ignoring the fact that international law and practice in relation to torture place greater emphasis on the role of States and their duties in order to enable proceedings to be completed. The complainant notes that the State party places the burden of proof on the victim alone, even though the supporting evidence, such as legal files, registers of police custody and visits, and so on, is in the sole hands of the State party and unavailable to the complainant. Referring to European case law,[12] the complainant points out that the European Court and Commission call on States parties, in the case of allegations of torture or ill-treatment, to conduct an effective investigation into the allegations of ill-treatment and not to content themselves with citing the theoretical arsenal of options available to the victim to lodge a complaint.

Consideration of the merits

10.1 The Committee has examined the complaint, by taking due account of all the information provided to it by the parties, in accordance with article 22, paragraph 4, of the Convention.

10.2 The Committee took note of the State party's observations of 3 April 2003 challenging the admissibility of the complaint. It notes that the points raised by the State party are not such as to prompt reconsideration of the Committee's decision on admissibility, notably owing to the lack of new or additional information from the State party on the matter of investigations voluntarily carried out by the State party (see para. 7.2). The Committee therefore does not consider that it should review its decision on admissibility.

10.3 The Committee therefore proceeds to examine the merits of the complaint, and notes that the complainant alleges violations by the State party of article 1, article 2, paragraph 1, article 4, article 5, article 11, article 12, article 13, article 14, article 15 and article 16 of the Convention.

10.4 Article 12 of the Convention, the Committee notes that article 12 of the Convention places an obligation on the authorities to proceed automatically to a prompt and impartial investigation whenever there is reasonable ground to believe that an act of torture or ill-treatment has been committed, no special importance being attached to the grounds for the suspicion.[13]

10.5 The Committee notes that the complainant maintains that he complained of acts of torture committed against him to the judge at his trials in 1992 and 1995. The complainant states that in 1992 he requested a medical examination, which was refused, and that in 1995 he sought the protection of the judge of the Tunis court of first instance against the torture inflicted on him daily at the prison. The Committee notes that the State party challenges the complainant's claim that he was denied a medical examination, without commenting on the treatment of which the complainant complained to the judge or

---

[11] Alternative report by FIDH to Tunisia's second periodic report to the Committee against Torture; communiqué issued on 20 February 2003 by the International Association for Support for Political Prisoners in Tunisia.

[12] Guide to Jurisprudence on Torture and Ill-Treatment – Article 3 of the European Convention for the Protection of Human Rights, Debra Long (APT); *Ribitsch* v. *Austria*; *Assenov* v. *Bulgaria*.
[13] Communication N° 59/1996 (*Encarnación Blanco Abad* v. *Spain*).

providing the results of the medical checks allegedly carried out on Mr. Abdelli while he was being held. The Committee also takes note of the State party's failure to comment on the precise allegations set out above relating to 1995. Lastly, the Committee notes the existence of detailed and substantiated information provided by the complainant concerning his hunger strikes in Tunis central prison in 1995 and in Grombalia prison from 28 November to 13 December 1997, mounted in order to protest against the treatment he had suffered and to secure medical care. The complainant refers to letters sent to the prisons administration following his hunger strikes, which produced no result. The Committee notes that the State party has not commented on this information. The Committee considers that these elements, taken together, should have been enough to trigger an investigation, which was not held, in breach of the obligation to proceed to a prompt and impartial investigation under article 12 of the Convention.

10.6 The Committee also observes that article 13 of the Convention does not require either the formal lodging of a complaint of torture under the procedure laid down in national law or an express statement of intent to institute and sustain a criminal action arising from the offence, and that it is enough for the victim simply to bring the facts to the attention of an authority of the State for the latter to be obliged to consider it as a tacit but unequivocal expression of the victim's wish that the facts should be promptly and impartially investigated, as prescribed by this provision of the Convention.[14]

10.7 The Committee notes, as already indicated, that the complainant explains that he did complain to judges in 1992 and 1995 of the treatment inflicted on him, resorted to hunger strikes and wrote to the prison authorities to complain about the conditions imposed on him. The Committee regrets that the State party has not responded or provided the necessary clarification on these points. Moreover, and notwithstanding the jurisprudence under article 13 of the Convention, the Committee notes the State party's position maintaining that the complainant should have made formal use of domestic remedies in order to lodge his complaint, for example by presenting to the court a certificate proving that a complaint had been lodged with the office of the public prosecutor, or displaying obvious traces of torture or ill-treatment, or submitting a medical report. On this latter point, to which the Committee wishes to draw its attention, it is clear that the complainant maintains that his request for a medical examination in 1992 was refused, and that the State party challenges this allegation on the grounds that the complainant enjoyed appropriate care and proper medical supervision, as stipulated in the prison regulations, throughout his stay in prison. The Committee observes that this response by the State party is categorical and general and does not necessarily answer the complainant's precise affirmation that he asked the judge in 1992 to order a medical examination. Finally, the Committee refers to its consideration of the report submitted by Tunisia in 1997, at which time it recommended that the State party should arrange for medical examinations to be organized systematically when allegations of abuse were made.

10.8 In the light of its practice relating to article 13 and the observations set out above, the Committee considers that the breaches enumerated are incompatible with the obligation stipulated in article 13 to proceed to a prompt investigation

10.9 Finally, the Committee considers that there are insufficient elements to make a finding on the alleged violation of other provisions of the Convention raised by the complainant at the time of adoption of this decision.

11. The Committee against Torture, acting under article 22, paragraph 7, of the Convention, is of the view that the facts before it disclose a violation of articles 12 and 13 of the Convention.

12. Pursuant to rule 112, paragraph 5, of its rules of procedure, the Committee urges the State party to conduct an investigation into the complainant's allegations of torture and ill-treatment, and to inform it, within 90 days from the date of the transmittal of this decision, of the steps it has taken in response to the Views expressed above.

---

[14] Communications N° 6/1990 (*Henri Unai Parot* v. *Spain*) and N° 59/1996 (*Encarnación Blanco Abad* v. *Spain*).

Communication N° 189/2001

Submitted by: Mr. Bouabdallah LTAIEF (represented by the non-governmental organization Vérité-Action)
Alleged victim: The complainant
State party: Tunisia
Declared admissible: 20 November 2002
Date of adoption of Views: 14 November 2003

Subject matter: torture of complainant by police and intelligence services

Procedural issues: exhaustion of domestic remedies; abuse of the right to lodge a complaint

Substantive issues: failure to take effective measures to prevent torture; failure to ensure that acts of torture are offences under State party criminal law; failure to institute legal proceedings against those responsible for torture; use of evidence obtained as a result of torture; lack of investigation of the acts of torture and examination of allegations of torture; sentence based on a confession obtained as a result of torture; cruel, inhuman and degrading treatment or punishment

Articles of the Convention: 1, 2 (1), 4, 5, 11, 12, 13, 14, 15, 16

1.1 The complainant is Mr. Bouabdallah Ltaief, a Tunisian citizen born on 2 June 1967 in Gabès, Tunisia, and a resident in Switzerland since 18 March 1999, where he obtained refugee status. He claims to have been the victim of violations by Tunisia of the provisions of article 1, article 2, paragraph 1, article 4, article 5, article 11, article 12, article 13, article 14, article 15 and article 16 of the Convention. He is represented by the non-governmental organization Vérité-Action.

1.2 Tunisia ratified the Convention against Torture and Other Cruel Inhuman or Degrading Treatment or Punishment and made the declaration under article 22 of the Convention on 23 September 1988.

The facts as submitted by the complainant

2.1 The complainant states that he was an active member of the Islamist organization ENNAHDA (formerly MTI). In July 1987, he was detained while on a camping trip with scouts. The complainant says that he asked the police officers if they were acting on the basis of a judicial warrant, but he was finally forced at gunpoint to remain silent. He states that, during his interrogation, he was deprived of food and sleep and subjected to intimidation by being forced to witness other detainees being tortured. He says that, despite requests to the local police, his family were unable to ascertain where he was being held and that his father was even detained himself for an entire day, because he had been making such representations.

2.2 While being held on Interior Ministry premises, in the cells of the national guard in Bouchoucha and in the police headquarters of Gabès governorate, the complainant maintains that he was subjected to eight torture sessions and provides a detailed description of these sessions.

2.3 He describes what is customarily known as the "roast chicken" position, in which the victim is stripped naked, his hands tied and his legs folded between his arms, with an iron bar placed behind his knees, from which he is then suspended between two tables and beaten, in particular on the soles of his feet. The complainant says that his torturers blew cigarette smoke into his face to choke him.

2.4 The complainant also claims to have been tortured in the "upside-down" position whereby the victim is stripped, hands tied behind his back and suspended from the ceiling by a rope tied to one or both of his feet, with his head hanging downwards. In this position he is kicked and struck with sticks and whips until he passes out. The complainant adds that his torturers tied a piece of string to his penis which they then repeatedly tugged, as if to tear his penis off.

2.5 The complainant claims to have been subjected to the "falka", in which the victim's feet are tied to a bar which is then lifted so that his torturers can lash the soles of his feet.

2.6 The complainant also claims to have been subjected to the "chair" torture, in which the victim is stripped and tied to a chair, with his hands behind his back, and beaten across the face, chest and abdomen. He says that his torturers mopped up his blood with paper which they then stuffed into his mouth to stifle his cries.

2.7 The complainant was also prevented from sleeping, from using the lavatory and from washing.

2.8 According to the complainant, following this torture and ill-treatment, he was twice admitted to the emergency service at Gabès hospital, but was unable to receive any visitors or to contact his family or his lawyer.

2.9 The complainant states that, in these conditions, he was forced to make confessions and that at the beginning of September 1987, he was placed in the 9 April prison in a solitary cell and deprived of any contacts with the outside world.

2.10 The complainant was then brought before the examining magistrate in the presence, for the first time, of his lawyers. The examining magistrate would not, however, allow any exchange of information to take place between the complainant and his lawyers, refused to let the lawyers speak, dictated the prosecution's case [1] against the complainant to his secretary, but was unable to get the complainant and his counsel to sign the transcript of the hearing.

2.11 The complainant's case then went before the State Security Court (Cour de Sûreté de l'Etat), where it continued for an entire month and, according to the complainant, was unanimously regarded by the international press as a complete travesty. The complainant says that, prior to the proceedings, the Director of State Security, Mr. Moncef Ben Gbila, attempted unsuccessfully to persuade him to give false testimony against other detainees, including officials of ENNAHDA, in exchange for his release. According to the complainant, during the proceedings, the magistrate of the State security court, Mr. Hechmi Zemmal, forced him to keep his statements brief, thus compromising his right to a defence. In addition, when the complainant was brought face to face with a witness who claimed to have been the victim of an act of violence committed by him, this witness, according to the complainant, repeatedly stated that the complainant was not the person in question. The defence counsel demanded that he be acquitted for lack of evidence, but the magistrate found that the witness had been affected by the shock of having to face his aggressor once again and, on 27 September 1987, sentenced the complainant to 10 years' immediate imprisonment and hard labour and 10 years' administrative supervision.[2]

2.12 The complainant stresses that, like other victims of torture, he was given no opportunity in the examination proceedings and the trial to describe his experiences of torture or to denounce those responsible. According to the complainant, judges brusquely interrupt to prevent anyone, even lawyers, mentioning this topic, and the fear of being subjected again to torture, if the detainee dares raise this issue with the judge, acts as a strong deterrent in the intimidation process.

2.13 The complainant was subsequently moved around repeatedly both within and between the country's various penitentiary establishments. Thus, he was held in isolation with three political prisoners, Fethi Jebrane, Mohamed Charrada and Faouzi Sarraj, in the Borj Erroumi prison in Bizerte, from 1987 to 1992; from 1992 to 1993, he was transferred to a common criminals' cell; from 1993 to 1994, he was held in solitary confinement in a small cell; and from 1994 to 1996 he was held together with two ENNAHDA officials—Habib Ellouz and Ajmi Lourimi—and then transferred to El Kef prison and to the central prison in Tunis, from 1996 to 1997.

2.14 The complainant says that the living standards and the treatment meted out to prisoners by the prison authorities made his imprisonment an intolerable ordeal. He refers to the prison crowding, the dirty conditions, the contagious diseases and the lack of medical care. He claims that the punishment cells in which he was held in the Borj Erroumi prison were extremely cramped, dark, with no water or WC, and very damp; his rations were limited to one piece of bread a day and he was forced to wear dirty, flea-infested clothes. He maintains that the political prisoners were subjected to discriminatory treatment, as part of a general policy of physical and mental aggression. In support of this claim he explains that he was repeatedly barred from having contact with others and from engaging in joint prayers. He adds that he was deprived of medical care, despite repeated requests, threats to go on hunger strike and his refusal to take exercise in the prison yard. According to the complainant, his family visits were restricted to 10 minutes and the women visitors were forced to remove their veils. The complainant adds that, in punishment cell N° 2 at Borj Erroumi prison, he was stripped naked and tied hand-and-foot to a cot for three days on end. He says that he was then subjected to this punishment again for a period of six days, after requesting medical care for kidney pains. In addition, the warders punched, slapped and kicked him. According to the complainant, in February 1994, the prison director beat him viciously while he was on hunger strike and had been placed in shackles and, in the process, broke his right arm. When the complainant returned from hospital, the prison director ordered him to be returned to the punishment cells, where he was left shackled for eight days, naked and without blankets, thereby aggravating his kidney pains. In El Kef prison, where he spent 10 days in the punishment cells, he had a blanket only from 10 p.m. to 6 a.m., despite the cold temperatures in the town, with the result that for the last three days he was unable to walk. Finally, a few days before his release, he was placed together with 24 other prisoners in Tunis central prison in a cell measuring only 3.5 metres by 2 metres. According to the complainant, with only one

---

[1] The complaint does not specify the accusations brought against the complainant.
[2] The complaint does not specify the reasons given for the finding against the complainant.

very small window high up on the cell wall, it was difficult to breathe, and the overcrowding was so bad that the detainees were unable even to sit.

2.15 The complainant explains that, in a bid to lessen the torture against him, including solitary confinement for periods of between 3 days and one and a half months, he was forced on at least 15 occasions to mount hunger strikes, lasting for periods of between 5 and 28 days.

2.16 On the day of his release, 24 July 1997, the complainant was escorted to the Bouchoucha detention centre, where he was questioned about his plans for the future as a militant and about his fellow detainees. According to the complainant, this questioning was followed by a session of mental harassment and threats. He says that he was released at 4 p.m. with instructions to report to the local police the moment he arrived in his home region of Gabès. There he was subjected to further questioning for a period of four hours. He was ordered to report twice a week to the regional police headquarters and daily at the local police station. According to the complainant, this administrative supervision was accompanied by police checks, including at night, of him and his family, the denial of his right to work and to study, refusal to issue a passport to his father and the confiscation of his brother's passport. He was also required to obtain permission from the local police for any movement away from his place of residence, a requirement which was accompanied by further questioning about his relatives and people with whom he had contacts. The complainant adds that he was detained for 48 hours in November 1998, during President Ben Ali's visit to Gabès governorate. He maintains that, whenever he had any contact with others living in the neighbourhood, both he and the people he met would be taken in for questioning.

2.17 Given this situation, the complainant explains that he then fled Tunisia for Switzerland, where he obtained refugee status.[3]

2.18 The complainant provides a list of people who subjected him to torture and ill-treatment.[4]

2.19 The complainant describes the consequences of the torture and ill-treatment that was inflicted on him, namely, an operation in 1988 to remove a fatty growth at the back of his head caused by violent blows administered under torture; scars of cigarette burns on his feet; kidney pains resulting from the detention conditions; and mental problems: he submits a medical certificate attesting to a neuropsychiatric disorder and showing that he has received medical treatment and psychotherapy at a Swiss psychiatric centre.

2.20 As to whether all domestic remedies have been exhausted, the complainant argues that, while such remedies might be provided for in Tunisian law, they are impossible in practice because of the bias of judges and the impunity granted to those responsible for violations. He adds that the regulations governing the activities of bodies which play a role in upholding human rights, such as the Higher Committee for Human Rights and Fundamental Freedoms and the Constitutional Council, prevent them from supporting complaints of torture. To back up his argument, he cites the reports of such non-governmental organizations as Amnesty International, the International Federation for Human Rights and Human Rights Watch.

The complaint

3.1 The complainant maintains that the Tunisian Government has breached the following articles of the Convention against Torture and Other Cruel, Inhuman or Degrading Treatment or Punishment:

> Article 1. The practices described above, such as "falka", the "roast chicken" position, the "upside-down" position, the "chair", etc., to which the complainant was subjected, constitute acts of torture.
>
> Article 2, paragraph 1. It is alleged that the State party not only failed to take effective measures to prevent torture, but even mobilized its administrative machinery and, in particular, its police force as an instrument of torture against the complainant.
>
> Article 4. It is alleged that the State party has not ensured that all the acts of torture to which the complainant has been subjected are offences under its criminal law.
>
> Article 5. It is alleged that the State party has instituted no legal proceedings against those responsible for torturing the complainant.
>
> Article 11. It is alleged that the authorities have not used their supervisory powers to prevent torture; instead, specific instructions have been given that torture is to be applied.
>
> Article 12. It is alleged that the State party has not carried out an investigation of the acts of torture committed against the complainant.
>
> Article 13. It is alleged that the State party has not effectively upheld the complainant's right to lodge a complaint with the competent authorities.
>
> Article 14. It is alleged that the State party has ignored the complainant's right to make a

---

[3] He entered Swiss territory on 18 March 1999. There is no indication of the date when he obtained refugee status.
[4] Available for information in the file.

complaint and has thereby deprived him of his right to redress and rehabilitation.

Article 15. It is alleged that on 27 September 1987 the complainant was sentenced to a prison term on the basis of a confession obtained as a result of torture.

Article 16. The repressive measures and practices described above, such as solitary confinement, violation of the right to medical care and the right to send and receive mail, restriction of family visits, etc., applied by the State party against the complainant constitute cruel, inhuman and degrading treatment or punishment.

3.2 The complainant also claims that his freedom of movement and his right to work were infringed by the administrative supervision measures applied against him, as was his right to pursue his studies.

State party's admissibility observations

4.1 On 4 December 2001, the State party challenged the admissibility of the complaint on the grounds that the complainant has neither employed nor exhausted available domestic remedies.

4.2 The State party points out that the complainant is a well-known activist of the illegal extremist movement ENNAHDA, which foments religious and racial hatred and practises violence. The State party explains that the complainant was sentenced on 27 September 1987 by the State Security Court to 10 years' immediate imprisonment and hard labour for having carried out a terrorist attack against Ali Bouhlila, by throwing sulphuric acid over his face and abdomen on 21 March 1987. According to the State party, the complainant was also found guilty, at the same trial, of aiding and abetting other terrorist acts.

4.3 The State party maintains that the complainant may still have recourse to the available domestic remedies, since, under Tunisian law, the limitation period for acts alleged to be, and characterized as, serious offences is 10 years.

4.4 The State party explains that, under the criminal justice system, the complainant may submit a complaint, from within Tunisia or abroad, to a representative of the Public Prosecutor's Office with jurisdiction in the area in question. He may also authorize a Tunisian lawyer of his own choice to submit such a complaint or request a foreign lawyer to do so with the assistance of a Tunisian colleague.

4.5 Under the same rules of criminal procedure, the Public Prosecutor will receive the complaint and institute a judicial inquiry. In accordance with article 53 of the Code of Criminal Procedure, the examining magistrate to whom the case is referred will hear the author of the complaint. In the light of this hearing, he may decide to hear witnesses, question suspects, undertake on-site investigations and seize physical evidence. He may also order expert studies and carry out any actions which he deems necessary for the uncovering of evidence, both in favour of and against the complainant, with a view to discovering the truth and verifying facts on which the trial court will be able to base its decision.

4.6 The State party explains that the complainant may, in addition, lodge with the examining magistrate during the pretrial proceedings an application for criminal indemnification for any harm suffered, over and above the criminal charges brought against those responsible for the offences against him.

4.7 If the examining magistrate deems that the public right of action is not exercisable, that the acts do not constitute a violation or that there is no prima facie case against the accused, he shall rule that there are no grounds for prosecution. If, on the other hand, the magistrate deems that the acts constitute an offence punishable by imprisonment, he shall send the accused before a competent court—which in the present instance, where a serious offence has been committed, would be the indictment chamber. All rulings by the examining magistrate are immediately communicated to all the parties to the proceedings, including the complainant who brought the criminal indemnification proceedings. Having been thus notified within a period of 48 hours, the complainant may, within four days, lodge an appeal against any ruling prejudicial to his interests. This appeal, submitted in writing or orally, is received by the clerk of the court. If there is prima facie evidence of the commission of an offence, the indictment chamber sends the accused before the competent court (criminal court or criminal division of a court of first instance), having given rulings on all the counts established during the proceedings. If it chooses, it may also order further information to be provided by one of its assessors or by the examining magistrate; it may also institute new proceedings, or conduct or order an inquiry into matters which have not yet been the subject of an examination. The decisions of the indictment chamber are subject to immediate enforcement.

4.8 A complainant seeking criminal indemnification may appeal on a point of law against a decision of the indictment chamber once it has been notified. This remedy is admissible when the indictment chamber rules that there are no grounds for prosecution; when it has ruled that the application for criminal indemnification is inadmissible, or that the prosecution is time-barred; when it has deemed the court to which the case has been referred to lack jurisdiction; or when it has omitted to make a ruling on one of the counts.

4.9 The State party stresses that, in conformity with article 7 of the Code of Criminal Procedure, the complainant may bring criminal indemnification proceedings before the court to which the case has been referred (criminal court or criminal division of the court of first instance) and, as appropriate, may lodge an appeal, either with the Court of Appeal if the offence in question is an ordinary offence, or with the criminal division of the Court of Appeal if it is a serious offence. The complainant may also appeal to the Court of Cassation.

4.10 Second, the State party maintains that the domestic remedies are effective.

4.11 According to the State party, the Tunisian courts have systematically and consistently acted to remedy deficiencies in the law, and stiff sentences have been handed down on those responsible for abuses and violations of the law. The State party says that, between 1 January 1988 and 31 March 1995, judgements were handed down in 302 cases involving members of the police or the national guard under a variety of counts, 227 of which fell into the category of abuse of authority. The penalties imposed varied from fines to terms of imprisonment of several years.[5]

4.12 The State party maintains that, given the complainant's political and partisan motives and his offensive and defamatory remarks, his complaint may be considered an abuse of the right to submit complaints.

4.13 The State party explains that the extremist movement of which the complainant is an active member has perpetrated a number of terrorist acts, including an attack in a hotel in Monastir, in August 1987, which caused a British tourist to lose both legs. Furthermore, this "movement" is not recognized under current Tunisian law.

4.14 The State party explains that the claims by the complainant demonstrate his political aims and confirm the biased and partisan nature of his allegations. Such is the case, according to the State party, when the complainant states that, in a State where the people do not have the right to express their views on the major issues of public life, legality is de facto diminished by the lack of any form of democratic oversight. The State party maintains, in addition, that the complaint contains offensive and defamatory remarks about the institutions of the Tunisian State, such as the complainant's statement that the entire administration is at the beck and call of the police apparatus, which turns the State into an effective instrument of torture.

---

[5] The examples cited by the State party are available for information in the file.

Complainant's comments on State party's observations

5.1 On 3 June 2002, the complainant challenged the State party's argument that he was supposedly unwilling to turn to the Tunisian justice system and make use of domestic remedies. He enumerates, by way of introduction, the efforts he made, to no avail, to approach the judicial and prison authorities with his complaints of ill-treatment, which made his situation worse, causing fear and reluctance to take action. He refers once again to the insurmountable obstacles placed in his way by the administrative supervision arrangements, which also embodied a definite threat of reprisals if he made a complaint.

5.2 The complainant believes that the recourse procedures are excessively protracted. He describes, in this context, how he drew the judge's attention to the torture inflicted on him, so that the judge would take the necessary steps to bring the culprits to justice—but to no avail. He adds that, over the last 20 or 30 years, complaints about deaths resulting from torture have been ignored, while to this day the torturers continue to enjoy the protection of the State.

5.3 The complainant also maintains that the available remedies are not likely to succeed. He says that he complained to the judge of ill-treatment against him and requested a medical check, but to no avail. It therefore seemed unlikely to him that he would obtain satisfaction from the judicial authorities. The complainant explains that his case with the judge was not an isolated instance and, in that context, submits an extract from a report by the Tunisian Committee for Human Rights and Freedoms. The complainant maintains that the judicial system is not independent and gave him no protection during his trial and conviction. He also cites extracts from reports by the International Federation for Human Rights and the Tunisian Committee for Human Rights and Freedoms in support of his observation that complaints of torture do not succeed and that the authorities exert pressure to prevent the lodging of such complaints. He also maintains that the administrative supervision under which he was placed, which involved constant supervision by a number of different authorities accompanied by acts of intimidation, was not a circumstance conducive to the lodging of complaints.

5.4 The complainant also challenges the State party's argument that a Tunisian lawyer can be instructed from abroad to lodge a complaint.

5.5 The complainant cites serious encroachments by the authorities on the free and independent exercise of the legal profession. According to him, lawyers who dare to defend complaints of torture are subject to harassment and other abuses, including prison sentences. As an example, he cites the cases of the lawyers Néjib Hosni, Béchir Essid and Anouar

Kosri, and quotes extracts from reports and statements by Amnesty International, the World Organization against Torture, the International Federation for Human Rights and the International Commission of Jurists. He adds, also on the basis of these reports by non-governmental organizations, that none of the complaints lodged by victims of torture over recent years, particularly following the promulgation in 1988 of article 13 bis of the Code of Criminal Procedure, providing for the possibility of medical visits, have been followed up. He also explains that, in certain cases, medical checks have been allowed after a long delay, once all traces of torture have disappeared, and that the checks are sometimes carried out by compliant doctors who will fail to find anything wrong with the detainees' physical condition, even if there are traces of torture. The complainant believes that, in these circumstances, it would not make much difference to appoint a lawyer. The complainant also stresses that the lodging of a complaint from abroad with the Tunisian authorities is likely to be covered by article 305, paragraph 3, of the Code of Criminal Procedure, which provides that "any Tunisian who commits any of the offences mentioned in article 52 bis of the Criminal Code abroad may also be prosecuted and brought to trial, even if the aforementioned offences are not punishable under the legislation of the State in which they were committed". The complainant believes that a complaint submitted by him from abroad could be construed as an insult against the regime, given that the State party has declared him to be a terrorist. Lastly, he explains that his situation as an asylum-seeker, then as a political refugee in Switzerland, precludes him from successfully concluding any proceedings that he might initiate, given the restrictions placed on contacts between refugees and the authorities in their own countries. He explains that severance of all relations with the country of origin is one of the conditions on which refugee status is granted, and that it plays an important role when consideration is being given to withdrawing asylum. According to the complainant, such asylum would effectively end if the refugee should once again, of his own volition, seek the protection of his country of origin, for example by maintaining close contacts with the authorities or paying regular visits to the country.

5.6 The complainant also challenges the affirmation by the State party of the existence of available remedies.

5.7 He argues that the State party has confined itself to repeating the procedure described in the Code of Criminal Procedure, which is far from being applied in reality, particularly where political prisoners are concerned. In support of his argument, the complainant cites reports by Amnesty International, Human Rights Watch, the World Organization against Torture, the National Consultative Commission on Human Rights in France and the National Council for Fundamental Freedoms in Tunisia. The complainant also refers to the Committee against Torture's concluding observations on Tunisia, dated 19 November 1998. He stresses that the Committee against Torture recommended, among other things, that the State party should, first, ensure the right of victims of torture to lodge a complaint without the fear of being subjected to any kind of reprisal, harassment, harsh treatment or prosecution, even if the outcome of the investigation does not prove their allegations, and to seek and obtain redress if those allegations are proven correct; second, ensure that medical examinations are automatically provided following allegations of abuse and that autopsies are performed following any deaths in custody; and third, ensure that the findings of all investigations concerning cases of torture are made public and that such information includes details of any offences committed, the names of the offenders, the dates, places and circumstances of the incidents and the punishment received by those found guilty. The Committee also noted that many of the regulations existing in Tunisia for the protection of arrested persons were not adhered to in practice. It also expressed its concern over the wide gap that existed between law and practice with regard to the protection of human rights, and was particularly disturbed by the reported widespread practice of torture and other cruel and degrading treatment perpetrated by security forces and the police, which, in certain cases, resulted in death in custody. The complainant also notes the lack of independence of the judicial system and the bodies set up to monitor application of the law. Lastly, he emphasizes that the State party's reply, in the current case, shows that no domestic investigation has been held into the rather detailed information contained in the complaint under consideration.

5.8 The complainant challenges the State party's argument that the domestic remedies are effective.

5.9 With regard to the 302 cases involving police or national guard officers against whom, according to the State party, sentences have been handed down, the complainant points out that there is no tangible proof that these cases, which have not been published or made public in any way, actually took place; that the 277 cases cited by the State party as examples of abuse of authority are not relevant to the case in question; and that the State party refers only to cases which do not tarnish the image of Tunisia and therefore include no case of inhuman or degrading treatment. He explains that the cases adduced by the State party took place during the period 1988–1995 and were covered by the concluding observations of the Committee against

Torture mentioned above. Lastly, citing extracts from reports by the Tunisian Committee for Human Rights and Freedoms and Amnesty International in particular, he draws attention to the immunity enjoyed by officials involved in acts of torture, some of whom have even been promoted. The complainant adds that Tunisia has helped Tunisian officials evade arrest warrants issued against them abroad on the basis of complaints by victims of torture

5.10 Finally, the complainant rejects the comments by the State party characterizing his complaint as an abuse of rights. He says that, with its references in this context to political commitment and terrorism, the State party is demonstrating its bias and, by extension, the impossibility of obtaining any remedy in Tunisia. The complainant also stresses that the prohibition of torture and inhuman or degrading treatment is a provision which admits of no exception, including for terrorists. He believes that, in its response to this complaint, the State party is resorting to a political manoeuvre which has no legal relevance and which constitutes an abuse of rights.

Additional State party admissibility information

6. On 8 November 2002, the State party again challenged the admissibility of the complaint. It maintains that the complainant's claims about recourse to the Tunisian justice system and the use of domestic remedies are baseless and unsupported by any evidence. It affirms that appeal procedures do not take an unreasonable time, and that proceedings in respect of the allegations made in the complaint are not time-barred, since the time limit for bringing proceedings in such cases is 10 years. Contrary to what the complainant alleges, the State party says that he can instruct a lawyer of his choice to lodge a complaint from abroad. It adds that the complainant's claims that a complaint lodged from abroad with the Tunisian authorities might be covered by article 305, paragraph 3, of the Code of Criminal Procedure, which permits the prosecution of those guilty of terrorist acts, are baseless. The State party maintains that domestic remedies before the Tunisian judicial authorities are not only possible in the current case but indeed effective, as shown by the fact that victims of violations in Tunisia have obtained satisfaction. Fourth, the State party argues that the complainant is abusing the right to lodge complaints by seeking to misrepresent and distort the points made in the State party's response of 4 December 2001.

Committee's admissibility decision

7.1 At its twenty-ninth session, the Committee considered the admissibility of the complaint, and on 20 November 2002 declared it admissible.

7.2 With regard to the issue of the exhaustion of domestic remedies, the Committee noted that the State party challenged the admissibility of the complaint on the grounds that the available and effective domestic remedies had not been exhausted. In the present case, the Committee noted that the State party had provided a detailed description both of the remedies available, under law, to any complainant and of cases where such remedies had been applied against those responsible for abuses and for violations of the law. The Committee considered, nevertheless, that the State party had not sufficiently demonstrated the relevance of its arguments to the specific circumstances of the case of this complainant, who claims to have suffered violations of his rights. It made clear that it did not doubt the information provided by the State party about members of the security forces being prosecuted and convicted for a variety of abuses. But the Committee pointed out that it could not lose sight of the fact that the case at issue dates from 1987 and that, given a statute of limitations of 10 years, the question arose of whether, failing interruption or suspension of the statute of limitations—a matter on which the State party had provided no information—action before the Tunisian courts would be disallowed. The Committee noted, moreover, that the complainant's allegations related to facts that had already been reported to the authorities. The Committee pointed out that to date it remained unaware of any investigations voluntarily undertaken by the State party. The Committee therefore considered it very unlikely in the present case that the complainant would obtain satisfaction by exhausting domestic remedies, and decided to proceed in accordance with article 22, paragraph 5 (b), of the Convention.

7.3 The Committee noted, in addition, the argument by the State party to the effect that the complainant's claim was tantamount to abuse of the right to lodge a complaint. The Committee considered that any report of torture was a serious matter and that only through consideration of the merits could it be determined whether or not the allegations were defamatory. Furthermore, the Committee believed that the complainant's political and partisan commitment adduced by the State party did not impede consideration of this complaint, in accordance with the provisions of article 22, paragraph 2, of the Convention.

7.4 Lastly, the Committee ascertained, as it is required to do under article 22, paragraph 5 (a), of the Convention, that the same matter has not been and is not being examined under another procedure of international investigation or settlement.

State party's merits observations

8.1 In its observations of 3 April 2003 and 25 September 2003, the State party challenges the complainant's allegations and reiterates its position regarding admissibility.

8.2 In relation to the allegations concerning the State party's "complicity" and inertia vis-à-vis "practices of torture", the State party indicates that it has set up preventive[6] and dissuasive[7] machinery to combat torture so as to prevent any act which might violate the dignity and physical integrity of any individual.

8.3 Concerning the allegations relating to the "practice of torture" and the "impunity of the perpetrators of torture", the State party considers that the complainant has not presented any evidence to support his claims. It emphasizes that, contrary to the complainant's allegations, Tunisia has taken all necessary legal and practical steps, in judicial and administrative bodies, to prevent the practice of torture and prosecute any offenders, in accordance with articles 4, 5 and 13 of the Convention. Equally, according to the State party, the complainant has offered no grounds for his inertia and failure to act to take advantage of the effective legal opportunities available to him to bring his case before the judicial and administrative authorities (see para. 6). Concerning the Committee's decision on admissibility, the State party emphasizes that the complainant cites not only "incidents" dating back to 1987, but also "incidents" dating from 1994, 1996 and 1997, that is, the time when the Convention against Torture was fully incorporated into Tunisian domestic law and when he reports "ill-treatment" that he claims to have suffered while being held in "Borj Erroumi prison", El Kef prison and Tunis prison. Hence the statute of limitations has not expired, and the complainant should urgently act to interrupt the limitation period, either by contacting the judicial authorities directly, or by performing an act which has the effect of interrupting the limitation. The State party also mentions the scope for the complainant to lodge an appeal for compensation for any serious injury caused by a public official in the performance of his duties,[8] noting that the limitation period stands at 15 years.[9] The State party points out that the Tunisian courts have always acted systematically to remedy deficiencies in the law on acts of torture (see para. 4.11). According to the State party, the complainant has merely put forward false, contradictory, not to say defamatory remarks.

8.4 As for the allegations of failure to respect guarantees relating to judicial procedure, the State party regards them as unfounded. It refers to the complainant's inertia and failure to act. According to the State party, the authorities did not prevent him from lodging a complaint before the courts—on the contrary, he opted not to make use of domestic remedies. As for the "obligation" of judges to ignore statements made as a result of torture, the State party cites article 15 of the Convention against Torture, and considers that it is incumbent on the accused to provide the judge with at least basic evidence that his statement has been made in an unlawful manner. In this way he would confirm the truth of his allegations by presenting a medical report or a certificate proving that he had lodged a complaint with the public prosecutor's office, or even by displaying obvious traces of torture or ill-treatment to the court. However, the State party points out that the complainant did not deem it necessary to lodge a complaint either during his detention or during his trial; this formed part of a strategy adopted by the ENNAHDA illegal extremist movement in order to discredit Tunisian institutions by systematically alleging acts of torture and ill-treatment but not making use of available remedies.

8.5 Concerning the allegations relating to the trial, the State party maintains that the complainant is mistaken in claiming that he did not sign the record of his questioning by the examining magistrate. According to the State party, his counsel did indeed speak on the substance of the matter, at the invitation of the examining magistrate, in accordance with the applicable rules of criminal procedure. The State party points out that the complainant was found guilty of throwing acid at his victim, among other offences, and that he admitted the act before the

---

[6] This includes instruction in human rights values in training schools for the security forces, the Higher Institute of the Judiciary and the National School for training and retraining of staff and supervisors in prisons and correctional institutions; a human-rights-related code of conduct aimed at senior law enforcement officials; and the transfer of responsibility for prisons and correctional institutions from the Ministry of the Interior to the Ministry of Justice and Human Rights.

[7] A legislative reference system has been set up: contrary to the complainant's allegation that the Tunisian authorities have not criminalized acts of torture, the State party indicates that it has ratified the Convention against Torture without reservations, and that the Convention forms an integral part of Tunisian domestic law and may be invoked before the courts. The provisions of criminal law relating to torture are severe and precise (Criminal Code, art. 101 bis).

[8] Under the Administrative Court Act of 1 June 1972, the State may be held responsible even when it is performing a sovereign act if its representatives, agents or officials have caused material or moral injury to a third person. The injured party may demand from the State compensation for the injury suffered, under article 84 of the Code of Obligations and Contracts, without prejudice to the direct liability of its officials vis-à-vis the injured parties.

[9] Administrative Court – judgement N° 1013 of 10 May 1003 and judgement N° 21816 of 24 January 1997.

examining magistrate and the court, where he expressed his regret, stating that his action had given rise to psychological problems due to a feeling of guilt and the ghastly nature of the act. As for the complainant's statement that he had taken steps to request a medical examination, without success, the State party points out that an examination is not ordered in response to a mere request, but requires the presence of indications which would justify such an examination. Accordingly the examining magistrate had rejected the complainant's request for a medical examination, since, according to the State party, the complainant displayed no obvious signs of violence.

8.6 Concerning the allegations relating to his confession, the State party considers baseless the complainant's claim that he was found guilty on the sole basis of his confession. It points out that, under the last paragraph of article 69 and article 152 of the Code of Criminal Procedure, a confession on the part of the accused cannot relieve the judge of the obligation to seek other evidence, while confessions, like all items of evidence, are a matter for the independent appreciation of the judge. On that basis, it is a constant of Tunisian case law that an accused cannot be found guilty on the sole basis of a confession.[10] Moreover, according to the State party, the complainant's allegation that he confessed under torture his membership of the ENNAHDA movement is contradicted by the certificate supplied by Mr. Ltaief to the Swiss authorities in support of his application for political asylum, since the certificate, from the "leader of the ENNAHDA movement", confirmed his membership of the "movement".

8.7 Concerning the allegations relating to prison conditions, and in particular the arrangements for transfers between one prison and another, which the complainant considers an abuse, the State party points out that, in keeping with the applicable regulations, transfers are decided upon in the light of the different stages of the proceedings, the number of cases and the courts which have competence for specific areas. The prisons are grouped in three categories: for persons held awaiting trial; for persons serving custodial sentences; and semi-open prisons for persons found guilty of ordinary offences, which are authorized to organize agricultural labour. According to the State party, as the complainant had changed his status from that of remand prisoner to that of a prisoner serving a custodial sentence, and bearing in mind the requirements as to investigations in his case or in other similar cases, he was transferred from one prison to another, in accordance with the applicable regulations. The conditions in which the complainant was held, wherever he was held, were in keeping with the prison regulations governing conditions for holding prisoners in order to ensure prisoners' physical and moral safety. The State party points out that prisoners' rights are scrupulously protected in Tunisia, without any discrimination, whatever the status of the prisoner, in a context of respect for human dignity, in accordance with international standards and Tunisian legislation. Medical, psychological and social supervision is provided, and family visits are allowed. The State party maintains that the conditions in which the complainant was held were in keeping with Tunisian regulations governing prison establishments, which conform to relevant international standards.

8.8 Contrary to the allegations that the medical consequences suffered by the complainant are due to torture, the State party rejects any causal link. It notes in particular that the medical certificate recording a neuropsychiatric disorder, which was produced by the complainant, dates from 29 July 1999, that is, some 10 years after the "incidents". The State party also cites the psychological problems to which the complainant referred in court (para. 8.5). In addition, according to the State party, the complainant, contrary to his allegations, enjoyed proper medical supervision and appropriate care during his stay at the prison of Borj Erroumi.

8.9 Concerning the allegations that he was denied visits, according to the State party the complainant regularly received visits from his brothers, his uncle, his father and his mother, in accordance with the prison regulations, as demonstrated by the visitors' records in the prisons in which he was held.

8.10 Concerning the allegations relating to article 11 of the Convention, the State party rejects them and refers to systematic monitoring[11] of compliance with rules, instructions, methods and practices of interrogation and provisions relating to the holding[12]

---

[10] Judgement N° 4692 of 30 July 1996, published in the Revue de Jurisprudence et Législation (R.J.L.); judgement N° 8616 of 25 February 1974 R.J.L. 1975; and judgement N° 7943 of 3 September 1973 R.J.L. 1974.

[11] In addition to legislation, protective institutional machinery has been set up by stages, including surprise visits to prisons by the Chairman of the Higher Committee for Human Rights and Fundamental Freedoms, and the creation on 31 July 2000 of a post of "judge for the enforcement of sentences" who is responsible for closely monitoring the enforcement of custodial sentences and conducting periodic visits to prisons.

[12] Act N° 99-90 of 2 August 1999 amended and supplemented a number of provisions of the Code of Criminal Procedure, and in particular reduced the length of police custody to three days, renewable once only for a further three days. Under the Act, criminal investigation officers may not hold a suspect for more than three days; they must notify the public prosecutor, who may, by written decision, extend the length of police custody once only for a further three days. The criminal investigation

and treatment of persons who have been arrested, detained or imprisoned.[13]

8.11 Concerning the allegations relating to the social position of Mr. Ltaief's family, the State party maintains that his family is not suffering any form of harassment or restrictions, that the family is living in decent circumstances, and that the complainant's father is receiving a pension.

Further observations by the complainant

9.1 In his observations dated 20 May 2003, the complainant sought to respond to each of the points contained in the above observations by the State party.

9.2 Concerning the preventive arrangements for combating torture, the complainant considers that the State party has confined itself to listing an arsenal of laws and measures of an administrative and political nature which, he says, are not put into effect in any way. To support this assertion he cites a report prepared by the non-governmental organization "National Council for Fundamental Freedoms in Tunisia" (CNLT).[14]

9.3 In relation to the establishment of a legislative reference system to combat torture, the complainant considers that article 101 bis of the Code of Criminal Procedure was adopted belatedly in 1999, in particular in response to the concern expressed by the Committee against Torture at the fact that the wording of article 101 of the Criminal Code could be used to justify serious abuses involving violence during questioning. He also claims that this new article is not applied, and attaches a list of the victims of repression in Tunisia between 1991 and 1998 prepared by the non-governmental organization "Vérité-Action". He also points out that the cases cited by the State party to demonstrate its willingness to act to combat torture relate only to accusations of abuse of authority and violence and assault, as well as offences under the ordinary law, and not to cases of torture leading to death or cases involving physical and moral harm inflicted on the victims of torture.

9.4 Concerning the practice of torture and impunity, the complainant maintains that torturers do enjoy impunity, and that in particular no serious investigation has been carried out into those suspected of committing crimes of torture. He considers that, in his own case, the State party's observations display a selective approach to the facts, by concluding that the allegations of ill-treatment date back to 1987, whereas the complainant recounts his "martyrdom" in prison from 1987 to 1997. The complainant also points out that, whereas a State governed by the rule of law should automatically follow up any report of a criminal act which may be regarded as a serious offence, the Tunisian authorities are content to accuse the alleged victims of terrorism and manipulation. The complainant also produces a list of complaints by Tunisian public figures which were recently reported and ignored by the authorities. He considers that he has drawn up a detailed account of his individual case, giving names, places, dates and treatment inflicted, but the State party contents itself with a blanket denial of such treatment. The complainant did not mention torturers because of their membership of the security forces, but because of specific and repeated attacks on his physical and moral integrity and his private and family life. The initiation of an investigation designed to check whether a person belonging to the security forces has committed acts of torture or other acts does not constitute a violation of the presumption of innocence but a legal step which is vital in order to investigate a case and, if appropriate, place it before the judicial authorities for decision. In relation to appeals before the courts, the complainant considers that the State party has confined itself to repeating the description of legal options open to victims set out in its previous submissions without responding to the last two sentences of paragraph 7.2 of the decision on admissibility. He reiterates that the theoretical legal options described by the State party are inoperative.

9.5 Concerning the claim of inertia and lack of action, the complainant considers that the State party is inconsistent in holding that acts of torture are regarded as serious offences in Tunisian law and accordingly prosecuted automatically, while awaiting a complaint by the victim before taking action. He also re-emphasizes his serious efforts to demand a medical examination and an investigation into the torture he had suffered, referring to the examining magistrate's refusal of his request for a medical examination, and the medical certificate indicating a neuropsychiatric disorder.

---

officer must inform the suspect of the measure being taken against him and its duration, and his rights under the law, notably the possibility of undergoing a medical examination during his period in custody. The officer must also inform one of the suspect's parents or children, brothers or sisters or spouse, as selected by him, of the measure being taken against him. These safeguards were further strengthened under the constitutional reform of 26 May 2002, which granted constitutional status to supervision of police custody by the judiciary, stipulating that this custodial measure could be imposed only by order of a court.

[13] The Act of 24 April 2001 on conditions for the imprisonment and treatment of detainees strengthened safeguards for the protection of prisoners and provided for prisoners to be prepared for a working life by offering them opportunities for paid employment.

[14] «Pour la réhabilitation de l'indépendance de la justice», April 2000–December 2001.

9.6 The complainant maintains that his counsel refused to sign the transcript of the questioning before the examining magistrate, thereby proving the abnormal conditions in which the proceedings took place. He also notes that by its own admission, but by means of legal reasoning which he finds strange, the State party acknowledges that the examining magistrate refused his request for a medical examination because of the absence of any obvious traces of violence. The complainant explains that holding an individual in pretrial detention beyond the time limits laid down by law for the purposes of concealing the traces of torture, and then denying him the right to a medical examination on the grounds that there were no obvious traces of torture, falls within a pattern of institutionalization of torture. Lastly, according to the complainant, the State party thereby acknowledges that it prevented him from initiating an elementary and obvious procedure which would provide him with the initial evidence he requires. He adds that in his extremely serious case, in which he was brought before a court of special jurisdiction (the State Security Court), this refusal deprived him of the last resort which would have enabled him to defend his interests. According to the complainant, given the serious charges made against him, the slightest doubt and the slightest allegation of ill-treatment should have triggered a process of checking. Furthermore, the examining magistrate's refusal to authorize a medical examination lessened the complainant's chances of resubmitting the request to the court (even though the request was indeed resubmitted).

9.7 Concerning the allegations relating to his confession, the complainant maintains that his confession was extracted under torture, and, citing the reports of CNLT, states that such methods are used in political trials and sometimes in trials involving offences under ordinary law. As for the State party's endeavours to detect signs of contradiction in his acknowledgement of membership of the ENNAHDA movement (para. 8.6), the complainant is surprised at this strange reasoning, and explains that his conviction related to an alleged attack using acid, and not membership of the ENNAHDA movement.

9.8 Concerning the conditions in which he was held, the complainant considers that the State party is taking refuge behind legal texts in order to dismiss his plentiful, specific and substantiated evidence. He explains that he was transferred for purposes of punishment, and not for any matter related to cases pending before the courts. He points out that the question of transferring him for the purposes of the investigation never arose, and calls on the State party to prove the contrary.

9.9 In relation to visits, the complainant considers that denial of visits constituted a form of revenge against him each time he sought to exercise a right and took action to that end, for example in the form of a hunger strike. He explains that the actual conditions in which the visits took place—the ill-treatment inflicted on the members of his family at the place of the visit and by the local police on their return home—constituted breaches of national and international standards.

9.10 Concerning the allegations relating to the provision of care, the complainant draws the Committee's attention to the medical certificate contained in his file, pointing out that it was supplied only 10 years after the incidents as that was the first available opportunity. He also notes that the State party, while it accepts the existence of psychological problems, but only on the grounds of an alleged feeling of guilt and not because of the torture he suffered, refuses to produce the file which would confirm the extent of the regrets of which the court was informed. Concerning the treatment cited by the State party, the complainant demands the production of his medical file by the State party.

9.11 In relation to administrative supervision, the complainant considers that any punishment, including those provided for in the Tunisian Criminal Code, may be characterized as inhuman and degrading if the goal pursued does not include the reconciliation of the offender with his social environment. He notes in particular that he was arbitrarily prevented from continuing his studies, during his 10 years in prison but above all afterwards. He deplores the fact that aside from a remark on the resumption of studies, the State party contented itself with a blanket denial of his assertions, without any supporting investigation or evidence. According to the complainant, administrative supervision serves only to bolster the police's stranglehold over the freedom of movement of former prisoners.

9.12 Concerning the situation of his family, the complainant records the suffering caused by the police surveillance and various forms of intimidation, ill-treatment during visits and the denial of passports for a period of years, continuing up to the present.

9.13 Concerning the application of article 11 of the Convention, the complainant considers that the State party once again contents itself with a theoretical description of its legal arsenal and a reference to the activities of the Higher Committee on Human Rights and Fundamental Freedoms, a non-independent institution. Citing documents issued by non-governmental organizations,[15] the complainant notes violations relating to the supervision of detention

---

[15] Alternative report by FIDH to Tunisia's second periodic report to the Committee against Torture; communiqué issued on 20 February 2003 by the International Association for Support for Political Prisoners in Tunisia.

and police custody, such as manipulation of the dates when arrests were recorded, and incommunicado detention. He notes that the State party has not responded to his precise allegations relating to his detention for over two months.

9.14 In relation to the ENNAHDA movement, the complainant maintains that the organization is well known for its democratic ideals and its opposition to dictatorship and impunity, contrary to the State party's explanations. In addition, he challenges the accusations of terrorism levelled by the State party, which in fact form part of a complete fabrication.

9.15 Lastly, according to the complainant, the State party is endeavouring to place the burden of proof on the victim, accusing him of inertia and failure to act, seeking protection behind a panoply of legal measures which theoretically enable victims to lodge complaints and evading its duty to ensure that those responsible for crimes, including that of torture, are automatically prosecuted. According to the complainant, the State party is thus knowingly ignoring the fact that international law and practice in relation to torture place greater emphasis on the role of States and their duties in order to enable proceedings to be completed. The complainant notes that the State party places the burden of proof on the victim alone, even though the supporting evidence, such as legal files, registers of police custody and visits, and so on, is in the sole hands of the State party and unavailable to the complainant. Referring to European case law,[16] the complainant points out that the European Court and Commission call on States parties, in the case of allegations of torture or ill-treatment, to conduct an effective investigation into the allegations of ill-treatment and not to content themselves with citing the theoretical arsenal of options available to the victim to lodge a complaint.

Consideration of the merits

10.1 The Committee examined the complaint, taking due account of all the information provided to it by the parties, in accordance with article 22, paragraph 4, of the Convention.

10.2 The Committee took note of the State party's observations of 3 April 2003 challenging the admissibility of the complaint. It notes that the points raised by the State party are not such as to prompt reconsideration of the Committee's decision on admissibility, notably owing to the lack of new or additional information from the State party on the matter of investigations voluntarily carried out by the State party (see para. 7.2). The Committee therefore does not consider that it should review its decision on admissibility.

10.3 The Committee therefore proceeds to examine the merits of the complaint, and notes that the complainant alleges violations by the State party of article 1, article 2, paragraph 1, article 4, article 5, article 11, article 12, article 13, article 14, article 15 and article 16 of the Convention.

10.4 The Committee recalls that article 12 of the Convention places an obligation on the authorities to proceed automatically to a prompt and impartial investigation whenever there is reasonable ground to believe that an act of torture or ill-treatment has been committed, no special importance being attached to the grounds for the suspicion.[17]

10.5 The Committee notes that the complainant maintains that in 1987, he complained to the examining magistrate of acts of torture inflicted on him and requested a medical examination in that regard, to no avail. The Committee also notes that the State party acknowledges that the examining magistrate rejected the complainant's request for a medical examination on the grounds that he displayed no obvious traces of violence. The Committee considers that the State party's reply referring to the lack of obvious traces of violence does not necessarily constitute a response to the complainant's complaint of acts of torture, which under the definition of torture set out in article 1 of the Convention give rise to "severe pain or suffering, whether physical or mental" and may leave non-obvious but real traces of violence. In that regard, the Committee notes the certificate produced by the complainant reporting a neuropsychiatric disorder. Lastly, the Committee takes note of the detailed and substantiated information provided by the complainant regarding the hunger strikes he carried out while in prison from 1987 to 1997, on at least 15 occasions, for periods of between 5 and 28 days, in protest at the treatment he had suffered. The Committee notes that the State party did not comment on this information. The Committee considers that these elements, taken together, should have been enough to trigger an investigation, which was not held, in breach of the obligation to proceed to a prompt and impartial investigation under article 12 of the Convention.

10.6 The Committee also observes that article 13 of the Convention does not require either the formal lodging of a complaint of torture under the procedure laid down in national law or an express statement of intent to institute and sustain a criminal action arising from he offence, and that it is enough for the victim simply to bring the facts to the

---

[16] Guide to Jurisprudence on Torture and Ill-Treatment – Article 3 of the European Convention for the Protection of Human Rights, Debra Long (APT); *Ribitsch* v. *Austria*; *Assenov* v. *Bulgaria*.

[17] Communication N° 59/1996 (*Encarnación Blanco Abad* v. *Spain*).

attention of an authority of the State for the latter to be obliged to consider it a tacit but unequivocal expression of the victim's wish that the facts should be promptly and impartially investigated, as prescribed by this article of the Convention.[18]

10.7 The Committee notes, as already indicated, that the complainant explains that he did complain to the examining magistrate of the treatment inflicted on him, and resorted to hunger strikes in protest at the conditions imposed on him. Yet notwithstanding the jurisprudence under article 13 of the Convention, the Committee notes the State party's position maintaining that the complainant should have made formal use of domestic remedies in order to lodge his complaint, for example by presenting to the court a certificate proving that a complaint had been lodged with the office of the public prosecutor, or displaying obvious traces of torture or ill-treatment, or submitting a medical report. On this latter point, to which the Committee wishes to draw its attention, it is clear that the complainant maintains that his request for a medical check was denied, and that the State party justifies this decision by citing the lack of obvious traces of violence. The Committee points out that this reply on the part of the State party does not necessarily answer the complainant's precise allegation of acts of torture which left actual traces, particularly of a neuropsychiatric nature. Finally, the Committee refers to its consideration of the report submitted by Tunisia in 1997, at which time it recommended that the State party should arrange for medical examinations to be organized systematically when allegations of abuse were made.

10.8 In the light of its practice relating to article 13 and the observations set out above, the Committee considers that the breaches enumerated are incompatible with the obligation stipulated in article 13 to proceed to a prompt investigation.

10.9 Finally, the Committee considers that there are insufficient elements to make a finding on the alleged violation of other provisions of the Convention raised by the complainant at the time of adoption of this decision.

11. The Committee against Torture, acting under article 22, paragraph 7, of the Convention, is of the view that the facts before it disclose a violation of articles 12 and 13 of the Convention against Torture and Other Cruel, Inhuman or Degrading Treatment or Punishment.

12. Pursuant to rule 112, paragraph 5, of its rules of procedure, the Committee urges the State party to conduct an investigation into the complainant's allegations of torture and ill-treatment, and to inform it, within 90 days from the date of the transmittal of this decision, of the steps it has taken in response to the Views expressed above.

---

[18] Communications N° 6/1990 (*Henri Unai Parot* v. *Spain*) and N° 59/1996 (*Encarnación Blanco Abad* v. *Spain*).

Communication N° 195/2002

Submitted by: Mafhoud Brada (represented by counsel, Ms. de Linares of the Action of Christians for the Abolition of Torture (ACAT))
Alleged victim: The complainant
State party: France
Declared admissible: 29 April 2003
Date of adoption of Views: 17 May 2005

Subject matter: deportation of complainant to Algeria with alleged risk of torture

Procedural issues: exhaustion of domestic remedies; failure to comply with request for interim measures

Substantive issue: risk of torture after deportation

Article of the Convention: 3

1.1 The complainant, Mr. Mafhoud Brada, a citizen of Algeria, was residing in France when the present complaint was submitted. He was the subject of a deportation order to his country of origin. He claims that his forced repatriation to Algeria constitutes a violation by France of article 3 of the Convention against Torture and Other Cruel, Inhuman or Degrading Treatment or Punishment. He is represented by Action of Christians for the Abolition of Torture, a non-governmental organization.

1.2 In accordance with article 22, paragraph 3, of the Convention, the Committee brought the complaint to the State party's attention by note verbale dated 19 December 2001. At the same time, the Committee, acting in accordance with rule 108, paragraph 9, of its rules of procedure, requested the State party not to deport the complainant to Algeria while his complaint was being considered. The Committee reiterated its request in a note verbale dated 26 September 2002.

1.3 In a letter dated 21 October 2002 from the complainant's counsel, the Committee was informed that the complainant had been deported to Algeria on 30 September 2002 on a flight to Algiers, and that he had been missing since his arrival in Algeria.

The facts as submitted by the complainant

2.1 The complainant, a fighter pilot since 1993, was a member of the Algerian air force squadron based in Bechar, Algeria. From 1994 on, the squadron was regularly used, as a back-up for helicopter operations, to bomb Islamist maquis areas in the region of Sidi Bel Abbes. The fighter aircraft were equipped with incendiary bombs. The complainant and other pilots were aware that the use of such weapons was prohibited. After seeing the destruction caused by these weapons on the ground in photographs taken by military intelligence officers—pictures of dead men, women, children and animals—some pilots began to doubt the legitimacy of such operations.

2.2 In April 1994, the complainant and another pilot declared, during a briefing, that they would not participate in bombing operations against the civilian population, in spite of the risk of heavy criminal sanctions against them. A senior officer then waved his gun at the complainant's colleague, making it clear to him that refusal to carry out missions "meant death". When the two pilots persisted in their refusal to obey orders, the same officer loaded his gun and pointed it at the complainant's colleague, who was mortally wounded as he tried to escape through a window. The complainant, also wishing to escape, jumped out of another window and broke his ankle. He was arrested and taken to the interrogation centre of the regional security department in Bechar third military region. The complainant was detained for three months, regularly questioned about his links with the Islamists and frequently tortured by means of beatings and burning of his genitals.

2.3 The complainant was finally released owing to a lack of evidence of sympathy with the Islamists and in the light of positive reports concerning his service in the forces. He was forbidden to fly and assigned to Bechar airbase. Explaining that servicemen who were suspected of being linked to or sympathizing with the Islamists regularly "disappeared" or were murdered, he escaped from the base and took refuge in Ain Defla, where his family lived. The complainant also alleges that he received threatening letters from Islamist groups, demanding that he desert or risk execution. He forwarded the threatening letters to the police.

2.4 Later, when the complainant was helping a friend wash his car, a vehicle stopped alongside them and a submachine gun burst was fired in their direction. The complainant's friend was killed on the spot; the complainant survived because he was inside the car. The village police officer then advised the complainant to leave immediately. On 25 November 1994, the complainant succeeded in fleeing his country. He arrived at Marseilles and met one of his brothers in Orléans (Indre). In August 1995, the complainant made a request for asylum, which was later denied by the French Office for the Protection of Refugees and Stateless Persons (OFPRA). Since the complainant had made the request without the assistance of counsel, he was unable to appeal the decision to the Refugee Appeals Commission.

2.5 The complainant adds that, since he left Algeria, his two brothers have been arrested and tortured. One died in police custody. Moreover, since his desertion, two telegrams from the Ministry of Defence have arrived at the complainant's home in Abadia, demanding that he report immediately to air force headquarters in Cheraga in connection with a "matter concerning him". In 1998, the complainant was sentenced in France to eight years' imprisonment for a rape committed in 1995. The sentence was accompanied by a 10-year temporary ban from French territory. As the result of a remission of sentence, the complainant was released on 29 August 2001.

2.6 Meanwhile, on 23 May 2001, the prefect of Indre issued an order for the deportation of the complainant. In a decision taken on the same day, he determined that Algeria would be the country of destination. On 12 July 2001, the complainant lodged an appeal with the Limoges Administrative Court against the deportation order and the decision to return him to his country of origin. In an order dated 29 August 2001, the court's interim relief judge suspended enforcement of the decision on the country of return, considering that the risks to the complainant's safety involved in a return to Algeria raised serious doubts as to the legality of the deportation decision. Nevertheless, in a judgement dated 8 November 2001, the Administrative Court rejected the appeal against the order and the designated country of return.

2.7 On 4 January 2002, the complainant appealed against this judgement to the Bordeaux Administrative Court of Appeal. He points out that such an appeal does not have suspensive effect. He also refers to recent case law of the Council of State which he maintains demonstrates the inefficacy of domestic remedies in two similar cases.[1] In those cases, which involved deportation to Algeria, the Council of State dismissed the risks faced by the persons concerned, but the Algerian authorities subsequently unearthed a death sentence passed *in absentia*. On 30 September 2002, the complainant was deported to Algeria on a flight to Algiers and has been missing since.

The complaint

3.1 The complainant considers that his deportation to Algeria is a violation by France of article 3 of the Convention in so far as there are real risks of his being subjected to torture in his country of origin for the reasons mentioned above.

3.2 The complainant, supported by medical certificates, also maintains that he suffers from a serious neuropsychiatric disorder that requires constant treatment, the interruption of which would adversely affect his health. His doctors have considered these symptoms to be compatible with his allegations of torture. Moreover, the complainant's body shows traces of torture.

The State party's admissibility observations

4.1 By note verbale dated 28 February 2002, the State party challenged the admissibility of the complaint.

4.2 As its main argument, the State claimed that the complainant had not exhausted domestic remedies within the meaning of article 22, paragraph 5, of the Convention. On the date that the complaint was submitted to the Committee, the appeal to the Bordeaux Administrative Court of Appeal against the judgement upholding the order to deport the complainant was still pending. Moreover, there were no grounds for concluding that the procedure might exceed a reasonable time.

4.3 With regard to the complainant's argument that such an appeal did not suspend the deportation order, the State party maintained that the complainant had the option of applying to the interim relief judge of the Administrative Court of Appeal for suspension of the order. Indeed, the complainant had successfully made such an appeal to the Limoges Administrative Court.

4.4 Secondly, the State party maintained that the complaint submitted to the Committee was not in keeping with the provision of rule 107, paragraph 1 (b), of the rules of procedure that "the communication should be submitted by the individual himself or by his relatives or designated representatives or by others on behalf of an alleged victim when it appears that the victim is unable to submit the communication himself, and the author of the communication justifies his acting on the victim's behalf". However, the procedural documents did not indicate that the complainant designated Action of Christians for the Abolition of Torture as his representative, and it had not been established that the complainant is unable to instruct that organization to act on his behalf. It therefore had to be ascertained whether or not the purported representative, who signed the complaint, was duly authorized to act on the complainant's behalf.

Comments by counsel

5.1 In a letter dated 21 October 2002, counsel set out her comments on the State party's comments as to admissibility.

---

[1] The complainant refers to the *Chalabi* and *Hamani* cases.

5.2 In relation to the exhaustion of domestic remedies, counsel pointed out that, in accordance with the general principles of international law, the domestic remedies which must be exhausted are those which are effective, adequate or sufficient, in other words, which offer a serious chance of providing an effective remedy for the alleged violation. In this case, the annulment proceedings instituted before the Bordeaux Administrative Court of Appeal were still pending. Since that procedure had no suspensive effect, the deportation order against the complainant was enforced on 30 September 2002. Domestic remedies thus proved ineffective and inadequate.

5.3 Moreover, since the complainant was under the protection of the Committee by virtue of its request to the State party not to send him back to Algeria while his application was being considered, he had not considered it worthwhile to launch additional domestic proceedings, in particular interim relief proceedings for suspension.

5.4 In any event, the enforcement of the deportation order despite the pertinent arguments raised in the proceedings before the Bordeaux Administrative Court of Appeal rendered the appeal ineffective. Even if the Court were now to grant the complainant's appeal, it was unrealistic to imagine that Algeria would return him to France.

5.5 In response to the complaint that rule 107, paragraph 1, of the Committee's rules of procedure had not been respected, counsel referred to a statement signed by the complainant in person on 29 November 2001 authorizing the Action of Christians for the Abolition of Torture to act on his behalf before the Committee.

The Committee's treatment of State party's failure to accede to request for interim measures

6.1 The Committee observed that any State party which made the declaration provided for under article 22 of the Convention recognized the competence of the Committee against Torture to receive and consider complaints from individuals who claimed to be victims of violations of one of the provisions of the Convention. By making this declaration, States parties implicitly undertook to cooperate with the Committee in good faith by providing it with the means to examine the complaints submitted to it and, after such examination, to communicate its comments to the State party and the complainant. By failing to respect the request for interim measures made to it, the State party seriously failed in its obligations under article 22 of the Convention because it prevented the Committee from fully examining a complaint relating to a violation of the Convention, rendering action by the Committee futile and its comments worthless.

6.2 The Committee concluded that the adoption of interim measures pursuant to rule 108 of the rules of procedure, in accordance with article 22 of the Convention, was vital to the role entrusted to the Committee under that article. Failure to respect that provision, in particular through such irreparable action as deporting an alleged victim, undermined protection of the rights enshrined in the Convention.

Committee's admissibility decision

7.1 The Committee considered the admissibility of the complaint at its thirtieth session and declared the complaint admissible on 29 April 2003.

7.2 Concerning the *locus standi* of Action of Christians for the Abolition of Torture, the Committee noted that the statement signed by the complainant on 29 November 2001 authorizing the organization to act on his behalf before the Committee was in the file submitted to it, and therefore considered that the complaint complied with the conditions set out in rules 98 (2) and 107 (1) of its rules of procedure.

7.3 On the exhaustion of domestic remedies, the Committee noted that on 2 January 2002 the complainant had appealed to the Bordeaux Administrative Court of Appeal against the ruling of the Limoges Administrative Court upholding the deportation order, and that that appeal had no suspensive effect. Concerning the State party's argument that the complainant had had, but did not pursue, the option of applying to the interim relief judge of the Bordeaux court to suspend enforcement of the deportation order, the Committee noted that the State party had not indicated that the complainant should make such application by a specific deadline, implying that the application could in theory have been made at any time up to the moment when the Administrative Court of Appeal ruled on the merits of the appeal.

7.4 The Committee also noted that the complaint did not constitute an abuse of the right to submit a communication and was not incompatible with the Convention.

7.5 The Committee also noted that on 30 September 2002, after communicating its comments on the admissibility of the complaint, the State party had enforced the order for the deportation of the complainant to Algeria.

7.6 In the circumstances, the Committee considered it ought to decide whether domestic remedies had been exhausted when examining the admissibility of the complaint. In its view it was unarguable that, since the deportation order had been enforced before the Administrative Court of Appeal reached a decision on the appeal, the complainant had, from the moment he was deported to Algeria, had no opportunity to pursue the option of applying for suspension.

7.7 The Committee noted that, when it called for interim measures of protection such as those that would prevent the complainant from being deported to Algeria, it did so because it considered that there was a risk of irreparable harm. In such cases, a remedy which remains pending after the action which interim measures are intended to prevent has taken place is, by definition, pointless because the irreparable harm cannot be averted if the domestic remedy subsequently yields a decision favourable to the complainant: there is no longer any effective remedy to exhaust after the action which interim measures were intended to prevent has taken place. In the present case, the Committee felt no appropriate remedy was available to the complainant now he had been deported to Algeria, even if the domestic courts in the State party were to rule in his favour at the conclusion of proceedings which were still under way after the extradition.

7.8 In the present case, according to the Committee, the essential purpose of the appeal was to prevent the deportation of the complainant to Algeria. In this specific case, enforcing the deportation order rendered the appeal irrelevant by vitiating its intended effect: it was inconceivable that, if the appeal went in the complainant's favour, he would be repatriated to France. In the circumstances, in the Committee's view, the appeal was so intrinsically linked to the purpose of preventing deportation, and hence to the suspension of the deportation order, that it could not be considered an effective remedy if the deportation order was enforced before the appeal concluded.

7.9 To this extent, the Committee was of the view that returning the complainant to Algeria despite the request made to the State party under rule 108 of the rules of procedure, and before the admissibility of the complaint had been considered, made the remedies available to the complainant in France pointless, and the complaint was accordingly admissible under article 22, paragraph 5, of the Convention.

State party submission on interim measures issue and on merits

8.1 The State party submitted its observations on 26 September and 21 October 2003.

8.2 Regarding interim measures (paras. 6.1 and 6.2) and the Committee's repeated view that "failure to respect a call for interim measures pursuant to rule 108 of the rules of procedure, in particular through such an irreparable action as deporting the complainant, undermines protection of the rights enshrined in the Convention", the State party registers its firm opposition to such an interpretation.

According to the State party, article 22 of the Convention gives the Committee no authority to take steps binding on States parties, either in the consideration of the complaints submitted to it or even in the present case, since paragraph 7 of the article states only that "The Committee shall forward its views to the State party concerned and to the individual". Only the Committee's rules of procedure, which cannot of themselves impose obligations on States parties, make provision for such interim measures. The mere failure to comply with a request from the Committee thus cannot, whatever the circumstances, be regarded as "undermining protection of the rights enshrined in the Convention" or "rendering action by the Committee futile". The State party explains that when receiving a request for interim measures, cooperating in good faith with the Committee requires it only to consider the request very carefully and try to comply with it as far as possible. It points out that until now it has always complied with requests for interim measures, but that should not be construed as fulfilment of a legal obligation.

8.3 Concerning the merits of the complaint and the reasons for the deportation, the State party considers the complaint to be unfounded for the following reasons. First, the complainant never established, either in domestic proceedings or in support of his complaint, that he was in serious danger within the meaning of article 3 of the Convention. The State party refers to the Committee's case law whereby it is the responsibility of an individual who claims he would be in danger if sent back to a specific country to show, at least beyond reasonable doubt, that his fears are serious. The Committee has also stressed that "for article 3 of the Convention to apply, the individual concerned must face a foreseeable and real risk of being subjected to torture in the country to which he/she is being returned, and that this danger must be personal and present"[2] and that invoking a general situation or certain specific cases is not sufficient. According to the State party, while the complainant describes himself as a fighter pilot and an officer of the Algerian armed forces who has deserted for humanitarian reasons, he provides no proof. To establish that he is a deserter he has merely presented the Committee with two telegrams from the Algerian air force addressed to his family home; both are extremely succinct and merely request him "to present himself to the air force authorities in Béchar for a matter concerning him", without further details or any mention of his rank or former rank. In the State party's view it is very difficult to believe that the complainant was unable to produce any other document to substantiate the fears he expressed.

---

[2] *U.S.* v. *Finland*, complaint N° 197/2002, Views adopted on 1 May 2003.

8.4 Secondly, even if the complainant did establish that he was a fighter pilot and a deserter, his account contains various contradictions and implausibilities that discredit the fears invoked. In particular, he maintains that in early March, when along with another pilot he refused to participate in bombing operations against the civilian population, he knew that he risked heavy penalties by refusing to obey orders; he points out that such penalties were more severe for officers and, given the situation in Algeria, would have been handed down in time of war and included the death penalty for officers. While the other pilot had been shot on the spot for disobeying orders, the complainant had apparently been released after only three months in prison for the same conduct, his only punishment, once he had been cleared of suspected Islamist sympathies, being that he was forbidden to fly and assigned to the airbase. When he deserted from the airbase and fled to his family's village, an attempt was supposedly made to kill the complainant with a submachine gun fired from an intelligence vehicle: his neighbour was killed on the spot while he himself—the sole target—escaped once again.

8.5 The State party considers that the complainant's personal conduct renders his claims implausible. While he claims to have deserted in 1994 on humanitarian grounds as a conscientious objector, consciously exposing himself to the risk of very severe punishment, his humanitarian concerns seem totally at odds with his violent criminal conduct on arrival in France and subsequently. Scarcely a year after supposedly deserting on grounds of conscientious objection, the complainant perpetrated a common crime of particular gravity, namely, aggravated rape under threat of a weapon, and while in prison for that crime showed he was a continuing danger to society by making two violent attempts to escape.

8.6 In any case, the State party maintains that the complainant's alleged fears cannot be held to represent a serious danger of torture and inhuman or degrading treatment within the meaning of article 3 of the Convention. The complainant maintained that he faced two kinds of danger in the event of being sent back to Algeria: one, the result of his deserting, consisting in the punishment laid down in the Algerian military criminal code for such cases; the other related to the possibility that he might in the future again be accused of Islamist sympathies. The State party considers that the danger of imprisonment and other criminal penalties for desertion does not in itself establish a violation of article 3 of the Convention since these are the legal punishments for an ordinary offence in the estimation of most States parties to the Convention. It is important to note that, although the complainant maintains that punishment in the event of desertion may in extreme cases extend to the death penalty, he does not claim that he himself would incur that penalty. In fact, according to the State party, he could not: it emerges from his own account that his desertion was an individual act, unrelated to combat operations, after he had been suspended from flying and assigned to the airbase, while it emerges both from his written submission and from details of Algerian legislation compiled by Amnesty International and submitted on the complainant's behalf that the death penalty might possibly be applicable only in the case of a group desertion by officers. Secondly, although the complainant maintains that he was suspected of Islamist sympathies and tortured under questioning after refusing to obey orders, the State party concludes from the Committee's case law[3] that past torture, even where it is established that it was indeed inflicted in circumstances coming within the scope of the Convention, does not suffice to demonstrate a real and present danger for the future. In the present case, the State party stresses that it emerges from the complainant's own written submission that he was acquitted of accusations of Islamist sympathies. The State party further considers that the potential danger of the complainant's facing fresh charges of Islamist sympathies in the future does not seem substantial within the meaning of article 3 of the Convention, nor yet credible in terms of his own account, which suggests that his service file was sufficient for the military authorities to clear him of all suspicion in this regard and he was acquitted of the charges. Besides, it is hardly credible that he would have been released and assigned to the airbase if the military authorities had still had the slightest doubt about the matter. Since they had kept him on the actual airbase, the military authorities had clearly been convinced that not the slightest suspicion of sympathy towards the Armed Islamist Group (GIA) could be held against him. Here the State party notes that no complaint admissible by the Committee could arise out of the complainant's allegations that he had received death threats from armed Islamist groups, since such threats by a non-governmental entity not occupying the country were in any case beyond the scope of the Convention. Similarly, the State party notes that, although the complainant shows with the help of medical certificates that he suffers from a neuro-psychiatric disorder, he does not establish that this disorder, about which he gives no details, could not be adequately treated in Algeria.

8.7 The State party maintains that the dangers alleged by the complainant were given a fair and thorough review under domestic procedures. It recalls the Committee's case law whereby it is for the courts of the States parties to the Convention, and not for the Committee, to evaluate the facts and

---

[3] Ibid.

evidence in a particular case, unless it can be ascertained that the manner in which such facts and evidence were evaluated was clearly arbitrary or amounted to a denial of justice.[4] The question before the Committee is whether the complainant's deportation to the territory of another State violated France's obligations under the Convention, which means that it should be asked whether, when the French authorities decided to enforce the deportation order against the individual in question, they could reasonably consider in the light of the information available to them that he would be exposed to real danger if sent home. In actual fact, the dangers the complainant said he would face should he be sent back to his country of origin had been successively reviewed in France four times in six years by three different administrative authorities and one court, all of which had concluded that the alleged dangers were not substantial. In a judgement of 8 November 2001, the Limoges Administrative Court rejected the appeal against the deportation order submitted by the complainant on 16 July 2001 and the decision establishing Algeria as the country of destination, opening the way to enforcement of the order. The court considered that the complainant's allegations "lacked any justification". The complainant, who appealed the judgement to the Bordeaux Administrative Court of Appeal on 4 January 2002, makes no claim to the Committee that the manner in which the evidence he produced was evaluated by the Court of Appeal "was clearly arbitrary or amounted to a denial of justice". The complainant's application for political refugee status to the French Office for the Protection of Refugees and Stateless Persons (OFPRA) had previously been rejected, on 23 August 1995, on the grounds that he had not submitted sufficient evidence to prove that he was personally in one of the situations for which article 1 (A) (2) of the Geneva Convention relating to the Status of Refugees provides. The complainant had subsequently refrained from submitting his case to the Refugee Appeals Commission (CRR), an independent jurisdiction which carries out de facto and de jure reviews of OFPRA decisions, thus acquiescing in the decision taken in this regard. The complainant's situation had again been reviewed by the Minister of the Interior on 19 December 1997 further to the circular of 24 June 1997 on the regularization of the residence status of certain categories of illegal aliens, which allows prefects to issue residence permits to individuals who claim to be at risk if returned to their country of origin. Once again, the complainant limited himself to stating that he was a former member of the Armed Forces who had deserted from the Algerian army and been threatened by the GIA. For want of details, and in the absence of any justification for his allegations, his application was rejected. Once more, the complainant did not contest this decision in the competent domestic court. Before determining Algeria as the country he should be deported to, the prefect of Indre had conducted a further review of the risks he would run if returned to that country.

8.8 In the State party's view, by the day the deportation order was enforced, the complainant's situation must be said to have been fairly reviewed without him showing that he would be in serious and present danger of torture or inhuman treatment if returned to Algeria. The State party argues that the complainant continues to fail to offer evidence of such danger to support his complaint to the Committee.

8.9 In the circumstances, the State party was persuaded that the complainant's appeal to the Committee was but a device to gain time, thus abusing the State party's tradition, hitherto always respected, of suspending enforcement of a deportation order pending the Committee's decision on the admissibility of a complaint.

8.10 The State party explains that, despite this delaying tactic, the French Government would have acceded to the Committee's request for interim measures, albeit non-binding ones, if keeping the complainant, a demonstrably dangerous common criminal, in France had not also presented a particularly disproportionate risk to public order and the safety of third parties when set against the absence of any real benefit the complainant could hope to derive from his appeal. It was a fact that, during his first year in France, the complainant had committed aggravated rape, threatening his victim with a weapon, for which crime he had been imprisoned in July 1995 and sentenced by the Loiret Criminal Court to 8 years' imprisonment and a 10-year judicial ban from French territory. He had furthermore demonstrated the firmly rooted and persistent nature of the danger he represented to public order by two violent attempts to escape during his imprisonment, in September 1995 and July 1997, each punished by a term of eight months' imprisonment. In a situation that was extremely prejudicial to public safety, the State party explains that it nevertheless delayed enforcement of the deportation order long enough for a final review of the complainant's situation, to see whether he could be kept in France as the Committee wished. Once again, he was found not to have substantiated his alleged fears; in the circumstances, there was no justification for continuing to hold in France an individual who had more than demonstrated that he was a danger to public order and whose complaint to the Committee was quite clearly no more than a ploy to gain time, despite the obvious good faith of the human rights associations which had supported his

---

[4] *G.K.* v. *Switzerland*, complaint N° 219/2002, Views adopted on 7 May 2003.

application. The State party particularly stresses that house arrest would not have provided any guarantee, given the complainant's violent history of escape attempts. In the circumstances, the State party concluded that sending the complainant back to his country of origin was not likely to give rise to a "substantial danger" within the meaning of article 3 of the Convention.

8.11 As to the complainant's current situation, the State party explains that the Algerian authorities, from whom the French Government requested information, reported on 24 September 2003 that he was living in his home district of Algeria.

Comments by counsel

9.1 Counsel submitted comments on the State party's submission on 29 October and 14 November 2003. On the binding nature of requests for interim measures, counsel recalls that in two cases[5] where States parties to the Convention carried out deportations contrary to the Committee's opinion, the Committee found that action further to its terms of reference, which could include the rules of procedure under which suspension had been requested, was a treaty obligation.

9.2 Concerning the reasons put forward by the State party for enforcing the deportation order, counsel maintains that the complainant trained as a fighter pilot in Poland. Furthermore, according to counsel, his criminal act and his two escape attempts a year earlier did not mean that he would not have rebelled against bombing operations on civilian populations: counsel describes the considerable unrest in the Algerian army at the time, as illustrated by the escape of an Algerian lieutenant to Spain in 1998. As for the State party's contention that the complainant had not shown he was in serious danger of being tortured if he were returned to Algeria, since past torture not sufficing to establish the existence of a real and present danger in the future, counsel contends that the complainant actually was tortured, that modesty made him very reticent about the after-effects on his genitals, that he had to be treated for related psychiatric problems, and that the administrative court had been told only very vaguely about the torture, while a medical certificate had been submitted to the Bordeaux Administrative Court of Appeal. As to the future, counsel submits that the possible charges against the complainant, aggravated by the facts of his desertion and flight to France, made the danger of torture, by the Algerian military security in particular, sufficiently substantial to be taken into consideration. The State party argues that the dangers alleged by the complainant had already been reviewed thoroughly and fairly under domestic procedures; counsel acknowledges that OFPRA rejected the complainant's application for refugee status—on what grounds counsel does not know, since the application was declined while the complainant was in prison. Counsel also acknowledges that the complainant did not refer his case to the Refugee Appeals Commission (CRR). She points out that the Limoges Administrative Court likewise refused to overturn the decision establishing Algeria as the country of return although the interim relief judge had suspended the decision. Lastly, the complainant's more detailed submission to the Bordeaux Administrative Court of Appeal should have urged the administration to greater caution and, thus, to suspend his deportation.

9.3 Concerning the danger represented by the complainant and the risk to public safety, counsel maintains that he committed a serious act, but did not thereby pose a serious risk to the general public. On 18 March 1999, the complainant married a French citizen and had a daughter. When he left prison, no immediate attempt was made to deport him, although the Administration could have again tried to do so. According to counsel, it was only following a chance incident, in the form of a dispute with security officers, that the deportation order was reactivated.

9.4 In relation to the complainant's present situation, counsel considers that the State party's information is incorrect. She states that neither she nor his family in France have any news of him and that his brother in Algiers denies that he is living at the address given by the State party. Even if the complainant was where the State party said, remote though it is, counsel questions why there is no word from him: it could indicate that he is missing.

Supplementary submissions by counsel

10. On 14 January 2004, counsel submitted a copy of the decision by the Bordeaux Administrative Court of Appeal of 18 November 2003 overturning the judgement of the Limoges Administrative Court of 8 November 2001 and the decision of 23 May 2001 in which the prefect of Indre ordered the complainant to be returned to his country of origin. Concerning the decision to expel the complainant, the Court of Appeal reasoned as follows:

"Considering

that [the complainant] claims that he was subjected to torture and, several times, to attempted murder on account of his desertion from the national army because of his opposition to the operations to maintain order directed against the civilian population;

---

[5] *Núñez Chipana* v. *Venezuela*, complaint N° 110/1998, Views adopted on 10 November 1998; and *T.P.S.* v. *Canada*, complaint N° 99/1997, Views adopted on 16 May 2000.

that in support of his submissions to the court and concerning the risks of inhuman or degrading treatments to which his return to this country [Algeria] would expose him, he has supplied various materials, and notably a decision of the United Nations Committee against Torture concerning him, which are of such a nature as to attest to the reality of these risks;

that these elements, which were not known to the prefect of Indre, have not been contradicted by the minister of the interior, internal security and local liberties, who despite the request addressed to him by the court, did not produce submissions in defence before the closure of proceedings;

that, in these circumstances, [the complainant] must be considered as having established, within the meaning of article 27 bis cited above of the ordinance of 2 November 1945 [providing that "an alien cannot be returned to a State if it is established that his life or liberty are threatened there or he would be exposed to treatment contrary to article 3 of the European Convention], that he is exposed in Algeria to treatments contrary to article 3 of the European Convention on Human Rights and Fundamental Freedoms;

that, as a result, his request for the annulment of the decision to return him to his State of origin taken by the prefect of Indre on 23 May 2001 is well-founded".

State party's further comments

11.1 On 14 April 2004, the State party contended that the question before the Committee was whether *refoulement* of the complainant to another State violated France's obligations under the Convention; in other words whether, when the French authorities decided to enforce the deportation order they could reasonably think, in the light of the information available to them, that Mr. Brada would be exposed to substantial danger if sent home. The State party alludes to the Committee's case law holding that an individual claiming to be in danger if returned to a specific country is responsible, at least beyond reasonable doubt, for establishing that his fears are substantial. According to the State party, however, the complainant had produced no evidence before either the administrative court or the administrative authorities to substantiate his alleged fears about being returned to Algeria. The interim relief judge of the Limoges Administrative Court, to whom the complainant appealed against the decision of 29 August 2001 to deport him to Algeria, suspended the decision as to where the complainant should be deported pending a final judgement on the merits, so as to protect the complainant's situation should his fears prove justified. Noting, however, that the complainant's allegations were not accompanied by any supporting evidence, the Administrative Court subsequently rejected the appeal in a ruling dated 8 November 2001.

11.2 Ruling on 18 November 2003 on the complainant's appeal against the ruling by the Limoges Administrative Court of 8 November 2001, the Bordeaux Administrative Court of Appeal found that, given the seriousness of his crimes, the prefect of Indre could legitimately have considered that the complainant's presence on French territory constituted a serious threat to public order, and that his deportation was not, in the circumstances, a disproportionate interference with his private and family life.

11.3 The court overturned the judgement of the Limoges Administrative Court and the decision by the prefect of Indre to remove the individual in question to his country of origin based on article 3 of the European Convention on Human Rights and article 27 bis of the order of 2 November 1945 prohibiting the deportation of an alien to a country where it is established that he would be exposed to treatment contrary to article 3 of the Convention.

11.4 According to the State party, particular emphasis should be placed on the fact that, in so doing, the Administrative Court of Appeal based its ruling on evidence which, it noted expressly, was new. It deduced that, in the circumstances, the complainant's allegations must be considered well-founded unless contradicted by the Minister of the Interior, and thus overturned the decision establishing the country of destination.

11.5 The State party stresses that the court's proviso—unless contradicted by the Ministry of the Interior—should not be understood to indicate that the administration was prepared to acknowledge that the complainant's submissions were compelling. The court was unable to take account of evidence produced by the administration for the defence only because of the rules on litigious proceedings deriving from article R.612.6 of the Code of Administrative Justice: the defence brief produced by the Ministry of the Interior reached the court some days after the termination of pretrial proceedings.

11.6 Furthermore, the State party explains that the key point on which the court based its decision is the very decision the Committee used to find the present complaint admissible. In pronouncing on admissibility, however, the Committee did not take any stand on the merits of the complaint, nor on the establishment by the complainant, beyond reasonable doubt, of the facts he invoked, since they could only be evaluated in the context of the decision on the merits of the complaint. The State party concludes that, given the reasoning behind it, the decision by the Administrative Court of Appeal does nothing to strengthen the complainant's position before the Committee.

11.7 This being so, the State party alludes to the Committee's recently reiterated view that it is for the courts of the States parties to the Convention, and not for the Committee, to evaluate the facts and evidence in a particular case, unless it can be ascertained that the manner in which such facts and evidence were evaluated was clearly arbitrary or amounted to a denial of justice.[6] The ruling by the Administrative Court of Appeal shows precisely that the manner in which the domestic courts examined the facts and evidence produced by the complainant cannot be regarded as clearly arbitrary or tantamount to a denial of justice.

11.8 In conclusion, the State party maintains that France cannot be held to have ignored its treaty obligations by removing the individual in question to his country of origin after checking several times, before arriving at that decision, that the complainant could not reasonably be considered to be exposed to danger if he was sent home. With regard to the Committee's case law, it cannot be supposed that the French authorities could reasonably have considered that he would be exposed to real danger in the event of being sent home when they decided to enforce the deportation order against him.

Comments by counsel

12. In her comments of 11 June 2004, counsel maintains that the State party violated article 3 of the Convention. She adds that she had had a telephone conversation with the complainant, who said he had been handed over by the French police to Algerian agents in the plane; on leaving Algiers airport in a van, he was handed over to the Algerian secret services who kept him in various different venues for a year and half before releasing him without documents of any kind, apparently pending a judgement, the judgement *in absentia* having been annulled. The complainant claims that he was severely tortured.

Consideration of the merits

13.1 The Committee must decide, pursuant to article 3, paragraph 1, of the Convention, whether there are substantial grounds for believing that the complainant would be in danger of being subjected to torture upon return to Algeria. The Committee observes, at the outset, that in cases where a person has been expelled at the time of its consideration of the complaint, the Committee assesses what the State party knew or should have known at the time of expulsion. Subsequent events are relevant to the assessment of the State party's knowledge, actual or constructive, at the time of removal.

13.2 In reaching this decision, the Committee must take into account all relevant considerations, pursuant to article 3, paragraph 2, of the Convention, including the existence of a consistent pattern of gross, flagrant or mass violations of human rights. The aim of the determination, however, is to establish whether the individual concerned would be personally at risk of being subjected to torture in the country to which he would return. It follows that the existence of a consistent pattern of gross, flagrant or mass violations of human rights in a country does not as such constitute a sufficient ground for determining that a particular person would be in danger of being subjected to torture upon his return to that country; additional grounds must exist to show that the individual concerned would be personally at risk. Similarly, the absence of a consistent pattern of gross violations of human rights does not mean that a person cannot be considered to be in danger of being subjected to torture in his or her specific circumstances. In deciding a particular case, the Committee recalls that, according to its General Comment on article 3 of the Convention, it gives "considerable weight" to the findings of national authorities.

13.3 At the outset, the Committee observes that at the time of his expulsion on 30 September 2002, an appeal lodged by the complainant with the Bordeaux Administrative Court of Appeal on 4 January 2002 was still pending. This appeal contained additional arguments against his deportation that had not been available to the prefect of Indre when the decision of expulsion was taken and of which the State party's authorities were, or should have, been aware still required judicial resolution at the time he was in fact expelled. Even more decisively, on 19 December 2001, the Committee had indicated interim measures to stay the complainant's expulsion until it had had an opportunity to examine the merits of the case, the Committee having established, through its Special Rapporteur on Interim Measures, that in the present case the complainant had established an arguable risk of irreparable harm. This interim measure, upon which the complainant was entitled to rely, was renewed and repeated on 26 September 2002.

13.4 The Committee observes that the State party, in ratifying the Convention and voluntarily accepting the Committee's competence under article 22, undertook to cooperate with it in good faith in applying and giving full effect to the procedure of individual complaint established thereunder. The State party's action in expelling the complainant in the face of the Committee's request for interim measures nullified the effective exercise of the right to complain conferred by article 22, and has rendered the Committee's final decision on the merits futile and devoid of object. The Committee thus concludes that in expelling the complainant in

---

[6] Op. cit.

the circumstances that it did the State party breached its obligations under article 22 of the Convention.

13.5 The Committee observes, turning to issue under article 3 of the Convention, that the Bordeaux Administrative Court of Appeal, following the complainant's expulsion, found upon consideration of the evidence presented, that the complainant was at risk of treatment in breach of article 3 of the European Convention, a finding which would could encompass torture (see para. 10.1 above). The decision to expel him was thus, as a matter of domestic law, unlawful.

13.6 The Committee observes that the State party is generally bound by the findings of the Court of Appeal, with the State party observing simply that the Court had not considered the State's brief to the court which arrived after the relevant litigation deadlines. The Committee considers, however, that this default on the part of the State party cannot be imputed to the complainant, and, moreover, whether the Court's consideration would have been different remains speculative. As the State party itself states (see para. 11.7) and with which the Committee agrees, the judgement of the Court of Appeal, which includes the conclusion that his expulsion occurred in breach of article 3 of the European Convention, cannot on the information before the Committee be regarded as clearly arbitrary or tantamount to a denial of justice. As a result, the Committee also concludes that the complainant has established that his removal was in breach of article 3 of the Convention against Torture and Other Cruel, Inhuman or Degrading Treatment or Punishment.

14. The Committee against Torture, acting under article 22, paragraph 7, of the Convention against Torture and Other Cruel, Inhuman or Degrading Treatment or Punishment, considers that the deportation of the complainant to Algeria constituted a breach of articles 3 and 22 of the Convention.

15. Pursuant to rule 112, paragraph 5, of its rules of procedure, the Committee wishes to be informed, within 90 days, of the steps the State party has taken in response to the Views expressed above, including measures of compensation for the breach of article 3 of the Convention and determination, in consultation with the country (also a State party to the Convention) to which the complainant was returned, of his current whereabouts and state of well-being.

Communication N° 207/2002

Submitted by: Mr. Dragan DIMITRIJEVIC (represented by counsel)
Alleged victim: The complainant
State party: Serbia and Montenegro
Date of adoption of Views: 24 November 2004

Subject matter: torture of complainant by police

Procedural issue: exhaustion of domestic remedies

Substantive issues: failure to take effective measures to prevent torture; lack of prompt and impartial investigation of acts of torture; cruel, inhuman and degrading treatment or punishment

Articles of the Convention: 1, 2 (1), 12, 13, 14, 16

1. The complainant is Mr. Dragan Dimitrijevic, a Serbian citizen of Roma origin born on 7 March 1977. He claims to have been the victim of violations by Serbia and Montenegro of articles 2, paragraph 1, read in conjunction with article 1; article 16, paragraph 1; and articles 12, 13 and 14 taken alone and/or together with article 16, paragraph 1, of the Convention. He is represented by the non-governmental organizations Humanitarian Law Center, based in Belgrade, and European Roma Rights Center, based in Budapest.

The facts as submitted by the complainant

2.1 The complainant was arrested on 27 October 1999 at around 11 a.m. at his home in Kragujevac, Serbia, in connection with the investigation of a crime. He was taken to the local police station located in Svetozara Markovica Street. Upon arrival he was handcuffed to a radiator and beaten up by several police officers, some of whom the complainant knew by their first names or their nicknames. The police officers kicked and punched him all over his body while insulting his ethnic origins and cursing his "gypsy mother". One of the officers struck the complainant with a big metal bar. Some time later the officers unfastened the complainant from the radiator and handcuffed him to a bicycle. Then they continued punching and beating him with their nightsticks and the metal bar. At one point the complainant began bleeding from his ears, despite which the beating continued until he was released at about 4.30 p.m.

2.2 As a result of the ill-treatment the author had to stay in bed for several days. He sustained injuries on both arms and legs, an open wound on the back of his head and numerous injuries all over his back. For several days following the incident he bled from his left ear and his eyes and lips remained swollen. Fearing reprisals by the police the complainant did not go to hospital for treatment. Consequently, there is no official medical certificate documenting the injuries referred to above. The complainant, however, has provided the Committee with written statements from his mother, his sister and a cousin indicating that the he was in good health when he was arrested and severely injured at the time of his release.

2.3 On 31 January 2000, the complainant, through counsel, filed a criminal complaint with the Kragujevac Municipal Public Prosecutor's Office alleging that he had been the victim of the crimes of slight bodily harm and civil injury, as provided for under articles 54 (2) and 66 of the Serbian Criminal Code respectively. As there was no response for almost six months following the submission of the complaint, the complainant wrote a letter to the Public Prosecutor's Office on 26 July 2000 requesting an update on the status of the case and invoking, in particular, article 12 of the Convention. By the time the complainant submitted his case to the Committee, i.e., more than 23 months after the submission of the criminal complaint, no response had been received from the Public Prosecutor.

2.4 The complainant claims that he has exhausted available domestic criminal remedies and refers to international jurisprudence according to which only a criminal remedy can be considered effective and sufficient in addressing violations of the kind at issue in the instant case. He also refers to the relevant provisions of the State party's Criminal Procedure Code (CPC) setting forth the obligation of the Public Prosecutor to undertake measures necessary for the investigation of crimes and the identification of the alleged perpetrators.

2.5 Furthermore, under article 153 (1) of the CPC, if the public prosecutor decides that there is no basis for the institution of a formal judicial investigation he must inform the complainant, who can then exercise his prerogative to take over the prosecution in the capacity of a "private prosecutor". However, the CPC sets no time limit in which the public prosecutor must decide whether or not to request a formal judicial investigation. In the absence of such decision the victim cannot take over the prosecution of the case on his own behalf. Prosecutorial inaction following a complaint filed by the victim therefore amounts to an insurmountable impediment in the exercise of the victim's right to act as a private prosecutor and to have his case heard before a court. Finally, even if there were a legal possibility for the victim himself to file for a formal judicial investigation because of the inaction of the public prosecutor, this would in effect be unfeasible if, as in the instant case, the police and the public prosecutor had failed to identify all of the alleged perpetrators beforehand. Article 158 (3) of the CPC provides that the person against whom a formal judicial investigation is requested must be identified by name, address and other relevant personal data. A contrario, such a request cannot be filed if the alleged perpetrator is unknown.

The complaint

3.1 The complainant claims that the acts described constitute a violation of several provisions of the Convention, in particular articles 2, paragraph 1, read in conjunction with article 1; article 16, paragraph 1; and articles 12, 13 and 14 taken alone and/or together with article 16, paragraph 1. Such acts were perpetrated with a discriminatory motive and for the purpose of extracting a confession or otherwise intimidating and/or punishing him. He also submits that his allegations should be interpreted in the context of the serious human rights situation in the State party and, in particular, the systematic police brutality to which Roma and others are subjected to. In evaluating his claim the Committee should take into account his Romani ethnicity and the fact that his membership in a historically disadvantaged minority group renders him particularly vulnerable to degrading treatment. All else being equal, a given level of physical abuse is more likely to constitute "degrading or inhuman treatment or punishment" when motivated by racial animus and/or coupled with racial epithets than when racial considerations are absent.

3.2 With respect to article 12 read alone or taken together with article 16, paragraph 1, of the Convention, the complainant claims that the State party's authorities failed to conduct a prompt, impartial and comprehensive investigation into the incident at issue, notwithstanding ample evidence that an act of torture and/or cruel, inhuman and degrading treatment or punishment had been committed. Public prosecutors seldom institute criminal proceedings against police officers accused of violence and/or misconduct even though such cases are in the category of those that are officially prosecuted by the State. When the victims themselves or NGOs on their behalf file complaints against police misconduct, public prosecutors as a rule fail to initiate proceedings. They generally restrict themselves to requesting information from the police authorities and, when none is forthcoming, they take no further action. Judicial dilatoriness in proceedings involving police brutality often results in the expiration of the time period envisaged by law for the prosecution of the case. Notwithstanding the proclaimed principle of the independence of the judiciary, practice makes clear that public prosecutor's offices do not operate on this principle and that both they and the courts are not independent of the agencies and offices of the Ministry of Internal Affairs. This is especially true with respect to incidents of police misconduct.

3.3 With respect to article 13 of the Convention the complainant submits that the right to complain implies not just a legal possibility to do so but also the right to an effective remedy for the harm suffered. In view of the fact that he has received no redress for the violations at issue he concludes that his rights under article 13 taken alone and/or in conjunction with article 16, paragraph 1, of the Convention have been violated.

3.4 The complainant further claims that his rights under article 14 taken alone and/or in conjunction with article 16, paragraph 1, of the Convention have been violated. By failing to provide him with a criminal remedy the State party has barred him from obtaining "fair and adequate compensation" in a civil lawsuit, "including the means for as full a rehabilitation as possible." Pursuant to domestic law, the complainant had the possibility of seeking compensation by way of two different procedures: (1) criminal proceedings, under article 103 of the Criminal Procedure Code, that should have been instituted on the basis of his criminal complaint, or (2) in a civil action for damages under articles 154 and 200 of the Law on Obligations. Since no formal criminal proceedings followed as a result of his complaint with the Public Prosecutor, the first avenue remained closed to him. As regards the second avenue, the author filed no civil action for compensation given that it is standard practice of the State party's courts to suspend civil cases for damages arising out of criminal offences until prior completion of the respective criminal proceedings. Had the complainant decided to sue for damages immediately following the incident, he would have faced another insurmountable procedural impediment caused by the inaction of the public prosecutor office. Namely, articles 186 and 106 of the Civil Procedure Code stipulate that both parties to a civil action, the plaintiff and the respondent, must be identified by name, address and other relevant personal data. Since the complainant to date remains unaware of this information and as it was exactly the duty of the public prosecutor's office to establish these facts, instituting a civil action for compensation would have clearly been procedurally impossible and thus rejected by the civil court.

State party's admissibility and merits submissions

4. The complaint with its accompanying documents was transmitted to the State party on 17 April 2002. Since the State party did not respond to the Committee's request, under rule 109 of the rules of procedure, to submit information and observations in respect of the admissibility and merits of the complaint within six months, a reminder was addressed to it on 12 December 2002. On 20 October 2003, the State party informed the Committee that the Ministry on Human and Minority Rights was still in the process of collecting data from the relevant authorities with a view to responding on the merits of the complaint. Such response, however, has not been received by the Committee.

Issues and proceedings before the Committee

5.1 The Committee notes the State party's failure to provide information with regard to the admissibility or merits of the complaint. In the circumstances, the Committee, acting in accordance with rule 109, paragraph 7, of its rules of procedure, is obliged to consider the admissibility and the merits of the complaint in the light of the available information, due weight being given to the complainant's allegations to the extent that they have been sufficiently substantiated.

5.2 Before considering any claims contained in a complaint, the Committee against Torture must decide whether or not the complaint is admissible under article 22 of the Convention. In the present case the Committee has ascertained, as it is required to do under article 22, paragraph 5 (a), of the Convention, that the same matter has not been and is not being examined under another procedure of international investigation or settlement. With respect to the exhaustion of domestic remedies, the Committee took note of the information provided by the complainant about the criminal complaint which he filed with the public prosecutor. The Committee considers that the insurmountable procedural impediment faced by the complainant as a result of the inaction of the competent authorities rendered the application of a remedy that may bring effective relief to the complainant highly unlikely. In the absence of pertinent information from the State party the Committee concludes that the domestic proceedings, if any, have been unreasonably prolonged. With reference to article 22, paragraph 4, of the Convention and rule 107 of the Committee's rules of procedure the Committee finds no other obstacle to the admissibility of the complaint. Accordingly, it declares the complaint admissible and proceeds to its examination on the merits.

5.3 The complainant alleges violations by the State party of article 2, paragraph 1, in connection with article 1, and of article 16, paragraph 1, of the Convention. The Committee notes in this respect the description made by the complainant of the treatment he was subjected to while in detention, which can be characterized as severe pain or suffering intentionally inflicted by public officials in the context of the investigation of a crime, and the written testimonies of witnesses to his arrest and release that the complainant has provided. The Committee also notes that the State party has not contested the facts as presented by the complainant, which took place more than five years ago. In the circumstances the Committee concludes that due weight must be given to the complainant's allegations and that the facts, as submitted, constitute torture within the meaning of article 1 of the Convention.

5.4 Concerning the alleged violation of articles 12 and 13 of the Convention, the Committee notes that the public prosecutor never informed the complainant about whether an investigation was being or had been conducted after the criminal complaint was filed on 31 January 2000. It also notes that the failure to inform the complainant of the results of such investigation, if any, effectively prevented him from pursuing "private prosecution" of his case before a judge. In these circumstances the Committee considers that the State party has failed to comply with its obligation, under article 12 of the Convention, to carry out a prompt and impartial investigation wherever there is reasonable ground to believe that an act of torture has been committed. The State party also failed to comply with its obligation, under article 13, to ensure the complainant's right to complain and to have his case promptly and impartially examined by the competent authorities.

5.5 As for the alleged violation of article 14 of the Convention the Committee notes the complainant's allegations that the absence of criminal proceedings deprived him of the possibility of filing a civil suit for compensation. In view of the fact that the State party has not contested this allegation and given the passage of time since the complainant initiated legal proceedings at the domestic level, the Committee concludes that the State party has also violated its obligations under article 14 of the Convention in the present case.

6. The Committee, acting under article 22, paragraph 7, of the Convention, is of the view that the facts before it disclose a violation of articles 2, paragraph 1, in connection with article 1; 12; 13; and 14 of the Convention against Torture and Other Cruel, Inhuman or Degrading Treatment or Punishment.

7. The Committee urges the State party to conduct a proper investigation into the facts alleged by the complainant and, in accordance with rule 112, paragraph 5, of its rules of procedure, to inform it, within 90 days from the date of the transmittal of this decision, of the steps taken in response to the Views expressed above.

Communication N° 212/2002

Submitted by: Mr. Kepa Urra Guridi (represented by counsel, Mr. Didier Rouget)
Alleged victim: The complainant
State party: Spain
Date of adoption of Views: 17 May 2005

Subject matter: torture of complainant by police

Procedural issues: exhaustion of domestic remedies; status of "victim"

Substantive issues: torture; failure to take effective measures to prevent torture; failure to ensure that all acts of torture are offences under criminal law of the State party; right to obtain redress

Articles of the Convention: 1, 2, 4, 14

1. The author of the complaint, submitted on 8 February 2002, is Kepa Urra Guridi, a Spanish national born in 1956. He alleges that he is a victim of a violation by Spain of articles 2, 4 and 14 of the Convention against Torture and Other Cruel, Inhuman or Degrading Treatment or Punishment. The complainant is represented by counsel, Mr. Didier Rouget.

The facts as submitted by the complainant

2.1 On 22 January 1992, the Spanish Civil Guard launched a police operation in Vizcaya province to dismantle the so-called "Bizkaia combat unit" of the organization Euskadi Ta Askatasuna (ETA). In all, 43 people were arrested between then and 2 April 1992; many of them have reportedly been tortured and held incommunicado. The complainant was arrested on 22 January 1992 by Civil Guard officers as part of these operations.

2.2 The complainant alleges that, in the course of his transfer to the Civil Guard station, the officers took him to a piece of open ground where they subjected him to severe abuse. He was stripped, handcuffed, dragged along the ground and beaten. He states that after six hours of interrogation, he had to be taken to hospital because his pulse rate was very high, he could not speak, he was exhausted and unconscious, and was bleeding from his mouth and nose. The hospital doctors ascertained that he had injuries to his head, face, eyelids, nose, back, stomach, hip, arms and legs. He also had a neck injury which left him unable to move. The complainant maintains that this serious ill-treatment can be categorized as torture within the meaning of article 1 of the Convention.

2.3 The complainant filed suit with Vizcaya Provincial Court alleging that he had been tortured, and on 7 November 1997 the court found three civil guards guilty of torture. Each officer received a prison sentence of four years, two months and one day, was disqualified from serving in State security agencies and units for six years and one day, and suspended from duty for the duration of his prison sentence. Under the terms of the sentence, the civil guards were ordered to pay compensation of 500,000 pesetas to the complainant. The court held that the injuries sustained by the complainant had been caused by the civil guards in the area of open country where he was taken following his arrest.

2.4 The public prosecutor's office appealed the sentence to the Supreme Court, asking for the charges to be reviewed and the sentences reduced. In its judgement of 30 September 1998, the Supreme Court decided to reduce the civil guards' prison sentence to one year. In its judgement, the Supreme Court held that the civil guards had assaulted the complainant with a view to obtaining a confession about his activities and the identities of other individuals belonging to the Bizkaia combat unit. It took the view that "fact-finding" torture of a degree exceeding cruel or degrading treatment had been established, but held that the injuries suffered by the complainant had not required medical or surgical attention: the first aid the complainant had received was sufficient. The Court considered that a sentence of one year's imprisonment was in proportion to the gravity of the offence.

2.5 While the appeal was pending before the Supreme Court, one of the civil guards continued to work in French territory as an anti-terrorism coordinator with the French security forces, and with the authorization of the Ministry of the Interior embarked on studies with a view to promotion to the grade of Civil Guard commander.

2.6 The Ministry of Justice initiated proceedings to have the three convicted civil guards pardoned. The Council of Ministers, at its meeting of 16 July 1999, granted pardons to the three civil guards, suspending them from any form of public office for one month and one day. Notwithstanding this suspension, the Ministry of the Interior kept one of the civil guards on active duty in a senior post. The pardons were granted by the King in decrees published in Spain's Official Gazette.

2.7 The complainant alleges that he has exhausted all available domestic remedies and has not submitted the matter to any other procedure of international investigation.

The complaint

3.1 The complainant alleges that article 2 of the Convention has been violated because the various acts of the Spanish political and judicial authorities effectively legitimize the practice of torture, leading torturers to believe that they are virtually immune from prosecution, and demonstrating that the authorities condone serious ill-treatment that can be classified as torture.

3.2 The complainant alleges a violation of article 4 of the Convention. He argues that an example should be made of State officials found guilty of torture. According to him, both the reductions in prison terms and the pardons granted to the torturers violate the right of victims to obtain effective justice. He claims that the authorities of the State party, by taking decisions that effectively reduce the sentences and the actual punishment meted out to State officials convicted of torture, have violated article 4 of the Convention.

3.3 He further claims that there has been a violation of article 14 of the Convention, since the pardoning of the civil guards is tantamount to denying the fact of the complainant's torture and suffering. According to the complainant, the State party should have redressed the wrong he had suffered as a victim of torture and taken steps to ensure that such acts did not happen again. He adds that the pardon accorded to the torturers encourages the practice of torture within the Civil Guard. According to the complainant, remedial measures cover all the damages suffered by the victim, including restitution, compensation, rehabilitation, satisfaction and guarantees of non-repetition, as well as prevention, investigation, and punishment of the persons responsible. In this regard, he cites the studies carried out by the United Nations Commission on Human Rights on the impunity of perpetrators of violations of human rights and on the right to restitution, compensation and rehabilitation for victims of grave violations of human rights, as well as the judgement of the Inter-American Court of Human Rights in the case of *Velásquez Rodríguez v. Honduras*.

3.4 The complainant believes that systematic practice in the State party, exemplified by failure to investigate cases of torture promptly and impartially, protracted investigations, the imposition of minimum sentences, the retention in the security bodies of persons accused of torture and the promotion, decoration and pardoning of persons accused of torture, allows torture to go unpunished. He refers to the conclusions and recommendations of the Committee with reference to the second, third and fourth periodic reports submitted by the State party, in which it expressed concern at the lenient sentences imposed on persons accused of torture and recommended that the State party impose appropriate punishments.

State party's admissibility and merits observations

4.1 The State party considers the complaint inadmissible because it says that the complainant has failed to exhaust domestic remedies. It argues that the complainant should have appealed against the royal decrees of 1999 that granted the pardons. It states that both the Supreme Court and the Court of Jurisdictional Disputes have held that a pardon may be subject to judicial review. It adds that the Convention against Torture has been incorporated into domestic law and may be invoked directly before the courts and, if the complainant maintains that granting pardons violates the Convention, he should have put this argument to the Spanish courts.

4.2 As to the merits, the State party maintains that the victim of a crime has no right to block a pardon, the granting of which is a prerogative of the King acting in accordance with the Constitution. It claims that, according to the position adopted by the human rights treaty bodies, victims have no right to ask for anyone to be convicted, and accordingly it would be a contradiction to grant them the right to block a pardon. When a crime is investigated ex officio, the granting of a pardon does not provide for the victim's involvement and, therefore, the interests of the victim of the crime are unaffected. The State party adds that it was the civil guards themselves who requested the pardon.

4.3 The State party claims that the complainant received the full compensation awarded to him by the court.

4.4 The State party indicates that, until such time as a guilty verdict was handed down in the complainant's case, the accused went about their business as normal, which included one of them taking a course of studies with a view to promotion, as anyone is legally entitled to do in the absence of measures affecting their rights. Upon conviction, the civil guards lodged an application for pardon with the Vizcaya provincial court, with the request that the sentence should not be carried out until a decision had been reached on their request for a pardon. Although the court did not manage to order execution of the sentence, the complainant could have asked it to. Once the pardon had been granted, the civil guards were suspended from duty for one month and one day.

Complainant's comments

5.1 On the admissibility of the complaint, the complainant indicates that, in the circumstances of his case, there were no domestic remedies against the granting of a pardon. He adds that neither the 1870 statute on pardons nor the position adopted by the Constitutional Court permits a private individual to object to a pardon. He cites the Constitutional Court judgement of 5 October 1990, which says that pardons "as a gesture of grace, shall be decided upon by the executive and granted by the King. Such decisions shall not be examined on their merits by the courts, including this Constitutional Court". The complainant maintains that the most recent judgements of the Constitutional Court, those handed down between January and March 2001, did not introduce a means of appealing against pardons but merely gave the sentencing court a certain degree of procedural control. The victim is not informed that a pardon has been granted and is thus denied the opportunity to appeal. The complainant states that the pardons procedure specifies that the victim of the pardoned crime should be given a hearing. He objected to the pardons when consulted, but his views were not binding.

5.2 On the merits, the complainant maintains that the pardon granted by the authorities to civil guards convicted of torture is incompatible with the purpose and object of the Convention, inasmuch as it calls into question the absolute nature of the prohibition of torture and other cruel, inhuman or degrading treatment. Granting pardons creates a climate of impunity that encourages State officials to commit further acts of torture. When the pardon was granted, the accused's sense of impunity was validated by the Spanish authorities' common practice of pardoning individuals accused of torture. The State party should have redressed the wrongs suffered by the complainant and taken steps to ensure that such torture would not happen again. The complainant insists that the pardon granted to the civil guards denies the very existence of the torture and ill-treatment of which he was the victim.

Issues and proceedings before the Committee

6.1 Before examining the merits of a communication, the Committee against Torture must determine whether it is admissible under article 22 of the Convention.

6.2 The State party is of the view that the communication is inadmissible because domestic remedies have not been exhausted. It claims that, if the complainant considers that his rights under the Convention have been violated by the pardoning of the three civil guards, he ought to have put this argument to the Spanish courts. The complainant maintains that there were no available and effective means to challenge the granting of a pardon.

6.3 The Committee observes that the State party confined itself to asserting that recent decisions by the courts permit the judicial review of pardons, and that the Convention against Torture can be invoked before the domestic courts; it did not indicate what specific remedies were available to the complainant, nor what degree of judicial review pardons would be subject to. The Committee notes that, although the injured party may not be a party to pardon proceedings in a material sense, he or she can be heard if he or she opposes the pardon, and that, according to the State party, the injured party has no right as such to request that no pardon be allowed. The Committee recalls that it is necessary to exhaust only those remedies that have a reasonable chance of success, and is of the view that, in the present case, the complainant did not have such remedies available. Accordingly, the Committee considers the communication admissible under article 22, paragraph 5 (b), of the Convention.

6.4 The Committee notes that the complainant has alleged violations of articles 2 and 4 of the Convention, maintaining that the State party has failed in its obligations to prevent and punish torture. These provisions apply to the extent that the acts of which the complainant was a victim are considered to be torture within the meaning of article 1 of the Convention. The Committee takes note of the complainant's allegation that his treatment constituted torture within the meaning of the Convention. In the Committee's view, however, it is unnecessary to rule on whether the treatment meted out to the complainant was consistent with the concept of torture within the meaning of article 1 of the Convention, since the State party has not contradicted the complainant's allegation that he was tortured. The Committee notes that the courts that tried the complainant's case concluded that he had indeed been tortured. The Committee must, however, rule on the State party's argument that the complainant does not have a right to object to the granting of the pardon, and that the complainant therefore does not qualify as a victim in the meaning of article 22, paragraph 1, of the Convention. The Committee points out that the State party has not denied that the complainant was tortured, allowing criminal proceedings to be brought against the civil guards who injured the complainant and accepting that the treatment suffered by the complainant was described during the trial as torture, and that three people were in principle found guilty.

6.5 The Committee accordingly considers that the complaint raises issues of importance in connection with article 2, paragraph 1, article 4, paragraph 2, and article 14, paragraph 1, of the Convention, which should be examined on their merits.

6.6 As to the alleged violation of article 2 of the Convention, the Committee notes the complainant's argument that the obligation to take effective measures to prevent torture has not been honoured because the pardons granted to the civil guards have the practical effect of allowing torture to go unpunished and encouraging its repetition. The Committee is of the view that, in the circumstances of the present case, the measures taken by the State party are contrary to the obligation established in article 2 of the Convention, according to which the State party must take effective measures to prevent acts of torture. Consequently, the Committee concludes that such acts constitute a violation of article 2, paragraph 1, of the Convention. The Committee also concludes that the absence of appropriate punishment is incompatible with the duty to prevent acts of torture.

6.7 With regard to the alleged violation of article 4, the Committee recalls its previous jurisprudence to the effect that one of the purposes of the Convention is to avoid allowing persons who have committed acts of torture to escape unpunished. The Committee also recalls that article 4 sets out a duty for States parties to impose appropriate penalties against those held responsible for committing acts of torture, taking into account the grave nature of those acts. The Committee considers that, in the circumstances of the present case, the imposition of lighter penalties and the granting of pardons to the civil guards are incompatible with the duty to impose appropriate punishment. The Committee further notes that the civil guards were not subject to disciplinary proceedings while criminal proceedings were in progress, though the seriousness of the charges against them merited a disciplinary investigation. Consequently, the Committee considers that there has been a violation of article 4, paragraph 2, of the Convention.

6.8 As to the alleged violation of article 14, the State party indicates that the complainant received the full amount of compensation ordered by the trial court and claims that the Convention has therefore not been violated. However, article 14 of the Convention not only recognizes the right to fair and adequate compensation but also imposes on States the duty to guarantee compensation for the victim of an act of torture. The Committee considers that compensation should cover all the damages suffered by the victim, which includes, among other measures, restitution, compensation, and rehabilitation of the victim, as well as measures to guarantee the non-repetition of the violations, always bearing in mind the circumstances of each case. The Committee concludes that there has been a violation of article 14, paragraph 1, of the Convention.

7. The Committee against Torture, acting under article 22, paragraph 7, of the Convention, decides that the facts before it constitute a violation of articles 2, 4 and 14 of the Convention.

8. In pursuance of rule 112, paragraph 5, of its rules of procedure, the Committee urges the State party to ensure in practice that persons responsible for acts of torture are appropriately punished, to ensure that the author receives full redress and to inform it, within 90 days from the date of the transmittal of this decision, of all steps taken in response to the Views expressed above.

Communication N° 214/2002

Submitted by: M.A.K. (represented by counsel, Mr. Reinhard Marx)
Alleged victim: The complainant
State party: Germany
Declared admissible: 30 April 2003
Date of adoption of Views: 12 May 2004

Subject matter: deportation of complainant to Turkey with alleged risk of torture

Procedural issue: exhaustion of domestic remedies

Substantive issue: risk of torture after deportation

Article of the Convention: 3

1.1 The complainant is M.A.K., a Turkish national of Kurdish origin, born in 1968, currently residing in Germany and awaiting expulsion to Turkey. He claims that his forcible return to Turkey would constitute a violation by the Federal Republic of Germany of article 3 of the Convention against Torture and Other Cruel, Inhuman or Degrading Treatment or Punishment. He is represented by counsel.

1.2 On 11 September 2002, the Committee forwarded the complaint to the State party for comments and requested, under rule 108, paragraph 1, of the Committee's rules of procedure, not to extradite the complainant to Turkey while his complaint was under consideration by the Committee. The Committee indicated, however, that this request could be reviewed in the light of observations provided by the State party on the admissibility or on the merits. The State party acceded to this request.

1.3 On 11 November 2002, the State party submitted its observations on the admissibility of the complaint together with a motion asking the Committee to withdraw its request for interim measures, pursuant to rule 108, paragraph 7, of the Committee's rules of procedure. In his comments, dated 23 December 2002, on the State party's observations on admissibility, counsel asked the Committee to maintain its request for interim measures until a final decision on the complaint has been taken. On 4 April 2002, the Committee, through its Rapporteur on new communications and interim measures, decided not to withdraw its request for interim measures.

The facts as submitted by the complainant

2.1 The complainant arrived in Germany in December 1990 and claimed political asylum on 21 January 1991, stating that he had been arrested for a week in 1989 and tortured by the police in Mazgirt because of his objection to the conduct of superiors during military service. As a PKK sympathiser, he was being persecuted and his life was in danger in Turkey. On 20 August 1991, the Federal Agency for the Recognition of Foreign Refugees (*Bundesamt für die Anerkennung ausländischer Flüchtlinge*) rejected the complainant's application on the basis of inconsistencies in his counts.

2.2 The complainant appealed the decision of the Federal Agency before the Wiesbaden Administrative Court which dismissed the appeal on 7 September 1999. On 17 April 2001, the Higher Administrative Court of Hessen refused leave to appeal from that judgement.

2.3 On 7 December 2001, the City of Hanau issued an expulsion order against the complainant, together with a notification of imminent deportation. The expulsion was based on the fact that the complainant had been sentenced by penal order, dated 16 January 1995, of the District Court of Groß-Gerau to a suspended prison term of four months for participation in a highway blockade organized by PKK sympathisers in March 1994.

2.4 On 17 January 2001, the complainant applied to the Federal Agency to reopen proceedings in his case, arguing that he had been trained by the PKK in a camp in the Netherlands in 1994, with a view to joining the PKK's armed forces in southeast Turkey, a duty from which he had been exempted at his subsequent request. He further claimed that the Turkish authorities knew about his PKK activities and, in particular, his participation in the highway blockade, on the basis of his conviction for joint coercion of road traffic.

2.5 By decision of 6 February 2002, the Federal Agency rejected the application to reopen asylum proceedings, stating that the complainant could have raised these fresh arguments in the initial proceedings, and that his submissions lacked credibility. On 26 February 2002, the complainant appealed this decision before the Frankfurt Administrative Court, where proceedings were still pending in this regard at the time of the initial submission of the complaint.

2.6 The complainant's application for provisional court relief against his deportation to Turkey was rejected by the Frankfurt Administrative Court on 21 March 2002, essentially based on grounds identical to those of the Federal Agency.

2.7 On 16 April 2002, an informational hearing of the complainant was held at the Federal Agency, during which the complainant stated that, prior to his training at the Dutch PKK camp, he had been introduced to the public of the Kurdish Halim-Dener-Festival, celebrated in September 1994 in the Netherlands, as part of a group of 25 "guerrilla candidates". He had not raised the issue during initial asylum proceedings since he feared punishment for PKK membership (the PKK is illegal under German law).

2.8 The complainant's application to reconsider its decision denying provisional court relief was rejected by the Frankfurt Administrative Court on 18 June 2002. The court reiterated that the late submission, as well as various details in the description of his alleged PKK activities, undermined the complainant's credibility. Thus, it was considered questionable whether the PKK would publicly present its guerrilla candidates, knowing that the Turkish secret service observed events such as the Halim-Dener-Festival. Moreover, following political and ideological training in Europe, PKK members were generally obliged to undergo immediate military training in Southeast Turkey.

2.9 On 22 July 2002, the complainant lodged a constitutional complaint with the Federal Constitutional Court against the decisions of the Frankfurt Administrative Court of 21 March and 18 June 2002, claiming violations of his constitutionally protected rights to life and physical integrity, equality before the law as well as his right to be heard before the courts. In addition, he filed an urgent application for an interim decision granting protection from deportation for the duration of the proceedings before the Federal Constitutional Court. By decision of 30 August 2002 of a panel of three judges, the Federal Constitutional Court dismissed the complaint as well as the urgent application, on the basis that "the complainant solely objects to the assessment of facts and evidence by the lower courts without specifying any violation of his basic rights or rights equivalent to basic rights".

The complaint

3.1 The complainant claims that substantial grounds exist for believing that he would be at a personal risk of being subjected to torture in Turkey, and that Germany would, therefore, be violating article 3 of the Convention if he were returned to Turkey. In support of his claim, he submits that the Committee has found the practice of torture to be systematic in Turkey.

3.2 The complainant argues that the Federal Agency and the German courts overemphasized the inconsistencies in his statements during the initial asylum proceedings, which were not in substance related to his subsequent claim to reopen proceedings on the basis of new information. He admits his failure to mention his PKK activities during initial proceedings. However, he could have reasonably expected the Turkish authorities' knowledge of his participation in the highway blockade to establish sufficient grounds for recognition as a refugee. His participation in the blockade could easily be inferred from his conviction of joint coercion in road traffic, since the judicial records exchanged between German and Turkish authorities indicate the date of a criminal offence. In the absence of witnesses of his participation in the PKK training course, which was to be kept secret, he claims the benefit of doubt for himself. He refers to the Committee's General Comment 1, which provides that, for purposes of article 3 of the Convention, the risk of torture "does not have to meet the test of being highly probable".

3.3 Moreover, the complainant refers to the written testimony by a Mr. F.S., dated 6 July 2002, in which the witness declared that he had travelled to the Kurdish festival in the Netherlands in 1994 together with the complainant, who had publicly declared to participate in the PKK.

3.4 The complainant explains the apparent contradiction between the PKK's policy of secrecy and the public presentation of 25 guerrilla candidates in front of 60,000 to 80,000 people at the Halim-Dener-Festival with the campaign, initiated by Abdullah Öcalan in March 1994, of demonstrating the Organization's presence and capacity to enforce its policies throughout Europe. His exemption from the duty to undergo military PKK training was only temporary, pending a final decision to be taken in May 1995. In any event, inconsistencies in the official PKK policy could not be raised against him.

3.5 As regards the burden of proof within national proceedings, the complainant submits that, pursuant to section 86 of the Code of Administrative Court Procedure, the administrative courts must investigate the facts of a case ex officio. He was therefore under no procedural obligation to prove his PKK membership. By stating that he took part in a PKK training course from September 1994 to January 1995, the complainant considers to have complied with his duty to cooperate with the courts.

3.6 As to the Turkish authorities' knowledge of his PKK membership, the complainant contends that there can be no doubt that the Turkish secret service observed the events taking place at the Halim-Dener-Festival in 1994. Moreover, he claims to have seen one of his training officers at the Maastricht camp, called "Yilmaz", on Turkish television after his arrest by Turkish police. "Yilmaz" reportedly agreed to cooperate with Turkish authorities, thereby placing the participants of the training camp at risk of having their identities revealed. The complainant further claims that one of his neighbour villagers told him that another participant of the training camp, called "Cektar", to whom he had close contact during the course, was captured by the Turkish army. It can be reasonably assumed, according to the complainant, that "Cektar" was handed over to the police for interrogation and tortured in order to extract information on PKK members from him.

3.7 The complainant concludes that, upon return to Turkey, he would be seized by Turkish airport police, handed over to specific police authorities for interrogation, and gravely tortured by those authorities. From previous views of the Committee he infers that the Committee found instances of torture by Turkish police likely to happen when the authorities were informed about a suspect's collaboration with the PKK.

3.8 The complainant submits that even if he had committed a criminal offence under German law by adhering to the PKK, this could not absolve the State party from its obligations under article 3 of the Convention.

3.9 The complainant claims to have exhausted all available domestic remedies. His complaint is not being examined under another procedure of international investigation or settlement.

The State party's admissibility observations

4.1 On 11 November 2002, the State party submitted its observations on the admissibility of the complaint, asking the Committee to declare it inadmissible for failure to exhaust domestic remedies, pursuant to article 22, paragraph 5, of the Convention.

4.2 The State party argues that domestic remedies which need to be exhausted include the remedy of a constitutional complaint, as held by the European Court of Human Rights in several cases concerning Germany.[1] Although the complainant lodged a constitutional complaint on 22 July 2002, he failed to exhaust domestic remedies, since this complaint was not sufficiently substantiated to be accepted for adjudication. In particular, the complainant failed to state why the challenged decisions infringed his constitutionally protected rights. It follows from the *ratio decidendi* of the decision of the Federal Constitutional Court, dated 30 August 2002, that he "solely object[ed] to the assessment of facts and evidence by the lower courts".

4.3 The State party submits that domestic remedies cannot be exhausted by means of an inadmissible complaint which patently fails to comply with the admissibility criteria under national procedural law.[2] In the present case, the State party does not see any circumstances which would justify an exemption from the requirement to exhaust domestic remedies, given that the constitutional complaint combined with the application for a provisional order, pending the final decision of the Federal Constitutional Court, provided the complainant with an effective remedy.

Complainant's comments

5.1 In his response dated 9 December 2002, the complainant challenges the State party's interpretation of the Constitutional Court's decision of 30 August 2002. He argues that the Court explicitly or implicitly ruled his constitutional complaint inadmissible, arguing that it did not distinguish between aspects of admissibility and merits. However, as the complaint satisfied the admissibility criteria of Section 93 of the Federal Constitutional Court Act, indicating the basic rights claimed to be infringed as well as the manner in which the lower courts' decisions violated these rights, it follows that the Federal Constitutional Court did not reject it as inadmissible "but with reference to the merits of the case".

5.2 The complainant submits that the constitutional complaint is not an additional appeal but constitutes an extraordinary remedy, allowing the Constitutional Court to determine whether basic

---

[1] *Djilali* v. *Germany*, application N° 48437/99; *Thieme* v. *Germany*, application N° 38365/97; *Teuschler* v. *Germany*, application N° 47636/99; *Tamel Adel Allaoui et al.* v. *Germany*, application N° 44911/98.
[2] See Section 92 of the Federal Constitutional Court Act.

rights have been infringed by the lower courts, when these fail to comply with their duty to ensure the enjoyment of such basic rights. However, the questions whether the requirement to exhaust all available domestic remedies includes recourse to this specific remedy, and whether this requirement is not met if a constitutional complaint is rejected as inadmissible, is immaterial in the complainant's opinion, since his constitutional complaint was not declared inadmissible by the Federal Constitutional Court in the first place.

5.3 The complainant argues that compliance with specific particularities of the German Constitution is not a prerequisite to lodge a complaint under a universal treaty-based procedure, such as the individual complaint procedure under article 22 of the Convention.

5.4 Lastly, the complainant submits that the domestic remedies rule must be applied with a certain degree of flexibility, and that only effective remedies must be exhausted. In the absence of a suspensive effect, the constitutional complaint cannot be considered an effective remedy in cases of imminent deportation.

Additional State party admissibility observations

6.1 On 10 March 2003, the State party submitted its additional observations on the admissibility of the complaint. While conceding that the Federal Constitutional Court did not explicitly state whether the constitutional complaint was inadmissible or ill-founded, the State party reiterates that the wording of the operative part of the Federal Constitutional Court's decision of 30 August 2002 allowed the inference that the complainant's constitutional complaint was unsubstantiated and therefore inadmissible. Hence, the complainant failed to comply with the procedural requirements for lodging a constitutional complaint.

6.2 The State party objects to the complainant's argument that a constitutional complaint has no suspensive effect, arguing that such effect can be substituted by means of an urgent application for interim relief, under Section 32 of the Federal Constitutional Court Act.

Decision on admissibility

7.1 At its thirtieth session, the Committee considered the question of the admissibility of the complaint and ascertained that the same matter had not been, and was not being, examined under another procedure of international investigation or settlement. In so far as the State party argued that the complainant had failed to exhaust domestic remedies, since his constitutional complaint did not meet the procedural requirements as to the substantiation of the claims, the Committee considered that, as an international instance which supervises States parties' compliance with their obligations under the Convention, it is not in a position to pronounce itself on the specific procedural requirements governing the submission of a constitutional complaint to the Federal Constitutional Court, unless such a complaint is manifestly incompatible with the requirement to exhaust all available domestic remedies, laid down in article 22, paragraph 5 (b), of the Convention.

7.2 The Committee noted that the complainant had lodged a constitutional complaint with the Federal Constitutional Court on 22 July 2002, which had been dismissed by the Court by formal decision dated 30 August 2002. In the absence of a manifest failure to comply with the requirement in article 22, paragraph 5 (b), of the Convention, the Committee was satisfied that, in the light of the circumstances of the case and in conformity with general principles of international law, the complainant had exhausted all available domestic remedies.

7.3 Accordingly, the Committee decided on 30 April 2003, that the complaint was admissible.

State party's merits observations

8.1 By note verbale of 24 February 2003, the State party submitted its observations on the merits of the complaint, arguing that the complainant had failed to substantiate a personal risk of torture in the event of his deportation to Turkey.

8.2 By reference to the Committee's General Comment 1 on the interpretation of article 3 of the Convention, the State party stresses that the burden is on the complainant to present an arguable case for establishing a personal and present risk of torture. It considers the complainant's Kurdish origin or the fact that he sympathizes with the PKK insufficient for that purpose.

8.3 The State party submits that the different versions about the severity of the torture allegedly suffered by the complaint after his arrest in Turkey raise doubts about his credibility. While he had first stated, before the Federal Agency, that he had been insulted and thrown into dirty water, he later, before the Wiesbaden Administrative Court, supplemented his allegations to the effect that he had been lifted up with his hands tied behind his back and a stick placed under his arms.

8.4 For the State party, the author failed to prove his PKK membership, or any remarkable political activities, during exile. In particular, the letter by Mr. F.S. merely stated that the complainant had participated in cultural and political activities in Germany, without specifying any of them. Moreover, the State party argues that the mere claim to be a PKK member is not as such sufficient to substantiate a personal danger of being tortured, in the absence of a prominent role of the complainant within that

Organization. Out of the more than 100,000 persons proclaiming themselves PKK members during the "self-incriminating campaign" in 2001, not a single case of subsequent persecution by Turkish authorities was reported.

8.5 While conceding that participation in PKK training for a leadership role might subject a party member to personal danger upon return to Turkey, the State party denies that the complainant ever participated in such training; he did not raise this claim during his hearing before the Wiesbaden Administrative Court in 1999. It considers the complainant's explanation that he wanted to keep this participation confidential, as required by the PKK, and because PKK membership was punishable under German law, implausible, because: (a) the contradiction between the alleged confidentiality of his training and the fact that the complainant had allegedly been introduced to a wide Kurdish community at the Halim-Dener-Festival; (b) the unlikelihood that the complainant would consider an imminent danger of torture the "lesser of two evils" compared to a conviction for PKK membership in Germany; (c) the fact that, despite the dismissal of his asylum claim by the Wiesbaden Administrative Court on 7 September 1999, he did not reveal his participation in PKK training on appeal to the Higher Administrative Court of Hessen; and (d) the obvious need to supplement his claims for purposes of a new asylum application after the expulsion order of 7 December 2001 had become final and binding.

8.6 The State party submits that, even assuming that the complainant had been introduced as a "guerrilla candidate" at the festival in 1994, his subsequent failure to continue the training, let alone to fight in Southeast Turkey, prevented him from occupying a prominent position within PKK.

8.7 While not excluding the possibility that the complainant's conviction of "joint coercion in road traffic" was communicated to the Turkish authorities under the international exchange of judicial records, the State party submits that the place of the offence could only be deduced indirectly from the information concerning the competent court. Even if his participation in the highway blockade could be revealed on the basis of this information, such low-profile activity was unlikely to trigger any action on the part of the Turkish authorities.

8.8 As to the burden of proof in national proceedings, the State party argues that the German courts' obligation to investigate the facts of a case only relates to verifiable facts. The Federal Agency and courts complied with this obligation by pointing out inconsistencies in the complainant's description of events and by providing him with opportunities to clarify these inconsistencies in two hearings before the Federal Agency and one before the Administrative Court of Wiesbaden.

Comments by the complainant

9.1 On 27 March and 10 May 2003, the complainant commented on the State party's merits submission, arguing that the issue before the Committee is not whether his allegations during the first set of asylum proceedings were credible, but whether knowledge by the Turkish authorities of his participation in the PKK training course would subject him to a personal and foreseeable risk of torture upon return to Turkey.

9.2 The complainant justifies inconsistencies between his initial and later submissions to the German authorities with the preliminary character, under the Asylum Procedure Law of 1982 (replaced in 1992), of his first statement before the immigration police. This, according to the police translator, had to be confined to one handwritten page, outlining the reasons for his asylum application. In his agent's letter of 7 February 1991, as well as his interview of 5 May 1991, the complainant explained in detail that, after his military service, he became a PKK sympathizer and was arrested together with other PKK activists during a demonstration. The letter also states that the police tortured him and the others during arrest to extract information on other PKK sympathizers.

9.3 The complainant recalls that complete accuracy can seldom be expected from victims of torture; his statements in the initial set of asylum proceedings should not be used to undermine his credibility with regard to his later claims.

9.4 With regard to the second set of asylum proceedings, the complainant submits that, in its decision of 18 June 2002, the Frankfurt Administrative Court itself recognized his dilemma, as he could not reveal his PKK membership without facing criminal charges in Germany. His expectation to be recognized as a refugee on the basis of his participation in the highway blockade rather than his PKK membership was therefore plausible and in conformity with the predominant jurisprudence at the time of his hearing before the Wiesbaden Administrative Court, under which refugee status was generally granted to Kurdish claimants who participated in PKK-related highway blockades.

9.5 Regarding his failure to continue PKK training after completing the course in the Netherlands, the complainant refers to a letter dated 16 February 2003 from the International Association for Human Rights of the Kurds (IMK), which confirms that the PKK had conducted training activities in the Netherlands from 1989 on, and that participants of training courses were often ordered to wait at their domicile for further instructions, or even exempted from the duty to undergo military training in Turkey.

9.6 While conceding that the Committee normally requires evidence of PKK membership, the complainant argues that the standard of proof must be applied reasonably, taking into consideration exceptional circumstances. He reiterates that the risk of torture that must be established by a complainant must not be one of high probability but rank somewhere between possibility and certainty. He claims that the written statement and a supplementary affidavit of 4 April 2003 by F.S., describing the complainant's introduction as a guerrilla candidate at the Halim-Dener-Festival, corroborate his allegations. He concludes that his statements are sufficiently reliable to shift the burden of proof to the State party.

9.7 The complainant cites a number of German court decisions which are said to acknowledge the risk that PKK suspects run of being subjected to torture after deportation to Turkey. This risk was not mitigated by the fact that he failed to take part in the PKK's armed combat. Rather, the Turkish police would try, including through torture, to extract information from him concerning other participants of the training course, PKK officials in Germany and other European countries.

9.8 The complainant reiterates that the Turkish authorities know of his participation in PKK training, as he was a member of a relatively small group of guerrilla candidates. He recalls that the Committee has repeatedly held that membership in an oppositional movement can draw the attention of the country of origin to a complainant, placing him at a personal risk of torture.

9.9 By reference to reports of, inter alia, the Human Rights Foundation of Turkey, the complainant submits that, despite the efforts of the new Turkish government to join the European Union, torture is still widespread and systematic in Turkey, in particular with regard to suspected PKK members.

Additional submissions by the parties

10.1 On 29 October 2003, the State party contests the complainant's credibility and that he faces a risk of torture in Turkey. It submits that the complainant did not describe the severity of the alleged torture to the Federal Agency for the Recognition of Foreign Refugees on 2 May 1991, but only eight and a half years later during the appeal proceedings. This raises fundamental doubts about his credibility, which is further undermined by his inability to explain the extent and prominence of his political activities for the PKK in exile.

10.2 The State party contests that the complainant's expectation to be recognized as a refugee merely on the basis of his conviction for participation in a highway blockage was reasonable. It cites two judgements denying refugee status to asylum-seekers in similar circumstances.

10.3 As regards the standard of proof, the State party submits that a complainant should be expected to present the facts of the case in a credible and coherent manner, unlike in the present case.

10.4 Lastly, the State party argues that the human rights situation in Turkey has improved significantly. The Turkish Government has demonstrated its intention to facilitate the unproblematic return of former members or followers of PKK and to respect their fundamental rights by adopting the Act on Reintegration into Society on 29 July 2003. At the same time, the scope of application of Section 169 of the Turkish Criminal Code was reduced considerably, resulting in the discontinuance of numerous criminal proceedings against PKK supporters. In the past three years, not a single is reported where an unsuccessful asylum-seeker who returned to Turkey from Germany was tortured "in connection with former activities." The State party indicates that it would monitor the complainant's situation after his return.

11.1 On 30 January 2004, the complainant reiterates that inconsistencies in his first application for asylum are irrelevant for the assessment of his new claims in the second set of proceedings. His second asylum application was based on his participation in a PKK training course as well as the Turkish authorities' knowledge of the same.

11.2 For the complainant, the Sate party has conceded that training for a PKK leadership role can place a member at danger upon return to Turkey. It should therefore accept his claim that his activities for the PKK and his introduction as a guerrilla candidate place him at such risk.

11.3 As to the reasons for the late disclosure of his participation in the PKK training course, the complainant reiterates that, on the basis of the unanimous jurisprudence of the administrative courts in Hessen, where he resides, he could reasonably expect to be recognized as a refugee on account of his participation in the highway blockage. The diverging jurisprudence of administrative courts in other regions of the State party was either of more recent date or was unknown to him at the material time during the first set of asylum proceedings.

11.4 The complainant argues that, in any event, the late disclosure of these activities does not undermine his credibility on the whole. He invokes the benefit of doubt, arguing that he presented sufficient evidence to substantiate his participation in the PKK training course in a credible and coherent manner.

11.5 Regarding the general human rights situation in Turkey, the complainant submits: (a) that the armed conflict between the Turkish army and PHH/Kadek forces is ongoing; (b) that, according to the Human Rights Foundation of Turkey, the number of reported cases of torture has increased in 2003 totalling 770; (c) that, despite the reduction of the maximum length of incommunicado detention to four days, torture is still widespread and systematic, although methods such as beating or "Palestinian hanging" have been replaced by more subtle methods which leave no trace, such as solitary confinement or denial of access to clean drinking water and sanitary facilities; (d) that none of the twenty complaints related to alleged cases of torture which had been submitted in 2003 by the "Izmir Bar Association Lawyers' Group for the Prevention of Torture" were investigated; and (e) that the 2003 Act on Reintegration in Society requires former PKK members to disclose their knowledge about other PKK members and that persons refusing to disclose such information are often subjected to ill-treatment by the authorities.

11.6 The complainant concludes that there are no sufficient safeguards to ensure that he would not be tortured upon return, either during initial interviews by the police or if he refuses to cooperate with the Turkish authorities by disclosing information on the PKK.

11.7 The main proceedings concerning the complainant's application to reopen asylum proceedings are still pending before the Administrative Court of Frankfurt. In the absence of suspensive effect, these proceedings would not stay his deportation, if the Committee decided to withdraw its request for interim measures. Since it is unlikely for the Frankfurt Administrative Court to order the reopening of asylum proceedings, after having rejected the complainant's application for interim relief, the only means to prevent his expulsion would be a final decision of the Committee, with a finding of a violation of article 3.

12.1 On 15 March 2004, the State party confirmed that the Administrative Court of Frankfurt had not taken a decision on the complainant's appeal against the Federal Agency's decision of 6 February 2002 not to reopen asylum proceedings and that this appeal has no suspensive effect. Although the complainant was free to formulate another application for interim court relief, such application would have little prospects of success unless it was based on new facts.

12.2 The State party recalls that it has complied with the Committee's request not to expel the complainant pending a final decision on his complaint, despite the final rejection of his first asylum application, the rejection by the Federal Agency to reopen asylum proceedings and the dismissal by the Frankfurt Administrative Court of his request for interim relief. Against this background, the State party requests the Committee to adopt a decision on the merits of the complaint at its earliest convenience.

Issues and proceedings before the Committee

13.1 The issue before the Committee is whether the forced return of the author is Turkey would violate the State party's obligation under article 3 of the Convention not to expel or to return a person to another State where there are substantial grounds for believing that he would be in danger of being subjected to torture.

13.2 The Committee must decide, pursuant to paragraph 1 of article 3, whether there are substantial grounds for believing that the author would be in danger of being subjected to torture upon return to Turkey. In reaching this decision, the Committee must take into account all relevant considerations, pursuant to article 3, paragraph 2, including the existence of a consistent pattern of gross, flagrant or mass violations of human rights. In this regard, the Committee notes the State party's argument that the Turkish Government acted to improve the human rights situation, including through the enactment of the Reintegration into Society Act in 2003 and the discontinuance of numerous criminal proceedings against PKK supporters. It also notes the complainant's argument recent legislative changes have not reduced the number of reported incidents of torture in Turkey (770 cases in 2003), and further recalls its conclusions and recommendations on the second periodic report of Turkey, in which it expressed concern about "[n]umerous and consistent allegations that torture and other cruel, inhuman or degrading treatment of detainees held in police custody are apparently still widespread in Turkey."[3]

13.3 The aim of the present determination, however, is to establish whether the complainant would be personally at risk of being subjected to torture in Turkey after his return. Even if a consistent pattern of gross, flagrant or mass violations of human rights existed in Turkey, such existence would not as such constitute a sufficient ground for determining that the complainant would be in danger of being subjected to torture after his return to that country; specific grounds must exist indicating that he would be personally at risk. Similarly, the absence of a consistent pattern of gross violations of human rights does not mean that a person cannot be considered to be in danger of being subjected to torture in his or her specific circumstances.

---

[3] Committee against Torture, 30th session (28 April–16 May 2003), Conclusions and recommendations of the Committee against Torture: Turkey (CAT/C/CR/30/5, para. 5 (a)).

13.4 In the present case, the Committee notes that the State party draws attention to a lack of evidence about the complainant's participation in a PKK training camp in the Netherlands in 1994, and to his failure to raise this claim until late in the asylum proceedings. It equally notes the complainant's explanations relating to the difficulty of presenting witnesses from the PKK, his fear to reveal his claimed PKK membership, punishable under German law, as well as the documentation and testimony he submitted in support of his claims.

13.5 On the burden of proof, the Committee recalls that it is normally for the complainant to present an arguable case and that the risk of torture must be assessed on grounds that go beyond mere theory and suspicion. Although the risk does not have to meet the test of being highly probable, the Committee considers that the complainant has not provided sufficiently reliable evidence which would justify a shift of the burden of proof to the State party. In particular, it observes that the affidavit by F.S. merely corroborates the complainant's claim that he was introduced as a "guerrilla candidate" at the Halim-Dener-Festival, without proving this claim, his participation in the training camp or PKK membership. Similarly, the letter dated 16 February 2003 of the International Association for Human Rights of the Kurds, while stating that it was not implausible that the complainant had temporarily been exempted from military PKK training in Turkey, falls short of proving these claims. In the absence of a prima facie case for his participation in the PKK training camp, the Committee concludes that the complainant cannot reasonably claim the benefit of the doubt regarding these claims. Moreover, the Committee observes that it is not competent to pronounce itself on the standard of proof applied by German tribunals.

13.6 With regard to the complainant's conviction for participation in a highway blockade by PKK sympathizers in March 1994, the Committee considers that, even if the Turkish authorities knew about these events, such participation does not amount to the type of activity which would appear to make the complainant particularly vulnerable to the risk of being subjected to torture upon return to Turkey.

13.7 Regarding the complainant's allegation that he was tortured during police arrest in Mazgirt (Turkey), the Committee observes that these allegations refer to events dating from 1989 and thus to events which did not occur in the recent past.[4] In addition, the complainant has not submitted any medical evidence which would confirm possible after-effects or otherwise support his claim that he was tortured by Turkish police.

13.8 The Committee emphasizes that considerable weight must be attached to the findings of fact by the German authorities and courts and notes that proceedings are still pending before the Frankfurt Administrative Court with regard to his application to reopen asylum proceedings. However, taking into account that the Higher Administrative Court of Hessen dismissed the complainant's first asylum application by a final decision, the complainant's fresh claims relating to his alleged participation in a PKK training camp have not been sufficiently corroborated (see para. 13.5) to justify further postponing the Committee's decision on his complaint, pending the outcome of the proceedings before the Frankfurt Administrative Court. In this regard, the Committee notes that both parties have requested the Committee to make a final determination on the complaint (see paras. 11.7 and 12.2) and emphasizes that the complainant exhausted domestic remedies in the proceedings for interim relief and that only this part of the second set of asylum proceedings had suspensive effect.

13.9 The Committee concludes that, in the specific circumstances of the case, the complainant has failed to establish a foreseeable, real and personal risk of being tortured if he were to be returned to Turkey. The Committee welcomes the State party's readiness to monitor the complainant's situation following his return to Turkey and requests it to keep the Committee informed about said situation.

14. The Committee against Torture, acting under article 22, paragraph 7, of the Convention against Torture and Other Cruel, Inhuman or Degrading Treatment of Punishment, concludes that the State party's decision to return the complainant to Turkey does not constitute a breach of article 3 of the Convention.

---

[4] See Committee against Torture, General Comment 1: Implementation of article 3 of the Convention in the context of article 22, 21 November 1997, para. 8 (b).

Communication N° 219/2002

Submitted by: Ms. G.K. (represented by counsel)
Alleged victim: The complainant
State party: Switzerland
Date of adoption of Views: 7 May 2003

Subject matter: extradition of complainant to Spain with alleged risk of torture

Procedural issue: none

Substantive issues: risk of torture after extradition; statement made under torture

Articles of the Convention: 3, 15

1.1 The complainant is G.K., a German national, born on 12 January 1956, at the time of the submission of the complaint held at the police detention centre at Flums (Switzerland), awaiting her extradition to Spain. She claims that her extradition to Spain would constitute a violation by Switzerland of articles 3 and 15 of the Convention against Torture and Other Cruel, Inhuman or Degrading Treatment or Punishment. She is represented by counsel.

1.2 On 22 October 2002, the Committee forwarded the complaint to the State party for comments and requested, under rule 108, paragraph 1, of the Committee's rules of procedure, not to extradite the complainant to Spain while her complaint was under consideration by the Committee. The Committee indicated, however, that this request could be reviewed in the light of new arguments presented by the State party or on the basis of guarantees and assurances from the Spanish authorities. The State party acceded to this request.

1.3 By note verbale of 8 November 2002, the State party submitted its observations on the admissibility and merits of the complaint; it also asked the Committee to withdraw its request for interim measures, pursuant to rule 108, paragraph 7, of the Committees rules of procedure. In his comments, dated 9 December 2002, counsel asked the Committee to maintain its request for interim measures, pending a final decision on the complaint. On 6 January 2003, the Committee, through its Special Rapporteur, decided to withdraw its request for interim measures.

The facts as presented by the complainant

2.1 In 1993, the complainant worked as a language teacher in Barcelona, where she became involved with one Benjamin Ramos Vega, a Spanish national. During that time, the complainant and Mr. Ramos Vega both rented apartments in Barcelona, one at *calle Padilla*, rented on 21 April 1993 in Mr. Ramos Vega's name, and one at *calle Aragon*, rented on 11 August 1993 in the complainant's name and for the period of one year. According to counsel, the complainant had returned to Germany by October 1993.

2.2 On 28 April 1994, Felipe San Epifanio, a convicted member of the commando "Barcelona" of the Basque terrorist organization "Euskadi ta Askatasuna" (ETA), was arrested by Spanish police in Barcelona. The judgement of the *Audiencia Nacional*, dated 24 September 1997, sentencing him and other ETA members to prison terms, states that, upon his arrest, Mr. San Epifanio was thrown to the floor by several policemen after he had drawn a gun, thereby causing him minor injuries which reportedly healed within two weeks. Based on his testimony, the police searched the apartment at *calle Padilla*[1] on 28 April 1994, confiscating firearms and explosives stored by the commando. Subsequent to this search, Mr. Ramos Vega left Spain for Germany.

2.3 The *Juzgado Central de Instrucción N° 4 de Madrid* issued an arrest warrant, dated 23 May 1994, against both the complainant and Mr. Ramos Vega under suspicion of ETA collaboration as well as possession of firearms and explosives. A writ was issued on 6 February 1995 by the same examining judge indicting the complainant and Mr. Ramos Vega of the above offences for having rented "under their name, the apartments at the streets *Padilla* and *Aragon*, respectively, places which served as a refuge and for the hiding of arms and explosives, which the members of the commando had at their disposition for carrying out their actions."[2]

2.4 On 10 March 1995, the Berlin public prosecutor's office initiated criminal proceedings against the complainant, following a request by the Spanish Ministry of Justice. However, the German authorities decided to discontinue proceedings on 23 November 1998, in the absence of a reasonable suspicion of an offence punishable under German law. In a letter to the Spanish authorities, the Berlin public prosecutor's office stated that the apartment at *calle Padilla*, where the firearms and explosives had been found, had not been rented by the complainant but by Mr. Ramos Vega, while only a bottle filled with lead sulphide—which is not used for the

---

[1] Apparently, the apartment was rented but not inhabited by Mr. Ramos Vega.
[2] Translation by the Secretariat.

production of explosives—had been found in the complainant's apartment at *calle Aragon*.

2.5 Subsequent to Mr. Ramos Vega's extradition to Spain in 1996, the *Audiencia Nacional*, by judgement of 24 September 1997, convicted him of collaboration with an armed group and falsification of licence plates in relation with terrorist activities ("*con agravante de relación con actividades terroristas*"), sentencing him to two terms of imprisonment, one of seven years and the second of four years and three months. However, the *Audiencia Nacional* acquitted him of the charges in relation to the storage of firearms and to the possession of explosives due to lack of proof that he known about the existence of these materials, noting that he had rented the apartment at *calle Padilla* at the request and for the use of a friend, Dolores Lopez Resina ("Lola"). The judgement states that, immediately following the search of that apartment, the convict assisted the escape of several members of the commando "Barcelona" by renting, and changing the license plates of, a car which he, together with these members, used to leave Barcelona.

2.6 The complainant was arrested by Swiss police when crossing the Austrian-Swiss border at St. Margrethen on 14 March 2002, on the basis of a Spanish search warrant, dated 3 June 1994. She was provisionally detained, pending a final decision on her extradition to Spain. During a hearing on 20 March 2002, she refused to consent to a simplified extradition procedure. By diplomatic note of 22 April 2002, Spain submitted an extradition request to the State party, based on an international arrest warrant dated 1 April 2002, issued by the *Juzgado Central de Instrucción N° 4* at the *Audiencia Nacional*. This warrant is based on the same charges as the original arrest warrant and the writ of indictment against both the complainant and Mr. Ramos Vega.

2.7 By letter of 7 June 2002, the complainant, through counsel, asked the Federal Office of Justice to reject the extradition request of the Spanish Government, claiming that by referring the criminal proceedings to the German authorities, Spain had lost the competence to prosecute the complainant, thus precluding the complainant's extradition to that country.[3] Moreover, the fact that the Spanish authorities, in their extradition request to the State party, had deliberately not revealed who actually rented the apartment at *calle Padilla*, indicated that the complainant was to be tried for political rather than juridical reasons. Since political offences were not extraditable,[4] counsel argued that, contrary to the general rule that decisions on extraditions were purely a formal matter, the State party was obliged to examine whether a reasonable suspicion of an offence existed with respect to the complainant, in the absence of any link with the firearms and explosives found in the *calle Padilla* apartment, or with the escape vehicle. In counsel's opinion, the complainant's extradition is also precluded by the fact that the Spanish arrest warrant was based on testimony which had allegedly been extracted from Mr. San Epifanio by torture.

2.8 By decision of 8 August 2002, the Federal Office of Justice granted the Spanish extradition request, subject to the condition that the complainant was not to be tried for political motivations to commit the alleged offences and that the severity of punishment was not to be increased on the basis of such a motivation. This decision was based on the following considerations: (1) that the examination of reciprocal criminal liability was based on the facts set out in the extradition request, the evaluation of facts and evidence and matters of innocence or guilt being reserved to the Spanish courts; (2) that no issue of *ne bis in idem* arose since the German authorities, for lack of territorial competence, had not exhaustively dealt with these questions; (3) that the charges brought against the complainant were not of a purely political nature; (4) that the complainant was not at direct and personal risk of being tortured during incommunicado detention following her extradition to Spain, because she could already engage the services of a lawyer in Spain prior to her extradition and because she enjoyed diplomatic protection by Germany; and (5) that even if Mr. San Epifanio's testimony had been extracted by torture, this was not the only evidence on which the charges against the complainant had been based.

2.9 On 8 September 2002, counsel lodged an administrative court action with the Federal Tribunal against the decision of the Federal Office of Justice to extradite the complainant. In addition to the reasons stated in his motion of 7 June 2002, he criticized that the Spanish extradition request lacked the necessary precision required by article 14, paragraph 2, of the European Convention of Mutual Legal Assistance in Criminal Matters (1959)[5] since it was essentially based on the arrest warrant of 1994 and failed to take into account the results of the subsequent criminal proceedings in Germany as well as in Spain. In particular, it did not clarify that the apartment at *calle Padilla* was rented by Mr. Ramos

---

[3] Pursuant to article 9 of the European Convention on Extradition to which Germany, Switzerland and Spain are parties, "[e]xtradition my be refused if the competent authorities of the requested party have decided either not to institute or to terminate proceedings in respect of the same offence or offences".

[4] See article 3 (1) of the European Convention on Extradition.

[5] See also ibid., article 12 (2) (b).

Vega exclusively, that the latter had been acquitted of the charges relating to the storage of firearms and possession of explosives by the *Audiencia Nacional*, and that the powder found in the apartment at *calle Aragon* was lead sulphide which could not be used for the production of explosives. The facts established in the extradition request were, therefore, to be disregarded; the request itself was abusive and had to be rejected. With respect to article 3 of the Convention against Torture and Other Cruel, Inhuman or Degrading Treatment or Punishment, counsel submitted that, although in theory the complainant enjoyed diplomatic protection by Germany and could already engage the services of a lawyer of her choice in Spain prior to her extradition, these rights could in practice only be exercised after incommunicado detention had ended. Regarding article 15 of the Convention, counsel criticized that the Spanish extradition request failed to indicate on which additional evidence the charges against the complainant had been based. In so far as the evidence was found indirectly through Mr. San Epifanio's testimony, counsel claims that the theory of the "tainted fruits of the poisonous tree" precludes the use of such evidence by the Swiss courts.

2.10 By letter of 20 September 2002, the Federal Office of Justice asked the Federal Tribunal to dismiss the complainant's legal action. Counsel responded to this motion by letter, dated 15 October 2002, in which he maintained and further explained his arguments.

2.11 The Swiss section of Amnesty International sent an amicus curiae brief, dated 2 October 2002, on behalf of the complainant to the Federal Tribunal, stating that Spanish legislation provided for the possibility of keeping suspects of terrorist offences in incommunicado detention for a period up to five days during which they could only be visited by a legal aid lawyer, and that such detention increased the risk of torture and maltreatment. Although torture was not systematically inflicted by the *Policía Nacional* or the *Guardia Civil*, instances of massive maltreatment of ETA suspects still occurred, including sexual assaults, rape, blows to the head, putting plastic bags over the head ("la bolsa"), deprivation of sleep, electric shocks, threats of execution etc. Amnesty International considered it indispensable for the State party to make the complainant's extradition to Spain subject to the following assurances: (1) that under no circumstances the complainant should be handed over to the *Guardia Civil* or the *Policía Nacional*, but that she be placed directly under the authority of the *Audiencia Nacional* in Madrid; (2) that the complainant be granted direct and unlimited access to a lawyer of her choice; and (3) that she be brought before a judge as soon as possible following her extradition to Spain.

2.12 By judgement of 21 October 2002, the Federal Tribunal dismissed the complainant's action, upholding the decision of the Federal Office of Justice to grant the Spanish extradition request. The Tribunal based itself on the facts set out in the extradition request and concluded that the complainant was punishable under Swiss law (either as a participant in or as a supporter of a terrorist organization pursuing the objective to commit politically motivated crimes of violence) as well as under Spanish law. The Tribunal did not pronounce itself on the complainant's challenges as to the facts contained in the extradition request, ruling that questions of facts and evidence were for the Spanish courts to decide. Moreover, since ETA was not merely a group struggling for political power by employing legitimate means, the Tribunal did not consider the complainant's participation in or, respectively, her support of ETA a political offence within the meaning of article 3 of the European Convention on Extradition. The fact that criminal proceedings against the complainant had been closed by the Berlin public prosecutor's office for lack of a reasonable suspicion of an offence did not, in the Tribunal's opinion, bar the Swiss authorities from extraditing her to Spain because the decision to close proceedings was not based on material grounds and had been taken by a third State.[6] With respect to the alleged risk of torture following the complainant's extradition to Spain, the Tribunal held that Spain, being a democratic State and a member of the pertinent regional and universal human rights conventions, could not be presumed to systematically practise torture. Moreover, the Tribunal rejected the claim that the charges against the complainant were primarily based on testimony extracted by torture, in the absence of any supporting evidence.[7]

2.13 According to counsel's information, the complainant was extradited to Spain after the Committee, on 6 January 2003, decided to withdraw its request for interim measures.

The complaint

3.1 Counsel claims that following an extradition to Spain, the complainant would be at risk of being tortured during a maximum of five days of incommunicado detention and that Switzerland would, therefore, be violating article 3 of the Convention if she were extradited to Spain. In substantiation of this claim, counsel refers to several

---

[6] Cf. article 9 of the European Convention on Extradition.
[7] In that regard, the Federal Tribunal argues that, according to the complainant herself, the criminal proceedings initiated by Mr. San Epifanio against the police had been closed by the Spanish authorities.

reports[8] on instances of torture inflicted on suspected members or supporters of ETA as well as to the Committee's views on communication N° 63/1997 (*Josu Arkauz Arana* v. *France*)[9] concerning the extradition of an ETA suspect from France to Spain, where the Committee stated that "notwithstanding the legal guarantees as to the conditions under which it could be imposed, there were cases of prolonged detention incommunicado, when the detainee could not receive the assistance of a lawyer of his choice, which seemed to facilitate the practice of torture."[10] Counsel also submits that, in the absence of guarantees from the Spanish authorities, the author could not, in practice, obtain access to a lawyer of her choice and to diplomatic protection by Germany until after incommunicado detention had ended. Furthermore, counsel argues that the numerous reports on cases of torture and maltreatment in Spanish prisons indicated a consistent pattern of gross, flagrant or mass violations of human rights, a finding which was reinforced by the fact that ETA suspects had been killed in the past by death squads (*Grupos Antiterroristas de Liberación/GAL*) linked to the former Spanish Government. In counsel's view, the complainant's personal risk of being tortured was increased by the fact that the Spanish extradition request had been based on false charges, which indicated that Spain was unwilling to grant the complainant a fair trial. In the absence of any clear evidence against the complainant, it was not excluded that Spanish police would try to extract a confession by torture.

3.2 Counsel claims that by granting the Spanish extradition request which exclusively relied on Felipe San Epifanio's testimony, extracted by torture, and on the evidence found on the basis of this testimony in the apartment at *calle Padilla*, the State party violated article 15 of the Convention. Counsel argues that the use in extradition proceedings of evidence obtained as a result of torture runs counter to the spirit of the Convention since it provides the authorities of the requesting State with an incentive to disregard the prohibition of torture. By granting the Spanish extradition request, the Federal Office of Justice de facto accepted the evidence obtained through torture.

The State party's admissibility and merits observations

4.1 On 8 November 2002, the State party submitted its observations on the admissibility and merits of the complaint. It does not contest the admissibility of the complaint.

4.2 The State party reiterates that questions of facts and evidence as well as of innocence or guilt cannot be examined in an extradition procedure, these matters being reserved to the trial courts. Since the complainant was free to invoke her arguments before the Spanish courts, an extradition to Spain was possibly even in her own interest because it provided her with an opportunity to be released from prison following an acquittal.

4.3 With regard to the complainant's claim under article 3, the State party submits that isolated cases of maltreatment in Spanish prisons fall short of attesting to a systematic practice of torture in that country. Moreover, the complainant had failed to establish that she was at a concrete and personal risk of being tortured if extradited to Spain. In particular, the case of *Josu Arkauz Arana*, who had been extradited to Spain on the basis of a purely administrative procedure, which had subsequently been found illegal by the Administrative Court of Pau, in the absence of any intervention of a judicial authority and of the possibility for the author to contact his family or lawyer, was not comparable to the complainant's situation: While the particular circumstances of Josu Arkauz Arana's extradition to Spain had placed him in a situation where he had been particularly vulnerable to possible abuse, the complainant had enjoyed the benefits of a judicial extradition procedure ensuring respect for her human rights and fundamental freedoms. According to the State party, the same guarantees applied in Spain which, being a member to the Convention against Torture and Other Cruel, Inhuman or Degrading Treatment or Punishment as well as to the Optional Protocol to the International Covenant on Civil and Political Rights and the European Convention, was subject to the scrutiny of the supervising bodies of these instruments, which provided the complainant with a preventive guarantee not to be tortured. Moreover, the complainant enjoyed diplomatic protection by Germany and could avail herself of the services of a lawyer of her choice already hired from Switzerland. The State party could also mandate its own Embassy in Spain to monitor the complainant's conditions of detention. The international attention drawn to the case provided a further guarantee against any risk of torture.

4.4 With respect to the complaint's claim under article 15 of the Convention, the State party submits that nothing establishes that Felipe San Epifanio's testimony had been extracted by torture. The

---

[8] Human Rights Committee, Concluding observations on the second periodic report of Spain; European Committee for the Prevention of Torture and Inhuman or Degrading Treatment or Punishment, Reports on visits to Spain in 1997, 1998 and 2000; Amnesty International, Annual Report 2001.
[9] Views adopted on 9 November 1999.
[10] Ibid., para. 11.4.

complainant herself had stated that the criminal proceedings initiated by Mr. San Epifanio had been closed. Again, it was for the criminal courts in Spain and not for the Swiss extradition authorities to pronounce themselves on the admissibility of evidence.

Complainant's comments

5.1 In his response to the State party's submission, counsel maintains that the complainant would be at personal risk of being tortured if extradited to Spain. Such a risk was indicated by several precedents, in particular the cases of Felipe San Epifanio and Agurtzane Ezkerra Pérez de Nanclares, another convicted member of the commando "Barcelona" who had allegedly been tortured during incommunicado detention. Counsel submits a letter, dated 4 May 1994, addressed to the *Juzgado de Instrucción N° 4 (Bilbao)*, in which Felipe San Epifanio brought criminal charges against the police, stating that the police arrested him by immobilizing him on the ground, where he received blows and kicks on his entire body, including blows to his head with a gun. Although the wounds had been stitched at hospital, no thorough medical examination had been carried out. Instead, the police allegedly had continued to maltreat him during incommunicado detention, beating him repeatedly. The following days, Mr. San Epifanio had been questioned on his links with ETA and individual members of that organization without the assistance of a lawyer. During the four days of incommunicado detention, he had allegedly been denied sleep and had not received any solid food but only large amounts of water. Counsel argues that the examining judge's decision to close criminal proceedings initiated by Mr. San Epifanio reflects the extent of impunity enjoyed by alleged torturers of ETA suspects.[11]

5.2 Counsel reiterates that numerous human rights reports provide evidence of the existence of a consistent pattern of gross, flagrant or mass violations of human rights in Spain. In particular, he cites the Committee's most recent concluding observations relating to Spain[12] in which it expressed its concern about the dichotomy between Spanish official statements denying the occurrence of torture or maltreatment except in isolated cases, and the information received from non-governmental sources indicating the persistence of cases of torture and maltreatment by Spanish security forces. Moreover, the Committee noted that Spain maintained its legislation providing for incommunicado detention for up to a maximum of five days during which the detainee neither had access to a lawyer or a medical doctor of his choice, nor to his family. Counsel submits that diplomatic protection is inaccessible during that period.

5.3 With respect to the admissibility of Mr. San Epifanio's testimony, counsel submits that the prohibition in article 15 of the Convention applies not only to criminal proceedings in Spain but also to the complainant's extradition proceedings in Switzerland. This follows from the wording of article 15 which obliges the State party to "ensure that any statement which is established to have been made as a result of torture shall not be invoked as evidence in any proceedings". Counsel challenges the State party's argument that it had not been established that Mr. San Epifanio's testimony had been extracted by torture, arguing that the requirements as to the evidence for this torture claim should not be overly strict.[13]

Issues and proceedings before the Committee

6.1 Before considering any claim contained in a communication, the Committee against Torture must decide whether or not it is admissible under article 22 of the Convention. The Committee has ascertained, as it is required to do under article 22, paragraph 5 (a), of the Convention, that the same matter has not been, and is not being, examined under another procedure of international investigation or settlement. In the present case, the Committee also notes that all domestic remedies have been exhausted and that the State party has not objected to the admissibility of the communication. It therefore considers that the communication is admissible and proceeds to the examination to the merits of the case.

6.2 With regard to the complainant's claim under article 3, paragraph 1, of the Convention, the Committee must determine whether the author's deportation to Spain violated the State party's obligation, under that article, not to expel or return a person to another State where there are substantial grounds for believing that he would be in danger of being subjected to torture. In doing so, the Committee must take into account all relevant considerations with a view to determining whether the person concerned is in personal danger, including the existence, in the State concerned, of a consistent pattern of gross, flagrant or mass violations of human rights.

---

[11] In the complaint, dated 18 October 2002, counsel stated that the examining judge had considered that the facts submitted by Mr. San Epifanio fell short of constituting a criminal offence, despite the fact that a medical examiner had found several haematoma and open wounds on his body after his detention incommunicado had ended.

[12] See Committee against Torture, 29th session (11–22 November 2002), Conclusions and recommendations of the Committee against Torture: *Spain* (CAT/C/CR/29/3).

[13] This argument is contained in the complaint, dated 18 October 2002.

6.3 The Committee recalls that during the consideration of the fourth periodic report submitted by Spain under article 19 of the Convention, it noted with concern the dichotomy between the assertion of the Spanish Government that, isolated cases apart, torture and ill-treatment do not occur in Spain and the information received from non-governmental sources which is said to reveal instances of torture and ill-treatment by the State security and police forces.[14] It also expressed concern about the fact that incommunicado detention up to a maximum of five days has been maintained for specific categories of particularly serious offences, given that during this period, the detainee has no access to a lawyer or to a doctor of his choice, nor is he able to contact his family.[15] The Committee considered that the incommunicado regime facilitates the commission of acts of torture and ill-treatment.[16]

6.4 Notwithstanding the above, the Committee reiterates that its primary task is to determine whether the individual concerned would personally risk torture in the country to which he or she would return. It follows that the existence of a consistent pattern of gross, flagrant or mass violations of human rights in a country does not as such constitute sufficient grounds for determining that the particular person would be in danger of being subjected to torture upon his return to that country; additional grounds must be adduced to show that the individual concerned would be personally at risk. Conversely, the absence of a consistent pattern of gross violations of human rights does not mean that a person cannot be considered to be in danger of being subjected to torture in his or her specific circumstances.

6.5 As to the complainant's personal risk of being subjected to torture following extradition to Spain, the Committee has noted the complainant's arguments that the Spanish extradition request was based on false accusations, that, as an ETA suspect, she was at a personal risk of being tortured during incommunicado detention, in the absence of access to a lawyer of her choice during that time, that other persons had been subjected to torture in circumstances that she considers to be similar to her case, and that diplomatic protection by Germany as well as the prior designation of a lawyer constituted protections against possible abuse during incommunicado detention in theory only. It has equally noted the State party's submission that, in addition to the above-mentioned protections, the international attention drawn to the complainant's case, as well as the possibility for her to challenge torture or ill-treatment by the Spanish authorities before the Committee and other international instances, constitute further guarantees preventing Spanish police from subjecting her to such treatment.

6.6 Having regard to the complainant's reference to the Committee's views in the case of *Josu Arkauz Arana*, the Committee observes that the specific circumstances of that case, which led to the finding of a violation of article 3 of the Convention, differ markedly from the circumstances in the present case. The deportation of *Josu Arkauz Arana* "was effected under an administrative procedure, which the Administrative Court of Pau had later found to be illegal, entailing a direct handover from police to police, without the intervention of a judicial authority and without any possibility for the author to contact his family or his lawyer."[17] By contrast, the complainant's extradition to Spain was preceded by a judicial review, by the Swiss Federal Tribunal, of the decision of the Federal Office of Justice to grant the Spanish extradition request. The Committee notes that the judgement of the Federal Court, as well as the decision of the Federal Office, both contain an assessment of the risk of torture that the complainant would be exposed to following an extradition to Spain. The Committee, therefore, considers that, unlike in the case of *Josu Arkauz Arana*, the legal guarantees were sufficient, in the complainant's case, to avoid placing her in a situation where she was particularly vulnerable to possible abuse by the Spanish authorities.

6.7 The Committee observes that possible inconsistencies in the facts on which the Spanish extradition request was based, cannot as such be construed as indicating any hypothetical intention of the Spanish authorities to inflict torture or ill-treatment on the complainant, once the extradition request was granted and executed. In so far as the complainant claims that the State party's decision to extradite her violated articles 3 and 9 of the European Convention on Extradition of 1957, the Committee observes that it is not competent *ratione materiae* to pronounce itself on the interpretation or application of that Convention.

6.8 Lastly, the Committee notes that, subsequent to the complainant's extradition to Spain, it has received no information on torture or ill-treatment suffered by the complainant during incommunicado detention. In the light of the foregoing, the Committee finds that the complainant's extradition to Spain did not constitute a violation by the State party of article 3 of the Convention.

---

[14] Committee against Torture, 29th session (11–22 November 2002), Conclusions and recommendations of the Committee against Torture: *Spain* (CAT/C/CR/29/3, para. 8).
[15] CAT/C/CR/29/3, para. 10.
[16] CAT/C/CR/29/3, para. 10.

[17] Communication N° 63/1997, *Josu Arkauz Arana* v. *France*, Views adopted on 9 November 1999, para. 11.5.

6.9 With regard to the alleged violation of article 15 of the Convention, the Committee has noted the complainant's arguments that, in granting the Spanish extradition request, which was, at least indirectly, based on testimony extracted by torture from Felipe San Epifanio, the State party itself had relied on this evidence, and that article 15 of the Convention applied not only to criminal proceedings against her in Spain, but also to the extradition proceedings before the Swiss Federal Office of Justice as well as the Federal Court. Similarly, the Committee has noted the State party's submission that the admissibility of the relevant evidence was a matter to be decided by the Spanish courts.

6.10 The Committee observes that the broad scope of the prohibition in article 15, proscribing the invocation of any statement which is established to have been made as a result of torture as evidence "in any proceedings", is a function of the absolute nature of the prohibition of torture and implies, consequently, an obligation for each State party to ascertain whether or not statements admitted as evidence in any proceedings for which it has jurisdiction, including extradition proceedings, have been made as a result of torture.[18]

6.11 At the same time, the Committee notes that, for the prohibition in article 15 to apply, it is required that the statement invoked as evidence "is established to have been made as a result of torture". As the complainant herself stated, criminal proceedings initiated by Felipe San Epifanio against his alleged torturers were discontinued by the Spanish authorities. Considering that it is for the complainant to demonstrate that her allegations are well-founded, the Committee concludes that, on the basis of the facts before it, it has not been established that the statement of Mr. San Epifanio, made before Spanish police on 28 April 1994, was obtained by torture.

6.12 The Committee reiterates that it is for the courts of the States parties to the Convention, and not for the Committee, to evaluate the facts and evidence in a particular case, unless it can be ascertained that the manner in which such facts and evidence were evaluated was clearly arbitrary or amounted to a denial of justice. The Committee considers that the State party's decision to grant the Spanish extradition request does not disclose a violation by the State party of article 15 of the Convention.

7. Consequently, the Committee against Torture, acting under article 22, paragraph 7, of the Convention against Torture and Other Cruel, Inhuman or Degrading Treatment or Punishment, concludes that the extradition of the complainant to Spain did not constitute a breach of either article 3 or 15 of the Convention.

---

[18] See communication N° 193/2001, *P.E.* v. *France*, Views adopted on 21 November 2002 (para. 6.3).

Communication N° 233/2003

Submitted by: Mr. Ahmed Hussein Mustafa Kamil Agiza (represented by counsel, Mr. Bo Johansson, of the Swedish Refugee Advice Centre)
Alleged victim: The complainant
State party: Sweden
Declared admissible: 19 May 2004
Date of adoption of Views: 20 May 2005

Subject matter: deportation of complainant to Egypt with alleged risk of torture

Procedural issues: abuse of process; delay in submitting complaint;

Substantive issues: justifiability of diplomatic assurances; risk of torture on deportation; effective use of right of individual communication; right to an effective remedy for breach of the Convention; right to effective, independent and impartial review

Articles of the Convention: 3, 16, 22

1. The complainant is Ahmed Hussein Mustafa Kamil Agiza, an Egyptian national born on 8 November 1962, detained in Egypt at the time of submission of the complaint. He claims that his removal by Sweden to Egypt on 18 December 2001 violated article 3 of the Convention. He is represented by counsel, who provides as authority to act a letter of authority issued by the complainant's father. The complainant himself, detained, is allegedly not allowed to sign any documents for external purposes without special permission from the Egyptian State prosecutor, and according to counsel such a permit cannot be expected.

The facts as presented by the complainant

2.1 In 1982, the complainant was arrested on account of his family connection to his cousin, who had been arrested for suspected involvement in the assassination of the former Egyptian President, Anwar Sadat. Before his release in March 1983, he was allegedly subjected to torture. The complainant, active at university in the Islamic movement, completed his studies in 1986 and married Ms. Hannan Attia. He avoided various police searches, but encountered difficulties, such as the arrest of his attorney, when he brought a civil claim in 1991 against the Ministry of Home Affairs, for suffering during his time in prison.

2.2 In 1991, the complainant left Egypt for Saudi Arabia on security grounds, and thereafter to Pakistan, where his wife and children joined him. After the Egyptian embassy in Pakistan refused to renew their passports, the family left in July 1995 for Syria under assumed Sudanese identities, in order to continue to Europe. This plan failed and the family moved to Iran, where the complainant was granted a university scholarship.

2.3 In 1998, the complainant was tried in Egypt for terrorist activity directed against the State before a "Superior Court Martial" in absentia, along with over one hundred other accused. He was found guilty of belonging to the terrorist group "Al Gihad", and was sentenced, without possibility of appeal, to 25 years' imprisonment. In 2000, concerned that improving relations between Egypt and Iran would result in his being returned to Egypt, the complainant and his family bought air tickets, under Saudi Arabian identities, to Canada, and claimed asylum during a transit stop in Stockholm, Sweden, on 23 September 2000.

2.4 In his asylum application, the complainant claimed that he had been sentenced to "penal servitude for life" in absentia on account of terrorism linked to Islamic fundamentalism,[1] and that, if returned, he would be executed as other accused in the same proceedings allegedly had been. His wife contended that, if returned, she would be detained for many years, as the complainant's wife. On 23 May 2001, the Migration Board sought the opinion of the Swedish Security Police on the case. On 14 September 2001, the Migration Board held a "major enquiry" with the complainant, with a further enquiry following on 3 October 2001. During of the same month, the Security Police questioned the complainant. On 30 October 2001, the Security Police advised the Migration Board that the complainant held a leading position in an organization guilty of terrorist acts and was responsible for the activities of the organization. The Migration Board thus forwarded the complainant's case, on 12 November 2001, to the Government for a strength of the decision under chapter 7, section 11 (2) (2), of the Aliens Act. In the Board's view, on the information before it, the complainant could be considered entitled to claim refugee status; however, the Security Police's assessment, which the Board saw no reason to question, pointed in a different direction. The balancing of the complainant's possible need for protection against the Security

---

[1] Counsel explains the variation with the actual sentence on the basis that a 25-year sentence amounted to the same as few could be expected to endure that length of time in prison.

Police's assessment, thus had to be made by the Government. On 13 November 2001, the Aliens Appeals Board, whose view the Government had sought, shared the Migration Board's assessment of the merits and also considered that the Government should decide the matter. In a statement, the complainant denied belonging to the organization referred to in the Security Police statement, arguing that one of the designated organizations was not a political organization but an Arab-language publication. He also claimed that he had criticized Usama Bin Laden and the Afghan Taliban in a letter to a newspaper.

2.5   On 18 December 2001, the Government rejected the asylum applications of the complainant and of his wife. The reasons for these decisions are omitted from the text of this decision at the State party's request and with the agreement of the Committee. Accordingly, it was ordered that the complainant be deported immediately and his wife as soon as possible. On 18 December 2001, the complainant was deported, while his wife went into hiding to avoid police custody.

2.6   On 23 January 2002, the Swedish Ambassador to Egypt met the complainant at Mazraat Tora prison outside Cairo.[2] The same day, the complainant's parents visited him for the first time. They allege that they when they met him in the warden's office, he was supported by an officer and near breakdown, hardly able to shake his mother's hand, pale and in shock. His face, particularly the eyes, and his feet were swollen, with his cheeks and bloodied nose seemingly thicker than usual. The complainant allegedly said to his mother that he had been treated brutally upon arrest by the Swedish authorities. During the eight-hour flight to Egypt, in Egyptian custody, he allegedly was bound by hands and foot. Upon arrival, he was allegedly subjected to "advanced interrogation methods" at the hand of Egyptian State security officers, who told him the guarantees provided by the Egyptian Government concerning him were useless. The complainant told his mother that a special electric device with electrodes connected to his body was utilized, and that electric shocks were utilized if he did not respond properly to orders.

2.7   On 11 February 2002, a correspondent for Swedish radio visited the complainant in prison. According to him, the complainant walked with difficulty but he could not see any sign of torture. In response to a question by counsel, the correspondent stated that he had explicitly asked the complainant if he had been tortured, and that he had replied that he could not comment. After the initial visit, the Ambassador or other Swedish diplomats were permitted to visit the complainant on a number of occasions. Counsel states that what can be understood from the diplomatic dispatches up to March 2003, is that the complainant had been treated "relatively well", and that he had not been subjected to torture even if the prison conditions were harsh.

2.8   On 16 April 2002, the complainant's parents again visited him. He allegedly told his mother that after the January visit further electric shocks had been applied, and that for the last ten days he had been held in solitary confinement. His hands and legs had been tied, and he had not been allowed to visit a toilet. At a following visit, he told his parents that he was still in solitary confinement but no longer bound. He was allowed to visit a toilet once a day, and the cell was cold and dark. With reference to a security officer, he was said to have asked his mother, "do you know what he does to me during the nights?" He had also been told that his wife would soon be returned to Egypt and that she and his mother would be sexually assaulted in his presence. Thereafter, the complainant's parents visited him once a month until July 2002 and then every fortnight. According to counsel, the information available is that he is held in a two square metre cell, which is artificially cooled, dark and without a mattress to sleep on. His toilet visits are said to be restricted.

2.9   In December 2002, the complainant's Egyptian lawyer, Mr. Hafeez Abu Saada, the head of an Egyptian human rights organization with knowledge of local conditions of detention and interrogation methods, met in Cairo with Mr. Thomas Hammarberg, head of the Olaf Palme International Centre. Mr. Abu Saada expressed his belief that the complainant had been subjected to torture.

2.10   On 5 March 2003, the Swedish Ambassador met the complainant with a human rights envoy from the Swedish Ministry of Foreign Affairs. The complainant allegedly stated for the first time that he had been subjected to torture. In response to the question as to why he had not mentioned this before, he allegedly responded, "It does no longer matter what I say, I will nevertheless be treated the same way".

The complaint

3.1   Counsel claims that the reason that he lodged the complainant over one and a half years after the complainant's removal was that for a long period it was uncertain who was able to represent him. Counsel contends that the original intention had been for lawyer who had represented the complainant in domestic proceedings in Sweden to submit the

---

[2] Counsel states that the following information concerning the complainant's whereabouts and well-being originates from Swedish diplomatic sources, the complainant's parents, a Swedish radio reporter and the complainant's Egyptian attorney.

complaint; "due to the circumstances", that lawyer found himself "unable to fulfil the commission" and transferred the case to present counsel "some months ago". Counsel adds that it had been difficult to obtain the complainant's personal consent to lodge a complaint.

3.2 As to the merits, counsel argues that the complainant's removal to Egypt by Sweden violated his right under article 3 of the Convention. He bases this proposition both on what was known at the time the complainant was expelled, as viewed in the light of subsequent events. He contends that it has been satisfactorily established that the complainant was in fact subjected to torture after his return.

3.3 Counsel argues that torture is a frequently used method of interrogation and punishment in Egypt, particularly in connection with political and security matters, and that accordingly the complainant, accused of serious political acts, was at substantial risk of torture. In counsel's view, the State party must have been aware of this risk and as a result sought to obtain a guarantee that his human rights would be respected. Counsel emphasizes, however, that no arrangements had been made prior to expulsion as to how the guarantees in question would be implemented after the complainant's return to Egypt. Counsel refers to the judgement of the European Court of Human Rights in *Chahal* v. *United Kingdom*,[3] where the Court found a guarantee provided by the Indian Government to be, of its own, insufficient protection against human rights violations.

3.4 Subsequent events are said to bear out this view. Firstly, Amnesty International expressed concerns about the complainant's situation in communiqués dated 19 and 20 December 2001, 10, 22 January, and 1 February 2002. Secondly, the conclusions drawn by the State party as a result of its visits should be discounted because they took place in circumstances which were deficient. In particular, the visits were short, took place in a prison which is not the one where the complainant was actually detained, were not conducted in private and without the presence of any medical practitioners or experts. Thirdly, independent evidence tends to corroborate that torture did occur. Weight should be attached to the complainant's parents' testimony as, although supervised, not every word was recorded as it was with the official visits and there was opportunity for him to share sensitive information, especially when bidding his mother farewell. In the course of these visits, supervision lessened, with persons entering and leaving the room. Counsel argues it would not be in the parents' or the complainant's interests for them to have overrepresented the situation, as this would needlessly put him at risk of prejudicial treatment as well as distress the complainant's family still in Sweden. In addition, the parents, elderly persons without political motivation, would thereby be placing themselves at risk of reprisal.

3.5 Furthermore, the complainant's Egyptian lawyer is well qualified to reach his conclusion, after meeting with the complainant, that he had been tortured. Mr. Hammarberg, for his part, considers this testimony reliable. In advice dated 28 January 2003 provided by Mr. Hammarberg to counsel, the former considered that there was prima facie evidence of torture. He was also of the view that there were deficiencies in the monitoring arrangements implemented by the Swedish authorities, given that during the first weeks after return there were no meetings, while subsequent meeting were neither in private nor with medical examinations undertaken.

3.6 For counsel, the only independent evidence on the question, that of the radio correspondent's visit, confirms the above conclusions, as the complainant declined to answer a direct question as to whether he had been tortured. He would not have done this had he not feared further reprisals. The complainant also informed the Swedish Ambassador directly on 5 March 2003 that he had been subjected to torture, having by that point allegedly given up any hope that the situation would change.

3.7 Counsel concludes that the complainant's ability to prove torture has been very limited, though he has done his best to inform on his experiences in prison. He has been unable to present a full statement of his experiences or corroborative evidence such as medical reports.

The State party's admissibility and merits submissions

4.1 By submission of 5 December 2003, the State party contests both the admissibility and the merits of the complaint. It regards complaint as inadmissible (i) for the time elapsed since the exhaustion of domestic remedies, (ii) as an abuse of process, and (iii) as manifestly ill-founded.

4.2 While accepting that neither the Convention not the Committee's case law prescribe a definitive timeframe within which a complaint must be submitted, the State party submits that in light of the content of rule 107 (f) of the Committee's rules of procedure, this cannot mean that a complaint could *never* be time-barred. The State party refers to the six-month limit applicable to cases submitted to the European Court of Human Rights, including with respect to expulsion cases arising under article 3 of the European Convention, and the strong rationale of legal certainty for both complainants and States underlying that rule. The State party argues that this principle of legal certainty must be considered as

---
[3] Judgement of 15 November 1996.

one of the fundamental principles inherent in the international legal order. As the Convention as well as the European Convention are both important parts of international human rights law, it would be natural for one regime to seek guidance from another on an issue on which the former is silent. In view of rule 107 (f) of the Committee's rules,[4] therefore, a six-month limit could arguably serve as a point of departure for the Committee.

4.3 With respect to the present case, the State party argues that no convincing information has been provided for the delay of over one and a half years in submission of the complaint. As counsel derives his authority to act from the complainant's father rather than the complainant himself, there is no reason why this could not have been obtained at an earlier stage. Nor does it appear that any attempt was made shortly after expulsion to obtain authority to act from this or another relative, such as the complainant's wife in Sweden. The State party refers to the complaint submitted by the same counsel on behalf of the complainant's wife in December 2001,[5] where it was argued that her situation was so closely linked to that of the present complaint that it was impossible to argue her case without referring to his. The arguments advanced in her case show that counsel was well acquainted with the circumstances presently invoked, and he should not be allowed to argue that the delay was due to his involvement with the family's case until a much later stage. There is, in the State party's view, no reason why the present complainant could not have been included in the first complaint submitted in December 2001. Accordingly, the State party argues that in the interests of legal certainty, the time that has elapsed since exhaustion of domestic remedies is unreasonably prolonged, and the complaint is inadmissible pursuant to article 22, paragraph 2, of the Convention and rule 107 (f).

4.4 The State party also argues that the complaint discloses an abuse of the right of submission, disputing whether the complainant can be considered to have justifiable interest in having his complaint considered by the Committee. The factual basis of the current complaint is the same as that submitted on his wife's behalf in December 2001,[6] with the crucial issue in both cases relating to the guarantees issued by the Egyptian authorities prior to and for the purpose of the expulsion of the complainant and his family. In its decision on that case, after having assessed the value of the guarantees and finding no violation of the Convention, the Committee already dealt with the very issue raised by the present complaint. The issue should accordingly be considered *res judicata*.

4.5 Furthermore, within the framework of the proceedings concerning the complaint by the complainant's wife, the same extensive information has been submitted concerning his past activities, present whereabouts and conditions of detention. As both complaints were submitted by the same counsel, the present complaint places an unnecessary burden both on the Committee and the State party. Accordingly, the complainant does not have a demonstrable interest in having his complaint examined by the Committee. It should thus be regarded as an abuse of the right of submission and inadmissible pursuant to article 22, paragraph 2, of the Convention and rule 107 (b).[7]

4.6 Finally, the State party considers the complaint manifestly unfounded, as the complainant's claims fail to rise to the basic level of substantiation required in light of the arguments on the merits set out below. It should thus be declared inadmissible under article 22, paragraph 2, of the Convention and rule 107 (b).

4.7 On the merits, the State party sets out the particular mechanisms of the Aliens Act 1989 applicable to cases such as the complainant's. While asylum claims are normally dealt with by the Migration Board and, in turn, the Aliens Appeals Board, under certain circumstances either body may refer the case to the Government, while appending its own opinion. This constellation arises if the matter is deemed to be of importance for the security of the State or otherwise for security in general, or for the State's relations with a foreign power (chapter 7, section 11(2)(2), of the Act). If the Migration Board refers a case, it must first be forwarded to the Aliens Appeals Board which provides its own opinion on the case.

4.8 An alien otherwise in need of protection on account of a well-founded fear of persecution at the hand of the authorities of another State on account of a reason listed in the Convention on the Status of Refugees (under chapter 3, section 2, of the Act) may however be denied a residence permit in certain

---

[4] Rule 107 (f) provides: "With a view to reaching a decision on the admissibility of a complaint, the Committee, its Working Group or a rapporteur designated under rules 98 or 106, para. 3, shall ascertain: … (f) That the time elapsed since the exhaustion of domestic remedies is not so unreasonably prolonged as to render consideration of the claims unduly difficult by the Committee or the State party."
[5] *Hanan Ahmed Fouad Abd El Khalek Attia* v. *Sweden*, case N° 199/2002, Decision adopted on 17 November 2003.
[6] Ibid.

[7] Rule 107 (b) provides: "With a view to reaching a decision on the admissibility of a complaint, the Committee, its Working Group or a rapporteur designated under rules 98 or 106, para. 3, shall ascertain: … (b) That the complaint is not an abuse of the Committee's process or manifestly unfounded."

exceptional cases, following an assessment of that alien's previous activities and requirements of the country's security (chapter 3, section 4 of the Act). However, *no* person at risk of torture may be refused a residence permit (chapter 3, section 3 of the Act). In addition, if a person has been refused a residence permit and has had an expulsion decision issued against him or her, an assessment of the situation at the enforcement stage must be made to avoid that an individual is expelled to face, inter alia, torture or other cruel, inhuman or degrading treatment or punishment.

4.9 The State party recalls United Nations Security Council resolution 1373 of 28 September 2001, which enjoins all United Nations Member States to deny safe haven to those who finance, plan, support or commit terrorist acts, or themselves provide safe haven. The Council called on Member States to take appropriate measures, consistent with international human rights and refugee law, to ensure asylum-seekers have not planned, facilitated, or participated in, terrorist acts. It also called upon Member States to ensure, in accordance with international law, that the institution of refugee status is not abused by perpetrators, organizers or facilitators of terrorist acts. In this context, the State party refers to the Committee's statement of 22 November 2001, in which it expressed confidence that responses to threats of international terrorism adopted by States parties would be in conformity with their obligations under the Convention.

4.10 The State party also recalls the interim report[8] submitted in July 2002 by the Special Rapporteur of the Commission on Human Rights on the question of torture and other cruel, inhuman or degrading treatment or punishment, submitted in accordance with resolution 56/143 of 19 December 2001. In his report, the Special Rapporteur urged States "to ensure that in all appropriate circumstances the persons they intend to extradite, under terrorist or other charges, will not be surrendered unless the Government of the receiving country has provided an unequivocal guarantee to the extraditing authorities that the persons concerned will not be subjected to torture or any other forms of ill-treatment upon return, and that a system to monitor the treatment of the persons in question has been put into place with a view to ensuring that they are treated with full respect for their human dignity" (para. 35).

4.11 As to the facts of the present case, the State party details the information obtained by its Security Police, which led it to regard the complainant as a serious security threat. At the State party's request, this information, while transmitted to counsel for the complainant in the context of the confidential proceedings under article 22 of the Convention, is not set out in the Committee's public decision on the present complaint.

4.12 The State party observes that on 12 December 2001, after referral of the case from the Migration and Aliens Appeals Boards, a State secretary of its Ministry of Foreign Affairs met with a representative of the Egyptian Government in Cairo. At the State party's request and with the Committee's agreement, details of the identity of the interlocutor are deleted from the text of the decision. As the State party was considering excluding the complainant from protection under the Refugee Convention, the purpose of the visit was to determine the possibility, without violating Sweden's international obligations, including those arising under the Convention, of returning the complainant and his family to Egypt. After careful consideration of the option to obtain assurances from the Egyptian authorities with respect to future treatment, the State party's Government concluded it was both possible and meaningful to inquire whether guarantees could be obtained to the effect that the complainant and his family would be treated in accordance with international law upon return to Egypt. Without such guarantees, return to Egypt would not be an alternative. On 13 December 2002, requisite guarantees were provided.

4.13 The State party then sets outs in detail its reasons for refusing, on 18 December 2001, the asylum claims of the complainant and his wife. These reasons are omitted from the text of this decision at the State party's request and with the agreement of the Committee.

4.14 The State party advises that the complainant's current legal status is, according to the Egyptian Ministries of Justice and Interior, that he presently serves a sentence for his conviction, in absentia, by a military court for, among other crimes, murder and terrorist activities. His family provided him with legal representation, and in February 2002, a petition for review of the case was filed with the President. By October 2002, this had been dealt with by the Ministry of Defence and would soon be handed to the President's office for decision. Turning to the monitoring of the complainant's situation after his expulsion, the State party advises that his situation has been monitored by the Swedish embassy in Cairo, mainly by visits approximately once every month. As of the date of submission, there had been seventeen visits.[9] On most occasions, visitors have included the Swedish Ambassador, and several on

---

[8] A/57/173.

[9] These took place on 23 January, 7 March, 14 April, 27 May, 24 June, 22 July, 9 September and 4 November 2002, as well as 19 January, 5 March, 9 April, 14 May, 9 June, 29 July, 25 August, 30 September and 17 November 2003.

other visits a senior official from the Ministry of Foreign Affairs.

4.15 According to the embassy, these visits have over time developed into routine, taking place in the prison superintendent's office and lasting an average 45 minutes. At no time has the complainant been restrained in any fashion. The atmosphere has been relaxed and friendly, with the visitors and the complainant being offered soft drinks. At the end of the June 2002 visit, embassy staff observed the complainant in seemingly relaxed conversation with several prison guards, awaiting return to detention. At all times he has been dressed in clean civilian clothes, with well-trimmed beard and hair. He appeared to be well-nourished and not to have lost weight between visits. At none of the visits did he show signs of physical abuse or maltreatment, and he was able to move around without difficulty. At the request of the Ambassador, in March 2002, he removed his shirt and undershirt and turned around, disclosing no sign of torture.

4.16 In the embassy's report of the first (January 2002) visit, the complainant did not seem to hesitate to speak freely, and told the Ambassador that he had no complaints as to his treatment in prison. Asked whether he had been subjected to any kind of systematic abuse, he made no claim to such effect. When asked during the April 2002 visit whether he had been in any way maltreated, he noted that he had not been physically abused or otherwise maltreated. During most visits he had complaints concerning his general health, concerning a bad back, gastric ulcer, kidney infection and thyroid gland, causing inter alia sleeping problems. He had seen a variety of internal and external medical specialists, and had had an MRI spinal examination, physiotherapy for his back and an X-ray thyroid gland examination. The X-ray revealed a small tumour for which he will undergo further tests. In August 2003, he expressed to the Ambassador, as he had done before, his satisfaction with the medical care received. At the November 2003 visit, he advised that a neurologist had recommended a back operation. He has received regular medication for various health problems.

4.17 During the May and November 2002 visits, the complainant remarked adversely about the general conditions of detention. He referred to the absence of beds or toilets in the cell, and that he was being held in a part of the prison for unconvicted persons. According to him, this generally improved after December 2002, when he was no longer kept apart from other prisoners and could walk in the courtyard. In January 2003, he was moved on health grounds to a part of the prison with a hospital ward. In March 2003, in response to a question, he said he was treated neither better nor worse than other prisoners; general prison conditions applied. At no subsequent visits did he make such complaints.

4.18 On 10 February 2002, that is at an early stage of detention, the Swedish national radio reported on a visit by one of its correspondents with the complainant in the office of a senior prison official. He was dressed in dark-blue jacket and trousers, and showed no external signs of recent physical abuse, at least on his hands or face. He did have some problems moving around, which he ascribed to a long-term back problem. He complained about not being allowed to read and about lack of a radio, as well as lack of permission to exercise.

4.19 Further issues that have been brought up regularly between the complainant and embassy staff are visits from family and lawyers. Following the June 2002 visit, a routine of fortnightly family visits appeared to have been established. At the time of submission this routine continued, though visits in May and June 2003 were restricted for security reasons. The complainant remarked that he had only received two visits from his lawyer, in February and March 2002. He had not requested to see his lawyer as he considered it meaningless. This issue was raised in the embassy's follow-up meetings with Egyptian Government officials, who affirmed that the complainant's lawyer is free to visit and that no restrictions apply.

4.20 As the complainant on several occasions and in reply to direct questions, stated he had not suffered abuse, the Ambassador concluded after the November 2002 visit that, although the detention was mentally trying, there was no indication that the Egyptian authorities had breached the guarantees provided. The State party details certain allegations subsequently made by the complainant and the actions it took in response thereto. At the request of the State party and with the Committee's agreement, details of these matters are not included in the text of this decision.

4.21 As to the application of the Convention, the State party observes that the present case differs from most article 3 complaints before the Committee in that the expulsion has already taken place. The wording of article 3 of the Convention however implies that the Committee's examination of the case must focus on the point in time when the complainant was returned to his country of origin. Events that have taken place or observations made thereafter may naturally be of interest in establishing whether the guarantees provided have been respected, and this bears on the assessment of the State party's Government that the complainant would not be treated contrary to the Convention was in fact correct. But while such developments are relevant, the State party maintains that the principal question in the current complaint is whether or not its authorities had reason to believe, at the time of the complainant's expulsion on 18 December 2001, that substantial grounds existed for believing him to be at risk of torture.

4.22 The State party refers to the Committee's constant jurisprudence that an individual must show a foreseeable, real and personal risk of torture. Such a risk must rise beyond mere theory or suspicion, but does not have to be highly probable. In assessing such a risk, a standard which is incorporated into Swedish law, the guarantees issued by the Egyptian Government are of great importance. The State party recalls the Committee's decision on the complaint presented by the complainant's wife where the same guarantees were considered effective,[10] and refers to relevant decisions of the European organs under the European Convention on Human Rights.

4.23 In *Aylor-Davis* v. *France* (judgement of 20 January 1994), it was held that guarantees from the receiving country, the United States, were found to eliminate the risk of the applicant being sentenced to death. The death penalty could only be imposed if it was actually sought by the State prosecutor. By contrast, in *Chahal* v. *United Kingdom*, the Court was not persuaded that assurances from the Indian Government that a Sikh separatist "would enjoy the same legal protection as any other Indian citizen, and that he would have no reason to expect mistreatment of any kind at the hand of the Indian authorities" would provide an adequate guarantee of safety. While not doubting the Indian Government's good faith, it appeared to the Court that despite the efforts inter alia of the Indian Government and courts to bring about reform, violations of human rights by members of the security forces in Punjab and elsewhere in India remained a recurrent problem. The case law thus suggests that guarantees may be accepted where the authorities of the receiving State can be assumed to have control of the situation.

4.24 Applying this test, the State party argues that the current case is more in line with *Aylor-Davis*. The guarantees were issued by a senior representative of the Egyptian Government. The State party points out that if assurances are to have effect, they must be issued by someone who can be expected to be able to ensure their effectiveness, as, in the State party's view, was presently the case in light of the Egyptian representative's senior position. In addition, during the December 2001 meeting between the Swedish State secretary and the Egyptian official, it was made clear to the latter what was at stake for Sweden: as article 3 of the Convention is of absolute character, the need for effective guarantees was explained at length. The State secretary reaffirmed the importance for Sweden to abide by its international obligations, including the Convention, and that as a result specific conditions would have to be fulfilled in order to make the complainant's expulsion possible. It was thus necessary to obtain written guarantees of fair trial, that he would not be subjected to torture or other inhuman treatment, and that he would not be sentenced to death or executed. The trial would be monitored by the Swedish embassy in Cairo, and it should be possible to visit the complainant, even after conviction. Moreover, his family should not be subjected to any kind of harassment. It was made clear that Sweden found itself in a difficult position, and that Egypt's failure to honour the guarantees would impact strongly on other similar European cases in the future.

4.25 The State party expands on the details of these guarantees. They are omitted from the text of this decision at the request of the State party, and with the consent of the Committee. The State party points out that the guarantees are considerably stronger than those provided in *Chahal* and are couched much more affirmatively, in positive terms of prohibition. The State party recalls that Egypt is a State party to the Convention, has a constitutional prohibition on torture and acts of, or orders to torture, are serious felonies under Egyptian criminal law.

4.26 For the State party, it is of interest in assessing the complaint whether the guarantees have been and are being respected. It recalls the allegations of ill-treatment made by the complainant's mother, and subsequently by non-governmental organizations, including the mother's description of his physical condition at her first visit on 23 January 2002. The State party's Ambassador's visit the same day immediately followed the mother's visit, and the Ambassador observed no signs of physical abuse. As observed, he seemed to speak freely, made no complaints about torture, and in response to a direct question on systematic abuse in prison, made no claim to that effect. The State party thus argues the allegation of ill-treatment on that date has been effectively refuted by its Ambassador's observations.

4.27 The State party asserts that judging from the numerous reports provided by the Ambassador, embassy staff and the senior official of its Ministry of Foreign Affairs, the guarantees provided have proved effective vis-à-vis the complainant. Allegations made by him to the contrary have not been substantiated, and on numerous occasions, he confirmed to the Swedish Ambassador that he had not been tortured or ill-treated. The allegations of March 2003 were refuted by the Egyptian authorities. The complainant receives the medical care he requires as a result of his health problems, and legal assistance has been provided to him by his family. That his lawyer so far may not have taken sufficient action to achieve review of sentence is of no relevance to the current complaint. In addition, his family visits him regularly. On the whole, considering the inherent constraints of detention, the

---
[10] Ibid.

complainant appears to be in fairly good health. The State party concludes that as the allegations of torture have not been substantiated, they cannot form the basis of the Committee's assessment of the case. The State party also points out that the case has been widely reported in national media and has received international attention. The Egyptian authorities can be assumed to be aware of this, and are likely to ensure as a result he is not subjected to ill-treatment.

4.28 The State party recalls that in its decision on the complaint of the complainant's wife,[11] the Committee appeared to make a prognosis for her in the light of the information about the effectiveness of the guarantees regarding her husband, the present complainant, to whom she had linked her case solely on the basis of her relationship to him. The Committee declared itself "satisfied by the provision of guarantees against abusive treatment" and noted that they were "regularly monitored by the State party's authorities in situ." It went on to observe that Egypt "is directly bound properly to treat prisoners within its jurisdiction." In the State party's view, therefore, the Committee's conclusion that she had not made out a breach of article 3 in her complaint is of "essential importance" to the present complaint.

4.29 In conclusion, the State party argues that by obtaining the guarantees in question from the competent Egyptian official, it lived up to its commitments under the Convention while at the same time as fulfilling its obligations under Security Council resolution 1373. Prior to expelling the complainant, appropriate guarantees were obtained from the official best placed to ensure their effectiveness. The guarantees correspond in content to the requirements of the Special Rapporteur (see para. 4.10 above), while a monitoring mechanism was put into place and has been functioning for almost two years. Therefore, the complainant has not substantiated his claims that the guarantees have, in practice, not been respected. Should the Committee come to another conclusion, the crucial question is what the State party's Government had reason to believe at the time of the expulsion. As the complainant has not substantiated his claim under article 3, his removal to his country of origin was not in breach of that provision.

Counsel's comments

5.1 By letter of 21 January 2004, counsel disputed the State party's submissions both on admissibility and merits. On the State party's arguments concerning timely submission of the complaint, he argues that it was unclear for a long period who was entitled to represent the complainant. Counsel argues that his prior lawyer had been unable to arrange for a power of attorney to be signed prior to the complainant's rapid removal, and that the prior lawyer considered his responsibilities at an end once the complainant had been removed. Counsel argues that once the complainant had been removed and could not be consulted directly, it was necessary to obtain more information about his situation, before carefully evaluating, together with his parents, whether it would be productive to file a complaint on his behalf. Counsel argues that the circumstances in the complaint brought by the complainant's wife were "completely different", as she had remained in Sweden and thus an urgent communication was necessary in order to prevent removal. In the present case, the complainant had already been expelled, and there was no urgent need to submit the complaint before a careful evaluation of its substance. He also points out that the six-month limit for submission refers only to complaints presented under the European Convention, and that there is no difficulty in the existence of different treaty regimes. In any case, counsel argues that the issue of principle before the Committee in terms of the satisfactory protection afforded by diplomatic assurances is so important that it should consider the case rather than declare it inadmissible.

5.2 Counsel denies that the complaint constitutes an abuse of the right of submission. While conceding that many of the "basic factors" in the cases of the complainant and his wife are the same and that the circumstances "coincide to a considerable degree", the current complainant is the individual at most serious risk of torture. His wife, who by contrast based her claim simply as a close relative to a person sought for terrorist activities, is in a subsidiary position facing a less serious risk than her husband. As a result there are "major differences" between the two cases and the complaint should thus not be declared inadmissible on this ground. Counsel also rejects the characterization of the case as manifestly ill-founded.

5.3 On the merits, counsel refers, for a general picture of the gross, flagrant and widespread use of torture by Egyptian authorities to reports of several human rights organizations. The human rights report of the Swedish Ministry of Foreign Affairs itself refers to frequent torture by Egyptian police, especially in terrorism-related investigations. Counsel argues that the complainant was not involved in any terrorist activities, and rejects any applicability of Security Council resolution 1373. In any event, this resolution could not override other international obligations such as the Convention. Counsel denies that the complainant participated in terrorist activities, including through those organizations that the Security Police claimed he was involved in. In any case, allegations of involvement with terrorist organizations would only have served to heighten the existing interest of the

---

[11] Ibid.

Egyptian authorities in the complainant, an individual convicted of terrorist offences, and this aggravating circumstance exacerbating the risk of torture should have been considered by the State party prior to expelling him.

5.4 For counsel, the key issue is not whether a guarantee was given by a Government official, but rather whether it can be implemented and, if so, how. The guarantee in question was obtained at short notice, vague in its terms and provided no details on how the guarantees would be given effect with respect to the complainant; nor did the Egyptian Government provide, or the Swedish authorities request, any such information. Neither did the Swedish authorities conceive an effective and durable arrangement for monitoring, conducting the first visit over a month after the complainant's removal. This arrangement, coming shortly after the Committee had requested interim measures of protection with respect to the complainant's wife, appeared to be an ad hoc reaction rather than part of a properly conceived monitoring plan. Counsel reiterates his criticisms of the effectiveness of the monitoring arrangements, observing that standard routines in such cases applied by organizations such as the International Committee of the Red Cross had not been met. In addition, the Swedish authorities apparently did not seek to call any medical expertise, particularly after the complainant's direct allegation of torture in March 2003. Counsel contends that differences between the complainant's testimony to his parents on one hand, and to Swedish authorities, unknown to him and accompanied by Egyptian authorities, on the other, are explicable.

5.5 Counsel criticizes the Committee's decision on the complaint presented by the complainant's wife, as the information that her husband had suffered ill-treatment, was based on a variety of sources and could not be dismissed as unfounded. Counsel disputes the State party's interpretation of the jurisprudence of the European organs, viewing the content of the current guarantee and that offered by India in *Chahal* as "basically the same". He observes that the Court did not doubt the good faith of the Indian Government, but regarded the fundamental problem as human rights violations committed at the operational level by the security forces. In the present case, similarly, even assuming the same good will at the political level on the part of Egyptian authorities such as the representative with whom the guarantees were agreed, the reality at the lower operational levels of the State security services and other authorities with whom the complainant was in contact is that torture is commonplace. The *Aylor-Davis* case, by contrast, is inapposite as the guarantee there was offered by a State the circumstances of which cannot be compared to those appertaining in Egypt.

5.6 With respect to the State party' statement that the Egyptian authorities rejected the allegations made by the complainant in March 2003, counsel observes that any contrary reaction would have been surprising, and that such refutation does not disprove the complainant's allegation. In counsel's view, the burden of proof to show ill-treatment did not occur rests with the State party, with the most effective capacity to present evidence and conduct appropriate supervision. Counsel submits that the State party has not discharged this burden.

5.7 While accepting that Egypt is a State party to the Convention, counsel observes that this formal act is regrettably no guarantee that a State party will abide by the commitments assumed. As to the prophylactic effect of media publicity, counsel argues that there was some coverage of the cases of the complainant and his wife around the time of the former's removal, but that thereafter interest has been limited. In any case, there is reason to doubt whether media coverage has any such protective effect, and even where coverage is intensive, its positive effect may be doubted.

5.8 Counsel submits that if the Committee were to accept guarantees such as those offered in the present case as sufficient protection against torture, one could not discount that large scale deportations could take place after some standard form of assurance provided by States with poor human rights records. At least in circumstances where there was a limited will and capability on the part of the removing State appropriately to monitor the consequences, the results could readily be wide scope for authorities of the receiving State to engage in and conceal torture and ill-treatment. As a result, counsel invites the Committee to find that there was (i) a violation by the State party of article 3 of the Convention at the time of the complainant's expulsion, in the light both of the information then available and of subsequent events, and (ii) that he has been subjected to torture after removal.

Supplementary submissions by the parties

6.1 By letter of 20 April 2004, counsel advised that on 18 February 2004, the complainant met his mother in prison. He informed her that he had been threatened by interrogation officers that he could be killed or tortured, and the same day lodged a complaint that he had been tortured. On 19 February 2004, he was transferred to Abu-Zabaal prison some 50 kilometres from Cairo, against which he protested by hunger strike lasting 17 days. He was allegedly placed in a small punitive isolation cell measuring 1.5 square metres in unhygienic conditions, receiving a bottle of water a day. On 8 March 2004, representatives of the Swedish embassy visited him with unknown results. On 20 March 2004, following unsuccessful attempts by the complainant's mother to visit him, it was announced that no family visits would be permitted outside major holidays due to his status as a security prisoner with special restrictions. On 4 April 2004, he was returned to Masra Torah prison. On 10 April 2004, a retrial began before the 13th superior military court on charges of joining and leading an illegal group or organization and criminal conspiracy, to which the complainant pleaded not guilty. A representative of Human Rights Watch was admitted, but family, journalists and representatives of the Swedish embassy were not. The complainant's lawyer requested an adjournment in order that he could read the 2000 pages of charging material and prepare a defence. As a result, the trial was adjourned for three days, with the lawyer permitted only to make handwritten notes. In counsel's view, this information demonstrates that the complainant had been tortured in the past, has been threatened therewith and faces a considerable risk of further torture. It also shows he has been treated in cruel and inhumane manner as well as denied a fair trial.

6.2 By further letter of 28 April 2004, counsel advised that on 27 April 2004 the complainant had been convicted and sentenced to 25 years' imprisonment. He also contended that the court rejected a request from the complainant for a medical examination as he had been tortured in detention. In counsel's view, the complainant's statement to the court and the court's rejection of his request constitute a further clear indication that he had been subjected to torture.

7.1 By submission of 3 May 2004, the State party responded to counsel's letter of 20 April 2004. The State party advised that since the last (seventeenth) visit reported to the Committee on 5 December 2003, four further visits on 17 December 2003, 28 January 2004, 8 March 2004 and 24 March 2004 had taken place. The State party advised that from December 2003 to January 2004, the complainant's situation remained broadly the same, with him taking up law studies. While complaining that his two cellmates disturbed peace and quiet required for study, he managed to prepare for examinations that took place in the facility in January 2004. The reportedly maximum security Abu-Zabaal facility to which he was transferred was said to be a more customary facility for prisoners sentenced to long terms. At the same time, the prison director advised that the complainant had been ordered to spend 15 days in isolation as a disciplinary sanction for having attempted to instigate a rebellion amongst Masra Torah inmates. The State party had obtained separate corroborating evidence that (i) the complainant had attempted to start a prison riot by "shouting words calling for disobedience against the instructions and regulation of the prison" and that (ii) restrictions had been imposed on correspondence and visiting rights, for a period of three months. The State party observed that the complainant was found guilty of one of the two offences with which he was charged, namely having held a leading position in, and being responsible for, the terrorist organization *Islamic Al-Fath Vanguards*. He was sentenced to life imprisonment, hard labour (abolished in 2003) not being imposed. He is currently in Masra Torah prison awaiting decisions as to future placement.

7.2 The State party maintained its earlier positions with respect to the admissibility of the complaint, as well as to the merits, that is, that the complainant has not substantiated his claims that the Egyptian authorities have not respected the guarantees in practice. It recalled that the crucial question is what the State party had reason to believe, in light of the guarantees given, at the time of the expulsion. The State party thus submitted that it has been in full conformity with its obligations under the Convention.

8.1 By letter of 3 May 2004, counsel argued that he had initially only been supplied with a redacted version of the diplomatic report supplied after the first ambassadorial meeting in 23 January 2002 with the complainant. Counsel contended that the full report had just been provided to him by a lawyer representing a third party deported at the same time as the complainant. Counsel contends that according to this report the complainant informed the Ambassador that he had been tortured (in the form of beating by prison guards) and subjected to cruel and degrading treatment (in the form of blindfolding, solitary confinement in a very small cell, sleep deprivation and refusal of prescribed medication). Counsel argued that the State party had not supplied this information to the Committee. Counsel further provided a report by Human Rights Watch critical of diplomatic assurances in this context,[12] as well as a statement dated 27 April 2004 of the Egyptian Organization for Human Rights critical of the complainant's retrial.

8.2 By letter of 4 May 2004, counsel provided his translation of the diplomatic report described. After describing a forced posture during the air transport to Egypt, the complainant is said to have told the Ambassador at the first meeting, in the presence of Egyptian officials, that he had been "forced to be blindfolded during interrogation, kept in too narrow cells, 1.50 x 1.50 metres during the same period, lack of sleep due to supervision in cells, a delay of ten days before [he] once gets access to his anti-gastric drugs (after medical examination), that [he] had been beaten by prison guards during transport to and from interrogation and threats from interrogation offices that it could affect his family if he did not tell everything about his time in Iran". The Ambassador

---

[12] Human Rights Watch, "Empty promises: diplomatic assurances no safeguard against torture", April 2004.

concluded that he could not evaluate the veracity of these statements, but did not understand the claim to be of any form of systematic, physical torture. Counsel viewed this newly disclosed information as a clear indication that the complainant had been subjected to torture. Counsel also argued that the real reason that the complainant had been transferred to the Abu-Zaabal facility was because he had lodged a complaint of threatened torture. He also contended that the complainant was denied "real and fair possibilities" to prepare his defence and observed that the State party did not address issues arising from the complainant's trial.

8.3   By a further letter of 4 May 2004, counsel provided a statement of the same day by Human Rights Watch entitled "Suspected Militants Unfair Trial and Torture Claim Implicate Sweden", in which the complainant's retrial as well as the State party's monitoring arrangements were criticized. Counsel also provided a letter to him by a Human Rights Watch researcher purporting to confirm the contents of the unredacted first diplomatic report described above and concluding that there were credible allegations of ill-treatment.

8.4   By submission of 5 May 2004, the State party advised that it considered the Committee to be in a position to take a decision on the admissibility and, if necessary, the merits of the complaint on the basis of the Convention and the information before the Committee. Accordingly, it did not intend to make additional submissions beyond those already made on 3 May 2004. It observed in conclusion that counsel's letter of 4 May 2004 raised, inter alia, issues falling outside the scope of the Convention.

Committee's admissibility decision

9.1   At its 32nd session, the Committee considered the admissibility of the communication. The Committee ascertained, as it was required to do under article 22, paragraph 5 (a), of the Convention, that the same matter had not been and was not being examined under another procedure of international investigation or settlement.

9.2   On the State party's argument that the present complaint was an abuse of process which rendered it inadmissible, the Committee observed that the complaint submitted on behalf of the complainant's wife in order to prevent her removal had necessarily been filed with dispatch, and had concerned, at least at the time of the Committee's decision, the issue of whether *at that point* the circumstances were such that her removal would be a violation of article 3 of the Convention. In reaching the conclusion that removal of the complainant's wife would not breach article 3, the Committee had considered the chronology of events up to the time of its decision, a necessarily wider enquiry than that at issue in the present case, which was focused upon the situation of the complainant at the time of his expulsion in December 2001. Indeed, the Committee had observed in its decision on the original complaint that it was not being presented with the issue of whether the present complainant's removal itself breached article 3. The two complaints related to different persons, one already removed from the State party's jurisdiction at the time of submission of the complaint and the other still within its jurisdiction pending removal. In the Committee's view, the complaints were thus not of an essentially identical nature, and it did not consider the current complaint to be a simple resubmission of an already decided issue. While submission of the present complaint with greater dispatch would have been preferable, the Committee considered that it would be inappropriate to take so strict a view that would consider the time taken in obtaining authorization from the complainant's father as so excessively delayed as amounting to an abuse of process.

9.3   As to the State party inadmissibility argument grounded on rule 107 (f), the Committee observed that this rule required the delay in submission to have made consideration of the case "unduly difficult". In the present case, the State party had had ready access to the relevant factual submissions and necessary argumentation, and thus, while the timing of submission of the two complaints may have been inconvenient, consideration of the present complaint could not be said to have been made unduly difficult by the lapse of 18 months from the date of the complainant's expulsion. The Committee thus rejected the State party's argument that the complaint is inadmissible on this ground.

9.4   The Committee noted that Egypt has not made the declaration provided for under article 22 recognizing the Committee's competence to consider individual complaints against that State party. The Committee observed, however, that a finding, as requested by the complainant, that torture had in fact occurred following the complainant's removal to Egypt (see para. 5.8), would amount to a conclusion that Egypt, a State party to the Convention, had breached its obligations under the Convention without it having had an opportunity to present its position. This separate claim against Egypt was thus inadmissible *ratione personae*.

9.5   In terms of the State party's argument that the remaining complaint was insufficiently substantiated, for purposes of admissibility, the Committee considered that the complainant had presented a sufficiently arguable case with respect to Sweden for it to be determined on the merits. In the absence of any further obstacles to the admissibility of the complaint advanced by the State party, the Committee accordingly was ready to proceed with the consideration of the merits.

9.6 Accordingly, the Committee against Torture decided that the complaint was admissible, in part, as set out in paragraphs 9.2 to 9.5 above.

Supplementary submissions by the parties

10.1 By letter of 20 August 2004, counsel for the complainant made additional submissions on the merits of the case, providing additional details on the complainant's retrial in April 2004. He stated that the complainant's defence counsel was only provided with copies of parts of the criminal investigation that had been conducted, despite a request to be able to photocopy the investigation records. When the trial was resumed on 13 April, the complainant was only able to speak to his counsel for about 15 minutes. The State called a colonel of the State Security Investigation Sector to testify against the complainant, to the effect that the complainant had had a leading position since 1980 in the Jamaa group, as well as links since 1983 with Ayman al Zawahiri, a central figure of the group. He further testified that the complainant had attended training camps in Pakistan and Afghanistan, and participated in weapons training sessions. Upon cross-examination, the colonel stated that the Jamaa leadership continually changes, that his testimony was based on secret information, that the sources thereof could not be revealed due to risks to their lives and that he (the colonel) had had a supplementary role in the investigation alongside other officers whom he did not know. According to counsel for the complainant, the court in its verdict of 27 April 2004 rejected the complainant's request for a forensic medical examination made during the trial, but referred to a medical examination report by the prison doctor which indicated that the complainant had suffered injuries in prison.

10.2 Counsel refers to a Swedish television broadcast of 10 May 2004 on entitled "Kalla Fakta", examining the circumstances of the expulsion of the complainant and another individual.[13] The programme stated that the two men had been handcuffed when brought to a Stockholm airport, that a private jet of the United States of America had landed and that the two men were handed over to a group of special agents by Swedish police. The agents stripped the clothes from the men's bodies, inserted suppositories of an unknown nature, placed diapers upon them and dressed them in black overalls. Their hands and feet were chained to a specially designed harness, they were blindfolded and hooded as they were brought to the plane. Mr. Hans Dahlgren, State Secretary at the Foreign Ministry, stated in an interview that the Egyptian Government had not complied with the fair trial component of the guarantees provided.

10.3 According to counsel for the complainant, following this programme, the Swedish Foreign Ministry sent two senior representatives to Egypt to discuss with the Egyptian Government how the two deportees had been treated. Results of the meeting are not known apart from an Egyptian denial of maltreatment and that an investigation under Egyptian leadership, but with international participation and medical expertise, would be involved. Three separate investigations in Sweden have also resulted and are ongoing: (i) a *proprio motu* investigation by the Chief Ombudsman to determine whether the actions taken were lawful, (ii) a criminal investigation by the Stockholm public prosecutor, upon private complaint, on whether Swedish Security Police committed any crime in connection with the deportation, and (iii) an investigation by Parliament's Constitutional Committee into the lawfulness of the Swedish handling of the cases.

10.4 On 15 June 2004, the Aliens Appeals Board granted the complainant's wife and her five children permanent resident status in Sweden on humanitarian grounds. Later in June, the Egyptian Government through prerogative of mercy reduced the complainant's 25-year sentence to 15 years of imprisonment. According to counsel for the complainant, the complainant last met Swedish representatives in July 2004. For the first time, the meeting was wholly private. After the meeting, he met his mother and told her that prior to the meeting he had been instructed to be careful and to watch his tongue, receiving from an officer the warning "don't think that we don't hear, we have ears and eyes."

10.5 As at 20 August 2004, the date of the submissions, there was no information as to the announced inquiry in Egypt.[14] However, that day, the Swedish Minister of Foreign Affairs announced in a radio broadcast the receipt of a Note from the Egyptian Government rejecting all allegations of the complainant's torture and considering an international inquiry unnecessary and unacceptable. The Minister of Foreign Affairs also considered there reason to be self-critical concerning the Swedish handling of the case.

10.6 Counsel submits that the retrial fell patently short of international standards, being conducted in a military court with limited time and access available to the defence resulting in a conviction based on

---

[13] Counsel has supplied a transcript of the programme.

[14] Counsel supplies a public statement by Amnesty International, dated 28 May 2004, entitled "Sweden : Concerns over the treatment of deported Egyptians" calling for an "international, wide-ranging, independent and impartial investigation " (EUR 42/001/2004), and, to similar effect, a statement by Human Rights Watch, dated 27 May 2004, entitled "Sweden: torture inquiry must be under U.N. auspices."

weak and insufficient evidence.[15] The failure to respect this portion of the guarantee, as conceded by State Secretary Dahlgren, raised of itself serious doubts as to the fulfilment of the remaining commitments. Counsel states that the complainant told his mother that he is irregularly sent to hospital for his back damage, there being no indication that he has been examined by a forensic physician. In counsel's view, the information already made known, coupled with the finding by the prison doctor that the complainant had suffered medical injuries (see para. 8.1, supra) and the refusal of the Egyptian authorities to allow an international investigation, together show that he has been subjected to torture. The burden to prove the contrary must rest upon the State party, with its commensurately greater resources and influence upon proceedings.

10.7 Reiterating his previous arguments, counsel contends that the complainant faced substantial risks of torture at the time of expulsion irrespective of the guarantees obtained from a country with a record such as Egypt. Counsel refers in this connection to a report on Sweden, dated 8 July 2004, of the Council of Europe, where criticism was expressed on the use of guarantees.[16] Alternatively, counsel argues that the steps taken to prevent and monitor the guarantees were insufficient. In addition to the arguments already raised, no detailed plans or programmes featuring matters such as special orders on permissible interrogation techniques, confirmation that subordinate personnel were aware and would adhere to the guarantees or a post-expulsion treatment and trial plan were implemented.

11.1 By submission of 21 September 2004, the State party responded, observing that further visits since its last submissions of 3 May 2004 took place on 4 May, 2 June, 14 July and 31 August 2004. Each visit, excepting the most recent, took place in Masra Torah prison where the complainant appears to be serving sentence. The most recent visit took place at the Cairo university hospital. The State party refers to the complainant's improved legal situation, with the reduction to fifteen years' imprisonment subject, according to the complainant, to further reduction in the event of good behaviour. An assessment thereof is conducted automatically by the Egyptian Ministry for Interior Affairs. The complainant's health situation has also improved since May when he fell ill with pneumonia. Upon his return to Masra Torah prison on 4 April 2004, his previous treatments and medication were resumed. In late August 2004, he underwent surgery at the Cairo university hospital on spinal discs. The neurosurgeon involved informed the embassy on 31 August that the operation had taken five hours, involving microsurgery, but had been successful and without complications. According to the physician, the back problems were of a type which could befall anyone and had no apparent cause.

11.2 Concerning general conditions at Masra Torah prison, the complainant offered embassy staff no particular complaints when asked. Family visits have resumed upon his return to that prison. He was pleased to be informed of the permanent residence granted his wife and children, and has continued with his law studies and exams.

11.3 Following renewed allegations of ill-treatment by the complainant's counsel, his Egyptian lawyer and NGOs, the State party's Government made further investigative efforts. On 18 May 2004, it dispatched Ms. Lena Hjelm-Wallén, former Minister of Foreign Affairs and Deputy Prime Minister, as special envoy to Egypt, accompanied by the Director General for Legal Affairs of the Swedish Ministry for Foreign Affairs. The envoy met with the Egyptian Deputy Minister of Justice and the Minister in charge of the General Intelligence Service (GIS), voicing the State party's concerns over the alleged ill-treatment in the first weeks following the complainant's return to Egypt. She requested an independent and impartial inquiry on the allegations, including international medical expertise. The Egyptian Government dismissed the allegations as unfounded, but agreed to undertake an investigation. Subsequently, on 1 June 2004, the Swedish Minister of Foreign Affairs dispatched a letter to the Egyptian Minister in charge of the GIS, suggesting that in order for the Egyptian investigation to receive the widest possible international acceptance, it should be

---

[15] Counsel cites in support a public statement by Human Rights Watch, dated 4 May 2004, entitled "Sweden/Egypt: suspected militant's unfair trial and torture claims implicate Sweden."

[16] Report by Mr. Alvaro Gil-Robles, Commissioner for Human Rights, on his visit to Sweden (21–23 April 2003), CommDH(2004)13, stating, at para. 19: "The second point relates to the use of diplomatic assurances regarding the treatment of deported aliens in the countries to which they are returned. This example, which is not unique to Sweden, clearly illustrates the risks of relying on diplomatic assurances. The weakness inherent in the practice of diplomatic assurances lies in the fact that where there is a need for such assurances, there is clearly an acknowledged risk of torture and ill-treatment. Due to the absolute nature of the prohibition of torture or inhuman or degrading treatment, formal assurances cannot suffice where a risk nonetheless remains. As the United Nations Special Rapporteur on Torture has noted, such assurances must be unequivocal and a system to monitor such assurances must be in place. When assessing the reliability of diplomatic assurances, an essential criterion must be that the receiving state does not practice or condone torture or ill-treatment, and that it exercises effective control over the acts of non-State agents. In all other circumstances it is highly questionable whether assurances can be regarded as providing indisputable safeguards against torture and ill-treatment."

carried out with or by an independent authority, involving the judiciary and medical expertise, and preferably international expertise with recognized expertise in investigation of torture. She also professed willingness to allow a Swedish official, such as senior police officer or prosecutor, to assist. She added that it was crucial that the fight against terrorism be carried out with full respect for the rule of law and in conformity with international human rights obligations. In his answer of late July 2004, the responsible Egyptian Minister refuted the allegations of ill-treatment as unfounded, referring without detail to Egyptian investigations. While confirming the reduction of the complainant's sentence, he gave no direct answer to the Swedish request for an independent investigation.

11.4 The State party states that its Government is not content with the Egyptian response. In the process of considering possible further action, it is of the utmost importance that the Government receives a confirmation that such action will be in line with the complainant's own wishes, as further measures should not risk affecting his legal interests, safety or welfare adversely in any way. It is also necessary, in the circumstances, for the Egyptian Government to concur and cooperate in any further investigative efforts.

11.5 The State party reiterated its previous submissions based on a deficient retrial are outside the scope of the present case, concerned with whether the complainant's return to Egypt was in breach of the absolute ban on torture. It reiterates that the complainant has not substantiated his claim that he was ill-treated following return, and, thus, that the guarantees provided were not respected. The State party recalls that the crucial issue for decision is what its Government, in view of the guarantees received, had reason to believe at the time of the expulsion. Accordingly, the State party has complied with its obligations under the Convention, including article 3.

11.6 By letter of 16 October 2004, counsel responded to the State party's supplementary submissions, pointing out that the circumstances of the four visits from May to August 2004 described by the State party remained unclear but that it is likely that Egyptian officials were present and it would be difficult to speak freely. The situation may have been different for the hospital visit. Counsel criticizes the State party for stating that it appeared that Masra Torah prison was the detention facility for sentence, arguing that as it is well known that the complainant was serving sentence at the Esquebahl Torah prison, the State party appeared to be ill-informed on the circumstances of his detention.

11.7 Counsel observes argues that the complainant's back condition was already diagnosed, as moderate, in Sweden. These problems deteriorated after his return and in 2003 he was brought to a Cairo hospital for examination, where he was recommended for surgery. Only a year later was "absolutely necessary" surgery actually carried out. He stayed for eleven days in hospital under supervision and received controlled visits from family. Although far from recovered, he was then returned to prison in an ordinary transport vehicle rather than an ambulance. Counsel argues that the State party knew of but neglected to tend to the complainant's medical condition for two and a half years, and in that time exposed him to treatment such as being kept in "very small" cells and with arms being tied behind the back. Apart from itself causing severe pain, such treatment seriously risked exacerbating his medical condition.

11.8 Counsel argues that the reduction in sentence does not affect how the complainant has been treated, is being and will be treated until release. As to law studies, it is not known whether and how the complainant has been able to pass any exams. Counsel rejects that there has been a significant improvement of the complainant's situation during the summer of 2004, conceding only that the situation is an improvement on that just after his return, arguing that as late as March 2004 the complainant was detained in a very small cell without adequate hygiene facilities and proper access to water. There remains a considerable risk the complainant will be subjected to torture or treatment approximating it. In any event, counsel argues that the complainant's present condition does not establish how he was treated in the past.

11.9 Counsel points out that the complainant's Egyptian attorney has lodged a request for review of verdict to the Highest State Security Court, on grounds that the trial Military Court misjudged the evidence, that the preliminary investigation was afflicted with serious shortcomings, that defence rights were violated at trial and that during the investigation the complainant had been subjected to violence and torture. The attorney has also lodged a special complaint with the Egyptian Minister of the Interior, the Chief Public Prosecutor and the Director-General of the Prison Institutions, alleging improper treatment of the complainant during his hospitalization, including being chained to the bed and rendered immobile on medical grounds, and being returned to prison prior to recuperation.

11.10 Counsel argues that after the publicity generated by the television broadcast referred to in paragraph 10.2, supra, the State party shifted its position from a firm denial that torture had taken place to the "more reluctant position" shown by the measures it then took by way of dialogue with Egypt. Counsel points out Egypt's curt dismissal as unfounded of the allegations giving rise to the

Swedish requests for an investigation, without so much as supplying any detail of the investigation allegedly conducted. This strongly suggests the complainant was in fact tortured, as Egypt would benefit significantly from being able to demonstrate to other countries, through an independent investigation showing the complainant had not been tortured, that Egypt could safely be entrusted with the return of sensitive prisoners and to abide by assurances given.

11.11 Counsel refers to the State party's apparent unwillingness to further press the Egyptian authorities, with the State party citing possible prejudices to the complainant's legal interests or welfare. This suggests the State party accepts, in contrast to its earlier view, that the complainant is at risk of external pressure in the event of an insistence on an independent investigation. In fact, the complainant, through his relatives, has repeatedly made known his desire for the fullest possible defence of his interests.

11.12 Counsel goes on to refer to relevant case law in national jurisdictions. In the case of Mr. Bilasi-Ashri, the Egyptian Government refused to accept a detailed set of assurances, including post-return monitoring, requested by the Austrian Minister of Justice following a decision to that effect by an Austrian court of appeal. In the case of Ahmed Zakaev, a British extradition court found that a real risk of torture was not discounted by assurances given in open court by a Russian deputy minister overseeing prisons. Counsel argues that a similarly rigorous approach, with effective protection provided by the legal system, ought to have been followed in the complainant's case.

11.13 Counsel expands on the earlier reference to involvement of the United States of America in the complainant's case in paragraph 10.2, *supra*, referring to a book entitled "Chain of Command" by Seymour Hersh. This contended that "the Bromma action" (referring to the airport from which the complainant was removed) was carried out by members of the Special Access Program of the United States Department of Defense who were engaged in returning terrorist suspects to their countries of origin utilizing "unconventional methods". It is said that the complainant's removal was one of the first operations carried out under this programme and described by an operative involved as "one of the less successful ones". In counsel's view, this third State involvement at the removal stage in an anti-terrorism context should have confirmed what the State party already knew from its knowledge of the common use of torture in Egypt and the complainant's particular vulnerability, that is, that a real risk of torture existed at the time of his removal, in breach of article 3.

11.14 By further letter of 16 November 2004, counsel provided a copy of a Human Rights Watch report to the Committee entitled "Recent Concerns regarding the Growing Use of Diplomatic Assurances as an Alleged Safeguard against Torture". The report surveys recent examples of State practice in the area of diplomatic assurances by Germany, the United States of America, the Netherlands, the United Kingdom and Canada. The report argues that such assurances are increasingly viewed as a way of escaping the absolute character of non-refoulement obligations, and are expanding from the anti-terrorism context into the area of refugee claims. It contends that assurances tend to be sought only from countries where torture is a serious and systematic problem, which thus acknowledges the real risk of torture presented in such cases.

11.15 In the light of national experience, the report concludes that assurances are not an adequate safeguard for a variety of reasons. Human rights protection is not amenable to diplomacy, with its tendency to untransparent process and to place the State to State relationship as the primary consideration. Such assurances amount to trusting a systematic abuser who otherwise cannot be trusted to abide by its international obligations. It also amounts to giving a systematic abuser a "pass" with respect to an individual case when torture is otherwise widespread. Finally, the effectiveness of post-return monitoring is limited by the undetectability of much professionally inflicted torture, the absence of medical expertise from typical monitoring arrangements, the unwillingness of torture victims to speak out for fear of retribution, and the unwillingness of either the sending State or the receiving State to accept any responsibility for exposing an individual to torture.

11.16 In conclusion, the report refers to the October 2004 report to the General Assembly of the United Nations Special Rapporteur on Torture, who argued that, as a baseline, diplomatic assurances should not be resorted to in circumstances where torture is systematic, and that if a person is a member of a specific group that is routinely targeted and tortured, this factor must be taken into account. In the absence of either of these factors, the Special Rapporteur did not rule out the use of assurances provided that they reflect an unequivocal guarantee that is meaningful and verifiable.

12.1 By letter of 11 March 2005, the State party provided additional submissions on the merits of the complaint. It observed that the Swedish embassy in Cairo had continued to monitor the complainant's situation, with further visits taking place in Toraj prison on 3 October 2004, 21 November 2004, 17 January 2005 and 2 March 2005. The State party notes for the sake of clarity that there are several buildings on the prison grounds, one of which is called Masra and another Estekbal. The complainant has been detained, and visits have taken place, in both parts of the prison compound at different points in time.

12.2 With respect to his legal situation, the complainant stated that he had instructed his Egyptian lawyer to lodge a petition with the President of Egypt for a new trial in a civil court, invoking Egypt's undertaking prior to his expulsion from Sweden that he was to be given a fair trial. He had not met with the lawyer in person; his mother appeared to be the one giving instructions to the lawyer. According to the complainant, she had subsequently been informed by the lawyer that the petition had been lodged. However, the complainant was not very hopeful with regard to the outcome of such a petition.

12.3 Concerning the health situation, the complainant was recovering according to plan from the back surgery he underwent in August 2004 at the university hospital in central Cairo. Back at the Torah prison, he had spent some time in the prison hospital before returning to a normal cell. He had received physiotherapy treatment and a so-called MRI-examination, where his back had been x-rayed. He complained about the lack of further physiotherapy sessions which, he stated, had to be held at the hospital. This was due to the fact that the necessary equipment was not available in the prison. In order to further strengthen his back, he had been scheduled for special magnetic treatment.

12.4 With regard to the issue of the general conditions of detention, the State party observes that by March 2005 the complainant was placed in a cell of his own. He continued to receive visits from his mother, who brought him books, clothes and extra food. She also appeared to be providing him with information about his family in Sweden on a regular basis. However, he complained that his request to call his wife and children had been denied. Moreover, it was his intention to continue with his law studies. He had managed to pass further exams during the autumn.

12.5 In addition to the measures described in its last submissions to the Committee on 21 September 2004, the State party states that it had made further efforts to bring about an investigation into the ill-treatment allegedly suffered by the complainant at the hands of the Egyptian authorities during the initial stage of the detention. In a new letter of 29 September 2004 to the Egyptian Minister in charge of the GIS, the Swedish Minister of Foreign Affairs, Ms. Laila Freivalds, responded to the answer given by him in July of that year. Ms. Freivalds remarked that the letter she had received in July 2004 contained no information on the type of investigations that had been carried out by the Egyptian authorities and on which the Egyptian Minister's conclusions were based. She concluded, in her turn, that under the circumstances she did not exclude that she would have to revert to him on the same matter at a later stage.

12.6 In the course of the Swedish embassy's visit to the complainant on 3 October 2004, the question of the complainant's position in respect of further inquiries into the allegations of ill-treatment was raised again. When the issue had been raised with him for the first time (during the visit of 14 July 2004), the complainant's prison sentence had recently been reduced to 15 years and he was concerned that new investigations might have a negative impact on the chances of further reductions being made as a consequence of good behaviour on his part. On 3 October 2004, however, the complainant's position had changed. He then declared that he was in favour of an independent inquiry and said that he was willing to contribute to such an inquiry.

12.7 In view of the importance attached by the State party to the complainant's own wishes in this regard, the State party regarded the complainant's new position as making way for further measures on its part. Since the envisaged inquiry would naturally require the additional approval and cooperation of the Egyptian Government, the Swedish Ambassador to Egypt was instructed on 26 October 2004 to raise this issue with the Egyptian Foreign Ministry at the highest possible level. The Ambassador consequently met with the Egyptian Minister of Foreign Affairs on 1 November 2004. The Ambassador conveyed the message that the Swedish Government continued to be concerned about the allegations that the complainant had been exposed to torture and other ill-treatment during the initial period following his return to Egypt. The need for a thorough, independent and impartial examination of the allegations, in accordance with the principle of the rule of law and in a manner that was acceptable to the international community, was stressed by the Ambassador. In response, the latter was informed of the Minister's intention to discuss the matter with the Minister in charge of the GIS. The Egyptian Minister of Foreign Affairs, however, anticipated two problems with regard to an international inquiry. Firstly, there was no tradition in Egypt when it came to inviting representatives of the international community to investigate domestic matters of this character. It would probably be viewed as an unwelcomed interference with internal affairs. Secondly, attempting to prove that ill-treatment had not occurred could pose a problem of a more technical nature, particularly in view of the fact that several years had passed since the ill-treatment allegedly took place.

12.8 As a follow-up to the meeting with the Minister of Foreign Affairs, the State party informs that its Ambassador met with the Undersecretary of State of the GIS on 22 November and 21 December 2004. During the first of these meetings, the undersecretary of State mentioned that Egypt was anxious to comply, as far as possible, with the Swedish Government's request for an inquiry. However, during the second meeting, the Ambassador was handed a letter by the Minister in charge of the GIS containing the Egyptian Government's formal answer to the renewed Swedish request for an inquiry. The content of the letter was similar to that of the previous letter from the same Minister in July 2004. Thus, the allegations concerning ill-treatment of the complainant were again refuted as unfounded. Furthermore, no direct answer was provided to the request that an independent inquiry be conducted.

12.9 The matter was again brought up by Ms. Freivalds in connection with a visit to Stockholm on 15 February 2005 by the Egyptian Deputy Minister of Foreign Affairs responsible for multilateral issues. Ms. Freivalds informed the Egyptian Deputy Minister of the complainant's case and the allegations made regarding his ill-treatment. She stressed that it ought to be a common interest for Sweden and Egypt to look into those allegations and asked the Deputy Minister to use his influence with the Egyptian authorities in favour of the Swedish position. The Deputy Minister assured her that he would raise the issue upon his return to Cairo.

12.10 The State party also points out that the issue of an international inquiry was raised with the United Nations High Commissioner for Human Rights, Ms. Louise Arbour, when she visited Stockholm in December 2004. On that occasion, Ms. Freivalds made clear that the Swedish Government would welcome any efforts that might be undertaken by the High Commissioner to investigate the allegations that the complainant had been subjected to torture or other forms of ill-treatment while in detention in Egypt. The State party also observes that the investigation initiated by the Swedish Chief Parliamentary Ombudsman into the circumstances surrounding the execution of the Government's decision to expel the complainant from Sweden has not yet concluded.

12.11 The State party recalls that already in May 2004, counsel for the complainant provided the Committee with a written account of the embassy's report of its first visit on 23 January 2002 to the complainant after his return to Egypt. A copy of the report was submitted by counsel to the Committee in August 2004. In the State party's view, therefore, the Committee had thus been provided with all the information of relevance for its examination of the present case. Prior to explaining the fact that the report was not fully accounted for by the Government in its initial observations of 5 December 2003, the State party provides the following translation of the relevant portion of the Ambassador's report:

12.12 "Agiza and [name of another person] had just been transferred to the Torah prison after having been interrogated for 30 days at the security service's facilities in another part of Cairo. Their treatment in the Torah prison was 'excellent'. However, they had a number of complaints that related to the time period between their apprehension in Sweden and the transfer to the Torah: excessive brutality on the part of the Swedish police when they were apprehended; forced to remain in uncomfortable positions in the airplane during the transport to Egypt; forced to be blindfolded during the interrogation period; detention in too small cells 1.5 x 1.5 metres during the same period; lack of sleep due to surveillance in the cells; a delay of ten days before Agiza, following a medical examination, had access again to his medication for gastric ulcer; blows from guards while transported to and from interrogation; threats from interrogator that there could be consequences for Agiza's family if he did not tell everything about his time in Iran etc. It is not possible for me to assess the veracity of these claims. However, I am able to note that the two men did not, not even on my direct questions, in any way claim that they had been subjected to any kind of systematic, physical torture and that they consider themselves to be well treated in the Torah prison."

12.13 The State party argues that it has been aware of difficulties experienced by the Committee in the past with regard to upholding respect for the confidentiality of its proceedings. For that reason, the State party formulated its submissions with great care when they involved the unveiling of information that has been classified under the Swedish Secrecy Act. For the State party, it was a question of balancing the need to reveal information in order to provide the Committee with the correct factual basis for the proper administration of justice, on the one hand, and the need to protect the integrity of Sweden's relations with foreign powers, the interests of national security and the security and safety of individuals, on the other.

12.14 The State party argues that its position in this regard should be seen against the background of the experience gained from the proceedings relating to the case of *Hanan Attia*.[17] In the State party's view, it became clear during those proceedings that the concerns in respect of confidentiality, which existed already at that time, were not unfounded. In that case, the Committee offered the State party in September 2002 the opportunity to withdraw its initial

---

[17] Op. cit.

observations of 8 March 2002 and to submit a new version in view of the fact that the Committee could not guarantee that "any of the information submitted by the parties to the case would not be disclosed in any of its decisions or views on the merits of the case". Furthermore, in January 2003 counsel for Hanan Attia appended a briefing note from Amnesty International in London to his own observations, from which it was clear that counsel had made the State party's observations of 8 March 2002 available to Amnesty International.

12.15 The State party argues that its concerns with regard to the Committee's ability to uphold respect for the confidentiality of its proceedings were reflected in its repeated requests and comments concerning the confidentiality of the information that was in fact included in the initial observations of 5 December 2003 in the present case. However, in the light of the foregoing, the conclusion was drawn that only part of the classified information found in the Security Police's written opinion of 30 October 2001 to the Migration Board could be revealed. Another conclusion was that the information contained in the embassy's report from its first visit on 23 January 2002 to the complainant in detention should not be fully accounted for either. The reason for the latter conclusion was that it could not be ruled out that the information concerning ill-treatment provided by the complainant during the embassy's first visit would later be found in the public domain and thus become known to the Egyptian authorities.

12.16 The State party concludes that for these reasons not all the information that emerged at the embassy's first visit was revealed to the Committee. If such unconfirmed information had been released at that stage, and with the indirect assistance of the Swedish Government, this could have resulted in reprisals against the complainant. The risk for reprisals was not deemed to be insignificant, irrespective of whether the information was correct or not. If the information regarding the complainant's ill-treatment was correct—although such treatment did not appear to amount to torture within the meaning of the Convention—this would have meant that the diplomatic assurances had not had the intended effect to protect him against treatment in breach of Sweden's international obligations, including treatment prohibited under article 3 of the European Convention on Human Rights. In such a case, there was an apparent risk that the disclosure of the information would put the complainant at risk of further ill-treatment and maybe even of torture. On the other hand, if the disclosed information was incorrect, this could have had a negative impact on the relations between Sweden and Egypt. In turn, it could have led to problems as far as the embassy's monitoring efforts were concerned. In this situation, when the different risks involved were assessed, the conclusion was reached that the best course of action would be to await the report of the embassy's next visit.

12.17 The State party points out that according to the embassy's report from its second meeting with the complainant in the detention facility, there were at that time no indications of torture or other ill-treatment. However, even prior to the third visit on 14 April 2002, information was circulating to the effect that the complainant's mother had stated publicly that her son had been tortured after his return to Egypt. The embassy's report from the first visit on 23 January 2002 confirmed the information submitted by the complainant's mother, namely that the visit when she had allegedly noticed signs of ill-treatment on her son's body had been interrupted by the Swedish Ambassador's first visit. The fact that the Ambassador had reported that he had not been able to see any signs of physical abuse on that very same day led the State party to doubt the veracity of the claims made by the complainant's mother and affected its assessment of the credibility of the complainant's own information to the Ambassador the same day.

12.18 The State party observes that there was no new information from the complainant regarding ill-treatment during the following year and the view that the information submitted during the embassy's first visit had been incorrect gradually gained in strength. It was essential that the embassy's opportunities to carry out the monitoring on a regular basis were not hampered, which could have been the result if the State party had forwarded unconfirmed or incorrect information to the Committee already during the first months of 2002. Considering the situation in April 2002 when the contents of a letter by the complainant's mother became known, it was therefore, on balance, not deemed appropriate to supplement, at that time, the information already submitted by the State party regarding the embassy's first visit in its observations of 8 March 2002.

12.19 A different assessment was made by the State party when the complainant, on 5 March 2003, repeated his complaints about ill-treatment at the hands of the Egyptian authorities during the initial stages of his detention. The allegations were much more serious this time and included claims that he had been subjected to torture involving the use of electricity. The mere fact that the complainant came back more than a year later to what had allegedly occurred already at the beginning of the detention period contributed to the fact that a different assessment was made in March 2003. The allegations of torture were therefore immediately raised with representatives of the relevant Egyptian authorities, who refuted them categorically. The State party accounted for the information submitted by the complainant, and the Egyptian authorities' reactions to it, in its submissions to the Committee of 26 March 2003. It should be reiterated that the information in issue was considerably more serious than that provided by the complainant a year earlier and that it concerned the same time period.

12.20 The State party further contends that by March 2003 the reasons for confidentiality were not as weighty as before. Even if the information from the embassy's tenth visit on 5 March 2003 would have ended up in the public domain despite the fact that the proceedings before the Committee were confidential according to the applicable provisions in the Convention and the Committee's own rules of procedure, the damaging effects were no longer considered to be as serious as before. Following the State party's initial submissions to the Committee, information had already been in circulation that—if correct—amounted to a breach on the part of Egypt of the diplomatic assurances. Moreover, the issue of torture had already been raised with the Egyptian authorities in March 2003. Furthermore, the monitoring carried out by the embassy had been going on for more than a year by that time and had become routine for both the Egyptian authorities, the embassy and the complainant himself. It was thus no longer likely that there would be a negative impact on the monitoring so that it would be more difficult in the future to ensure the continued effectiveness of the assurances. The State party also stresses that the allegations made by the complainant during the first embassy visit did not amount, in its view, to torture within the meaning of the Convention. It is, however, clear that the ill-treatment complained of at that time would have amounted to inhuman and maybe also cruel treatment, had the allegations been substantiated.

12.21 The State party refers the Committee to the recent decision of the Grand Chamber of the European Court on Human Rights, on 4 February 2005, in the case of *Mamatkulov et al.* v. *Turkey*. This case concerned the applicants' extradition in March 1999 to Uzbekistan under a bilateral treaty with Turkey. Both applicants had been suspected of homicide, causing injuries to others by the explosion of a bomb in Uzbekistan and an attempted terrorist attack on the President of Uzbekistan. Following their extradition, they were found guilty of various offences and sentenced to twenty and eleven years' imprisonment respectively.

12.22 Before the European Court, the applicants claimed that Turkey had violated inter alia article 3 of the European Convention. In defence, Turkey invoked assurances concerning the two applicants given by the Uzbek authorities. According to those assurances, which were provided by the public prosecutor of the Republic of Uzbekistan, the applicants would not be subjected to acts of torture or sentenced to capital punishment. The assurances also contained the information that Uzbekistan was a party to the Convention against Torture and accepted and reaffirmed its obligation to comply with the requirements of the provisions of the Convention "as regards both Turkey and the international community as a whole". Officials from the Turkish embassy in Tashkent had visited the applicants in their respective places of detention in October 2001. They were reportedly in good health and had not complained about their prison conditions. Turkey also invoked medical certificates drawn up by military doctors in the prisons where the applicants were held.

12.23 The State party observes that the European Court assessed the existence of the risk primarily with reference to those facts which were known or ought to have been known to the State party at the time of the extradition, with information coming to light subsequent to the extradition potentially being of value in confirming or refuting the appreciation that had been made by the State party of the well-foundedness or otherwise of a complainant's fears. The Court concluded that it had to assess Turkey's responsibility under article 3 by reference to the situation that obtained on the date of the applicants' extradition, i.e., on 27 March 1999. While taking note of reports of international human rights organizations denouncing an administrative practice of torture and other forms of ill-treatment of political dissidents and the Uzbek regime's repressive policy towards such dissidents, the Court furthermore stated that, although those findings described the general situation in Uzbekistan, they did not support the specific allegations made by the applicants in the case and required corroboration by other evidence. Against the background of the assurances obtained by Turkey and the medical reports from the doctors in the Uzbek prisons in which the applicants were held, the Court found that it was not able to conclude that substantial grounds existed at the relevant date for believing that the applicants faced a real risk of treatment proscribed by article 3 of the European Convention.

12.24 The State party invites the Committee to adopt the same approach. It points out that assurances similar to those in the case before the European Court were indeed obtained by the Swedish Government in the instant case. Although the guarantees given in this case did not refer to Egypt's obligations under the Convention against Torture, this is of no particular consequence since Egypt, like Uzbekistan, is in fact bound by the Convention. It is doubtful whether the value of assurances should be considered to be increased simply because they include a reference to a state's human rights obligations. The important factor must be that the State in issue has actually undertaken to abide by the provisions of a human rights convention by becoming party to it. The fact that Egypt was a party to the Convention against Torture was known to the State party when it obtained the diplomatic assurances in this case and subsequently decided to expel the complainant.

12.25 The State party goes on to argue that the assurances obtained in the present case must be regarded as carrying even more weight than those in the case against Turkey since they were issued by the person in charge of the Egyptian security service. It is difficult to conceive of a person better placed in Egypt to ensure that the diplomatic guarantees would actually have the intended effect, namely to protect the complainant against treatment in breach of Sweden's obligations under several human rights instruments.

12.26 The State party acknowledges that no medical certificates have been invoked in the present case. However, the medical certificates obtained in the Turkish case had been issued by Uzbek military doctors working in the prisons where the applicants in that case were detained. In the State party's view, such certificates are of limited value in view of the fact that they had not been issued by experts who could be perceived as truly independent in relation to the relevant State authorities. Moreover, in the current case, the absence of corresponding medical certificates must reasonably be compensated by the monitoring mechanism put in place by the Swedish Government. To this date, almost thirty visits to the complainant in detention have been made by its embassy in Cairo. The visits have taken place over a period of time that amounts to over three years. This should be compared to the single visit by two officials from the Turkish embassy in Tashkent more than two and a half years after the extradition of the applicants in the case examined by the European Court.

12.27 By letter of 7 April 2005, counsel for the complainant made further submissions. As to his medical care, counsel argues that treatment following the complainant's surgery in August 2004 was interrupted prior to full recovery, and he was denied medical treatment in the form of micro-electric stimulation that he required.

12.28 Counsel observes that in December 2004 and January 2005, the expulsion of the complainant and a companion case was debated in the Swedish parliament and media. The Prime Minister and the Minister of Immigration stated that the expellees were terrorists and their removal was necessary to prevent further attacks and deny safe haven. According to counsel, these statements were presented to the complainant by Egyptian officials during an interrogation. For counsel, this demonstrates that the Egyptian security services are still interrogating the complainant and seeking to extract information, exposing him to ongoing risk of torture.

12.29 Counsel provides the conclusions (in Swedish with official English summary) dated 22 March 2005 of the investigations of the Parliamentary Ombudsman into the circumstances of deportation from Sweden to Cairo, with an emphasis on the treatment of the expellees at Bromma Airport. According to the Ombudsman's summary, a few days prior to 18 December 2001 the Central Intelligence Agency offered the Swedish Security Police the use of an aircraft for direct expulsion to Egypt. The Security Police, after apparently informing the Minister of Foreign Affairs, accepted. At midday December 18, the Security Police was informed that American security personnel would be onboard the aircraft and they wished to perform a security check on the expellees. It was arranged for the check to be conducted in a police station at Bromma airport in Stockholm.

12.30 Immediately after the Government's decision in the afternoon of December 18, the expellees were apprehended by Swedish police and subsequently transported to Bromma airport. The American aircraft landed shortly before 9.00 p.m. A number of American security personnel, wearing masks, conducted the security check, which consisted of at least the following elements. The expellees had their clothes cut up and removed with a pair of scissors, their bodies were searched, their hands and feet were fettered, they were dressed in overalls and their heads were covered with loosely fitted hoods. Finally, they were taken, with bare feet, to the airplane where they were strapped to mattresses. They were kept in this position during the entire flight to Egypt. It had been alleged that the expellees were also given a sedative per rectum, which the Ombudsman was unable to substantiate during the investigation. The Ombudsman found that the Security Police had remained passive throughout the procedure. The Ombudsman considered that, given that the American offer was received only three months after the events of 11 September 2001, the Security Police could have been expected to inquire whether the American offer involved any special arrangements with regard to security. No such inquiry was made, not even when the Security Police had been informed of the fact that American security personnel would be present and wished to perform a security check. When the actual content of the security check became obvious as it was performed at Bromma airport, the attending Swedish police personnel remained passive.

12.31 In the Ombudsman's view, the investigation disclosed that the Swedish Security Police lost control of the situation at the airport and during the transport to Egypt. The American security personnel took charge and were allowed to perform the security check on their own. Such total surrender of power to exercise public authority on Swedish territory was, according to the Ombudsman, clearly contrary to Swedish law. In addition, at least some of the coercive measures taken during the security check were not in conformity with Swedish law. Moreover, the treatment of the expellees, taken as a whole, must be considered to have been inhuman and thus unacceptable and may amount to degrading treatment within the meaning of article 3 of the European Convention for the Protection of Human Rights and Fundamental Freedoms. The Ombudsman emphasized that the inhuman treatment to which the expellees were subjected could not be tolerated. The Security Police should have decided to discontinue the expulsion proceedings and deserved severe criticism for its handling of the case.

12.32 Counsel observes that the Ombudsman declined to bring charges against any individuals, as it was not possible to hold any individual to account before a court. Counsel contends that, at least, the prolonged hooding amounted to torture, and that what occurred on the aircraft could also be formally imputed to Sweden. Counsel argues that in the prevailing atmosphere the State party ought to have been sceptical of American motives in offering to transport the expellees to Egypt and been reluctant to accept the Egyptian guarantees provided.

12.33 By letter of 12 April 2005, the State party also provided the summary of the Ombudsman's report, as "background information in full understanding that the execution of the Government's decision to expel the complainant from Sweden is not part of the case now pending before the Committee, which deals with the issue of the diplomatic assurances by Egypt with regard to the complainant."

12.34 By letter of 21 April 2005, counsel for the complainant submitted final remarks. He criticizes the modalities of the State party's most recent visits on the same basis as the earlier visits. As to medical care, the complainant has been re-examined twice at the facility that performed the 2004 surgery and may require further surgery. Concerning the proposed international investigation, counsel argues that the only reason for Egypt's refusal to cooperate lies in its breach of the guarantees provided.

12.35 Counsel rejects the State party's reasons for concealing part of the initial Ambassadorial report from the Committee, arguing that they can only be relevant to protect the complainant from Egyptian reprisals concerning his outspokenness as to the torture suffered. The complainant's statement was made in the presence of the prison warden and other officials, and the Ambassador raised the issue with the Ministry of Foreign Affairs. In any event, having already endured reprisals, there was nothing left for the State party to protect against in withholding information. Mistreatment of the author was already in the public domain through the complainant's mother and Amnesty International shortly after January 2002. Counsel argues that the State party's position also reflects "weak confidence" in the integrity of the Egyptian guarantees. Counsel also questions how national security could be affected by public knowledge of the complainant's allegations. In sum, the only plausible reason to conceal the information was to avoid inconvenience and embarrassment on the part of the State party.

12.36 Concerning his transmittal of information supplied in the context of the article 22 process to non-governmental organizations, counsel argues that at the time he saw no obstacle to doing so, neither the Convention nor the Committee's rules proscribing, in his view, such a course. He did not intend to disseminate the information to the media or the broader public. Following the Committee's advice that complaint information was confidential, counsel argues his capacity to defend the complainant was significantly reduced, particularly given the disparity of resources available to the State party. In any event, the State party has shared other confidential intelligence information with the Committee, belaying its concerns that sensitive information would be inappropriately disseminated. Counsel argues that the conduct described is, contrary to the Ambassador's characterization, torture as understood by the Committee, bearing in mind that the complainant may have been reluctant to disclose the totality of circumstances to the Ambassador and that more severe elements emerged through the testimony of his mother.

12.37 With respect to the European Court's decision in *Mamatkulov et al.*, counsel seeks to distinguish the instant case. He emphasizes however that in both cases the speed with which the removal was undertaken denied an effective exercise of a complaint mechanism, a circumstances that for the European Court disclosed a violation of article 34 of the European Convention. In counsel's view, the *Mamatkulov* Court was unable to find a violation of article 3 of the European Convention as, in contrast to the present case, there was insufficient evidence before the Court. A further distinction is that the treatment at the point of expulsion clearly pointed, in the current case, to the future risk of torture. Given the prophylactic purpose of article 3, it cannot be correct that an expelling State simply transfers, through the vehicle of diplomatic assurances, responsibility for an expellee's condition to the receiving State.

12.38 Finally, counsel supplies to the Committee a report, dated 15 April 2005, by Human Rights Watch, entitled "Still at Risk: Diplomatic Assurances no Safeguard against Torture", surveying the contemporary case law and experiences of diplomatic assurances and concluding that the latter are not effective instruments of risk mitigation in an article 3 context. Concerning the current case, Human Rights Watch argues that "there is credible, and in some instances overwhelming, evidence that the assurances were breached" (at 59).

Issues and proceedings before the Committee

Consideration of the merits

13.1 The Committee has considered the merits of the complaint, in the light of all information presented to it by the parties, pursuant to article 22, paragraph 4, of the Convention. The Committee acknowledges that measures taken to fight terrorism, including denial of safe haven, deriving from binding Security Council resolutions are both legitimate and important. Their execution, however, must be carried out with full respect to the applicable rules of international law, including the provisions of the Convention, as affirmed repeatedly by the Security Council.[18]

Substantive assessment under article 3

13.2 The issue before the Committee is whether removal of the complainant to Egypt violated the State party's obligation under article 3 of the Convention not to expel or to return a person to another State where there are substantial grounds for believing that he or she would be in danger of being subjected by the Egyptian authorities to torture. The Committee observes that this issue must be decided in the light of the information that was known, or ought to have been known, to the State party's authorities *at the time* of the removal. Subsequent events are relevant to the assessment of the State party's knowledge, actual or constructive, at the time of removal.

13.3 The Committee must evaluate whether there were substantial grounds for believing that the complainant would be personally in danger of being subjected to torture upon return to Egypt. The Committee recalls that the aim of the determination is to establish whether the individual concerned was personally at risk of being subjected to torture in the country to which he was returned. It follows that the existence of a consistent pattern of gross, flagrant or mass violations of human rights in a country does not as such constitute a sufficient ground for determining that a particular person was in danger of being subjected to torture upon his return to that country; additional grounds must exist to show that the individual concerned was personally at risk. Similarly, the absence of a consistent pattern of gross violations of human rights does not mean that a person could not be considered to be in danger of being subjected to torture in his or her specific circumstances.

13.4 The Committee considers at the outset that it was known, or should have been known, to the State party's authorities at the time of the complainant's removal that Egypt resorted to consistent and widespread use of torture against detainees, and that the risk of such treatment was particularly high in the case of detainees held for political and security reasons.[19] The State party was also aware that its own security intelligence services regarded the complainant as implicated in terrorist activities and a threat to its national security, and for these reasons its ordinary tribunals referred the case to the Government for a decision at the highest executive level, from which no appeal was possible. The State party was also aware of the interest in the complainant by the intelligence services of two other States: according to the facts submitted by the State party to the Committee, the first foreign State offered through its intelligence service an aircraft to transport the complainant to the second State, Egypt, where to the State party's knowledge, he had been sentenced in absentia and was wanted for alleged involvement in terrorist activities. In the Committee's view, the natural conclusion from these combined elements, that is, that the complainant was at a real risk of torture in Egypt in the event of expulsion, was confirmed when, immediately preceding expulsion, the complainant was subjected on the State party's territory to treatment in breach of, at least, article 16 of the Convention by foreign agents but with the acquiescence of the State party's police. It follows that the State party's expulsion of the complainant was in breach of article 3 of the Convention. The procurement of diplomatic assurances, which, moreover, provided no mechanism for their enforcement, did not suffice to protect against this manifest risk.

13.5 In light of this assessment, the Committee considers it appropriate to observe that its decision in the current case reflects a number of facts which were not available to it when it considered the largely analogous complaint of *Hanan Attia*,[20] where, in particular, it expressed itself satisfied with the assurances provided. The Committee's decision in that case, given that the complainant had not been expelled, took into account the evidence made available to it up to the time the decision in that case was adopted. The Committee observes that it did not

---

[18] Security Council resolution 1566 (2004), third and sixth preambular paragraphs, resolution 1456 (2003), paragraph 6, and resolution 1373 (2001), paragraph 3 (f).

[19] See, among other sources, the Report of the Committee against Torture to the General Assembly (A/51/44), paras. 180–222, and the Committee's Conclusions and Recommendations on the fourth periodic report of Egypt (CAT/C/CR/29/4).
[20] Op. cit.

have before it the actual report of mistreatment provided by the current complainant to the Ambassador at his first visit and not provided to the Committee by the State party (see para. 14.10 below); the mistreatment of the complainant by foreign intelligence agents on the territory of the State party and acquiesced in by the State party's police; the involvement of a foreign intelligence service in offering and procuring the means of expulsion; the progressively wider discovery of information as to the scope of measures undertaken by numerous States to expose individuals suspected of involvement in terrorism to risks of torture abroad; the breach by Egypt of the element of the assurances relating to guarantee of a fair trial, which goes to the weight that can be attached to the assurances as a whole; and the unwillingness of the Egyptian authorities to conduct an independent investigation despite appeals from the State party's authorities at the highest levels. The Committee observes, in addition, that the calculus of risk in the case of the wife of the complainant, whose expulsion would have been some years after the complainants, raised issues differing from to the present case.

Procedural assessment under article 3

13.6 The Committee observes that the right to an effective remedy for a breach of the Convention underpins the entire Convention, for otherwise the protections afforded by the Convention would be rendered largely illusory. In some cases, the Convention itself sets out a remedy for particular breaches of the Convention,[21] while in other cases the Committee has interpreted a substantive provision to contain within it a remedy for its breach.[22] In the Committee's view, in order to reinforce the protection of the norm in question and understanding the Convention consistently, the prohibition on refoulement contained in article 3 should be interpreted the same way to encompass a remedy for its breach, even though it may not contain on its face such a right to remedy for a breach thereof.

13.7 The Committee observes that in the case of an allegation of torture or cruel, inhuman or degrading treatment having occurred, the right to remedy requires, after the event, an effective, independent and impartial investigation of such allegations. The nature of refoulement is such, however, that an allegation of breach of that article relates to a future expulsion or removal; accordingly, the right to an effective remedy contained in article 3 requires, in this context, an opportunity for effective, independent and impartial review of the decision to expel or remove, once that decision is made, when there is a plausible allegation that article 3 issues arise. The Committee's previous jurisprudence has been consistent with this view of the requirements of article 3, having found an inability to contest an expulsion decision before an independent authority, in that case the courts, to be relevant to a finding of a violation of article 3.[23]

13.8 The Committee observes that, in the normal course of events, the State party provides, through the operation of the Migration Board and the Aliens Appeals Board, for review of a decision to expel satisfying the requirements of article 3 of an effective, independent and impartial review of a decision to expel. In the present case, however, due to the presence of national security concerns, these tribunals relinquished the complainant's case to the Government, which took the first and at once final decision to expel him. The Committee emphasizes that there was no possibility for review of any kind of this decision. The Committee recalls that the Convention's protections are absolute, even in the context of national security concerns, and that such considerations emphasise the importance of appropriate review mechanisms. While national security concerns might justify some adjustments to be made to the particular process of review, the mechanism chosen must continue to satisfy article 3's requirements of effective, independent and impartial review. In the present case, therefore, on the strength of the information before it, the Committee concludes that the absence of any avenue of judicial or independent administrative review of the Government's decision to expel the complainant does not meet the procedural obligation to provide for effective, independent and impartial review required by article 3 of the Convention.

Frustration of right under article 22 to exercise complaint to the Committee

13.9 The Committee observes, moreover, that by making the declaration under article 22 of the Convention, the State party undertook to confer upon persons within its jurisdiction the right to invoke the complaints jurisdiction of the Committee. That jurisdiction included the power to indicate interim measures, if necessary, to stay the removal and preserve the subject matter of the case pending final decision. In order for this exercise of the right

---

[21] See articles 12 to 14 in relation to an allegation of torture.

[22] See *Dzemajl* v. *Yugoslavia*, case N° 161/2000, Decision adopted on 21 November 2002, at para. 9.6: "The positive obligations that flow from the first sentence of article 16 of the Convention include an obligation to grant redress and compensate the victims of an act in breach of that provision. The Committee is therefore of the view that the State party has failed to observe its obligations under article 16 of the Convention by failing to enable the complainants to obtain redress and to provide them with fair and adequate compensation."

[23] *Arkauz Arana* v. *France*, case N° 63/1997, Decision adopted on 9 November 1999, paras. 11.5 and 12.

of complaint to be meaningful rather than illusory, however, an individual must have a reasonable period of time before execution of a final decision to consider whether, and if so to in fact, seize the Committee under its article 22 jurisdiction. In the present case, however, the Committee observes that the complainant was arrested and removed by the State party immediately upon the Government's decision of expulsion being taken; indeed, the formal notice of decision was only served upon the complainant's counsel the following day. As a result, it was impossible for the complainant to consider the possibility of invoking article 22, let alone seize the Committee. As a result, the Committee concludes that the State party was in breach of its obligations under article 22 of the Convention to respect the effective right of individual communication conferred thereunder.

State party's failure to cooperate fully with the Committee

13.10 Having addressed the merits of the complaint, the Committee must address the failure of the State party to cooperate fully with the Committee in the resolution of the current complaint. The Committee observes that, by making the declaration provided for in article 22 extending to individual complainants the right to complain to the Committee alleging a breach of a State party's obligations under the Convention, a State party assumes an obligation to cooperate fully with the Committee, through the procedures set forth in article 22 and in the Committee's rules of procedure. In particular, article 22, paragraph 4, requires a State party to make available to the Committee all information relevant and necessary for the Committee appropriately to resolve the complaint presented to it. The Committee observes that its procedures are sufficiently flexible and its powers sufficiently broad to prevent an abuse of process in a particular case. It follows that the State party committed a breach of its obligations under article 22 of the Convention by neither disclosing to the Committee relevant information, nor presenting its concerns to the Committee for an appropriate procedural decision.

14. The Committee against Torture, acting under article 22, paragraph 7, of the Convention against Torture and Other Cruel, Inhuman or Degrading Treatment or Punishment, decides that the facts before it constitute breaches by the State party of articles 3 and 22 of the Convention.

15. In pursuance of rule 112, paragraph 5, of its rules of procedure, the Committee requests the State party to inform it, within 90 days from the date of the transmittal of this decision, of the steps it has taken in response to the Views expressed above. The State party is also under an obligation to prevent similar violations in the future.

Appendix

Separate Opinion of Committee member Mr. Alexander Yakovlev (dissenting, in part)

I respectfully disagree with the majority's finding on the article 3 issues. The Committee establishes, correctly, the time of removal as the key point in time for its assessment of the appropriateness, from the perspective of article, of the complaint's removal. As is apparent from the Committee's decision, the bulk of the information before it relates to events transpiring after expulsion, which can have little relevance to the situation at the time of expulsion.

It is clear that the State party was aware of its obligations under article 3 of the Convention, including the prohibition on refoulement. Precisely as a result, it sought assurances from the Egyptian Government, at a senior level, as to the complainant's proper treatment. No less an authority than the former Special Rapporteur of the Commission on Human Rights on Torture, Mr. van Boven, accepted in his 2002 report to the Commission on Human Rights the use of such assurances in certain circumstances, urging States to procure "an unequivocal guarantee ... that the persons concerned will not be subjected to torture or any other forms of ill-treatment upon return". This, which is precisely what the State party did, is now faulted by the Committee. At the time, the State party was entitled to accept the assurances provided, and indeed since has invested considerable effort in following up the situation in Egypt. Whatever the situation may be if the situation were to repeat itself today is a question that need not presently be answered. It is abundantly clear however at the time that the State party expelled the complainant, it acted in good faith and consistent with the requirements of article 3 of the Convention. I would thus come to the conclusion, in the instant case, that the complainant's expulsion did not constitute a violation of article 3 of the Convention.

[signed]

Alexander Yakovlev

Communication N° 238/2003

Submitted by: Mr. Z.T. (N° 2) (represented by counsel, Mr. Thom Arne Hellerslia)
Alleged victim: The complainant
State party: Norway
Declared admissible: 14 November 2003
Date of adoption of Views: 14 November 2005

Subject matter: deportation of complainant to Ethiopia with alleged risk of torture

Procedural issues: exhaustion of domestic remedies; request for an oral hearing pursuant to rule 111, paragraph 4, of the rules of procedure

Substantive issue: risk of torture after deportation

Article of the Convention: 3

1. The author of the communication is Z.T., an Ethiopian national born on 16 July 1962 and currently residing in Norway, where his request for asylum has been denied and he faces removal. He claims that he would risk imprisonment and torture upon return to Ethiopia and that his forced return would therefore constitute a violation by Norway of article 3 of the Convention. He is represented by counsel.

The facts as presented by the complainant

2.1 The complainant is of Amharic ethnic origin. During his high school in Addis Ababa, he participated in several demonstrations supporting Colonel Mengistu. When Mengistu came to power in February 1977, thousands of youth, including the complainant, were sent to rural areas as part of a literacy campaign. Disappointed with the regime, the complainant began to work for the Ethiopian People's Revolutionary Party (EPRP).

2.2 The EPRP started to organize resistance against the Mengistu regime by calling students and youth back from the rural areas to Addis Ababa. In 1977, the conflicts between the various political groups resulted in the so-called "Red Terror", the brutal eradication of all opposition to the governing Provincial Military Administrative Council (PMAC) and random killings. An estimated 100,000 people were killed. The complainant, who had been distributing pamphlets and putting up posters in Addis Ababa on behalf of the EPRP, was arrested and taken to a concentration camp, together with thousands of other youth, where he was held for one year between 1980 and 1981. While in the camp he was subjected to fake executions and brainwashing. According to the complainant, the "Red Terror" ended when the regime was convinced that all EPRP leaders were dead. Many political prisoners, including the complainant, were then freed.

2.3 After his release, the complainant went underground and continued work for the EPRP. He states that the Mengistu regime carefully followed the movements of previous political prisoners to suppress a revival of the opposition. In 1986/87, the complainant was arrested in a mass arrest and taken to Kerchele prison, where he remained for four years. According to him, the prisoners were forced to walk around naked and were subjected to ill-treatment in the form of regular beatings with clubs. While imprisoned, he suffered from tuberculosis.

2.4 In May 1991, the Mengistu regime fell and the Ethiopian People's Revolutionary Democratic Front (EPRDF) came to power. Once freed, the complainant tried to contact members of the EPRP, but all his contacts had left. He then started to work for the Southern Ethiopian Peoples Democratic Coalition (SEPDC), a new coalition of 14 regional and national political opposition parties. According to a translation supplied by the complainant, in early 1994 a warrant for his arrest was issued for interrogation on the basis of political activity. In February 1995, he was on his way to deliver a message to Mr. Alemu Abera, a party leader, when he was caught by the police in Awasa.

2.5 The complainant states that he was kept in detention for 24 hours in Awasa and then transferred to the central prison of Addis Ababa. After three days, he was taken to Kerchele prison where he was kept for one year and seven months. He was never tried nor had contact with a lawyer. The treatment in prison was similar to what he had experienced during his first imprisonment. He says that he was taken to the torture room and threatened with execution if he did not cooperate. He believes that the only reason he was not severely tortured like many other prisoners was that he was already in a weak physical condition. While in prison he developed epilepsy.

2.6 On 5 October 1996, the complainant managed to escape when he was taken to the house of one of the high-ranking guards to make some repairs. Through a friend, the complainant managed to get the necessary papers to leave the country and requested asylum in Norway on 8 October 1996.

2.7 On 18 June 1997, the Directorate of Immigration turned down his application for asylum, mainly on the basis of a report made by the Norwegian Embassy in Nairobi, on the basis of contradictory information said to have been given by the complainant and his mother, and discrepancies in his story. He appealed on 3 July 1997. The appeal was rejected by the Ministry of Justice on 29 December 1997 on the same grounds. On 5 January 1998, a request for reconsideration was made which again was rejected by from the Ministry of Justice on 25 August 1998.

2.8 According to the complainant, his right to free legal assistance had been exhausted and the Rådgivningsgruppa (Advisory Group) agreed to take his case on a voluntary basis. On 1 and 9 September 1998, the Advisory Group made additional requests for reconsideration and deferred execution of the expulsion decision, which were rejected on 16 September 1999. The complainant has submitted to the Committee, in this regard, copies of 16 pieces of correspondence between the Advisory Group and the Ministry of Justice, including a medical certificate from a psychiatric nurse indicating that the complainant suffers from post-traumatic stress syndrome. The date of expulsion was finally set for 21 January 1999.

2.9 For the complainant, all the inconsistencies in his story can be explained by the fact that during the initial interrogation he agreed to be questioned in English, not having been informed that he could have an Amharic interpreter present. Since the difference in years between the Ethiopian and Norwegian calendar is approximately eight years, when he tried to calculate the time in Norwegian terms and translate this into English, he became confused. The communication was further complicated by the fact that in Ethiopia the day starts at the equivalent of 6 o'clock in the morning in Norway. That meant that when the complainant said "2 o'clock", this should have been interpreted as "8 o'clock".

2.10 During the interrogation, the complainant referred to the Southern Ethiopian People's Democratic Coalition (SEPDC) as the "Southern People's Political Organization" (SPPO), which does not exist. This error was due to the fact that he only knew the name of the organization in Amharic.

The complaint

3. The complainant argues that he would be in danger of being imprisoned and tortured if he were to return to Ethiopia. He claims that, during the asylum procedure, the immigration authorities did not seriously examine the merits of his asylum claim and did not pay enough attention to his political activities and his history of detention.

Committee's admissibility decision relating to the complainant's earlier complaint N° 127/1999

4. On 25 January 1999, the complainant lodged his initial complaint [N° 127/1999] with the Committee, alleging his expulsion by Norway to Ethiopia would violate article 3 of the Convention. On 19 November 1999, in light of the submissions of the parties, the Committee declared the complaint inadmissible for failure to exhaust domestic remedies.[1] The Committee reasoned as follows:

7.2 The Committee notes that the State party challenges the admissibility of the communication on the grounds that all available and effective domestic remedies have not been exhausted. It further notes that the legality of an administrative act may be challenged in Norwegian courts, and asylum-seekers who find their applications for political asylum turned down by the Directorate of Immigration and on appeal by the Ministry of Justice have the opportunity to request judicial review before Norwegian courts.

7.3 The Committee notes that according to information available to it, the complainant has not initiated any proceedings to seek judicial review of the decision rejecting his application for asylum. Noting also the complainant's information about the financial implications of seeking such review, the Committee recalls that legal aid for court proceedings can be sought, but that there is no information indicating that this has been done in the case under consideration.

7.4 However, in the light of other similar cases brought to its attention and in view of the limited hours of free legal assistance available for asylum-seekers for administrative proceedings, the Committee recommends to the State party to undertake measures to ensure that asylum-seekers are duly informed about all domestic remedies available to them, in particular the possibility of judicial review before the courts and the opportunity of being granted legal aid for such recourse.

7.5 The Committee notes the complainant's claim about the likely outcome were the case to be brought before a court. It considers, nevertheless, that the complainant has not presented enough substantial information to support the belief that such remedy would be unreasonably prolonged or unlikely to bring effective relief. In the circumstances, the Committee finds that the requirements under article 22, paragraph 5 (b), of the Convention have not been met.

---

[1] *Z.T.* v. *Norway*, complaint N° 127/1999, Decision adopted on 19 November 1999.

Complainant's renewed complaint

5.1 On 31 June 2001, the complainant filed a new complaint before the Committee, arguing that the grounds upon which the Committee had declared the case inadmissible no longer applied. He stated that, on 24 January 2000, he had applied for legal aid, which was rejected by the County Governor of Aust-Agder on 5 July 2000. On 14 March 2001, the Ministry of Labour and Administration rejected his appeal against the County Governor's decision. As to the possibility of retaining his own lawyer, in view of his precarious pecuniary situation, he would be unable to afford either the necessary legal fees and filing costs, or an award of costs, if unsuccessful. Nor could he represent himself, as he scarcely speaks Norwegian and lacks knowledge of the relevant rules of procedural and substantive law. Accordingly, the complainant argued that in practice, there was no "available" or "effective" remedy which he could pursue, and that the complaint should therefore be declared admissible.

5.2 On 21 August 2002, the renewed complaint was registered as complaint N° 238/2003 and transmitted to the Government of the State party for comments on its admissibility.

State party's admissibility submissions on the new complaint

6.1 On 27 March 2003, the State party contested the admissibility of the renewed complaint, arguing that paragraph 7.3 of the Committee's original inadmissibility decision could be read in two ways. On the one hand, reading the second sentence in isolation would suggest that once legal aid was sought, admissibility would have to be reconsidered. On the other, the first sentence suggested a complainant must initiate judicial review proceedings, and a failure to do so—even following denial of legal aid—disposed of the issue. In the State party's view, the latter approach was most logical, and was supported by the context of the decision's paragraph 7.2, which rehearsed the arguments on the availability and effectiveness of judicial review. In this light, the first sentence of paragraph 7.3, read in conjunction with 7.5, constitutes the conclusive response of the Committee, and the second sentence inter alia bearing the word "also" was superfluous additional reasoning.

6.2 Even if the Committee held the complaint inadmissible simply for failure to seek legal aid, the complaint would not, according to the State party, become admissible simply because legal aid was subsequently sought, as other reasons of inadmissibility may still apply. In particular, the State party submitted that judicial review was still an "available" remedy to be exhausted. There was no basis for exempting applicants from the obligation to exhaust domestic remedies for lack of financial means, as such an approach had no basis in the text of article 22, paragraph 5, of the Convention. The State party argued that, in any legal system, civil proceedings are generally financed by the parties, and that the framers of the Convention, aware of this approach, made no exception for applicants without resources. Such an approach would interfere with the principle of exhaustion of domestic remedies.

6.3 In the State party's view, were the Committee to do so, States would either (i) have to provide legal aid to a much greater extent than is currently practised or required under international conventions, or (ii) accept the Committee's competence to review administrative decisions rejecting asylum claims without the domestic courts having had the opportunity to review those cases. As to the former option, few States would accept such an approach: civil legal aid is a scarce resource anywhere, and is subject to strict conditions (if available at all). Thus, in view of the large number of asylum applications rejected yearly, a State party would have to take the unlikely step of greatly increasing resources supplied to legal aid schemes.

6.4 The result of such a step would be that the Committee de facto makes itself the first review instance in a vast number of cases, and result in significant growth in the Committee's caseload. In Norway alone, 9000 asylum applications were rejected at last instance in 2002, and most asylum-seekers would claim, as did the current complainant, to be of modest means and unable to access the legal system. There could thus be major consequences for the Committee.

6.5 Administering such an exception would create great difficulties of law and fact for the Committee. It would have to set precise criteria concerning financial ability, and presumably some economic standards that could not be exceeded by applicants claiming impecuniosity. The Committee would have to develop methods to ensure that an applicant does not actually exceed these standards. It would be difficult for States parties to rebut an applicant's allegation of lack of resources, as pertinent information is rarely available. Likewise, in the present case, the State party had ascertained, through tax records, that the complainant had only very modest incomes in the last few years, and it could not scrutinise his financial situation any further. It had no knowledge of any assets abroad, nor any possessions in Norway which could be realized to finance review proceedings.

6.6 In the State party's view, only detailed regulations established in advance could deal with such problems, which would merely underpin the absence of such an exception in the Convention. A decision of admissibility would be a significant innovation in the Committee's case law and a considerable departure from the domestic remedies rule interpreted by treaty bodies. Only the jurisprudence of the Human Rights Committee revealed some very limited exceptions.

Complainant's comments

7.1 By letter of 26 May 2003, the complainant rejected the State party's submissions. He stated that he only receives a welfare check for basic daily needs, in addition to housing support, which would not suffice for raising private counsel. His counsel before the Committee was acting pro bono in respect of those proceedings only. Neither he nor others could be expected to operate pro bono in respect of any judicial review proceedings.

7.2 As to the original reasons for inadmissibility, the complainant submitted it was clear that both elements were criteria on which the conclusion was founded. This was confirmed by the context of paragraph 7.4 of the original case. Were it otherwise, it would have been pointless for the Committee to make any remarks on the legal aid question. As both parties had made submissions on the legal aid issue, paragraph 7.3 was necessary to address those points and was thus far from superfluous. At a minimum, the decision should be reviewed to clarify whether, and on what conditions, judicial review is an available remedy even in the absence of legal aid.

7.3 Turning to whether judicial review must be pursued despite the absence of legal aid, the complainant pointed out that article 22, paragraph 5, only requires available and effective remedies to be exhausted by a complainant. Were the complainant to represent himself, with little knowledge of Norwegian law or language, against skilled lawyers of the State, domestic remedies would not be "effective" within the meaning of article 22.

7.4 The complainant argued that human rights treaties must be interpreted so as to make them effective. If complaints are held inadmissible for non-exhaustion in circumstances where domestic remedies are, in fact, unavailable, a victim has remedies neither at the national nor international level.

7.5 The complainant invoked the jurisprudence of the Human Rights Committee, which had found communications admissible under the Optional Protocol to the International Covenant on Civil and Political Rights in circumstances where legal aid was unavailable.[2]

7.6 The complainant observed that in Norway, many people received legal aid in different categories of cases. He easily satisfied the economic criteria. Thus, in support of his claim for legal aid, he invoked the doctrine of "positive obligations" for the State party to prevent human rights violations, as part of the general obligation to secure effectively the right to *non-refoulement*. The complainant pointed out that if a right to legal aid existed, it would certainly be considered relevant to an assessment of the exhaustion of domestic remedies, and thus the unavailability of legal aid should be treated similarly.

7.7 The complainant rejected the State party's misgivings about the results of holding the present case admissible. Firstly, it would not result in all unsuccessful asylum-seekers pleading before the Committee. A possible violation of article 3 would arise only in few cases. In any event, the outcome on the merits would be a more important guide to the future. The Committee should thus be wary of the adverse consequences advanced by the State party against an interpretation consistent with the Convention's purpose.

7.8 On the facts of his case, the complainant noted that the State party had not disputed the details of his income. In the Norwegian legal aid scheme, the authorities were satisfied with a declaration from the applicant along with a print of tax records, and the State party should not hold the Committee to a stricter standard. In any event, as the Human Rights Committee's experience has shown, the consequences are manageable, and the advantage—greater protection of Convention rights for those who would otherwise go without any protection—is obvious. The complainant thus requested the Committee to declare the case admissible.

Committee's admissibility decision on the new complaint

8.1 During its 31st session, in November 2003, the Committee considered the admissibility of the renewed complaint. It observed, at the outset, that the question of whether a complainant had exhausted domestic remedies that are available and effective, as required by article 22, paragraph 5, of the Convention, could not be determined *in abstracto*, but had to be assessed by reference to the circumstances of the particular case. In its initial decision, the Committee had accepted that judicial review, in the State party's courts, of an administrative decision to reject asylum was, in

---

[2] The complainant cited *Campbell* v. *Jamaica*, case N° 248/1987, Views adopted on 30 March 1992; *Little* v. *Jamaica*, case N° 283/1988, Views adopted on 24 July 1989; *Ellis* v. *Jamaica*, case N° 276/1988, Views adopted on 28 July 1992; *Wright* v. *Jamaica*, case N° 349/1989, Views adopted on 27 July 1992; *Currie* v. *Jamaica*, case N° 377/1989, Views adopted on 29 March 1994; *Hylton* v. *Jamaica*, case N° 600/1994, Views adopted on 16 August 1996; *Gallimore* v. *Jamaica*, case N° 680/1996, Views adopted on 23 July 1999; and *Smart* v. *Trinidad and Tobago*, case N° 672/1995, Views adopted on 29 July 1998.

principle, an effective remedy. The Committee noted that a precondition of effectiveness, however, was the ability to access the remedy, and, in this case, as the complainant had not pursued an application for legal aid, he had not shown that judicial review was closed, and therefore unavailable, to him, within the meaning of article 22, paragraph 5, of the Convention.

8.2 In the present case, the complainant had since been denied legal aid. Had legal aid been denied because the complainant's financial resources exceeded the maximum level of financial means triggering the entitlement to legal aid, and he was thus able to provide for his own legal representation, then the remedy of judicial review could not be said to be unavailable to him. Alternatively, in some circumstances, it might be considered reasonable, in the light of the complainant's language and/or legal skills, that s/he represented himself or herself before a court.

8.3 In the present case, however, it was unchallenged that the complainant's language and/or legal skills were plainly insufficient to expect him to represent himself, while, at the same time, his financial means, as accepted by the State party for purposes of deciding his legal aid application, were also insufficient for him to retain private legal counsel. If, in such circumstances, legal aid was denied to an individual, the Committee considered that it would run contrary to both the language of article 22, paragraph 5, as well as the purpose of the principle of exhaustion of domestic remedies and the ability to lodge an individual complaint, to consider a potential remedy of judicial review as "available", and thus declaring a complaint inadmissible if this remedy was not pursued. Such an approach would deny an applicant protection before the domestic courts *and* at the international level for claims involving a most fundamental right, the right to be free from torture. Accordingly, the consequence of the State party's denial of legal aid to such an individual was to open the possibility of examination of the complaint by an international instance, though without the benefit of the domestic courts first addressing the claim. The Committee thus concluded that, since the complainant applied unsuccessfully for legal aid, the initial reasons for inadmissibility no longer applied.

8.4 On 14 November 2003, the Committee declared the case admissible, since the reasons for inadmissibility referred to in its previous decision of 19 November 1999 on the initial complaint N° 127/1999 were no longer applicable and no other grounds for inadmissibility had been advanced. The Committee accordingly invited the State party to supply its submissions on the merits of the renewed complaint.

State party's merits submissions on the new complaint

9.1 On 23 July 2004, the State party submitted that it considered its submissions on the merits of the renewed complaint to address the same matter as dealt with under complaint N° 127/1999, and invoked as relevant its submissions on the merits regarding the initial complaint The State party maintained that it observes relevant international standards both in its legal practices and in its administrative proceedings. On 1 January 2001, the State party established a quasi-judicial organ independent of the political authorities, known as Immigration Appeals Board and mandated to handle appeals against all decisions taken by the Directorate of Immigration, including asylum cases. It submitted that the Appeals Board maintained a large number of highly qualified employees, among them a country expert for Ethiopia who undertook a visit to Ethiopia as late as in February 2004, and cooperated closely with the special immigration officer in the Norwegian Embassy in Nairobi.

9.2 Since the State party's submission of 31 March 1999, the Immigration Appeals Board had, on its own initiative, undertaken another examination of the case before the Committee and, on 12 March 2004, upheld the decision to reject the complainant's asylum application. The Board's conclusion was based on its findings that there are no substantial grounds for believing that the complainant, upon return to Ethiopia, would be personally in danger of being subjected to torture or other forms of ill-treatment. The State party accordingly submitted that returning the complainant to Ethiopia would not constitute a violation of article 3 of the Convention.

9.3 Among the factors contributing to a personal risk of the complainant to be subjected to torture upon return to Ethiopia was the complainant's degree of involvement in political activities in the early 1990s in Ethiopia. The State party submitted that the information provided by the complainant in that regard lacked credibility, as it contained numerous contradictions and as his explanations changed throughout the history of this case. According to the information provided by the complainant in his asylum interview on 19 and 20 October 1996, he had been arrested on 20 February either in 1992 or 1993 (Gregorian calendar) and had been imprisoned for one year and seven months, after which he claimed to have fled directly to Norway. However, he did not arrive in Norway until October 1996; the State party concluded that his safe and voluntary stay in Ethiopia for another two years after his imprisonment was incompatible with his alleged fear of persecution.

9.4 The State party further submitted that an inquiry conducted by the Norwegian Embassy in

Ethiopia with former leader of the SEPDC coalition, revealed that the latter had not heard of the complainant himself nor of two of the three SPPO leaders who the complainant claimed to have worked for. Upon learning of the former leader's statements, the complainant changed his statements and confirmed that it was in fact the SEPDC coalition he had been a member of and had assisted, and that the confusion resulted from a mistranslation. The State party argued that the confusion between a single political party (the SPPO) and a 14-party coalition (the SEPDC) could not simply be attributed to problems of translation.

9.5 The State party dismissed the credibility of the complainant's claims on the basis of fundamental contradictions between the complainant's claims and those of his mother who was interviewed by the Norwegian Embassy in Ethiopia. After the complainant learned that his mother had informed the Norwegian authorities of his prior imprisonment for his membership of the EPRP, he claimed to have been arrested several times, a fact which he had not previously mentioned. Further discrepancies between his account and that of his mother included the identity of his siblings and his places of residence at different stages in his life, which the State party regarded as undermining the complainant's credibility further.

9.6 The State party noted that in his asylum interview, the complainant had stated that he had never been subjected to any kind of physical torture, but that he had been threatened in a way akin to psychological torture. Two years later, however, when requesting the annulment of the Ministry of Justice's negative decision concerning his asylum claim, he claimed to have been subjected to torture in the form of baton blows to his head. The State party maintained that the late submission of such a crucial fact further undermined the credibility of the complainant's claims. It further argued that his contraction of epilepsy was not, contrary to the arguments advanced by the complainant, a result of the torture he allegedly suffered, but that it more likely emerged from his infection with a tapeworm. The State party finally argued that the contradictions and inconsistencies in the complainant's story cannot, as maintained by the complainant, be reasonably attributed to post-traumatic stress disorder (PTSD), as the complainant's allegation to be suffering from PTSD had been submitted late and had not been substantiated beyond a declaration by a nurse purely based on the complainant's own account.

9.7 The State party did not regard the support letter from the EPRP's Norwegian group, certifying that the complainant was a victim of imprisonment and political persecution in Ethiopia, as sufficient evidence for the claim that the complainant had been politically active in his home country or that he was viewed with suspicion by the authorities. In the State party's experience, exile organizations had a tendency routinely to issue "confirmations" to country people requesting them. The State party contended that EPRP's Norwegian section had only limited knowledge of the complainant's case.

9.8 In the State party's view, accepting that complete accuracy is seldom to be expected from potential victims of torture, the credibility of the complainant's claim was nonetheless comprehensively undermined by the evident contradictions and inconsistencies set out. Moreover, even if the complainant's account of his political persecution in the past had been true, given the current situation in Ethiopia, there was no basis for holding that he would now be of particular interest to the Ethiopian authorities. The State party therefore concluded that the assessment of the available information and material made by the Norwegian authorities was correct, and that those assessments warranted the conclusion that there were no substantial grounds for believing that the complainant would be at a personal and real risk of being subjected to torture or other ill-treatment if returned to Ethiopia.

Complainant's comments

10.1 By letter of 5 November 2004, the complainant noted that the State party's rejection of his claim that he would risk being tortured upon return to Ethiopia was based on its allegations of inconsistencies in his account. He referred to the Committee's case law, according to which neither inconsistencies in an applicant's story, provided they did not raise doubts about the general veracity of the claim,[3] nor late submissions,[4] automatically constituted obstacles to the protection guaranteed by article 3 of the Convention. He pointed out that the Committee has rejected similar arguments advanced by the State party in *Tala* v. *Sweden*,[5] and that it found, for example in *Mutombo* v. *Switzerland*,[6] that "even if there are doubts about the facts adduced by the [complainant], [the Committee] must ensure that his security is not endangered." He further submitted that the risk of torture invoking protection under article 3 must go beyond mere theory or suspicion,

---

[3] *Kisoki* v. *Sweden*, complaint N° 41/1996, Views adopted on 8 May 1996, *Alan* v. *Switzerland*, complaint N° 21/1995, Views adopted on 8 May 1996, and *I.A.O.* v. *Sweden*, complaint N° 65/1997, Views adopted on 6 May 1998.
[4] *Khan* v. *Canada*, complaint N° 15/1994, Views adopted on 15 November 1994, and *Tala* v. *Sweden*, complaint N° 43/1996, Views adopted on 15 November 1996.
[5] Ibid.
[6] Case N° 13/1993, Views adopted on 27 April 1994, para. 9.2.

whereas the wording of article 3 does not demand a demonstration of a "high probability" that torture will occur. He also recalled that the reasons for the danger of being tortured should have been established before or after the flight of the involved person, or as a combination of both.[7]

10.2 The complainant argued that his identity as well as his involvement in politics and his imprisonment for his political activities, both under the former and under the present regime, had been established beyond reasonable doubt. The information provided by his mother confirmed that he disappeared about four years ago, which corresponded to the period of his last imprisonment and his political underground work. His political activities in Ethiopia and his persecution by the Ethiopian authorities were further confirmed by the support letters from the EPRP's Norwegian section. The complainant also submitted a copy of an arrest warrant of 25 March 1994, when he worked for SEPDC, showing that he was wanted for interrogation. The complainant's continued involvement in the EPRP's Norwegian section was also acknowledged in a support letter from that organization. According to the complainant, his name appeared in the headlines of the Norwegian media several times in that context.[8] All of these facts could not, in the complainant's view, be overshadowed by the alleged inconsistencies in his case.

10.3 Regarding the allegations of inconsistencies and of the complainant intentionally presenting false information, the complainant recalls that he had initially given his account under adverse conditions. Having recently arrived in Norway and been kept in a security cell for some hours before his interrogation, and suffering from PTSD, his uncertainty and fear were worsened by the behaviour of the interrogation officer and the translator who allegedly ridiculed him. Moreover, the complainant communicated his surprise that the interrogation focused mainly on his family background and his departure from Ethiopia (11 pages of the protocol), rather than on what the complainant regards as material to his reasons for seeking asylum (1.5 pages), such as his political involvement and his fear of being returned to Ethiopia.

10.4 Regarding his family and personal history, the complainant submitted that related inconsistencies concern questions of minor importance, whereas the main facts provided by him, such as his family members' names and place of their home, were correct.

10.5 Concerning his alleged persecution in the past, the complainant claimed that, following his first asylum interrogation, he submitted additional details rather than, as the State party alleges, providing another account altogether. In fact, the complainant had, during the asylum interrogation, submitted only those details he deemed relevant, and submitted further facts once informed by the Advisory Group of their importance. The State party's claim that the complainant had said in the interrogation that he was arrested "only" once was false.

10.6 The complainant confirmed that he had stated in the asylum interview to have been "active in", rather than being "a member" of, the SEPDC, whose title he translated freely into English by retaining the main concepts of the organization. The State party's assumption that the former SEPDC leader it interviewed knew all the members of the SEPDC was, in the complainant's view, rebutted by the former's stated willingness to investigate further into the case. The fact that the complainant mainly operated underground in an illegal organization supports the former SEPDC leader's unawareness of the complainant's work as well as his claim that activists were not formally registered. The complainant notes that the State party has not informed the Committee or the complainant about any possible verification work undertaken by it, such as further contact with the former SEPDC leader or the verification of the detailed description of the Kerchele prison in Addis Ababa provided by the complainant.

10.7 Concerning past incidents of torture, the complainant submits that he was beaten during his long imprisonment in the 1980s, whereas he was not subjected to physical torture during his last imprisonment in the 1990s. However, he claims to have been tortured mentally in custody, and witnessed the torture of Abera, one of his political leaders, by the police.

10.8 The complainant submits that he faces a substantial risk of being tortured if returned to Ethiopia. Information provided by Human Rights Watch and United States Department of State reports of 2003 leave little doubt that there is a consistent pattern of gross, flagrant and mass violations of human rights in Ethiopia, a country which still produces refugees. That the complainant has been politically active in two major opposition movements and escaped from prison eight years ago under the present regime, as well as his continued involvement as an "active member" in the EPRP in Norway[9] all render him at a risk of being tortured if returned. Since Ethiopia has not recognized the Committee's competence to act under article 22 of

---

[7] The complainant here refers to *Aemei* v. *Switzerland*, complaint N° 34/1995, Views adopted on 9 May 1997.
[8] The complainant supplies no further detail as to the sources or content of these media reports.

[9] The complainant provides no details as to what political activities he undertook in Norway.

the Convention, the complainant will have no possibility of bringing a complaint before the Committee if tortured upon return.

Supplementary submissions by the parties

11.1 On 6 April 2005, the State party submitted additional observations regarding the Immigration Appeals Board's decision of 12 March 2004. It states that its decision to review the complainant's case was taken by the Board on its own initiative, without any formal request by the complainant. While the Committee's admissibility decision of 14 November 2003 was the cause for the review, there was no obligation upon the Board to do so. The State party points out that the final decision of 29 December 1997 has now been reviewed four times in total by the Norwegian authorities, who each time did not find substantial grounds for believing that he would be at a substantial, present and personal risk of torture if returned to Ethiopia.

11.2 By letter of 22 April 2005, the complainant responded to the State party's supplementary submission, criticizing the procedure followed by the Immigration Appeals Board concerning its most recent decision of 12 March 2004. He accepts that the decision entailed "an extensive deliberation of the case", but states that due to a change in counsel the decision was apparently not received by him. He argues that he should have been provided with prior notice of the hearing and should have been provided with the Board's decision.

Disposition of procedural issue

12.1 On 10 November 2004, the complainant applied to the Committee, under rule 111, paragraph 4, of the Committee's rules of procedure, for leave to submit oral testimony to the Committee. He argued that he had not had not had opportunity to present his case in person before the domestic decision-making bodies in his case, nor had he appeared before the courts. Given that a major reason for the rejection of his claim was an assessment of his credibility, an issue that can be well tested in oral testimony, he contended that oral testimony before the Committee would provide it with a basis to assess his credibility.

12.2 On 26 November 2004, at its 33rd session, the Committee rejected the complainant's application under rule 111, paragraph 4.

Examination of the merits

13.1 The issue before the Committee is whether the removal of the complainant to Ethiopia would violate the State party's obligation under article 3 of the Convention not to expel or to return a person to another State where there are substantial grounds for believing that he or she would be in danger of being subjected to torture. The Committee must evaluate whether there are substantial grounds for believing that the complainant would be personally in danger of being subjected to torture upon return to Ethiopia. In assessing this risk, the Committee must take into account all relevant considerations, pursuant to article 3, paragraph 2, of the Convention, including past incidents of torture or the existence of a consistent pattern of gross, flagrant or mass violations of human rights. However, the Committee recalls that the aim of such determination is to establish whether the individual concerned would be personally at a foreseeable and real risk of being subjected to torture in the country to which he or she would return.

13.2 The Committee has considered the periods of imprisonment suffered by the complainant in the 1980s and 1990s and his allegation that he was subjected to beatings, to maltreatment and psychological torture in Ethiopia in the past on account of his political activities. It notes the interest of the Ethiopian authorities in his person apparently demonstrated by an arrest warrant dating from 1994. The Committee has finally noted the complainant's submissions about his involvement in the Norwegian section of the EPRP. Nevertheless, in the Committee's view, the complainant has failed to adduce evidence about the conduct of any political activity of such significance that would still attract the interest of the Ethiopian authorities at the current time, nor has he submitted any other tangible evidence to demonstrate that he continues to be at a personal risk of being tortured if returned to Ethiopia.

13.3 The Committee finds accordingly that, in view of the lengthy period of time that has elapsed since the events described by the complainant, the information submitted by the complainant, including the low-level nature of his political activities in Ethiopia and Norway, coupled with the nature and extent of inconsistencies in the complainant's accounts, is insufficient to establish his claim that he would personally be exposed to a substantial risk of being subjected to torture if returned to Ethiopia at the present time.

14. In the light of the above, the Committee against Torture, acting under article 22, paragraph 7, of the Convention against Torture and Other Cruel, Inhuman or Degrading Treatment or Punishment, concludes that the decision of the State party to return the complainant to Ethiopia would not constitute a breach of article 3 of the Convention.

Communication N° 258/2004

Submitted by: Mostafa Dadar (represented by counsel)
Alleged victim: The complainant
State party: Canada
Date of adoption of Views: 23 November 2005

Subject matter: deportation of complainant to Iran with alleged risk of torture

Procedural issue: none

Substantive issue: risk of torture after deportation

Article of the Convention: 3

1.1 The complainant is Mr. Mostafa Dadar, an Iranian national born in 1950, currently detained in Canada and awaiting deportation to Iran. He claims that his deportation would constitute a violation of article 3 of the Convention against Torture. The Convention entered into force for Canada on 24 July 1987. The complainant is represented by counsel, Mr. Richard Albert.

1.2 In accordance with article 22, paragraph 3, of the Convention, the Committee transmitted the complaint to the State party on 30 November 2004. Pursuant to rule 108, paragraph 1, of the Committee's rules of procedure, the State party was requested not to expel the complainant to Iran while his case was pending before the Committee. The State party acceded to such request.

Factual background

2.1 From 1968 to 1982 the complainant was a member of the Iranian Air Force, where he obtained the rank of captain. In December 1978, when rioting and widespread protests in the country was at its peak, and prior to the installation of the Ayatollah Khomeini, he was given the responsibility of commander of martial law at "Jusk" Air Force Base. He claims that he was given that assignment, inter alia, because he was an outspoken opponent of Ayatollah Khomeini and strongly loyal to the Shah.

2.2 On 13 February 1979, after Ayatollah Khomeini became President of Iran, he was arrested and kept in Q'asr prison in Tehran for almost 3 months. He was frequently interrogated and beaten. On 2 May 1979, he was released and soon afterwards was assigned to an Air Force base in Mehrabad, Tehran.

2.3 In December 1980, he was expelled from the Air Force on allegations of being loyal to the monarchist regime, but in February 1981, he was called back to service. He retained his rank of captain and was assigned to "Karaj" radar station in Tehran. In July 1981, he was expelled a second time from the Air Force, due to the fact that he had expressed sentiments of loyalty to the Shah. Subsequently, he became involved with the National Iranian Movement Association ("NIMA"), which staged an unsuccessful coup d'état against the Khomeini regime in 1982. In March 1982, in the aftermath of the coup d'état, many NIMA members were executed. The complainant was arrested, taken to Evin prison in Tehran and severely tortured. He was also kept incommunicado. On 9 July 1982, he was subjected to a false execution. On three occasions, authorities called his brother informing him of the complainant's execution. The complainant provides copy of a newspaper article referring to his detention and trial.

2.4 In December 1984, he was found guilty of an attempt against the security of the State and transferred to Mehr-Shar prison, near the city of Karaj. According to the complainant, this prison is partially underground and he was deprived of sunlight for most of the time. In May 1985, he was transferred to Gezel Hessar prison, where his health deteriorated drastically and he became paralyzed from the waist up.

2.5 In July 1987, he got a two-day medical pass to exit the prison in order to obtain medical treatment. At that time, some members of his family were in contact with a pro-monarchist organization known as the Sepah Royalist Organization, based in London. Arrangements had been made through Sepah for removing him from Iran. During his two-day release he fled to Pakistan with his wife.

2.6 The UNHCR Office in Karachi issued the complainant with an identity card and referred him to Canada, which permitted him to enter Canada with his wife as a permanent resident on 2 December 1988.

2.7 The complainant states that, while in Pakistan, he was actively involved in operations on behalf of the Shah. He provides copy of four letters from the Military Officer of the Shah, dated between 1987 and 1989, referring to his activities. The last one, dated 24 January 1989, states the following: "We would like to congratulate your landing in Canada as a permanent resident. We appreciate your sense of duty and thank you. We do not have any activity in Canada or any other country like Canada which would require your services. Certainly, you would be called to a tour of duty any time we need you." He also provides copy of a letter dated 4 April 2005 from the Secretariat of Reza Pahlavi stating: "Given Mr. Mostafa Dadar's background and extended high profile political activities, his return to Iran under existing circumstances will indeed subject him to methods used frequently by the intolerant clerics in Iran, namely, immediate imprisonment, torture and eventually execution".

2.8 In Canada, the complainant was treated for severe depression, anxiety and suicidal tendencies. He was diagnosed with chronic post-traumatic stress disorder, as a result of the treatment to which he was subjected while in prison. The complainant is now divorced from his wife, with whom he has two Canadian-born children.

2.9 On 31 December 1996, the complainant was convicted of aggravated assault and sentenced to 8 years in prison. The assault was upon a woman the complainant had recently befriended and resulted in her being hospitalized in intensive care and in the psychiatric ward for several weeks, unable to speak or walk. She sustained permanent disability. At trial the complainant pleaded not guilty. He has maintained this position ever since. He lists a number of irregularities that occurred at the trial. He says, for instance, that the judge did not take into consideration the fact that he had been found in a sleepy and drug-induced stupor at the crime scene. He had just woken up from a drug-induced sleep having ingested a high quantity of sedatives prior to the time the assault occurred. The New Brunswick Court of Appeal dismissed his appeal. A motion for leave to appeal to the Supreme Court of Canada was dismissed in 1999.

2.10 The complainant indicates that, while in detention in Canada, he was offered to meet with the Canadian Intelligence and Security Service (CSIS). After the death of Zahra Kazemi, an Iranian-born Canadian photojournalist who died in detention in Iran in 2003, he provided accurate information to the CSIS about her place of arrest and detention, the kind of torture she was subjected to, the hospital where she was taken to, etc. He had obtained such information telephonically through his sources in Iran. The complainant provides this information as evidence of his involvement with the opposition forces in Iran.

2.11 On 30 October 2000 the Minister of Citizenship and Immigration issued a Danger Opinion pursuant to the Immigration Act, declaring the complainant to be a danger to the public. As a result, on 18 June 2001 he was ordered deported. On 20 August 2001, he filed an Application for Judicial Review of the Minister's Danger Opinion citing a breach of his entitlement to procedural fairness among other grounds. On 5 November 2001, the Minister consented to the application and the danger opinion was quashed. On 11 April 2002, the complainant was granted conditional release by the National Parole Board. On 15 May 2002, he was ordered detained by the Department of Citizenship and Immigration, pursuant to s. 103 of the former Immigration Act, because it was believed that he posed a danger to the Canadian public.[1] He has remained in detention to date.

2.12 On 21 November 2002, the Minister of Citizenship and Immigration issued a second Danger Opinion. This Opinion was quashed by an Order of the Federal Court of Canada of 8 July 2003.

2.13 On 8 March 2004, the Minister issued a third Danger Opinion, which was upheld after the complainant filed an Application for Judicial Review. This opinion indicates that the complainant had been convicted of the following offences: Theft under $5000 in December 1995, for which he was fined $100; assault of his wife, on 12 July 1995, for which he was sentenced to four days in prison and one year probation; aggravated assault, on 14 January 1997, for which he was sentenced to eight years imprisonment. The Opinion acknowledged a Correctional Services of Canada Detention Review report dated 18 October 2001 and stated: "This report also indicates that the risk that Mr. D. poses to the general population is low but rises to moderate if he is in a 'conflicted' domestic relationship."

2.14 Regarding the risk of torture the Minister states the following: "I cannot, however, disregard the country conditions present in Iran at this time when considering whether or not a person who has been found to be a Convention refugee may be 'refouled'. I also cannot ignore the material prepared by the Immigration and Refugee Board concerning the lack of force of the monarchist movement in Iran at this time. While there is no doubt in my mind that the human rights situation in Iran is precarious, it is my opinion that Mr. D. would be of limited interest to Iranian authorities due to his former membership in this organization; though I do acknowledge that he claims that he is still a supporter of this movement. He left Iran some 17 years ago and was imprisoned 21 years ago. (…) In the event that I am in error and Mr. D. would be subjected to torture, death or to cruel and unusual treatment or punishment, I am guided by the principles expressed by the Supreme Court of Canada in the case of Suresh. In Suresh, the Supreme Court noted: (…) 'We do not exclude the possibility that in exceptional circumstances, deportation to face torture might be justified'".

2.15 The complainant indicates that the Correctional Services of Canada (CSC) is the main agency to make determinations in regard to the future risk of offenders if they were to be released to society. A report completed by a CSC parole officer

---

[1] At that time, a valid Danger Opinion was not yet in place, the first Danger Opinion having already been quashed.

is one of the most objective tools available to the CSC for determining if the subject of the report will pose any danger to the public if he was to be released. The reporting procedure governing risk assessment is based on file materials, psychological assessments, programme performances, etc. The complainant report concluded that there were no reasonable grounds to believe that he was likely to commit an offence resulting in serious harm prior to the expiration of his sentence according to the law.

2.16 The complainant also sent to the Committee copies of two psychological assessment reports according to which he represented a low risk to the general public and a moderate risk in the context of a spousal relationship.

2.17 The complainant challenges the Danger Opinion in that it states that there has not been a politically motivated arrest or execution of monarchists in Iran since 1996. He says that the founder of the Iran Nation Party, a monarchist political organization, and five of his colleagues were summarily executed in Tehran by members of the Iranian intelligence service in 1998. Monarchists in Iran are very active, but are unwilling to engage in a campaign of terror to achieve their goals.

2.18 The complainant further states that the Danger Opinion is based, in large part, on allegations made by his ex-wife. Such allegations should be regarded as being tainted by strong animosity against the complainant, by reason of their marital separation and divorce.

2.19 The complainant applied for judicial review of the third Danger Opinion. On 12 October 2004, the Federal Court of Canada upheld the Opinion. On 22 February 2005, the complainant filed an application for release on humanitarian and compassionate grounds. On 31 March 2005, he filed an application pursuant to s. 84 (2) of the Immigration and Refugee Protection Act for release as a foreign national who has not been removed from Canada within 120 days after the Federal Court determines a certificate to be reasonable.

The complaint

3. According to the complainant, there are substantial grounds for believing that he would be subjected to torture if returned to Iran, in violation of article 3 of the Convention. He refers to reports indicating that torture is practised extensively in Iran. Should the complainant be removed to that country, attempts to extract information from him will jeopardize not only the complainant's own life, but also the lives of several others in Iran who at one time or another aided or cooperated with him in his activities against the Iranian regime.

State party's admissibility and merits submissions

4.1 In its submission of 24 March 2005, the State party indicates that it does not challenge the admissibility of the complaint on the ground of non-exhaustion of domestic remedies. It notes, however, that the complainant had not made an application under s 25 (1) of the Immigration and Refugee Protection Act, despite the fact that, in his submission to the Committee, he had expressed his intention to do so. However, the State party claims that the case is inadmissible because the complainant failed to establish a prima facie violation of article 3 of the Convention. If the Committee concluded that the communication was admissible, the State party submits, on the basis of the same arguments, that the case is without merit.

4.2 The State party indicates that in July 1995 the complainant was convicted of assault against his former wife, Ms. J. They separated in 1995. They have two children who live with the mother. By court order, the complainant is not permitted access to the children out of concern for their safety and well being. In December 1995 he was convicted of theft of an amount under $5000 and was fined $100. In January 1997, he was convicted of aggravated assault upon his then girlfriend and sentenced to eight years of imprisonment. The assault occurred while he was on probation with respect to the 1995 assault conviction.

4.3 Throughout the appeal process, the complainant asserted that he did not commit the offence. However, he has made several statements which effectively amount to admitting his crimes, and has even expressed remorse for the victim. The State party refers, in this respect, to the submissions made by the complainant relating to the Ministerial Opinion Report dated 30 October 2000.

4.4 The Ministerial Opinion Report, dated 15 October 2000, concluded that there was little doubt that the complainant received harsh and inhuman treatment when he was in Iran. Relying on the *1999 United States Country Report on Human Rights Practices,* the Opinion also observed that he could face harsh and inhuman treatment upon his return. However, the Opinion determined that the risk that the complainant represented to Canadian society outweighed any risk that he might face upon his return to Iran. As a result of the Report, the complainant was ordered deported on 18 June 2001. On 14 November 2001, due to procedural defects, the Federal Court ordered the Opinion set aside, and referred the matter back for redetermination.

4.5 A second Ministerial Opinion Report was issued against the complainant on 21 November 2002. The Risk Assessment given in the Request of Minister's Opinion, dated 17 July 2002, was that there were no substantive grounds to believe that the complainant would face torture, and that it was unlikely that he would be subject to other cruel, inhuman and degrading treatment or punishment, should he be removed to Iran. This assessment was based on the fact that the complainant did not provide details of his current involvement with the NIMA organization, that it had been 20 years since participating in the failed coup, and 16 years since he had left Iran. On 21 November 2002, the Minister gave his opinion. He noted that the situation in Iran had ameliorated somewhat, but that there was a risk that the complainant could be rearrested due to his prison escape and again subjected to torture. It concluded, however, that the significant risk to the public in Canada had to be given greater weight than the risk that the complainant may be rearrested and tortured upon his return to Iran. On 8 July 2003, due to procedural defects, the Federal Court of Canada ordered the Opinion set aside and referred the matter back for redetermination.

4.6   A third Ministerial Opinion Report was issued on 8 March 2004. It concluded that the complainant, like other returnees, may be subjected to a search and to extensive questioning upon return to Iran for evidence of anti-government activities abroad. However, in itself, this did not establish any serious risk that he would face torture or other cruel, inhuman or degrading treatment or punishment. The report recalled that it had been 21 years since the complainant was imprisoned for his political activities and that there had been a large reform movement in Iran since 1997. Furthermore, it was difficult to accept that the complainant maintained any high profile within Iranian society. The Opinion also referred to the situation of pro-monarchists in Iran citing two papers that were prepared by the Research Directorate of the Immigration and Refugee Board in March 2000 and October 2002. The first one concluded that the monarchists were no longer organized and active in Iran. The second stated that monarchist demonstrations were dispersed using tear gas and clubs and that some individuals were arrested. The Opinion concluded that the complainant would be of limited interest to Iranian authorities due to his former membership in a pro-monarchist organization which no longer posed a threat to the current regime.

4.7   The report also pointed out to certain inconsistencies regarding the circumstances of the complainant's escape from prison. In a Community Assessment document dated 1 September 1998 the complainant's former wife stated that he was sentenced to two years' imprisonment and was released within that time frame, less 22 days for good behaviour. Furthermore, a psychological report dated 8 December 1988 indicated that the complainant went to Pakistan after release from jail.

4.8   The Ministerial Opinion report also indicated that the complainant had presented no specific evidence to establish that he did remain politically active while in Canada. He had not suggested that the Iranian authorities had actively sought him out at any time and there was no mention of any harassment by Government officials towards his family members. Taken into consideration that he had been incarcerated for a number of years and, prior to that, lead what was apparently an isolated existence, it was unlikely that he had remained politically active in any significant way.

4.9   The State party concludes that the complainant did not prima facie establish substantial grounds for believing that his removal to Iran will have the foreseeable consequence of exposing him to a real and personal risk of being tortured. While it does not dispute that the complainant was at one time involved in a failed coup d'état or that he was imprisoned as a result of his participation in the coup, he has not shown that he faces any risk of torture if he is removed to Iran by reason of his past association with the NIMA. He has provided a newspaper clipping written in Persian and a letter from the Secretariat of Reza II. Both date back to 1988. He has provided no recent material to suggest that Iranian authorities have any interest or intention to prosecute or detain him and subject him to any treatment contrary to article 3. His participation in an attempted coup that took place over 20 years ago cannot be viewed as having occurred in the recent past.

4.10   The complainant has provided no evidence to suggest that members of his family in Iran have been the victims of retribution by the Iranian authorities because of his alleged political opinions, nor on account of any involvement in his alleged escape from prison and subsequent departure from Iran. In fact, all that remains is the complainant's bare assertion that he will be tortured or executed upon his return. Given the complainant's continuing equivocation with respect to whether he did or did not commit aggravated assault, as well as other inconsistencies that were noted by the Federal Court in its reasons for dismissing the complainant's application for judicial review, the State party submits that the complainant is not credible and that reliance should not be placed on his word alone.

4.11   Regarding the complainant's activities since leaving Iran, all the complainant has provided is his own unreliable statement that he continued his political involvement in Canada. In the absence of credible and recent evidence, it is impossible to conclude that he faces a danger that is personal, present and foreseeable. Finally, while the human rights situation in Iran remains problematic, the complainant has provided no evidence in support of his allegations that he himself is at any risk of torture.

4.12 The State party submits that three risk assessments were conducted prior to the determination that the complainant was a danger to the public and should be removed from Canada. The complainant had the opportunity to make submissions about the risks he would face on three separate occasions. He used these opportunities and made extensive submissions in relation to his particular circumstances. In none of the three separate assessments was the conclusion reached that the complainant faced a substantial risk of torture if he were to be removed to Iran. In fact, in the most recent assessment, it was determined that the Iranian authorities would have a minimal interest in him. This finding was upheld by the Federal Court.

4.13 The State party contends that the Committee should not substitute its own findings on whether there were substantial grounds for believing that the complainant would be in personal danger of being subjected to torture upon return, since the national proceedings disclose no manifest error or unreasonableness and were not tainted by abuse of process, bad faith, manifest bias or serious irregularities. It is for the national courts of the States parties to the Convention to evaluate the facts and evidence in a particular case and the Committee should not become a "fourth instance" competent to re-evaluate findings of fact or to review the application of domestic legislation.

4.14 Alternatively, if the communication were declared admissible, the State party requests the Committee to conclude, based on the same submissions, that the communication is without merit.

Complainant's comments

5. By letter of 11 July 2005, the complainant contends that the Ministerial Opinion of 8 March 2004 is based, in large part, on allegations made by his ex-wife. However, her statements must be regarded as being tainted by strong animosity against him by reason of their marital separation and divorce. He provides examples of statements made by her in other to demonstrate that she is not a credible witness. For instance, in statements before the police she feigned that she did not know the complainant's girlfriend; this was not true, as both women had a prior acquaintance that predated the assault. According to a police report dated 23 May 1996, police arrived at her residence on 27 April 1996 after she called them alleging that the complainant had threatened her. However, despite such allegations the complainant was not charged. The inference is that the complainant did not threaten her and that her allegations to the police were false.

Additional submissions by the parties

6.1 By submission of 29 July 2005, the State party enumerates the list of sources that were consulted in the preparation of the Ministerial Opinion with respect to the role of monarchists in Iran. Reports and publications from the United Nations, the United States Department of State, as well as non-governmental organizations have documented human rights abuses in Iran, including the use of torture against particular groups. These groups generally include: prominent political dissidents, journalists, women, youth and religious minorities. There is scarce mention of monarchists in such reports. What little discussion there is of monarchists is limited to the period immediately following the 1979 Revolution. The complainant refers to a list of individuals belonging to the NIMA who were allegedly executed. However, the date of the executions was 9 November 1982.

6.2 The complainant refers to the 1998 killing of Dariush and Parvaneh Forouhar, founders of the Iran Nation Party, as an example of a recent incident of torture perpetrated against monarchists in Iran. While the State party is not in a position to comment on the circumstances that led to the killing, neither the 2004 United States State Department Report relied on by the complainant, nor any other report found by the Government of Canada describe the Forouhars or the Iran Nation Party as "hard-core monarchists". Rather, they are described as "prominent political activists" or "prominent critics of the Government". Moreover, according to Human Rights Watch, Mr. Forouhar was also a former political prisoner under Shah Pahlavi, the founder of the monarchist movement. This casts doubt on the complainant's assertion that the Forouhars were part of a "hard-core monarchist political organization". The State party concludes that the link between the Forouhars and the monarchists has not been made out.

6.3 The State party offers information about other alleged monarchists aiming to demonstrate that there have not been any politically motivated arrests or prosecutions of monarchists in Iran over the past several years. Furthermore, the complainant, by his own account, has not been involved with monarchists since he left Pakistan in 1988. As a result, his involvement cannot be said to rise to a level of prominence that would attract the attention of Iranian authorities.

Additional submission of the complainant

7.1 By letter of 27 September 2005, the complainant refers to one of the Danger Opinions, which used sources according to which, in February 2001, the Iranian police used tear gas to disperse a demonstration by monarchists and that dozens of demonstrators were arrested and a number of others were injured. He also submits that the Forouhars, although political prisoners under the Shah Pahlavi, are now pro-monarchist. He names other alleged monarchists or pro-monarchists who were arrested after July 1999, accused of organizing a protest against the Iranian regime and executed on 15 March 2003.

7.2 There are two major groups in Iran which oppose the present regime, namely the MEK and the monarchists. The MEK has been involved in terrorist activities and is therefore a less legitimate replacement for the current regime. Monarchists operate several television stations in different countries and are actively involved in disseminating information criticizing the current Iranian regime.

7.3 The complainant reiterates his involvement with monarchists since 1988. He refers to the letters of 24 January 1989 and 4 April 2005 (see para. 2.7) and states that he is an officer on-call for the monarchists. He reiterates that on 20 June 2003 he was interviewed by the Canadian Security and Intelligence Service, who offered to engage his services.

7.4 Regarding the sources referred to by the State party, the complainant submits that the majority of international human rights organizations have not had direct contact with prisoners of the Iranian regime that would allow them to accurately gauge the extent of the regime's brutality against its detractors, including monarchists.

7.5 The complainant refers to the poor human rights record of Iran and cites the 2002 Amnesty International Report, according to which torture and ill-treatment, including of prisoners of conscience, continued to be used.

Issues and proceedings before the Committee

8.1 Before considering any claims contained in a complaint, the Committee against Torture decides whether or not it is admissible under article 22 of the Convention. The Committee has ascertained, as it is required to do under article 22, paragraph 5 (a), of the Convention, that the same matter has not been and is not being examined under another procedure of international investigation or settlement. The Committee further notes that the State party does not challenge the admissibility of the complaint on the ground of non-exhaustion of domestic remedies and that the complainant has sufficiently substantiated his allegations for purposes of admissibility. Accordingly, the Committee considers the complaint admissible and proceeds to its consideration on the merits.

8.2 The issue before the Committee is whether the removal of the complainant to Iran would violate the State party's obligation under article 3 of the Convention not to expel or to return a person to another State where there are substantial grounds for believing that he or she would be in danger of being subjected to torture.

8.3 In assessing the risk of torture, the Committee takes into account all relevant considerations, including the existence in the relevant State of a consistent pattern of gross, flagrant or mass violations of human rights. However, the aim of such determination is to establish whether the individual concerned would be personally at risk in the country to which he would return. It follows that the existence of a consistent pattern of gross, flagrant or mass violations of human rights in a country does not as such constitute a sufficient ground for determining that a particular person would be in danger of being subjected to torture upon his or her return to that country; additional grounds must exist to show that the individual concerned would be personally at risk. Similarly, the absence of a consistent pattern of gross violations of human rights does not mean that a person cannot be considered to be in danger of being subjected to torture in his or her specific circumstances.

8.4 The Committee recalls its General Comment on article 3, which states that the Committee is to assess whether there are substantial grounds for believing that the complainant would be in danger of torture if returned, and that the risk of torture must be assessed on grounds that go beyond mere theory or suspicion. The risk need not be highly probable, but it must be personal and present.

8.5 In assessing the risk of torture in the present case, the Committee notes that the complainant claims to have been tortured and imprisoned on previous occasions by the Iranian authorities because of his activities against the current regime and that, after his arrival in Canada, he was diagnosed with chronic post-traumatic stress disorder. This is not contested by the State party.

8.6 Although the complainant's torture and imprisonment occurred between 1979 and 1987, i.e., not in the recent past, the complainant claims that he is still involved with the Iranian opposition forces. The State party has expressed doubts about the nature of such involvement. However, there are no clear indications, from the information before the Committee, that such involvement is inexistent. In this regard, the complainant has submitted a number of letters referring to his activities as a member of the monarchist opposition group. In one of them, fears are expressed that he might be imprisoned, tortured and eventually executed if he returns to Iran under existing circumstances. The complainant has also submitted information in support of his claim that the monarchists are still active inside and outside the country and that they continue to be persecuted in Iran. Furthermore, the State party has not denied that the complainant cooperated with the Canadian Intelligence and Security Service in 2003. The complainant submitted such information to the Committee as evidence of his continuing involvement with Iranian opposition forces.

8.7 The Committee is aware of the human rights situation in Iran and notes that the Canadian authorities also took this issue into consideration when assessing the risk that the complainant might face if he were returned to his country. In this regard, it notes that, according to such authorities, there is no doubt that the complainant would be subjected to questioning if returned to Iran, as are all persons returned through deportation. In the Committee's view, the possibility of being questioned upon return increases the risk that the complainant might face.

8.8 The Committee notes that the complainant's arguments and his evidence to support them, have been considered by the State party's authorities. It also notes the State party's observation that the Committee is not a fourth instance. While the Committee gives considerable weight to findings of fact made by the organs of the State party, it has the power of free assessment of the facts arising in the circumstances of each case. In the present case, it notes that the Canadian authorities made an assessment of the risks that the complainant might face if he was returned and concluded that he would be of limited interest to the Iranian authorities. However, the same authorities did not exclude that their assessment proved to be incorrect and that the complainant might indeed be tortured. In that case, they concluded that their finding regarding the fact that the complainant presented a danger to the Canadian citizens should prevail over the risk of torture and that the complainant should be expelled from Canada. The Committee recalls that the prohibition enshrined in article 3 of the Convention is an absolute one. Accordingly, the argument submitted by the State party that the Committee is not a fourth instance cannot prevail, and the Committee cannot conclude that the State party's review of the case was fully satisfactory from the perspective of the Convention.

8.9 In the circumstances, the Committee considers that substantial grounds exist for believing that the complainant may risk being subjected to torture if returned to Iran.

9. The Committee against Torture, acting under article 22, paragraph 7, of the Convention against Torture and Other Cruel, Inhuman or Degrading Treatment or Punishment, concludes that the deportation of the complainant to Iran would amount to a breach of article 3 of the Convention.

10. The Committee urges the State party, in accordance with rule 112, paragraph 5, of its rules of procedure, to inform it, within 90 days from the date of the transmittal of this decision, of the steps taken in response to the Views expressed above.

Communication N° 262/2005

Submitted by: V.L. (not represented by counsel)
Alleged victim: The complainant
State party: Switzerland
Date of adoption of Views: 20 November 2006

Subject matter: deportation of complainant to Belarus with alleged risk of torture

Procedural issue: none

Substantive issue: risk of torture after deportation

Articles of the Convention: 3, 22

1.1 The complainant is V.L., born in 1946, a Belarusian citizen currently living in Switzerland, pending her return to Belarus. She does not invoke specific provisions of the Convention against torture and other cruel, inhuman or degrading treatment or punishment, but her complaint appears to raise issues under article 3 thereof. She is not represented by counsel.

1.2 On 14 January 2005, the Committee, through its Rapporteur on New Complaints and Interim Measures, transmitted the complaint to the State party and requested it, under rule 108, paragraph 1, of its rules of procedure, not to return the complainant to Belarus while her case is under consideration by the Committee. The Rapporteur indicated that this request could be reviewed in the light of new arguments presented by the State party. The State party acceded to this request by note of 25 February 2005.

Factual background

2.1 The complainant's husband stood in local elections in Belarus in 1995 and in 2000. In a letter to the editor of a newspaper, he criticized the president of the country. He was then interrogated several times by the office of security and the police. He was also attacked by four unknown men in April 2000. The police advised him to cease his political activities. He left Minsk and stayed with relatives from July 2000 to June 2001. He left the country on 7 June 2001 and went to Belgium where he applied for asylum. His application was rejected and he travelled to Switzerland on 18 December 2002. In the meantime, the complainant herself remained behind in Belarus and was frequently interrogated about her husband's whereabouts. On 12 September 2002, her passport was taken away from her. She left the country on 16 December 2002 and joined her husband in Switzerland on 18 December 2002.

2.2 The complainant, together with her husband, applied for asylum in Switzerland on 19 December 2002. Both based their claims on the alleged political persecution of the husband by the Belorussian authorities. These claims were not considered to be credible by the Swiss Federal Office for Refugees (BFF) which considered that the documents submitted by the claimants were not genuine. Consequently, the applications were rejected on 14 August 2003 and the complainant and her husband were ordered to leave the country by 9 October 2003.

2.3 On 11 September 2003, the complainant and her husband appealed to the Swiss Asylum Review Board (ARK). The ARK rejected the appeal on 15 September 2004. The complainant requested a revision of the decision on 11 October 2004, in which she mentioned for the first time that she had suffered sexual abuses by members of the police ("Miliz"). She urged the Swiss authorities to reconsider her asylum application on its own right, rather than as part of her husband's claims, explaining that they now lived separately. It was only after the couple's arrival in Switzerland that the complainant informed her husband of the sexual abuses. He reacted with insults and humiliating remarks and forbade her to mention the sexual abuses to the Swiss authorities. By letter dated 15 October 2004, the ARK requested further information on the request for revision because the reasons invoked for the revision of the appeal decision were not sufficient. On 21 October 2004, the complainant elaborated on the grounds for revision. She now claimed that prior to her departure from Belarus, she had been interrogated and raped by three officers of the police who wanted information about the whereabouts of her husband. These officers also beat her and penetrated her with objects. A subsequent medical examination in a hospital confirmed bruises and damage to her sexual organs. The complainant was then treated medically and could not return to her workplace for more than three weeks.

2.4 Following this incident, the complainant complained to the officer-in-charge of the department whose officials had sexually abused her. Thereafter, she received threats from several officers of this department. One officer followed her home, asking her to withdraw her complaint. There were constant night visits to her home and searches by the police. One day, the same officers who had previously raped her kidnapped her in front of her office, and drove her to an isolated place where she was raped again. The officers threatened to mutilate and kill her. On 12 September 2002, she was called to the police offices, where her passport was taken away. Following these events, she became depressed and went into hiding. The threats and intimidations, coupled with the previous sexual abuses, motivated her flight from Belarus.

2.5 The complainant claims that her failure to mention the rape in her initial interview with the BFF was due to the fact that she had considered it humiliating and an affront to her personal dignity. Furthermore, the psychological pressure from her husband prevented her from mentioning the sexual abuses. She explained that her husband had disappeared in October 2004 and his whereabouts are unknown to her. Now that he had left the country, she was however willing to provide details about the events described above and a medical certificate.

2.6 In its decision of 1 December 2004, the ARK acknowledged that in principle, rape was a relevant factor to be considered in the asylum procedure, even when reported belatedly, and that there may be psychological reasons for victims not to mention it in the first interview. However, the complainant's claims did not appear plausible to the ARK, since, according to it, the complainant had neither substantiated nor proven psychological obstacles to at least mentioning the rape in the initial interview. Nor had her story or her behaviour been otherwise convincing. The ARK also expressed suspicion about the "sudden ability of the complainant to provide details about the alleged rape". It was unconvinced that the complainant would be threatened with persecution or inhuman treatment upon return, and concluded that there were no legal obstacles to her return to Belarus.

2.7 On 7 December 2005, the complainant sent to the ARK a medical report, demonstrating that she had suffered sexual abuses before she left Belarus. By letter of 14 December 2005, the ARK replied that her case was closed. She wrote again to the ARK on 7 January 2005 explaining why she disagreed with its decision of 1 December 2004. She was informed on 11 January 2005 that she would be removed from the country on 20 January 2005.

The complaint

3. The complainant submits that, from the documents submitted by the complainant, it is clear that she justifiably fears persecution by the police in Belarus. She does not invoke specific provisions of the Convention against torture and other cruel, inhuman or degrading treatment or punishment, but her complaint appears to raise issues under article 3.

State party's admissibility submissions

4.1 By note verbale of 25 February 2005, the State party challenges the admissibility of the complaint. It submits that the complainant's letter dated 12 January 2005 cannot be considered to be a complaint within the meaning of article 22 of the Convention. It recalls that under rule 107, paragraph (a), of the Committee's rules of procedure, the complainant must claim to be a victim of a violation by the State party concerned of the provisions of the Convention. Under paragraph (b), the Committee shall ascertain that the complaint is not an abuse of the Committee's process or manifestly unfounded. It notes that the complainant merely forwards the documents concerning her asylum application and requests the Committee "to render me the help and assistance in [...] the decision of my question of protection", rather than identifying any error on the part of the national authorities when confirming the removal decision. It argues that the complainant failed to demonstrate that she would face a risk of torture upon her return to Belarus. In the absence of any claim of a violation, the State party considers it impossible to comment on the complainant's submission.

4.2 The State party concludes that the complainant's letter cannot be considered as a communication within the meaning of article 22 of the Convention. In the event that it was nevertheless considered as such, it invites the Committee to declare it inadmissible for failing to disclose violations of the Convention, or as amounting to an abuse of the right of submission, or as being manifestly unfounded under rule 107, paragraph (b), of the rules of procedure.

Complainant's comments

5. By letter of 12 March 2005, the complainant presents her comments on the State party's submission on the admissibility of the communication. She provides more detail on the sequence of events leading to her departure from Belarus. She also sends a medical report dated 4 July 2002 of the 7th urban polyclinic in Minsk. The report states that the complainant has suffered a trauma and damage to her sexual organs.

State party's merits submissions

6.1 By note verbale of 24 June 2005, the State party reaffirms its challenge to the admissibility of the communication; subsidiarily, it submits the following arguments on the merits. The State party first recalls its obligations under article 3 of the Convention, and recalls that the Committee has specified the conditions of application of this provision in its jurisprudence and in its General Comment 1 of 21 November 1997.

6.2 Under article 3, paragraph 2, of the Convention, the Committee must take into account all relevant considerations including the existence in the State concerned of a consistent pattern of gross, flagrant or mass violations of human rights. The State party submits that it must be determined whether the individual concerned would be *personally* at risk of being subjected to torture in the country to which he or she would return. It follows that the existence of a consistent pattern of human rights violations in a country does not as such constitute a sufficient ground for determining that a particular person would be in danger of being subjected to torture upon his return to that country.[1] Consequently, additional grounds must be adduced to show that the risk of torture can be qualified as "foreseeable, real and personal."[2] The State party notes that the situation in Belarus cannot of itself constitute a sufficient ground for concluding that the complainant would be in danger of being subjected to torture upon her return to that country.[3] The State party contends that the complainant has not demonstrated that she would face a "foreseeable, real and personal" risk of being subjected to torture upon her return to Belarus.

6.3 Under General Comment 1, whether the complainant has been tortured or ill-treated in the past must be taken into account so as to assess the risk of being subjected to torture upon return to her country. The complainant claims that she was raped several times in 2002, the first time by three police officers as part of an interrogation as to the whereabouts of her husband and the second, as a result of her reporting the first rape to the authorities. She fears that her return would come immediately to the knowledge of the police and that she would be ill-treated again, or even raped. In order to support the claims that she was raped in 2002, she sent to the Committee a medical report dated 4 July 2002 of the 7th urban polyclinic in Minsk. For the State party, it

---

[1] See communication N° 94/1997, *K.N.* v. *Switzerland*, decision adopted on 19 May 1998, para.10.2.

[2] Ibid, para.10.5. See also communication N° 100/1997, *J.U.A.* v. *Switzerland*, decision adopted on 10 November 1998, paras. 6.3 and 6.5.

[3] See also communication N° 106/1998, *N.P.* v. *Australia*, decision adopted on 6 May 1999, para. 6.5.

is surprising that the complainant did not present this essential piece of evidence in the ordinary procedure, nor in the procedure for revision before the ARK. According to the complainant, because she was expecting a new interview, she sent this medical report only after reception of the decision of the ARK of 1 December 2004. The State party does not consider this explanation to be convincing. It notes that, on the one hand, the ARK asked the complainant to specify her request for revision and to make it more substantial, and that, on the other hand, the complainant herself replied that she found it necessary to provide the required information in writing. In these circumstances, the State party recalls that the complainant and her husband provided false and/or falsified means of evidence in the ordinary asylum procedure, and that the husband's claim of persecution was considered not credible by the national authorities. It considers that the medical report cannot support the rape allegation.

6.4 According to General Comment 1, the complainant's previous political activities in the country of origin must be taken into in order to assess the risk of her being subjected to torture upon return to that country. The State party notes that the complainant has not been politically active in Belarus. The sole political activities which were invoked were those of her husband who allegedly stood in the local elections in 1995 and 2000, and criticized the Head of State. The State party concludes that the complainant has not established that she would face a risk of torture because of her own political activities.

6.5 With regard to the credibility of the complainant, the State party notes that she mentions grounds not invoked before the national authorities during the asylum procedure, and that she made reference to the sexual abuses by the police only in her request for revision of 11 October 2004. On explicit request from the ARK, she completed her request for revision on 21 October 2004. It is only on this occasion that she specified that members of the police raped her several times in 2002 and that she was subsequently seriously threatened by the police, notably because she reported the crime. The complainant has never supported her allegations with evidence. According to the complainant, she did not dare mentioning the rapes during the ordinary procedure because her husband forbade her to talk about them. The State party argues that, even though this explanation could be accepted for the period preceding the complainant's separation from her husband, it cannot be considered as convincing for the subsequent period. In particular, it cannot explain why the complainant did not provide any evidence to the ARK during the revision procedure. Furthermore, the evidence provided by the complainant and her husband to support their claims during the asylum procedure were essentially false and/or falsified. In the light of the above, the State party doubts the authenticity of the medical report provided in the present procedure only on 12 March 2005.

6.6 Finally, the State party submits that the complainant's claims are full of factual inconsistencies, which undermines her credibility. According to her, the rapes she was subjected to in 2002 had a direct link with the political activities of her husband. However, the national authorities have found the allegations related to her husband's persecution not to be credible. Since the complainant has always claimed that her husband's activities were the sole cause for her own persecution, these allegations are without any basis.

6.7 The State party concludes that nothing indicates that there are serious grounds to fear that the complainant would be seriously and personally exposed to torture upon her return to Belarus.

Additional comments by the complainant

7.1 By letter of 28 July 2005, the complainant responds that although she was not an active political figure, she supported the political activities of her husband, and that her belonging to a family where there is opposition to the Government makes her politically active. In response to the State party's contention that she has not mentioned the threat of arrest upon return to Belarus in the initial asylum application, she claims that she had mentioned that risk in her first interview upon arrival in Switzerland on 14 February 2003, but also at several other times. She adds that these comments were sent to the Committee in the annexes to her initial communication.

7.2 The complainant argues that there is a consistent pattern of gross, flagrant or mass violations of human rights in Belarus and that she is thus afraid of facing persecution upon her return. She mentions that opponents to the authorities regularly disappear in Minsk and Vitebsk, and that many people are falsely imprisoned. Regarding the question whether there is a real and personal risk of being subjected to torture upon her return, she recalls that she has received on several occasions specific threats to put her in prison and even, to kill her. She adds that upon her return to Belarus, she would have to go to the police for registration of her personal documents, which is compulsory. Consequently, members of the police would learn immediately that she was back. In order to demonstrate that she faces a real risk of ill-treatment, she recalls that there have been numerous night visits of members of the police to her home, searches, interrogations, acts of violence against her which were corroborated by a medical report and that her political activity consisted in distributing pre-election propaganda materials.

7.3 With regard to the delay in presenting the medical report to the national authorities of the State party, the complainant claims that the report was still in Belarus. When her case was reconsidered, her daughter found the medical report at the complainant's home in Belarus and sent it to the complainant by fax on 17 November 2004.

7.4 With regard to the absence of persecution of the complainant's husband, the complainant argues that the State party is mistaken, and that, if there were no threats against her husband, he would have returned to Belarus. Instead, he is now in Belgium.

7.5 On the issue of credibility of her claims, the complainant explains that in her application for revision dated 11 October 2004, she mentioned only briefly the sexual abuses she had suffered because she was expecting to be called for a new interview. Concerning the availability of means of evidence to support her allegations, she recalls that the complaint she made to the police has been suspended because she had left the country. The documents concerning her complaint are confidential and she cannot have access to them from Switzerland.

Issues and proceedings before the Committee

8.1 Before considering any claim contained in a communication, the Committee against Torture must decide whether or not it is admissible under article 22 of the Convention. The Committee has ascertained, as it is required to do under article 22, paragraph 5 (a), of the Convention, that the same matter has not been, and is not being, examined under another procedure of international investigation or settlement. In the present case, the Committee also notes that all domestic remedies have been exhausted and that the complainant has sufficiently substantiated the facts and her claims, for purposes of admissibility. With regard to the State party's argument that the complainant's letter does not constitute a complaint within the meaning of article 22 of the Convention, the Committee considers that while the complainant does not specifically mention article 3 of the Convention in her initial submission, she has made clear that she should not be returned to Belarus because she faces a risk of further instances of rape by militia authorities upon return. Considering that she was not represented by counsel and in the light of the seriousness of the allegation, the Committee recalls that it has been its constant practice to treat similar communications as complaints within the meaning of article 22 of the Convention.[4] It therefore considers that the communication is admissible and proceeds to an examination on the merits of the case.

8.2 The Committee must determine whether the forced return of the complainant to Belarus would violate the State party's obligations under article 3, paragraph 1, of the Convention not to expel or return ('refouler') an individual to another State where there are substantial grounds for believing that he or she would be in danger of being subjected to torture.

8.3 The Committee must evaluate whether there are substantial grounds for believing that the complainant would be personally in danger of being subjected to torture upon return to Belarus. In assessing this risk, the Committee must take into account all relevant considerations, pursuant to article 3, paragraph 2, of the Convention, including the existence, in the State concerned, of a consistent pattern of gross, flagrant or mass violations of human rights. However, the Committee recalls that the aim of its determination is to establish whether the individual concerned would be personally at risk of being subjected to torture in the country to which he or she would return. It follows that the existence of a consistent pattern of gross, flagrant or mass violations of human rights in a country does not as such constitute a sufficient ground for determining that a particular person would be in danger of being subjected to torture upon his or her return to that country. Additional grounds must be adduced to show that the individual concerned would be personally at risk. Conversely, the absence of a consistent pattern of gross violations of human rights does not necessarily mean that a person cannot be considered to be in danger of being subjected to torture in his or her specific circumstances.

8.4 The Committee is aware of the poor human rights situation in Belarus. The police alleged to have harassed, sexually abused and raped the complainant acts under the Ministry of the Interior and has been responsible for numerous instances of torture across the country, including against persons who participated in alternative election campaigns. The Special Rapporteur on the situation of human rights in Belarus has noted several attacks on members of the political opposition.[5] The Committee itself has cited numerous allegations of torture and ill-treatment by Belarus authorities, the absence of an independent procurator, the failure to conduct prompt, impartial and full investigations into claims of torture, and the absence of an independent

---

[4] See for instance communication N° 248/2004, *A.K.* v. *Switzerland*, decision adopted on 8 May 2006.

[5] See the Report of the Special Rapporteur on the situation of human rights in Belarus, Adrian Severin (E/CN.4/2006/36, paras. 51–54). See also the Report of the Working Group on Arbitrary Detention (Mission to Belarus) (E/CN.4/2005/6/Add.3, paras. 58–60).

judiciary.[6] The Special Rapporteur on Violence against Women has noted the increasing number of reports of violence against women including rape in Belarus, and the "rather frequent" reports of abuse, including sexual attacks, by female detainees.[7] According to data released by the Belarus Ministry of Labor and Social Security in 2004, over 20 percent of women reported experiencing sexual abuse at least once. In the first ten months of the year 2005, the Ministry of Interior reported a 17 percent increase in reports of rape from the year before.[8]

8.5   The Committee recalls its General Comment 1 on article 3, which states that the Committee is to assess whether there are substantial grounds for believing that the complainant would be in danger of torture if returned, and that the risk of torture must be assessed on grounds that go beyond mere theory or suspicion. The risk need not be highly probable, but it must be personal and present.

8.6   As to the State party's assertion that the earlier finding that some of the original documents submitted in the joint asylum application were falsified, and that this undermines the complainant's credibility, the Committee considers that the evidence that the husband, and not the complainant, was in control of what was presented in support of the original joint asylum application, cuts against attributing responsibility to her for such defects on this basis alone. As to the State party's claim that the medical report from the hospital summarizing and supporting the allegation of rape is also falsified, the Committee notes that the State party concluded this on the sole ground that the earlier documents submitted by the husband in support on the joint asylum application were deemed to be falsified (see para. 6.5 above) and has not adduced any further evidence or argument to support this claim. Noting that the date and the detailed information about the severe injury to the complainant's sexual organs by insertion of blunt objects contained in the medical report from Belarus correspond to the information contained in her submissions, the Committee does not question the authenticity of this document.

8.7   As to the State party's argument that the complainant has not established that she would face a risk of torture because of her own political activities, the Committee observes that while the complainant is now separated from her husband, this will not prevent the authorities from harming her. This complainant has explained that she participated in distributing pre-election propaganda when in Belarus. The complainant is now separated but not divorced from her husband; to the authorities, she remains a source of contact and a means of pressuring him. Moreover, according to a recent United States State Department Human Rights Country Report, cases of harassment of divorced women because of their former husband's activities are not unknown in Belarus.[9] In any case, while the complainant contends that she was detained and raped the first time because of her husband's political activities in Belarus, the Committee notes that she was raped for a second time because she had made a complaint about the initial rape. Upon return to Belarus, the complainant would thus be at risk of ill-treatment independently of her relationship to her husband. Her report against the police accusing them of night visits, searches, violence and rape could easily make the complainant vulnerable to reprisals by the police anywhere in Belarus. As the Special Representative of the Secretary-General on human rights defenders has argued, women human rights defenders face gender-specific forms of hostility, harassment and repression such as sexual harassment and rape.[10] The police in Belarus function in a highly uniform and hierarchical system with a top-down rule; in current political conditions, it is hard to assess that any one location is safer than another. For all those reasons, the complainant would be of interest to the local police.

8.8   The State party has argued that the complainant is not credible because the allegations of sexual abuse and the medical report supporting these allegations were submitted late in the domestic proceedings. The Committee finds, to the contrary, that the complainant's allegations are credible. The complainant's explanation of the delay in mentioning the rapes to the national authorities is totally reasonable. It is well-known that the loss of privacy and prospect of humiliation based on revelation alone of the acts concerned may cause both women and men to withhold the fact that they have been subject to rape and/or other forms of sexual abuse until it appears absolutely necessary. Particularly for women, there is the additional fear of shaming and rejection by their partner or family members. Here the complainant's allegation that her husband reacted to the complainant's admission of rape by humiliating her and forbidding her to

---

[6] See Concluding Observations of the Committee against Torture: Belarus (A/56/44), para. 45 (d).
[7] See the Report of the Special Rapporteur on violence against women, its causes and consequences, Radhika Coomaraswamy: international, regional and national developments in the area of violence against women (1994–2003) (E/CN.4/2003/75/Add.1, para. 1901).
[8] As cited in the United States Department of State Country Report on human rights practices (2005), 8 March 2006.

[9] See the United States Department of State Country Report on human rights practices (2005), 8 March 2006.
[10] See the Report of the Special Representative of the Secretary-General on human rights defenders (E/CN.4/2002/106, para. 91).

mention it in their asylum proceedings adds credibility to her claim. The Committee notes that as soon as her husband left her, the complainant who was then freed from his influence immediately mentioned the rapes to the national authorities in her request for revision of 11 October 2004. Further evidence of her psychological state or psychological "obstacles," as called for by the State party, is unnecessary. The State party's assertion that the complainant should have raised and substantiated the issue of sexual abuse earlier in the revision proceedings is insufficient basis upon which to find that her allegations of sexual abuse lack credibility, particularly in view of the fact that she was not represented in the proceedings.

8.9 With regard to the State party's argument that there are many inconsistencies in the complainant's claims, the Committee notes that this argument has not been substantiated since the State party has not specified what these inconsistencies were.

8.10 In assessing the risk of torture in the present case, the Committee considers that the complainant was clearly under the physical control of the police even though the acts concerned were perpetrated outside formal detention facilities. The acts concerned, constituting among others multiple rapes, surely constitute infliction of severe pain and suffering perpetrated for a number of impermissible purposes, including interrogation, intimidation, punishment, retaliation, humiliation and discrimination based on gender. Therefore, the Committee believes that the sexual abuse by the police in this case constitutes torture even though it was perpetrated outside formal detention facilities. Moreover, the authorities in Belarus appear to have failed to investigate, prosecute and punish the police for such acts. This failure to act increases the risk of ill-treatment upon the complainant's return to Belarus, since the perpetrators of the rapes have never been investigated and can mistreat the complainant again in all impunity. There is thus substantial doubt, based on the particular facts of this case, as to whether the authorities in Belarus will take the necessary measures to protect the complainant from further harm.

8.11 In the circumstances, the Committee considers that substantial grounds exist for believing that the complainant may risk being subjected to torture if returned to Belarus.

9. The Committee against Torture, acting under article 22, paragraph 7, of the Convention against Torture and Other Cruel, Inhuman or Degrading Treatment or Punishment, concludes that the complainant's removal to Belarus by the State party would constitute a breach of article 3 of the Convention.

10. The Committee urges the State party, in accordance with rule 112, paragraph 5, of its rules of procedure, to inform it, within 90 days from the date of the transmittal of this decision, of the steps taken in response to the Views expressed above.

Communication N° 279/2005

Submitted by: C.T. and K.M. (represented by counsel)
Alleged victim: The complainants
State party: Sweden
Date of adoption of Views: 17 November 2006

Subject matter: deportation of complainants to Rwanda with alleged risk of torture

Procedural issue: none

Substantive issue: risk of torture after deportation

Article of the Convention: 3

1.1 The complainants are C.T., a citizen of Rwanda, of Hutu ethnicity, and her son, K.M., born in Sweden in 2003, both awaiting deportation from Sweden to Rwanda. Although the complainants do not invoke specific articles of the Convention, their claims appear to raise issues under article 3 of the Convention against Torture and Other Cruel, Inhuman or Degrading Treatment or Punishment. They are represented by counsel.[1]

1.2 On 9 September 2005, the Committee requested the State party not to deport the complainants to Rwanda while their case is pending before the Committee, in accordance with rule 108, paragraph 1, of the Committee's rules of procedures. On 7 November 2005, the State party acceded to the Committee's request.

---

[1] The complainants have been represented by counsel since 22 March 2006, after the initial submission to the Committee.

Factual background[2]

2.1 Before the first named complainant's arrival in Sweden on 17 October 2002, she lived in Kigali. She and her brother had become members of the PDR-Ubuyanja party sometime between February and May 2002. In April 2002, they attended a meeting of the party. Following this meeting, the leaders of this party, Mr. Bizimungu and Mr. Ntakirutinka, were arrested. In May 2002, the first named complainant and her brother were arrested and she was imprisoned in a container in Remera in Kigali, with six other women. She has not seen her brother since. She was interrogated about her own involvement and that of her brother's in the PDR-Ubuyanja party. She was repeatedly raped, under the threat of execution, and became pregnant with her son K.M., the second named complainant, who was born in Sweden.

2.2 In October 2002, a soldier helped her escape and took her to a religious order, which helped her organize her flight to Sweden. On 17 October 2002, she arrived in Sweden and requested asylum. On 23 March 2004, her request was denied by the Migration Board on grounds of lack of credibility and developments in Rwanda following the elections of 2003. In 2003, her son was born. On 29 June 2005, the Migration Board's decision was confirmed on appeal to the Aliens Appeals Board. On 7 September 2005, the Aliens Appeals Board denied a new application.

The complaint

3.1 The first named complainant claims that if returned to Rwanda, she will be immediately detained and tortured by the Rwandan Directory of Military Intelligence (DMI), on account of her membership of the PDR-Ubuyanja party. She would be raped again and interrogated in order to make her reveal how she escaped. She fears that she and her son could even be killed.

3.2 She further claims that she will be tried by the gacaca courts, which were set up by the Government to avenge the genocide of 1994. She claims to be one of the 760,000 Hutus who are due to be tried by these courts, in particular for her alleged involvement in a massacre at Kigali Hospital.

State party's admissibility and merits observations

4.1 On 19 June 2006, the State party provided its submission on the admissibility and the merits. It submits that the complaint is inadmissible as manifestly ill-founded, and sets out the relevant provisions of the Aliens Act, pointing out that several provisions reflect the same principle as that laid down in article 3, paragraph 1, of the Convention. The national authority conducting the asylum interview is naturally in a good position to assess the information submitted by asylum-seekers. On 9 November 2005, temporary amendments were enacted to the 1989 Aliens Act. On 15 November 2005, these amendments entered into force and were to remain in force until the entry into force of a new Aliens Act on 31 March 2006. The temporary amendments introduced additional legal grounds for granting a residence permit with respect to aliens against whom a final refusal-of-entry or expulsion order has been issued. According to the new Chapter 2, section 5 b of the Aliens Act, if new circumstances come to light concerning enforcement of a refusal-of-entry or expulsion order that has entered into force, the Swedish Migration Board, acting upon an application from an alien or of its own initiative, may grant a residence permit, inter alia, if there is reason to believe that the intended country of return will not be willing to accept the alien or if there are medical obstacles to enforcing the order.

4.2 Furthermore, a residence permit may be granted if it is of urgent humanitarian interest for some other reason. When assessing the humanitarian aspects, particular account shall be taken of whether the alien has been in Sweden for a long time and if, on account of the situation in the receiving country, the use of coercive measures would not be considered possible when enforcing the refusal-of-entry or expulsion order. Further special considerations shall be given to a child's social situation, his or her period of residence in and ties to the State party, and the risk of causing harm to the child's health and development. It must also be considered whether the alien committed crimes and a residence permit may be refused for security reasons. Decisions made by the Migration Board under Chapter 2, Section 5 b, as amended, are not subject to appeal.

4.3 On the facts, the State party provides the reasoning behind the Migration Board's decision to reject the application for refugee status under chapter 3, section 2 of the Aliens Act, for residence permits as aliens otherwise in need of protection under chapter 3, section 3 and for residence permits on humanitarian grounds under chapter 2, section 4, paragraph 1, subparagraph 5. It considered that: the general political situation in Rwanda did not per se constitute a ground to grant the complainants asylum; according to the EU special representative in the region there had been positive developments in Rwanda following the general elections in 2003; the PDR-Ubuyanja party was banned before the elections in 2003 and unknown persons previously

---

[2] The complainants do not describe the facts in detail themselves: the following account is a summary of the facts as described by the first named complainant to the Swedish immigration authorities and set out in the immigration authorities' decisions.

suspected of involvement in the party or persons who have been active in the party at a low level cannot be considered to run any risk of persecution or harassment; and the credibility of certain of the first-named complainant's statements was doubtful. The State party submits that, while both the Migration Board and Aliens Appeals Board found reason to question the credibility of certain statements made by the first named complainant, this was not the decisive factor for their decisions. Indeed, the Migration Board found that irrespective of the factors which detracted from the complainant's credibility, the developments in Rwanda after the 2003 elections had been such as to render it unlikely that she would be at risk of persecution due to her membership of the PDR-Ubuyanja party.

4.4 Since the new application to the Aliens Appeal Board was denied on 7 September 2005, another new application was lodged on 23 September 2005. On 21 November 2005, it was transferred from the Aliens Appeals Board to the Migration Board for determination, in accordance with the temporary legislation contained in chapter 2, section 5 b of the 1989 Aliens Act. On 3 March 2006, the Migration Board denied the application, as the medical certificates furnished by the complainants (including a psychologist's certificate of 31 July 2005) did not show that the first named complainant suffered from such a serious mental illness or comparable condition that she could be granted a residence permit on medical grounds. As regards the second named complainant, who was then nearly three years, the Board was of the view that he had not developed such close ties with Sweden that he could be granted a residence permit on that ground. On 16 March 2006, the complainants lodged an additional application with the Migration Board for a residence permit under the temporary legislation contained in chapter 2, section 5 b of the 1989 Aliens Act. On 15 August 2006, the State party subsequently informed the Committee that by a decision of 5 July 2006, the Board found that the complainants were not entitled to residence permits. While it considered medical and psychological opinions not previously presented to the Swedish authorities, it found that no new circumstances had emerged and that there was no medical obstacle to enforcing the expulsion order. In addition, concerning the second named complainant, it found that he had not developed such ties to Sweden that he should be granted a residence permit.

4.5 On the merits, the State party endorses the finding of both the Migration Board and the Aliens Appeal Board that the first named complainant was vague in her statement regarding her involvement in the PDR-Ubuyanja party. She did not provide details about the party, with the exception of the name of the party leader, former President Pasteur Bizimungu, and that of the secretary general, former Minister Charles Ntakirutina. She did not give a detailed account of the activities and programme of the party but merely stated that the party wished to "rebuild the country and give everyone their rights". In addition, she amended the information she gave with respect to when she became a member of the party during the proceedings. Initially, she claimed to have become a member in May 2002, after attending a meeting. However, after her first application was turned down by the Migration Board, she amended the statement and claimed to have become a member at an earlier stage, in February or March 2002. The State party notes would like to point to the fact that the amended statement is inconsistent with the statement before the Migration Board that she attended a party meeting in April 2002 to become a member.

4.6 The State party highlights the fact that, although there are several international reports, regarding the arrest of PDR-Ubuyanja members, there are no such reports to support the claim that the first named complainant and her brother were arrested and detained. The State party also notes that, according to international reports, many of the individuals who were arrested due to their alleged involvement in the party have been released. Only a small number of people have been sentenced to imprisonment by criminal courts because of their involvement in the party.

4.7 As to the document invoked as evidence by the complainant drawn up by Pelicicn Dufitumukiza, a former representative of LIPRODHOR,[3] the State party notes that there is a factual inconsistency in this document if compared to what the complainants have stated both in the national proceedings and before the Committee. Mr. Dufitumukiza refers to a LIPRODHOR journal from July 2001, according to which from that day there is no member of the C.T. family still alive. However, the complainants claim that the first named complainant and her brother were arrested in the spring of 2002, i.e., almost a year after the date of the journal in which LIPRODHOR claims to have found information regarding her case. It is not clear from the document who informed LIPRODHOR about the abduction of the first complainant and her brother.

4.8 As to the claim relating to the gacaca tribunals, the State party submits that, while the system has been the subject of criticism from a human rights perspective, the international community at large, including the European Union, has given it its support. Regarding the allegation that the first named complainant is in fear of facing trial before

---

[3] The State party acknowledges that this is Rwanda's largest human rights organization.

the gacaca tribunals for participation in the genocide in 1994, the State party draws the Committee's attention to the fact that this allegation was made for the first time in the so-called new application filed before the Aliens Appeals Board on 23 September 2005, and then only by reference to an attached letter from a M.U. to the first complainant. The complainants have not provided any details regarding this allegation either before the national authorities or before the Committee, and there is no conclusive evidence, substantiating the alleged fear. The submitted documents drawn up by Mr. Joseph Matata, a representative of Centre du lutte contre "impunité et l'injustice au Rwanda," only refer to the gacaca tribunals in general and do no support the allegation that the first complainant personally would be at risk. The only evidence in support of this claim is the letter from M.U., referred to above. The letter, which is undated and unsigned, does not give any specific details of the alleged criminal investigation or of any pending criminal charges in Rwanda that concern the first named complainant. In addition, it does not appear from the letter who the author is or how he or she received the information. In the State party's view, the letter cannot therefore be regarded as reliable evidence that, in case of expulsion, the first named complainant would risk indictment for genocidal acts before the gacaca tribunals, let alone that she would be at risk of torture.

4.9 The State party recalls the Committee's jurisprudence that while past torture is one of the elements to be taken into account when examining a claim under article 3 of the Convention, the aim of the examination is to determine whether the complainants would risk being subjected to torture if returned to their country at the present time.[4] Thus, even if it were to be established that the first named complainant had been subjected to ill-treatment in 2002, it does not prove her claim that their removal to Rwanda would expose them to a foreseeable, real and personal risk of being tortured thereby constituting a violation of article 3. The State party acknowledges that reports had been made that military troops, until their withdrawal in October 2002, abducted women and children from villages they raided to perform labour, military services and sexual services.

4.10 The State party submits that even if the first named complainant had proved that she was a member of the PDR-Ubuyanja party, and that she was arrested and detained and managed to escape, the political situation in Rwanda has undergone significant changes since the complainants' arrival in Sweden, especially since the 2003 elections. The party is a proscribed political party and its activities are subject to monitoring by the authorities. However, there is no objective evidence to show that ordinary members or relatives of members of the party are at risk from the authorities According to her own statement, she only attended one party meeting. If the first named complainant had become a member of the party, it must have been at a very low level and thus she would not be at risk from the authorities. For these reasons, the State party concludes that the complainants have not shown that there is a foreseeable real and personal risk of torture if returned to Rwanda.

Complainant's comments

5.1 On 28 September 2006, the complainants refer to the Migration Board decision of 5 July 2006, and highlight its finding that there was no medical obstacle to returning the complainants to Rwanda. However, it did not consider what the effects of being expelled would have on their health in Rwanda. The Board made this decision despite a medical report, of 2 June 2006, which confirmed the first complainant's claims of rape and diagnosed her as suffering from PTSD.

5.2 As to the State party's claim that the first named complainant's lack of detail regarding the PDR-Ubuyanja party demonstrates her lack of credibility, the complainants argue that a document in Danish entitled "PDK......Parti Démocratique pour le Renouveau-Ubuyanja (PDR-Ubuyanja) Udlaendingestyrelsen", dated 19 June 2003, which provided background information on this party, was available to the Migration Board. According to this document, the PDR-Ubuyanja party never developed into a fully fledged party: No party programme was ever published, no membership cards issued and no formal membership list established. Interest in supporting the party was shown by attending the few private meetings that were organized. In April 2002, the first named complainant attended a meeting in Kigali with her brother, where they met and were recruited by Mr. Ntakirutinka. The DMI would have known that the first named complainant's brother was Mr. Ntakirutinka's employee, and would, on that basis alone, have singled out both brother and sister for arrest. The same document also stated that persons who were related to members or were suspected to be members themselves would have difficulties in Rwanda, as they might be aware of PDR-Ubuyanja documents of interest to the authorities.

5.3 According to the complainants, the Swedish authorities paid little attention to the position of the UNHCR outlined in its paper of January 2004, published after the elections of 2003. It stated that early in 2004, almost two years after the arrest of Pastor Bizimungu and Mr. Ntakirutinka, those

---

[4] *X, Y and Z* v. *Sweden*, complaint N° 61/1996, Views adopted on 6 May 1998, para. 11.2

associated with the PDR-Ubuyanja party were at greatest risk inside the country . On the issue of victims of rape, the complainants quote from the paper arguing that, "The crime of rape itself and the manner in which it was committed qualify as a serious form of torture and may warrant continued international protection… The victims should favourably be considered for the granting of refugee status on the ground that their refusal to return to Rwanda is due to compelling reasons arising from previous persecution…"

5.4 The first named complainant provides an account of what happened to her while in detention and a letter from a woman, who allegedly was detained at the same time, and corroborates her claim that she was tortured during her detention. Since then, this woman has received refugee status in France. According to the complainants, this evidence was not presented during the domestic proceedings, as upon receipt the first named complainant's "case had been finally rejected and there was talk of an amnesty for families with children so she set her hopes on that."

5.5 As to the State party's argument that the statement from M.U. was undated and unsigned, the complainants explain that only the English translation was handed in to the Swedish authorities and attach for the Committee's attention the original handwritten letter signed by M.U. and M.U. was the first named complainant's neighbour in Kigali. When the complainant feared that she would be sent back to Rwanda, she contacted M.U. and M.U. expressed concern about her safety should she be expelled to Rwanda because M.U. had heard that her name had been mentioned in the gacaca procedure as one of the suspects involved in the massacre of Tutsis at the CHK hospital in Kigali in April 1994. Afterwards, M.U. wrote his letter, which is signed in the original. On 13 August 2006, C.T. telephoned M.U., as a result of which M.U. sent an e-mail to explain why it was not possible to obtain a document with the first named complainant's name on it as one of the suspects. M.U. wrote that the list is confidential and has not been published for fear that suspects will abscond. M.U. has not responded to a further request for information, to provide the name of the person that heard that the complainant was a suspect, the date this occurred etc.

5.6 As to the State party's argument that the first named complainant only raised the fact that she was accused before the gacaca court at a late stage, the complainants argue that this can be explained by the fact that the gacaca process has been going through various developments and that in 2005, more extensive witness material was gathered. It was only upon contact with M.U. that she was informed of this information. Regarding the procedure before the gacaca courts, the complainants refer to a report by Penal Reform International of June 2006, which states inter alia that the gacaca "raises serious misgivings regarding the situation of accused persons."

5.7 As to the argument that no evidence exists that PDR-Ubuyanja party members were arrested or detained since 2003, counsel states that he represented a Rwandan asylum-seeker before the Swedish authorities who had been subjected to torture while being interrogated on his involvement in the PDR-Ubuyanja party in 2004. This individual was considered credible and was granted refugee status by the Swedish authorities in 2005. As to the fact that neither the first named complainant nor her brother were cited as detainees on any of the Amnesty lists, the complainants submit that these lists were incomplete and that, according to the Danish document referred to, "some of the detainees on the Amnesty list had in reality no connection with RDR-Ubuyanja".

5.8 According to the complainants, the discrepancy in the dates in the letter from the representative of the LIPRODHOR was a typographical error and a new certificate is submitted to the Committee with the correct date. Finally, the complainants submit that a return to Rwanda in light of the heinous circumstances of the first complainant's pregnancy, where they have no immediate family, may have serious consequences for C.T.'s son as his mother may not be able to give him the help and support that he needs. He is currently attending a preschool and is being investigated to ascertain whether he suffers from a form of autism.

Issues and proceedings before the Committee

Consideration of admissibility

6.1 Before considering any claims contained in a communication, the Committee against Torture must decide whether or not it is admissible under article 22 of the Convention. The Committee has ascertained, as it is required to do under article 22, paragraph 5 (a), of the Convention, that the same matter has not been and is not being examined under another procedure of international investigation or settlement. It notes the State party's confirmation, in the submission of 15 August 2006, that domestic remedies have been exhausted.

6.2 The Committee finds that no further obstacles to the admissibility of the complaint exist, declares it admissible and thus proceeds to its consideration on the merits.

Consideration of the merits

7.1 The issue before the Committee is whether the removal of the complainants to Rwanda would violate the State party's obligation under article 3 of the Convention not to expel or to return a person to another State where there are substantial grounds for believing that he or she would be in danger of being subjected to torture.

7.2 In assessing the risk of torture, the Committee takes into account all relevant considerations, including the existence in the relevant State of a consistent pattern of gross, flagrant or mass violations of human rights. However, the aim of such determination is to establish whether the individuals concerned would be personally at risk in the country to which he or she would return. It follows that the existence of a consistent pattern of gross, flagrant or mass violations of human rights in a country does not as such constitute a sufficient ground for determining that a particular person would be in danger of being subjected to torture upon his or her return to that country; additional grounds must exist to show that the individual concerned would be personally at risk. Similarly, the absence of a consistent pattern of gross violations of human rights does not mean that a person cannot be considered to be in danger of being subjected to torture in his or her specific circumstances.

7.3 The Committee recalls its General Comment 1 on article 3, which states that the Committee is obliged to assess whether there are substantial grounds for believing that the complainant would be in danger of being subjected to torture were he/she to be expelled, returned or extradited, the risk of torture must be assessed on grounds that go beyond mere theory or suspicion. However, the risk does not have to meet the test of being highly probable. The risk need not be highly probable, but it must be personal and present. In this regard, in its jurisprudence the Committee has determined that the risk of torture must be foreseeable, real and personal.

7.4 The Committee notes the claim that if the complainants are returned to Rwanda they will be detained and tortured, on the basis of the first named complainant's involvement in the PDR-Ubuyanja party, for which reason she was detained and subjected to torture. She also fears that she may be tried before the gacaca courts. On this latter issue, without wishing to consider whether the gacaca courts meet international standards of due process, the Committee considers that fear of a future trial before them is in itself insufficient to amount to a reasonable fear of torture.

7.5 As to the first named complainant's claim of past torture due to her political activism, the Committee notes that the State party questions her credibility due to her vagueness, inconsistency and lack of evidence in her account of and involvement in the PDR-Ubuyanja party and the argument that she would not suffer torture given the developments after the elections in 2003. The Committee notes that the State party did not contest, during the domestic proceedings, nor in its submission to the Committee, the first named complainant's claim (supported by two medical reports) that she was repeatedly raped in detention, as a result of which she became pregnant, and gave birth to her son in Sweden. In fact, on a review of the decisions of the domestic authorities, it would appear that these medical reports were not taken into account at all and that the issue of whether or not the complainant had been raped and the consequences thereof for her and her son were not considered. Thus, on the basis of the medical evidence provided, and the State party's failure to dispute the claim, the Committee considers that the first named complainant was repeatedly raped in detention and as such was subjected to torture in the past. On examining the dates of her detention and the date of birth of her son, the Committee considers it without doubt that he was the product of rape by public officials, and is thus a constant reminder to the first named complainant of her rape.

7.6 On the State party's general argument that the first named complainant is not credible, the Committee recalls its jurisprudence that complete accuracy is seldom to be expected by victims of torture and that such inconsistencies as may exist in the complainant's presentation of the facts are not material and do not raise doubts about the general veracity of her claims, especially since it has been demonstrated that she was repeatedly subjected to rape in detention.[5] The Committee also takes into account the revised letter from LIPRODHOR (para. 5.8), the authenticity of which has not been contested by the State party, which attests to the first named complainant's arrest along with her brother by the Directory of Military Intelligence.

7.7 As to the general situation in Rwanda, the Committee considers that information provided by the complainants demonstrates that ethnic tensions continue to exist, thus increasing the likelihood that the first named complainant may be subjected to torture on return to Rwanda. For the above reasons, the Committee considers that substantial grounds exist for believing that the complainants would be in danger of being subjected to torture if returned to Rwanda.

8. The Committee against Torture, acting under article 22, paragraph 7, of the Convention against Torture and Other Cruel, Inhuman or Degrading Treatment or Punishment, concludes that the removal of the complainants to Rwanda would amount to a breach of article 3 of the Convention.

---

[5] *Alan* v. *Switzerland*, case N° 21/1995, Decision adopted on 8 May 1996, *Tala* v. *Sweden*, case N° 43/1996, Decision adopted 15 November 1996, *Kisoki* v. *Sweden*, case N° 41/1996, Decision adopted on 8 May 1996.

9. The Committee urges the State party, in accordance with rule 112, paragraph 5, of its rules of procedure, to inform it, within 90 days from the date of the transmittal of this decision, of the steps taken in response to the Views expressed above.

Communication N° 280/2005

Submitted by: Gamal El Rgeig (represented by counsel)
Alleged victim: The complainant
State party: Switzerland
Date of adoption of Views: 15 November 2006

Subject matter: deportation of complainant to Libyan Arab Jamahiriya with alleged risk of torture

Procedural issue: none

Substantive issue: risk of torture after deportation

Article of the Convention: 3

1.1 The complainant is Gamal El Rgeig, a Libyan national born in 1969, currently residing in Switzerland where he submitted an application for asylum on 10 June 2003; the application was rejected on 5 March 2004. He claims that his deportation to the Libyan Arab Jamahiriya would constitute a violation by Switzerland of his rights under article 3 of the Convention against Torture and Other Cruel, Inhuman or Degrading Treatment or Punishment. He is represented by counsel.

1.2 On 16 September 2005, in accordance with rule 108, paragraph 1, of its rules of procedure, the Committee, acting through its Rapporteur for new complaints and interim measures, requested the State party to suspend the expulsion of the complainant while his complaint was being considered. In a note verbale dated 27 October 2005, the State party informed the Committee that it acceded to this request.

The facts as submitted by the complainant

2.1 In February 1989, the complainant was arrested for his "political activities" and was held at the Abu Salim prison for six years, without ever having been accused or tried. He claims that, during his detention, he was repeatedly subjected to ill-treatment and acts of torture.

2.2 The complainant was released in 1995 and allegedly continued to be harassed by the security forces. He claims to have been summoned regularly to the security office where he was threatened and tortured and, in 2000, State agents allegedly burst into his home to confiscate his computer. He alleges that, following that incident, he was arrested and tortured on several occasions. The last arrest took place in 2002, and on that occasion the acts of torture were more severe.

2.3 In March 2003, he learned that one of his friends, who had been imprisoned at the same time as the complainant and for the same reasons, had been sent to prison again because his name appeared on a list. The complainant concluded that his name also appeared on that list. Following these events, the complainant left the Libyan Arab Jamahiriya for Egypt, where he claims to have obtained an Italian visa through "an acquaintance" at the Italian Embassy. He arrived in Italy, and from there proceeded to Switzerland. On 10 June 2003, upon his arrival in Switzerland, he filed an application for asylum and produced official documents indicating that he had been imprisoned for six years, as well as one of the summonses, dated December 1997, that he had received after his release.

2.4 The complainant states that he continued his political activities in Switzerland, where he maintained contact with various organizations and associations campaigning for human rights in the Libyan Arab Jamahiriya. He claims that he received two letters from his family informing him that the security forces had come looking for him on several occasions and that they had threatened members of his family. Following those events, his family was forced to move.

2.5 On 5 March 2004, the complainant's application for asylum was rejected by the Federal Office for Refugees, now the Federal Office for Migration, which ordered his expulsion from Swiss territory by 30 April 2004. The complainant notes that the Federal Office for Refugees acknowledged that he had been imprisoned without trial, but concluded that it had not been established that he had been tortured and persecuted after his release in 1995. On 5 April 2004, the complainant lodged an appeal against this decision and, on 7 July 2004, the Swiss Asylum Review Board rejected the appeal, considering that there were many factual inconsistencies in the complainant's allegations and that his presentation of the facts was not believable. The Commission therefore upheld the decision of the Federal Office for Refugees, ordering the complainant's return under threat of expulsion.

2.6 On 8 September 2005, the Geneva Police Commissioner issued an order for the administrative detention of the complainant. On 9 September 2005, the Cantonal Aliens Appeal Board (*Commission cantonale de recours en matière de police des étrangers*) upheld the order for the complainant's detention for a period of one month, that is, until 8 October 2005. On 19 September 2005, the complainant appealed to the Geneva Administrative Tribunal against the decision of the Geneva Cantonal Aliens Appeal Board of 9 September 2005, which upheld the order for his administrative detention. Attached to his appeal to the Administrative Tribunal were letters in support of his application for asylum from non-governmental organizations that deal with the Libyan Arab Jamahiriya and political refugees in Switzerland. The complainant was released on an unspecified date, and on 27 September 2006, the Administrative Tribunal decided to strike his appeal from the list of cases, since it was no longer necessary.[1]

The complaint

3. According to the complainant, the Federal Office for Refugees acknowledged that he had been imprisoned for six years without trial but considered that he had not succeeded in proving that he had been persecuted between 1995 and 2003, whereas it had been impossible to adduce the evidence to that effect. The Swiss authorities had apparently not examined the recent reports published by various international observers concerning cases of detention and torture in the Libyan Arab Jamahiriya. The complainant maintains that there are substantial grounds for believing that he would be subjected to torture if he were returned to the Libyan Arab Jamahiriya and that, consequently, his expulsion to that country would constitute a violation by Switzerland of article 3 of the Convention.

State party's merits observations

4.1 In a note verbale dated 27 October 2005, the State party declared that it did not contest the admissibility of the complaint, and on 16 March 2006, it submitted its observations on the merits. With regard to the effectiveness of the appeal to the Administrative Tribunal of Geneva Canton, the State party observes that the sole subject of that procedure was the lawfulness of the administrative detention, and that it did not affect the binding nature of the decision of the Federal Office for Migration ordering the complainant's expulsion. The State party concludes that the appeal to the Administrative Tribunal can therefore not be deemed effective, and recalls that it has not contested the admissibility of the complaint.

4.2 The State party emphasizes that the complainant does not adduce any relevant new evidence that would enable him to challenge the decision of the Asylum Review Board. It notes that, following a thorough examination of the complainant's allegations, the Board, like the Federal Office for Migration, was not convinced that the complainant ran a serious risk of being persecuted if he was returned to the Libyan Arab Jamahiriya.

4.3 Having recalled the Committee's jurisprudence and its General Comment 1 on the implementation of article 3, the State party endorses the grounds cited by the Asylum Review Board substantiating its decisions to reject the complainant's application for asylum and to uphold his expulsion. It recalls the Committee's jurisprudence whereby the existence of a consistent pattern of gross, flagrant or mass violations of human rights does not constitute sufficient reason for concluding that a particular individual is likely to be subjected to torture on return to his or her country, and that additional grounds must therefore exist before the likelihood of torture can be deemed to be, for the purposes of article 3, paragraph 1, "foreseeable, real and personal".

4.4 The State party maintains that, since the complainant was released on 2 March 1995, there is no temporal link between the complainant's detention and his flight in 2003; this was allegedly confirmed by the complainant during his registration hearing on 13 June 2003. At the hearing, the complainant confirmed that he had not had any problem with the authorities after his release and had left the Libyan Arab Jamahiriya because he had been unable to find work there. He added that he was "afraid of going back to prison". These assertions apparently contradict the statements made by the complainant during his cantonal hearing, where he claimed that he had been continually persecuted after his release in 1995 owing to his dissemination of ideas relating to freedom of expression and a multiparty system. Even if the complainant later changed the reasons for his flight by referring to persistent harassment and ill-treatment because of his political convictions, the situation of dissidents in the Libyan Arab Jamahiriya does not in itself make it possible to conclude that he is likely to be subjected to torture on return to his country. The State party adds that the complainant has not provided the least shred of evidence that would make it possible to conclude that the security forces had continued to harass or maltreat him after his release. The 1997 summons instructing the complainant to report to the El Barak security office cannot alter this conclusion.

4.5 The State party recalls that the complainant not only remained in the Libyan Arab Jamahiriya for eight years after his release but also that he returned

---

[1] On this subject, see also para. 5.1 of this decision.

after a trip to Egypt in 2001. On that occasion, in spite of the fact that the complainant, according to his own allegations, had been forbidden to travel by the authorities, no proceedings were instituted against him, although the authorities had stamped his passport on his departure and return to the country. The State party also finds it surprising that the complainant had been able to obtain a passport without any difficulty in August 1998.

4.6 The State party notes that there were a number of inconsistencies in the supporting documents from non-governmental organizations attached to the complainant's appeal to the Asylum Review Board and that, in particular, contrary to the statements made by the complainant during the cantonal hearing to the effect that he had always worked alone, some of these documents maintain that he had been active in political groups. For the most part, these documents mention only that the complainant had been imprisoned between 1989 and 1995.

4.7 The State party also takes note of the two letters from members of the complainant's family, dated 5 March 2004 and 6 June 2005, in which they claimed that they were being harassed by the security forces and felt forced to move. It notes that the complainant himself had never felt such a need. The State party finds it surprising that the complainant did not inform the Asylum Review Board of the existence of the letter of 5 March 2004 when he submitted further observations concerning his appeal.

4.8 The State party concludes that the application is completely unfounded and requests the Rapporteur for new complaints and interim measures to lift the interim measures and the Committee to consider the complaint at its earliest convenience.

Complainant's comments

5.1 The complainant notes that the appeal lodged with the Geneva Administrative Tribunal has been withdrawn because it is no longer necessary following his release.

5.2 He reiterates the facts, particularly his detention for six years in the Libyan Arab Jamahiriya and the torture to which he was subjected. He refers to a medical certificate issued in April 2006 by a physician of the Geneva University Hospitals who specializes in the treatment of victims of torture and war attesting to the existence of physical and psychological after-effects that are consistent with the complainant's allegations.

5.3 The complainant recalls that, in Switzerland, he continued to take part in activities to promote human rights in the Libyan Arab Jamahiriya and participated in a public demonstration, and that the Libyan services in Geneva closely monitor this type of activity. He claims that he was continually questioned about his actions when he was still in the Libyan Arab Jamahiriya and that his actions in Switzerland were clearly under surveillance. Moreover, he states that his family is regularly questioned about his activities and whereabouts. The complainant refers to a letter dated 5 March 2004 from a friend who visited his family in the Libyan Arab Jamahiriya and who claimed that they were being harassed by the security forces, and advised him not to return home. He refers to a detailed report of the Swiss section of Amnesty International on the deportation of Libyan asylum-seekers to their country of origin.

5.4 The complainant submits the following documents: the decision of the Geneva Administrative Tribunal of 26 September 2005; an attestation from the Libyan internal security service dated 17 May 2003; a copy of a letter from his friend dated 5 March 2004; attestations of support from Libyan non-governmental organizations, as well as copies of several reports of international non-governmental organizations; and the observations and recommendations of the Committee against Torture on reports submitted by the Libyan Arab Jamahiriya in 1999 and 2005.

5.5 With regard to the alleged factual inconsistencies, the complainant denies that they have any bearing on the merits of the case. He claims that his only error is to have stated, at the time of his first interview in Switzerland, that he had left the Libyan Arab Jamahiriya because he could not find any work there. He had felt very ill at ease during that interview and had not been able to express himself clearly. Moreover, he had not really understood what was taking place and what was expected of him: he had been constantly encouraged to be brief. He had nevertheless added that he had always lived in fear in the Libyan Arab Jamahiriya. As can be ascertained from the reports of several international and non-governmental organizations, the situation in the Libyan Arab Jamahiriya has not improved. The complainant considers that, in so far as he had been tortured and persecuted when he lived in the Libyan Arab Jamahiriya, where his family continues to be threatened, and in view of the fact that he is under surveillance in Switzerland, he will again be subjected to torture if he is expelled.

Issues and proceedings before the Committee

Consideration of admissibility

6. Before considering any claim contained in a communication, the Committee must decide whether or not it is admissible under article 22 of the Convention. The Committee has ascertained, as it is required to do under article 22, paragraph 5 (a), of the Convention, that the same matter has not been, and is not being, examined under another procedure of international investigation or settlement. In the

present case, the State party has not contested admissibility. The Committee therefore considers that the complaint is admissible.

Consideration of the merits

7.1 With regard to the merits, the Committee must rule on whether the return of the complainant to the Libyan Arab Jamahiriya would constitute a violation of the obligation of the State party, under article 3 of the Convention, not to expel or return a person to a State where there are substantial grounds for believing that he would be in danger of being subjected to torture.

7.2 The Committee must determine, pursuant to article 3, paragraph 1, whether there are substantial grounds for believing that the complainant would be in danger of being subjected to torture if he was returned to the Libyan Arab Jamahiriya. In order to take such a decision, the Committee must take account of all relevant considerations, in accordance with article 3, paragraph 2, including the existence of a consistent pattern of gross, flagrant or mass violations of human rights. However, the aim of such an analysis is to determine whether the complainant runs a personal risk of being subjected to torture in the country to which he would be returned. The Committee recalls its established jurisprudence whereby the existence in a country of a consistent pattern of gross, flagrant or mass violations of human rights does not as such constitute sufficient grounds for determining that a particular person would be in danger of being subjected to torture on return to that country.[2] Additional grounds must be adduced to show that the individual concerned would be personally at risk. Conversely, the absence of a consistent pattern of flagrant violations of human rights does not mean that a person might not be subjected to torture in his or her specific circumstances.

7.3 The Committee recalls its General Comment 1 on the implementation of article 3, in which it states that it is obliged to assess whether there are substantial grounds for believing that the complainant would be in danger of being subjected to torture if he or she were returned to the country concerned, and that the existence of such a risk must be assessed on grounds that go beyond mere theory or suspicion. While the risk does not have to meet the test of being highly probable, the danger must be personal and present. It also notes that the State party contends that there is no temporal link between the complainant's detention and his flight from the country, and that the complainant's statements contain many inconsistencies and contradictions. It takes note of the information supplied by the complainant in that regard, particularly that he had been ill at ease during his first interview, as well as the documents supporting his application for asylum in Switzerland.

7.4 Nevertheless, and leaving aside his past activities, the complainant has submitted to the Committee in connection with this communication attestations from organizations of Libyan refugees in Europe indicating the support he has provided to their organizations, as well as his earlier political activities before he left the Libyan Arab Jamahiriya, and his relations with opposition religious movements which are banned in the Libyan Arab Jamahiriya and whose members are persecuted. The complainant has also referred to meetings with representatives of the Libyan consular authorities in Geneva, who had objected to his having lodged a request for political asylum. Lastly, he has submitted a copy of a medical certificate dated 24 April 2006 in which a specialist in post-traumatic disorders from a Geneva hospital identified a causal link between the complainant's bodily injuries, his psychological state and the ill-treatment he described at the time of his medical examination. According to this doctor, in his present psychological state, the complainant does not appear capable of coping with a forcible return to the Libyan Arab Jamahiriya, and such coercive action would entail a definite risk to his health. The State party has made no comments in this regard. In the specific circumstance of this case, and in particular in the light of the findings in the above-mentioned medical report on the presence of serious after-effects of the acts of torture inflicted on the complainant, his political activities subsequent to his departure from the Libyan Arab Jamahiriya (as described in paras. 2.4 and 5.3 above), and the persistent reports concerning the treatment generally meted out to such activists when they are forcibly returned to the Libyan Arab Jamahiriya, the Committee considers that the State party has not presented to it sufficiently convincing arguments to demonstrate a complete absence of risk that the complainant would be exposed to torture if he were to be forcibly returned to the Libyan Arab Jamahiriya.

8. The Committee against Torture, acting under article 22, paragraph 7, of the Convention, is of the view that the forcible return of the complainant to the Libyan Arab Jamahiriya would constitute a breach by Switzerland of his rights under article 3 of the Convention.

9. In pursuance of rule 112, paragraph 5, of its rules of procedure, the Committee invites the State party to inform it, within 90 days from the date of the transmittal of these Views, of the steps it has taken in accordance with the above observations.

---

[2] See, for example, *S.S.H.* v. *Switzerland*, communication N° 254/2004, decision adopted on 15 November 2005, para. 6.3.

Communication N° 282/2005

Submitted by: S.P.A. (represented by counsel)
Alleged victim: The complainant
State party: Canada
Date of adoption of Views: 7 November 2006

Subject matter: deportation of complainant to Iran with alleged risk of torture

Procedural issue: non-substantiation of allegations

Substantive issue: risk of torture after deportation

Articles of the Convention: 3, 16

1.1 The complainant is S.P.A., an Iranian national born in 1954 in Tonkabon, Iran, currently residing in Canada, from where she faces deportation. She claims that her return to Iran would constitute a violation by Canada of articles 3 and 16 of the Convention against Torture and Other Cruel, Inhuman or Degrading Treatment. She is represented by counsel.

1.2 In accordance with article 22, paragraph 3, of the Convention, the Committee transmitted the communication to the State party on 27 September 2005, and requested it, under rule 108, paragraph 1, of the Committee's rules of procedure, not to expel the complainant to Iran while her complaint is under consideration by the Committee. The State party subsequently informed the Committee that the complainant had not been deported.

The facts as presented by the complainant

2.1 The complainant obtained a nursing degree in 1986 in Iran, and became a supervisory nurse at the Rejai Hospital and a lecturer at the Islamic Azad University of Mahal Salas Tonkabon. One of her responsibilities was the purchase of nursing supplies, including bones and cadavers for teaching purposes. Sometime in late 1999, she noticed the poor quality of bones delivered: they showed signs of fractures and it was obvious to her that the individuals had suffered trauma before their deaths. The complainant advised M., the supplier, that she could not use the bones, upon which she wrote a report to the Dean of the University. The next set of bones provided were in perfect condition. Upon querying the origin of this later set of bones, the complainant was informed by M. that the first set were taken from "anti revolutionary groups" while the second were obtained by raiding an Armenian cemetery. The complainant was distressed by this information and went to the Magistrate for Islamic law to discuss the matter, which she believed was a religious one. The Magistrate advised that he would look into the matter.

2.2 On subsequent occasions the complainant noted that the cadavers delivered were of light skin, and on enquiry was told they had been taken from a Baha'i cemetery. She complained again to the Magistrate, who told her that he had ordered that bodies be taken from the Baha'i cemetery, as their religion was below Islam. The complainant argued with him and was accused of being an anti-revolutionary. That evening, the complainant was arrested without charge in her home and taken to a basement room belonging to the Ministry of Intelligence and Security, where she was interrogated while blindfolded. Despite her explanations, she was accused of insulting the Islamic religion, was tortured and beaten. She was kept in a cell and interrogated every night, still blindfolded. She was beaten with sticks and wires, kicked, insulted and taunted. She was given electric shocks and forced to stand for hours without sleep. The injuries on her head were particularly severe and kept bleeding, and her toes were bruised and bloody.

2.3 After two months and because of her bleeding, she was put into a car one night after midnight and taken for medical care. On the way, the driver stopped, got out of the car and left it unlocked. The complainant got out of the car and climbed into the back seat of the first car which was parked near by. She managed to tell the driver her name and address and asked him to take her home, before she lost consciousness. The driver of the car recognized her, and took her to Rasht where her wounds were tended to. The complainant fell in and out of consciousness. When she recovered she was told that she was in Kermanshar and in a safe place. Those who took care of her for several months advised her to leave Iran. They assisted her in obtaining her passport from her family and through a smuggler she travelled to Dubai and then to Colombia. She advised the smuggler that she did not wish to stay in Colombia and therefore travelled to Turkey, Greece, Spain, Jamaica, Mexico and then Canada. Upon her arrival in Canada on 10 September 2001 she made a claim for refugee status.

2.4 She was subsequently informed by relatives in Iran that the authorities were looking for her and that they had been to her sister's house with several summons for her arrest. They had threatened her daughter and asked to speak to her husband. She was also informed that the driver who was taking her from her detention place to obtain medical care had been bribed, and was supposed to take her back to her family. As she had escaped, her family had not known her whereabouts for a month and a half, at which time the people in Kermanshar had contacted them. Finally, the complainant was told that the people in Kermanshar had been paid by her family to care for her and help her to leave Iran.

2.5 The complainant's application for refugee status on the basis of her political opinion was rejected on 2 May 2003. On 23 May 2003, she filed an application for leave and judicial review of this decision, which was denied on 16 September 2003. On 25 March 2004 she filed an application for consideration under section 25(1) of the Immigration and Refugee Protection Act (humanitarian and compassionate grounds application, 'H&C'), providing new evidence that she had been employed as the Supervisor of Nursing and an Instructor at the University of Mahal Salas Tonekabon. She also submitted a pre-removal risk assessment ('PRRA') application on 13 August 2004, and subsequently submitted new evidence in the form of letters from her daughter and sister, and a court summons dated 22 December 2003 from the Tehran Islamic Revolutionary Court, requiring her to attend court on 6 January 2004. The H&C and PRRA applications were denied by the same officer and notified to the complainant on 16 August 2005. An application for leave and judicial review of the PRRA and H&C decisions was filed in the Federal Court on 25 August 2004. Her application for stay of removal was denied on 26 September 2005.

2.6 The complainant was scheduled to be deported to Iran on 27 September 2005. The application for leave to apply for judicial review of both the PRRA and H&C decisions was subsequently dismissed on 1 December 2005.

The complaint

3.1 The complainant argues that she would be imprisoned, tortured or even killed if returned to Iran, in violation of articles 3 and 16 of the Convention. This is based on the fact she is a known perceived opponent of the Iranian regime and the fact a passport was applied for on her behalf, thereby alerting the Iranian authorities of her imminent return. There is a court summons in her name, and as she missed the court date, based on objective country information there will most likely be a warrant for her arrest. Counsel refers to the United Kingdom Country Report from the Immigration and Nationality Directorate Home Office from October 2003, which states that the traditional court system in Iran is not independent and is subject to Government and religious interference. The report states that trials in the Revolutionary Courts, where crimes against national security and other principal offences are heard, are notorious for their disregard of international standards of fairness. Revolutionary Court judges act as prosecutor and judge in the same case, and judges are chosen for their ideological commitment to the system. Indictments lack clarity and refer to undefined offences such as 'anti-revolutionary behaviour'. Counsel claims that those accused of 'anti-revolutionary behaviour' are dealt with unfairly once detained: although the Constitution prohibits arbitrary arrest and detention, there is reportedly no legal time limit on incommunicado detention, nor any judicial means to determine the legality of the detention. Further, female prisoners are repeatedly raped or otherwise tortured while in detention, and there are widespread reports of extra judicial killings, torture, harsh prison conditions, and disappearances.

3.2 Counsel submits a medical certificate dated 22 June 2005 based on the complainant's Personal Information Form and a clinical interview and exam performed on 17 June 2005, which concludes that there is evidence of multiple scars on her body. Significant wounds are on her face and scalp, and are consistent with a mechanism of blunt trauma as described by her. The irregular depressed scar on the top of her head is said to be consistent with her description of a lesion that was left open and sutured at a later date. The scars on her arms and legs are more non-specific but are consistent with blunt trauma. The bilateral toenail onycholysis is typical for post-traumatic nail injury and could certainly have resulted from being stepped on repeatedly as she has described. The medical report concludes that her psychological history is consistent with post-traumatic stress disorder-chronic.

3.3 Counsel argues that the PRRA officer did not assess the risk as the officer seemed to determine that the complainant was not credible, despite this independent physician's report that her injuries were consistent with the information provided in her Personal Information Form. Further, counsel highlights that the PRRA officer did not determine that the warrant for the complainant's arrest was not genuine.

State party's admissibility and merits observations

4.1 On 27 June 2006, the State party argues, on article 3, that the communication is inadmissible as manifestly unfounded as the complainant has not substantiated her allegations even on a prima facie basis. Her communication is based on the same story that competent domestic tribunals have determined to lack credibility and plausibility. On article 16, the complainant has made no attempt to substantiate her claim and it is therefore also inadmissible as manifestly unfounded. Apart from the complete absence of evidence on this point, according to the Committee's jurisprudence, the potential aggravation of a complainant's state of health possibly caused by deportation does not amount to the type of cruel, inhuman or degrading treatment envisaged by article 16.[1]

4.2 With regard to the scope of article 3, the State party recalls that it refers to "substantial grounds" for believing that a person would be in danger of being subjected to torture, and that the Committee's General Comment on article 3 places the burden on the complainant to establish that she would be in danger of being torture. The grounds on which a claim is established must be substantial and must "go beyond mere theory or suspicion", as confirmed by the Committee in numerous decisions. Consideration of the relevant factors leads to the conclusion that there are no substantial grounds for believing that the complainant would be in danger of being subject to torture. In particular, her credibility is highly suspect and her claim inconsistent and implausible. There are no credible reasons to consider that she fits the personal profile of someone who would be of interest to the Iranian authorities or particularly vulnerable if returned to Iran.

4.3 With regard to the credibility and plausibility of the allegations and the Committee's scope of review, the State party concedes that the Committee does not expect complete accuracy from the complainant. What is required is that the evidence may be considered "sufficiently substantiated and reliable."[2] Nevertheless, important inconsistencies in the present case are "pertinent to the Committee's deliberations as to whether the complainant would be in danger of being tortured upon return."[3] It is not the role of the Committee to weigh evidence or reassess findings of fact by domestic courts, tribunals or decision makers.[4] The complainant's allegations and supporting evidence are identical to that submitted to competent, impartial domestic tribunals and decision makers and that were found not to support a finding of risk in Iran. The analysis of the evidence and the conclusions drawn by the Immigration Refugee Board as well as by the PRRA officer who assessed the risk to which she may be exposed if returned to Iran were appropriate and well-founded.

4.4 The State party recalls that the Committee cannot review credibility findings "unless it is manifest that the evaluation was arbitrary or amounted to a denial of justice". The complainant made no such allegations and the material submitted does not support a finding that the Board's decision suffered from such defects.[5] Nothing suggests that domestic authorities had any doubts concerning their assessment, nor is there any evidence that the domestic authorities' review was anything other than fully satisfactory: the complainant is simply dissatisfied with the results of the domestic proceedings and the prospects of deportation, but made no allegations or produced any evidence that the proceedings were in any way deficient. Accordingly there are no grounds on which the Committee could consider that it is necessary for it to re-evaluate the findings of fact and credibility made by the domestic tribunals. Nevertheless, should be Committee be inclined to assess the credibility of the complainant, a focus on some of the more important issues clearly supports a finding that the complainant's story simply cannot be believed.

4.5 With regard to her role at the University, the complainant asserted in her Personal Information Form that she was in charge of purchasing all supplies necessary for the nursing faculty and that the University had an arrangement for six years with the supplier of bones. However, in the oral testimony, she stated that she was in charge of ordering bones and that these began to be ordered in 1998, only one year before her problems began. With regard to her arrest and torture, she stated in her Personal Information Form that she recognized the voice of her first cousin, a member of the Ministry, as one of her interrogators. However, in the oral testimony, she stated that her first cousin was among those who arrested her.

4.6 With regard to the complainant's account of her escape, the State party shares the IRB's assessment that it was "unbelievable" and "exaggerated and implausible." In any case, even if it were accepted that the man who was driving her to the medical centre had been bribed by her family, it is implausible that he would leave to allow her to get into another car which coincidentally belonged to someone who recognized her, and that this stranger would not take her to a hospital if she was bleeding and had fainted. It is also not plausible that she would live in a house full of strangers yet not know even after four months of living with them who they were or what their names were, and would not ask to contact her family during all that time.

4.7 With regard to her exit from Iran, the complainant's Personal Information Form indicated

---

[1] The State party refers to communication N° 183/2001, *B.S.S.* v. *Canada*, Views adopted on 12 May 2004, para. 10.2.
[2] The State party refers to communication N° 34/1995, *Aemei* v. *Switzerland*, Views adopted on 9 May 1997, para. 9.6.
[3] Communication N° 148/1999, *A.K.* v. *Australia*, Views adopted on 5 May 2004, para. 6.2; and communication N° 106/1998, *N.P.* v. *Australia*, Views adopted on 6 May 1999, para. 6.6.
[4] The State party refers, inter alia, to communication N° 148/1999, *A.K.* v. *Australia*, Views adopted on 5 May 2004, para. 6.4.

[5] The State party refers, inter alia, to communication N° 223/2002, *S.U.A.* v. *Sweden*, Views adopted on 22 November 2004, para. 6.5.

that strangers helped her obtain her passport from her family. However, in her oral testimony, she claimed that she left Iran with a false passport. She claims that she needed an exit visa; it was implausible that she would have received such a visa if she was escaping the authorities. The State party shares the finding of the IRB that it is "practically impossible to leave Iran through the Tehran airport if a person is sought by the Iranian authorities. It is also almost impossible to obtain false passports because of the many check-ups conducted before getting on the plane". The complainant has not submitted any evidence that would be capable of casting doubt on this finding.

4.8 With regard to the delay in seeking refugee protection, the complainant travelled for two months through Colombia, Turkey, Greece, Spain, Jamaica and Mexico, before coming to Canada and filing a refugee claim. The delay in making a refugee claim detracts from her credibility. Under domestic and international refugee law jurisprudence, a delay in filing a refugee claim is a relevant factor to be taken into account in assessing whether the complainant has a subjective and objective fear of persecution.

4.9 With regard to the existence of a summons, although the refugee claim was made in September 2001, the complainant failed to present documentary evidence to corroborate her claim before it was heard in November 2002. Although she was in telephone contact with her family, she did not tell the IRB if there was an arrest warrant out in her name, and it was not until her claim was rejected that she submitted, as part of her PRRA application, a "summons" dated 22 December 2003. It is implausible that a summons would be issued more than two years after the complainant's alleged escape from detention. If the authorities had been looking for her since her escape, it is implausible that her family would have simply destroyed the other notices of summons as their letters claim, nor even mentioned the existence of the notices during their phone conversations with her. The State party thus shares the PRRA officer's findings about the minimal probative weight of the purported summons. In addition, there is no evidence or allegation that any member of her family was detained or mistreated. With regard to the existence of an arrest warrant, the State party emphasizes that there is no such warrant despite the complainant's claims.

4.10 As far as the medical evidence is concerned, the complainant produced a medical report dated 22 June 2005 in support of her PRRA application. The PRRA Officer did not consider the report to be probative of future risk, because the physician's opinion was based on his/her consideration of the complainant's Personal Information Form and a clinical interview. The existence of scars does not, by itself, establish that the complainant had been a victim of torture in the past or would face a substantial risk of torture in the future. In the light of the complainant's overall lack of credibility and the implausibility of central aspects of her claim, particularly since it is unsupported by other independent and reliable evidence, the alleged cause of the scarring is implausible. Most significantly, the scarring, while perhaps evidence of past torture is insufficient to substantiate that the complainant would be at risk of torture *in the future*.

4.11 Finally, although the State party concedes that the general human rights situation in Iran is poor and deteriorating, it notes that because the country to which the complainant would be returned is Iran does not by itself constitute sufficient grounds for determining that she would be in danger of being subjected to torture upon her return.[6]

Complainant's comments

5.1 On 6 September 2006, the complainant argues that the jurisdiction of the Committee *does* include an independent review of the facts.[7] Its role would be redundant if it were merely to follow the decisions of domestic tribunals without any independent assessment of the case.[8] Further, the IRB, the only comprehensive evaluation of her case, failed to recognize the effects of torture or trauma on a person's ability to recount her story. With regard to her credibility, the complainant argues that the evidence of four independent medical and psychological experts as well as letters from the Vancouver Association for Survivors of Torture about her psychological state and the scars on her body corroborate her account of being tortured. She recalls that torture affects one's ability to recount traumatic experiences in a coherent and consistent manner, and that complete accuracy is seldom to be expected from victims of torture, especially those suffering post-traumatic stress disorder.

5.2 With regard to the State party's argument that the complainant's case has been reviewed by "competent, domestic tribunals", and firstly as to the Immigration and Refugee Board ('IRB'), the complainant notes that there is no reference whatsoever to training of IRB members on the effects of trauma or torture. There is also no reference to training on how IRB members understand or use medical and psychological reports as a tool in the assessment of credibility. The complainant recalls that at no time during the hearing did the IRB member appear to recognize that she displayed classic symptoms of trauma. The IRB

---

[6] The State party refers, inter alia, to communication N° 256/2004, *M.Z. v. Sweden*, Views adopted on 12 May 2006, para. 9.6.
[7] Counsel refers to communication N° 258/2004, *Dadar v. Canada*, Views adopted on 23 November 2005, para. 8.8.
[8] Ibid.

member who heard her refugee application on 28 November 2002 had limited, if any, expertise in the effects of trauma or torture. Consequently, the member was distracted by minor inconsistencies in the testimony and failed to give due weight to the expert report of a psychologist, which was filed with the IRB on 10 September 2003. Since the IRB member found the complainant not credible, the psychological assessment was ignored. In other words, the Member assessed the complainant's credibility without considering the effects of depression and PTSD, then dismissed the psychological report as irrelevant.

5.3 While the State party argues that the complainant benefited from several reviews by independent, competent tribunals after the refugee hearing, she submits that this is a misleading description of the process for failed refugee claimants. Indeed, judicial review is an extremely narrow remedy, available only on technical legal grounds, and applicants must obtain leave from the Court before they can proceed to judicial review. From 1998 to 2004, the Federal Court denied leave in 89 per cent of cases. Of the 11 per cent who were granted leave, only 1.6 per cent of negative decisions by the IRB were overturned by the Federal Court.

5.4 With regard to the PRRA, the complainant recalls that its scope is limited to "new evidence", not arguments that the initial decision by the IRB was wrong, and that in 2003 only 2.6 per cent of PRRA applications were approved. She also recalls that she submitted new evidence which her family had sent her and that had not been available at the time of the IRB hearing. She filed a medical report confirming the scars on her body, evidence that she worked at Azad University, and a writ of summons issued by the Tehran Islamic Revolutionary Court. The PRRA officer rejected her application in July 2005 on the basis of lack of corroborating evidence. She emphasized that her jurisdiction was limited to review of "new evidence" and refused to consider the newly available documents relating to the complainant's employment at the University because, in her opinion, the documents should have been obtained *before* the refugee hearing and therefore could not be considered as new evidence. In fact, the documents were found in storage at the complainant's mother's home.

5.5 While the PRRA officer did not contest that there was significant, unusual scarring on the complainant's head, scalp and body, she dismissed the medical report because the doctor's opinion was based on a "clinical interview" with the complainant and a review of her Personal Information Form. These comments reflect a complete lack of training or understanding about the nature of medical evidence. Thus, the complainant argues that crucial medical and psychological evidence have never been properly considered at any stage of the refugee process. The dismissal by the PRRA officer of the medical evidence was arbitrary, unreasonable and completely incorrect. As to the writ of summons, the PRRA officer accorded it "minimal weight", drawing on research concerning criminal proceedings in Iran. This is an inappropriate comparison as the writ indicates that it was issued by the Islamic Revolutionary Court, which presides over religious matters.

5.6 With regard to the H&C decision, the complainant recalls that the Committee has noted its limitations[9] and that in the present case the H&C review and the PRRA were performed by the same officer. In her decision on the H&C, the officer referred to her findings in the PRRA and many of the paragraphs in the PRRA are copied verbatim in the H&C. It is submitted that the H&C was not an independent review and suffered from the same flaws as the PRRA.

5.7 With regard to inconsistencies in her testimony, the complainant submits that none of them go to the heart of her account and that her overall account has always been consistent. She recalls that the Committee has frequently acknowledged that complete accuracy is seldom to be expected by victims of torture.[10] It has also held that a medical diagnosis of post-traumatic stress disorder is a relevant factor in considering whether inconsistencies detract from a claimant's credibility.[11] Finally, as to the delay in seeking protection, the Convention for the protection of refugees does not require that a refugee seek protection in the first State to which he flees.

5.8 With regard to the human rights situation in Iran, the complainant recalls that the Committee has previously taken note of the serious human rights situation in Iran in finding that an applicant should not be *refouled* to that country.[12] She submits that the situation in Iran has not improved, and recalls that the General Assembly has recently expressed serious concern at the continuing human rights violations taking place there.[13] The Committee has persuasive evidence corroborating that the complainant was tortured by the Iranian authorities,

---

[9] Counsel refers to communication N° 133/1999, *Enrique Falcon Ríos* v. *Canada*, Views adopted on 23 November 2004.
[10] Counsel refers to communications N° 21/1995, *Ismail Alan* v. *Switzerland*, Views adopted on 8 May 1996; and N° 41/1996, *Pauline Muzonzo Paku Kisoki* v. *Sweden*, Views adopted on 8 May 1996.
[11] Counsel refers to communication N° 43/1996, *Kaveh Yaragh Tala* v. *Sweden*, Views adopted on 15 November 1996.
[12] Ibid., para. 10.4.
[13] Counsel refers to resolution 60/171, adopted in March 2006.

and in Iran a history of detention and torture is a significant indicator of future risk.[14]

Issues and proceedings before the Committee

Admissibility considerations

6.1 Before considering any claims contained in a communication, the Committee must decide whether or not the communication is admissible under article 22 of the Convention. The Committee has ascertained, as it is required to do so under article 22, paragraph 5 (a), of the Convention that the same matter has not been and is not being examined under another procedure of international investigation or settlement.

6.2 The Committee notes that the State party has raised an objection to admissibility based on the fact that the complainant, in its view, has not substantiated her allegations even on a prima facie basis and that therefore the communication is manifestly unfounded. As to the complainant's claims under article 16 of the Convention, the Committee notes that no arguments or evidence have been submitted in substantiation of this claim, and therefore the Committee concludes that this claim has not been substantiated for the purposes of admissibility. This part of the communication is thus inadmissible.

6.3 As to the allegations made pursuant to article 3 of the Convention, the Committee is of the opinion that the arguments before it raise substantive issues which should be dealt with on the merits and not on admissibility alone. The Committee therefore declares the communication admissible as to the allegations made under article 3 of the Convention.

Consideration of the merits

7.1 The issue before the Committee is whether the forced return of the complainant to Iran would violate the State party's obligation pursuant to article 3, paragraph 1, of the Convention not to expel or return ('refouler') an individual to another State where there are substantial grounds for believing that he or she would be in danger of being subjected to torture upon return to Iran. In reaching this decision, the Committee must take into account all relevant considerations, pursuant to article 3, paragraph 2, of the Convention including the existence of a consistent pattern of gross, flagrant or mass violations of human rights. The aim of the determination, however, is to establish whether the individual concerned would be personally at risk of being subjected to torture in the country to which he or she would return. It follows that the existence of a consistent pattern of gross, flagrant or mass violations of human rights in a country does not as such constitute a sufficient ground for determining that a particular person would be in danger of being subjected to torture upon his return to that country; additional grounds must exist to show that the individual concerned would be personally at risk. Similarly, the absence of a consistent pattern of gross violations of human rights does not mean that a person cannot be considered to be in danger of being subjected to torture in his or her specific circumstances.

7.2 The Committee recalls its General Comment 1 on article 3,[15] which states that it is to assess whether there are "substantial grounds for believing that the author would be in danger of torture" if returned, and that the risk of torture "must be assessed on grounds that go beyond mere theory or suspicion". The risk need not be "highly probable", but it must be "personal and present". In this regard, in previous decisions, the Committee has determined that the risk of torture must be "foreseeable, real and personal."[16]

7.3 In assessing the risk of torture in the present case, the Committee notes that the complainant has claimed that she was arrested and detained for around two months in early 2001 by Iranian authorities, and that during this period she was tortured. It also notes the complainant's contention that there is a foreseeable risk that she would be tortured if returned to Iran, on the basis of her previous detention and torture, the fact the State party applied for a passport for her, and the court summons which, according to the complainant, will result in an arrest warrant as she did not appear before the court as required.

7.4 The Committee also notes the complainant's argument that the PRRA, H&C and subsequent judicial review procedures are flawed, as the officer who concluded both procedures deemed that the court summons and proof of the complainant's employment as a nurse were not "new evidence" which she had to take into account during the PRRA. On this point the Committee considers that the judicial review procedure, while limited to appeal on points of law, did examine whether there were any irregularities in the PRRA and/or H&C determinations.

7.5 The State party has pointed to inconsistencies and contradictions in the complainant's testimonies which, in its opinion, cast doubt on the veracity of her allegations. The State party has specifically highlighted inconsistencies relating to the

---

[14] Referring to the *Tala* case, where the Committee held that "his history of detention and torture should be taken into account when determining whether he would be in danger of being subjected to torture upon his return".

[15] A/53/44, annex XI, adopted on 21 November 1997.
[16] Communication N° 203/2002, *A.R.* v. *Netherlands*, Views adopted on 21 November 2003, para. 7.3.

complainant's story on her role at the University, her arrest, torture, and escape from detention, her exit from Iran and delay in seeking refugee protection, and finally the summons for court and the lack of evidence of an arrest warrant. The Committee draws the attention of the parties to its General Comment 1 according to which the burden to present an arguable case is on the author of a complaint. Here, the Committee notes that the complainant has provided a court summons and documents purporting to refer to her employment at the University. However the Committee deems that the complainant has not submitted sufficient details or corroborating evidence to shift the burden of proof. In particular, she has not adduced satisfactory evidence or details relating to her detention or escape from detention. Further, she has failed to provide plausible explanations for her failure or inability to provide certain details which would have been of relevance to buttress her case, such as her stay for over three months in Kermanshah and the names of those who helped her to escape. Finally, the Committee deems that she has failed to provide plausible explanations for her subsequent journey through seven countries, including some asylum countries, prior to finally claiming refugee status in Canada.

7.6 The Committee notes that the complainant's arguments, and the evidence to support them, have been presented to the State party's courts. The Committee reiterates in this regard that it is for the courts of the State parties to the Convention, and not the Committee, to evaluate facts and evidence in a particular case. It is for the appellate courts of States parties to the Convention to examine the conduct of a case, unless it can be ascertained that the manner in which the evidence was evaluated was clearly arbitrary or amounted to a denial of justice, or that the officers had clearly violated their obligations of impartiality. In this case, the material before the Committee does not show that the State party's review of the complainant's case suffered from such defects.

7.7 Finally, the Committee, whilst noting with concern the numerous reports of human rights violations, including the use of torture, in Iran, must reiterate that for the purposes of article 3 of the Convention, the individual concerned must face a foreseeable, real and personal risk of being tortured. On the basis of the above, the Committee considers that the complainant has not substantiated that she would personally face such a real and imminent risk of being subjected to torture upon her return to Iran.

7.8 The Committee against Torture, acting under article 22, paragraph 7, of the Convention, considers that the complainant has not substantiated her claim that she would be subjected to torture upon return to Iran and therefore concludes that the complainant's removal to that country would not constitute a breach of article 3 of the Convention.

Communication N° 300/2006

Submitted by: Adel Tebourski (represented by counsel)
Alleged victim: The complainant
State party: France
Date of adoption of Views: 1 May 2007

Subject matter: deportation of complainant to Tunisia with alleged risk of torture

Procedural issue: failure to comply with request for interim measures of protection

Substantive issue: risk of torture after deportation

Articles of the Convention: 3 and 22

1.1 The complainant, Adel Tebourski, a Tunisian national, was residing in France when the present complaint was submitted and was the subject of a deportation order to his country of origin. He claims that his forced repatriation to Tunisia constitutes a violation of article 3 of the Convention against Torture. The complainant is represented by counsel, Lucile Hugon, from Action by Christians for the Abolition of Torture (ACAT).

1.2 In accordance with article 22, paragraph 3, of the Convention, the Committee brought the complaint to the State party's attention in a note verbale dated 27 July 2006. At the same time the Committee, pursuant to rule 108, paragraph 9, of its rules of procedure, requested the State party not to deport the complainant to Tunisia while his complaint was being considered. The Committee reiterated this request in a note verbale dated 28 July 2006.

1.3 The Committee was informed by counsel that the complainant had been deported to Tunisia on 7 August 2006.

The facts as submitted by the complainant

2.1 In 1985, the complainant left Tunisia for Belgium, where he pursued his studies. On 26 November 2001, he was arrested in northern France, following the assassination of Ahmed Shah Massoud on 9 September 2001 in Afghanistan. Massoud, the leader of the Northern Alliance forces in Afghanistan, was assassinated by Abdessatar Dahmane and Bouraoui El Ouaer (who also died in the attack). The trial of the complainant and his alleged accomplices began in March 2005 before the Paris Criminal Court. The complainant stood accused of having organized the departure of volunteers for Pakistan and Afghanistan. His role was confined to procuring false papers such as visas and passports. He denies any knowledge of the plans of his friend Abdessatar Dahmane, from whom he had heard nothing in the months leading up to Massoud's assassination.

2.2 On 17 May 2005, the Paris Criminal Court sentenced the complainant to six years' imprisonment for "criminal conspiracy in connection with a terrorist enterprise" and to deprivation of his civil, civic and family rights for a period of five years. He received a remission of sentence for good conduct. He held dual French-Tunisian nationality, which he had acquired in 2000 after marrying a French national in 1995. Pursuant to a decree of 19 July 2006, he was stripped of his French nationality, and he was served the same day with a ministerial deportation order, motivated by "the imperative requirements of State security and public safety". On 22 July 2006, he was released from Nantes prison and taken straight to the Mesnil-Amelot administrative detention centre.

2.3 On 25 July 2006, the complainant filed an application for asylum in France. This application was reviewed under the urgent procedure that allows the French Office for the Protection of Refugees and Stateless Persons (OFPRA) to take a decision within 96 hours. On 28 July 2006, OFPRA rejected the asylum application. On the same day, the complainant lodged an appeal against this decision with the Refugee Appeals Board. This appeal does not have suspensive effect.

2.4 In an appeal filed on 24 July 2006, the complainant asked the interim relief judge at the Paris Administrative Court to take interim measures pending a review of the legality of the ministerial deportation order. In a ruling dated 25 July 2006, this request was rejected. In an appeal lodged on 26 July 2006, the complainant requested annulment of the ministerial deportation order. In a ruling dated 4 August 2006, the interim relief judge rejected the request for a stay of execution of the decision. In an appeal lodged on 1 August 2006, the complainant requested annulment of the decision establishing Tunisia as the destination country. In a ruling dated 5 August 2006, the interim relief judge rejected the request for a stay of execution of the decision, and the complainant was finally deported to Tunisia on 7 August 2006.

2.5 On 17 October 2006, the Refugee Appeals Board turned down the complainant's appeal, having due regard to the nature and gravity of the acts committed which, in the Board's view, justify his exclusion from the status of refugee pursuant to article 1 (F) of the 1951 Geneva Convention. However, the Board noted that the complainant "could have had reason to fear that he would be retried for the same offences for which he had already been convicted and punished, should he return to his country" and "the fact that, after his deportation to Tunisia, he remained at liberty but had been placed under close police surveillance without being arrested must be regarded as evidence of a desire on the part of the Tunisian authorities to disguise their true intentions towards him, particularly in view of the attention which this case has attracted in the international media."

The complaint

3.1 The complainant alleges a violation of article 3 of the Convention. He cites the Tunisian Criminal Code, the Military Code of Pleadings and Penalties, and the anti-terrorist law of 10 December 2003, which prescribe penalties for activities carried out outside Tunisia. He argues that he will be convicted and imprisoned again for the acts for which he has already served a sentence in France.

3.2 The complainant argues that terrorism cases involving Tunisian nationals provoke a particularly strong reaction in Tunisia. Several individuals convicted under article 123 of the Code of Military Pleadings and Penalties or the anti-terrorist law of 10 December 2003 have been severely tortured after being deported by a third country to Tunisia. The complainant cites several examples of Tunisians who were allegedly subjected to torture or ill-treatment after arriving in Tunisia. He recalls that many persons accused of engaging in activities relating to terrorism are often tortured by the Tunisian authorities in order to extract confessions from them. He further recalls that conditions of detention in Tunisia are inhuman and degrading, without giving further details.

3.3 The complainant contends that the Tunisian authorities cannot be ignorant of his conviction in France, since it was the subject of numerous press articles. His family in Tunisia contacted two lawyers to try to ascertain whether proceedings against the complainant had already been instituted in Tunisia. The two lawyers were unable to obtain this information from the clerks of the courts concerned.

The State party's admissibility and merits observations

4.1 On 18 October 2006, the State party submitted its observations on the admissibility and merits of the complaint. It argued that it is inadmissible, because the complainant did not appeal against the decisions taken by the interim relief judge (see para. 2.4 above). Likewise, the appeals on the substance of the case are still pending before the Paris Administrative Court and, consequently, the complainant has not exhausted all domestic remedies.

4.2 On the merits, the State party considers the complaints brought by the complainant to be manifestly unfounded. At no point did he provide material and irrefutable evidence of the threats that he would allegedly face upon return to Tunisia. In the first place, during the procedure prior to the decision to establish Tunisia as the country of destination, he evinced no specific arguments that would have led the French authorities to conclude that his personal security would not be assured in his country of origin. Secondly, he failed to provide solid evidence to OFPRA when it reviewed his request for asylum. In its decision of 28 July 2006, that body found that there was no evidence to suggest that the complainant would face personal persecution if he returned to a country to which he had in any case returned several times since 1985.

4.3 The State party invoked the decision handed down by the interim relief judge at the Paris Administrative Court on 29 July 2006, in which the judge found that, even if the acts for which the complainant had been convicted in France could, under a Tunisian law of 10 December 2003, be grounds for bringing proceedings against him, that circumstance alone could not be construed as constituting inhuman and degrading treatment, since the complainant did not risk being sentenced to death and there was no evidence that the conditions in which he might be detained amounted to inhuman or degrading treatment. The State party submits that the different French administrative and judicial authorities to which the complainant applied conducted a thorough and balanced review of his situation under conditions free from any form of arbitrariness, in accordance with the requirements of the Committee.[1]

4.4 The State party emphasizes that, in so far as the complainant was unable to show that the fears cited in the event of his return to Tunisia were well founded, there was no justification for deferring the removal from France of a person who had proved himself highly dangerous to public order. It recalls that the Paris Criminal Court, in its judgement of 17 May 2005, stressed that the complainant was highly dangerous because of his subversive activities. It was because of this manifest danger and the demonstrable absence of risks in the event of his return to Tunisia that the State party considered it necessary promptly to remove the complainant from the country, balancing the imperatives of State security with the guarantees afforded by the Convention.

4.5 The State party stresses that it intends to respond favourably to requests from the Committee against Torture for stays of execution, even though, under rule 108 of the rules of procedure, such requests are not legally binding on States parties. However, it does consider that where, as in the present case, requests appear to it to be manifestly unfounded, it has a responsibility, having ensured beyond reasonable doubt that the interested parties do not face an individual and proven risk of ill-treatment, to remove foreigners whose presence poses a grave threat to public order and national security.

Complainant's comments

5.1 On 18 December 2006, the complainant recalled that the purpose of the appeal to the interim relief judge for the imposition of interim measures was to prevent his deportation to Tunisia. In such a case, a remedy that remains pending after the deportation is, by definition, pointless.[2] The same argument applies to remedies pending before the Paris Administrative Court. The very fact that the deportation was carried out demonstrates the ineffectiveness of these remedies, which cannot thenceforth be exhausted by the complainant.

5.2 Regarding the State party's contention that the complainant did not provide evidence of the threats that he would face if he returned to his country of origin, the complainant recalls that the Refugee Appeals Board recognized, in its decision of 17 October 2006, that he feared persecution. He further recalls that he provided the French courts with sufficient evidence to raise serious doubts as to the legality of the deportation decision.

5.3 Regarding the so-called "demonstrable absence of risks in the event of his return to Tunisia", the complainant stresses that he frequently has to call his counsel from a public telephone box. Although he was not arrested upon or after his arrival in Tunisia, he is under constant surveillance (wiretapping and being followed). His personal belongings are still being withheld. He still has no Tunisian identity papers, in spite of his many attempts to procure some. He has learned from a friend of his brother who works for the police that an

---

[1] See communication N° 219/2003, *G.K.* v. *Switzerland*, Views adopted on 7 May 2003, para. 6.12.

[2] See communication N° 195/2002, *Brada* v. *France*, Views adopted on 17 May 2005, para. 7.8.

internal message was sent out to all Tunisian police stations and offices when he arrived in Tunisia, giving instructions that he should not be arrested under any pretext in the weeks that followed, probably because of the media attention surrounding the case.

Additional observations of the State party

6.1 On 1 February 2007, the State party submitted that the Refugee Appeals Board's decision of 17 October 2006 merely confirmed the decision taken by OFPRA on 28 July 2006, denying the complainant refugee status. The Board noted that "while he did not directly commit terrorist acts, Mr. Adel Tebourski knowingly participated in their organization". The State party furthermore informs the Committee that, pursuant to a ruling of 15 December 2006, the Paris Administrative Court dismissed on the merits the complainant's appeal for annulment of the decision by the Minister of the Interior establishing Tunisia as the destination country. In that ruling, the court noted that "the evidence in the case does not show that Mr. Tebourski, who has been living in Europe since the mid-1980s, is currently the subject of criminal proceedings brought by the Tunisian authorities".

6.2 In response to the complainant's allegation that the French authorities refused to deport him to a country other than Tunisia, the State party recalls that the complainant at no time designated a country that could take him and to which he could be legally admitted. In these circumstances, he could only be sent to his country of origin, given that his presence on French soil constituted a grave threat to public order and the safety and security of the State.

6.3 The State party informs the Committee that, while no provision of the Convention requires it to do so, it has nonetheless contacted the Tunisian authorities, through the diplomatic channel, in order to obtain information on the complainant's circumstances since his return to Tunisia. The Committee will be informed of the outcome of this initiative at the earliest opportunity.

Issues and proceedings before the Committee

Consideration of admissibility

7.1 The Committee ascertained that the communication satisfies the conditions of admissibility set out in article 22, paragraphs 1, 2 and 5 (a), of the Convention, namely, that it concerns a State party which has made the declaration under article 22, and that, in so far as it alleges a breach of article 3 of the Convention against a named and identifiable individual, it is not anonymous, does not constitute an abuse of the right of submission to the Committee and is not incompatible with any provisions of the Convention.

7.2 The Committee also ascertained that the same matter, i.e., France's failure to comply with article 3 of the Convention by deporting to Tunisia a person who alleges that he risks being tortured, has not been and is not being examined under another investigation or settlement procedure.

7.3 Regarding domestic remedies, the Committee noted with interest the observations of the State party, which considers the complaint to be inadmissible, because the complainant failed to exhaust all domestic remedies (cf. para. 4.1 above). However, the Committee notes in this regard that, on 26 July 2006, the complainant lodged a non-suspensive appeal with the Paris Administrative Court for an annulment of the ministerial enforcement order. It also notes that, on 1 August 2006, the complainant appealed to the same court for annulment of the decision by the Minister of the Interior to establish Tunisia as the destination country. The complainant also asked the interim relief judge to impose interim protection measures, which the judge refused to do. On 15 December 2006, the Paris Administrative Court dismissed the two appeals for annulment. The complainant could doubtless have appealed this decision before the Paris Administrative Court. However, given that the expulsion order was executed on 7 August 2006, the Committee is entitled to find that a remedy which remains pending after the act which it was designed to avert has already taken place has, by definition, become pointless, since the irreparable harm can no longer be avoided, even if a subsequent judgement were to find in favour of the complainant.

7.4 In light of the foregoing, the Committee considers that it has grounds to conclude that, from the moment that the complainant was deported to Tunisia under the conditions in which that took place, it was very unlikely that the remaining remedies cited by the State party would have given him satisfaction. The Committee also notes that if the exercise of domestic remedies is to be effective and not illusory, an individual must be allowed a reasonable length of time before execution of the final decision to exhaust such remedies. The Committee notes that in the present case the complainant was stripped of his nationality by the State party on 19 July 2006, the consequence of which was to make him an immigrant in an irregular situation who was liable to expulsion. Despite the steps he took (cf. paras. 2.3 and 2.4 above), the complainant was expelled just three weeks after this decision. All remedies which remain open to the complainant following his expulsion are by definition pointless. The Committee therefore declares the complaint admissible.

Consideration of the merits

8.1 The Committee must determine whether, in deporting the complainant to Tunisia, the State party violated its obligation under article 3 of the Convention not to expel, return ("refouler") or extradite a person to another State where there are substantial grounds for believing that he would be in danger of being subjected to torture. The Committee stresses that it must take a decision on the question in the light of the information which the authorities of the State party had or should have had in their possession *at the time* of the expulsion. Subsequent events are useful only for assessing the information which the State party actually had or could have deduced at the time of expulsion.[3]

8.2 To justify its refusal to comply with the Committee's decision requesting it not to deport the complainant to Tunisia while his case was being considered by the Committee, the State party puts forward four arguments:

- The danger which the complainant posed to the domestic public order;
- The absence of a risk that the individual concerned would be tortured if returned to Tunisia;
- The fact that the individual concerned, while opposing his deportation to Tunisia, did not suggest another host country;
- The non-legally binding character for States parties of protection measures decided by the Committee pursuant to rule 108 of the rules of procedure.

In this regard, the Committee affirms that the purpose of the Convention in article 3 is to prevent a person from being exposed to the *risk* of torture through refoulement, expulsion or extradition "to another State where there are substantial grounds for believing that he would be in danger of being subjected to torture", regardless of the character of the person, in particular the danger he poses to society.

8.3 In other words, article 3 of the Convention offers absolute protection to anyone in the territory of a State party which has made the declaration under article 22. Once this person alludes to a risk of torture under the conditions laid down in article 3, the State party can no longer cite domestic concerns as grounds for failing in its obligation under the Convention to guarantee protection to anyone in its jurisdiction who fears that he is in serious danger of being tortured if he is returned to another country.

8.4 In the present case, the matter having been brought to the Committee's attention after the alleged or real exhaustion of domestic remedies, even if the Committee takes into consideration all the comments which the State party has submitted on this communication, the declaration made by the State party under article 22 confers on the Committee alone the power to assess whether the danger invoked is serious or not. The Committee takes into account the State party's assessment of the facts and evidence, but it is the Committee that must ultimately decide whether there is a risk of torture.

8.5 By establishing Tunisia as the destination for the complainant, in spite of the latter's explicit request not to be returned to his country of origin, the State party failed to take account of the universally accepted practice in such cases, whereby an alternative solution is sought with the agreement of the individual concerned and the assistance of the Office of the United Nations High Commissioner for Refugees and a third country willing to receive the individual who fears for his safety.

8.6 The Committee also notes that the Convention (art. 18) vests it with competence to establish its own rules of procedure, which become inseparable from the Convention to the extent they do not contradict it. In this case, rule 108 of the rules of procedure is specifically intended to give meaning and scope to articles 3 and 22 of the Convention, which otherwise would offer asylum-seekers claiming a serious risk of torture purely relative, not to say theoretical, protection.

8.7 The Committee therefore considers that, by expelling the complainant to Tunisia under the conditions in which it did and for the reasons adduced, thereby presenting the Committee with a fait accompli, the State party not only failed to demonstrate the good faith required of any party to a treaty, but also failed to meet its obligations under articles 3 and 22 of the Convention.

9. The Committee against Torture, acting under article 22, paragraph 7, of the Convention against Torture and Other Cruel, Inhuman or Degrading Treatment or Punishment, concludes that the deportation of the complainant to Tunisia was a violation of articles 3 and 22 of the Convention.

10. In conformity with article 112, paragraph 5, of its rules of procedure, the Committee wishes to be informed, within 90 days, of the steps taken by the State party to respond to these Views, to make reparation for the breach of article 3 of the Convention, and to determine, in consultation with the country (also a State party to the Convention) to which he was deported, the complainant's current whereabouts and the state of his well-being.

---

[3] See communication N° 233/2003, *Agiza* v. *Sweden*, Views adopted on 20 May 2005, para. 13.2.

AUTHOR AND VICTIM INDEX

	A = author *V = victim* *A, V =* *author's* *name as* *victim*	*State party*	*Communication number*	*Page*
A				
A.A.	A, V	Azerbaijan	247/2004	3
Abdelli, Imed	A, V	Tunisia	188/2001	120
Aemei, Seid Mortesa	A, V	Switzerland	34/1995	21
Agiza, Ahmed Hussein Mustafa Kamil	A, V	Sweden	233/2003	177
Arkauz Arana, Josu	A, V	France	63/1997	43
B				
Blanco Abad, Encarnación	A, V	Spain	59/1996	37
Brada, Mafhoud	A, V	France	195/2002	146
C				
C.T.	A, V	Sweden	279/2005	221
D				
Dadar, Mostafa	A, V	Canada	258/2004	209
Dimitrijevic, Danilo	A, V	Serbia and Montenegro	172/2000	89
Dimitrijevic, Dragan	A, V	Serbia and Montenegro	207/2002	155
Dimitrov, Jovica	A, V	Serbia and Montenegro	171/2000	85
Dzemajl, Hajrizi et al.	A, V	Yugoslavia	161/2000	78
E				
El Rgeig, Gamal	A, V	Switzerland	280/2005	227
Elmi, Sadiq Shek	A, V	Australia	120/1998	70
G				
G.K.	A, V	Switzerland	219/2002	170
Guengueng, Suleymane et al.	A, V	Senegal	181/2001	99
H				
Halimi-Nebzibi, Qani	A, V	Austria	8/1991	12
K				
K.M.	A, V	Sweden	279/2005	221
L				
Ltaief, Bouabdallah	A, V	Tunisia	189/2001	133
M				
M.A.K.	A, V	Germany	214/2002	162
Mutombo, Balabou	A, V	Switzerland	13/1993	15

	A = author V = victim A, V = author's name as victim	State party	Communication number	Page
N				
Nikolić, Ljiljana	A, V	Serbia and Montenegro	174/2000	92
Nikolić, N.	V	Serbia and Montenegro	174/2000	92
Nikolić, Slobodan	A, V	Serbia and Montenegro	174/2000	92
Núñez Chipana, Cecilia Rasana	A, V	Venezuela	110/1998	62
R				
Ristic, Milan	V	Yugoslavia	113/1998	65
Ristic, Radijove	A	Yugoslavia	113/1998	65
S				
S.P.A.	A, V	Canada	282/2005	231
T				
T.A.	A, V	Canada	273/2005	7
Tala, Kaveh Yaragh	A, V	Sweden	43/1996	27
Tapia Páez, Gorki Ernesto	A, V	Sweden	39/1996	31
Tebourski, Adel	A, V	France	300/2006	237
Thabti, Dhaou Belgacem	A, V	Tunisia	187/2001	107
T.P.S.	A, V	Canada	99/1997	51
U				
Urra Guridi, Kepa	A, V	Spain	212/2002	158
V				
V.L.	A, V	Switzerland	262/2005	215
Z				
Z.T.	A, V	Norway	238/2003	201